DEEP LEARNING
CRASH COURSE

DEEP LEARNING CRASH COURSE

A Hands-On, Project-Based Introduction to Artificial Intelligence

by Giovanni Volpe, Benjamin Midtvedt,
Jesús Pineda, Henrik Klein Moberg,
Harshith Bachimanchi, Joana B. Pereira,
and Carlo Manzo

no starch
press®

San Francisco

Printed in the United States of America

First printing

29 28 27 26 25   1 2 3 4 5

ISBN-13: 978-1-7185-0392-2 (print)
ISBN-13: 978-1-7185-0393-9 (ebook)

 Published by No Starch Press®, Inc.
245 8th Street, San Francisco, CA 94103
phone: +1.415.863.9900
www.nostarch.com; info@nostarch.com

Publisher: William Pollock
Managing Editor: Jill Franklin
Production Manager: Sabrina Plomitallo-González
Production Editor: Miles Bond
Developmental Editors: Annie Choi and Ryan Frankel
Cover Illustrator: Garry Booth
Interior Design: Octopod Studios
Technical Reviewer: Wylie Ahmed
Copyeditor: Sharon Wilkey
Proofreader: Audrey Doyle

Library of Congress Control Number: 2025027767

For customer service inquiries, please contact info@nostarch.com. For information on distribution, bulk sales, corporate sales, or translations: sales@nostarch.com. For permission to translate this work: rights@nostarch.com. To report counterfeit copies or piracy: counterfeit@nostarch.com. The authorized representative in the EU for product safety and compliance is EU Compliance Partner, Pärnu mnt. 139b-14, 11317 Tallinn, Estonia, hello@eucompliancepartner.com, +3375690241.

About the Authors

Giovanni Volpe is a professor in the physics department of the University of Gothenburg, Sweden, and head of the Soft Matter Lab. His research interests include deep learning, brain connectivity, statistical mechanics, and soft matter. He has authored more than 200 articles and reviews on these topics and has co-authored two books. He has also developed several software packages for microscopy (DeepTrack), deep learning (Deeplay), and brain connectivity (BRAPH).

Benjamin Midtvedt earned his PhD at the University of Gothenburg with a focus on enhancing microscopy through deep learning. His research has centered on the development of accessible and practical AI optimized to the needs of the user. He has also been the lead developer of several Python-based open source deep learning frameworks, including DeepTrack and Deeplay.

Jesús Pineda earned his PhD in physics at the University of Gothenburg with a focus on the intersection of deep learning and computer vision. He has co-authored several articles in high-impact journals on the application of deep learning to glean insights from microscopy data. He is also a core developer of the deep learning software packages DeepTrack and Deeplay.

Henrik Klein Moberg received his PhD from Chalmers University of Technology, Sweden, where he specialized in the integration of AI with the physical sciences. His research focused on applying deep learning techniques to nanofluidic microscopy and nanophotonics, aiming to enhance the precision and efficiency of these technologies. He has also organized and spoken at numerous conferences related to AI and scientific data analysis.

Harshith Bachimanchi completed his PhD at the University of Gothenburg on the integration of holographic microscopy and deep learning to better understand marine microorganisms. He has applied deep learning techniques and experimental optics to track both biological and synthetic particles, enhancing our understanding of these complex systems. He has also developed simulations demonstrating the applications of deep learning in microscopy.

Joana B. Pereira is an associate professor at Karolinska Institute, Sweden, where she focuses on investigating new biomarkers for neurodegenerative disorders, in particular Alzheimer's disease. Since 2020, she has organized an annual interdisciplinary conference called Emerging Topics in Artificial Intelligence in San Diego, California. She is the scientific coordinator for NeurotechEU and winner of the 2021 de Leon Prize for best neuroimaging article on Alzheimer's disease.

Carlo Manzo is an associate professor at the University of Vic, Spain, where he leads the Quantitative Bioimaging Lab. His research is dedicated to the analysis of biophysical processes, merging deep learning techniques with state-of-the-art imaging technologies to achieve single-molecule sensitivity. He is the founder of the Anomalous Diffusion challenge and winner of the 2017 E. Pérez Payá Prize from the Sociedad de Biofísica de España.

About the Technical Reviewer

Wylie Ahmed is a CNRS researcher at the Laboratoire de Physique Théorique and the Centre de Biologie Intégrative at the University of Toulouse, France, where he leads the Soft, Living, and Active Matter Lab. His research focuses on biological physics, statistical mechanics, and nonequilibrium systems, using a combined experimental and theoretical approach. In 2023, he received the Irwin Oppenheim Award from the American Physical Society.

BRIEF CONTENTS

Acknowledgments xix
Introduction xxi
Chapter 1: Building and Training Your First Neural Network 1
Chapter 2: Capturing Trends and Recognizing Patterns with Dense Neural Networks 51
Chapter 3: Processing Images with Convolutional Neural Networks 95
Chapter 4: Enhancing, Generating, and Analyzing Data with Autoencoders 167
Chapter 5: Segmenting and Analyzing Images with U-Nets 209
Chapter 6: Training Neural Networks with Self-Supervised Learning 251
Chapter 7: Processing Time Series and Language with Recurrent Neural Networks 279
Chapter 8: Processing Language and Classifying Images with Attention and Transformers .. 325
Chapter 9: Creating and Transforming Images with Generative Adversarial Networks 375
Chapter 10: Implementing Generative AI with Diffusion Models 425
Chapter 11: Modeling Molecules and Complex Systems with Graph Neural Networks 475
Chapter 12: Continuously Improving Performance with Active Learning 529
Chapter 13: Mastering Decision-Making with Deep Reinforcement Learning 557
Chapter 14: Predicting Chaos with Reservoir Computing 601
Conclusion 623
Index 625

CONTENTS IN DETAIL

ACKNOWLEDGMENTS   **xix**

INTRODUCTION   **xxi**

Who Should Read This Book? xxiii
This Book's Approach xxiii
Setting Up Your Learning Environment xxiv
Obtaining the Data and Code Used in This Book xxv
What's in This Book? xxv
Online Resources xxviii
Time to Start Your Journey xxviii

1
BUILDING AND TRAINING YOUR FIRST NEURAL NETWORK   **1**

Classifying Data with a Single Neuron 2
    Classifying 1D Data 3
    Classifying 2D Data 11
    Adding a Bias as Another Dimension 17
    Using Weight Regularization to Stabilize the Training 18
Using Different Activation Functions 19
Classifying Data with a Two-Layer Neural Network 20
    Implementing a Dense Neural Network 22
    Training with Error Backpropagation 25
    Attempting an Impossible Classification 30
Classifying Data with a Three-Layer Neural Network 31
Project 1A: Classifying Handwritten Digits **34**
    Using the MNIST Digit Dataset 34
    Implementing the Neural Network 36
    Training and Testing 38
    Making Improvements 41
    Performing Failure Analysis 46
Summary 48
Seminal Works and Further Reading 48

2
**CAPTURING TRENDS AND RECOGNIZING PATTERNS WITH DENSE
NEURAL NETWORKS**   **51**

Regressing Data with a Single Neuron 52
    Regressing 1D Data 52
    Regressing 2D Data 57

Regressing Data with a Two-Layer Neural Network 61
    Implementing a Dense Neural Network.................................. 62
    Training with Error Backpropagation 63
Training Using Batches.. 65
    Plotting Predictions vs. Ground Truth 65
    Training with Mini-Batches 67
    Tracking Training Metrics 69
    Randomizing the Batches 71
Dividing Data into Multiple Datasets 73
    Splitting the Data 74
    Training and Validating the Neural Network 75
Project 2A: Emulating a Physical System **79**
    Loading the Theoretical and Geometrical–Optics Optical Forces 80
    Loading and Preparing the Training Data 84
    Implementing the Neural Network 87
    Implementing Data Loaders 88
    Training the Neural Network 88
    Evaluating Performance 91
Summary 92
Seminal Works and Further Reading 93

3
PROCESSING IMAGES WITH CONVOLUTIONAL NEURAL NETWORKS   95

Understanding Convolutions 96
    Convolving 1D Data 96
    Convolving 2D Data 98
    Using Convolutions in a Neural Network 100
Implementing Neural Networks in PyTorch 100
    Defining Convolutional Layers 102
    Adding ReLU Activation.. 104
    Adding Pooling Layers... 105
    Using Upsampling Layers 106
    Transforming Images 108
    Using Dense Layers to Classify Images 109
Project 3A: Classifying Malaria-Infected Blood Smears **110**
    Loading the Malaria Dataset 111
    Classifying with Dense Neural Networks 115
    Classifying with Convolutional Neural Networks 118
    Checking the Values of the Filters 120
    Visualizing Activations of Convolutional Layers.......................... 121
    Visualizing Heatmaps 124
Project 3B: Localizing Microscopic Particles **128**
    Loading the Videos.. 128
    Manually Annotating the Videos 130
    Implementing a Convolutional Neural Network........................... 134

Training with Annotated Data 135
Simulating the Training Data 137
Training with Simulated Data 143

Project 3C: Creating DeepDreams 145
Loading an Image. 146
Loading a Pretrained Neural Network 147
Implementing the DeepDreams Algorithm 149
Using Multiple Layers at Once 156

Project 3D: Transferring the Style of Images 158
Loading the Content and Style Images. 158
Loading a Pretrained Neural Network 159
Implementing Style Transfer 160
Creating an Image in Gaudí's Style 163

Summary 164
Seminal Works and Further Reading 165

4
ENHANCING, GENERATING, AND ANALYZING DATA WITH
AUTOENCODERS   167

Understanding Encoder-Decoders 168
Implementing a Denoising Encoder-Decoder 169
Generating the Data 169
Creating a Simulated Dataset 172
Defining and Training the Encoder-Decoder 173
Denoising the Image 173
Checking for Absence of Mode Collapse 175
Checking Generalization Capabilities 176
Retraining 177

Project 4A: Generating Images with Variational Autoencoders 179
Understanding Variational Autoencoders 179
Loading the MNIST Dataset 181
Training the Variational Autoencoder 182
Generating Images with the Decoder. 183
Clustering Images with the Encoder 186

Project 4B: Morphing Images with Wasserstein Autoencoders 188
Understanding Wasserstein Autoencoders 188
Loading the Fashion-MNIST Dataset. 189
Training the Wasserstein Autoencoder 191
Reconstructing the Fashion-MNIST Images 192
Creating New Images 192
Morphing Images 193

Project 4C: Detecting Anomalies in ECG Data 195
Understanding Anomaly Detection 196
Loading the ECG Dataset 196
Defining and Training the Autoencoder. 199
Testing with Normal and Anomalous ECGs 200
Detecting Anomalies 201

Summary 206
Seminal Works and Further Reading 207

5
SEGMENTING AND ANALYZING IMAGES WITH U-NETS   209

Introducing U-Nets 210
Understanding Semantic Segmentation with U-Nets 211
Segmenting Images of Biological Tissues 212
    Loading the Segmented Tissue Images 213
    Creating the Data Pipelines 214
    Defining and Training the U-Net 216
    Plotting the Training Metrics 219
    Preventing Overfitting 220
    Evaluating the Trained U-Net 222
Project 5A: Detecting Quantum Dots in Fluorescence Images 224
    Loading the Image 224
    Simulating Quantum Dots 225
    Defining and Training the U-Net 231
    Evaluating the Trained U-Net 232
Project 5B: Counting Cells 234
    Loading the Dataset 234
    Creating a Pipeline... 235
    Simulating the Cell Images 237
    Implementing and Training the U-Net.............................. 244
    Testing the Trained U-Net 245
Summary 248
Seminal Works and Further Reading 248

6
TRAINING NEURAL NETWORKS WITH SELF-SUPERVISED
LEARNING   251

Understanding Self-Supervised Learning 252
    Self-Supervised Contrastive Learning 252
    Self-Supervised Non-Contrastive Learning 253
    Self-Supervised Geometric Learning 254
Determining the Position of a Particle in an Image...................... 255
    Creating the Dataset 255
    Learning from Translations 257
    Learning from Flipping the Image 262
    Improving Performance with LodeSTAR 265
Project 6A: Localizing Mouse Stem Cells with LodeSTAR 268
    Using the Cell Tracking Challenge Dataset........................ 268
    Preparing the Training Crop....................................... 271
    Creating the Training Pipeline and Data Loader 272
    Training the Neural Network 273
    Evaluating Performance 274

Summary 277
Seminal Works and Further Reading 278

7
PROCESSING TIME SERIES AND LANGUAGE WITH RECURRENT NEURAL NETWORKS 279

Understanding Recurrent Neural Networks 279
    Using a Comb Filter 280
    Understanding a Simple Recurrent Neural Network 281
Predicting Temperature with Recurrent Neural Networks 282
    Loading the Jena Climate Dataset 282
    Preprocessing the Data 284
    Implementing a Commonsense Benchmark 287
    Determining the Computational Device 287
    Predicting with a Simple Recurrent Neural Network 288
    Stacking Multiple Recurrent Layers 293
    Using Gated Recurrent Units 294
    Using Long Short-Term Memory Networks 296
Project 7A: Translating with Recurrent Neural Networks **299**
    Preparing the Bilingual Dataset 299
    Defining the Sequence-to-Sequence Application 308
    Loading Pretrained Embeddings 316
    Training the Sequence-to-Sequence Application 318
    Testing the Model Performance 319
    Evaluating the Model with the BLEU Score 321
Summary 322
Seminal Works and Further Reading 323

8
PROCESSING LANGUAGE AND CLASSIFYING IMAGES WITH ATTENTION AND TRANSFORMERS 325

Understanding Attention 326
    Implementing Dot-Product Attention 326
    Visualizing Attention 331
    Making the Attention Mechanism Trainable 333
    Implementing Other Attention Mechanisms 335
Project 8A: Using Attention to Improve Language Translation **336**
    Incorporating Attention 337
    Training and Testing the Seq2Seq Model with Attention 339
    Interpreting the Attention Matrix 340
Project 8B: Performing Sentiment Analysis with a Transformer **342**
    Breaking Down Multi-Head Attention 342
    Understanding the Transformer Structure 344
    Loading the IMDb Dataset 345
    Preprocessing the Reviews 347

Defining the Data Loaders 349
Building an Encoder-Only Transformer 350
Training the Model 356
Evaluating the Trained Model 356
Project 8C: Classifying Images with a Vision Transformer **358**
Using the CIFAR-10 Dataset 358
Data Preprocessing 360
Building the ViT Model 361
Training and Evaluating the ViT Model 363
Improving the ViT Model with CutMix 364
Using a Pretrained ViT Model 370
Summary 372
Seminal Works and Further Reading 373

9
CREATING AND TRANSFORMING IMAGES WITH GENERATIVE ADVERSARIAL NETWORKS   375

Understanding GANs 376
Discriminating Between Real and Fake Data 377
Generating Realistic Fake Data 378
Training a GAN 379
Generating Digits with a GAN 379
Loading the MNIST Dataset with PyTorch 380
Defining the Generator and Discriminator 381
Training the GAN 382
Plotting the Intermediate Results 386
Plotting the Training Losses 388
Project 9A: Generating Digits with a Conditional GAN **389**
Defining the Conditional Generator and Discriminator 390
Training the Conditional GAN 392
Plotting the Generated Digits 393
Project 9B: Virtually Staining a Biological Tissue **394**
Downloading the Human Motor Neurons Dataset 394
Creating a Dataset 395
Instantiating the Generator and Discriminator 400
Compiling the Conditional GAN 402
Training the Conditional GAN 403
Evaluating the Trained Conditional GAN 408
Project 9C: Converting Between Holographic and Bright-Field Microscopy Images **409**
Understanding CycleGANs 410
Using the Holo2Bright Dataset 411
Instantiating the CycleGAN Generators and Discriminators 414
Training the CycleGAN 416
Evaluating the Trained CycleGAN 421
Summary 423
Seminal Works and Further Reading 423

10
IMPLEMENTING GENERATIVE AI WITH DIFFUSION MODELS   425

Understanding Diffusion 426
Breaking Down Denoising Diffusion Probabilistic Models 427
     Modeling the Forward Diffusion Process 428
     Deriving the Fast Forward Process 429
     Modeling the Reverse Diffusion Process 430
Generating Digits with a Diffusion Model 432
     Loading the MNIST Dataset 432
     Implementing the Forward Diffusion Process 433
     Applying the Reverse Diffusion Process 435
     Defining the Positional Encoding Function 436
     Instantiating the Attention U-Net 438
     Training the Diffusion Model 439
     Sampling Images from Fixed Noise 444
Project 10A: Generating Bespoke Digits **446**
     Guiding the Diffusion Model 446
     Defining the Conditional Attention U-Net 447
     Training the Conditional Diffusion Model 448
     Plotting the Intermediate Training Results 448
Project 10B: Generating Images from Text Prompts **450**
     Providing a Conditional Text Input 450
     Defining the Conditional Attention U-Net 457
     Training the Conditional Diffusion Model 458
     Plotting the Intermediate Training Results 459
     Training with the CLIP Tokenizer and CLIP Text Encoder 460
Project 10C: Generating Super-Resolution Images **463**
     Downloading the BioSR Dataset 463
     Managing the Dataset 464
     Preprocessing the Images 465
     Creating the Training and Test Datasets 465
     Adapting the Diffusion Process for Super-Resolution 466
     Defining the Conditional Attention U-Net 467
     Training the Conditional Diffusion Model 468
Summary 471
Seminal Works and Further Reading 471

11
MODELING MOLECULES AND COMPLEX SYSTEMS WITH GRAPH NEURAL NETWORKS   475

Understanding Graph Convolutions 476
Predicting Molecular Properties with Graph Convolutions 479
     Implementing a Graph Convolution Layer 480
     Representing a Molecule as a Graph 482
     Using the ZINC Dataset 483
     Applying a Graph Convolutional Network 486

Training the Graph Convolutional Network 489
Evaluating the Graph Convolutional Network 491
Predicting Molecular Properties with Message Passing.............................. 491
Implementing a Message-Passing Layer 492
Implementing a Message-Passing Network.. 495
Training and Evaluating the Message-Passing Network 496
Project 11A: Simulating Complex Physical Phenomena **497**
Working with the SAND Dataset 497
Building a Graph Network–Based Simulator 500
Building the Dataset 502
Training the Model 507
Testing the Model 508
Simulating the System 509
Project 11B: Identifying Cell Trajectories **511**
Exploring the Cell-Tracking Data... 512
Creating a Graph from Segmented Images 514
Building a Training Dataset 519
Making MAGIK 521
Evaluating Performance... 522
Summary 526
Seminal Works and Further Reading 527

12
CONTINUOUSLY IMPROVING PERFORMANCE WITH ACTIVE LEARNING

529

Understanding Active Learning... 530
Performing Binary Classification.. 531
Creating a Dataset with Two Groups of Data Points 531
Classifying the Data Points with a Logistic Regression 532
Implementing the Active Learning Process................................. 533
Comparing Random and Uncertainty Sampling Strategies 538
Performing Multiclass Classification 539
Creating a Dataset with Three Groups of Data Points 540
Implementing the Active Learning Process with Multiple Classes 541
Comparing Sampling Strategies 545
Project 12A: Classifying MNIST Digits with Active Learning **547**
Training a Baseline Model 547
Implementing Multiple Active Learning Strategies 548
Comparing the Performance of the Active Learning Strategies................ 553
Summary 555
Seminal Works and Further Reading 556

13
MASTERING DECISION-MAKING WITH DEEP REINFORCEMENT LEARNING   557

Understanding Reinforcement Learning and Q-Learning 558
Implementing Tetris 561
    Constructing a Simplified Tetris 561
    Playing Tetris with the Command Line 568
    Playing Tetris with a Pygame Graphical Interface 569
Making an Agent Play Tetris with Q-Learning 573
    Adapting the Actions of Tetris for Q-Learning 573
    Implementing the Q-Learning Agent 574
    Training the Q-Learning Agent 581
    Training with a Random Tile Sequence 584
Making an Agent Play Tetris with Deep Q-Learning 585
    Understanding Deep Q-Learning 586
    Implementing the Deep Q-Learning Agent 587
    Training the Deep Q-Learning Agent 595
Summary 598
Seminal Works and Further Reading 598

14
PREDICTING CHAOS WITH RESERVOIR COMPUTING   601

Introducing Reservoir Computing 601
Defining the Lorenz System 602
    Numerically Integrating the Lorenz System 603
    Visualizing Time Evolution 604
    Visualizing the Lorenz Attractor 606
    Demonstrating the Butterfly Effect 607
Implementing a Reservoir Computer 610
    Setting Up the Reservoir 610
    Preparing the Training and Validation Data 612
    Training the Reservoir Computer 613
    Evaluating the Performance of the Reservoir Computer 616
Summary 619
Seminal Works and Further Reading 620

CONCLUSION   623

INDEX   625

ACKNOWLEDGMENTS

Writing a book on deep learning is a lot like training a neural network. It's an endless cycle of tweaking parameters, second-guessing decisions, and resisting the urge to rage-quit and take up gardening instead, like when we decided to switch all the code from TensorFlow to PyTorch after completing the first draft of the book, because who doesn't love rewriting everything from scratch?

Fortunately, we weren't alone in this process. Along the way, we had the support, advice, and much-needed sarcasm of many brilliant people who kept us from overfitting to our own ideas (and reminded us to occasionally get some sleep). This book is as much a result of their contributions as it is of our own efforts.

First of all, we'd like to thank all the students who survived our deep learning courses over the years—starting at ETH Zurich and making stops at the Institute of Photonic Sciences (ICFO), the Singapore-MIT Alliance for Science and Technology, Sorbonne University, FEMTO-ST, Chalmers University of Technology, the University of Gothenburg, and more. Your curiosity, feedback, and unyielding patience have continuously improved not just the courses themselves but also the material that inspired this book. You all made sure we stayed on our toes and constantly reminded us that "just one more line of code" rarely ends at just one line; it's often the start of a debugging rabbit hole that only bottomless cups of coffee can conquer.

A special shout-out to Lucio Isa at ETH, who casually suggested we organize a PhD course, accidentally setting off a chain of events that ultimately led to this book. Lucio, this is all your fault!

Also, a big thank-you to our scientific collaborators and colleagues, whose brilliant ideas, tough questions, and occasional well-timed reality checks kept us from disappearing completely into the deep learning abyss. Your insights and feedback sharpened our work, inspired many of the examples and metaphors scattered throughout these pages, and reminded us that no matter how deep the neural network, there's always room for one more layer of constructive criticism. It turns out that arguing about activation functions and the philosophical implications of AI over coffee is, in fact, a legitimate path to progress. We couldn't have done it without you—at least not without sounding a lot more confused.

Huge thanks to No Starch Press and its team for believing in this idea and for not laughing us out of the room when we first pitched it with the improbable title "Hello, Deep Learning!" In particular, thanks to Bill Pollock, founder and president of NSP, for immediately backing the project after our very first chat. Thanks also to Jill Franklin, managing editor, for guiding us with infinite patience and ensuring that every page reached the highest standard of quality. Special thanks to Miles Bond for expert production editing, and to Sharon Wilkey for meticulous copyediting, both of whom significantly improved the clarity and quality of our text. Big thanks to Annie Choi and Ryan Frankel for their meticulous editing, which not only smoothed out our typos and occasional questionable grammar choices but also clarified the meaning of entire sections that, as it turned out, weren't as crystal clear as we thought.

We're also grateful to Wylie Ahmed for his razor-sharp technical review, making sure our equations actually worked and our code wouldn't make anyone's computer spontaneously combust.

A big thank-you also to the European Research Council under the European Union's Horizon 2020 research and innovation program and the Knut and Alice Wallenberg Foundation for their funding that has permitted us to dedicate a substantial amount of time to writing this book.

And, of course, to our families and friends—thanks for putting up with us and enduring our late-night coding sessions, countless eureka moments, and occasional existential crises, and for pretending to understand why we were doing what we were doing for the past couple of years. Without your unwavering support, this book might still exist, but it would have taken much longer and made far less sense.

Thank you all!

INTRODUCTION

The deep learning revolution has arrived, and it's changing our lives in ways we never imagined. From everyday conveniences to groundbreaking innovations, deep learning is at the core of many of the technologies shaping our future. Whether you're ordering food, planning your commute, or searching for a playlist, deep learning is optimizing these experiences behind the scenes. But its impact goes far beyond these everyday tasks.

Today, deep learning is enabling scientists to design drugs tailored to specific receptors, accelerating medical breakthroughs and transforming health care. Large language models (LLMs) like GPT-4 are capable of generating text and writing code, revolutionizing fields like education, programming, and research. Deep learning is even reshaping social interactions, sometimes in unsettling ways, such as AI-powered chatbots serving as virtual companions or romantic partners.

Whether you need to learn deep learning for your career or are just curious about how it works, this book is for you. It covers everything from basic concepts to advanced problem-solving tools, equipping you to understand deep learning so that you can go from being a passive user to someone who can control and optimize this technique for your own unique needs.

Although the terms *deep learning, machine learning*, and *artificial intelligence* are often used interchangeably, they're different. *Artificial intelligence (AI)* refers to any technique used to create systems capable of performing cognitive tasks that usually require human intelligence, such as recognizing faces, understanding speech, making complex decisions, or translating languages. Examples of AI that don't involve machine learning include rule-based systems and expert systems used in medical diagnosis (remember IBM Watson?).

Machine learning is a branch of AI where computers use algorithms to learn from data and make predictions. Importantly, not all forms of machine learning fall under deep learning—for example, the decision trees and support vector machines that were popular in the early 2000s.

In turn, *deep learning* is a branch of machine learning that uses neural networks, typically with many layers of artificial neurons (hence the term *deep*). The ability of deep learning to learn directly from data makes it effective for solving a wide range of problems, from recognizing objects in images and videos, to translating spoken and written languages, to playing complex strategy games like Go. Notable applications encompass advanced conversational agents like ChatGPT, image-generation models like DALL-E, and protein structure prediction tools like AlphaFold.

With its foundation in neural network research from the 1950s to the 1980s, deep learning gained momentum after breakthroughs in the early 2000s and exploded in popularity in the mid-2010s. This revolution was fueled by gamers and social networks. As increasingly powerful graphics processing units (GPUs) were developed for gaming, social media provided a gold mine of data for training models. The turning point came in 2012 when a deep learning model, AlexNet, won the ImageNet Large Scale Visual Recognition Challenge. ImageNet is a large database of annotated images. The competition involves developing models to accurately classify and detect objects within these images. AlexNet's success demonstrated the potential of deep learning, leading to its widespread adoption in just a few years.

The rapid development of AI brought about by these transformations has led to all sorts of sensational conjectures: the utopian remaking of society, vast economic disruption, and even humanity's extermination. In this environment, understanding AI has never been more crucial, and the best way to grasp its nuances is through direct experience. This direct experience should also convince you that, despite predictions of doom and gloom, the most creative and purposeful aspects of our lives and careers will likely remain uniquely human for a long time.

This book is designed for those eager to dive into deep learning through practical, hands-on experience, without assuming any prior knowledge of deep learning. Each chapter is structured around examples and projects that are computationally manageable on standard hardware yet realistic in scope. Even so, readers will understand and implement the latest advancements in the field, such as diffusion models for generating high-resolution images and vision transformers (ViTs) for image classification.

Who Should Read This Book?

Whether you're an engineer optimizing models, a scientist seeking new data analysis tools, a doctor looking to automate diagnostics, an artist exploring psychedelic image transformations, or simply an AI enthusiast wanting to learn more, you'll find something here for you.

To get the most out of this book, you'll need a basic understanding of programming, ideally in Python, which is the language we'll use throughout this book. If you have experience in other programming languages like C/C++, Matlab, or R, you'll be able to quickly familiarize yourself with Python.

If you know how to write a for loop and define a function, you're ready to start. You should also be comfortable working with data structures like lists, dictionaries, and sets, as well as using libraries such as NumPy and Matplotlib for numerical data manipulation and visualization. You should also be familiar with reading and writing files, handling exceptions, and debugging your code efficiently by using tools like print statements or debugging environments. If you've written programs using classes and objects, you're ahead of the game. Along the way, you'll encounter more-advanced concepts, like context managers and hooks, as needed. By the end of this book, you'll not only gain a strong grasp of deep learning but also become a better programmer.

If you'd like an introduction to Python, consider *Python Crash Course*, 3rd edition, by Eric Matthes (No Starch Press, 2023). Another great companion to this practical guide is *Deep Learning: A Visual Approach* by Andrew Glassner (No Starch Press, 2021), which provides intuitive explanations of the key deep learning concepts.

Beyond programming, some familiarity with high school–level math will be helpful, particularly with concepts like basic algebra, probability, and statistics. However, for a deeper understanding of the algorithms and models discussed in later chapters, knowledge of linear algebra and calculus will be important. While readers with prior exposure will find it easier to grasp the more advanced concepts, don't worry if you're rusty or new to these topics; we'll introduce the necessary concepts you need at the intuitive level as we go along, without overwhelming you with too much mathematical notation.

If you're looking to bolster your mathematical foundations specifically for deep learning applications, consider reading *Math for Deep Learning* by Ronald T. Kneusel (No Starch Press, 2021) or *Machine Learning with Neural Networks: An Introduction for Scientists and Engineers* by Bernhard Mehlig (Cambridge University Press, 2021).

This Book's Approach

We believe that the best way to learn deep learning is by coding. For this reason, this book is organized around self-contained examples and projects that progress from simple to complex. As a result, you'll receive all the benefits of sequential learning while also having the freedom to explore each topic independently.

As you embark on this journey, it's important to recognize that deep learning frameworks continuously evolve, but their core principles remain consistent. This book primarily uses PyTorch, currently the most popular deep learning framework, along with Lightning and Deeplay for added convenience. However, the fundamental concepts, techniques, and insights you will gain are transferable across various frameworks. In an ever-evolving landscape, they will empower you to choose the best tools for your projects as well as transition between them, easing your learning curve when the next deep learning framework emerges.

Setting Up Your Learning Environment

Before diving into deep learning, you'll have to set up your learning environment. For software, you'll need Python. Python is an accessible, versatile programming language widely used in data science and machine learning because of its readability and extensive libraries. To install Python, you need to download the latest stable version from the official website (*https://www .python.org*). On the official Python documentation page (*https://docs.python .org*), you'll find detailed installation instructions for Microsoft Windows, Apple macOS, and Linux.

You'll also need various deep learning libraries, which you can install as they get imported in each example. The Python libraries you'll most frequently use are NumPy, essential for numerical computations and array operations, and Matplotlib, for creating visualizations and plots. You can easily install these libraries via the Python package manager by typing `pip install numpy matplotlib` in your terminal or command prompt.

Python code can be written in any text editor and executed directly from the command line or terminal without compiling, making development quick and interactive. While simple text editors can be sufficient, using dedicated resources greatly enhances productivity and provides useful tools for debugging, version control, and code management. In particular, Jupyter Notebooks (*https://jupyter.org*) provide interactive interfaces for executing Python code block by block, ideal for exploratory analysis and visualization.

It might also be helpful to use dedicated development environments, such as Visual Studio Code (VS Code, *https://code.visualstudio.com*), which is a powerful, lightweight code editor that supports Python through numerous extensions, including linting, debugging, and Git integration. Online environments like Google Colab (*https://colab.research.google.com*) and Kaggle Notebooks (*https://www.kaggle.com/code*) will allow you to run Python code and notebooks directly from your browser.

For hardware, any computer with a recent, powerful GPU will be sufficient. Most examples will run in minutes, although the more computationally expensive ones might take a few hours. While you can use a central processing unit (CPU) for most tasks, some examples (especially those involving generative adversarial networks, or GANs, and diffusion models) become too computationally expensive without a GPU. You can run those examples in Google Colab or Kaggle, which provide free (although limited) access to powerful cloud hardware resources like GPUs and tensor processing units (TPUs).

Obtaining the Data and Code Used in This Book

You can find all necessary data and example code in the book's GitHub repository at *https://github.com/DeepTrackAI/DeepLearningCrashCourse*. To get started, here are some guidelines to download and set up the repository.

To set up manually from GitHub, follow these steps:

1. Visit the repository page.
2. Click **Code** and select **Download ZIP**.
3. Extract the ZIP file in your desired folder.

To download using GitHub Desktop, follow these steps:

1. Download and install GitHub Desktop from *https://desktop.github.com*.
2. Open GitHub Desktop and sign in with your GitHub account.
3. Click **Clone a repository from the Internet**.
4. Enter the repository URL, *https://github.com/DeepTrackAI/Deep LearningCrashCourse*, and select a local path to clone it to.
5. Click **Clone**.

To download using the command line, take these steps:

1. Open your terminal or command prompt.
2. Navigate to the directory where you want to clone the repository.
3. Run the command `git clone https://github.com/DeepTrackAI/DeepLearningCrashCourse.git`.

Once you have downloaded the repository, navigate to the relevant chapter folders to find the code and data for each project. For further instructions, read the README files within each folder.

What's in This Book?

Each chapter of this book progressively builds your understanding of deep learning. The first two chapters provide a fundamental introduction to neural networks, assuming no prior knowledge—essential reading for those new to the field. Best studied sequentially, the following chapters progress through increasingly advanced topics, including state-of-the-art techniques and innovations. The final three chapters are more independent, highlighting complementary methods essential to a well-rounded understanding of deep learning as a whole.

Most chapters include hands-on projects designed to be self-contained so you can focus on the topics that interest you most or that align with your goals. Here's a closer look at each chapter's content:

Chapter 1: Building and Training Your First Neural Network   You'll explore the basics of neural networks, starting with single neurons and gradually building up to multilayer dense networks. You'll learn about activation functions, weight regularization, and training using backpropagation, culminating in the practical project of classifying handwritten digits from the MNIST dataset.

Chapter 2: Capturing Trends and Recognizing Patterns with Dense Neural Networks   You'll focus on regression problems, which involve predicting continuous values rather than categories, thus using neural networks to predict continuous outputs. Starting with simple single-neuron models, you'll progress to complex multilayer networks, learning about mini-batch training and evaluation metrics to improve and validate your models. You'll then apply your acquired knowledge to simulate data by using a digital twin.

Chapter 3: Processing Images with Convolutional Neural Networks Convolutional neural networks are powerful tools for image-processing tasks. You'll learn the fundamentals of convolutions with 1D and 2D data. Then, you'll implement these networks in PyTorch, combining convolutional, activation, pooling, and upsampling layers. This chapter's projects include classifying malaria-infected blood smears, localizing microscopic particles, creating DeepDreams, and transferring the style of images.

Chapter 4: Enhancing, Generating, and Analyzing Data with Autoencoders   You'll encounter encoder-decoder architectures, essential tools for tasks involving data compression and generation. Through practical examples, you'll explore denoising autoencoders, variational autoencoders, and Wasserstein autoencoders, which will teach you how to manipulate and generate data in latent spaces as well as how to detect anomalies.

Chapter 5: Segmenting and Analyzing Images with U-Nets   U-Nets are specialized neural networks designed for image-transformation tasks. You'll learn their architecture and training process through projects such as segmenting images of biological tissues, detecting diffraction-limited features in fluorescence images, and counting cells in biomedical datasets.

Chapter 6: Training Neural Networks with Self-Supervised Learning Self-supervised learning uses the data itself to generate labels for training. You'll explore techniques to exploit symmetries in data, using methods like translations and reflections to improve model performance. Projects focus on particle localization.

Chapter 7: Processing Time Series and Language with Recurrent Neural Networks   Recurrent neural networks are crucial for analyzing sequential data. You'll see the implementation of basic recurrent neural networks, gated recurrent units (GRUs), and long short-term memory (LSTM) networks, applying them to time-series forecasting, such as temperature prediction. You'll also use them to implement a simple text translator.

Chapter 8: Processing Language and Classifying Images with Attention and Transformers   Transformers using attention mechanisms have revolutionized sequence-processing tasks, especially in natural language processing (NLP). You'll learn how attention and transformers work and apply them in tasks like sentiment analysis and image classification, using state-of-the-art models like ViT. You'll also use the attention mechanism to improve the text translator implemented in Chapter 7.

Chapter 9: Creating and Transforming Images with Generative Adversarial Networks   Generative adversarial networks (GANs) are powerful tools for generating synthetic data. You'll learn the architecture and training process of GANs, with practical projects including generating new images from the MNIST dataset, virtually staining a biological tissue, and transforming microscopic images.

Chapter 10: Implementing Generative AI with Diffusion Models Diffusion models provide a powerful framework for data representation and exploration, often exceeding the performance of GANs. This chapter introduces these models and their applications, such as generating new images from the MNIST dataset, generating images from text prompts, and improving the resolution of microscopic images.

Chapter 11: Modeling Molecules and Complex Systems with Graph Neural Networks   Graph neural networks extend neural networks to graph-structured data. You'll explore the basics of graph convolutions and message passing, applying graph neural networks to tasks like predicting molecular properties, simulating complex physical phenomena, and identifying trajectories.

Chapter 12: Continuously Improving Performance with Active Learning   Active learning strategies are essential for efficient model training, optimizing the use of labeled data. You'll discover active learning techniques and their implementation, focusing on how to continuously improve models by selecting the most informative data points for training.

Chapter 13: Mastering Decision-Making with Deep Reinforcement Learning   Reinforcement learning is used for optimizing strategies in dynamic environments. You'll learn the fundamentals of reinforcement learning by teaching an agent to play the classic game of *Tetris*.

Chapter 14: Predicting Chaos with Reservoir Computing   Reservoir computing is a framework for dealing with complex, chaotic systems. You'll gain an understanding of the principles of reservoir computing and apply them to predict chaotic time series, gaining insights into the dynamics of nonlinear systems.

Online Resources

For additional support and resources, you can visit the book's GitHub repository at *https://github.com/DeepTrackAI/DeepLearningCrashCourse*. Here, you'll find tips, code examples, and extra materials that complement the content of each chapter.

In addition, all figures from the book are available in color through the online resources. Readers who purchase the book directly from No Starch Press receive the color ebook automatically, but those who purchase it through other online retailers or in bookshops may not. To ensure everyone has access to the clearest visual material, the color images can be freely downloaded from the book's GitHub repository.

If you run into any issues or have questions, the GitHub repository offers a discussion forum where you can seek help and engage with the authors and other readers. You can also use the Issues section to ask questions, report problems, and clarify any confusion about the code examples. This interactive platform ensures that you have continuous support throughout your learning journey, allowing you to fully benefit from the hands-on approach of this book.

Your feedback is invaluable. Please feel free to contribute your thoughts and suggestions on the GitHub repository. Your input will help improve the materials and provide a better learning experience for everyone.

Time to Start Your Journey

Now it's time to embark on your quest to understand deep learning. As you dive into the concepts and projects within this book, you'll gain not only the knowledge and practical skills necessary to wield powerful deep learning tools but also a nuanced understanding of the technology's potential and pitfalls that will help you navigate the fascinating world of AI. Whether you're driven by curiosity, passion, or ambition, this journey will empower you to play an active role in the deep learning revolution—and maybe even shape its future. So, roll up your sleeves, fire up your neural networks, and let's get started!

1

BUILDING AND TRAINING YOUR FIRST NEURAL NETWORK

In this chapter, you'll learn how to implement an artificial neuron and connect multiple neurons into a dense neural network. Then you'll train dense neural networks to classify points in a plane by implementing the backpropagation algorithm.

This training method is an example of *supervised learning*, a type of machine learning that trains a model on labeled data. In supervised learning, each input is associated with an output, or target, and the neural network learns by iteratively adjusting its parameters to minimize the difference between its predictions and the actual outputs.

By the end of this chapter, you'll be able to build a dense neural network to classify the images of handwritten digits in the Modified National Institute of Standards and Technology (MNIST) dataset—a classic initiation for anyone working in deep learning. Mastering the MNIST dataset classification isn't just a deep learning milestone but also a stepping stone to more-advanced topics like regression, paving your way toward further exploration and more-advanced applications in the chapters ahead.

Classifying Data with a Single Neuron

An *artificial neuron* is a computational unit inspired by the biological neurons found in many multicellular animals. Figure 1-1 illustrates a biological neuron.

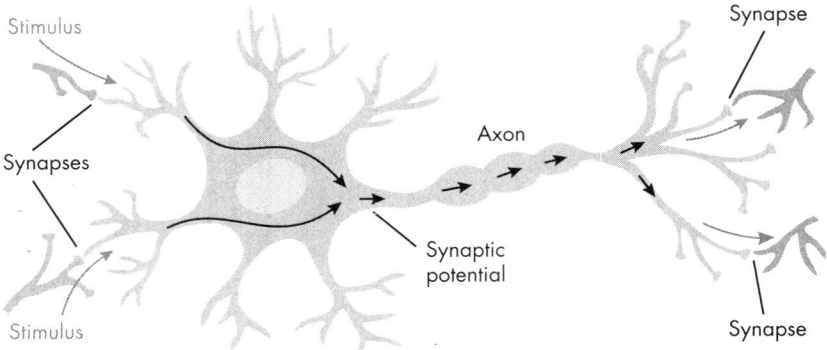

Figure 1-1: A biological neuron

Biological neurons are electrically excitable cells that receive stimulus signals from other neurons through their synapses. When the synaptic potential of a biological neuron exceeds a certain threshold, that neuron emits an electric signal that, in turn, can excite or inhibit other neurons.

Figure 1-2 shows an artificial neuron that emulates this behavior. This is a simple computational unit that responds to input signals with an output activation. The output activation is typically a nonlinear function.

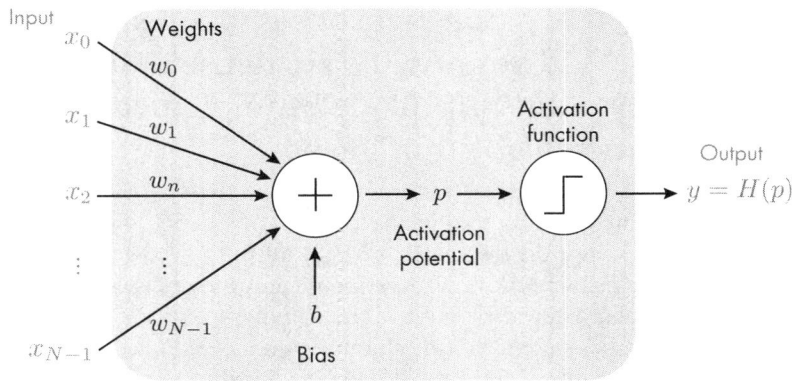

Figure 1-2: An artificial neuron

The artificial neuron shown in Figure 1-2 works in this way:

1. It receives a vector of inputs, $\mathbf{x} = (x_0, \ldots, x_{N-1})$ (corresponding to the synaptic signals received by a biological neuron).

2. It calculates its activation potential (corresponding to the synaptic potential)

$$p = \mathbf{w} \cdot \mathbf{x} + b \qquad (1.1)$$

where $\mathbf{w} \cdot \mathbf{x} = \sum_{0}^{N-1} w_n x_n$ is the weighted sum of the inputs, $\mathbf{w} = (w_0, \ldots, w_{N-1})$ is the vector of the weights, and b is a *bias* that shifts the activation function, enabling more flexibility.

3. Finally, the artificial neuron returns a binary output that is the result of the activation function operating on the activation potential (corresponding to the emitted signal)

$$y = H(p) \qquad (1.2)$$

where H is the Heaviside step function so that $y = 0$ if $p \leq 0$, and $y = 1$ if $p > 0$.

In the rest of this section, you'll write the Python code to implement a single neuron and solve the problem of classifying the points in a line or in a plane into two classes, denoted by the labels 0 and 1. You'll implement this neuron from scratch, step-by-step, using Python's basic NumPy library as well as the Matplotlib library for visualization.

Classifying 1D Data

Using a text editor, open the one-dimensional (1D) dataset from the *data_class _1d_clean.csv* file containing *comma-separated values*, often abbreviated as *CSV* (hence the *.csv* file extension). The first line is the header, which indicates the label of each column. The first column contains the input data. The second column contains the respective classification into the two classes 0 and 1, which are the output, or *target*, data.

Loading the Data

Before you can analyze the data, you need to load it. Start by writing the `load_data_1d(filename)` function shown in Listing 1-1.

```
import csv
from numpy import asarray

def load_data_1d(filename):
    """Load 1D data."""
❶ with open(filename) as file:
        reader = csv.reader(file)
        header = next(reader)
        data = []
        for row in reader:
            data.append(row)
        data = asarray(data).astype(float)
    x = data[:, 0]  # Input
```

```
y = data[:, 1]  # Output/target/ground truth
return (x, y)
```

Listing 1-1: The function to load the 1D data

This function returns the input (x) and output (y) data in the form of NumPy arrays. They both have the same shape, with a single dimension that corresponds to the number of samples in the dataset. (The with statement ❶ ensures that the file is automatically closed when the code execution is done with it.)

It's convenient to create a Python package containing the load_data_1d() function. To do so, simply place it in a file named *loader.py* in the same folder as your code. Then you can import it via the following statement:

```
from loader import load_data_1d
```

You can then use this function to load the data with

```
(x, y_gt) = load_data_1d(filename="data_class_1d_clean.csv")
```

which saves the input data in the variable x and the output data in the variable y_gt, where gt stands for *ground truth*, which corresponds to the expected results. Using this variable name permits you to distinguish it from the predictions made by the neuron, which you'll denote as y_p, where p stands for *predicted*.

Verifying and Visualizing the Data

Before proceeding further, it's good practice to verify that the data has been loaded correctly. First, you can verify that the lengths of the input and output data are equal by using the commands print(len(x)) and print(len(y_gt)), which should both print 10. Then you can also print their values with print("x:", x) and print("y_gt:", y_gt), which should display this:

```
x: [ 0.69890926 -0.66948353 -1.26176998 -0.39901233 -0.06169857 -0.55097679
 -1.48984407 -0.07923319  0.9727034   0.43455583]
y_gt: [1. 0. 0. 0. 1. 0. 0. 1. 1. 1.]
```

Note that these are all floating-point numbers, even though y_gt acquires only values of 0 and 1.

Finally, plot the data using the plot_data_1d() function in Listing 1-2.

```python
import matplotlib.pyplot as plt

def plot_data_1d(x, y_gt):
    """Plot 1D data."""
    plt.scatter(x, y_gt, s=20, c="k")
    plt.xlabel("x0", fontsize=24)
    plt.ylabel("y", fontsize=24)
    plt.tick_params(axis="both", which="major", labelsize=16)
    plt.show()
```

Listing 1-2: The function to plot the 1D data

It's also convenient in this case to create a Python package by placing the plot_data_1d() function in a file named *plotting.py*. You can then import and use it with Listing 1-3.

```
from plotting import plot_data_1d

plot_data_1d(x, y_gt)
```

Listing 1-3: Plotting the 1D data

This listing generates the plot shown in Figure 1-3.

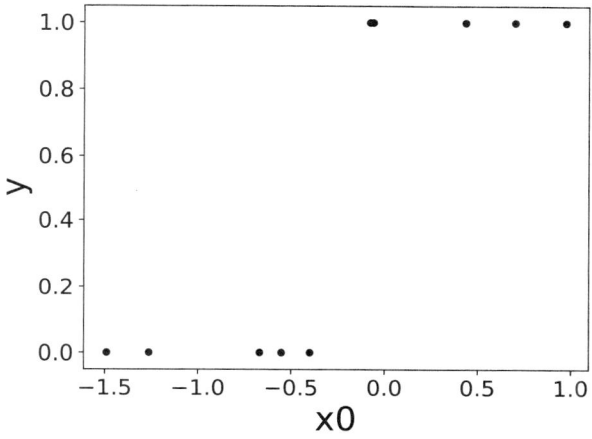

Figure 1-3: The 1D data for classification

Upon examining this plot, you can easily deduce the simulation model that produced this dataset. The model uses a step function that assigns values beneath a certain threshold to 0, while assigning those above it to 1.

Implementing a Single Neuron

You can now implement your first artificial neuron by using the code shown in Listing 1-4.

```
def neuron_clas_1d(w0, x):
    """Artificial neuron for 1D classification."""
    return (w0 * x > 0).astype(int)
```

Listing 1-4: An artificial neuron for 1D classification

This function represents a single neuron with one input (x) and one weight (w0). This neuron returns a binary output equal to 1 (true) if w0 * x > 0, and equal to 0 (false) otherwise. Since the result of the w0 * x > 0 operation is a logical value, it needs to be converted to a numerical form for further use in the neural network; this is done by the astype(int) function.

You can randomly initialize the weight of the neuron via Listing 1-5.

```
from numpy.random import default_rng

rng = default_rng()
w0 = rng.standard_normal()
```

Listing 1-5: Initializing the weight of the neuron

This code first creates an instance of the default Python random-number generator (rng). Next, it creates the w0 weight for the neuron sampled from a standard normal distribution by using rng.standard_normal() to return a Gaussian random number with zero mean and unitary variance.

You obtain the prediction of this neuron for the x input by using the randomly initialized w0 weight with Listing 1-6.

```
y_p = neuron_clas_1d(w0, x)
```

Listing 1-6: Obtaining a prediction from the neuron

This code returns the prediction y_p of the class corresponding to x. Note that this calculates the predictions of the neuron for all the inputs contained in the NumPy array x at the same time.

Now let's test how well this neuron performs its task (even though your expectations shouldn't be very high, as the neuron is randomly initialized). To do this, you can expand the plot_data_1d() function in Listing 1-2 to also plot the predicted results as crosses, resulting in the plot_pred_1d() function in Listing 1-7, which you should also add to your *plotting.py* Python package.

```
def plot_pred_1d(x, y_gt, y_p):
    """Plot 1D data and predictions."""
    --snip--
    plt.scatter(x, y_gt, s=20, c="k", label="ground truth")
    plt.scatter(x, y_p, s=100, c="tab:orange", marker="x", label="predicted")
    plt.legend(fontsize=20)
    --snip--
```

Listing 1-7: The function to plot both the 1D data and the predictions (by modifying Listing 1-2)

NOTE *In this listing, bold highlights changes from the earlier version of the code. We'll use this convention in modified listings throughout the book so you can quickly spot what's new.*

Then import this function and use it to plot the predictions of the neuron with Listing 1-8.

```
from plotting import plot_pred_1d

plot_pred_1d(x, y_gt, y_p=neuron_clas_1d(w0, x))
```

Listing 1-8: Plotting both the 1D data and the predictions

In this way, you should get a plot similar to Figure 1-4.

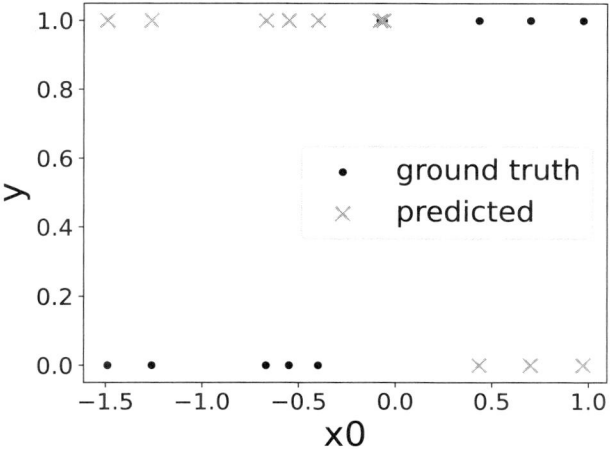

Figure 1-4: Predictions from a randomly initialized neuron

Since the neuron is randomly initialized, its prediction will often be wrong. In fact, since the neuron output is binary, it can produce only two sets of results depending on the sign of w0.

Training the Neuron

If you want to get useful predictions, you need to train your neuron. Given two sets of points to be classified, you can train the weights (and bias, if present) of your artificial neuron iteratively by following these steps:

1. Initialize the weights $\mathbf{w}$ (and bias b) with random values (typically, it's good if these values are of order 1 to ease convergence). This was done when initializing the weight of the neuron in Listing 1-5. (In the case you are currently considering, the neuron has the single w0 weight and no bias.)

2. Choose at random a point $\mathbf{x}$ from one of the two sets, and call $\tilde{y}$ the corresponding desired output (which can assume a value of 0 or 1).

3. Calculate the output with the current weights (and bias), using Equations 1.1 and 1.2—that is, $y = H(\mathbf{w} \cdot \mathbf{x} + b)$.

4. If $y = \tilde{y}$, the prediction is correct. So, you don't need to do anything. Just iterate from step 2.

5. If $y \neq \tilde{y}$, the prediction is incorrect. So, you should update the weights as $\mathbf{w} \to \mathbf{w} - \eta(y - \tilde{y})\mathbf{x}$ (and the bias as $b \to b - \eta(y - \tilde{y})$), where $\eta \in (0, 1]$ is the *learning rate*. Then iterate from step 2.

Listing 1-9 implements this algorithm to train a single neuron with one input and a binary output (and without bias).

```
num_samples = len(x)
num_train_iterations = 100
eta = .1  # Learning rate

for i in range(num_train_iterations):
❶   selected = rng.integers(0, num_samples)  # Select random sample
    x0_selected = x[selected]
    y_gt_selected = y_gt[selected]

    y_p_selected = neuron_clas_1d(w0, x0_selected)  # Neuron prediction

    error = y_p_selected - y_gt_selected  # Calculate error

    w0 = w0 - eta * error * x0_selected  # Update neuron weight

    print(f"i={i} w0={w0:.2f} error={error:.2f}")
```

Listing 1-9: Training a single neuron for binary classification

The two most important parameters of the training are the number of iterations (num_train_iterations), set to 100, which is sufficient for this problem as determined through trial and error, and the *learning rate* (eta), set to .1. During each iteration, the code selects a random sample among the available ones ❶ (returning a random integer between 0 and number_samples - 1, extremes included) and prints the intermediate results of the training at the end of the iteration. You'll notice that the error is always +1, 0, or -1, reflecting the binary nature of the classification results, and the value of w0 becomes stably positive after a while, indicating the convergence of the learning algorithm.

NOTE   *The learning rate is a very important parameter. When setting it, there's a trade-off between the rate of convergence and the risk of overshooting. If the learning rate is too high, the learning process will jump over minima. If the rate is too low, the learning process will take too long to converge or get stuck in undesirable local minima. Therefore, to achieve faster convergence while avoiding oscillations and local minima, the learning rate is often varied during training either in accordance with a learning rate schedule or by using an adaptive learning rate.*

You can now plot the performance of the trained neuron with the plot_pred_1d() function (Listing 1-8), which generates Figure 1-5.

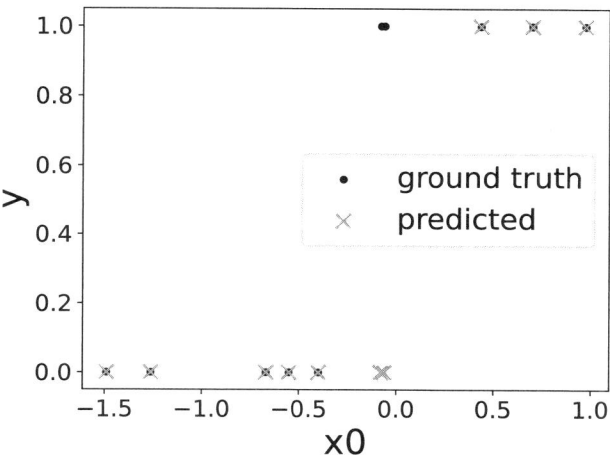

Figure 1-5: Predictions by a trained neuron

These results are a marked improvement over the performance of the untrained neuron you saw in Figure 1-4.

NOTE   *Code Example 1-1, "Classifying 1D Data with a Single Neuron," is available at* https://github.com/DeepTrackAI/DeepLearningCrashCourse. *Navigate to the* Ch01_DNN_classification *folder and then* ec01_1_neuron_class_1d. *The* neuron_class_1d.ipynb *notebook provides a complete code example that loads the data contained in* data_class_1d_clean.csv, *trains a neuron to classify it, and finally uses it to predict the classification of the data in* data_class_1d_clean_test.csv. *This code also requires* loader.py, *which contains the* load_data_1d() *function, and* plotting.py, *which contains the* plot_data_1d() *and* plot_pred_1d() *functions.*

EXERCISES

1-1: To observe the lack of training variability, randomly initialize and train the neuron several times. Why is the trained neuron's performance always the same?

1-2: The neuron can never perfectly predict the data in *data_class_1d _clean.csv*. This is because this neuron is far too simple: With only one trainable parameter (w0), it can converge to only the Heaviside step function or its opposite. So, the output values corresponding to the points at $x = -0.061 \ldots$ and $x = -0.079 \ldots$ are systematically predicted as 0 instead of 1. How can this problem be overcome?

1-3: Retrain the neuron, making the learning rate smaller (for example, eta = 0.01) or larger (for example, eta = 1). How is the training process affected?

1-4: Use the trained neuron to analyze the test data provided in *data _class_1d_clean_test.csv*, which has been generated with the same underlying simulation model used for the training data (but hasn't been seen by the neuron during its training).

Classifying Noisy Data

Now let's consider some noisier data. Load the dataset in the *data_class_1d _noisy.csv* file as follows:

```
(x, y_gt) = load_data_1d(filename="data_class_1d_noisy.csv")
```

The left side of Figure 1-6 shows what you get when you plot the data with the `plot_data_1d()` function, as shown in Listing 1-3.

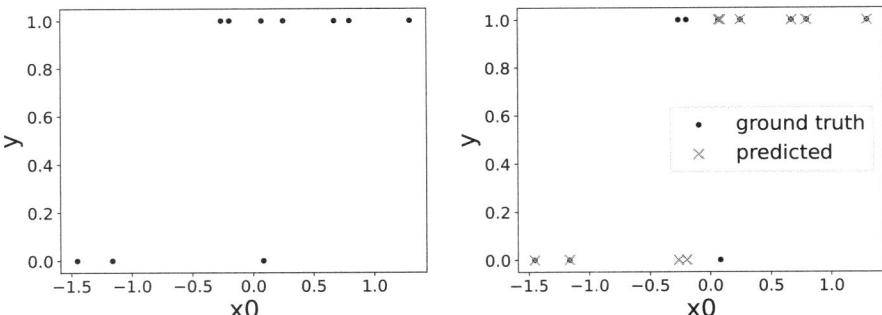

Figure 1-6: The 1D noisy data (left) and the prediction of a trained neuron (right)

Note the absence of a sharp change between the two classes, which is a consequence of the noise added to the underlying simulation model.

Now you can repeat the initialization (Listing 1-5) and the training (Listing 1-9) of the neuron. By plotting the predictions of the trained neuron via the `plot_pred_1d()` function (Listing 1-8), you should get results similar to those shown on the right side of Figure 1-6, which show good agreement between the predictions and the ground truth.

EXERCISE

1-5:   Use the trained neuron to analyze the test data in *data_class_1d _noisy_test.csv*, which has been generated with the same underlying simulation model as the training data.

Attempting to Classify More-Complex Data

Let's further challenge your neuron by considering a more complex dataset. As you may have already noticed, so far you've used only *convex datasets*, or datasets with a single change point between the two classes of the underlying model. Furthermore, the change point has always been around the origin. In fact, these conditions are necessary to get a good classification with the simple neuron you've been using until now because it can only separate the input data into two classes corresponding to positive and negative inputs.

To deal with some more-complex data, load *data_class_1d_nonconvex.csv* with the following code:

```
(x, y_gt) = load_data_1d(filename="data_class_1d_nonconvex.csv")
```

When you plot this data with the plot_data_1d() function, as shown in Listing 1-3, you should get the scatterplot on the left side of Figure 1-7.

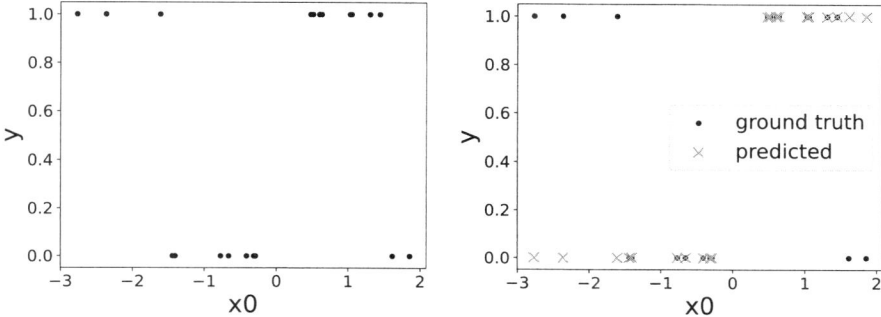

Figure 1-7: The 1D non-convex data (left) and the prediction of a trained neuron (right)

The plot now has at least three change points. Therefore, a single neuron can't learn to distinguish the two classes in this dataset. You can try anyway by initializing the neuron (Listing 1-5), training it (Listing 1-9), and plotting its predicted output with the plot_pred_1d() function (Listing 1-8). This should result in a rather unsuccessful attempt, similar to the predictions from a trained neuron shown on the right side of Figure 1-7.

EXERCISES

1-6:   Use the trained neuron to analyze the test data in *data_class_1d _nonconvex_test.csv*, which has been generated with the same underlying simulation model.

1-7:   Play with the underlying simulation model. Generate your own data and explore how well the neuron works for various cases. Try convex and non-convex as well as noisy and non-noisy data. Try also to move the position(s) of the change point(s).

Classifying 2D Data

Now that you know how to classify 1D data, you can analyze higher-dimensional datasets, such as the dataset in *data_class_2d_clean.csv*. When you open it with a text editor, you should see that the first and second columns contain the input data, which are the two input variables corresponding to the vector $\mathbf{x} = (x_0, x_1)$. The third column contains the respective classification into the two classes 0 and 1.

Loading the Data

First, you need to upgrade the load_data_1d() function in Listing 1-1 to deal with an arbitrary number of inputs. Listing 1-10 shows the modified load_data() function.

```
import csv
from numpy import asarray, reshape

def load_data(filename):
    """Load multidimensional data."""
    with open(filename) as file:
        --snip--
❶  x = data[:, 0:-1]   # Input
❷  num_samples = data.shape[0]
❸  y = reshape(data[:, -1], (num_samples, 1))   # Output/target/ground truth
    return (x, y)
```

Listing 1-10: The function to load multidimensional data (by modifying Listing 1-1)

This code selects as input all data in the *.csv* file except the last column ❶. The resulting two-dimensional (2D) NumPy array has a shape equal to the number of samples (rows) times the number of inputs (columns). The code then extracts the number of samples ❷. Finally, it selects as output the last column and reshapes it into a 2D NumPy array with a shape equal to the number of samples (rows) times 1 (column) to make the subsequent processing of the data easier ❸.

Now add the load_data() function to *loader.py* and import it:

```
from loader import load_data
```

Then you can load the dataset contained in *data_class_2d_clean.csv*:

```
(x, y_gt) = load_data(filename="data_class_2d_clean.csv")
```

Note that this function still works for the special case where the input data is 1D, such as *data_class_1d_clean.csv*, which you can verify by rerunning the listings in the previous section with this function instead of load_data_1d() (but you'll need to update the print statement in Listing 1-9 as shown in Listing 1-18).

Verifying and Visualizing the 2D Data

Again, it's good practice to inspect the data. First, print out the data via print("x:", x) and print("y_gt:", y_gt), which should display this:

```
x: [[ 1.13210319 -1.4066463 ]
 [-1.09042665  1.92715243]
 --snip--
 [-0.54700911 -0.15378581]]
y_gt: [[0.]
 [1.]
 --snip--
 [1.]]
```

Then you can generate a 2D scatterplot of the data with the plot_data_2d() function shown in Listing 1-11, which you should add to *plotting.py*.

```
import matplotlib.pyplot as plt

def plot_data_2d(x, y_gt):
    """Plot 2D data."""
❶  plt.scatter(x[:, 0], x[:, 1], c=y_gt, s=50)
❷  plt.colorbar()
    plt.axis("equal")
    plt.xlabel("x0", fontsize=24)
    plt.ylabel("x1", fontsize=24)
    plt.tick_params(axis="both", which="major", labelsize=16)
    plt.show()
```

Listing 1-11: The function to plot the 2D data

This function color-codes the class of each point by assigning it its ground-truth value, y_gt, as the color parameter, c ❶, and it visualizes the color bar next to the plot ❷.

To import this function and use it to plot the figure, use Listing 1-12.

```
from plotting import plot_data_2d

plot_data_2d(x, y_gt)
```

Listing 1-12: Visualizing the 2D data with a scatterplot

Figure 1-8 shows the resulting scatterplot. The class assignment is indicated by the colors of the points.

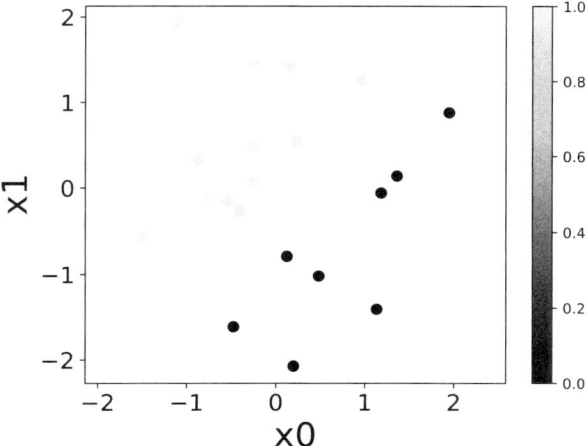

Figure 1-8: A scatterplot of the 2D data for classification

In this scatterplot, you can discern the dataset's underlying model, where a straight line (not depicted) separates the two classes of points. Points above this line are designated as 1, while those below it are marked as 0.

Upgrading the Neuron with Multiple Inputs

Now you need to upgrade your neuron to have two inputs instead of one by modifying Listing 1-4 to add an extra input, leading to Listing 1-13.

```
def neuron_clas_2d(w, x):
    """Artificial neuron for multidimensional classification."
    return (x @ w > 0).astype(int)
```

Listing 1-13: The artificial neuron with multiple inputs (by modifying Listing 1-4)

This code implements a single neuron with multiple inputs (the x NumPy array), an equal number of weights (the w NumPy array), and one binary output (acquiring values 0 or 1). The code x @ w calculates the dot product between the input and the weights, which can be written in a more explicit way as x[0] * w[0] + x[1] * w[1] (so that x @ w > 0 represents all the points of the plane above the line passing by the origin of the coordinate system with slope -w[0] / w[1]).

You can randomly initialize the neuron's weights with Listing 1-14.

```
--snip--
w = rng.standard_normal(size=(2,))
```

Listing 1-14: Initializing the weights of the neuron for 2D classification (by modifying Listing 1-5)

Compared to Listing 1-5, this code adds a second weight for the second input.

To obtain a prediction from this neuron, use Listing 1-15.

```
y_p = neuron_clas_2d(w, x)
```

Listing 1-15: Obtaining a prediction from the neuron for 2D classification (by modifying Listing 1-6)

Then add the predictions by this neuron to the scatterplot of the data by using the plot_pred_2d() function shown in Listing 1-16, obtained by slightly modifying Listing 1-11. Also add the plot_pred_2d() function to the package *plotting.py*.

```
def plot_pred_2d(x, y_gt, y_p):
    """Plot 2D data and predictions."""
    --snip--
    plt.scatter(x[:, 0], x[:, 1], c=y_gt, s=50, label="ground truth")
    plt.scatter(x[:, 0], x[:, 1], c=y_p, s=100, marker="x", label="predicted")
    plt.legend(fontsize=20)
    --snip--
```

Listing 1-16: The function to plot the 2D data and predictions (by modifying Listing 1-11)

Now import this function and use it to plot the predictions of the neuron, as shown in Listing 1-17.

```
from plotting import plot_pred_2d

plot_pred_2d(x, y_gt, y_p=neuron_clas_2d(w, x))
```

Listing 1-17: Plotting both the 2D data and predictions

You should see a plot similar to the one shown in Figure 1-9.

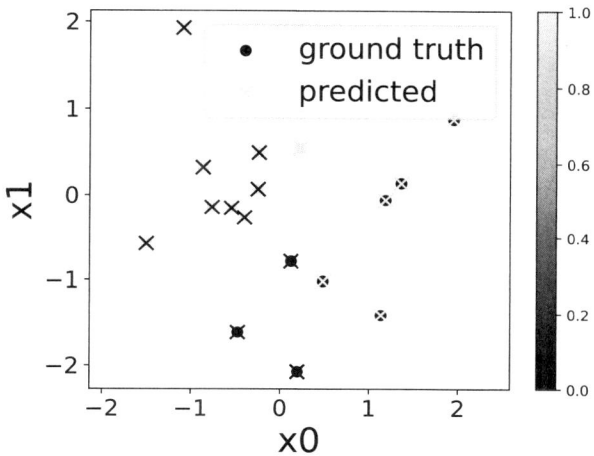

Figure 1-9: Predictions from a randomly initialized neuron

For the randomly initialized neuron, the output is pretty much unrelated to the actual ground truth, as the coefficients are chosen randomly. However, the output isn't completely random, as there's a clear decision boundary. This boundary is the result of the linear equation defined by the weights, which segregates the input plane into two halves, each corresponding to one class of the output.

Training with Two Inputs

Now you can train this neuron with Listing 1-18, which is a small variation on the training code provided in Listing 1-9.

```
--snip--
for i in range(num_train_iterations):
    selected = rng.integers(0, num_samples)  # Select random sample
    x_selected = x[selected]
    y_gt_selected = y_gt[selected]

    y_p_selected = neuron_clas_2d(w, x_selected)  # Neuron prediction
```

```
    error = y_p_selected - y_gt_selected  # Calculate error

    w = w - eta * error * x_selected  # Update neuron weights

❶ print(f"i={i} w0={w[0]:.2f} w1={w[1]:.2f} error={error[0]:.2f}")
```

Listing 1-18: Training the neuron with two inputs (by modifying Listing 1-9)

Note that this code alters the print statement by changing w0 and error to w[0] and error[0] ❶, which is necessary because they are now NumPy arrays as a consequence of the changes to the load_data() function.

The neuron's performance rapidly improves during the training. You can plot the performance of the trained neuron with the plot_pred_2d() function (Listing 1-17). You should get a scatterplot similar to Figure 1-10.

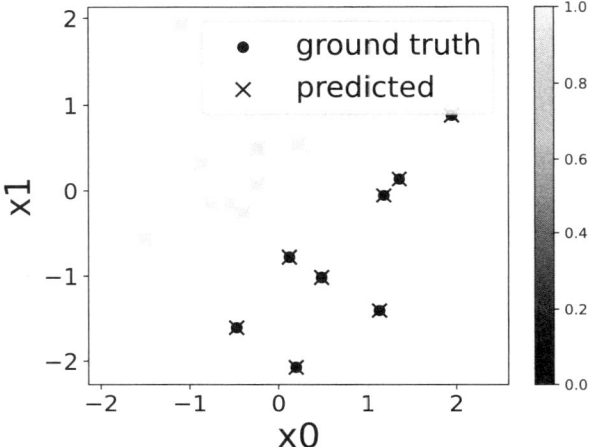

Figure 1-10: Predictions by a trained neuron

This scatterplot shows that the data contained in *data_class_2d_clean.csv* (color of the dots) and the predictions of a trained neuron (color of the crosses) are in excellent agreement with each other.

NOTE *Code Example 1-2, "Classifying 2D Data with a Single Neuron," is available at https://github.com/DeepTrackAI/DeepLearningCrashCourse. Navigate to the* Ch01_DNN_classification *folder and then* ec01_2_neuron_class_2d. *The* neuron_class_2d.ipynb *notebook provides a complete code example that loads the data contained in* data_class_2d_clean.csv, *trains a neuron to classify it, and finally uses it to predict the classification of the data in* data_class_2d_clean_test.csv. *Note that this code also requires* loader.py *containing the* load_data() *function and* plotting.py *containing the* plot_data_2d() *and* plot_pred_2d() *functions.*

1-8: Use the trained neuron to analyze the test data in *data_class_2d _clean_test.csv* generated with the same underlying simulation model.

1-9: Repeat the same training on the noisy data in *data_class_2d _noisy.csv*, and then test the trained neuron on the data in *data_class _2d_noisy_test.csv*.

1-10: Repeat the same training on the data corresponding to classes that are convex—meaning that at least one of the two classes of points is convex, which can be assessed by checking that any two points in the class are joined by a line segment completely contained within the class itself. Examples of such data are in *data_class_2d_convex_clean.csv* and *data_class _2d_convex_noisy.csv*. After training, test the trained neuron on the data in *data_class_2d_convex_clean_test.csv* and *data_class_2d_convex_noisy _test.csv*.

1-11: Repeat the same training on some data corresponding to the non-convex classes in *data_class_2d_nonconvex.csv*. Test the trained neuron on the *data_class_2d_nonconvex_test.csv* dataset.

1-12: Play with the underlying simulation model. Generate your own data and test how well the neuron works for various cases. Try convex and non-convex classes as well as noisy and non-noisy data.

Adding a Bias as Another Dimension

Until now we have disregarded the bias in the neuron (the b in Equation 1.1). Introducing a bias into the neuron allows it to shift the activation function to the left or right. This shift enables the neuron to represent patterns that aren't origin centered, thereby increasing its flexibility and accuracy.

A bias can be added as an additional input with a constant value—for example, equal to +1. To do so, first you need to update the neuron initialization and activation by altering Listing 1-13 as shown in Listing 1-19.

```
def neuron_clas_2d_bias(w, b, x):
    """Artificial neuron with a bias for multidimensional classification."""
    return (x @ w + b > 0).astype(int)
```

Listing 1-19: The artificial neuron with a bias (by modifying Listing 1-13)

Then you need to initialize the bias with Listing 1-20.

```
b = rng.standard_normal()
```

Listing 1-20: Initializing the bias of the neuron

You also need to update the training procedure, altering Listing 1-18 as shown in Listing 1-21.

```
--snip--
for i in range(num_train_iterations):
    --snip--
    y_p_selected = neuron_clas_2d_bias(w, b, x_selected)  # Neuron prediction
    --snip--
    b = b - eta * error  # Update neuron bias

    print(f"i={i} w0={w[0]:.2f} w1={w[1]:.2f} b={b[0]:.2f} err={error[0]:.2f}")
```

Listing 1-21: Training the neuron with the bias (by modifying Listing 1-18)

Now you can repeat the analyses performed in the previous sections by using a neuron with a bias.

EXERCISE

1-13:   Revisit the predictions made in the previous sections by using a neuron with a bias. Verify that the predictions improve, especially when the change point isn't at the origin (for the 1D data) or the line separating the two classes doesn't pass by the origin (for the 2D data).

Using Weight Regularization to Stabilize the Training

Before moving on to more-complex neural network architectures that use more than a single neuron, let's consider *weight regularization*, which permits you to keep the values of the weights in check during the training.

As you might have noticed in the previous examples, the weights often decrease during training to very small values. Thus, since the output is binary, the relative size of the error increases to very large values. Consequently, the weights can change a lot in a single iteration, wreaking havoc on the neuron training.

More generally, having runaway weights (toward either small or large values) is a major problem in the training of any neural network. To prevent this issue, it's possible to regularize the weights. For example, you can *normalize* the weights periodically with a small modification to Listing 1-18 as shown in Listing 1-22.

```
from numpy import sqrt
--snip--
for i in range(num_train_iterations):
    --snip--
    w = w - eta * error * x_selected  # Update neuron weights
    w = w / sqrt(w[0] ** 2 + w[1] ** 2)  # Weight regularization
    --snip--
```

Listing 1-22: Training the neuron with weight regularization (by modifying Listing 1-18)

Dividing the weights by their norm ensures that the norm of the weight vector remains unitary in every iteration, which is equivalent to constraining the weight vector to move on a (hyper)circle.

NOTE *Here, you've used the Euclidean norm, or* L_2 *norm, of the vector, which for a vector $x = (x_0, x_1)$ is:*

$$\|\mathbf{x}\|_2 = \sqrt{x_0^2 + x_1^2}$$

In machine learning, the L_1 norm is often used, corresponding to:

$$\|\mathbf{x}\|_1 = |x_0| + |x_1|.$$

Generally, the L_p norm is defined as

$$\|\mathbf{x}\|_p = \left(|x_0|^p + |x_1|^p \right)^{1/p}$$

for $p \geq 1$.

EXERCISES

1-14:   Repeat the previous training and analysis of 2D data by using weight regularization (why not also for the 1D data case?). Compare these new results with those without regularization.

1-15:   Perform the regularization with the L_1 norm of the weight vector. What differences do you notice? What happens when you use other L_p norms with $p > 1$?

Using Different Activation Functions

Instead of using the Heaviside step function activation, it's possible and often convenient to use other activation functions:

Sigmoid   A smooth, S-shaped function that squashes its input into the range [0,1]

Hyperbolic tangent (tanh)   A smooth function that squashes its input into the range [−1,1]

Linear function   A function that returns the input unmodified

ReLU (rectified linear unit)   A continuous function often used for computational efficiency, given the ease with which it can be calculated together with its derivative

Leaky ReLU   A variation on the ReLU that can help avoid the vanishing gradient problem in deep neural networks

These activation functions are shown in Figure 1-11.

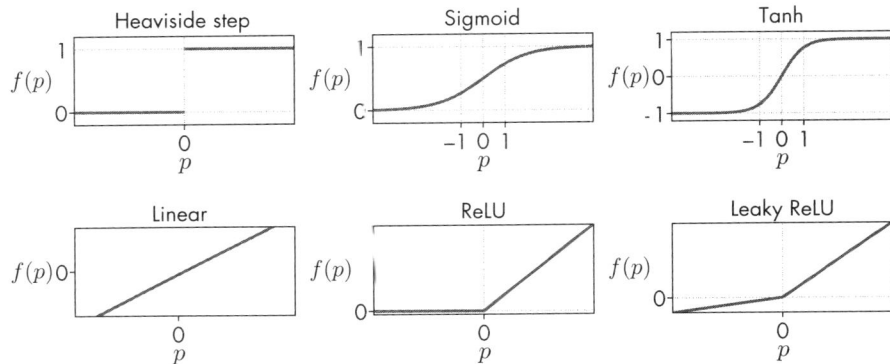

Figure 1-11: Common activation functions

These alternative functions have the advantage of being continuous, so you can use the artificial neuron not only for classification tasks but also for regression tasks (as you'll see in Chapter 2). Furthermore, they're differentiable almost everywhere, which will become important when you use the backpropagation algorithm to train complex neural networks in the next sections.

Nevertheless, even when using these functions, a single artificial neuron is able to classify only datasets that can be separated by a single change point in 1D and by a single straight line in 2D (and by a hyperplane in higher dimensions) because it performs a linear operation computing a weighted sum of its inputs followed by a nondecreasing operation, which translates to a linear decision boundary in the input space. Nonlinearly separable data can't be accurately classified by such a boundary, requiring more-complex models with multiple neurons arranged in layers, as you'll see in the following sections.

EXERCISE

1-16: Revisit all the examples in the previous sections, using various activation functions. Note the corrections you need to implement in order to accommodate continuous activation functions.

Classifying Data with a Two-Layer Neural Network

In this section, you'll see how multiple artificial neurons can be combined into more-complex architectures to perform more-complex tasks. For example, you can start considering a two-layer network, made of artificial neurons with Heaviside step function activation, such as that shown in Figure 1-12. The first layer is usually referred to as the *hidden* layer, whereas the last is called the *output* layer.

NOTE *The number of layers determines the depth of a network. As you'll see later, increasing the number of hidden layers enhances the representational capacity of the network. A network is typically considered "deep" when it contains two or more hidden layers, allowing for more-complex data representations. However, networks with only two or three layers may still be regarded as shallow compared to modern deep learning models, which often contain dozens or even hundreds of layers.*

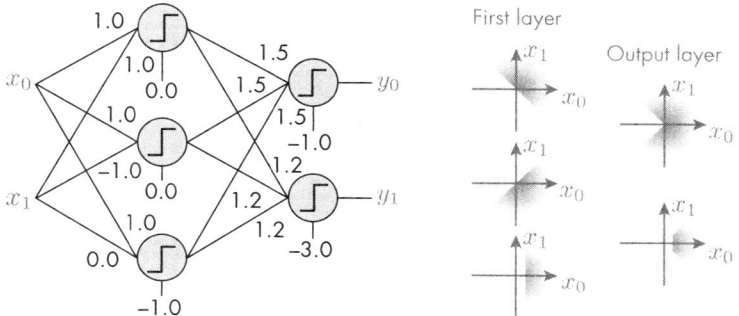

Figure 1-12: A two-layer dense neural network

In Figure 1-12, the annotations near the connections denote the weights, while those beneath each neuron represent the biases. The depicted network features a first hidden layer composed of binary neurons that each execute a linear separation, dividing the input plane into distinct half-planes. Subsequently, the output layer—comprising two neurons—synthesizes these regions into more-complex shapes. Specifically, the first neuron in the output layer combines the outputs from the first layer to create the final partitioning of the plane, whereas the second neuron intersects them.

This process is illustrated on the right side of Figure 1-12: The first column illustrates how each neuron in the first layer bisects the plane, and the second column demonstrates the complex partitioning achieved by the output layer through the combination and intersection of these bisected regions.

This two-layer neural network is an example of a *dense neural network*. A dense neural network consists of multiple stacked layers of neurons. Each neuron in a layer receives inputs from all neurons in the previous layer and sends outputs to all neurons in the following layer, in a classical feed-forward architecture. Dense neural networks are also known as *fully connected neural networks* or *multilayer perceptrons*.

EXERCISES

1-17: Implement the two-layer neural network with the fixed weights illustrated in Figure 1-12 and verify that it works to separate the points of the plane as shown.

(continued)

> **1-18:** Use a two-layer neural network to implement the logic gates by figuring out the appropriate weights yourself. Show that it's possible to implement NOT, AND, OR, and NAND, but not XOR. Can you figure out why XOR is not possible? Can any of these logic gates be implemented using a single neuron?

Implementing a Dense Neural Network

As usual, you'll start by loading the data. Use the `load_data()` function in Listing 1-10 to load the data into *data_class_2d_convex_clean*:

```
from loader import load_data

(x, y_gt) = load_data(filename="data_class_2d_convex_clean.csv")
```

Then plot the data with the `plot_data_2d()` function as shown in Listing 1-12, which should show the plot in Figure 1-13.

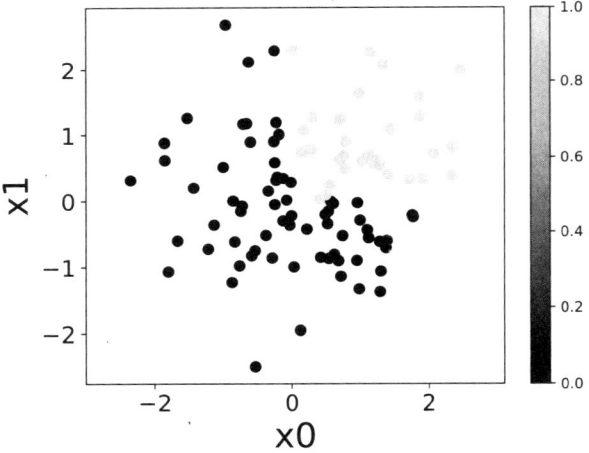

Figure 1-13: A scatterplot of the 2D data with a convex class

As you've seen in Exercise 1-10, this data can't be classified by a single neuron; you'll need to implement a two-layer dense neural network. As a first step, you need to implement the sigmoidal activation function, as shown in Listing 1-23.

```
from numpy import exp

def sigmoid(x):
    """Sigmoid function."""
    return 1 / (1 + exp(-x))
```

Listing 1-23: The sigmoidal activation function

This code defines the sigmoidal function (shown in Figure 1-11), which will be the activation function of each neuron.

You can then implement the dnn2_clas() function in Listing 1-24 to define the neural network.

```
def dnn2_clas(wa, wb, x):
    """Two-layer dense neural network for classification."""
    x_a = x  # Input layer 1
    p_a = x_a @ wa  # Activation potential layer 1
    y_a = sigmoid(p_a)  # Output layer 1

    x_b = y_a  # Input layer 2
    p_b = x_b @ wb  # Activation potential layer 2
    y_b = sigmoid(p_b)  # Output layer 2 (output neuron)

    y_p = y_b  # Network prediction

    return y_p
```

Listing 1-24: The two-layer dense neural network (detailed calculation)

This function implements a two-layer dense neural network that takes the x array as input and returns the continuous output in the y_p array, which takes values between 0 and 1.

The implementation of this neural network can be made more compact, as shown in Listing 1-25.

```
def dnn2_clas(wa, wb, x):
    """Two-layer dense neural network for classification."""
    return sigmoid(sigmoid(x @ wa) @ wb)
```

Listing 1-25: The two-layer dense neural network (compact calculation, by modifying Listing 1-24)

The calculation of the neural network output from the value of the input and of its weight matrices is now done in a single expression, instead of the previous explicit calculation.

You can now define the number of neurons with Listing 1-26.

```
num_neurons = 3
```

Listing 1-26: Defining the number of neurons in the hidden layer

Although num_neurons is set to 3, you can change it.

Now you need to randomly initialize the weight matrices between the inputs and the first layer (wa) and between the first layer and the output (wb) via Listing 1-27.

```
from numpy.random import default_rng

rng = default_rng()
```

```
❶ wa = rng.standard_normal(size=(2, num_neurons))  # Input weights layer 1
❷ wb = rng.standard_normal(size=(num_neurons, 1))  # Input weights layer 2
```

Listing 1-27: Initializing the weight matrices

Since you have two inputs, three neurons in the first layer, and one neuron in the output layer, the weight matrices have dimensions 2×3 ❶ and 3×1 ❷, respectively.

Next, obtain the predictions by this neural network with Listing 1-28.

```
y_p = dnn2_clas(wa, wb, x)
```

Listing 1-28: Obtaining predictions by the dense neural network

Note that the predicted output y_p of this network is a continuous value from 0 to 1, so the class assignment won't be sharp but will have a probabilistic flavor to it.

Plot the output above the ground truth with Listing 1-29.

```
--snip--
plot_pred_2d(x, y_gt, y_p=dnn2_clas(wa, wb, x))
```

Listing 1-29: Plotting the 2D data and the predictions of a two-layer neural network (by modifying Listing 1-17)

This should generate a scatterplot that looks like Figure 1-14.

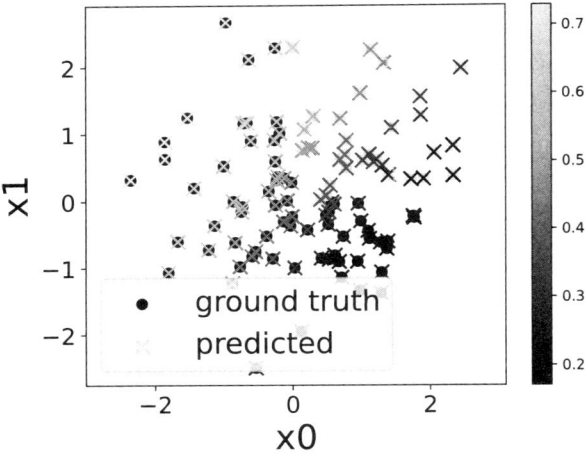

Figure 1-14: Predictions by a randomly initialized two-layer network

Since the output is now a continuous function, the predicted results (color of the crosses) acquire the whole range of values in the color bar. As usual, the predictions are random, so there is no agreement between the ground truth and the neural network prediction—as you should expect given the random initialization of the weights.

Training with Error Backpropagation

Now you need to train this simple neural network. This training aims to minimize the neural network's error, quantified by the *loss function*. This mathematical formula measures the difference between the network's predicted outputs and the actual target values; the goal of training is to find the weight configuration that results in the lowest possible loss.

Conceptually, training involves evaluating the performance of each individual weight within the network to understand its impact on the final output. For example, you might slightly increase the value of a weight and observe the effect on the network's output. If the adjustment results in a closer match to the actual target, the change has decreased the loss function, indicating a step in the right direction. Conversely, if the loss increases, you know to adjust the weight in the opposite direction. This process, repeated across all weights in the network, forms the basis of learning.

For every iteration, each weight is adjusted slightly in the direction that reduces the overall error of the network. This is known as *gradient descent*, where *gradient* refers to the slope of the loss function (representing the direction and rate of change of the error with respect to the weight), and *descent* indicates that the process seeks to move downward toward a minimum error.

You can perform gradient descent efficiently using the very powerful *backpropagation algorithm*, which is arguably the main technique responsible for the widespread success of deep learning. Similarly to the algorithm you used to train a single artificial neuron, it works by iteratively updating each weight.

NOTE   *The backpropagation algorithm computes the gradient of the loss function with respect to each weight by the chain rule, computing the gradient one layer at a time, and iterating backward from the last layer to avoid redundant calculations of intermediate terms in the chain rule. This implies that the activation functions at all neurons need to be differentiable almost everywhere (for example, all the activation functions in Figure 1-11 except the Heaviside step function).*

In the next section, you'll see a simple mathematical derivation of the backpropagation algorithm. If you prefer, you can skip this derivation and jump directly to the implementation provided in Listings 1-30 and 1-31.

Mathematical Derivation

Consider a simple two-layer neural network with N inputs, Q neurons in the hidden layer, and M neurons in the output layer, as shown in the left panel of Figure 1-15.

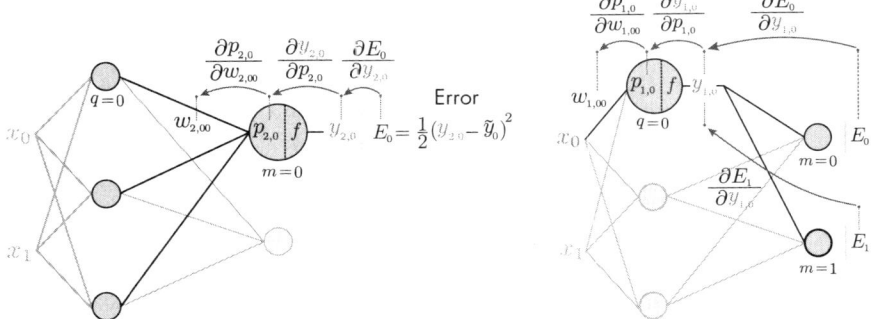

Figure 1-15: Error backpropagation

All neurons have the same (differentiable) activation function $f(p)$, where p is their input potential (the weighted sum of their inputs). Use as the loss function the *mean squared error (MSE)* of the output:

$$E = \frac{1}{2} \sum_{m=0}^{M-1} \left(y_{2,m} - \tilde{y}_m \right)^2 \tag{1.3}$$

Here, $y_{2,m}$ is the output of the mth neuron in the output layer (the subscript 2 indicates the second layer), and $\tilde{y}_m$ is the target value for the mth output.

Now you need to calculate the error gradient with respect to the weights. Start by considering the weight $w_{2,qm}$ between the qth hidden neuron and the mth output neuron (again the subscript 2 indicates the second layer). The error gradient is

$$\frac{\partial E}{\partial w_{2,qm}} = \frac{\partial E}{\partial y_{2,m}} \frac{\partial y_{2,m}}{\partial p_{2,m}} \frac{\partial p_{2,m}}{\partial w_{2,qm}}$$

$$= \underbrace{\left(y_{2,m} - \tilde{y}_m \right) f'(p_{2,m})}_{\delta_{2,m}} y_{1,q}$$

$$= \delta_{2,m} y_{1,q} \tag{1.4}$$

where

$$p_{2,m} = \sum_{q=0}^{Q-1} w_{2,qm} y_{1,q}$$

is the activation potential of the mth output neuron (the subscript 1 indicates the first layer), and $y_{1,q}$ is the output of the qth hidden neuron, which can be calculated as

$$\frac{\partial p_{2,m}}{\partial w_{2,qm}} = y_{1,q}$$

Therefore, you can update these weights as

$$\Delta w_{2,qm} = -\eta \frac{\partial E}{\partial w_{2,qm}}$$

$$= -\eta \, \delta_{2,m} y_{1,q} \tag{1.5}$$

where η is the learning rate and the minus sign indicates that you want to decrease the error.

In an analogous way, you can calculate the error gradient with respect to the weights of the connections between the inputs and the neurons in the hidden layer (right panel in Figure 1-15). You obtain

$$\frac{\partial E}{\partial w_{1,nq}} = \frac{\partial E}{\partial y_{1,q}} \frac{\partial y_{1,q}}{\partial p_{1,q}} \frac{\partial p_{1,q}}{\partial w_{1,nq}}$$

$$= \frac{\partial E}{\partial y_{1,q}} f'(p_{1,q}) x_n \tag{1.6}$$

where $p_{1,q} = \sum_{n=0}^{N-1} w_{1,nq} x_n$ is the activation potential of the qth hidden neuron and x_n is the nth input. Comparing this formula with the previous one, you should notice that, instead of the known errors $(y_{2,m} - \tilde{y}_m)$, there are now the derivatives

$$\frac{\partial E}{\partial y_{1,q}}$$

which you must calculate by backpropagating the errors (hence the name) from the output layer to each hidden neuron:

$$\frac{\partial E}{\partial y_{1,q}} = \sum_{m=0}^{M-1} \frac{\partial E}{\partial y_{2,m}} \frac{\partial y_{2,m}}{\partial p_{2,m}} \frac{\partial p_{2,m}}{\partial y_{1,q}}$$

$$= \sum_{m=0}^{M-1} \underbrace{(y_{2,m} - \tilde{y}_m) f'(p_{2,m})}_{\delta_{2,m}} w_{2,qm}$$

$$= \sum_{m=0}^{M-1} \delta_{2,m} w_{2,qm} \tag{1.7}$$

Therefore, the weights need to be updated as follows:

$$\Delta w_{1,nq} = -\eta \underbrace{f'(p_{1,q}) \sum_{m=0}^{M-1} \delta_{2,m} w_{2,qm}}_{\delta_{1,q}} x_n$$

$$= -\eta \, \delta_{1,q} x_n \tag{1.8}$$

Implementation

To implement the backpropagation algorithm, you need the first derivative of the sigmoid function, shown in Listing 1-30.

```
def d_sigmoid(x):
    """Derivative of sigmoid function."""
    return sigmoid(x) * (1 - sigmoid(x))
```

Listing 1-30: The derivative of the sigmoid function

Then you need to update the training cycle provided in Listing 1-18, as shown in Listing 1-31.

```
from numpy import reshape, sum, transpose
--snip--
❶ num_train_iterations = 10 ** 5
--snip--
for i in range(num_train_iterations):
    # Select random sample
    selected = rng.integers(0, num_samples)
❷   x_selected = reshape(x[selected], (1, -1))
❸   y_gt_selected = reshape(y_gt[selected], (1, -1))

❹   # Detailed neural network calculation
    x_selected_a = x_selected  # Input layer 1
    p_a = x_selected_a @ wa  # Activation potential layer 1
    y_selected_a = sigmoid(p_a)  # Output layer 1

    x_selected_b = y_selected_a  # Input layer 2
    p_b = x_selected_b @ wb  # Activation potential layer 2
    y_selected_b = sigmoid(p_b)  # Output layer 2 (output neuron)

    y_p_selected = y_selected_b

    # Update weights
    error = y_p_selected - y_gt_selected

    delta_b = error * d_sigmoid(p_b)
    wb = wb - eta * delta_b * transpose(x_selected_b)

    delta_a = sum(wb * delta_b, axis=1) * d_sigmoid(p_a)
    wa = wa - eta * delta_a * transpose(x_selected_a)

❺   if i % 100 == 0:
        print(f"{i} y_p={y_p_selected[0, 0]:.2f} error={error[0, 0]:.2f}")
```

Listing 1-31: Training with error backpropagation (by modifying Listing 1-18)

You've now increased the training interactions from 10^2 to 10^5 ❶ in order to get a proper training (try out intermediate values such as 10^3 and 10^4 to see what happens). Note that the number of samples has also increased.

In each training iteration, the code extracts the input ❷ and ground-truth output ❸ in vectorial form so that they have a shape equal to 1 by the number of inputs and 1 by the number of outputs, respectively. This makes the code more readable and more easily generalizable to higher-dimensional inputs.

Then it performs a detailed calculation of the predicted output ❹, as shown in Listing 1-24. This is necessary because the error backpropagation uses some of the intermediate results in this calculation. Finally, the current state of the network is printed once in a while (every 100 iterations) to avoid slowing the training or running out of memory because of the textual output ❺.

You can finally plot the network predictions after training:

```
plot_pred_2d(x, y_gt, y_p=dnn2_clas(wa, wb, x))
```

You should get results similar to those shown in Figure 1-16.

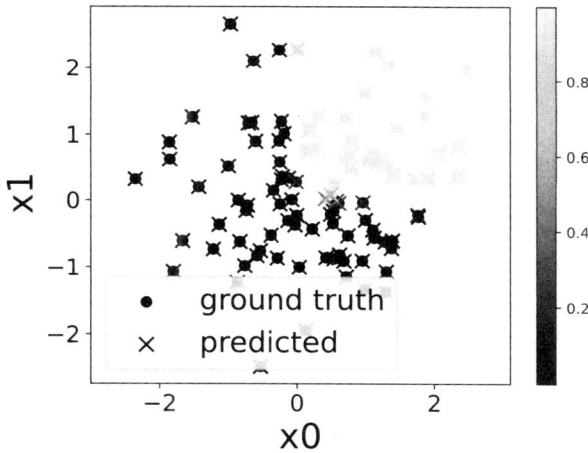

Figure 1-16: Predictions by a trained two-layer neural network

Thanks to the training, the predictions (color of the crosses) and the ground truth (color of the circles) are in very good agreement.

NOTE   *Code Example 1-3, "Classifying 2D Data with a Two-Layer Neural Network," is available at* https://github.com/DeepTrackAI/DeepLearningCrashCourse. *Navigate to the* Ch01_DNN_classification *folder and then* ec01_3_dnn2_class. *The* dnn2_class.ipynb *notebook provides a complete code example that loads the data in the* data_class_2d_convex_clean.csv *file, trains a two-layer neural network to classify it, and finally uses it to classify the test data in the* data_class_2d _convex_clean_test.csv *file. Note that this code also requires* loader.py *containing the* load_data() *function and* plotting.py *containing the* plot_data_2d() *and* plot_pred_2d() *functions.*

Attempting an Impossible Classification

Finally, let's consider an impossible case, which can't be solved by a neural network with two layers (one hidden layer plus the output layer) and will require deeper neural networks with multiple hidden layers.

Load the even more complex dataset *data_class_2d_nonconvex.csv*:

```
(x, y_gt) = load_data(filename="data_class_2d_nonconvex.csv")
```

Then plot the data with the plot_data_2d() function (Listing 1-12), which should give you Figure 1-17.

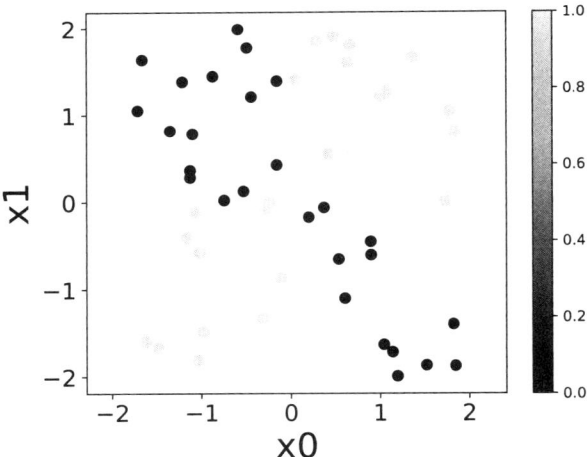

Figure 1-17: Even more complex 2D data

You can clearly see that this dataset can't be classified by a neural network with a single hidden layer such as those you've explored in this section. This is an impossible task because the classification region can't be obtained by the union (or intersection) of half-planes, but instead requires an additional layer capable of combining these two operations.

EXERCISES

1-23: Attempt an impossible classification and verify that the neural network can't correctly predict the data contained in *data_class_2d _nonconvex.csv*.

1-24: Use the data in *data_class_2d_nonconvex.csv* to train an ensemble of two-layer neural networks. Show that it's possible to combine their outputs to classify the data (for example, by multiplying them). Test this approach on the test data provided in *data_class_2d_nonconvex_test.csv*.

Classifying Data with a Three-Layer Neural Network

Neural networks with more layers can perform even more complex classifications. In fact, as the number of layers increases, the neural network becomes capable of classifying more and more complex shapes in the plane.

In this section, you'll see how a neural network with three layers can be used to classify more-complex datasets, like that shown in Figure 1-17. Figure 1-18 shows a three-layer neural network made of neurons with step-function activation.

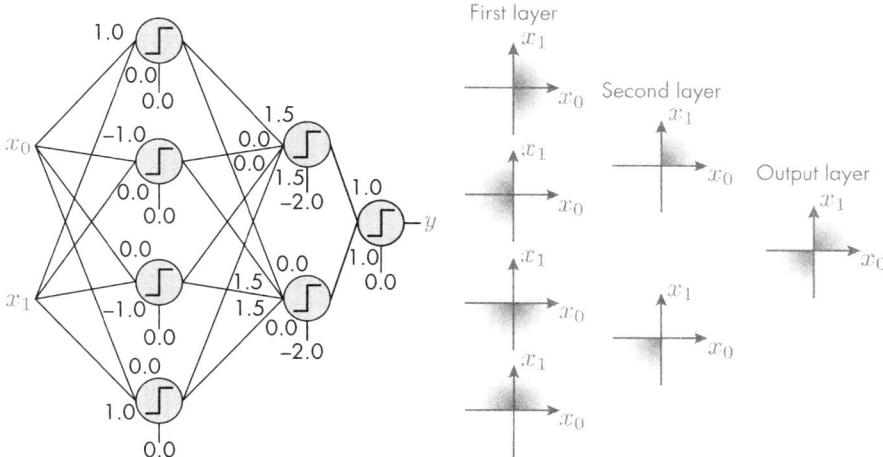

Figure 1-18: A three-layer dense neural network

The annotations near the connections indicate the respective weights, and those below the neurons indicate their biases. Each of the four neurons in the first layer partitions the plane into two half-planes. The two neurons in the second layer then combine these half-planes in various forms. Finally, the neuron in the output layer further elaborates these results.

Deep neural networks can also be realized using neurons with continuous activation functions, leading to even more interesting results. In particular, this permits the neural network to perform not only classifications but also regressions, as you'll see in Chapter 2. In fact, with enough layers and neurons, a neural network becomes able to approximate any function.

To implement a three-layer neural network, change Listing 1-25 as shown in Listing 1-32.

```
--snip--
def dnn3_clas(wa, wb, wc, x):
    """Three-layer dense neural network for classification."""
    return sigmoid(sigmoid(sigmoid(x @ wa) @ wb) @ wc)
```

Listing 1-32: The three-layer dense neural network (by modifying Listing 1-24)

This code implements a three-layer dense neural network for which you need to define the number of neurons in the hidden layers:

```
num_neurons_1 = 7
num_neurons_2 = 5
```

The neural network will have two inputs (x), seven neurons in the first layer (num_neurons_1), five neurons in the second layer (num_neurons_2), and one continuous output (with values from 0 to 1). You can change the number of neurons in the hidden layers.

Then initialize the weight matrices with Listing 1-33.

```
--snip--
❶ wa = rng.standard_normal(size=(2, num_neurons_1))
❷ wb = rng.standard_normal(size=(num_neurons_1, num_neurons_2))
❸ wc = rng.standard_normal(size=(num_neurons_2, 1))
```

Listing 1-33: Initializing the weight matrices of the three-layer neural network (by modifying Listing 1-27)

Since you have two inputs, seven neurons in the first layer, five neurons in the second layer, and one neuron in the output layer, the weight matrices have dimensions 2×7 ❶, 7×5 ❷, and 5×1 ❸.

Now you can obtain the predictions by this neural network:

```
y_p = dnn3_clas(wa, wb, wc, x)
```

The problem then becomes finding the optimal weights for the neural network. The formulas for the error backpropagation you've seen in the previous section can be straightforwardly generalized to update the weights in deeper neural networks. You can train the neural network by modifying Listing 1-31 as shown in Listing 1-34.

```
--snip--
for i in range(num_training_iterations):
    --snip--
    y_selected_b = sigmoid(p_b)  # Output layer 2

    x_selected_c = y_selected_b  # Input layer 3
    p_c = x_selected_c @ wc  # Activation potential layer 3
    y_selected_c = sigmoid(p_c)  # Output layer 3 (output neuron)

    y_p_selected = y_selected_c

    # Update weights
    error = y_p_selected - y_gt_selected

    delta_c = error * d_sigmoid(p_c)
    wc = wc - eta * delta_c * transpose(x_selected_c)

    delta_b = sum(wc * delta_c, axis=1) * d_sigmoid(p_b)
    wb = wb - eta * delta_b * transpose(x_selected_b)

    delta_a = sum(wb * delta_b, axis=1) * d_sigmoid(p_a)
    --snip--
```

Listing 1-34: Training the three-layer neural network with error backpropagation (by modifying Listing 1-31)

Now revisit the previous examples and test how they work with a deeper, three-layer neural network. In particular, by using a three-layer neural network, you should now be able to classify the *data_class_2d_nonconvex.csv* dataset, shown in Figure 1-17, which is impossible to classify with a two-layer neural network.

EXERCISES

1-27: Determine the minimum number of layers and neurons as well as their weights to correctly classify the data in *data_class_1d_nonconvex.csv*.

1-28: Mathematically derive the error backpropagation formulas for neural networks with three layers. Then generalize these formulas to an arbitrary number of layers.

Project 1A: Classifying Handwritten Digits

You'll now build a neural network to classify images. Then you'll use it to tackle the classical problem of classifying the handwritten digits in the MNIST dataset. You'll also learn to use confusion matrices, a common graphical tool to gain insights into the performance of a classifier.

Using the MNIST Digit Dataset

Recognizing the handwritten digits of the MNIST dataset (*http://yann.lecun.com/exdb/mnist/*), constructed by Yann LeCun and Corinna Cortes in 1998, is a classical benchmark for machine learning. The task consists of recognizing handwritten digits from 0 to 9 in 28×28–pixel images. The dataset contains 60,000 training images and 10,000 test images.

Importing the Data

You can download the MNIST images from the GitHub repository (*https://github.com/DeepTrackAI/MNIST_dataset*), as shown in Listing 1-35. This requires an active internet connection.

```
import os

if not os.path.exists("MNIST_dataset"):
 ❶ os.system("git clone https://github.com/DeepTrackAI/MNIST_dataset")

❷ train_path = os.path.join("MNIST_dataset", "mnist", "train")
❸ train_images_files = sorted(os.listdir(train_path))
```

Listing 1-35: Downloading the MNIST dataset

This code downloads the MINST digits into the folder *MNIST_dataset* ❶. The Python os.path.join() function creates the path to the folder containing the training images to make the path platform independent ❷, and sorted() sorts the list alphabetically, again to ensure that the order is platform independent ❸. You can verify that this list contains 60,000 images with print(len(train_images_files)). The first digit in the filename of each image is the ground-truth value of the digit so that the images are called *0_000000.png*, *0_000001.png*, . . . , *1_000000.png*, and so on.

Since the MNIST dataset is small enough to be held in memory, you can load all the images at once using Listing 1-36.

```
import matplotlib.pyplot as plt

train_images = []
for file in train_images_files:
    image = plt.imread(os.path.join(train_path, file))
    train_images.append(image)
```

Listing 1-36: Loading the digit images in memory

Use `print(len(train_images))` to double-check that the resulting list contains 60,000 images. You can further verify that the images have 28×28 pixels with `print(train_images[0].shape)`.

Since the digit is encoded as the first character of the filename, you can extract the ground-truth digits from the filenames via Listing 1-37.

```
train_digits = []
for file in train_images_files:
    filename = os.path.basename(file)
    digit = int(filename[0])
    train_digits.append(digit)
```

Listing 1-37: Extracting the ground-truth digits

Verify that there are 60,000 ground-truth digits with `print(len(train_digits))`.

Visualizing the Data

Now let's use Listing 1-38 to visualize some of the MNIST digits and their respective ground-truth labels.

```
import numpy as np

fig, axs = plt.subplots(nrows=3, ncols=10, figsize=(20, 6))
for ax in axs.ravel():
    idx_image = np.random.choice(60000)
    ax.imshow(train_images[idx_image], cmap="Greys")
    ax.set_title(f"Label: {train_digits[idx_image]}", fontsize=20)
    ax.axis("off")
plt.show()
```

Listing 1-38: Plotting 30 MNIST digits together with their ground-truth labels

These digits and labels are shown in Figure 1-19.

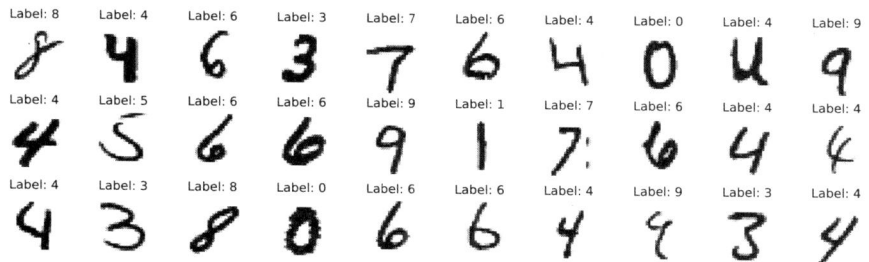

Figure 1-19: The images and ground-truth labels for 30 MNIST digits

By visually inspecting the digits, you can check that they have been correctly imported and that their labels are correct.

Implementing the Neural Network

You'll now define the neural network to classify the digits by using the
MultiLayerPerceptron class from the Deeplay Python library. This class makes
defining and training the neural network much easier (but less instructive!)
than doing it from scratch, as you've done when implementing the two-layer
and three-layer neural networks in the previous sections.

You can start with a small dense neural network with two hidden layers
of 32 neurons each, using Listing 1-39.

```
import deeplay as dl
from torch.nn import Sigmoid

mlp_template = dl.MultiLayerPerceptron(
    in_features=28 * 28, hidden_features=[32, 32], out_features=10,
)
❶ mlp_template[..., "activation"].configure(Sigmoid)
❷ mlp_model = mlp_template.create()
```

Listing 1-39: Defining a dense neural network

This code defines a dense neural network with 784 = 28 × 28 inputs (one
for each pixel in the digit image, in_features). This network has two hidden
layers with 32 neurons each (hidden_features), with sigmoid activation ❶
instead of the default ReLU activation; you can easily change the depth
and breadth of the neural network by altering the value of hidden_features.
The output layer has 10 neurons (out_features), one for each digit, also with
sigmoid activation ❶. The code then creates a concrete PyTorch instance of
this neural network ❷.

When you print a summary of the neural network with print(mlp_model),
you get the following:

```
MultiLayerPerceptron(
  (blocks): LayerList(
    (0): LinearBlock(
    ❶ (layer): Linear(in_features=784, out_features=32, bias=True)
      (activation): Sigmoid()
    )
    (1): LinearBlock(
    ❷ (layer): Linear(in_features=32, out_features=32, bias=True)
      (activation): Sigmoid()
    )
    (2): LinearBlock(
    ❸ (layer): Linear(in_features=32, out_features=10, bias=True)
      (activation): Sigmoid()
    )
  )
)
```

This summary lets you confirm the parameters used to initialize this network, including the number of input features (in_features=784 ❶), the hidden layers' dimensions (out_features=32 for both hidden layers ❶ ❷), and the number of output features (out_features=10 ❸). You can also see that the neural network has three dense layers (Linear) with sigmoid activations. Furthermore, you can print the number of trainable parameters with

```
print(f"{sum(p.numel() for p in mlp_model.parameters())} trainable parameters")
```

which tells you that this small neural network has 26,506 parameters (weights) to optimize.

Next, you need to assign the neural network a loss function and an *optimizer*, which defines an algorithm to update the weights of the neural network during training. This is sometimes known as *compiling* the neural network. You can do this with Listing 1-40.

```
from torch.nn import MSELoss

classifier_template = dl.Classifier(
    model=mlp_template, num_classes=10, make_targets_one_hot=True,
    loss=MSELoss(), optimizer=dl.SGD(lr=.1),
)
classifier = classifier_template.create()
```

Listing 1-40: Compiling the neural network

This code loads the configuration of the dense neural network (model=mlp _template). It sets the number of classes to 10 (num_classes=10), aligning with the 10 possible digits. It also specifies that the ground-truth digits are to be transformed into *one-hot vectors* (make_targets_one_hot=True), a binary encoding format where the index corresponding to the digit is marked with a 1, while all other indices are 0, effectively creating a unique binary representation for each digit. Finally, it sets the loss function to the mean squared error loss (Equation 1.3, loss=MSELoss()) and the optimizer to *stochastic gradient descent (SGD)* (optimizer=dl.SGD(lr=.1)), which refines the model's parameters by moving against the gradient of the loss function, computed from random data subsets—consistent with the methods you've used thus far.

When you print the summary of the classifier with print(classifier), you get the following additional information:

```
Classifier(
  (loss): MSELoss()
  (train_metrics): MetricCollection(
    (MulticlassAccuracy): MulticlassAccuracy(),
    prefix=train
  )
  (val_metrics): MetricCollection(
    (MulticlassAccuracy): MulticlassAccuracy(),
    prefix=val
  )
```

```
  (test_metrics): MetricCollection(
    (MulticlassAccuracy): MulticlassAccuracy(),
    prefix=test
  )
  (model): MultiLayerPerceptron(
    --snip--
  )
  (optimizer): SGD[SGD](lr=0.1)
)
```

This addition to the summary specifies the loss function; the metrics used for the training, validation, and testing; and the optimizer.

Training and Testing

Before proceeding to train the neural network, you need to create a *data loader*, which is an object that manages the data to be passed to the neural network. The simplest way to create a data loader from data already in memory is to create a list of (*sample, ground_truth*) tuples. This can easily be achieved using the Python native function zip(), as shown in Listing 1-41.

```
train_images_digits = list(zip(train_images, train_digits))
train_dataloader = dl.DataLoader(train_images_digits, shuffle=True)
```

Listing 1-41: Defining the data loader

Shuffling the training data (shuffle=True) prevents bias and ensures that the model is exposed to the samples in a varied order, reducing overfitting risks.

You should also create a *trainer*. This object manages the training and evaluation—for example, deciding what hardware to use (CPU or GPU) and when to stop training, save the model, log the training, and evaluate the metrics. You can do this with

```
trainer = dl.Trainer(max_epochs=1, accelerator="auto")
```

which creates a trainer for a single *epoch* (a single pass through the entire training set) and with automatic hardware acceleration (it'll use a GPU if available and, otherwise, a CPU).

You can finally train the neural network:

```
trainer.fit(classifier, train_dataloader)
```

This code trains the neural network for one epoch—that is, iterating only once through the entire dataset. Depending on your hardware, this code can take from a few to several minutes to run. Be patient! As you'll use increasingly complex neural networks, the training times will be even longer.

Calculating Accuracy

To evaluate how well the neural network performs, you need a new set of images and corresponding ground-truth labels. This is to ensure that the trained model performs as expected on images it has never seen before.

NOTE   *As the size of a neural network grows, so does its ability to memorize every image in the input data instead of formulating generalizable rules from common patterns. This phenomenon is known as overfitting, which you'll see in detail in Chapter 2.*

This set of images and labels is known as the *test dataset* (also sometimes called the *validation dataset*), which you'll learn about in more detail in Chapter 2. As you've seen, the MNIST dataset has 10,000 annotated images set aside for testing. You can load and flatten this test data using Listing 1-42.

```
test_path = os.path.join("MNIST_dataset", "mnist", "test")
test_images_files = sorted(os.listdir(test_path))

test_images, test_digits = [], []
for file in test_images_files:
    image = plt.imread(os.path.join(test_path, file))
    test_images.append(image)

    filename = os.path.basename(file)
    digit = int(filename[0])
    test_digits.append(digit)

test_images_digits = list(zip(test_images, test_digits))
❶ test_dataloader = dl.DataLoader(test_images_digits, shuffle=False)
```

Listing 1-42: Loading the test data

Note that the test data doesn't need to be shuffled ❶.

In deep learning and machine learning, the *accuracy* provides a measure of a model's performance by indicating the proportion of correct predictions it makes. You can compute the accuracy of the neural network model as follows:

```
trainer.test(classifier, test_dataloader)
```

This code evaluates the performance of `classifier` on the test dataset provided by `test_dataloader`. It calculates the accuracy as the number of correct predictions divided by the total number of predictions, providing a straightforward metric for the model's capability to generalize to unseen data.

You should get an accuracy of about 0.67. This accuracy isn't great, but don't worry, you'll substantially improve it in the next sections.

Visualizing Performance with a Confusion Matrix

You can use confusion matrices to visualize any errors the neural network is making and to gain insights that can help you improve its architecture and training *hyperparameters*. These control how the model is structured and learns.

Hyperparameters, unlike the trainable parameters that the model optimizes during training, are set before the training process begins and include values like the number of layers and neurons, the learning rate, the batch size, and the number of epochs. These settings dictate the model's learning behavior and are crucial for fine-tuning performance, but they don't change through backpropagation like trainable parameters do.

A *confusion matrix* is a square matrix with a number of rows and columns equal to the number of classes in the classification problem—10 in this case. Each row and each column corresponds to one class in the classification problem, ordered arbitrarily but equally for the two axes. In this case, the classes have a natural ordering, which is the order of the digits. An element $c_{i,j}$ of the confusion matrix represents the number of times the neural network assigned the predicted class j to the actual class i. For example, in our case, $c_{3,5}$ corresponds to the number of times the neural network (incorrectly) classified an image depicting the digit 3 as the digit 5. This representation makes it easy to see which classes the model is most commonly confusing—hence the name.

NOTE *We've chosen to define the confusion matrix with the ground-truth digit assigned to the first axis and the predicted digit assigned to the second axis, but the opposite is also a valid (and common) choice.*

You can plot the confusion matrix with the `plot_confusion_matrix()` function shown in Listing 1-43.

```
from seaborn import cubehelix_palette, heatmap

def plot_confusion_matrix(classifier, dataloader):
    """Plot confusion matrix."""
    confusion_matrix = np.zeros((10, 10), dtype=int)
❶ for image, gt_digit in dataloader:
        predictions = classifier(image)
        max_prediction, pred_digit = predictions.max(dim=1)
        np.add.at(confusion_matrix, (gt_digit, pred_digit), 1)

    plt.figure(figsize=(10, 8))
❷ heatmap(confusion_matrix, annot=True, fmt=".0f", square=True,
        cmap=cubehelix_palette(light=0.95, as_cmap=True), vmax=150)
    plt.xlabel("Predicted digit", fontsize=15)
    plt.ylabel("Ground truth digit", fontsize=15)
    plt.show()
```

Listing 1-43: The function to plot the confusion matrix

For simplicity, this code uses the Python package Seaborn, which simplifies the visualization of common statistical measures, but a similar effect can be achieved using `matplotlib.matshow`. The confusion matrix is computed by iterating through all the images in the test dataset ❶.

Among the various possible options to plot the confusion matrix ❷, this code uses `annot=True` to show the value of each element as text on top of a color, `fmt=".0f"` to define how the annotation text should be formatted for visual clarity, `square=True` to plot the confusion matrix as a square instead of a rectangle, and `vmax=150` to constrain the color bar to show only values up to 150, which increases the contrast for values not on the diagonal (which are typically comparatively small, at least if the classifier works well).

You can plot the confusion matrix of this first attempt at training the network:

```
plot_confusion_matrix(classifier, test_dataloader)
```

This should plot a confusion matrix similar to that shown in Figure 1-20.

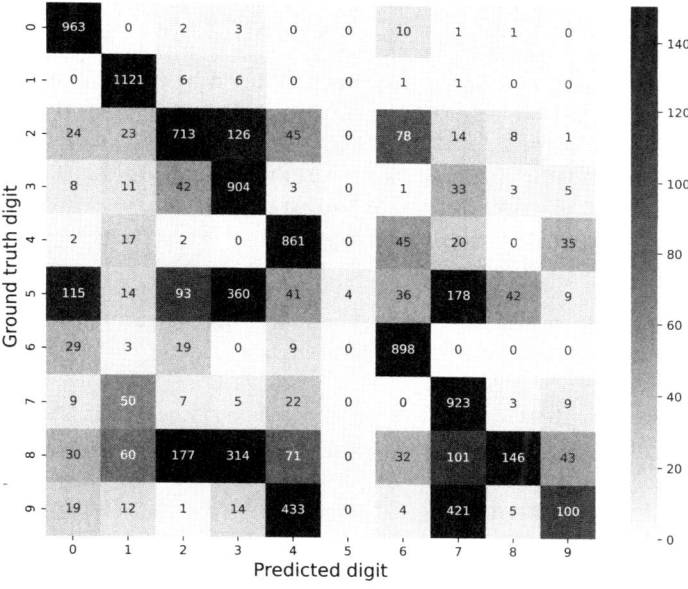

Figure 1-20: A confusion matrix of the first neural network

The 5s, 8s, and 9s are the hardest digits to classify for this neural network. The 2s are also quite hard. However, these difficulties may not be consistent across training sessions because of variations in the weight initialization, data shuffling, and other stochastic elements in the training process.

Making Improvements

In this section, you'll proceed to improve your neural network and its training, as is usual in developing machine learning solutions. By gradually trying some new (and fundamental) ideas (covered in more detail in the following chapters), you'll see how they affect the network's performance, and you'll gain valuable intuition about which hyperparameters are most relevant. Specifically, you'll alter the output activation of the network, the activation functions of the neurons, and the training process itself.

Output Representation

Using a proper output normalization function can significantly enhance the neural network's performance. Presently, the network assigns a value from 0 to 1 to each digit, which you can interpret as a probability. However, since each image represents a single digit, the output probabilities across all possible digit classes should sum to 1 to reflect the exclusive nature of the classifications. This adjustment ensures that the network's output represents a proper probability distribution over the digit classes, which can be crucial for the network to provide more confident and accurate predictions.

This adjustment is typically done using *softmax activation*, defined as

$$y_{\text{norm},m} = \frac{e^{y_m}}{\sum_{m=0}^{9} e^{y_m}} \tag{1.9}$$

where y_m are the linear outputs produced by the final layer's neurons before any activation is applied, often referred to as *logits*, and $y_{\text{norm},m}$ are the normalized outputs.

You can use softmax activation by modifying the architecture of the network and its compilation, as shown in Listing 1-44.

```
from torch.nn import Softmax

❶ classifier_template[..., "activation#-1"].configure(Softmax, dim=-1)
classifier_softmax = classifier_template.create()

trainer_softmax = dl.Trainer(max_epochs=1, accelerator="auto")
trainer_softmax.fit(classifier_softmax, train_dataloader)

trainer_softmax.test(classifier_softmax, test_dataloader)
```

Listing 1-44: Using a softmax output activation

This code uses a softmax activation in the output layer ❶ (here, indicated by the index -1 in "activation#-1").

You should achieve an accuracy of about 0.77. You can plot the confusion matrix of this second attempt:

```
plot_confusion_matrix(classifier_softmax, test_dataloader)
```

This should produce a confusion matrix similar to that shown in Figure 1-21.

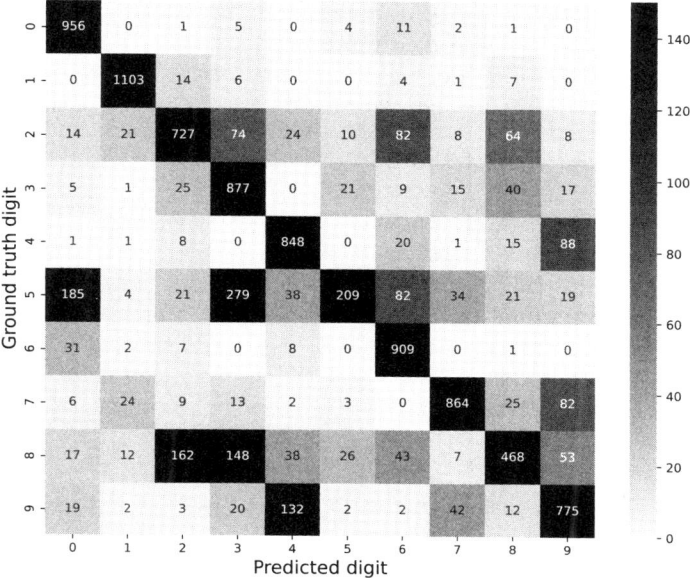

Figure 1-21: A confusion matrix of the second neural network

The same digits (5s, 8s, and 9s) are still being confused as in the previous attempts, though to a lesser extent. You can hypothesize that these digits are universally harder to distinguish.

Even though you are still using the MSE loss here, it is more common to pair a softmax output layer with a loss function known as *categorical cross-entropy loss*, defined as

$$L_{ce} = -\sum_{m=0}^{9} \tilde{y}_m \log y_{norm,m} \qquad (1.10)$$

where $\tilde{y}_m$ are the ground-truth one-hot-encoded classes. A useful property of categorical cross-entropy is that minimizing it is equivalent to maximizing the likelihood estimation. However, to use categorical cross-entropy, the predictions need to be constrained from 0 to 1, and must sum to 1, which is ensured by the softmax activation.

Activation Functions

You can further enhance the performance of your neural network by modifying the activation functions of the neurons. Activation functions play a crucial role in introducing nonlinearity into the network, allowing it to discover and learn more-complex patterns in the data.

While sigmoidal functions have traditionally been used, they suffer from the problem of vanishing gradients for large positive or negative input values, which can slow the learning process using backpropagation or even prevent the network from learning at all. The ReLU function has emerged as a popular alternative because of its ability to maintain a strong gradient for positive input values, thus accelerating the learning process and leading to better performance on complex tasks.

With this in mind, you should proceed to update the network's activation functions from sigmoid to ReLU, as detailed in Listing 1-45.

```
from torch.nn import ReLU

❶ classifier_template[..., "activation#:-1"].configure(ReLU)
classifier_relu = classifier_template.create()

trainer_relu = dl.Trainer(max_epochs=1, accelerator="auto")
trainer_relu.fit(classifier_relu, train_dataloader)

trainer_relu.test(classifier_relu, test_dataloader)
```

Listing 1-45: Changing the activation functions of the neurons to ReLU

This code sets the activation functions of all neurons to ReLU, except for the output layer ❶ (as indicated by the range :-1 in "activation#:-1").

You should now have an accuracy of around 0.94. You can plot the corresponding confusion matrix:

```
plot_confusion_matrix(classifier_relu, test_dataloader)
```

This should generate a confusion matrix similar to that in Figure 1-22.

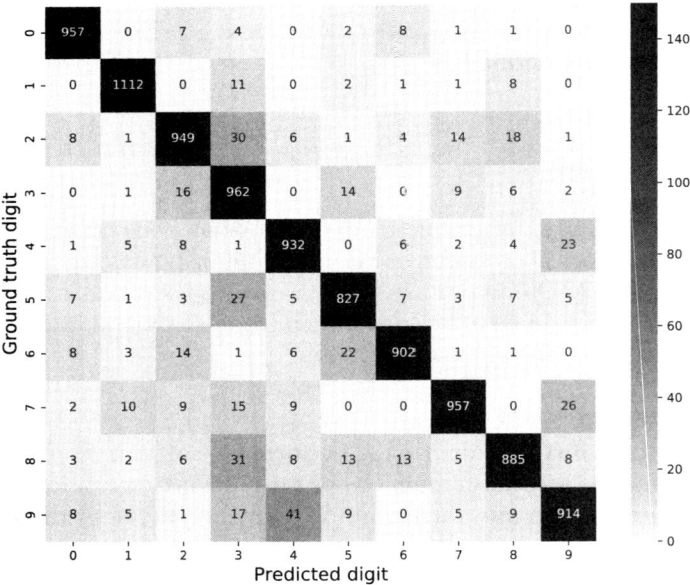

Figure 1-22: A confusion matrix of the third neural network

This shows a net improvement of the quality of the network predictions.

Mini-Batches and Optimizer

Batch size and training length are the next hyperparameters you can play with to see how they affect performance. Using a batch size larger than 1 allows the neural network to calculate the gradients from the average of many samples at once. This, in turn, achieves two results. First, it improves the computational efficiency of the training, allowing you to train on more data in the same amount of time. Second, it stabilizes the training by better approximating the optimal direction to update each weight in each training step.

However, this isn't to say that a larger batch size is always better. For example, the increased stochasticity from smaller batch sizes can help the neural network escape local minima in the optimization landscape.

You'll start by increasing the batch size:

```
train_dataloader_batch = dl.DataLoader(train_images_digits, shuffle=True,
                                       batch_size=32)
```

This creates a new data loader with a batch size of 32.

The choice of optimizer can also have a major impact on the training. Using plain SGD for updating weights is straightforward but generally not optimal because it can be inefficient and slow to converge, often getting stuck in suboptimal points of the complex loss landscape.

Modern deep learning almost universally uses extensions such as *root mean squared propagation (RMSprop)* or *Adam* (D.P. Kingma and J. Ba, "Adam: A Method for Stochastic Optimization," arXiv preprint 1412.6980, 2014). The main advantage of these alternatives is that they change the learning rate for each weight individually during training. Each algorithm has its own way of doing so, but using some type of *momentum* is common. For example, a weight that is updated in the same direction multiple times in a row will gain momentum and take larger steps at each iteration, while a weight that changes direction frequently will have less momentum and take smaller steps.

You can use RMSprop as shown in Listing 1-46. Having increased the batch size, you can also increase the number of epochs to take advantage of the faster training.

```
❶ classifier_template.configure(optimizer=dl.RMSprop(lr=0.001))
  classifier_rmsprop = classifier_template.create()

❷ trainer_rmsprop = dl.Trainer(max_epochs=10, accelerator="auto")
  trainer_rmsprop.fit(classifier_rmsprop, train_dataloader_batch)

  trainer_rmsprop.test(classifier_rmsprop, test_dataloader)
```

Listing 1-46: Changing the optimizer and increasing the number of epochs

This code sets the optimizer to RMSprop ❶ with a learning rate of 0.001 and increases the number of epochs to 10 ❷.

You should now get an accuracy of around 0.97. You can plot the relative confusion matrix:

```
plot_confusion_matrix(classifier_rmsprop, test_dataloader)
```

The confusion matrix should look similar to that shown in Figure 1-23.

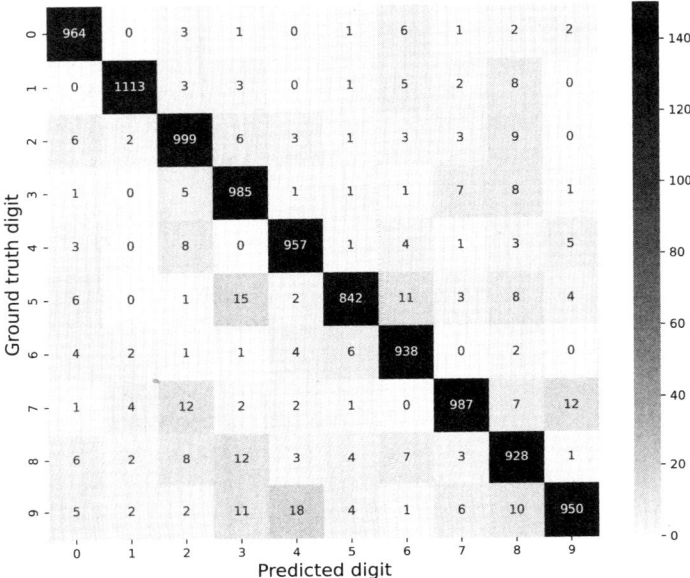

Figure 1-23: A confusion matrix of the fourth neural network

Compared to the initial network in Figure 1-20, the errors are fewer and much more evenly distributed.

Performing Failure Analysis

Finally, you can learn a lot by checking for which inputs the network fails. In fact, this can give you further insights into which digits are still difficult for the neural network to classify, thereby suggesting ways to improve its performance. You can select and plot a few inaccurately predicted digits by using Listing 1-47.

❶ num_images_x_digit = 3

```
plt.figure(figsize=(10, num_images_x_digit))

num_fails_x_digit = np.zeros(10, int)
for image, gt_digit in test_dataloader:
    gt_digit = int(gt_digit)

    if num_fails_x_digit[gt_digit] < num_images_x_digit:
```

```
            predictions = classifier_rmsprop(image)
            max_prediction, pred_digit = predictions.max(dim=1)

            if pred_digit != gt_digit:
                num_fails_x_digit[gt_digit] += 1

                plt.subplot(num_images_x_digit, 10,
                            (num_fails_x_digit[gt_digit] - 1) * 10 + gt_digit + 1)
                plt.imshow(image.squeeze(), cmap="Greys")
                plt.annotate(str(int(pred_digit)), (.8, 1), (1, 1),
                            xycoords="axes fraction", textcoords="offset points",
                            va="top", ha="left", fontsize=20, color="red")
                plt.axis("off")

        if (num_fails_x_digit >= num_images_x_digit).all():
            break

plt.tight_layout()
plt.show()
```

Listing 1-47: Failure analysis

This code selects the first three ❶ misclassified images for each digit and plots them.

Figure 1-24 shows some of the errors made by the trained network (note that the model you train will likely make different errors).

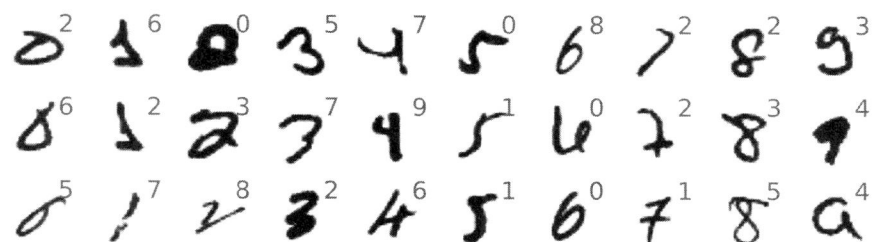

Figure 1-24: Misclassified digits

Some of these misclassified digits are indeed written relatively sloppily, so the confusion is somewhat understandable.

NOTE *Code Example 1-A, "Classifying the MNIST Digits," is available at* https://github .com/DeepTrackAI/DeepLearningCrashCourse. *Navigate to the* Ch01_DNN _classification *folder and then* ec01_A_mnist. *The* mnist.ipynb *notebook provides a complete code example that loads the MNIST digits, trains a fully connected neural network with two hidden layers to classify them, and analyzes where the trained network fails.*

Summary

In this chapter, you explored dense neural networks, putting together artificial neurons to solve classification problems. You began by discovering the essence of an artificial neuron, inspired by its biological counterpart. This knowledge laid the foundation to build more-complex neural networks, harnessing the power of interconnected artificial neurons.

You learned about supervised learning, using labeled datasets to train your neural networks. In a classical supervised learning approach, neural networks are trained using labeled datasets containing inputs and corresponding outputs (or targets). In the training process, the connection weights between the neurons are iteratively adjusted until the neural network learns to associate the correct output to each input. This is typically done using backpropagation. Using the backpropagation algorithm, you implemented the iterative process of adjusting connection weights, ensuring that your network learned the correct input-output associations.

Finally, you applied your newly acquired knowledge to classify the handwritten digits of the MNIST dataset, a rite of passage in the deep learning community.

Now that you have a firm understanding of classification using dense neural networks, you're ready to move to the next chapter, where you'll expand your neural network toolkit by exploring regression.

Seminal Works and Further Reading

The concept of artificial neurons was introduced in 1943 by Warren S. McCulloch and Walter Pitts in "A Logical Calculus of the Ideas Immanent in Nervous Activity," published in *The Bulletin of Mathematical Biophysics* (volume 5, pages 115–133). This work laid the theoretical basis for neural computation, presenting a simple yet fundamental model of a biological neuron, which became a precursor of artificial neurons.

Building on this foundation, Frank Rosenblatt in 1958 developed the perceptron model in his work "The Perceptron: A Probabilistic Model for Information Storage and Organization in the Brain," published in *Psychological Review* (volume 65, pages 386–408). This article introduced one of the earliest formal models of an artificial neuron: the *perceptron*, which is a simple binary classifier that models an artificial neuron by combining weighted input signals, applying an activation function, and producing an output based on whether the result exceeds a certain threshold.

In 1960, Bernard Widrow and Marcian E. Hoff introduced the adaptive linear element (ADALINE) in "Adaptive Switching Circuits," published in the 1960 *IRE WESCON Convention Record* (pages 96–104). They modified the learning process of the perceptron by adjusting the weights rather than changing the activation function.

Paul John Werbos made a significant breakthrough in 1974 with his doctoral thesis "Beyond Regression: New Tools for Prediction and Analysis in the Behavioral Sciences," completed at Harvard University. This work is often credited as the first formal introduction of the backpropagation algorithm to efficiently train multilayer neural networks by using the chain rule to compute gradients.

The next critical advance came in 1986 when David E. Rumelhart et al. published "Learning Representations by Back-Propagating Errors" in *Nature* (volume 323, pages 533–536). This work introduced a practical version of backpropagation, which enabled the efficient training of multilayer perceptrons by minimizing the error between predicted and actual outputs. Coauthor Geoffrey E. Hinton was awarded a share of the 2024 Nobel Prize in Physics for his pioneering work on neural networks.

Further extending the theoretical capabilities of neural networks, George Cybenko's "Approximation by Superpositions of a Sigmoidal Function," published in 1989 in *Mathematics of Control, Signals, and Systems* (volume 2, pages 303–314), demonstrated that a sufficiently large multilayer perceptron with sigmoidal activation functions could approximate any continuous function.

In parallel, Kurt Hornik et al. expanded on Cybenko's theorem in "Multilayer Feedforward Networks Are Universal Approximators," published in 1989 in *Neural Networks* (volume 2, pages 359–366). They demonstrated that multilayer perceptrons with general nonlinear activation functions could approximate any Borel measurable function.

Finally, in 2006, Geoffrey E. Hinton et al. revisited multilayer perceptron architectures and introduced techniques to pretrain multilayer perceptrons in an unsupervised manner in "A Fast Learning Algorithm for Deep Belief Nets," published in *Neural Computation* (volume 18, pages 1,527–1,554). This approach helped address the challenges of vanishing gradients, paving the way for effectively training deeper architectures.

CHALLENGE PROJECTS

1-1: MNIST classification from scratch Implement a dense neural network from scratch and train it to classify the MNIST digits. Evaluate how well it works, along the lines of what you've done in this chapter's project.

1-2: Fashion MNIST The Fashion MNIST dataset is a large, freely available database of fashion images commonly used for training and testing various machine learning systems. Implement a dense neural network to classify these images, along the lines of what you've done to classify the MNIST digits.

2

CAPTURING TRENDS AND RECOGNIZING PATTERNS WITH DENSE NEURAL NETWORKS

In this chapter, you'll learn how to use artificial neurons and dense neural networks for capturing trends and patterns through regression—a fundamental technique in the world of predictive analytics and modeling. While classification is used to predict discrete categories or classes (like the 10 digits), *regression* infers the continuous relationships between the input data (like positions) and target data (like forces), allowing neural networks to capture the underlying trends in datasets.

By the end of this chapter, you'll be able to use regression with neural networks to identify patterns and approximate unknown functions, predicting continuous outcomes based on input data in areas such as financial forecasting, climate modeling, and market trend analysis. You'll also learn some new concepts in deep learning, including batch training, and best practices for data management, particularly the division of data into training, validation, and test sets.

You'll then apply this knowledge to a concrete project to speed up the simulation of an optically trapped particle, which is often used in biophysics labs to exert and measure microscopic forces. In this way, you'll gain the skills to use neural networks to emulate a complex system, creating a *digital twin* of a system, which simulates the system without the need to model all its details.

Regressing Data with a Single Neuron

As in Chapter 1, let's start by implementing a single-neuron regressor to explore its potential in detail.

Regressing 1D Data

Using a text editor, open the 1D dataset in the *data_reg_1d_clean.csv* file. The first line is the header, and the subsequent lines contain the data points with the input and output values in the first and second columns, respectively. You can now proceed to analyze this dataset as you did in Chapter 1.

Loading and Visualizing the Data

Use the load_data() function from *loader.py* (Listing 1-10) to load the dataset:

```
from loader import load_data

(x, y_gt) = load_data(filename="data_reg_1d_clean.csv")
```

As usual, it's good practice to verify that the data has been loaded correctly by using print("x:", x) and print("y_gt:", y_gt), which should display this:

```
x: [[-0.79053779]
 [-1.39344279]
 --snip--
 [-0.00933567]]
y_gt: [[-0.2952689 ]
 [-0.59672139]
 --snip--
 [ 0.09533216]]
```

Finally, you can plot the data with the plot_data_1d() function from *plotting.py* (Listing 1-2) as shown in Listing 2-1.

```
from plotting import plot_data_1d

plot_data_1d(x, y_gt)
```

Listing 2-1: Plotting the 1D data for regression

This code plots Figure 2-1.

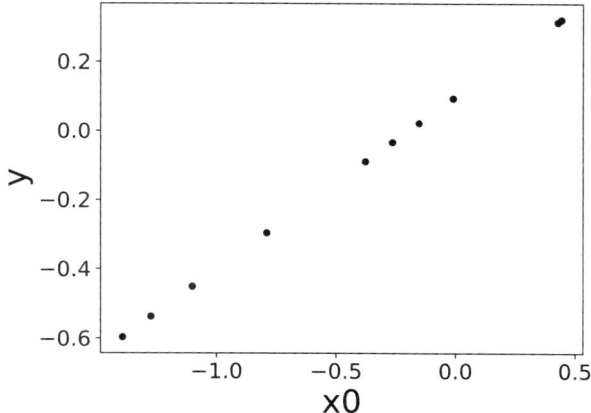

Figure 2-1: The 1D data for regression

This plot shows that the data falls neatly along a diagonal line.

Implementing a Single Neuron

You can now implement a neuron to perform a linear regression, using the code in Listing 2-2.

```
def neuron_reg_1d(w0, x):
    """Artificial neuron for 1D regression."""
    return w0 * x
```

Listing 2-2: A linear neuron for regression

This function implements a single linear neuron with one continuous input (x) and one continuous output. The weight of the neuron (w0) provides the proportionality factor defining the regression between the neuron input and its output, which essentially tunes the response of the neuron to its input.

You should now randomly initialize the neuron weight with Listing 2-3.

```
from numpy.random import default_rng

rng = default_rng()
w0 = rng.standard_normal()
```

Listing 2-3: Initializing the weight of the neuron

The value of w0 is randomly initialized with a normal distribution.
Then you can use Listing 2-4 to obtain the predictions of this neuron.

```
y_p = neuron_reg_1d(w0, x)
```

Listing 2-4: Obtaining a prediction from the neuron

You can also plot the predictions with the plot_pred_1d() function (Listing 1-7) from *plotting.py* as shown in Listing 2-5.

```
from plotting import plot_pred_1d

plot_pred_1d(x, y_gt, y_p=neuron_reg_1d(w0, x))
```

Listing 2-5: Plotting both the 1D data and the neuron's predictions

You should get a plot similar to Figure 2-2.

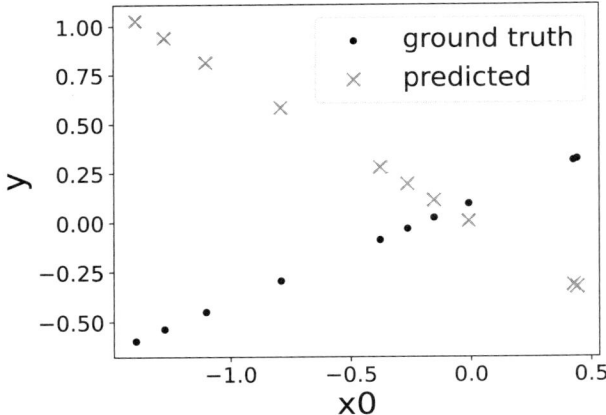

Figure 2-2: Predictions from a randomly initialized neuron

These are not very good predictions, which is to be expected from a regression model with a random proportionality factor.

Training the Neuron

To improve the performance of this neuron, you need to train it. You can do this by using the SGD updated for linear regression, as implemented in Listing 2-6.

```
num_samples = len(x)
num_train_iterations = 100
eta = .1  # Learning rate

for i in range(num_train_iterations):
    selected = rng.integers(0, num_samples)  # Select random sample
    x0_selected = x[selected]
    y_gt_selected = y_gt[selected]

    y_p_selected = neuron_reg_1d(w0, x0_selected)  # Neuron prediction

    error = y_p_selected - y_gt_selected  # Calculate error

❶   w0 = w0 - eta * error * x0_selected  # Update neuron weight

    print(f"i={i} w0={w0[0]:.2f} error={error[0]:.2f}")
```

Listing 2-6: Training of a single neuron for linear regression

This code is very similar to Listing 1-9, which you used to train the classifier neuron in Chapter 1. The main difference is that the ground truth is now a continuous function instead of a binary classification. This iterative optimization process minimizes the square error (error ** 2) because the weight update is proportional to the negative derivative of the squared error with respect to the weight ❶, guiding the neuron toward lower error values with each iteration.

If you plot the predictions of the trained neuron with the plot_pred_1d() function (Listing 2-5), you should obtain something similar to Figure 2-3.

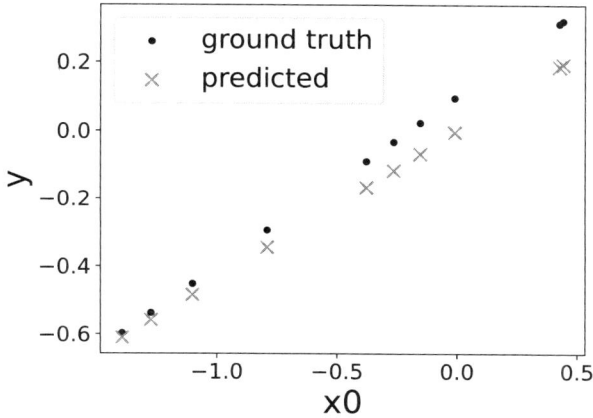

Figure 2-3: Much improved predictions by a trained neuron

Thanks to the training, the performance of the trained neuron has greatly improved so that the predictions lie very close to the desired ground-truth values.

NOTE *Code Example 2-1, "Regressing 1D Data with a Single Neuron," is available at* https://github.com/DeepTrackAI/DeepLearningCrashCourse. *Navigate to the* Ch02_DNN_regression *folder and then* ec02_1_neuron_reg_1d. *The* neuron_reg_1d.ipynb *notebook provides a complete code example that loads the data contained in* data_reg_1d_clean.csv, *trains a neuron to fit it, and finally uses the neuron to predict the values of the data in* data_reg_1d_clean_test.csv. *Note that this code also requires* loader.py *containing the* load_data() *function and* plotting.py *containing the* plot_data_1d() *and* plot_pred_1d() *functions.*

EXERCISES

2-1: Randomly initialize and train the neuron several times. Observe the variability of the performance of the trained neuron. What generates such variability?

(continued)

2-2: The neuron in Listing 2-2 can never perfectly predict the data contained in *data_reg_1d_clean.csv*. This is because this neuron is far too simple: With only one trainable parameter (w0), it can converge to only a regression function with intercept at the origin (0, 0). Therefore, any deviations from such a line cannot be modeled. How can this problem be overcome?

2-3: Repeat the training of the neuron, making the learning rate smaller (for example, eta = 0.01) or larger (for example, eta = 1). How is the training process affected?

2-4: Use the trained neuron to analyze the test data generated with the same underlying model provided in the *data_reg_1d_clean_test.csv* test dataset.

2-5: Real data usually presents some noise, so it's worthwhile for you to explore the performance of the neuron on noisy data such as that in *data_reg_1d_noisy.csv*. Once you've trained the neuron, use it to analyze the test data in *data_reg_1d_noisy_test.csv*, which is generated with the same underlying model.

Attempting to Regress More-Complex Data

If you want to consider a more challenging dataset, load the nonlinear data in *data_reg_1d_nonlinear.csv*:

```
(x, y_gt) = load_data(filename="data_reg_1d_nonlinear.csv")
```

If you plot this data with the plot_data_1d() function (Listing 2-1), you get the left side of Figure 2-4.

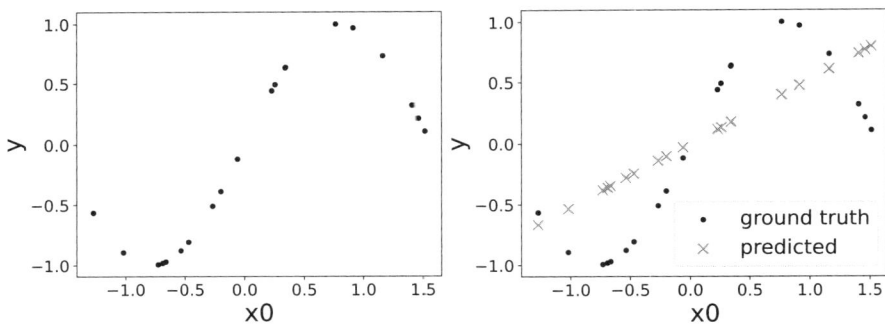

Figure 2-4: The 1D nonlinear data (left) and the prediction of a trained neuron (right)

This data is nonlinear, different from the various datasets you've used until now that had always been generated with a linear underlying function with intercept around $(0, 0)$. A single neuron with a linear activation function won't be able to approximate this dataset satisfactorily because it lacks the necessary complexity to model the nonlinearity of the data.

That said, you can still give it a try and initialize the neuron (Listing 2-2), train it (Listing 2-6), and plot the predicted output via the plot_pred_1d() function (Listing 2-5). You should get a plot similar to the right side of Figure 2-4. The neuron generates data along a line passing through the origin, which is the best approximation the neuron can produce, given its limitations.

EXERCISES

2-6: Use the trained neuron to analyze the test data generated with the same underlying model provided in *data_reg_1d_nonlinear_test.csv*.

2-7: Play with the model underlying the data. Generate your own data and test how well the neuron works in various cases. Try linear and non-linear as well as noisy and non-noisy data. Try also moving the position of the intercept.

Regressing 2D Data

Building on your experience with 1D data, you can now move on to regress multidimensional data.

Loading and Visualizing the Data

Load the 2D data from *data_reg_2d_clean.csv*:

```
from loader import load_data

(x, y_gt) = load_data(filename="data_reg_2d_clean.csv")
```

As always, it's good practice to inspect the data, first by printing it with `print("x:", x)` and `print("y_gt:", y_gt)`, which should display this:

```
x: [[ 0.09539425  0.62586094]
 [ 1.38026523  1.66483856]
 --snip--
 [-0.34130321  0.26006667]]
y_gt: [[ 0.7304667 ]
 [ 0.48457333]
 --snip--
 [ 0.80136988]]
```

The input data corresponds to vectors $\mathbf{x} = (x_0, x_1)$, while the corresponding output data is constituted by a single value per vector.

Now plot the data by using the `plot_data_2d()` function from *plotting.py* (Listing 1-11) as shown in Listing 2-7.

```
from plotting import plot_data_2d

plot_data_2d(x, y_gt)
```

Listing 2-7: Plotting the 2D data for regression

This code color-codes the value of each point in a 2D scatterplot. The resulting plot is shown in Figure 2-5.

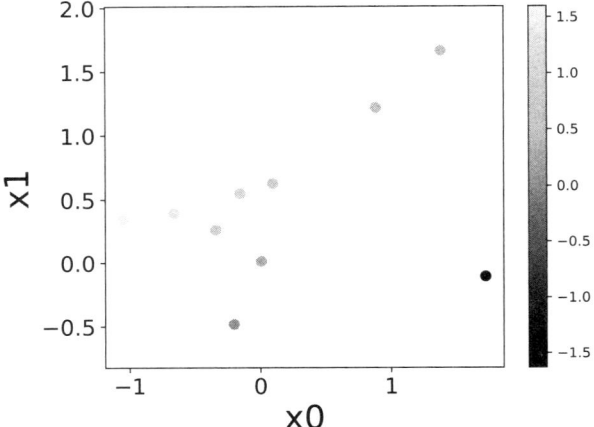

Figure 2-5: The 2D data for regression

The data points seem to ascend from smaller values in the lower-right corner to larger values in the upper-left corner.

Upgrading the Neuron with Multiple Inputs

Now you need to upgrade the neuron from one to two inputs. You can do this by modifying Listing 2-2 to add an extra input, as shown in Listing 2-8.

```
def neuron_reg_2d(w, x):
    """Artificial neuron for multidimensional regression."""
    return x @ w
```

Listing 2-8: The artificial neuron with multiple inputs (by modifying Listing 2-2)

This code implements a linear neuron with multiple inputs (the x NumPy array), an equal number of weights (the w NumPy array), and a linear continuous output, calculated as the scalar product between the input vector and the weight vector.

Next, initialize the weights of the neuron with Listing 2-9.

```
--snip--
w = rng.standard_normal(size=(2,))
```

Listing 2-9: Initializing the weight of the neuron for 2D regression (by modifying Listing 2-3)

Then you can get a prediction from the neuron, using Listing 2-10.

```
y_p = neuron_reg_2d(w, x)
```

Listing 2-10: Obtaining a prediction from the neuron for 2D regression (by modifying Listing 2-4)

Finally, plot the predictions of this neuron and compare them with the ground truth via the plot_pred_2d() function from *plotting.py* (Listing 1-16), as shown in Listing 2-11.

```
from plotting import plot_pred_2d

plot_pred_2d(x, y_gt, y_p=neuron_reg_2d(w, x))
```

Listing 2-11: Plotting both the 2D data and the neuron's predictions

Since the weights are chosen randomly, you can expect the predictions to be pretty much random as well.

Training with Two Inputs

You should now train this neuron using Listing 2-12.

```
--snip--
for i in range(num_train_iterations):
    selected = rng.integers(0, num_samples)  # Select random sample
    x_selected = x[selected]
    y_gt_selected = y_gt[selected]

    y_p_selected = neuron_reg_2d(w, x_selected)  # Neuron prediction

    error = y_p_selected - y_gt_selected  # Calculate error

    w = w - eta * error * x_selected  # Update neuron weights

    print(f"i={i} w0={w[0]:.2f} w1={w[1]:.2f} error={error[0]:.2f}")
```

Listing 2-12: Training the neuron with two inputs (by modifying Listing 2-6)

This code is a small variation on the training code shown in Listing 2-6.

The performance of the neuron rapidly improves during the training. You can plot the predictions of the trained neuron with the plot_pred_2d() function (Listing 2-11). You should get a scatterplot similar to that shown in Figure 2-6.

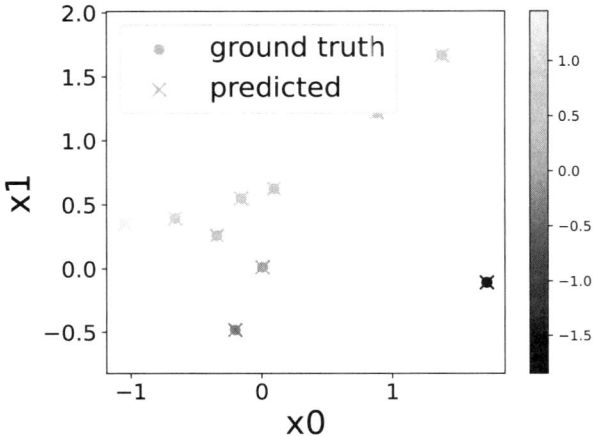

Figure 2-6: Predictions by a trained neuron

The values of the predictions encoded in the colors of the crosses are in excellent agreement with the values of the ground truth encoded in the colors of the dots.

NOTE *Code Example 2-2, "Regressing 2D Data with a Single Neuron," is available at* https://github.com/DeepTrackAI/DeepLearningCrashCourse. *Navigate to the* Ch02_DNN_regression *folder and then* ec02_2_neuron_reg_2d. *The* neuron_reg_2d.ipynb *notebook provides a complete code example that loads the data contained in* data_reg_2d_clean.csv, *trains a neuron to fit that data, and finally uses the neuron to predict the values of the data in* data_reg_2d_clean _test.csv. *Note that this code also requires* loader.py *containing the* load_data() *function and* plotting.py *containing the* plot_data_2d() *and* plot_pred_2d() *functions.*

EXERCISES

2-8: Use the trained neuron to analyze the test data generated with the same underlying model in *data_reg_2d_clean_test.csv*. What are the main differences you observe?

2-9: Repeat the same training on some noisy data such as that in *data _reg_2d_noisy.csv*. You can also test the trained neuron on the data in *data_reg_2d_noisy_test.csv*.

2-10: Repeat the same training on some nonlinear data, such as that in *data_reg_2d_nonlinear.csv*, and test the trained neuron on the data in *data_reg_2d_nonlinear_test.csv*.

2-11: Play with the model underlying the data. Generate your own data and test how well the neuron works for various cases. Try linear and nonlinear data as well as noisy and non-noisy data.

2-12: Just as you did for the classification in Chapter 1, you can now add a bias as an additional input with a constant value equal—for example, to +1. This will permit your neuron to also represent regression lines or planes that don't pass by the origin of the coordinate system. Use this neuron with a bias to revisit the predictions made in the previous section. Verify that the predictions improve, especially when the underlying model doesn't intercept the origin.

Regressing Data with a Two-Layer Neural Network

Similar to what you saw in the classification case in Chapter 1, a two-layer neural network can be more powerful and flexible than a single neuron for regression as well. In fact, while a single linear neuron can model only linear functions, a two-layer neural network with one hidden layer can also model nonlinear functions, allowing the network to represent more-complex relationships between inputs and outputs and to learn more-abstract features from the input data.

As usual, start by loading the data, in this case in *data_reg_2d_linear.csv*:

```
from loader import load_data

(x, y_gt) = load_data(filename="data_reg_2d_linear.csv")
```

You can use the plot_data_2d() function (Listing 2-7) to plot the data, generating Figure 2-7.

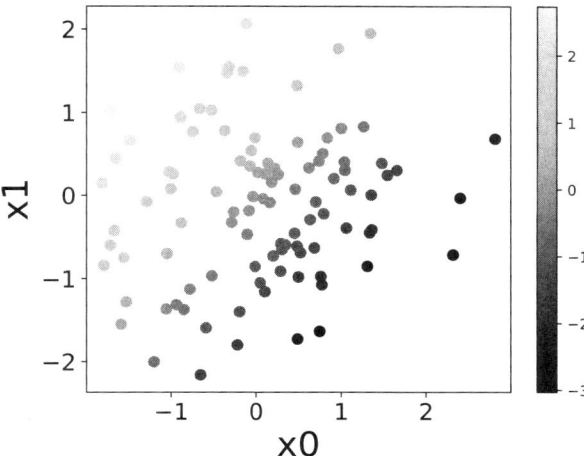

Figure 2-7: The scatterplot of the linear data

This scatterplot shows that the values of this dataset decrease from the top-left corner to the bottom-right corner. Note also that this is a larger dataset with 100 data points, which you can verify using print(len(x)) and print(len(y_gt)).

Implementing a Dense Neural Network

You can now implement a two-layer dense neural network for regression as shown in Listing 2-13.

```
def dnn2_reg(wa, wb, x):
    """Two-layer dense neural network for classification."""
    return sigmoid(x @ wa) @ wb
```

Listing 2-13: A two-layer dense neural network

This function implements a two-layer dense neural network with input x and an output that is nonlinear because the hidden layer has neurons with a `sigmoid()` activation function (Listing 1-23). You can define the number of neurons with

```
num_neurons = 3
```

which you can increase to strengthen the representational power of the neural network.

You need to randomly initialize the weight matrices, using Listing 2-14.

```
from numpy.random import default_rng

rng = default_rng()
❶ wa = rng.standard_normal(size=(2, num_neurons))  # Input weights layer 1
❷ wb = rng.standard_normal(size=(num_neurons, 1))  # Input weights layer 2
```

Listing 2-14: Initializing the weight matrices

Since you have two inputs, three neurons in the first layer, and one neuron in the output layer, the weight matrices between the inputs and the first layer ❶ and between the first layer and the output ❷ have dimensions 2×3 and 3×1, respectively.

You can now obtain this neural network's predictions with Listing 2-15.

```
y_p = dnn2_reg(wa, wb, x)
```

Listing 2-15: Obtaining predictions by the dense neural network

Use the `plot_pred_2d()` function to plot the predictions above the ground truth, as shown in Listing 2-16.

```
--snip--
plot_pred_2d(x, y_gt, y_p=dnn2_reg(wa, wb, x))
```

Listing 2-16: Plotting both the 2D data and the neuron's predictions (by modifying Listing 2-11)

As usual, you shouldn't expect much agreement between the ground truth and the predictions of the neural network, given the random initialization of the weights.

Training with Error Backpropagation

You can train this network by using the error backpropagation algorithm. To do so, you need to update the training cycle provided in Listing 2-12, resulting in Listing 2-17. (You also need the first derivative of the sigmoid function provided in Listing 1-30.)

```
from numpy import reshape, sum, transpose
--snip--
❶ num_train_iterations = 10 ** 5
--snip--
for i in range(num_train_iterations):
    # Select random sample
    selected = rng.integers(0, num_samples)
❷   x_selected = reshape(x[selected], (1, -1))
❸   y_gt_selected = reshape(y_gt[selected], (1, -1))

    # Detailed neural network calculation
    x_selected_a = x_selected  # Input layer 1
    p_a = x_selected_a @ wa  # Activation potential layer 1
    y_selected_a = sigmoid(p_a)  # Output layer 1

    x_selected_b = y_selected_a  # Input layer 2
    p_b = x_selected_b @ wb  # Activation potential layer 2
    y_selected_b = p_b  # Output layer 2 (output neuron)

    y_p_selected = y_selected_b  # Prediction

    # Update weights
    error = y_p_selected - y_gt_selected

    delta_b = error * 1
    wb = wb - eta * delta_b * transpose(x_selected_b)

    delta_a = sum(wb * delta_b, axis=1) * d_sigmoid(p_a)
    wa = wa - eta * delta_a * transpose(x_selected_a)

    if i % 100 == 0:
        print(f"{i} y_p={y_p_selected[0, 0]:.2f} error={error[0, 0]:.2f}")
```

Listing 2-17: Training with error backpropagation (by modifying Listing 2-12)

To get a proper training, you need to increase the training interactions to 10^5 ❶ from 10^2 (try out what happens with intermediate values such as 10^3 and 10^4).

In each training iteration, the code extracts the selected input ❷ and ground-truth output ❸ in vector form so that they have a shape equal to 1 by the number of inputs and 1 by the number of outputs, respectively. Then the code performs a detailed calculation of the predicted output, which produces the same result as sigmoid(x @ wa) @ wb in the definition of the neural network in Listing 2-13. Finally, the state of the network is printed every 100 epochs.

You can now plot the ground truth and predictions with Listing 2-16. You should get a scatterplot similar to Figure 2-8.

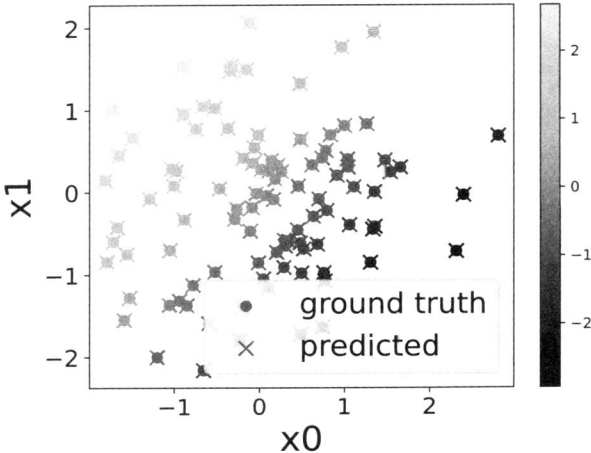

Figure 2-8: Predictions by a trained two-layer neural network

The network performance is very good, as shown by the agreement of the colors between the ground-truth dots and the prediction crosses.

NOTE   *Code Example 2-3, "Regressing 2D Data with a Two-Layer Neural Network," is available at* https://github.com/DeepTrackAI/DeepLearningCrashCourse. *Navigate to the* Ch02_DNN_regression *folder and then* ec02_3_dnn2_reg. *The* dnn2_reg.ipynb *notebook provides a complete code example that loads the data in* data_reg_2d_linear.csv, *trains a two-layer dense neural network to fit that data, and finally uses the network to predict the values of the data in* data_reg_2d_linear _test.csv. *Note that this code also requires* loader.py *containing the* load_data() *function and* plotting.py *containing the* plot_data_2d() *and* plot_pred_2d() *functions.*

EXERCISES

2-13:   Use the trained neural network to analyze the test data generated with the same underlying model provided in *data_reg_2d_linear_test.csv.*

2-14:   The two-layer neural network that you used in this section doesn't perform well on nonlinear data. To verify this, repeat the same analysis in this section with the nonlinear dataset in *data_reg_2d_nonlinear.csv.* Then test the trained network on the data in *data_reg_2d_nonlinear_test.csv.*

Training Using Batches

The way you present the training data to the neural network or artificial neuron matters a great deal. Until now, you've used *online training*, which presents only one sample to the neural network at each iteration, after which its weights and biases are updated.

However, it's often convenient to batch multiple training samples together and perform the update by using the average error signal. This is known as *batch training* (sometimes referred to as *mini-batch training*) and is more effective in avoiding local minima, as averaging across a batch of samples tends to smooth out the error landscape, leading to more stable and consistent gradient estimates. Additionally, this approach reduces oscillatory behaviors in the weight updates, since the averaging process mitigates the impact of outliers or noisy data, allowing for more controlled and directed adjustments toward the global minimum.

In an extreme case of batch learning, the whole training set is used in each iteration, which is known as *steepest-descent training*.

In general, you can achieve the best learning by using an intermediate batch size. Furthermore, as in the case of the learning rate, you can also vary the batch size (usually by increasing it) as the training progresses and moves toward more-stable global minima.

Plotting Predictions vs. Ground Truth

Start by loading the nonlinear data in *data_reg_2d_nonlinear.csv*:

```
from loader import load_data

(x, y_gt) = load_data(filename="data_reg_2d_nonlinear.csv")
```

You can use the two-layer neural network defined in Listing 2-13 (note that you also need the sigmoid function from Listing 1-23) but slightly larger, setting the following:

```
num_neurons = 10
```

Then randomly initialize the weights with Listing 2-14 and calculate the neural network's predictions with Listing 2-15.

As usual, you can plot these predictions above the ground truth via the plot_pred_2d() function (Listing 2-16). The resulting plot is shown on the left side of Figure 2-9.

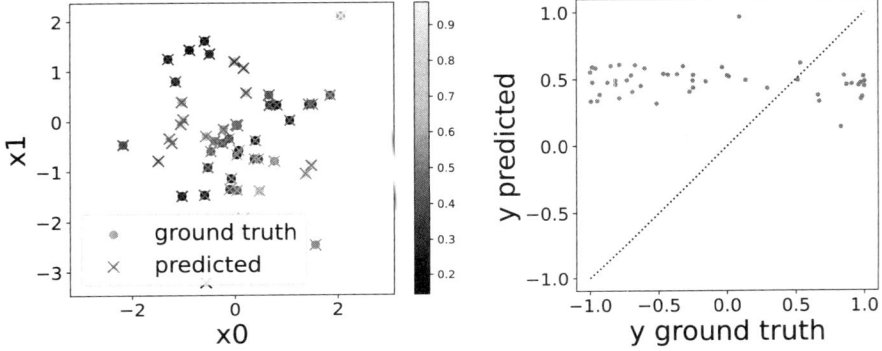

Figure 2-9: A scatterplot of predictions by a randomly initialized neural network (left) and a plot of the predictions versus ground-truth values (right)

As expected, using a randomly initialized neural network leads to random predictions that don't agree with the ground truth.

Innovating on the graphical representation of the results, you can now plot the predictions versus the ground-truth values. To do so, add the plot _pred_vs_gt() function, shown in Listing 2-18, to *plotting.py*.

```
def plot_pred_vs_gt(y_gt, y_p):
    """Plot prediction versus ground truth values."""
❶   plt.plot([-1, 1], [-1, 1], "k:")
    plt.scatter(y_gt, y_p, s=10)
    plt.axis("square")
    plt.xlabel("y ground truth", fontsize=24)
    plt.ylabel("y predicted", fontsize=24)
    plt.tick_params(axis="both", which="major", labelsize=16)
    plt.show()
```

Listing 2-18: The function to plot predictions versus ground-truth values

This function also plots the *bisectrix* of the plane ❶, a line representing the ideal scenario of the predicted values exactly matching the actual values, illustrating a perfect prediction.

Then import this function and plot the predictions versus ground truth, using Listing 2-19.

```
from plotting import plot_pred_vs_gt

plot_pred_vs_gt(y_gt, y_p=dnn2_reg(wa, wb, x))
```

Listing 2-19: Plotting the predictions versus ground-truth values

You should get a plot similar to the right side of Figure 2-9. As expected, the randomly initialized neural network generates random predictions, as you can tell from the scattering of the dots, which don't collapse on the bisectrix line as they would for a series of perfect predictions.

In general, the *prediction-versus-ground-truth plot* like the one shown in Figure 2-9 is a useful tool to evaluate the performance of a neural network. The plot's horizontal axis represents the true values (ground truth) of the data, while its vertical axis represents the network's predictions. A perfect prediction would result in a scatterplot with all the data points falling on the bisectrix line, indicating that the network's predictions perfectly match the ground-truth values.

However, in practice, the scatterplot will likely show some deviation from this line, indicating that the network's predictions aren't perfect. The degree of deviation can give insights into how well the network is performing and where it might be making mistakes. In this case, since the network is randomly initialized, the predictions are also random. Note, however, that even random predictions aren't necessarily uniformly distributed but can present a structure arising from the architecture of the network and the initialization of its weights and biases.

EXERCISE

2-18: Revisit the previous examples and plot the predictions versus the ground-truth values before and after training the neuron or neural network.

Training with Mini-Batches

You can now implement batch training, as shown in Listing 2-20, which builds on Listing 2-17 and uses the first derivative of the sigmoid function (Listing 1-30).

```
from numpy import mean, reshape, sum, transpose, zeros
--snip--
num_batches = 10
batch_size = int(num_samples / num_batches)
num_epochs = 10 ** 4
--snip--
```

```
for epoch in range(num_epochs):
    for batch_start in range(0, num_samples, batch_size):
        dwa = zeros(wa.shape)  # Initialize weight increments layer 1
        dwb = zeros(wb.shape)  # Initialize weight increments layer 2
    ❶ for selected in range(batch_start, batch_start + batch_size):
            x_selected = reshape(x[selected], (1, -1))
            y_gt_selected = reshape(y_gt[selected], (1, -1))
            --snip--
            # Update weight increments
            error = y_p_selected - y_gt_selected

            delta_b = error * 1
        ❷ dwb = dwb - eta * delta_b * transpose(x_selected_b)

            delta_a = sum(wb * delta_b, axis=1) * d_sigmoid(p_a)
        ❸ dwa = dwa - eta * delta_a * transpose(x_selected_a)

      ❹ wa = wa + dwa / batch_size  # Update weights layer 1
      ❺ wb = wb + dwb / batch_size  # Update weights layer 2

  ❻ y_p = dnn2_reg(wa, wb, x)
    mse_train = mean((y_p - y_gt) ** 2)

    print(f"epoch={epoch} MSE={mse_train:.4f}")
```

Listing 2-20: Training a neural network with mini-batches (by modifying Listing 2-17)

This script uses batches of samples to train a two-layer neural network.
Thus, the script introduces the number of batches (num_batches) and calculates the batch size (batch_size). The training iterates over the epochs and
over all the batches within each epoch. Within each batch, the script first
initializes the weight increments dwa and dwb to 0s; then it iterates over all
samples in the current batch ❶, adding to the weight increments the corresponding weight variations ❷ ❸; finally, it updates the weights by adding the
weight increments divided by the batch size ❹ ❺ (it's also possible not to divide, which leads to a faster but less stable convergence—similar to increasing
the learning rate). At the end of each epoch, the script calculates the predicted results for all samples in the training set ❻ and calculates and prints
out the corresponding MSE.

Figure 2-10 shows the predictions of a trained neural network. The left
side of the plot is obtained using the plot_pred_2d() function (Listing 2-16),
and the right side by using the plot_pred_vs_gt() function (Listing 2-19).

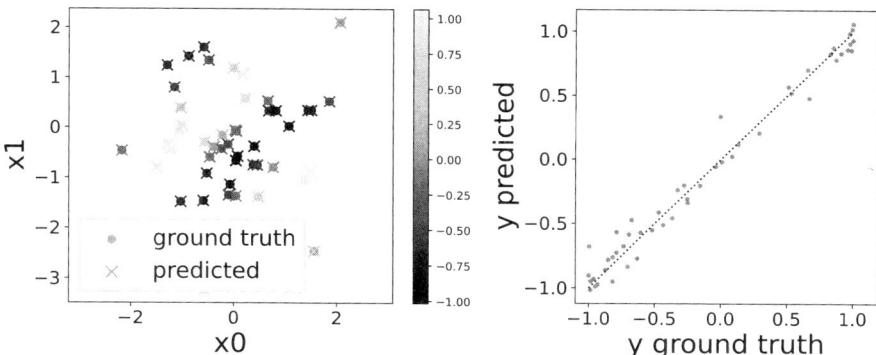

Figure 2-10: Predictions by a trained neural network using a scatterplot (left) and a prediction-versus-ground-truth plot (right)

The scatterplot on the left shows that there is now a decent agreement between the predictions of the network (color of the crosses) and the ground-truth values (color of the dots).

The prediction-versus-ground-truth plot on the right confirms this observation. In fact, the data points are now much closer to the dotted bisectrix line than for the untrained neural network (right side of Figure 2-9). This indicates that the trained network's predictions are more accurate and closer to the true values.

Tracking Training Metrics

The evolution of the MSE provides valuable information on the training process. Therefore, you can gain further insights into how the training is proceeding by storing the values of the MSE as a function of the epoch. You can do this by modifying Listing 2-20 as shown in Listing 2-21.

```
--snip--
mse_train = zeros((num_epochs,))
for epoch in range(num_epochs):
    --snip--
    y_predicted = sigmoid(x @ wa) @ wb
    mse_train[epoch] = mean((y_p - y_gt) ** 2)

    print(f"epoch={epoch} MSE = {mse_train[epoch]:.4f}")
```

Listing 2-21: Batch training storing the MSE (by modifying Listing 2-20)

You can now write the plot_mse() function to plot the evolution of the MSE during training, as shown in Listing 2-22 (but don't add it to *plotting.py* yet, as you'll soon update it).

```
def plot_mse(mse):
    """Plot MSE evolution during training."""
    fig, ax = plt.subplots(1, 2)
    fig.set_size_inches(10, 5)

    ax[0].plot(mse, c="tab:orange")
    ax[0].set_xlabel("epoch", fontsize=24)
    ax[0].set_ylabel("MSE", fontsize=24)
    ax[0].tick_params(axis="both", which="major", labelsize=16)

    ax[1].loglog(mse, c="tab:orange")
    ax[1].set_xlabel("epoch", fontsize=24)
    ax[1].set_ylabel("MSE", fontsize=24)
    ax[1].tick_params(axis="both", which="major", labelsize=16)

    plt.tight_layout()
    plt.show()
```

Listing 2-22: The function to plot the MSE evolution during training

Then use this function to plot the MSE:

```
plot_mse(mse_train)
```

The resulting plot should be similar to Figure 2-11.

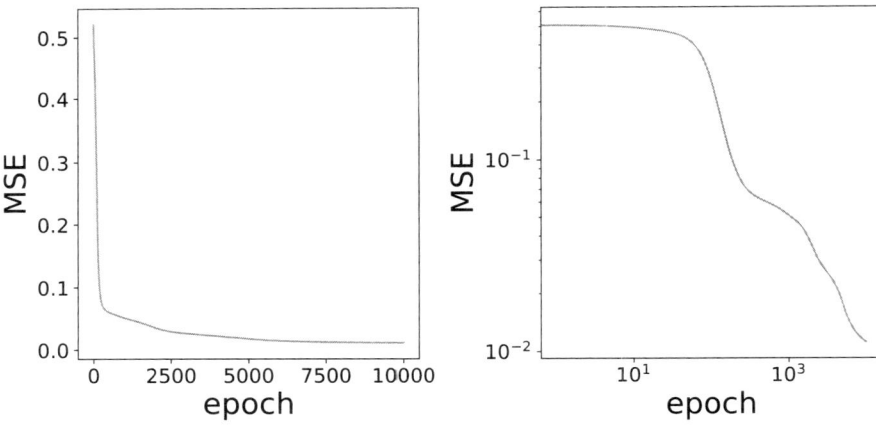

Figure 2-11: Evolution of the MSE during training

During training, the MSE steadily decreases, first quickly and then more slowly. Its evolution is plotted using both linear and logarithmic scales. The linear scale highlights absolute changes, while the logarithmic scale emphasizes relative changes.

Randomizing the Batches

Randomizing the order in which the samples are presented to the network in each training epoch is one last improvement that you can make to the batch training algorithm. Until now, the order of the training samples has been the same in each epoch. This can introduce unwanted biases in the trained neural network. The order randomization can be achieved by changing Listing 2-21 as shown in Listing 2-23.

```
from numpy import mean, reshape, sum, transpose, zeros
from numpy.random import permutation
--snip--
for epoch in range(num_epochs):
    # Permute samples
❶ permuted_order_samples = permutation(num_samples)
❷ x_permuted = x[permuted_order_samples]
❸ y_gt_permuted = y_gt[permuted_order_samples]

    for batch_start in range(0, num_samples, batch_size):
        --snip--
        for selected in range(batch_start, batch_start + batch_size):
            x_selected = reshape(x_permuted[selected], (1, -1))
            y_gt_selected = reshape(y_gt_permuted[selected], (1, -1))
            --snip--
```

Listing 2-23: Randomizing the sample order in batch training (by modifying Listing 2-21)

This code first calculates a permutation of the order of the samples ❶ and then applies the same permutation to both the inputs ❷ and ground truths ❸ used to train the network.

The resulting network performs better, which you can verify by plotting its predictions. More interestingly, the MSE now doesn't decrease monotonically as in Figure 2-11, because in each epoch the network is trained with a different sequence of the same samples.

To show the trend more clearly, you can update the plot_mse() function (Listing 2-22) by adding a black trend line, obtained as a smoothed version of the MSE evolution, as shown in Listing 2-24.

```
from numpy import convolve, full

def plot_mse(mse, smooth=11):
    """Plot MSE evolution during training with trend line."""
    mse_smooth = convolve(mse, full((smooth,), 1 / smooth), mode="valid")
    --snip--
    ax[0].plot(range(smooth // 2, len(mse) - smooth // 2), mse_smooth, "k--")
    --snip--
    ax[1].loglog(range(smooth // 2, len(mse) - smooth // 2), mse_smooth, "k--")
    --snip--
```

Listing 2-24: The function to plot the MSE evolution during training with its trend line (by modifying Listing 2-22)

This function uses 11 points for the smoothing convolution. Note that, when plotting the smoothed MSE, some of the initial and final points are skipped. In fact, the smoothing doesn't provide correct values for these points because of boundary conditions (alternatively, you could calculate a running average, which wouldn't create this problem but would lag behind the MSE).

You can now add this function to *plotting.py* and use it to plot the evolution of the MSE, as shown in Listing 2-25.

```
from plotting import plot_mse

plot_mse(mse_train)
```

Listing 2-25: Plotting the evolution of the training MSE

This should result in a plot similar to Figure 2-12.

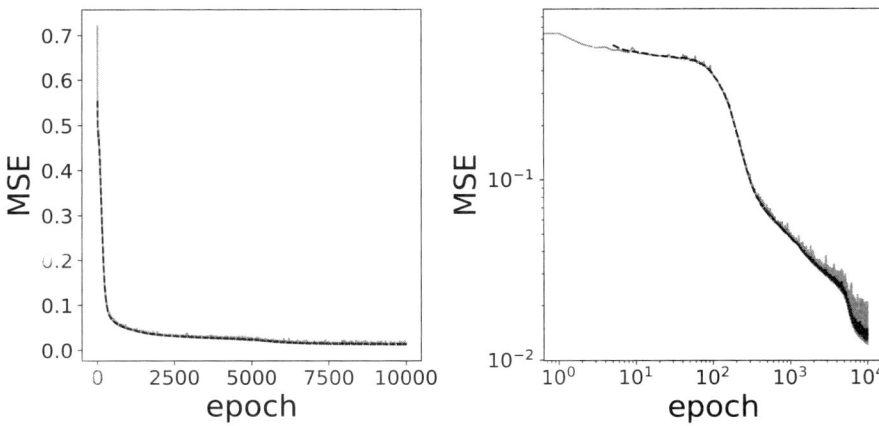

Figure 2-12: The evolution of training the MSE with randomized batches, and the trend line

The MSE now doesn't decrease steadily but tends to oscillate because of the randomization of the batches. The black dashed line represents a smoothed version of the MSE that allows you to see its trend more clearly.

NOTE

Code Example 2-4, "Fitting Data with a Neural Network Trained Using Batch Training," is available at https://github.com/DeepTrackAI/DeepLearning CrashCourse. *Navigate to the* Ch02_DNN_regression *folder and then* ec02_4 _dnn2_reg_batches. *The* dnn2_reg_batches.ipynb *notebook provides a complete code example that loads the data contained in the* data_reg_2d_nonlinear.csv *file, trains a two-layer neural network to fit the data with batch training, and finally uses the network to predict the values of the data in the file* data_reg_2d_nonlinear_test .csv. *Note that this code also requires* loader.py *containing the* load_data() *function and* plotting.py *containing the* plot_data_2d(), plot_pred_2d(), plot_pred_vs_gt(), *and* plot_mse() *functions.*

EXERCISES

2-20:   Show how the final MSE improves as you go from online training to batch training, and finally to randomized batch training. Compare these results with the performance of the trained neural network on the test set in *data_reg_2d_nonlinear_test.csv.*

2-21:   While it's a common practice to gradually decrease the learning rate during training, you can usually get a similar learning curve by increasing the batch size during training instead. Try this.

Dividing Data into Multiple Datasets

As with other machine learning techniques, when training neural networks, the available data is usually divided into multiple datasets. Three datasets are commonly used in the different stages of creating the machine learning model: training, validation, and testing.

The *training dataset* is a set of examples used to initially fit the parameters of the model—for example, the weights in a neural network. After being fit on the training dataset, the model should be able to make predictions on new, unseen data.

After training, the fitted model is used to predict the responses for the observations in the *validation dataset*, which provides an unbiased evaluation of a model fit while tuning the model's hyperparameters—for example, the number of hidden layers and neurons per layer in a neural network. Validation datasets can also be used for regularization by *early stopping* (stopping training when the error on the validation dataset starts to increase, as this is a sign of overfitting to the training dataset). However, this simple-sounding procedure is complicated in practice by the fact that the validation error may fluctuate during training, producing multiple local minima. This complication has led to the creation of many ad hoc rules for deciding when overfitting has truly begun.

Finally, the *testing dataset* is used to provide an unbiased evaluation of a final model fit. If the data in the test dataset is strictly not used in training (for example, in cross-validation), the test dataset is often referred to as a *holdout dataset*. (Confusing the terminology, the term *validation dataset* is sometimes used instead of *testing dataset*, or vice versa—for example, if the original dataset is partitioned into only two subsets.)

Deciding the sizes and strategies to split the available data among training, validation, and test datasets depends on the problem at hand and on the amount of available data. As a rule of thumb, often about 70 percent of the available data is used for training, and the rest is split between validation and testing.

Splitting the Data

You will now split the data. Start by loading the usual nonlinear data contained in the *data_reg_2d_nonlinear.csv* file:

```
from loader import load_data

(x, y_gt) = load_data(filename="data_reg_2d_nonlinear.csv")
```

This dataset contains 50 samples, which you can split into a training dataset (70 percent, 35 samples) and a validation dataset (30 percent, 15 samples) with Listing 2-26.

```
from numpy import delete, split
from numpy.random import choice

num_samples = len(x)
❶ split = .70

num_samples_train = int(split * num_samples)
❷ train_idx = choice(num_samples, num_samples_train, replace=False)

x_train = x[train_idx]  # Train inputs
y_gt_train = y_gt[train_idx]  # Train ground truths

x_val = delete(x, train_idx, axis=0)  # Validation inputs
y_gt_val = delete(y_gt, train_idx, axis=0)  # Validation ground truths
```

Listing 2-26: Splitting data into training and validation datasets

This code splits the data into a training dataset (70 percent of samples ❶) and a validation dataset (the remaining 30 percent of samples), randomly selecting the samples that should belong to the training dataset ❷, which is generally better than just taking the first initial 70 percent of the samples to avoid introducing unwanted biases.

You can now initialize a two-layer neural network. Run Listing 2-13 and set num_neurons = 10 (note that you'll also need the sigmoid function in

Listing 1-23), initialize its weights with Listing 2-14, and predict the results of the training and validation datasets with Listing 2-27.

```
y_p_train = dnn2_reg(wa, wb, x_train)
y_p_val = dnn2_reg(wa, wb, x_val)
```

Listing 2-27: Obtaining predictions for the training and validation datasets

Plot the predictions for the two datasets with the plot_pred_2d() function (Listing 2-11) to generate scatterplots, and the plot_pred_vs_gt() function (Listing 2-19) to generate the prediction-versus-ground-truth plots, as shown in Listing 2-28.

```
from plotting import plot_pred_2d, plot_pred_vs_gt

plot_pred_2d(x_train, y_gt_train, y_p=dnn2_reg(wa, wb, x_train))
plot_pred_vs_gt(y_gt_train, y_p=dnn2_reg(wa, wb, x_train))

plot_pred_2d(x_val, y_gt_val, y_p=dnn2_reg(wa, wb, x_val))
plot_pred_vs_gt(y_gt_val, y_p=dnn2_reg(wa, wb, x_val))
```

Listing 2-28: Plotting the predictions on the training and validation datasets

As usual, you can expect the resulting prediction to look quite random, since the network isn't trained yet.

Training and Validating the Neural Network

Proceed to train this neural network with Listing 2-29 (you'll also need the first derivative of the sigmoid function in Listing 1-30).

```
--snip--
num_samples_train = len(x_train)
❶ num_batches = 7
  batch_size = int(num_samples_train / num_batches)
  --snip--
  mse_train, mse_val = zeros((num_epochs,)), zeros((num_epochs,))
  for epoch in range(num_epochs):
      # Permute samples
      permuted_order_samples = permutation(num_samples_train)
      x_permuted = x_train[permuted_order_samples]
      y_gt_permuted = y_gt_train[permuted_order_samples]

      for batch_start in range(0, num_samples_train, batch_size):
          --snip--

      y_p_train = dnn2_reg(wa, wb, x_train)
      mse_train[epoch] = mean((y_p_train - y_gt_train) ** 2)

      y_p_val = dnn2_reg(wa, wb, x_val)
```

```
    mse_val[epoch] = mean((y_p_val - y_gt_val) ** 2)

    print(f"{epoch} MSE train={mse_train[epoch]:.4f} val={mse_val[epoch]:.4f}")
```

Listing 2-29: Training with the training dataset while monitoring the MSE (by modifying Listing 2-23)

This code introduces small changes to Listing 2-23 to switch from training on the full dataset (x and y_gt) to training only on the training dataset (x_train and y_gt_train), and to keep track of the evolution of the MSE for both training and validation datasets. Importantly, it adjusts the number of batches ❶ so that each batch still has an integer number of samples (a noninteger number of samples may generate an error).

You can then plot the training and validation MSE curves by using the plot_mse_train_vs_val() function shown in Listing 2-30.

```
def plot_mse_train_vs_val(mse_t, mse_v, smooth=11):
    """Plot training and validation MSE evolution during training."""
    mse_t_s = convolve(mse_t, full((smooth,), 1 / smooth), mode="valid")
    mse_v_s = convolve(mse_v, full((smooth,), 1 / smooth), mode="valid")
    --snip--
    ax[0].plot(mse_t, c="tab:orange", label="train")
    ax[0].plot(mse_v, ":", c="tab:green", label="validation")
    ax[0].plot(range(smooth // 2, len(mse_t) - smooth // 2), mse_t_s, "k--")
    ax[0].plot(range(smooth // 2, len(mse_v) - smooth // 2), mse_v_s, "k--")
    ax[0].legend(fontsize=16)
    --snip--
    ax[1].loglog(mse_t, c="tab:orange", label="train")
    ax[1].loglog(mse_v, ":", c="tab:green", label="validation")
    ax[1].loglog(range(smooth // 2, len(mse_v) - smooth // 2), mse_t_s, "k--")
    ax[1].loglog(range(smooth // 2, len(mse_v) - smooth // 2), mse_v_s, "k--")
    ax[1].legend(fontsize=16)
    --snip--
```

Listing 2-30: The function to plot the evolution of the training and validation MSE (by modifying Listing 2-24)

Also add this function to *plotting.py*, import it, and use it with Listing 2-31.

```
from plotting import plot_mse_train_vs_val

plot_mse_train_vs_val(mse_train, mse_val)
```

Listing 2-31: Plotting the evolution of the training and validation MSE

You should get a plot similar to Figure 2-13.

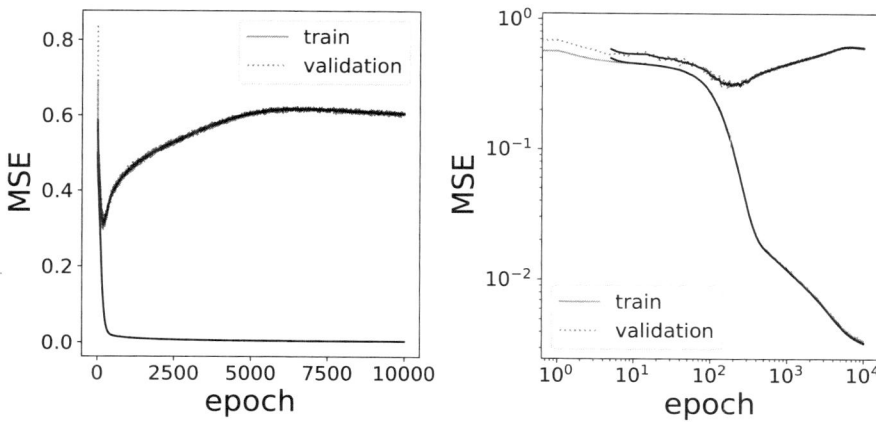

Figure 2-13: Evolution of the training and validation MSE

These curves show that the training MSE consistently decreases with the number of epochs, but the validation MSE at some point starts increasing. This is a common problem with neural networks (and indeed all supervised machine learning approaches) known as *overfitting*. Overfitting is a modeling error in statistics that occurs when a function is too closely aligned to a limited set of data points. As a result, the model is useful in reference only to its training dataset, and not to any other datasets, such as the validation dataset.

NOTE *Comparing the performance on training and validation data can also help detect underfitting. Underfitting occurs when the model is too simple and performs poorly on both the training and validation datasets. This happens when the model isn't able to capture the underlying patterns in the data. One way to detect underfitting is by observing that the model's performance on the training and validation datasets is similarly poor and doesn't improve even after training for many iterations.*

You can see the consequences of overfitting more clearly by plotting the predictions of the trained network on all datasets. To do this, you also need to load the test data in the *data_reg_2d_nonlinear_test.csv* test dataset:

```
(x_test, y_gt_test) = load_data(filename="data_reg_2d_nonlinear_test.csv")
```

Then compare the predictions and ground-truth values by using an extension of Listing 2-28, as shown in Listing 2-32.

```
--snip--
plot_pred_2d(x_test, y_gt_test, y_p=dnn2_reg(wa, wb, x_test))
plot_pred_vs_gt(y_gt_test, y_p=dnn2_reg(wa, wb, x_test))
```

Listing 2-32: Plotting the predictions on the training, validation, and testing datasets (by modifying Listing 2-28)

This code visualizes data and predictions through scatterplots and prediction-versus-ground-truth plots for the training, validation, and testing datasets. You should see plots similar to those in Figure 2-14.

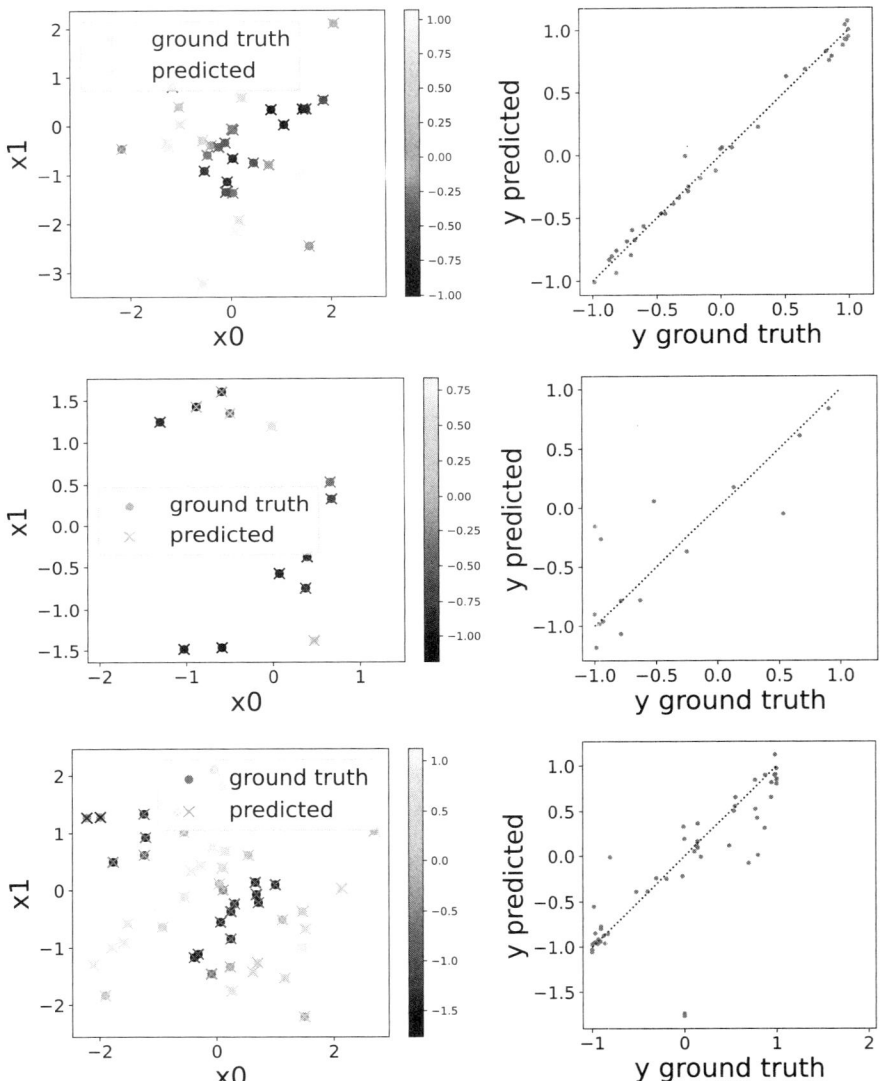

Figure 2-14: Training (first row), validation (second row), and testing (third row) predictions by a trained two-layer network

Notice that the spread of the data in the validation dataset is larger than in the training dataset. Furthermore, and more worryingly, the spread of the data on the testing dataset is even larger (note the different scales), which is a clear sign of overfitting.

NOTE *Code Example 2-5, "Training a Neural Network Splitting the Data," is available at* https://github.com/DeepTrackAI/DeepLearningCrashCourse. *Navigate to the* Ch02_DNN_regression *folder and then* ec02_5_dnn2_reg_split. *The* dnn2_reg_split.ipynb *notebook provides a complete code example that loads the data contained in the* data_reg_2d_nonlinear.csv *file and splits that data into a training, a validation, and a testing set. Then the code example trains a two-layer neural network via the training data while monitoring the training and validation MSE. Finally, it uses the trained network to predict the values of the test data (holdout dataset) in the* data_reg_2d_linear_test.csv *file. Note that this code also requires* loader.py *containing the* `load_data()` *function and* plotting.py *containing the* `plot_data_2d()`, `plot_pred_2d()`, `plot_pred_vs_gt()`, *and* `plot_mse_train_vs_val()` *functions.*

EXERCISES

2-22: With the data of the previous example, observe how the prediction quality and overfitting depend on the representational power of the network (for example, the number of layers and neurons).

2-23: Implement an early stopping strategy to prevent overfitting by monitoring the (smoothed) validation MSE and interrupting the training when it starts increasing. What practical problems do you encounter?

Project 2A: Emulating a Physical System

You'll now use a neural network to emulate a physical system. This approach embodies the concept of a *digital twin*, a virtual representation of a physical system that's created to mirror and predict a real-world system—or a more realistic and computationally expensive model of such a system. As you'll see, using a digital twin, you can get faster and more accurate simulations, thus enabling the study of more-complex physical systems that would otherwise be computationally impossible.

Specifically, you'll simulate the forces acting on a microscopic spherical particle held by an *optical tweezer*. Its laser light typically has a wavelength between 400 nanometers, or nm, (blue) and 1,064 nm (near infrared). Nowadays, optical tweezers are regularly used as microscopic force transducers in a variety of fields, including biology, physics, and nanotechnology. For example, they've been used to measure the forces involved in the mechanical properties of DNA, the behavior of motor proteins, and interactions at the cellular level, as well as to manipulate nanoparticles and to study the dynamics of colloidal systems.

Despite their importance, calculating the forces generated by optical tweezers remains a computationally challenging task, often relying on approximations that depend on the size of the particle. For particles much larger than the laser wavelength, the *geometrical–optics approximation* is commonly used; this method uses rays to describe an optical field, as illustrated in Figure 2-15.

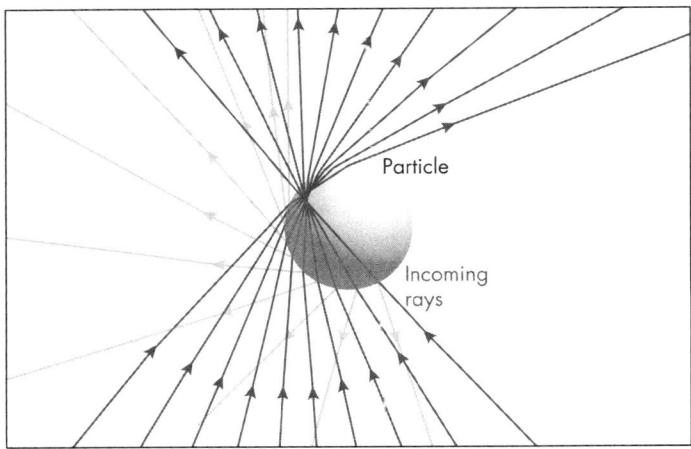

Figure 2-15: A focused light beam impinging on a spherical particle in the geometrical–optics approximation

The laser beam is represented as a collection of rays coming from the bottom of the figure and toward the spherical particle. When the rays reach the particle, they get partly reflected and partly transmitted. The force exerted on the particle is calculated from the reflection and refraction of each ray. This method requires dividing the laser beam into a large set of rays, leading to a trade-off between calculation speed and accuracy.

In the rest of this project, you'll see how to use a dense neural network to simulate the optical forces generated by the laser beam on the microscopic particle. This approach offers several advantages over the geometrical–optics approximation. One of its most significant benefits is the increased speed of neural network–based calculations (up to several orders of magnitude faster). Additionally, the neural network–based approach results in more-accurate simulations. You'll follow in the footsteps of David Bronte Ciriza and co-workers who in 2022 published "Faster and More Accurate Geometrical-Optics Optical Force Calculation Using Neural Networks" in *ACS Photonics* (volume 10, pages 234–241).

Loading the Theoretical and Geometrical–Optics Optical Forces

Download the data for this project from a GitHub repository as shown in Listing 2-33.

```
from os import path, system

if not path.exists("optical_forces_dataset"):
    system("git clone https://github.com/DeepTrackAI/optical_forces_dataset")
```

Listing 2-33: Downloading the optical forces dataset

This code downloads the optical forces dataset in the *optical_forces_dataset* folder. This folder contains optical forces calculated for a microsphere in an optical tweezer with these parameters: laser power P = 5 mW, refractive index of the medium n_m = 1.33 (water), refractive index of the particle n_p = 1.5 (glass), radius of the particle $R = 10^{-6}$ m, focal length f = 0.1 mm, numerical aperture NA = 1.3, and beam waist w_0 = 0.1 mm.

Theoretical Optical Forces

Conveniently, it's possible to calculate with an exact analytical formula the theoretical values of the optical force along the z-axis as a function of the z-coordinate, $f_z(z)$. These values will serve as the ground truth to which you'll compare the results obtained both with the geometrical–optics approximation and with the neural network. These are in the *fz_vs_z_theory.txt* file, which contains two columns corresponding to the z-position in micrometers and to the z-component of the optical force in piconewtons (pN). You can load this data with Listing 2-34.

```
import numpy as np

fz_vs_z_path = path.join("optical_forces_dataset", "fz_vs_z_theory.txt")

data_theo = []
with open(fz_vs_z_path, "r") as file:
    for line in file:
        row = []
        for number in line.split(","):
            ❶ row.append(float(number))
        data_theo.append(row)
data_theo = np.array(data_theo)

z_theo = data_theo[:, 0]
❷ fz_theo = data_theo[:, 1] * 1e3  # Conversion from pN to fN
```

Listing 2-34: Loading the theoretical data

This code loads the file with the theoretical data from the fz_vs_z_path path. Then it initializes the data_theo list to store the data; opens the file for reading; initializes the row list to store the numbers in a row; splits each line into individual numbers, which are separated by commas; appends these numbers to row after having converted them from string to float ❶; and, finally, appends row to data_theo. Note the conversion factor from piconewtons, which is how the data is saved in the file, to femtonewtons (fN) ❷, which is how you'll plot it later.

To print the number of positions and forces, use

```
print(f"Theory: {len(z_theo)} positions and {len(fz_theo)} forces")
```

which should print

```
Theory: 101 positions and 101 forces
```

confirming the number of data points you have for the theory.

Geometrical–Optics Optical Forces

The geometrical–optics data obtained by dividing the laser beam into 100 rays is in two pre-saved NumPy arrays contained in the *xyz_go_100rays.npy* and *fxyz_go_100rays.npy* files. The *xyz_go_100rays.npy* file contains a four-dimensional (4D) NumPy array with the x-, y-, and z-positions of the particle where the optical forces are calculated, while the *fxyz_go_100rays.npy* file contains a 4D NumPy array with the corresponding x-, y-, and z-components of the optical force at each position.

This data was simulated via the computational Optical Tweezers in Geometrical Optics (OTGO) toolbox. This toolbox was published in 2015 by Agnese Callegari and co-workers in "Computational Toolbox for Optical Tweezers in Geometrical Optics" in the *Journal of the Optical Society of America B* (volume 32, pages B11–B19).

You can load these files and extract the relevant positions and forces by using Listing 2-35.

```
xyz_go = np.load(path.join("optical_forces_dataset", "xyz_go_100rays.npy"))
z_go = xyz_go[50, 50, :, 2]  # Particle position - z-component

fxyz_go = np.load(path.join("optical_forces_dataset", "fxyz_go_100rays.npy"))
fz_go = fxyz_go[50, 50, :, 2]  # Optical force - z-component
```

Listing 2-35: Loading the geometrical–optics data

This code loads the two NumPy arrays from the files where they're stored. Then it selects the slices of the NumPy arrays corresponding to the positions and optical forces along the propagation axis of the optical beam.

Finally, to print the number of positions and forces, use

```
print(f"GO: {len(z_go)} positions and {len(fz_go)} forces")
```

which should print:

```
GO: 101 positions and 101 forces
```

Now verify that the theoretical positions fz_theo and the geometrical–optics positions fz_go are the same by checking that fz_theo == fz_go returns an array of true values.

Before proceeding further, use Listing 2-36 to plot the theoretical optical forces and those calculated with geometrical optics.

```
import matplotlib.pyplot as plt

plt.plot(z_go, fz_go, c="gray", linewidth=2, label="GO")
plt.plot(z_theo, fz_theo, c="k", linewidth=2, linestyle=":", label="theory")
plt.title("$F_z$ vs $z$ at $x=y=0$", fontsize=16)
plt.legend(fontsize=16)
plt.xlabel("$z$ [$\mu$m]", fontsize=16)
plt.ylabel("$F_z$ [fN]", fontsize=16)
```

```
plt.tick_params(axis="both", which="major", labelsize=8)
plt.show()
```

Listing 2-36: Comparing theoretical optical forces and optical forces calculated with geometrical optics

This code should generate Figure 2-16.

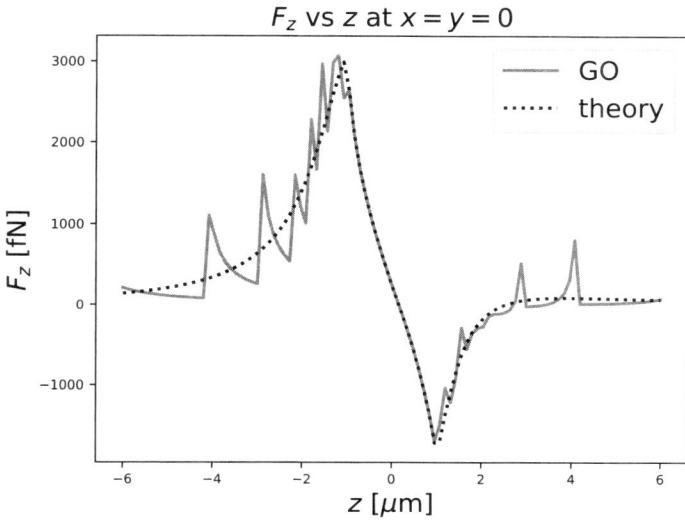

Figure 2-16: Comparison of theoretical optical forces versus optical forces calculated with geometrical optics

The gray solid line in Figure 2-16 shows the optical forces calculated with geometrical optics, while the black dashed line represents the exact model obtained from the theoretical calculation. Notice that the geometrical–optics line doesn't exactly follow the theoretical line. These artifacts depend on the finite number of rays and affect the accuracy of the geometrical–optics calculation.

NOTE *Notice the differences between text and binary file formats for data storage. Text files, typically saved with a .txt or .csv extension, contain human-readable text and are easily editable with standard text editors. They're favored for their simplicity and accessibility across various programming languages but are larger because of ASCII character storage and require manual data processing. NumPy binary files store data in a non–human readable binary format, usually with an .npy extension. They are more space and processing efficient, as you've seen with NumPy's np.save() and np.load() functions, but they require specific software or libraries for access, limiting their flexibility compared to text files.*

Loading and Preparing the Training Data

To train the neural network, we used the OTGO toolbox to simulate approximately 10^5 optical force data points around the optical tweezer's center. These are stored in the *sphere_100rays* directory in 101 files named *force_grid_3D=1.txt*, *force_grid_3D=2.txt*, and so on. Each row in these files consists of eight numbers with the format $[R, n_p, x, y, z, f_x, f_y, f_z]$, where $R \equiv 10^{-6}$ m is the particle radius, $n_p \equiv 1.5$ is its refractive index, (x, y, z) are the coordinates of its position (in meters), and (f_x, f_y, f_z) are the components of the optical force it experiences (in newtons).

From a Single File

To load this data, start by writing a function to load a single file, as shown in Listing 2-37.

```
def load_data_file(filename):
    """Load a datafile with optical forces."""
    data = []
    with open(filename, "r") as file:
        for line in file:
            row = []
❶         for number in line.split():
❷             row.append(float(number))
❸         data.append(row)
    return data
```

Listing 2-37: The function to load a single datafile containing optical forces

This function reads the data in the file into the data 2D list. The function splits each line into individual numbers separated by spaces ❶ and stores these numbers in the row 1D list ❷, which is eventually appended to data ❸. Finally, the function returns data, where each row represents a line in the file and each element in a row represents a number in that line.

You can now use this function with Listing 2-38.

```
data = load_data_file(path.join(
    "optical_forces_dataset", "sphere_100rays", "force_grid_3D=1.txt",
))
```

Listing 2-38: Loading a datafile with optical forces

Using print(data), you can have a look at the output of this function:

```
[[1e-06, 1.5, -4e-06, -4e-06, -6e-06, 0.0, 0.0, 0.0],
 [1e-06, 1.5, -4e-06, -4e-06, -5.88e-06, 0.0, 0.0, 0.0],
 [1e-06, 1.5, -4e-06, -4e-06, -5.76e-06, -3.72116747e-14, 1.00147531e-13,
    9.37947815e-14],
--snip--
```

Each row consists of eight numbers, as described at the end of the previous section. You need only the positions and forces, so you can edit the load_data_file() function (Listing 2-37) to remove the first two numbers, corresponding to the radius and refractive index. Furthermore, since the numerical values of the positions and forces are on the order of 10^{-6} (meters) and 10^{-15} (newtons), respectively, it's convenient to rescale them to make them of order 1, which is more suitable to train a neural network. You can do all this with the modified load_data_file() function in Listing 2-39.

```
def load_data_file(filename):
    --snip--
    with open(filename, "r") as file:
        for line in file:
            row, count = [], 0
            for number in line.split():
                if 2 <= count <= 4:
                 ❶ row.append(float(number) * 1e6)   # From m to um
                elif 5 <= count <= 7:
                 ❷ row.append(float(number) * 1e15)  # From N to fN
                count += 1
            data.append(row)
 ❸ return np.array(data)
```

Listing 2-39: The function to load a datafile with optical forces (by modifying Listing 2-39)

This function selects only the positions and forces and rescales them to make them of order 1. The function initializes the count counter to keep track of the number of elements in a row. It skips the first two elements in the row. Then it converts the next three numbers from string to float and rescales these positions into units of micrometers ❶. It converts the next three numbers from string to float and rescales these forces into units of femtonewtons ❷. Finally, it converts the output to a NumPy array ❸. Using this function with Listing 2-38 and printing the resulting data with print(data), you should see the following output:

```
[[  -4.          -4.         -6.          0.          0.
     0.        ]
 [  -4.          -4.         -5.88        0.          0.
     0.        ]
 [  -4.          -4.         -5.76      -37.2116747  100.147531
    93.7947815]
 --snip--
```

This is much more intuitive and easier to read than the previous output.

From All Files

You can now use Listing 2-40 to load all data into a single NumPy array iterating over all files.

```
data = np.empty((0, 6))
for i in range(1, 102):
    ❶ filename = path.join("optical_forces_dataset", "sphere_100rays",
                          f"force_grid_3D={i}.txt")
    ❷ data = np.append(data, load_data_file(filename), axis=0)
```

Listing 2-40: Loading all optical force data

This code uses the load_data_file() function to load all 101 datafiles into a single NumPy array. The data empty NumPy array is initialized with six columns corresponding to the three positions and three force components. Then the code determines the platform-independent path to the file ❶. Finally, the data is uploaded from the file and appended to the data array. The axis parameter in the np.append() function specifies the axis along which the values should be appended ❷; axis=0 means that the new values will be added as new rows in the array.

You can verify the number of data points that have been loaded with

```
print(f"{np.shape(data)[0]} data points with {np.shape(data)[1]} variables")
```

which prints

```
1030301 data points with 6 variables
```

confirming the exact number of data points available for training and validation.

Training and Validation Datasets

Finally, you need to split the data into training and validation datasets. You can do this with Listing 2-41.

```
train_split = .80
train_size = int(len(data) * train_split)

❶ np.random.shuffle(data)  # In-place shuffle

data_train, data_val = data[:train_size], data[train_size:]
xyz_train, fxyz_train = data_train[:, :3], data_train[:, 3:]
xyz_val, fxyz_val = data_val[:, :3], data_val[:, 3:]
```

Listing 2-41: Splitting the data into training and validation datasets

This script splits the data into training and validation datasets, where train_split represents the ratio of the data that should be used for training. The NumPy function shuffle() ❶ shuffles the data randomly in place and, only after having shuffled the data, separates the positions (xyz_train and xyz_val) from the forces (fxyz_train and fxyz_val).

Verify the size of the datasets with `print(f"{len(xyz_train)} training datapoints")` and `print(f"{len(xyz_val)} validation datapoints")`, printing `824240 training datapoints` and `206061 validation datapoints`. This confirms that the split is correct, as 80 percent of the data points are in the training set and 20 percent are in the validation set.

Implementing the Neural Network

You can now implement the neural network with Listing 2-42.

```
import deeplay as dl

mlp_model = dl.MultiLayerPerceptron(
    in_features=3, hidden_features=[256, 256, 256], out_features=3,
).create()
```

Listing 2-42: Implementing the neural network

This code implements the neural network that takes as inputs the position of the microscopic sphere and returns the predicted optical force that the optical tweezer exerts on the sphere. The `MultiLayerPerceptron` class from Deeplay creates a dense neural network with three inputs (in_features) corresponding to the coordinates of the particle position (x, y, z), three hidden layers (hidden_features) with 256 neurons each, and three outputs (out_features) corresponding to the three components of the force (f_x, f_y, f_z).

Finally, use `print(mlp_model)` to print the summary of the neural network and use `print(sum(p.numel() for p in mlp_model.parameters()))` to print the number of trainable parameters, which is 133,379.

Next, you need to compile the neural network to assign it a loss function and an optimizer, using Listing 2-43.

```
from torch.nn import MSELoss as MSE
from torchmetrics import MeanAbsoluteError as MAE

regressor = dl.Regressor(
    mlp_model, loss=MSE(), optimizer=dl.Adam(), metrics=[MAE()],
).create()
```

Listing 2-43: Compiling the neural network

This code adds the model you've just created to the `Regressor` class. Then it sets MSE as the loss function and Adam as the optimizer. It also adds mean absolute error (MAE) as a metric to be monitored during training. The MAE is a more straightforward indicator of how well you are doing with the force estimation, as it's expressed in units of femtonewton instead of femtonewton squared, as with the MSE.

Finally, print the summary of the compiled network with `print(regressor)`. It's good to get used to checking these summaries regularly to ensure that the code is implemented correctly.

Implementing Data Loaders

Now you need to define some data loaders. These streamline the process of feeding data into the training algorithm, ensuring efficient and organized access to the dataset during the training of your model. To do this, you need to define a custom dataset, as shown in Listing 2-44.

```
from torch.utils.data import Dataset

class GODataset(Dataset):
    """Geometrical optics dataset."""

    def __init__(self, r, f):
        """Initialize dataset."""
        self.r, self.f = r, f

    def __len__(self):
        """Return number of position-force couples."""
        return len(self.r)

    def __getitem__(self, i):
        """Get next position-force couple."""
        return (self.r[i].astype(np.float32), self.f[i].astype(np.float32))
```

Listing 2-44: Implementing a custom dataset

The GODataset class inherits from the PyTorch Dataset class and contains three mandatory methods: __init__() to initialize the dataset, __len__() to determine its length, and __getitem__() to retrieve individual samples. These methods are required by PyTorch to properly integrate the class with the data loader. An instance of GODataset contains pairs of input data (the positions r) and corresponding target data (the forces f).

You can now create instances of this dataset for the training and validation data and set up the corresponding data loaders, using Listing 2-45.

```
train_dataset = GODataset(xyz_train, fxyz_train)
train_dataloader = dl.DataLoader(train_dataset, batch_size=1024)

val_dataset = GODataset(xyz_val, fxyz_val)
val_dataloader = dl.DataLoader(val_dataset, batch_size=1024)
```

Listing 2-45: Setting up the data loaders for the training and validation data

The data loaders efficiently load and process the data in batches during the training and validation of the neural network.

Training the Neural Network

You can train the neural network with the code in Listing 2-46.

```
trainer = dl.Trainer(max_epochs=100, accelerator="auto")
trainer.fit(regressor, train_dataloader)
```

Listing 2-46: Training the neural network

This code uses the trainer.fit() method to train the neural network. The training runs for 100 epochs with hardware acceleration (for example, GPU) if available.

You might also want to monitor the training process. You can do this using a logger, as shown in Listing 2-47.

```
from lightning.pytorch.loggers import CSVLogger

trainer = dl.Trainer(
    max_epochs=100, accelerator="auto",
❶   logger=CSVLogger("logs", name="regressor"), log_every_n_steps=20,
)
❷ trainer.fit(regressor, train_dataloader, val_dataloader)
```

Listing 2-47: Training the neural network while logging the training metrics (by modifying Listing 2-46)

CSVLogger creates the *logs* folder, which in turn contains the *regressor* folder ❶. Inside this folder, the logger creates a new, progressively numbered folder for each training session, starting with the *0* folder, where it records various training metrics in the *metrics.csv* file every 20 training steps for both the training data and the validation data ❷.

You can access these results by using the Pandas library, as shown in Listing 2-48.

```
import pandas as pd

❶ version = 0
  logs = pd.read_csv(path.join("logs", "regressor", f"version_{version}",
                               "metrics.csv"))

  # Group by epoch and extract train loss and MAE
  train_epoch = logs[logs.train_loss_epoch.notnull()].epoch
❷ train_loss = logs[logs.train_loss_epoch.notnull()].train_loss_epoch
❸ train_mae = (logs[logs.trainMeanAbsoluteError_epoch.notnull()]
              .trainMeanAbsoluteError_epoch)

  # Group by epoch and extract val loss and MAE
  val_epoch = logs[logs.val_loss_epoch.notnull()].epoch
❹ val_loss = logs[logs.val_loss_epoch.notnull()].val_loss_epoch
❺ val_mae = (logs[logs.valMeanAbsoluteError_epoch.notnull()]
            .valMeanAbsoluteError_epoch)
```

Listing 2-48: Extracting the training metrics

This code extracts the data from the first version of the log ❶, which is created the first time the neural network is trained and held in the *0* folder. Subsequent versions will be numbered sequentially and held in the corresponding folders named *1, 2,* and so on. Within the *metrics.csv* file, the training loss (MSE) and MAE are contained in the train_loss_epoch ❷ and trainMeanAbsoluteError_epoch ❸ columns, while the validation loss (MSE) and MAE are contained in the val_loss_epoch ❹ and valMeanAbsoluteError_epoch ❺ columns.

You can use Listing 2-49 to plot the training history.

```
plt.plot(train_epoch, train_loss, label="train", c="gray", linestyle="--")
plt.plot(val_epoch, val_loss, label="val", c="orange")
plt.title("Loss (MSE)", fontsize=24)
plt.xlabel("Epoch", fontsize=16)
plt.ylabel("Loss (MSE) [fN$^2$]", fontsize=16)
plt.tick_params(axis="both", which="major", labelsize=8)
plt.legend(fontsize=16)
plt.show()

plt.plot(train_epoch, train_mae, label="train", c="gray", linestyle="--")
plt.plot(val_epoch, val_mae, label="val", c="orange")
plt.title("MAE", fontsize=24)
plt.xlabel("Epoch", fontsize=16)
plt.ylabel("MAE [fN]", fontsize=16)
plt.tick_params(axis="both", which="major", labelsize=8)
plt.legend(fontsize=16)
plt.show()
```

Listing 2-49: Plotting the training metrics

The resulting plot should be similar to Figure 2-17.

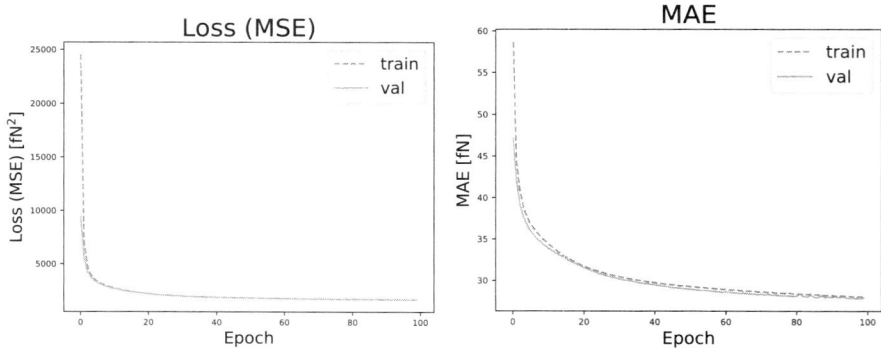

Figure 2-17: The training history with the MSE loss function (left) and the MAE (right) as a function of the training epoch

At the end of the training, the neural network should have an MAE on the order of about 30 fN. This is quite small compared with the characteristic value of the optical forces, which is in the thousands of femtonewtons, as shown in Figure 2-16. This means that you can safely use the forces predicted by the neural network when evaluating the optical forces generated by the optical tweezer.

Evaluating Performance

You can now compare the results of the neural network to the theory and geometrical–optics calculations shown in Figure 2-16. To do this, you need to first calculate the neural network predictions for the same z-positions as for the theory and geometrical–optics calculations, using Listing 2-50.

```
import torch

positions_nn = torch.zeros((z_theo.shape[0], 3))
positions_nn[:, 2] = torch.from_numpy(z_theo)
❶ positions_nn = positions_nn.to(regressor.device)

❷ forces_nn = regressor(positions_nn).cpu().detach().numpy()
fz_nn = forces_nn[:, 2]
```

Listing 2-50: Calculating the neural network predictions

Once positions_nn is prepared, this code moves it to the same device (CPU or GPU) that is being used by the neural network ❶. Then the code ensures that the neural network prediction is moved to the CPU and detached from the computational graph ❷. The *computational graph* is a representation of the operations and their corresponding gradients applied during the forward pass, including the model's weights and inputs, used for the backpropagation.

You can then expand Listing 2-36 to add the plotting of the neural network predictions, as shown in Listing 2-51.

```
plt.plot(z_go, fz_go, c="gray", linewidth=2, label="GO")
plt.plot(z_theo, fz_nn, c="orange", linewidth=2, label="NN")
plt.plot(z_theo, fz_theo, c="k", linewidth=2, linestyle=":", label="theory")
--snip--
```

Listing 2-51: Comparing theory, geometrical–optics calculations, and neural network predictions (by modifying Listing 2-36)

The resulting plot is shown in Figure 2-18.

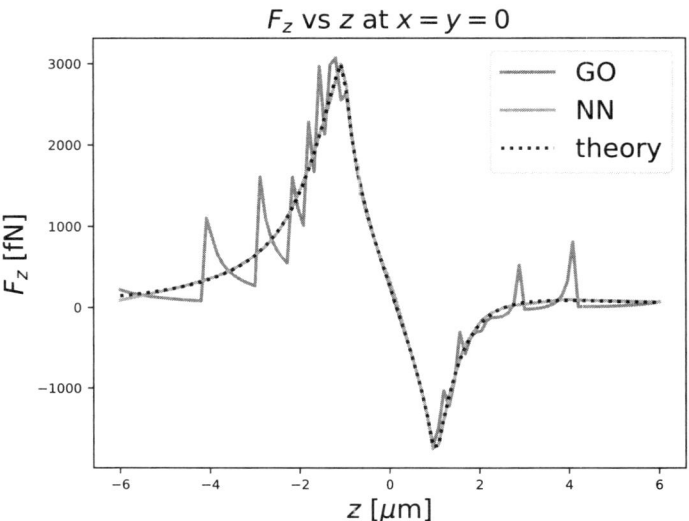

Figure 2-18: Comparison of theory, geometrical–optics (GO) calculations, and neural network (NN) predictions

The neural network provides more-accurate results than geometrical optics. In fact, geometrical optics introduces artifacts due to the division of the continuous laser beam into a finite number of rays. The neural network manages to remove these artifacts because it's designed to be complex enough to learn the smooth force profile, but not the superimposed fluctuating artifacts, achieving an accuracy higher than that of the training data.

NOTE *Code Example 2-A, "Simulating the Forces Acting on an Optically Trapped Particle," is available at* https://github.com/DeepTrackAI/DeepLearningCrash Course. *Navigate to the* Ch02_DNN_regression *folder and then* ec02_A_optical _forces. *The* optical_forces.ipynb *notebook provides a complete code example that loads a set of precalculated optical forces acting on a microsphere held by an optical tweezer and uses these forces to train a dense neural network to predict the optical forces as a function of the particle position.*

Summary

In this chapter, you used dense neural networks for regression, expanding your deep learning knowledge beyond classification. First, you implemented regression with a single neuron, exploring how to predict continuous outputs with both 1D and 2D data. This foundational step was vital to grasp the differences between classification and regression.

You then moved on to implementing more-complex neural networks. Starting with two-layer networks, you applied the principles from Chapter 1 in the context of regression. Through this, you gained hands-on experience in designing and training neural networks via error backpropagation, a concept you're now very familiar with.

A significant focus of this chapter has been on the practicalities of neural network training. You learned techniques such as training with mini-batches, tracking training metrics, and the importance of batch randomization. Understanding how to split datasets into training, validation, and testing sets was another crucial skill you learned. This knowledge is key to preventing overfitting and ensuring that your models generalize well to new data.

The culmination of this chapter was a comprehensive project emulating a physical system using neural networks. This project challenged you to apply all the concepts you learned to simulate the forces acting on an optically trapped particle. This is an example of how neural network regression can be effectively utilized to model complex phenomena. By training a neural network to estimate optical forces, this simulation demonstrates the real-world applicability of neural network regression in bridging the gap between theoretical concepts and practical, scientific applications.

Now that you have a solid understanding of how to use dense neural networks for both classification and regression, you're well prepared to dive into the next chapter, where you'll learn to use convolutional neural networks for image analysis—a key domain in the evolving landscape of deep learning.

Seminal Works and Further Reading

The exploration of improving training efficiency through batch size adjustments gained attention with the work by Samuel L. Smith et al. in their 2018 article "Don't Decay the Learning Rate, Increase the Batch Size," published in *Proceedings of the International Conference on Learning Representations* (ICLR 2018) and on arXiv (article number 1711.00489). This work demonstrated that increasing the batch size, instead of reducing the learning rate, could maintain training stability and efficiency as training progresses.

Project 2A draws on methods described in "Faster and More Accurate Geometrical-Optics Optical Force Calculation Using Neural Networks" by David Bronte Ciriza et al., published in 2022 in *ACS Photonics* (volume 10, pages 234–241). This work builds on the techniques in "Machine Learning Reveals Complex Behaviours in Optically Trapped Particles" by Isaac C.D. Lenton et al., published in 2020 in *Machine Learning: Science and Technology* (volume 1, article number 045009). These studies employ neural networks to accelerate the calculation of optical forces acting on microscopic particles and permitting the study of complex behaviors.

CHALLENGE PROJECTS

2-1: Digital twin for weather forecasting   Develop a dense neural network to create a digital twin for local weather forecasting. Using historical weather data (for example, temperature, pressure, humidity, wind speed),

(continued)

---

design and train a model to predict these parameters for the next day. Evaluate the model's accuracy and discuss its potential as a simple digital twin for weather prediction.

2-2: Building energy optimization with neural networks   Create a neural network model to optimize energy usage in a commercial building, taking into account weather, occupancy, and time factors. Your task is to gather relevant data, design the network for energy prediction, simulate scenarios for optimal energy use, and evaluate the model's effectiveness in reducing energy consumption while maintaining operational efficiency.

3

PROCESSING IMAGES WITH CONVOLUTIONAL NEURAL NETWORKS

In this chapter, you'll dive into convolutional neural networks, the primary tool for using deep learning for image analysis. You'll then apply this knowledge to classifying blood smears used to identify malaria and to measuring the position of microscopic particles from their images.

You'll begin by exploring how convolutions provide powerful tools to extract information from images. You'll learn to implement convolutional layers—the fundamental building blocks of convolutional neural networks. Then you'll discover how downsampling and upsampling layers are used to modify the spatial resolution of the feature maps generated by convolutional layers in advanced convolutional architectures. You'll also learn how to use heatmaps to better understand the workings of convolutional neural networks, showcasing the features they learn in an accessible and insightful way.

This chapter ends with two projects that demonstrate the creative potential of convolutional neural networks by generating artistic and visually stimulating outputs. The DeepDreams project demonstrates how to use convolutional neural networks to transform images into dreamlike scenes, showcasing the network's ability to amplify patterns in a visually intriguing way. Finally, the style transfer project explores how you can apply convolutional neural networks to merge the style of one image with the content of another, leading to captivating results.

Understanding Convolutions

A *convolution* is a blending process that combines two sets of data to produce a new set. Imagine you have a sequence of numbers (call this your main data) and a smaller set of numbers (think of this as a filter). You apply this filter to your main data by sliding it across, step-by-step.

At each step, you multiply the numbers in the filter with the numbers they cover in the main data, and then add these up to get a single number. This process is repeated across the entire main data sequence. The resulting series of numbers is your output—a transformed version of the original data that can highlight some of its properties.

This method is widely used in signal and image processing, where it helps in tasks like sharpening or blurring signals and images, as you'll see shortly.

Convolving 1D Data

To understand how a 1D convolution works, consider a sequence of values in a 1D signal. You may want to compute its *moving average*, which is derived at each point from its adjacent values in the sequence. You can implement this with a 1D convolution, as shown in Listing 3-1.

```
import numpy as np

signal = np.array([0, 2, 0, 2, 0, 2, 0, 2, 0])

filter1d = np.ones(2) / 2

❶ conv1d_length = signal.shape[0] - filter1d.shape[0] + 1
conv1d = np.zeros((conv1d_length,))
for i in range(conv1d_length):
  ❷ conv1d[i] = np.sum(signal[i:i + filter1d.shape[0]] * filter1d)
```

Listing 3-1: Implementing a moving average with a 1D convolution

This script calculates the moving average of a 1D signal by using a 1D convolution. It begins by defining the `signal` array with nine data points, representing the original 1D signal. Next, it creates the `filter1d` filter of length 2 with values [0.5, 0.5], indicating that each element within a two-point window of the signal will contribute equally to the average.

The convolution process starts by first determining the length of the output array ❶, which is calculated as the length of the signal minus the length of the filter plus 1. This calculation is essential to ensure that the convolution process covers the entire signal without exceeding its bounds. The reason for adding 1 is to account for the number of *valid complete placements* of the filter over the signal. The new `conv1d` array of this length is initialized to store the results. The script then performs the convolution operation by iteratively sliding the filter along the signal. At each step ❷, the script multiplies corresponding elements of the signal and the filter, sums them up, and stores the result in `conv1d`.

You can use `print(conv1d)` to print the resulting array, which represents the convolved signal:

```
[1 1 1 1 1 1 1 1]
```

This is a smoothed version of the original signal; while the original signal alternated 0s and 2s, the resulting signal is always 1.

Figure 3-1 illustrates this process. The signal on the left of the figure is convolved with a rectangular filter [0.5, 0.5] obtaining the averaged signal, corresponding to that calculated in Listing 3-1.

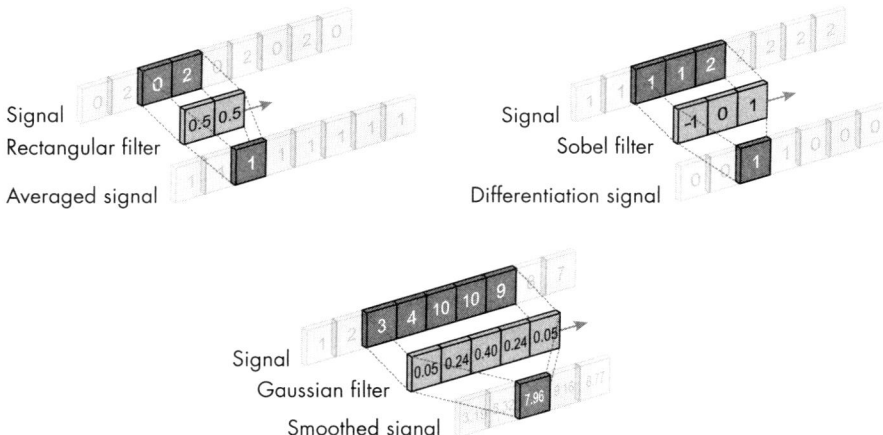

Figure 3-1: 1D convolutions of a signal with various filters

The other two panels of Figure 3-1 show the effect of convolving a signal with different filters. On the right, a signal is convolved with a *Sobel filter* of length 3 performing a differentiation operation often used to detect steps. Finally, at the bottom, another signal is convolved with a *Gaussian filter* of length 5 with unitary standard deviation obtaining another smoothed version of the signal.

Convolving 2D Data

To extend the concept of convolutions to higher dimensions, you'll now implement a 2D convolution using Listing 3-2.

```
❶ image = np.array([
    [1, 1, 0, 0, 1, 1, 0, 0, 1, 1],
    [1, 1, 0, 0, 1, 1, 0, 0, 1, 1],
    [0, 0, 1, 1, 0, 0, 1, 1, 0, 0],
    [0, 0, 1, 1, 0, 0, 1, 1, 0, 0],
])

❷ filter2d = np.ones((2, 2)) / 4

conv2d_height = image.shape[0] - filter2d.shape[0] + 1
conv2d_width = image.shape[1] - filter2d.shape[1] + 1
conv2d = np.zeros((conv2d_height, conv2d_width))
for i in range(conv2d_height):
    for j in range(conv2d_width):
        conv2d[i, j] = np.sum(
            image[i:i + filter2d.shape[0], j:j + filter2d.shape[1]] * filter2d
        )
```

Listing 3-2: Implementing a 2D convolution

This script convolves a 4×10–pixel (height by width) image ❶ with a 2×2–pixel filter ❷, using a procedure similar to that used for the 1D convolution. The 2D convolution process uses two nested for loops, which iterate over each pixel position in the image where the filter can be applied. At each position, the filter overlaps with a part of the image, and an element-wise multiplication followed by a sum is computed. This sum represents the convolved value at that specific location in the output array. This procedure is repeated across the entire image.

If you print the resulting convolution with print(conv2d), you get a smoothed version of the original image:

```
[[1.  0.5 0.  0.5 1.  0.5 0.  0.5 1. ]
 [0.5 0.5 0.5 0.5 0.5 0.5 0.5 0.5 0.5]
 [0.  0.5 1.  0.5 0.  0.5 1.  0.5 0. ]]
```

You can see that this output is a smoothed version of the original image from the gradual transitions in pixel values: Instead of abrupt shifts from 1 to 0 as in the original image, there is now an intermediate value of 0.5. This output is also an image with smaller dimensions (3×9 pixels) than the original image, corresponding to the valid *complete placements* of the filter over the image, which are areas where the filter fully fits within the original image boundaries during the convolution process.

Figure 3-2 illustrates this process.

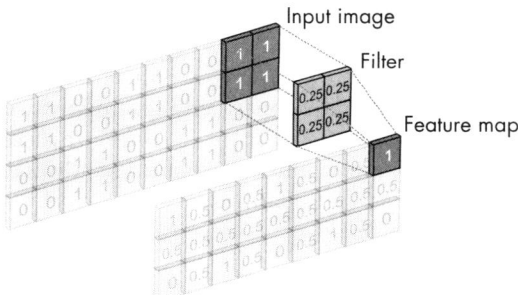

Figure 3-2: A 2D convolution of an image with a filter

The input image at the top is convolved with the filter, generating the convolved image at the bottom, which is often referred to as a *feature map*.

EXERCISES

3-5: Detect the edges in an image by convolving it with a 2D Prewitt filter. For example, use a filter with values [[-1, 0, 1], [-1, 0, 1], [-1, 0, 1]] to detect vertical edges, and a filter with values [[1, 1, 1], [0, 0, 0], [-1, -1, -1]] to detect horizontal edges. Alternatively, you could use 2D Sobel filters with values [[-1, 0, 1], [-2, 0, 2], [-1, 0, 1]] and [-1, -2, -1], [0, 0, 0], [1, 2, 1] for the same purposes.

3-6: Blur an image by convolving it with a 2D Gaussian filter. For example, use a Gaussian filter of size 5×5 with a standard deviation of 1.

3-7: Detect a specific pattern in an image by convolving it with a filter matching the pattern.

If the input image contains multiple color channels, such as in RGB (red, green, and blue) images, the convolution combines all the color channels, as shown in Figure 3-3.

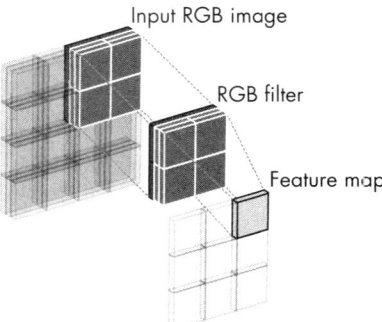

Figure 3-3: A 2D convolution of an RGB image with a filter

For a multichannel image, the image data is represented as a 3D array (height by width by channels), as shown by the input RGB image on the top left. The convolution operation uses a filter that extends through all the color channels. This filter performs the convolution across the height and width of the image, while simultaneously aggregating information from all the color channels. By combining all color channels, this convolution effectively integrates the spatial and color information, leading to a more comprehensive analysis of the image's features.

Using Convolutions in a Neural Network

Now that you've had a glimpse of the power of convolutions in analyzing signals and images, you're ready to integrate them within neural networks.

Convolutional layers consist of neural network layers containing multiple convolutions. They enable the construction of sophisticated neural network architectures to analyze signals and images. The versatility of convolutions in signal and image processing stems from their ability to perform varied operations with different filters, which is especially crucial in deep learning.

Filters are typically learned during training to achieve specific objectives, allowing for the extraction of significant features from signals and images. This adaptability through training explains why convolutions are a fundamental element in neural network architectures.

Implementing Neural Networks in PyTorch

In this section, you'll use PyTorch to explore some of the basic building blocks of neural network architectures. You'll see convolutional, activation, pooling, downsampling, and dense layers, as well as how to sequentially stack them to create a deep neural network.

Start by creating a sample image representing a checkerboard, using the code in Listing 3-3.

```
import torch

H, W, S = 12, 16, 4  # Height, width, square size
❶ image = torch.zeros(1, H, W)
for idx in range(0, H, S):
    for idy in range(0, W, S):
        ❷ image[0, idx:idx + S, idy:idy + S] = (-1) ** (idx // S + idy // S)
```

Listing 3-3: Creating a sample image

The image is stored in the image PyTorch *tensor* (a multidimensional array used by PyTorch to store and process data efficiently for deep learning models, which allows for optimized computations on GPUs). This tensor has three dimensions, corresponding to the number of color channels (1), the height (H), and the width (W) ❶. The image is a checkerboard with squares of size S = 4 taking as values either 1 or −1 ❷. This image has a single color channel, so you can think of it as grayscale.

You can now write the plot_image() function shown in Listing 3-4.

```
import matplotlib.pyplot as plt

def plot_image(image):
    """Render an image."""
❶   plt.imshow(image, cmap="gray", aspect="equal", vmin=-2, vmax=2,
                extent=[0, image.shape[1], 0, image.shape[0]])
    plt.colorbar()
❷   plt.xticks(range(0, image.shape[1] + 1))
❸   plt.yticks(range(0, image.shape[0] + 1))
❹   plt.grid(color="red", linewidth=1)
    plt.show()
```

Listing 3-4: The function to render an image

This function renders the image via the Matplotlib imshow() function with a grid highlighting its pixels ❹, ensuring that the grid lines are at the beginning and end of each pixel ❷ ❸. Even though the values of the image range from −1 to 1, the color bar limits are set from −2 to 2 ❶ to make this image directly comparable with the subsequent ones.

Now, use this function to plot the image you've created:

```
plot_image(image.squeeze())
```

When passing image to the plot_image() function, you need to eliminate the extra dimensions that are of size 1, which is done using the squeeze() method.

Figure 3-4 shows the rendered image.

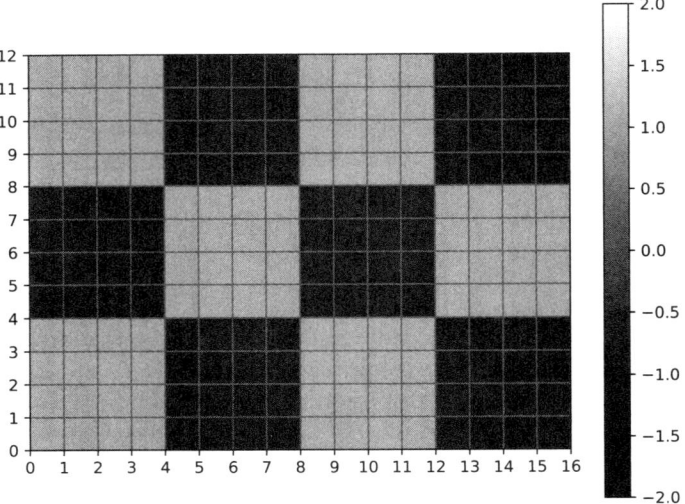

Figure 3-4: The sample image representing a checkerboard

The image is a checkerboard with three rows and four columns of 4×4-pixel squares with values -1 (dark gray) and 1 (light gray). In total, the image has 12×16 pixels (height by width).

Defining Convolutional Layers

You'll now define a convolutional layer, set the values of its filters, and apply it to the checkerboard image to see how it transforms, as shown in Listing 3-5.

```
import torch.nn as nn

conv = nn.Conv2d(in_channels=1, out_channels=2, kernel_size=(1, 3), bias=False)
❶ filters = torch.zeros(conv.out_channels, conv.in_channels, *conv.kernel_size)
❷ filters[0, 0, :, :] = torch.tensor([[1, 1, 1],]) / 3
❸ filters[1, 0, :, :] = torch.tensor([[-1, 0, 1],])
❹ conv.weight = nn.Parameter(filters)

❺ features_conv = conv(image.unsqueeze(0))
```

Listing 3-5: Implementing a convolutional layer in PyTorch

This code creates the conv convolutional layer with a single color channel (in_channels=1) and two filters (out_channels=2) with size kernel_size=(1, 3) (the terms *kernel* and *filter* are frequently used interchangeably), while setting the bias to 0 (bias=False). Similar to the bias in neurons discussed in Chapters 1 and 2, the bias in convolutional layers adds a constant offset to the output. In the rest of this section, you'll set the bias to 0 to focus on the convolutional operation.

By default, the filters of a convolutional layer are initialized to random numbers. In Listing 3-5, however, you set the filters by overwriting the randomly initialized ones. You first initialize a filters tensor with 0s, conforming to the shape required by the convolution layer ❶. The first index in filters corresponds to the filter number, and the second index to the channel number. Then you modify this tensor to define two specific kernels: the first, which is an averaging filter ❷, and the second, which is an edge-detection filter ❸. Finally, you set these custom kernels as weights in the convolutional layer ❹.

You can think of the output, features_conv, as a new image with two pseudo-color channels created by the kernels. Importantly, you need to batch the input image before passing it through the convolutional layer, which is a requirement of PyTorch (and most other deep learning frameworks). This involves adding an additional dimension to represent the batch size by using the unsqueeze(0) method ❺. To batch the image, in this case, you transform image, which is a 3D tensor of shape [1, 12, 16] (channels, height, width), into a 4D tensor of shape [1, 1, 12, 16], where the first dimension represents the batch.

To visualize the output feature maps, implement the plot_channels() function in Listing 3-6.

```
def plot_channels(channels, figsize=(15, 5)):
    """Render multiple channels."""
    fig, axs = plt.subplots(1, channels.shape[0], figsize=figsize)
    for channel, ax, i in zip(channels, axs, range(channels.shape[0])):
    ❶  im = ax.imshow(channel, cmap="gray", aspect="equal", vmin=-2, vmax=2,
                       extent=[0, channel.shape[1], 0, channel.shape[0]])
        plt.colorbar(im)
        ax.set_title(f"Channel {i}", fontsize=24)
        ax.set_xticks(range(0, channel.shape[1] + 1))
        ax.set_yticks(range(0, channel.shape[0] + 1))
    ❷  ax.grid(color="red", linewidth=1)
    plt.show()
```

Listing 3-6: The function to render the multiple channels of an image

For each channel of an image, this function renders the channel ❶ and overlays a grid to highlight the pixels ❷.

Now you can use this function to render the feature maps obtained by the convolution:

```
plot_channels(features_conv[0].detach())
```

When passing the feature maps to the plot_channels() function, you need to first extract the first (and, in this case, only) image of the batch and then use the detach() method to tell PyTorch that you don't require gradient calculation for the image (typically required for the backpropagation).

You should get Figure 3-5.

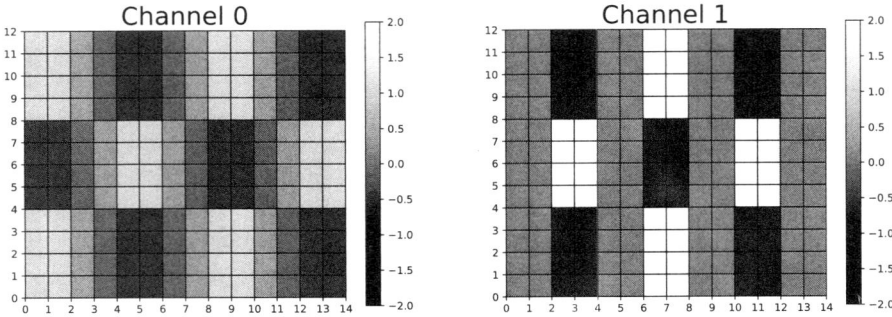

Figure 3-5: The feature maps obtained by convolutions with the filters

You can see two feature maps (channels), corresponding to the two filters in the convolutional layer you've defined in Listing 3-5. The first channel (Channel 0) corresponds to the feature map obtained by applying the averaging filter, which acts only along the horizontal direction. By averaging the intensity values, this filter produces a smoothing effect, reducing the distinction between adjacent horizontal regions.

The second channel (Channel 1) represents the feature map produced by the edge-detection filter. This filter highlights the horizontal transitions in intensity by accentuating edges perpendicular to the horizontal axis, as shown by the pronounced contrast between adjacent areas in the horizontal direction.

EXERCISES

3-8: Revisit the example in this section, using various filters. For example, use a vertical edge detector and a 3×3 Gaussian filter.

3-9: Until now, you've used grayscale images, but usually images have multiple colors. Revisit the example in this section, using an RGB image as input.

Adding ReLU Activation

You can now add a ReLU activation to the output of the convolutional layer:

```
relu = nn.ReLU()
model_relu = nn.Sequential(conv, relu)

features_relu = model_relu(image.unsqueeze(0))

plot_channels(features_relu[0].detach())
```

After creating a ReLU activation (relu), this code combines the convolutional layer and the ReLU activation via nn.Sequential(). The resulting output is rendered in Figure 3-6.

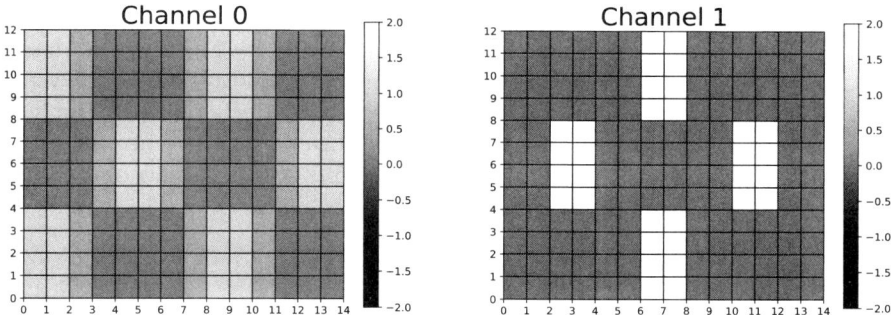

Figure 3-6: The image after convolution and ReLU activation

Comparing Figure 3-6 with Figure 3-5, you can see that all negative values have been converted to 0s.

Adding Pooling Layers

Pooling layers (also known as *downsampling layers*) reduce the spatial resolution of feature maps, downsampling the data. For example, you might add a pooling layer to the convolutional layer to reduce the computational load by decreasing the number of parameters and operations needed in the network. Furthermore, this approach helps in detecting larger-scale features by summarizing the presence of features in larger patches of the input image. You can implement a pooling layer with the following code:

```
pool = nn.MaxPool2d(kernel_size=(2, 1), stride=(2, 1))
model_pool = nn.Sequential(conv, pool)

features_pool = model_pool(image.unsqueeze(0))

plot_channels(features_pool[0].detach())
```

This code creates a *max pooling layer* (pool) with kernel_size=(2, 1), which means it extracts the maximum value over a window of 2 pixels in the vertical direction (height) and 1 pixel in the horizontal direction (width). The maximum extraction is executed with stride=(2, 1), which means that the window sequentially slides over the image with two steps in the vertical direction and one step in the horizontal one, effectively reducing the height by half and keeping the width the same. The code then combines the convolutional layer with the max pooling layer and plots the resulting feature maps, which are shown in Figure 3-7.

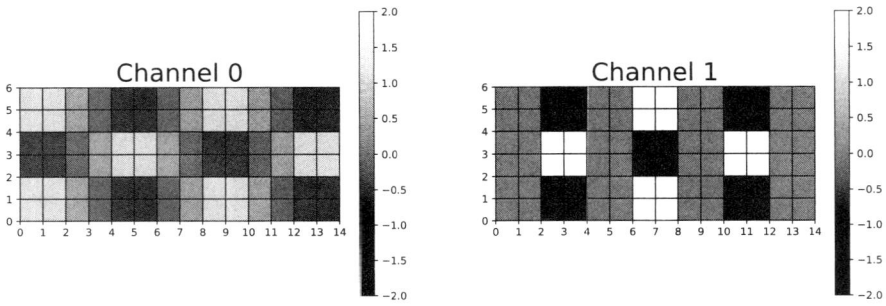

Figure 3-7: The image after convolution and pooling

By comparing Figure 3-7 with Figure 3-5, you'll notice that the pooled feature maps have half the height of those at the output of the convolutional layer. This reduction in dimensionality lessens the computational burden and helps in summarizing the information contained in larger patterns in the image.

Apart from max pooling, which selects the maximum value from the feature map within the pooling window, many alternative operations can be used by a pooling layer to downsample the feature maps. For example, *average pooling* computes the average value within the window, effectively smoothing the features; L_2-*norm pooling* calculates the square root of the sum of the squares of the pixel values, preserving the magnitude of large features; and *min pooling* selects the minimum value, useful when the absence of features is critical, as in background suppression or noise reduction.

EXERCISE

3-11: Revisit the given code to implement these alternative pooling operations; you can also change the kernel_size and stride. Observe how the output feature maps change.

Using Upsampling Layers

Upsampling layers (also known as *unpooling layers*) perform the inverse operation of pooling layers, increasing the spatial resolution of the feature maps. Understanding and utilizing both pooling and upsampling layers is crucial, as they are complementary techniques for manipulating feature maps: While pooling layers reduce dimensionality to improve computational efficiency and feature-detection robustness, upsampling layers restore or enhance the resolution, which is especially important for tasks like image segmentation or generating high-resolution outputs from lower-resolution inputs. You can implement an upsampling layer with the following code:

```
upsample = nn.Upsample(scale_factor=(2, 1))
model_upsample = nn.Sequential(conv, upsample)

features_upsample = model_upsample(image.unsqueeze(0))

plot_channels(features_upsample[0].detach(), figsize=(15, 8))
```

This code defines an upsampling layer (upsample) with scale_factor=(2, 1), which replaces each pixel by two vertically stacked pixels with the same value, thereby doubling the height of the feature maps while maintaining their original width. This upsampling layer is then combined with the convolutional layer and used to generate the output feature maps, which are rendered in Figure 3-8.

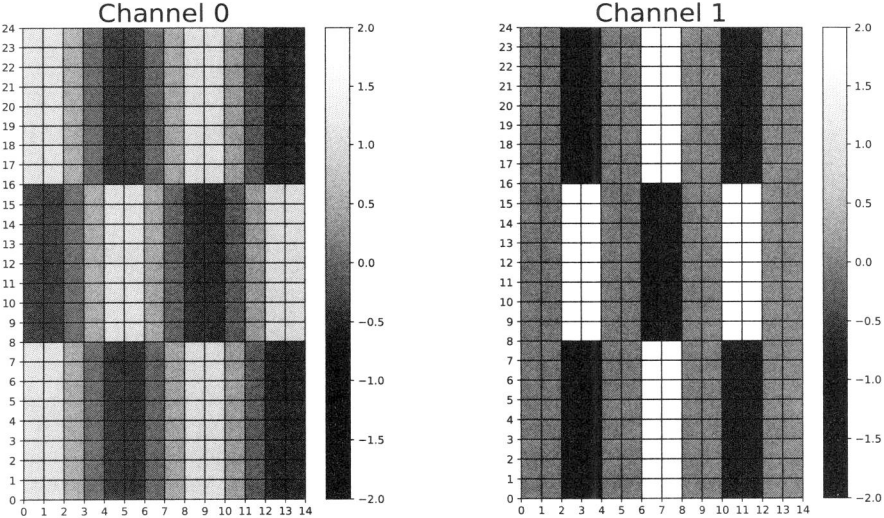

Figure 3-8: The image after convolution and upsampling

By comparing Figure 3-8 with Figure 3-5, you can verify that the upsampling has doubled the height of the feature maps, repeating each pixel twice along the vertical direction.

The upsampling method you've seen in this section uses a straightforward duplication approach that replicates pixels to enlarge the feature map. However, alternative upsampling techniques can offer different benefits. For example, *nearest neighbor upsampling* replicates the nearest pixel, potentially preserving sharper edges; *bilinear upsampling* uses linear interpolation, leading to smoother transitions; and *trilinear upsampling*, suitable for 3D data, interpolates in three dimensions.

EXERCISES

3-12: Experiment with different upsampling methods by modifying the upsampling layer in the given code. Observe and compare the effects on the spatial resolution and the overall appearance of the upsampled feature maps.

3-13: Perform subsequent pooling and upsampling operations on an image. What do you observe? How does the result depend on the order of the two operations? Try different combinations of pooling and upsampling layers.

Transforming Images

Now that you've learned about convolutional, activation, pooling, and up-sampling layers, you can combine them to construct complex convolutional architectures that transform images. This means applying operations to modify or analyze input images, crucial for tasks like image classification or object detection. The images being transformed will vary based on the application, such as facial recognition or medical imaging.

Listing 3-7 shows an example of a convolutional neural network for transforming images.

```
model_trans = nn.Sequential(
    nn.Conv2d(in_channels=1, out_channels=16, kernel_size=3),
    nn.ReLU(),
    nn.MaxPool2d(kernel_size=2, stride=2),
    nn.Conv2d(in_channels=16, out_channels=32, kernel_size=3),
    nn.ReLU(),
    nn.MaxPool2d(kernel_size=2, stride=2),
)
❶ image_trans = model_trans(image.unsqueeze(0))[0]
```

Listing 3-7: Implementing a convolutional neural network to transform an image

This code defines a neural network model named model_trans, which consists of two convolutional layers, each followed by a ReLU activation function and a max pooling layer.

The first convolutional layer has an input channel size of 1 (suitable for grayscale images) and an output channel size of 16, with a kernel size of 3 in both directions (kernel_size=3 is equivalent to kernel_size=(3, 3)). This is immediately followed by a ReLU activation function, which introduces nonlinearity in the network. Next, a max pooling layer with a kernel size of 2 and a stride of 2 in both directions reduces the spatial dimensions of the feature maps.

A similar sequence of convolutional layer, ReLU activation, and max pooling is repeated, with the second convolutional layer further increasing the number of output channels to 32.

When you use this network to process the usual input image, image, the result is a transformed image, image_trans ❶. Note that the first (and only, in this case) image is extracted from the batch. You can check the dimensions of the input and output with

```
print(f"Input image with {image.shape}")
print(f"Output image with {image_trans.shape}")
```

which prints:

```
Input image with torch.Size([1, 12, 16])
Output image with torch.Size([32, 1, 2])
```

The first indices indicate that the input image has one single color channel (it's grayscale), while the output image has 32 features. The second and third indices indicate that the input image has 12×16 pixels, but each of the output feature maps has only 1×2 pixels. Consequently, although the image has diminished in spatial resolution, it has simultaneously gained in the richness of its feature representation.

EXERCISES

3-14: Use Gaussian filters to get a smoothed, downsampled version of an image. Apply this to the MNIST digits.

3-15: Implement a code that enlarges an image through a series of upsampling and convolutional layers. Use Gaussian filters to smooth the upsampled image. Apply this to the MNIST digits.

3-16: Combine the reduction and enlargement of an image into a telescopic convolutional architecture. Apply this to the MNIST digits.

Using Dense Layers to Classify Images

You can also use convolutional neural networks for the classification of images. In this case, you typically need to flatten the feature maps obtained from the convolutional layers (known as the *convolutional base*) and couple them with a dense output layer (a *dense top*). For example, you can do this by expanding Listing 3-7 as shown in Listing 3-8.

```
model_clas = nn.Sequential(
    --snip--
    nn.MaxPool2d(kernel_size=2, stride=2),
    nn.Flatten(),
    nn.Linear(in_features=32 * 1 * 2, out_features=2),
```

```
    nn.Softmax(dim=1),
)
classification = model_clas(image.unsqueeze(0))
```

Listing 3-8: Implementing a convolutional neural network with a dense top to classify images (by modifying Listing 3-7)

This code adds a dense top to the convolutional base, transitioning from feature extraction to classification. The addition of a flattening layer reshapes the multidimensional output of the convolutional layers into a 1D tensor, which is a necessary step before feeding the data into fully connected layers. The flattening is followed by a dense layer with two output features, corresponding to a binary classification. Finally, a softmax activation is applied, obtaining some values that are often interpreted as the relative likelihoods of the two possible classes, though they aren't probabilities in the traditional statistical sense.

If you use this network to process the usual image, image, it results in a classification vector, classification. You can check the dimensions of the input and output with

```
print(f"Input image with {image.shape}")
print(f"Output classification with {classification.shape}")
```

which prints:

```
Input image with torch.Size([1, 12, 16])
Output classification with torch.Size([2])
```

The output classification has two values corresponding to two classes.

NOTE *Code Example 3-1, "Implementing Neural Networks in PyTorch," is available at https://github.com/DeepTrackAI/DeepLearningCrashCourse. Navigate to the Ch03_CNN folder and then ec03_1_cnn. The cnn.ipynb notebook provides a set of code examples to implement neural networks with PyTorch.*

EXERCISE

3-17: Use Prewitt or Sobel filters in the convolutional layers to construct a classifier capable of distinguishing between images predominantly featuring horizontal or vertical lines.

Project 3A: Classifying Malaria-Infected Blood Smears

Malaria is a blood disease transmitted by mosquitoes. It's commonly diagnosed by visually examining blood smears. The use of neural networks to automatically screen samples can help improve response time, decrease the workload of experts, and ensure reproducible results. In this project, you'll train neural networks to identify malaria-infected blood cells.

Loading the Malaria Dataset

The malaria dataset was published by Sivaramakrishnan Rajaraman and co-workers in 2018 in *PeerJ* (volume 6, article number e4568) and is publicly available. The dataset consists of 27,558 cell images with equal instances of uninfected and parasitized cells. You can download and extract the images with Listing 3-9.

```
import os
from torchvision.datasets.utils import _extract_zip, download_url

dataset_path = os.path.join(".", "blood_smears_dataset")
if not os.path.exists(dataset_path):
    url = "https://data.lhncbc.nlm.nih.gov/public/Malaria/cell_images.zip"
    download_url(url, ".")
    _extract_zip("cell_images.zip", dataset_path, None)
    os.remove("cell_images.zip")
```

Listing 3-9: Downloading and extracting the malaria dataset

This code downloads the zipped images, unzips them in the *blood_smears _dataset* folder, and finally removes the ZIP file.

Visualizing Blood Smears

You can use the `ImageFolder` class to load the images into a dataset, as shown in Listing 3-10.

```
from torchvision.datasets import ImageFolder

❶ base_dir = os.path.join(dataset_path, "cell_images")
dataset = ImageFolder(base_dir)
```

Listing 3-10: Loading the images into a dataset

This code populates the dataset with images. The base directory ❶ comprises two distinct folders, *Parasitized* and *Uninfected*, enabling you to categorize images under these specific labels. Consequently, the images are classified into two separate classes: parasitized cell images, assigned the value 0, and uninfected cell images, assigned the value 1, in alignment with their alphabetical ordering.

You can now have a look at a few images to gauge the best strategy to analyze the data. Write the `plot_blood_smears()` function shown in Listing 3-11.

```
import matplotlib.pyplot as plt
import numpy as np

def plot_blood_smears(dataset, parasitized):
    """Plot blood smears."""
    fig, axs = plt.subplots(3, 6, figsize=(16, 8))
    for ax in axs.ravel():
        image, label = dataset[np.random.randint(0, len(dataset))]
```

```
    ax.imshow(image)
    ax.set_title(f"Parasitized ({label})" if label == parasitized
            else f"Uninfected ({label})", fontsize=16)
plt.tight_layout()
plt.show()
```

Listing 3-11: The function to plot blood smears

Then use this function to plot examples of the images:

```
plot_blood_smears(dataset, parasitized=0)
```

This generates an image similar to that shown in Figure 3-9. The `parasitized` parameter indicates that the infected cells are labeled with 0s.

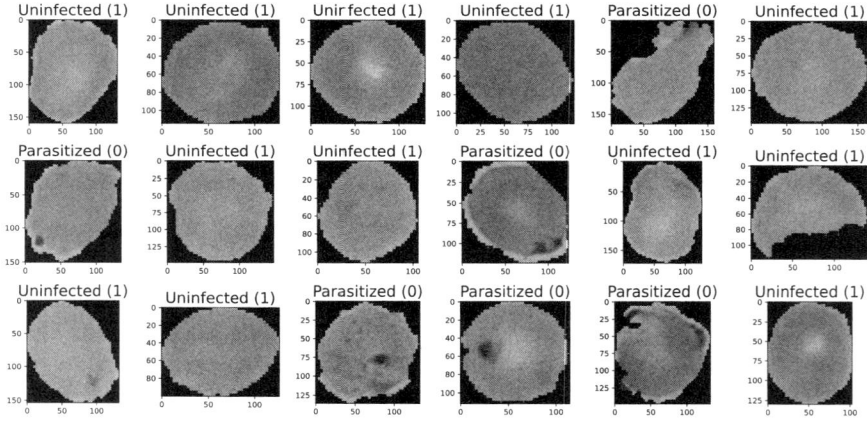

Figure 3-9: Samples of uninfected and parasitized blood-smear images

Notice that the infected cells present some spots due to the presence of the malaria plasmodium, which permits you to identify them. Also notice that the number of pixels in the images (on the order of tens of thousands of pixels) is quite large, so you'll likely need to downsample them significantly in order to be able to process them with a relatively small neural network.

Furthermore, the dimensions of the images aren't consistent; this is a problem if you want to use dense layers as part of the neural network architecture (either in a dense neural network or as the dense top of a convolutional architecture), because they require inputs of fixed length. Finally, in the medical literature, typically 1s signify the presence of a condition and 0s its absence, which is the opposite of the ground truth used in the dataset, where malaria-infected cells are denoted as 0s and uninfected cells with 1s. You'll take care of all these issues in the next section.

Transforming Images and Their Ground Truth

To take care of the identified issues, you'll need to transform the images and their labels. This can be done when creating `dataset`.

First, define a transformation to resize and normalize the images, as shown in Listing 3-12.

```
from torchvision.transforms import Compose, Resize, ToTensor

image_trans = Compose([Resize((28, 28)), ToTensor()])
```

Listing 3-12: Transformation for the images

This transformation will resize the image to 28×28 pixels and convert it to a PyTorch tensor (note that ToTensor() also normalizes the image values from 0 to 1).

You then need to create a transformation for the labels, as shown in Listing 3-13.

```
import torch

def label_trans(label):
    """Transform label."""
❶  return torch.tensor(1 - label).float().unsqueeze(-1)
```

Listing 3-13: Transformation for the labels

This defines a transformation to make the target label equal to 0 for the uninfected cells and to 1 for the parasitized ones ❶. Next, the code converts the label into a PyTorch tensor with tensor() and into a floating-point type with float(), enhancing the label's compatibility with PyTorch computational requirements. Finally, the code adds a new dimension to the tensor by using unsqueeze(-1), preparing it for batch processing in neural network models.

Next, update Listing 3-10 to make these transformations, as shown in Listing 3-14.

```
--snip--
dataset = ImageFolder(base_dir, transform=image_trans,
                        target_transform=label_trans)
```

Listing 3-14: Loading the images into a dataset while transforming images and labels (by modifying Listing 3-10)

This code assigns image_trans (Listing 3-12) to transform the input images and label_trans (Listing 3-13) to transform the labels.

Now you're ready to plot the transformed images and relative labels. You can't use the plot_blood_smears() function directly just yet because the images returned by dataset are PyTorch tensors and not NumPy arrays, but to address this, you can update the function as shown in Listing 3-15.

```
def plot_blood_smears(dataset, parasitized):
    """Plot blood smears for NumPy arrays and PyTorch tensors."""
    --snip--
    for ax in axs.ravel():
        image, label = dataset[randint(0, len(dataset))]
```

```
        if isinstance(image, torch.Tensor):
            image, label = image.numpy().transpose(1, 2, 0), label.numpy()
        ax.imshow(image)
        --snip--
```

Listing 3-15: The function to plot blood smears as either NumPy arrays or PyTorch tensors (by modifying Listing 3-11)

This revised function checks whether the image is a PyTorch tensor. If so, the function transforms the tensor into a NumPy array and transposes its dimensions so that the colors are the third dimension, as is normal for RGB images, using the transpose(1, 2, 0) method. The updated function also transforms the label from a PyTorch tensor to a NumPy array with the numpy() method. You can now use this function to plot the transformed images:

```
plot_blood_smears(dataset, parasitized=1)
```

The result should be similar to Figure 3-10. The parasitized parameter now indicates that the infected cells are those labeled with 1.

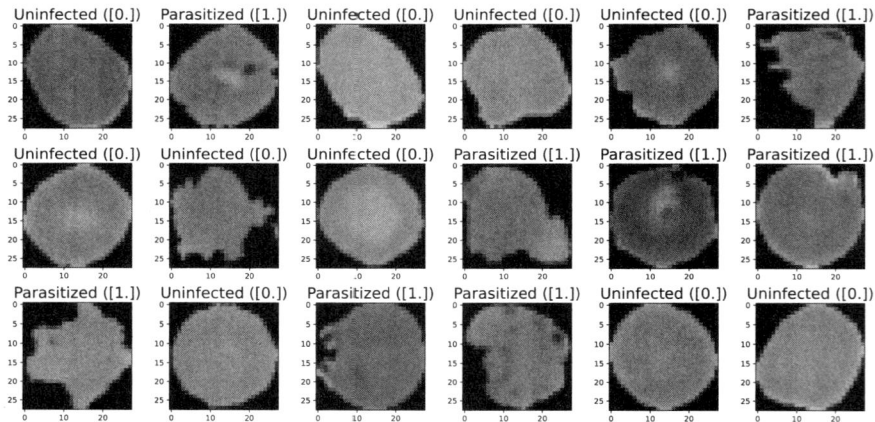

Figure 3-10: Samples of uninfected and parasitized blood-smear images after transformation

Now all the images are the same size, and the parasitized cell images are labeled as 1s and the uninfected cell images as 0s. Furthermore, you can see that the labels are NumPy arrays.

Splitting the Dataset and Defining the Data Loaders

You can now split the dataset into training (80 percent) and test (20 percent) sets with Listing 3-16.

```
train, test = torch.utils.data.random_split(dataset, [0.8, 0.2])
```

Listing 3-16: Splitting the dataset into training and test sets

Finally, define the data loaders for both sets, using Listing 3-17.

```
train_loader = torch.utils.data.DataLoader(train, batch_size=32, shuffle=True)
test_loader = torch.utils.data.DataLoader(test, batch_size=256, shuffle=False)
```

Listing 3-17: Defining the data loaders

This code defines the two data loaders. The batch size for the training data loader is set to 32, while a larger batch size of 256 is used for the test set. Another difference between the data loaders stems from the fact that it's best to shuffle the training data to improve training performance, while this isn't necessary for the test data.

Classifying with Dense Neural Networks

You can now implement a dense neural network to detect the presence of malaria infection, using Listing 3-18.

```
import deeplay as dl

dnn = dl.MultiLayerPerceptron(
    in_features=28 * 28 * 3, hidden_features=[128, 128], out_features=1,
    out_activation=torch.nn.Sigmoid,
)
```

Listing 3-18: Implementing the dense neural network

This code implements a dense neural network with one input for each pixel and color channel of the input image, two layers with 128 neurons, and a single sigmoidal output. You can use print(dnn) to check its detailed architecture.

Next, compile this neural network, assigning it a loss and an optimizer, as shown in Listing 3-19.

```
dnn_classifier = dl.BinaryClassifier(
    model=dnn, optimizer=dl.RMSprop(lr=0.001),
).create()
```

Listing 3-19: Compiling the dense neural network

This code compiles the dense neural network as a binary classifier, using RMSprop as an optimizer. You can use print(dnn_classifier) to print out the compiled network. This printout also contains information about the loss function and the tracked metrics.

The default loss of dl.BinaryClassifier is a *binary cross-entropy loss*, which is particularly well suited for scenarios where the output can be interpreted as a probability (that is, assuming values from 0 to 1 that sum up to 1). Its mathematical formulation is $L_{BCE} = -\left[y \log(p) + (1 - y) \log(1 - p)\right]$, where y

is the true label (0 or 1), and p is the predicted probability of the class with label 1. This loss function penalizes the predictions based on the divergence between the predicted probability and the actual label.

Furthermore, dl.BinaryClassifier uses *binary accuracy* as its default metric. This metric calculates the proportion of correct predictions by summing the true positives (TP) and true negatives (TN) and dividing by the total number of predictions. The formula is

$$\text{Accuracy} = \frac{\text{TP} + \text{TN}}{\text{TP} + \text{TN} + \text{FP} + \text{FN}}$$

where FP indicates false positives, and FN indicates false negatives.

Training

Next, train the dense neural network:

```
dnn_trainer = dl.Trainer(max_epochs=5, accelerator="auto")
dnn_trainer.fit(dnn_classifier, train_loader)
```

This code creates a trainer for the dense neural network with five epochs. This trainer uses error backpropagation to train the network via the fit() method.

Testing

Now let's test the trained dense neural network:

```
dnn_trainer.test(dnn_classifier, test_loader)
```

This code prints the final binary cross-entropy loss, which should be around 0.60, and the final binary accuracy, which should be around 0.68. This performance is better than chance (which would result in a binary accuracy of 0.50), but not very impressive. You'll greatly improve the performance in the next sections by using convolutional architectures.

Plotting the ROC Curve

The *ROC curve* is a way to evaluate the performance of a binary classifier. A binary classifier outputs a continuous value from 0 to 1, which is then converted to a binary classification by setting a *threshold* (or *cutoff*). This allows you to tune the behavior of the classifier. For example, it may be more acceptable on medical grounds to incorrectly classify an uninfected cell as parasitized than the other way around—in this case, it would be desirable to choose a lower threshold.

The ROC curve shows the relationship between the *true-positive rate (TPR)* and the *false-positive rate (FPR)* as the threshold is changed. Also known as *sensitivity*, or *recall*, the TPR is the proportion of positive samples that are correctly classified. The FPR, or *fallout*, is the proportion of negative samples that are incorrectly classified. The ROC curve is constructed by plotting TPR against FPR as the threshold is changed from 0 to 1. The *AUROC*, or area under the ROC curve, is a measure of classifier quality, with 0.5 being equivalent to a random classifier and 1 being a perfect classifier.

NOTE   *In case you're curious, the* receiver operating characteristic (ROC) *was developed during World War II for the analysis of radar signals. It was initially used to distinguish between signals (such as enemy aircraft) and noise (like birds or clouds) in radar technology. The ROC curve was later adopted in various fields, particularly in medicine and machine learning, to evaluate the performance of diagnostic tests and classification models by plotting the TPR against the FPR at various threshold settings.*

You can compute and plot the ROC curve with the `plot_roc()` function shown in Listing 3-20.

```
import torchmetrics as tm

def plot_roc(classifier, loader):
    """Plot ROC curve."""
❶  roc = tm.ROC(task="binary")
    for image, label in loader:
❷      roc.update(classifier(image), label.long())

❸  fig, ax = roc.plot(score=True)
    ax.grid(False)
    ax.axis("square")
    ax.set_xlim(0, 1)
    ax.set_ylim(0, 1)
    ax.legend(loc="center right")
    plt.show()
```

Listing 3-20: The function to calculate and plot the ROC curve of a classifier

This function uses the `ROC` class from TorchMetrics ❶ to calculate and plot the ROC curve. The labels are converted to the long format ❷, and the plot will include the AUROC value ❸.

You can then use this function to plot the ROC curve for the trained `dnn_classifier`:

```
plot_roc(dnn_classifier, test_loader)
```

Figure 3-11 shows the result.

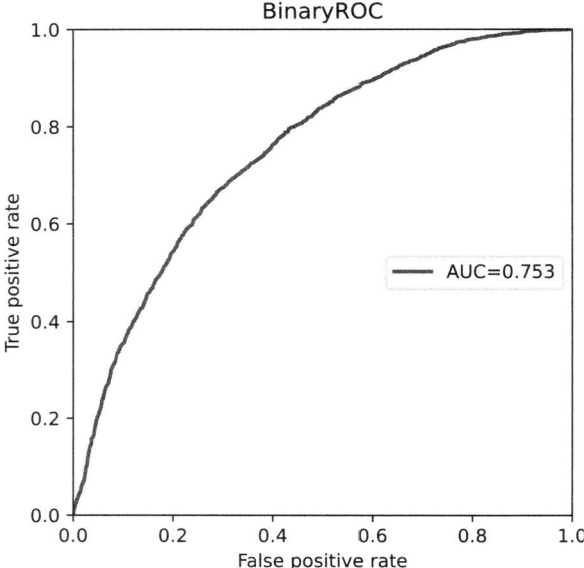

Figure 3-11: The ROC curve for the classifier, using the
dense neural network

You should get an AUROC of around 0.75, indicating a decent but not
exceptional ability to distinguish between the uninfected and parasitized
cells. For example, Figure 3-11 shows that you can correctly identify 90 percent of parasitized cells, as long as you are willing to accept mislabeling about
60 percent of the uninfected ones as false positives—probably not as good as
you'd like for medical tests.

Classifying with Convolutional Neural Networks

You can improve the performance of the classifier by using a convolutional
neural network with a dense top, as implemented by Listing 3-21.

```
conv_base = dl.ConvolutionalNeuralNetwork(
    in_channels=3, hidden_channels=[16, 16, 32], out_channels=32,
)
❶ conv_base.blocks[2].pool.configure(torch.nn.MaxPool2d, kernel_size=2)

connector = dl.Layer(torch.nn.AdaptiveAvgPool2d, output_size=1)

dense_top = dl.MultiLayerPerceptron(
    in_features=32, hidden_features=[], out_features=1,
    out_activation=torch.nn.Sigmoid,
)

cnn = dl.Sequential(conv_base, connector, dense_top)
```

Listing 3-21: Implementing a convolutional neural network with a dense top

This code creates a convolutional base (conv_base) with four layers of 16, 16, 32, and 32 filters. A max pooling layer is added between the second and third layers, with a kernel size of 2×2 (and implicitly a stride of 2 in both directions) ❶. The connector layer is created by using an average pooling layer that downsamples each one of the output filters to a single number. The code creates a dense top (dense_top) with 32 neurons and a single sigmoidal output. Finally, all these components are combined into a single convolutional neural network with a dense top (cnn).

You can visualize the overall architecture via print(cnn). In this architecture, the convolutional layers extract important features from the images, which can then be processed more effectively by the dense top.

Next, compile this neural network with Listing 3-22.

```
cnn_classifier = dl.BinaryClassifier(
    model=cnn, optimizer=dl.RMSprop(lr=0.001),
).create()
```

Listing 3-22: Compiling the convolutional neural network with a dense top

You are now ready to train your dense neural network.

Training

Train the convolutional neural network:

```
cnn_trainer = dl.Trainer(max_epochs=5, accelerator="auto")
cnn_trainer.fit(cnn_classifier, train_loader)
```

This code creates a trainer for the convolutional neural network, then calls the fit() method of the trainer to train the network.

Testing

Let's test the convolutional neural network:

```
cnn_trainer.test(cnn_classifier, test_loader)
```

This code prints the final binary cross-entropy loss, which should be around 0.12, and the final binary accuracy, which should be around 0.95. These results are much better than those with the dense neural network and, in absolute terms, are pretty good values for a binary classifier.

Plotting the ROC Curve

Now compute and display the ROC curve of this improved classifier:

```
plot_roc(cnn_classifier, test_loader)
```

You should see a ROC curve similar to that shown in Figure 3-12.

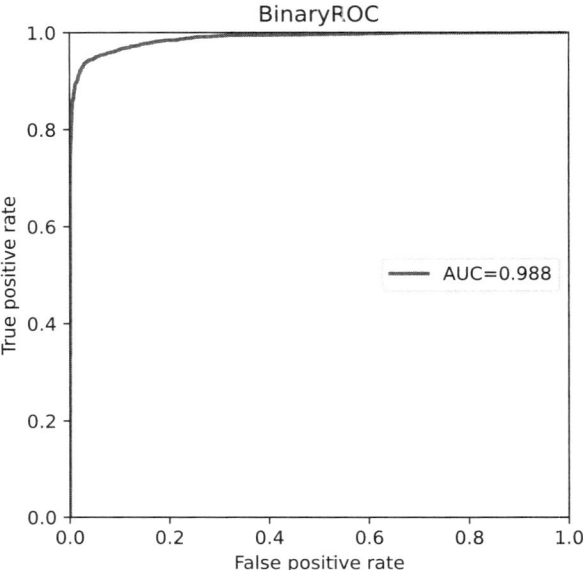

Figure 3-12: The ROC curve for the classifier, using the convolutional neural network with a dense top

This curve has an AUROC of about 0.99, which means that this is an excellent model capable of separating with high confidence the positive and negative classes.

Checking the Values of the Filters

Now that you've successfully trained a convolutional neural network to identify the malaria-infected cells, you might be curious to check the values of the filters that have been optimized in the training process. You can extract a filter as follows:

```
filter = cnn_classifier.model[0].blocks[0].layer.weight[15]
```

This accesses the model's first module, selects the initial block corresponding to the first convolutional layer, and selects the 16th filter. Then you can use print(filter) to print the filter values:

```
tensor([[[ 0.1500, -0.2196,  0.0505],
         [-0.0819,  0.0980,  0.0494],
         [ 0.0911, -0.0277, -0.1928]],

        [[-0.2429,  0.0118, -0.1666],
         [-0.0016,  0.2690,  0.1233],
         [ 0.1608,  0.2330, -0.1441]],
```

```
[[-0.1029,  0.0322, -0.0945],
 [-0.0732,  0.1109,  0.1606],
 [-0.0897,  0.0135, -0.2524]]], grad_fn=<SelectBackward0>)
```

This is a PyTorch tensor with dimensions 3 (number of color channels) by 3 (filter height) by 3 (filter width), just as you saw in Figure 3-3. Note that this tensor isn't detached from the computational graph, as indicated by grad_fn=<SelectBackward0>.

Printing out the values of the filters alone may not provide much clarity, as interpreting their specific functions can be challenging. Instead, it's more insightful to observe the activations associated with each filter when an image is processed through the neural network, which you'll do next.

Visualizing Activations of Convolutional Layers

Start by selecting an image from the dataset, using Listing 3-23.

```
from PIL import Image

im_ind = 0
image_filename = dataset.samples[im_ind][0]
image_hr = Image.open(image_filename)
image = image_trans(image_hr)
```

Listing 3-23: Loading an image from the dataset

This code retrieves the original image with index im_ind and applies the same transformation used in preprocessing (corresponding to Listing 3-12).

You can then verify whether this is an image of parasitized cells with print(label_trans(dataset.targets[im_ind])), which will print tensor([0.]) if the cells in the image are uninfected, or tensor([1.]) if they are parasitized.

To gain insights into the inner workings of a neural network, you can attach hooks to a specific layer of the network. *Hooks* are functions that can be set to execute at certain points during the forward or backward pass of the network. For example, you can use Listing 3-24 to access the activations in the forward pass of the neural network.

```
def hook_func(layer, input, output):
    """Hook for activations."""
❶ activations = output.detach().clone()
❷ print(f"Activations size: {activations.size()}")

layer = cnn_classifier.model[0].blocks[0].layer
❸ layer.register_forward_hook(hook_func)

❹ pred = cnn_classifier.model(image.unsqueeze(0))
```

Listing 3-24: Adding a hook to access the activations in the forward pass

This code defines the hook_func() function. Such a hook function takes three parameters: the layer itself, the input to the layer, and the output from the layer. The code then selects a layer to which it registers the hook ❸. When the network processes data, the hook is triggered during the forward pass ❹. This allows you to execute a custom function at that point, enabling you to observe or manipulate the activations. In this case, the hook will first detach from the current computation graph and clone the activations ❶ and then print the activation size ❷.

NOTE *Beyond visualizing activations, hooks can help significantly in debugging and analyzing neural networks.*

After utilizing the hook for its intended purpose, it's good practice to remove it from the network. This step is important because hooks, if left attached, can continue to execute on every forward pass, potentially leading to unintended side effects or performance issues. You can do this by modifying Listing 3-24 as shown in Listing 3-25.

```
--snip--
handle_hook = layer.register_forward_hook(hook_func)

try:
    pred = cnn_classifier.model(image.unsqueeze(0))
except Exception as e:
    print(f"An error occurred during model prediction: {e}")
finally:
  ❶ handle_hook.remove()
```

Listing 3-25: Adding and removing a hook in the forward pass (by modifying Listing 3-24)

This code saves the handle_hook reference to the hook handle returned when the code originally registers the hook. After the forward pass, the code uses this handle to remove the hook ❶. Furthermore, the evaluation of the neural network is enclosed inside a try-except construct to ensure that the hook removal is always executed, even if some errors occur during evaluation.

Next, write the plot_activations() function to visualize the activations, as shown in Listing 3-26.

```
def plot_activations(activations, cols=8):
    """Visualize activations."""
    rows = -(activations.shape[0] // -cols)

    fig, axs = plt.subplots(rows, cols, figsize=(2 * cols, 2 * rows))
    for i, ax in enumerate(axs.ravel()):
        ax.axis("off")
        if i < activations.shape[0]:
            ax.imshow(activations[i].numpy())
            ax.set_title(i, fontsize=16)
    plt.show()
```

Listing 3-26: The function to visualize the activations

You can now use this function within the hook, updating Listing 3-25 as shown in Listing 3-27.

```
def hook_func(layer, input, output):
    """Hook to plot activations."""
    activations = output.detach().clone()
    plot_activations(activations[0])
--snip--
```

Listing 3-27: Visualizing activations in the hook in the forward pass (by modifying Listing 3-25)

When passing activations to the plot_activations() function, this code uses [0] to select the first element of the activations tensor, representing the activations for the first image in the batch processed by the neural network.

Finally, make the last modification to Listing 3-27 to plot the activations of all convolutional layers, as shown in Listing 3-28.

```
--snip--
for block in cnn_classifier.model[0].blocks:
    layer = block.layer
    --snip--
```

Listing 3-28: Plotting the activations of all convolutional layers (by modifying Listing 3-27)

This final version of the code uses a for loop to plot the activations for each convolutional layer.

Figure 3-13 shows the activations of the first layer.

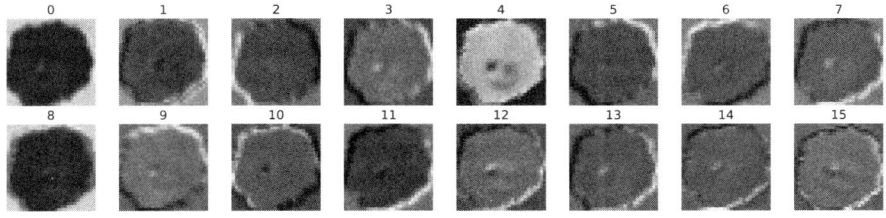

Figure 3-13: Activations of the first convolutional layer

These activations capture basic features, such as edges and simple textures, as is typical for the activations of the first layer of a convolutional neural network.

Figure 3-14 shows the fourth, and final, convolutional layer's activations.

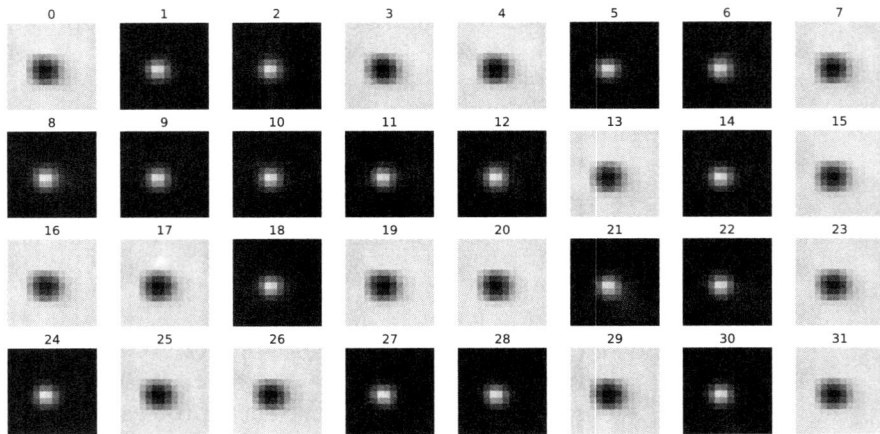

Figure 3-14: Activations of the fourth (last) convolutional layer

This last layer typically captures high-level content, representing full objects or specific parts that are relevant for making predictions. In fact, you can clearly see that the activations highlight the presence of a malaria plasmodium within the image, which then permits the dense top to classify the imaged cells as parasitized. You can also see that all the activations appear quite similar, suggesting that the convolutional network could likely be reduced in size—by decreasing the number of layers and features—without sacrificing performance.

By examining the progression from simple to complex feature detection across the layers, you gain valuable insights into how neural networks build a hierarchy of features, starting from basic edges and textures to more-complex patterns. By recognizing which types of features are extracted at each layer, you can make more-informed decisions about network architecture, such as the number of layers or their types, to better capture the relevant features for your specific task. These insights also aid in diagnosing and improving network performance, as you can pinpoint where the network might be failing to capture essential features or where it's focusing on irrelevant details.

Visualizing Heatmaps

Heatmaps give you a visual representation of which parts of the inputs are firing up your convolutional neural network, particularly in the later layers. They're like X-rays that show you what the model considers important in an image. In this section, you'll use an approach known as *Grad-CAM*, which stands for *gradient-weighted class activation mapping*, to generate these heatmaps.

First, you need to store the activations and the gradients corresponding to the layer for which you want to see the heatmap. You can do this by using hooks for both the forward and backward passes of the neural network, as shown in Listing 3-29.

```
hookdata = {}

def fwd_hook_func(layer, input, output):
    """Forward hook function."""
❶  hookdata["activations"] = output.detach().clone()

def bwd_hook_func(layer, grad_input, grad_output):
    """Backward hook function."""
❷  hookdata["gradients"] = grad_output[0].detach().clone()

layer = cnn_classifier.model[0].blocks[3].layer
handle_fwd_hook = layer.register_forward_hook(fwd_hook_func)
handle_bwd_hook = layer.register_full_backward_hook(bwd_hook_func)

try:
    pred = cnn_classifier.model(image.unsqueeze(0))
❸  pred.sum().backward()
except Exception as e:
    print(f"An error occurred during model prediction: {e}")
finally:
    handle_fwd_hook.remove()
    handle_bwd_hook.remove()
```

Listing 3-29: Implementing hooks for forward and backward passes

This code stores the activations and gradients from the last convolutional layer of the neural network. You initialize the hookdata dictionary to
store the activations ❶ and gradients ❷ captured by the hooks so that you'll
also be able to use them outside the hook functions themselves.

The fwd_hook_func() function is called during the forward pass to store
the activations ❶. These activations are detached from the current computation graph and cloned to ensure that they are preserved as they are at the
time of the forward pass.

The bwd_hook_func() function is another hook function called during the
backward pass. This function captures the gradients flowing back through
the layer immediately after the loss is calculated and the backward pass is
initiated. The first gradient tensor grad_output[0] is detached and cloned to
the dictionary ❷.

The two hooks are registered to the final convolutional layer, saving the
corresponding handle_fwd_hook and handle_bwd_hook handles. The prediction
obtained by the forward pass is used to call the backward() method ❸, initi-
ating the backward pass and triggering the backward hook. Here, the code
uses pred.sum().backward() instead of pred.backward() to combine all outputs
into a single scalar before computing gradients, which allows PyTorch to perform the backward pass without specifying a custom gradient vector. After
the forward and backward passes are complete, both the forward and backward hooks are removed.

Now you can combine activations and gradients to calculate the heatmap, as shown in Listing 3-30.

```
from torch.nn.functional import relu

activations = hookdata["activations"][0]
gradients = hookdata["gradients"][0]

pooled_gradients = gradients.mean(dim=[1, 2], keepdim=True)
❶ heatmap = relu((pooled_gradients * activations).sum(0)).detach().numpy()
```

Listing 3-30: Calculating the heatmap

This code pools the gradients via the `mean()` function, which averages them across the spatial dimensions (`dim=[1, 2]`). The use of `keepdim=True` results in a pooled gradient with the same number of channels as the original output, but with a spatial dimension of 1×1.

The heatmap is then calculated by multiplying these pooled gradients with the activations (pooled_gradients * activations) ❶. This operation is intended to weigh the activations by how much each channel contributed to the increase in the output. The sum(0) function aggregates these weighted activations across all channels, resulting in a single 2D heatmap.

Finally, the `relu()` function is applied to the aggregated heatmap to zero out any negative values, because you're interested in only the features that have a positive influence on the target class. Negative values would indicate pixels that decrease the output for the target class, which isn't useful for the heatmap. The heatmap is then detached from the computation graph and converted into a NumPy array for visualization purposes.

Visualize the heatmap with Listing 3-31.

```
from numpy import array
from skimage.exposure import rescale_intensity
from skimage.transform import resize

rescaled_image = rescale_intensity(array(image_hr), out_range=(0, 1))
resized_heatmap = resize(heatmap, rescaled_image.shape, order=2)
rescaled_heatmap = rescale_intensity(resized_heatmap, out_range=(0.25, 1))

plt.figure(figsize=(12, 5))

plt.subplot(1, 3, 1)
❶ plt.imshow(rescaled_image, interpolation="bilinear")
plt.title("Original image", fontsize=16)
plt.axis("off")

plt.subplot(1, 3, 2)
❷ plt.imshow(rescaled_heatmap.mean(axis=-1), interpolation="bilinear")
plt.title("Heatmap with Grad-CAM", fontsize=16)
plt.axis("off")
```

```
plt.subplot(1, 3, 3)
❸ plt.imshow(rescaled_image * rescaled_heatmap)
plt.title("Overlay", fontsize=16)
plt.axis("off")

plt.show()
```

Listing 3-31: Plotting a heatmap

This code rescales the image's intensity as well as the heatmap's size and intensity to match them. Then the code plots the image ❶, the heatmap ❷, and their overlay ❸. Figure 3-15 shows the resulting plots.

Figure 3-15: Input image (left), heatmap obtained with Grad-CAM (center), and overlay (right)

You can see how the neural network identifies the plasmodium present in the parasitized cell and then uses this as key information to classify the cell image. The original image on the left presents the cell as viewed under a microscope, with the features of interest being relatively indistinct to the unaided eye. The Grad-CAM image in the middle provides a heatmap that highlights the specific regions the neural network is focusing on, with warmer colors indicating areas of higher importance for the model's predictions. Here, the bright spot pinpoints the location of the plasmodium. The overlay image on the right combines these two, superimposing the heatmap onto the original image, thereby illustrating exactly where the plasmodium is situated within the cell.

And there you have it: a window into your model's mind. By analyzing these heatmaps, you can get a sense of the features your model is focusing on to make its decisions. This can be incredibly useful for debugging and understanding your neural network's behavior. For instance, if the heatmap highlights an area devoid of relevant features, like the corner of an image where only background is present rather than a plasmodium, this could indicate that the model is learning to focus on noise or artifacts rather than the meaningful patterns necessary for accurate predictions. Such a discrepancy would suggest that further data preprocessing is needed to remove noise, or that the model's architecture or training process requires adjustments to ensure that it learns to prioritize biologically relevant signals.

Code Example 3-A, "Classifying Blood Smears with a Convolutional Neural Network," is available at https://github.com/DeepTrackAI/DeepLearning CrashCourse. *Navigate to the* Ch03_CNN *folder and then* ec03_A_blood _smears. *The* blood_smears.ipynb *notebook provides the complete code example that loads the malaria dataset, trains a convolutional neural network with a dense top to classify the images of cells with and without malaria, analyzes where the trained network fails, and shows the network activations and heatmaps.*

Project 3B: Localizing Microscopic Particles

Determining the position of particles within an image is a fundamental task for microscopy. In this project, you'll build a neural network to determine the position of an optically trapped microparticle in a video.

Loading the Videos

Start by downloading the particle videos, using Listing 3-32.

```
import os

if not os.path.exists("particle_dataset"):
    os.system("git clone https://github.com/DeepTrackAI/particle_dataset")
```

Listing 3-32: Downloading the videos of an optically trapped particle

This code downloads the particle dataset into *particle_dataset*. This folder contains two videos with an optically trapped particle. One video is acquired with very low noise (*low_noise.avi*), and the other with very high noise (*high _noise.avi*). In both cases, an optically trapped microscopic particle jiggles around the center of the frame because of Brownian motion. This dataset was published in 2019 by Saga Helgadottir and co-workers in *Optica* (volume 6, pages 506–513).

Next, implement the load_video() function in Listing 3-33.

```
import cv2
import numpy as np

def load_video(path, frames_to_load, image_size):
    """Load video."""
    video = cv2.VideoCapture(path)

    data = []
    for _ in range(frames_to_load):
        _, frame = video.read()
        frame = cv2.normalize(frame, None, 0, 255, cv2.NORM_MINMAX)
        frame = cv2.cvtColor(frame, cv2.COLOR_BGR2GRAY) / 255
        frame = cv2.resize(frame, (image_size, image_size))
```

```
        data.append(frame)

    return np.array(data)
```

Listing 3-33: The function to load a video

This function takes as input the path to the video file, loads the video, and returns a NumPy array containing the extracted frames. After loading the video, the function returns `frames_to_load` frames. The code extracts each `frame`, normalizes its pixel values to the range 0 to 255, converts it to grayscale and normalizes the pixel values in the range 0 to 1, resizes it to `image_size` by `image_size` pixels, and stores the frame in the `data` list. Finally, the function returns the list of frames as a NumPy array.

Now use this function to load the first 100 frames for each video with Listing 3-34.

```
image_size = 51
video_low_noise = \
    load_video(os.path.join("particle_dataset", "low_noise.avi"),
            frames_to_load=100, image_size=image_size)
video_high_noise = \
    load_video(os.path.join("particle_dataset", "high_noise.avi"),
            frames_to_load=100, image_size=image_size)
```

Listing 3-34: Loading the first 100 frames of each video

Let's have a look at some of the frames, using Listing 3-35.

```
import matplotlib.pyplot as plt

fig, axs = plt.subplots(2, 6, figsize=(24, 8))
for i in range(6):
    axs[0, i].imshow(video_low_noise[i], cmap="gray", vmin=0, vmax=1)
    axs[0, i].text(0, 5, f"Frame {i}", color="white", fontsize=24)
    axs[0, i].axis("off")

    axs[1, i].imshow(video_high_noise[i], cmap="gray", vmin=0, vmax=1)
    axs[1, i].text(0, 5, f"Frame {i}", color="white", fontsize=24)
    axs[1, i].axis("off")
plt.subplots_adjust(wspace=0.1, hspace=0.1)
plt.show()
```

Listing 3-35: Plotting the first six frames of each video

This code plots the first six frames of each video, as shown in Figure 3-16.

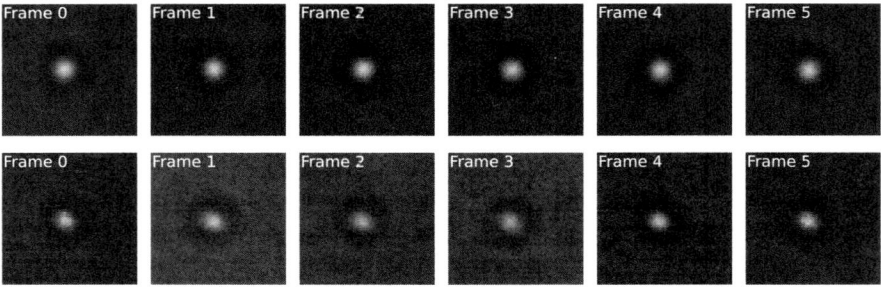

Figure 3-16: The first six frames of the low-noise (top) and high-noise (bottom) videos

In the top row, the frames are captured with high-quality illumination, so it's easy to identify the particle and locate its center. The particle is always close to the center of the frame because of the optical trap, but not exactly in the same position because it's continually shaken by the Brownian motion. In the bottom row, the same particle is captured with poor illumination. Now, it isn't so easy anymore to accurately locate the particle position, as you'll experience when trying to manually annotate this data in the next section.

Manually Annotating the Videos

To train a neural network, you need to know the ground truth. In this case, for each video frame, you need the corresponding particle position. A common way to get particle positions that can be used as a ground truth is to manually annotate some of the data and then use it for training and testing.

You can use the `ManualAnnotation` class shown in Listing 3-36 to do this.

```python
from matplotlib.widgets import Cursor

class ManualAnnotation:
    """Graphical interface for manual annotation."""

    def __init__(self, images):
        """Initialize manual annotation."""
        self.images, self.positions, self.i = images, [], 0
        self.fig, self.ax = plt.subplots(1, 1, figsize=(5, 5))
        self.fig.canvas.header_visible = False
        self.fig.canvas.footer_visible = False

    def start(self):
        """Start manual annotation."""
        self.im = self.ax.imshow(self.images[self.i], cmap="gray",
                                 vmin=0, vmax=1)
        self.text = self.ax.text(3, 5,
                                 f"Frame {self.i + 1} of {len(self.images)}",
                                 color="white", fontsize=12)
        self.ax.axis("off")
```

```
        self.cursor = Cursor(self.ax, useblit=True, color="red", linewidth=1)
        self.cid = self.fig.canvas.mpl_connect("button_press_event",
                                                self.onclick)
        self.next_image()
        plt.show()

    def next_image(self):
        """Get next image."""
        self.im.set_data(self.images[self.i])
        self.text.set_text(f"Frame {self.i + 1} of {len(self.images)}")
        self.fig.canvas.draw_idle()

    def onclick(self, event):
        """Save position on click."""
        self.positions.append([event.xdata, event.ydata])
        if self.i < len(self.images) - 1:
            self.i += 1
            self.next_image()
        else:
            self.fig.canvas.mpl_disconnect(self.cid)
            plt.close()
            return
```

Listing 3-36: The class to manually annotate the video frames with the particle position

This class creates an object that uses the Matplotlib library to create a simple graphical user interface (GUI) that allows you to record the position of the particle center by clicking it. The _init_() method initializes the GUI, setting up the figure and axes and preparing the image sequence for display. The start() method is where the actual GUI is displayed; it shows the first image and sets up the cursor for annotation. The next_image() method updates the display with the next frame in the sequence. The onclick() method captures the user's clicks, recording the position of the particle in each frame. This method also handles the progression to the next frame and concludes the annotation process when all frames have been processed.

You can use this class to annotate a subset of images, combining both low-noise and high-noise ones, as shown in Listing 3-37.

❶ ```%matplotlib ipympl

number_of_images_to_annotate = 100

dataset = np.concatenate([video_low_noise, video_high_noise], axis=0)
np.random.shuffle(dataset)
images_to_annotate = np.random.choice(
    np.arange(dataset.shape[0]), number_of_images_to_annotate, replace=False,
)

manual_annotation = ManualAnnotation(dataset[images_to_annotate])
```
```

```
manual_annotation.start()
annotated_images = manual_annotation.images
manual_positions = manual_annotation.positions
```

❷ `%matplotlib inline`

Listing 3-37: Manually annotating some video frames with the particle positions

This demonstrates the process of using the `ManualAnnotation` class for annotating a series of images with particle positions. Initially, the script sets up an interactive Matplotlib environment suitable for notebooks ❶. The script prepares a dataset for annotation by combining low-noise and high-noise video datasets and shuffling them to ensure variability. Then the script randomly selects a subset of `number_of_images_to_annotate` images from this combined dataset for annotation.

Subsequently, the script instantiates the `ManualAnnotation` object with the selected images and starts the annotation process. This opens a GUI for the user to manually annotate the particle positions in each image, shown in Figure 3-17.

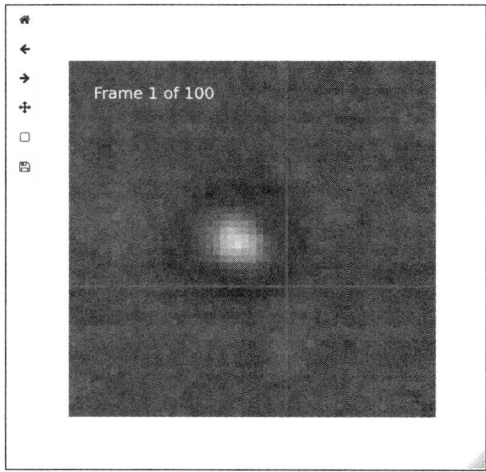

Figure 3-17: The GUI for manually annotating the video frames with the particle positions

After completing the annotation, the script retrieves the annotated images (`annotated_images`) and the corresponding manually recorded positions (`manual_positions`). Finally, the script switches back to the normal Matplotlib backend ❷, concluding the interactive session and returning to the standard plotting environment.

Save the annotated images and relative positions into files, using Listing 3-38.

```
if not os.path.exists("annotated_images.npy"):
    np.save("annotated_images.npy", np.array(annotated_images))
if not os.path.exists("manual_positions.npy"):
    np.save("manual_positions.npy", np.array(manual_positions))
```

Listing 3-38: Saving the annotated images and relative positions

This script saves the data as NumPy arrays into the *annotated_images.npy* and *manual_positions.npy* files, but only if these files don't already exist.

Now you need to define the data loaders to use the data in the training. To do this, you first need to define a custom dataset, as shown in Listing 3-39.

```
import torch

class AnnotatedDataset(torch.utils.data.Dataset):
    """Manually annotated dataset."""

    def __init__(self, file_images, file_positions):
        """Load annotated images and manual positions."""
        self.images = np.load(file_images)
        self.positions = np.load(file_positions)

    def __len__(self):
        """Return number of images."""
        return self.images.shape[0]

    def __getitem__(self, idx):
        """Get next image and annotated position."""
    ❶  im = torch.tensor(self.images[idx, np.newaxis, :, :]).float()
    ❷  pos = torch.tensor(self.positions[idx] / im.shape[-1] - 0.5).float()
        return [im, pos]
```

Listing 3-39: Implementing a custom dataset for the manually annotated particle data

This class inherits from the PyTorch Dataset class. It contains the particles' images and positions loaded from the files saved during the annotation process. When a new item is requested, the __getitem__() method of this class converts the image into a PyTorch tensor with an added new axis for the batch dimension and data type set to float for computational efficiency ❶. The __getitem__() method then normalizes the position by dividing it by the image width (im.shape[-1]), offsets the position by 0.5 to refer it to the center of the image (and not to its lower-left corner), and converts the position into a float PyTorch tensor ❷. Finally, the class combines the processed image tensor and the position tensor into a list to be returned.

Now that you've defined a custom dataset, create an instance of it

```
ann_dataset = AnnotatedDataset(file_images="annotated_images.npy",
                               file_positions="manual_positions.npy")
```

and use it to create the data loaders:

```
import deeplay as dl

train_ann_dataset, test_ann_dataset = \
    torch.utils.data.random_split(ann_dataset, [0.8, 0.2])

train_ann_dataloader = dl.DataLoader(train_ann_dataset, batch_size=1)
test_ann_dataloader = dl.DataLoader(test_ann_dataset, batch_size=1)
```

This code splits the annotated data into training and test sets so that 80 percent of the data is in the training set. Then the code creates a training data loader and a testing data loader.

Implementing a Convolutional Neural Network

Now you're ready to implement the neural network for classification with Listing 3-40.

```
cnn = dl.Sequential(
    dl.ConvolutionalNeuralNetwork(
        in_channels=1, hidden_channels=[16, 32], out_channels=64,
        pool=torch.nn.MaxPool2d(kernel_size=2), out_activation=torch.nn.ReLU,
    ),
    dl.Layer(torch.nn.MaxPool2d, kernel_size=2),
    dl.Layer(torch.nn.Flatten),
    dl.MultiLayerPerceptron(
        in_features=6 * 6 * 64, hidden_features=[32, 32], out_features=2,
        out_activation=torch.nn.Identity,
    ),
)
```

Listing 3-40: Implementing the convolutional neural network with a dense top

This code implements a convolutional neural network with a dense top that accepts as input an image of the particle and returns as output its predicted x- and y-coordinates. Before proceeding further, print out this neural network with print(cnn) and explore its details; it's indeed good practice to verify in the printout that the various layers and their properties match the way you set them up.

Next, compile the neural network with Listing 3-41.

```
from torchmetrics import MeanAbsoluteError as MAE

❶ cnn_regressor_template = dl.Regressor(
       model=cnn, loss=torch.nn.MSELoss(), optimizer=dl.Adam(), metrics=[MAE()],
   )
❷ cnn_ann_regressor = cnn_regressor_template.create()
```

Listing 3-41: Compiling the neural network

This code creates a template to use the neural network as a regressor ❶, setting up its loss function (`torch.nn.MSELoss()`), its optimizer (`dl.Adam()`), and a metric to be tracked (`MAE()`). Then the code creates a concrete instance of this template ❷. You can check the structure of this regressor with `print(cnn_ann_regressor)` and verify that its architecture and properties are as set up.

Training with Annotated Data

To train the neural network with the manually annotated data, use

```
cnn_ann_trainer = dl.Trainer(max_epochs=50, accelerator="auto")
cnn_ann_trainer.fit(cnn_ann_regressor, train_ann_dataloader)
```

which trains the neural network for 50 epochs with the manually annotated data.

Testing the Trained Neural Network

Next, evaluate the trained neural network performance:

```
test_ann_results = cnn_ann_trainer.test(cnn_ann_regressor, test_ann_dataloader)
MAE_ann = test_ann_results[0]["testMeanAbsoluteError_epoch"] * image_size
print(f"Mean pixel error (MAE): {MAE_ann:.3f} pixels")
```

This code tests the neural network against the test annotated data, then retrieves the MAE from the tracked metrics. This error is transformed from normalized units into pixels by multiplying it by `image_size`, and the result is printed. Depending on the consistency of your annotations, you might observe mean pixel errors varying from 0.2 to 2 pixels, indicating a substantial margin of error.

The observed error in this context relates to the precision *of your manual annotations.* Precision *here refers to the consistency or repeatability of your annotations. Higher error values indicate lower precision, suggesting that repeating annotations on the same image may yield significantly different positions. This concept of precision is distinct from the accuracy of the manual annotation process.* Accuracy *concerns how closely your annotations align with the actual ground-truth values. However, without access to these ground-truth values, it isn't possible to directly assess the accuracy of your manual annotations. Therefore, while you can gauge the precision of your work, assessing its accuracy remains a challenge in the absence of a known standard or reference.*

Repeating the annotation process with your family and friends could be a fascinating experiment to explore the variability and reliability of manual annotations. By involving multiple annotators, you can assess how different individuals perceive and mark the same set of images. This approach offers several benefits and insights, such as understanding the range of precision among different people, identifying potential biases in annotation, and determining whether certain images are consistently difficult to annotate.

Visualizing the Predictions

Finally, you can visualize the predictions of the trained network and compare them with your manual annotations, using Listing 3-42.

```
❶ indices = np.random.choice(np.arange(len(test_ann_dataset)), 6, replace=False)
❷ images = [test_ann_dataset[index][0] for index in indices]
❸ annotations = [test_ann_dataset[index][1] for index in indices]
❹ predictions = cnn_ann_regressor(torch.stack(images))

fig, axs = plt.subplots(1, 6, figsize=(25, 8))
for ax, im, ann, pred in zip(axs, images, annotations, predictions):
    ax.imshow(im.numpy().squeeze(), cmap="gray")

    ann = ann * image_size + image_size / 2
    ax.scatter(ann[0], ann[1], marker="+", c="g", s=500, linewidth=6,
            label="Annotation")

    pred = pred.detach().numpy() * image_size + image_size / 2
    ax.scatter(pred[0], pred[1], marker="x", c="r", s=500, linewidth=4,
            label="Prediction")

    ax.set_axis_off()
ax.legend(loc=(0.5, 0.8), framealpha=1, fontsize=24)
plt.show()
```

Listing 3-42: Comparing the predictions with the manual annotations

This code chooses some random frame indices ❶. Then it extracts the relative images ❷ and annotations ❸ and predicts the positions by using the neural network trained with the manual annotations ❹. The code then generates images that should look similar to those in Figure 3-18.

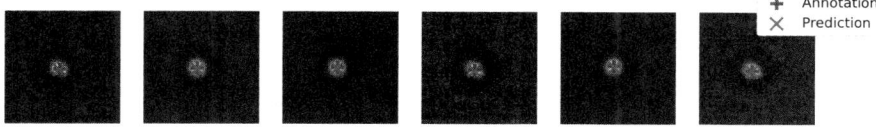

Figure 3-18: Particle images with annotated and predicted positions

The network has, in fact, learned to predict particle positions that are close to the manual annotations used for its training, as you can verify by observing that the annotation and prediction markers match.

Simulating the Training Data

You can enhance your neural network's performance by using simulated data rather than relying on manually annotated data. Manual annotations can be inconsistent because of differences in the way different people interpret data (*interobserver variability*) and because the same person may interpret data differently over time (*intraobserver variability*). Additionally, manually labeling data is often slow, effort intensive, and difficult to scale.

In contrast, using simulated datasets for training removes the inconsistencies associated with human annotations and enables the generation of substantially larger datasets. Such large datasets are vital for effectively training deep learning models.

To create simulated datasets that closely mimic experimental conditions, you need to carefully design them to incorporate a range of variable properties and realistic noise. This process requires simulating the various scenarios, conditions, and outliers that the neural network might encounter in real-world applications. You need to integrate factors such as differing lighting conditions and sensor noise to ensure that the dataset is comprehensive and challenging enough, replicating the complexity and unpredictability of real-world data as closely as possible.

Creating Particle Images

You'll use the DeepTrack2 library to generate simulated particle images, which will then be used to train your model. As you'll see, this method streamlines the training process while also potentially increasing the robustness and accuracy of the neural network.

Define the particle via the MieSphere class, as shown in Listing 3-43.

```
import deeptrack as dt

particle = dt.scatterers.MieSphere(
    position=(25, 25), z=0, radius=500e-9, refractive_index=1.37,
    position_unit="pixel",
)
```

Listing 3-43: Defining a microscopic particle with its physical parameters

This code defines the position of the particle in the image along the x- and y-axes, its z-coordinate, its radius in meters, its refractive index, and the units of the positions.

Next, you need to specify the optical device to image the particle. You'll use a bright-field microscope, implemented by the Brightfield class, as shown in Listing 3-44.

```
brightfield_microscope = dt.optics.Brightfield(
    wavelength=630e-9, NA=0.8, resolution=1e-6, magnification=15,
    refractive_index_medium=1.33, output_region=(0, 0, image_size, image_size),
)
```

Listing 3-44: Defining the optical device

This code defines the wavelength of the illuminating light in meters, the numerical aperture of the objective, the effective camera pixel size in meters, the magnification of the optical device, the refractive index of the medium where the particle is immersed, and the size of the camera sensor in pixels. These optical device parameters are defined such that they (loosely) match the experimental conditions in which the videos were acquired.

To create images of the particles, you need to combine brightfield _microscope with particle:

```
imaged_particle = brightfield_microscope(particle)
```

This code passes the particle to the bright-field microscope, creating the new imaged_particle pipeline that you'll use to create images of the particle. A *pipeline* is a series of steps or processes that allows for the systematic transformation, analysis, and interpretation of data.

Plot the simulated particle image with the plot_simulated_particles() function in Listing 3-45.

```
def plot_simulated_particles(image_pipeline):
    """Plot simulated particles."""
    fig, axs = plt.subplots(1, 6, figsize=(25, 8))
    for i, ax in enumerate(axs.flatten()):
        image = image_pipeline.update().resolve()
        ax.imshow(np.squeeze(image), cmap="gray")
        ax.set_xticks([])
        ax.set_yticks([])
    plt.show()
```

Listing 3-45: The function to plot the images of simulated particles

This function calls the update() method on the image_pipeline to get a new instance of the particle, and the resolve() method to resolve the simulation pipeline and to return the image of the particle. Then the function squeezes the resulting image to plot it.

You can plot multiple particle images obtained with this pipeline, using Listing 3-46.

```
plot_simulated_particles(imaged_particle)
```

Listing 3-46: Rendering images of the particle

Figure 3-19 shows the resulting examples of simulated particles.

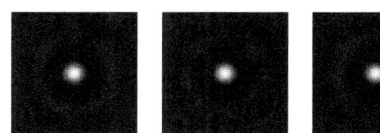

Figure 3-19: The simulated particle images

At the moment, the simulation pipeline is completely deterministic so that the particle will always have the same properties and be at the same position. This is why the six images are exactly the same. In the following section, you'll see how to make images of particles with a range of random properties.

Varying Particle Properties

To simulate images representative of the experimental dataset, you need to vary the particle's position, radius, and refractive index. You can do this by defining the particle's properties as functions that return a random value within a given range, updating Listing 3-43 as shown in Listing 3-47.

```
particle = dt.scatterers.MieSphere(
    position=lambda: np.random.uniform(image_size / 2 - 5,
                                        image_size / 2 + 5, 2),
    z=lambda: np.random.uniform(-1, -1),
    radius=lambda: np.random.uniform(500, 600) * 1e-9,
    refractive_index=lambda: np.random.uniform(1.37, 1.42),
    position_unit="pixel",
)
imaged_particle = brightfield_microscope(particle)
```

Listing 3-47: Simulating a particle with variable properties (by modifying Listing 3-43)

This code defines the particle's properties as lambda functions that return a random value within a given range. *Lambda functions* are small anonymous functions in programming that have a simple expression. The ranges are chosen to match the experimental conditions.

The position of the particle is a lambda function that returns two random values defined in the range from image_size / 2 - 5 to image_size / 2 + 5, its z-coordinate is a lambda function that returns a random value drawn from a uniform distribution defined in the range from −1 to 1, its radius is a lambda function that returns a random value in the range from 500 nm to 600 nm, and its refractive index is a lambda function that returns a random value defined in the range (1.37, 1.42). The code then resets imaged_particle to use the new particle.

When you plot examples of the resulting particle images with Listing 3-46, you should get particle images like those shown in Figure 3-20.

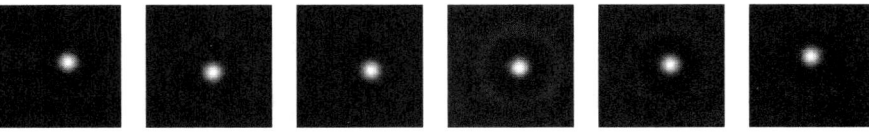

Figure 3-20: The simulated particle images with random parameters

These particle images are different each time `imaged_particle` is updated.

Generating Noisy Images

Although now the simulated images reproduce the variability encountered in experiments, they are still lacking the noise always present in experimental images. You can generate noisy images by adding a Poisson noise source to the simulation pipeline, as shown in Listing 3-48.

```
noise = dt.Poisson(
    min_snr=5, max_snr=20, background=1,
  ❶ snr=lambda min_snr, max_snr: np.random.uniform(min_snr, max_snr),
)
noisy_imaged_particle = imaged_particle >> noise

plot_simulated_particles(noisy_imaged_particle)
```

Listing 3-48: Adding noise to the simulation pipeline

This code adds noise to the simulated images of the particles, defining the minimum signal-to-noise ratio (SNR) as 5 and the maximum SNR as 20. Then a lambda function is defined to determine the SNR as a random value between the minimum and maximum SNR ❶, which is also a good example of a lambda function with two inputs. The code also defines the background intensity as 1, which is used to calculate the signal of the image. Finally, the code adds the noise source to the simulation pipeline by using the >> operator and plots some examples of the resulting images, shown in Figure 3-21.

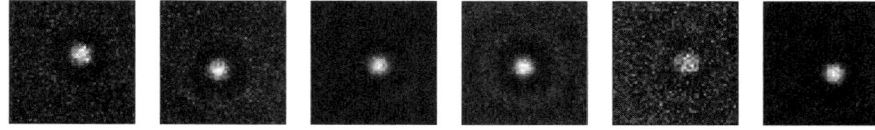

Figure 3-21: The simulated particle images with noise

Finally, to ensure that the neural network inputs are consistently scaled, facilitating more-stable and efficient learning, you should normalize the images to the range of 0 to 1 with Listing 3-49.

```
normalization = dt.NormalizeMinMax(lambda: np.random.uniform(0.0, 0.2),
                                   lambda: np.random.uniform(0.8, 1.0))
image_pipeline = noisy_imaged_particle >> normalization
```

Listing 3-49: Normalizing the simulated images

This code defines the normalization function, setting the minimum and maximum values of the normalization to random values in the range (0, 0.2) and (0.8, 1), respectively. Then the normalization function is added to the simulation pipeline via the >> operator.

Getting Particle Positions

Now you need to extract the particle's position from the simulated image to use as the ground truth when training the neural network:

```
pipeline = image_pipeline & particle.position
```

This code uses the & operator to create a pipeline to get both the simulated image and the particle position, which you can get as follows:

```
image, position = pipeline.update().resolve()
```

Then update the plot_simulated_particles() function to also plot the positions of the particles, as shown in Listing 3-50.

```
def plot_simulated_particles_with_positions(pipeline):
    """Plot simulated particles with positions."""
    --snip--
    for i, ax in enumerate(axes.flatten()):
        image, position = pipeline.update().resolve()
        ax.imshow(np.squeeze(image), cmap="gray")
        ax.scatter(position[1], position[0], s=500, facecolors="none",
                   edgecolor="g", linewidth=6)
        --snip--
```

Listing 3-50: The function to plot the images of simulated particles with their position (by modifying Listing 3-45)

Use this function to plot the simulated particles with their ground-truth positions:

```
plot_simulated_particles_with_positions(pipeline)
```

The resulting images should look like those in Figure 3-22.

Figure 3-22: The simulated particles with ground-truth positions

As expected, the ground-truth positions (plotted as circles) are perfectly at the center of the simulated images of particles, providing the data you need to train the neural network.

Preprocessing the Simulated Data

Modify the `AnnotatedDataset` class to work with the simulation pipeline instead of the annotated data, creating the `SimulatedDataset` class in Listing 3-51.

```
class SimulatedDataset(torch.utils.data.Dataset):
    """Dataset with simulated particles."""

    def __init__(self, pipeline, data_size):
        """Initialize simulated dataset."""
        images, positions = [], []
        for _ in range(data_size):
        ❶ image, position = pipeline.update().resolve()
        ❷ images.append(image), positions.append(position[[1, 0]])
        self.images, self.positions = np.array(images), np.array(positions)

    --snip--

    def __getitem__(self, idx):
        """Get next image and annotated position."""
    ❸ im = torch.tensor(self.images[idx]).float().permute(2, 0, 1)
    ❹ pos = torch.tensor(self.positions[idx] / im.shape[-1] - 0.5).float()
        return [im, pos]
```

Listing 3-51: Implementing a custom dataset for the simulated data (by modifying Listing 3-39)

In its initialization, this updated class creates the required number of simulations ❶, from which it saves as class attributes the images themselves and the relative ground-truth positions ❷. When getting an item, the __getitem__() method returns the image ❸ and the relative position ❹ already prepared as float PyTorch tensors.

Use this class to create the training and test data loaders, as shown in Listing 3-52.

```
train_sim_dataloader = dl.DataLoader(
    SimulatedDataset(pipeline=pipeline, data_size=10_000), batch_size=32,
)
test_sim_dataloader = dl.DataLoader(
    SimulatedDataset(pipeline=pipeline, data_size=100), batch_size=32,
)
```

Listing 3-52: Creating the data loaders for the simulated data

This code creates a training data loader with a dataset of 10,000 images, many more than what you could manually annotate in a reasonable amount of time. For the test dataset, you can still use just 100 images.

Training with Simulated Data

Now you're all set to train the neural network with simulated data:

```
cnn_sim_regressor = cnn_regressor_template.create()
cnn_sim_trainer = dl.Trainer(max_epochs=50, accelerator="auto")
cnn_sim_trainer.fit(cnn_sim_regressor, train_sim_dataloader)
```

This code creates a new instance of cnn_regressor_template and a new trainer and proceeds to train this second neural network with the simulated dataset.

Testing the Trained Neural Network

Test the trained neural network:

```
test_sim_results = cnn_sim_trainer.test(cnn_sim_regressor, test_sim_dataloader)
MAE_sim = test_sim_results[0]["testMeanAbsoluteError_epoch"] * image_size
print(f"Mean pixel error (MAE): {MAE_sim:.3f} pixels")
```

This code computes and prints the MAE of the neural network trained with simulated data, expected to be below 0.1 pixels. This represents a significant improvement in the neural network's precision compared to the model trained on manually annotated data. The improvement primarily stems from the systematic nature of the simulated data, which eliminates human-induced inconsistencies, as well as from the larger size of the dataset, which is crucial for deep learning models.

As an interesting exercise, you could analyze the impact of varying the size of the training dataset on the model's performance, gaining insights into the scalability and adaptability of the neural network to different data volumes.

Plotting the Predictions vs. the Ground Truth

To further evaluate the network's performance, you can plot the predicted particle positions versus the true particle positions, using Listing 3-53.

```
preds, gts = [], []
for image, position in iter(test_sim_dataloader):
❶  preds.append(cnn_sim_regressor(image))
❷  gts.append(position)
preds = torch.cat(preds, dim=0).detach().numpy()
gts = torch.cat(gts, dim=0).numpy()

fig, axs = plt.subplots(1, 2)
for i, ax, coordinate in zip([0, 1], axs, ["x", "y"]):
    gt, pred = gts[:][:, i], preds[:][:, i]
    ax.scatter(gt, pred, alpha=0.2)
    ax.plot([np.min(gt), np.max(gt)], [np.min(pred), np.max(pred)], c="k")
    ax.set_title(f"{coordinate}-coordinates")
    ax.set_xlabel("Prediction")
    ax.set_ylabel("Ground truth")
    ax.set_aspect("equal")
```

```
        ax.set_xlim([-0.07, 0.07])
        ax.set_ylim([-0.07, 0.07])
        ax.label_outer()
plt.show()
```

Listing 3-53: Plotting the predictions versus the ground truth

In the for loop, this code iterates over each item in the test data loader. For each item, the neural network predicts the particle position and appends it to the preds list ❶. Correspondingly, the actual ground-truth position from the data item is appended to the gts list ❷. After completing the loop, the lists of predictions and ground truths are concatenated into tensors and then converted into NumPy arrays for ease of handling and visualization. Finally, they are plotted in the predictions-versus-ground-truth plots shown in Figure 3-23.

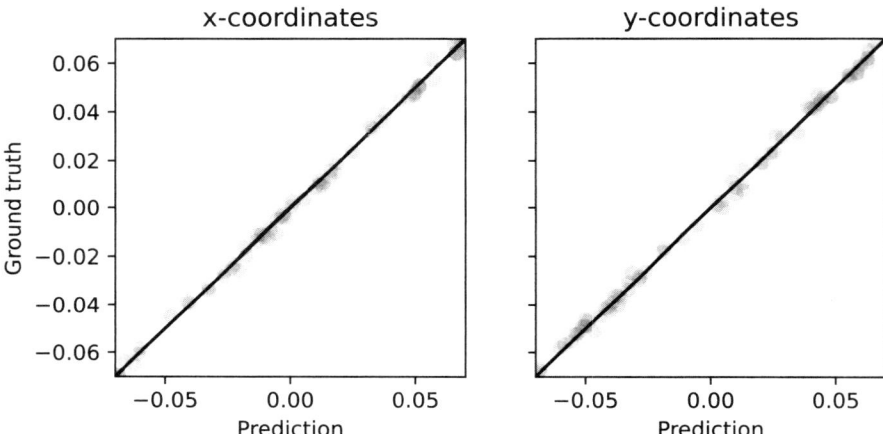

Figure 3-23: Ground-truth versus predicted positions

The predicted particle positions are in good agreement with the true particle positions, demonstrating the high quality of the training.

Comparing with the Annotated Data

Let's compare the positions obtained by the neural network trained on simulated data with your manual annotations:

```
test_ann_results_with_cnn_sim = \
    cnn_sim_trainer.test(cnn_sim_regressor, test_ann_dataloader)
MAE_ann_with_cnn_sim = (test_ann_results_with_cnn_sim[0]
                        ["testMeanAbsoluteError_epoch"] * image_size)
print(f"Mean pixel error (MAE): {MAE_ann_with_cnn_sim:.3f} pixels")
```

In this case, the MAE obtained from this test will strongly depend on your manual annotations.

As a last check, you can plot both the manual annotations and the network predictions on top of the experimental images, using Listing 3-54, which is a modification of Listing 3-42.

```
--snip--
predictions = cnn_sim_regressor(torch.stack(images))
--snip--
```

Listing 3-54: Plotting the predictions of the simulated data–trained neural network in comparison with the manual annotations (by modifying Listing 3-42)

Figure 3-24 shows the resulting images.

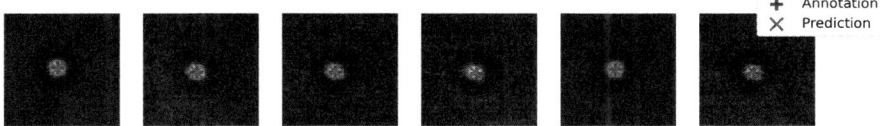

Figure 3-24: The manual annotations and predictions of the neural network trained on simulated data

The neural network predictions and the manual annotations are quite close—at least in this example, as this will strongly depend on the quality of your manual annotations.

NOTE *Code Example 3-B, "Localizing Microscopic Particles," is available at* https:// github.com/DeepTrackAI/DeepLearningCrashCourse. *Navigate to the* Ch03 _CNN *folder and then* ec03_B_particle_localization. *The* particle_localization .ipynb *notebook provides a complete code example that trains a convolutional neural network with a dense top, using annotated and simulated data, and then applies the trained neural network to experimental videos of an optically trapped particle.*

Project 3C: Creating DeepDreams

In this project, you'll explore *DeepDreams*—a concept conceived by Google engineer Alexander Mordvintsev. The fundamental question at the heart of DeepDreams is: How can an image be transformed to maximally activate a specific layer in a trained convolutional neural network?

This approach essentially flips the neural network training process on its head. Instead of tuning the weights of the network layers for optimal performance, you'll use backpropagation and gradient ascent to morph the input image into a form that highly activates a target layer. This method gives you a unique look into what a particular layer in a neural network is most responsive to, or "sees."

The DeepDreams algorithm has been aptly named for its ability to produce dreamlike, almost hallucinogenic imagery through a process of deliberate overprocessing. Interestingly, this process was named *Inceptionism*, which is a reference to InceptionNet, the first convolutional neural network used to generate DeepDreams, and the movie *Inception*.

For this project, you'll implement the DeepDreams algorithm and apply it to transform an image. Prior to starting this project, it's essential that you are already acquainted with the concepts introduced in Project 3A, particularly those relating to hooks and layer activations.

Loading an Image

You'll start by loading the image in the *neuraltissue_with_colorlabels.png* file. This image, sourced from the Drosophila ssTEM dataset at *https://figshare .com/articles/dataset/Segmented_anisotropic_ssTEM_dataset_of_neural_tissue/ 856713*, features a cross-section of neural tissue from the ventral nerve cord of a fruit fly larva (scientifically known as *Drosophila melanogaster*). Load the image with Listing 3-55.

```
from PIL import Image

image_file = "neuraltissue_with_colorlabels.png"
im = Image.open(image_file).convert("RGB").resize((256, 256))
```

Listing 3-55: Loading the image

This code uses Pillow, the common Python package for image processing, to load the image, convert it to RGB, and resize it from the original 1024×1024 pixels to 256×256 pixels for computational convenience.

Once the image is loaded, plot it by using Listing 3-56.

```
import matplotlib.pyplot as plt

plt.imshow(im)
plt.axis("off")
plt.show()
```

Listing 3-56: Plotting the image

Figure 3-25 shows the resulting image.

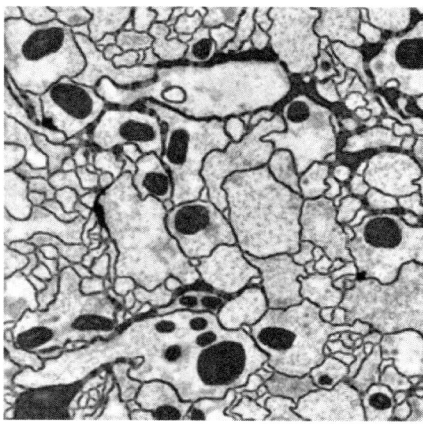

Figure 3-25: A transmission electron microscopy image of the neural tissue of a fruit fly larva

In the image, various neural structures are labeled with different shades to facilitate identification. In particular, the roundish shapes are the neuron mitochondria. Each pixel corresponds to a square with a side of length 18.4 nm (in the original image, before downsampling, it's 4.6 nm).

Loading a Pretrained Neural Network

To create DeepDreams, you need to use a pretrained network. So, you'll import the VGG16 model, a pretrained neural network known for its proficiency in image-recognition tasks, using Listing 3-57.

```
from torchvision.models import vgg16, VGG16_Weights

model = vgg16(weights=VGG16_Weights.IMAGENET1K_V1)
model.eval()
model.requires_grad_(False)
```

Listing 3-57: Loading the VGG16 pretrained neural network

This code loads the VGG16 model with weights trained on the ImageNet dataset. This large-scale, extensively annotated image database, designed for use in research on visual object recognition software, contains millions of images categorized according to a hierarchy of descriptive labels. The code then sets the model to evaluation mode with the eval() method and freezes all weights to prevent further changes with the requires_grad_(False) method.

When you print the VGG16 model with print(model), you get Listing 3-58.

```
VGG(
  (features): Sequential(
    (0): Conv2d(3, 64, kernel_size=(3, 3), stride=(1, 1), padding=(1, 1))
    (1): ReLU(inplace=True)
    (2): Conv2d(64, 64, kernel_size=(3, 3), stride=(1, 1), padding=(1, 1))
    (3): ReLU(inplace=True)
    (4): MaxPool2d(kernel_size=2, stride=2, padding=0, dilation=1, ...
    (5): Conv2d(64, 128, kernel_size=(3, 3), stride=(1, 1), padding=(1, 1))
    (6): ReLU(inplace=True)
    (7): Conv2d(128, 128, kernel_size=(3, 3), stride=(1, 1), padding=(1, 1))
    (8): ReLU(inplace=True)
    (9): MaxPool2d(kernel_size=2, stride=2, padding=0, dilation=1, ...
    (10): Conv2d(128, 256, kernel_size=(3, 3), stride=(1, 1), padding=(1, 1))
    (11): ReLU(inplace=True)
    (12): Conv2d(256, 256, kernel_size=(3, 3), stride=(1, 1), padding=(1, 1))
    (13): ReLU(inplace=True)
    (14): Conv2d(256, 256, kernel_size=(3, 3), stride=(1, 1), padding=(1, 1))
    (15): ReLU(inplace=True)
    (16): MaxPool2d(kernel_size=2, stride=2, padding=0, dilation=1, ...
    (17): Conv2d(256, 512, kernel_size=(3, 3), stride=(1, 1), padding=(1, 1))
    (18): ReLU(inplace=True)
    (19): Conv2d(512, 512, kernel_size=(3, 3), stride=(1, 1), padding=(1, 1))
    (20): ReLU(inplace=True)
```

```
    (21): Conv2d(512, 512, kernel_size=(3, 3), stride=(1, 1), padding=(1, 1))
    (22): ReLU(inplace=True)
    (23): MaxPool2d(kernel_size=2, stride=2, padding=0, dilation=1, ...
    (24): Conv2d(512, 512, kernel_size=(3, 3), stride=(1, 1), padding=(1, 1))
    (25): ReLU(inplace=True)
    (26): Conv2d(512, 512, kernel_size=(3, 3), stride=(1, 1), padding=(1, 1))
    (27): ReLU(inplace=True)
    (28): Conv2d(512, 512, kernel_size=(3, 3), stride=(1, 1), padding=(1, 1))
    (29): ReLU(inplace=True)
    (30): MaxPool2d(kernel_size=2, stride=2, padding=0, dilation=1, ...
  )
  (avgpool): AdaptiveAvgPool2d(output_size=(7, 7))
  (classifier): Sequential(
    (0): Linear(in_features=25088, out_features=4096, bias=True)
    (1): ReLU(inplace=True)
    (2): Dropout(p=0.5, inplace=False)
    (3): Linear(in_features=4096, out_features=4096, bias=True)
    (4): ReLU(inplace=True)
    (5): Dropout(p=0.5, inplace=False)
    (6): Linear(in_features=4096, out_features=1000, bias=True)
  )
)
```

Listing 3-58: Printout of the VGG16 model

The VGG16 model is structured hierarchically, starting with a features module composed of a series of convolutional (Conv2d) and ReLU (ReLU) layers. These layers progressively increase the number of feature maps, starting from 64 channels and going up to 512, with each convolutional layer using 3×3 kernel sizes and 1×1 strides, often followed by ReLU for nonlinear activation. This module also includes multiple max pooling layers (MaxPool2d) with a 2×2 kernel and a stride of 2, reducing the spatial dimensions after certain stages.

The avgpool module, which is an adaptive average pooling layer, follows the features module, resizing the output to a fixed size of 7×7, independent of the size of the input image—hence its adaptive nature.

Finally, the classifier module comprises three fully connected layers (Linear), each with 4,096 neurons (except the last one, which has 1,000 neurons corresponding to the classes of the ImageNet dataset), interspersed with ReLU activations and dropout layers to prevent overfitting.

When using the VGG16 model, it's crucial to normalize the input images by using the mean and standard deviation values specific to the ImageNet dataset's color channels. This ensures that the input data aligns with the data distribution the model was originally trained on. You can do this with Listing 3-59.

```
import numpy as np
import torch

mean = np.array([0.485, 0.456, 0.406], dtype=np.float32)
std = np.array([0.229, 0.224, 0.225], dtype=np.float32)
```

```
low = torch.tensor((- mean / std).reshape(1, -1, 1, 1))
high = torch.tensor(((1 - mean) / std).reshape(1, -1, 1, 1))
```

Listing 3-59: Defining the normalization parameters for VGG16

This code defines the normalization parameters. The `mean` array contains the mean values for the red, green, and blue channels, while the `std` array holds the standard deviations for these channels.

Implementing the DeepDreams Algorithm

Now that you've loaded the image you want to transform into a DeepDream and the neural network you want to use to do so, you can proceed to implement the DeepDreams algorithm.

Before actually implementing the algorithm, recall how a neural network works: When an image is fed into the network, the activations of the different layers of the neural network depend on which features they've been trained to detect. Early layers might detect simple features like edges and textures, while deeper layers recognize more-complex features like shapes or specific objects.

The DeepDreams algorithm reverses this process. Instead of using the network to detect features, the algorithm modifies the original image to amplify the features that the network detects. This is done by applying gradients to the image that transform it to increase the activation of certain layers. The core technique is *gradient ascent* in the input space. This technique involves asking the network's layers not just to detect features in an image but to enhance the features they detect. For example, if a cloud looks slightly like a bird, the DeepDreams algorithm will adjust the image to make it look even more like a bird.

The DeepDreams process is iterative. An image is put through the network, tweaked slightly to enhance its features, and then put through the network again, in a loop. With each pass through the network, the image is further modified to enhance its features—creating familiar shapes and patterns where none existed, often resulting in surreal, dreamlike images that have swirling patterns or fantastical creatures.

Using Gradient Ascent

First, you need to convert the image into a PyTorch tensor. You can do this with the `image_to_tensor()` function shown in Listing 3-60.

```
import torchvision.transforms as tt

def image_to_tensor(im, mean, std):
    """Convert image to tensor."""
    normalize = tt.Compose([tt.ToTensor(), tt.Normalize(mean, std)])
    return normalize(im).unsqueeze(0).requires_grad_(True)
```

Listing 3-60: The function to convert an image to a tensor

This function defines the `normalize` transformation sequence, which first converts the image into a tensor and then normalizes it via the provided mean and std values. The normalized image tensor is then expanded by one dimension via unsqueeze(0) to make it into a batch that can be passed to VGG16. Finally, gradient calculation is enabled for the image tensor via requires_grad _(True), which is essential to transform the image through gradient ascent.

Now use this function to convert the image into a PyTorch tensor:

```
im_tensor = image_to_tensor(im, mean, std)
```

Next, write the core of the DeepDreams algorithm, shown in Listing 3-61.

```
❶ layer = model.features[1]
iter_num = 100
eta = 0.1

hookdata = {}

def hook_func(layer, input, output):
    """Hook for activations."""
    hookdata["activations"] = output

for _ in range(iter_num):
    handle = layer.register_forward_hook(hook_func)
    try:
      ❷ _ = model(im_tensor)
    except Exception as e:
        print(f"An error occurred during model prediction: {e}")
    finally:
        handle.remove()

  ❸ loss = hookdata["activations"].mean()
  ❹ loss.backward()

    grad_mean = torch.mean(im_tensor.grad.data)
    grad_std = torch.std(im_tensor.grad.data)
  ❺ normalized_grad = (im_tensor.grad.data - grad_mean) / (grad_std + 1e-8)

  ❻ im_tensor.data = im_tensor.data + eta * normalized_grad

  ❼ im_tensor.grad.zero_()

  ❽ im_tensor.data.clamp_(low, high)
```

Listing 3-61: Performing the DeepDreams gradient ascent

This script calculates the DeepDreams version of the image that maximizes the activation of the first ReLU layer ❶ (the second layer of the features module of model).

The iterative process transforming the image by gradient ascent performs the following steps:

1. Applies a forward hook (defined by the `hook_func()` function) to capture layer activations ❷. No output is needed, as you need just the activations calculated in the forward pass and saved by the hook in `hookdata`.

2. Calculates the mean activation of the layer to be used as loss ❸.

3. Propagates the loss backward to calculate the gradients in the image ❹. No gradients are calculated for the VGG16 model, as it's set in evaluation mode and its weights are frozen.

4. Normalizes the gradient of the image ❺.

5. Updates the image based on the calculated gradients performing the gradient ascent ❻.

6. Clears the gradient in preparation of the next iteration ❼.

7. Clamps the image data to the bounds of the normalized image values to ensure that the image's pixel values are valid ❽.

NOTE *In implementing algorithms like DeepDreams, choosing the right number of iterations (`iter_num`) and step size (`eta`, which is quite similar to the learning rate that you've seen in the backpropagation algorithm) is crucial and often involves a bit of trial and error. Typically, `iter_num` ranges from 10 to 100, affecting the depth of the image transformation (more iterations lead to more-complex changes but could introduce noise). The value of `eta` is usually set from about 0.01 to 0.1 and dictates the magnitude of each image update. A larger step size makes more drastic changes per iteration, while a smaller step size results in subtler, more gradual alterations. The key is to balance these parameters to achieve meaningful transformations without excessively distorting the original image.*

Next, you need convert the image tensor back to the image format. You can do this with the `tensor_to_image()` function shown in Listing 3-62.

```
def tensor_to_image(image, mean, std):
    """Convert tensor to image."""
❶ denormalize = tt.Normalize(mean=- mean / std, std=1 / std)
   im_array = denormalize(image.data.clone().detach().squeeze()).numpy()
❷ im_array = np.clip(im_array.transpose(1, 2, 0) * 255, 0, 255)
❸ im_array = im_array.astype(np.uint8)
❹ return Image.fromarray(im_array, "RGB")
```

Listing 3-62: The function to convert a tensor back to an image

This function first defines a denormalization operation ❶, which reverses the effect of the previous normalization by using negative mean values and reciprocal standard deviation values. Next, the function applies the denormalization to the `image` tensor after cloning it, detaching it from the current computation graph, and squeezing it to remove the batch dimension. Finally, it converts `image` to the `im_array` NumPy array. This array is transposed to adjust the channel order from CHW (channels, height, width) to HWC ❷, scaled back to the original 0-to-255 range, clipped to ensure that the values stay within this range, and converted to an unsigned 8-bit integer format ❸. The final step is to create and return a Pillow `Image` from this array, specifying `RGB` as the color mode ❹.

Now use this function to convert the tensor back to the image format:

```
im_deepdream = tensor_to_image(im_tensor, mean, std)
```

Finally, you can render your first DeepDream, using Listing 3-63.

```
plt.imshow(im_deepdream)
plt.title("DeepDream for Layer 1")
plt.axis("off")
plt.show()
```

Listing 3-63: Plotting a DeepDream

You should get something similar to Figure 3-26.

DeepDream for Layer 1

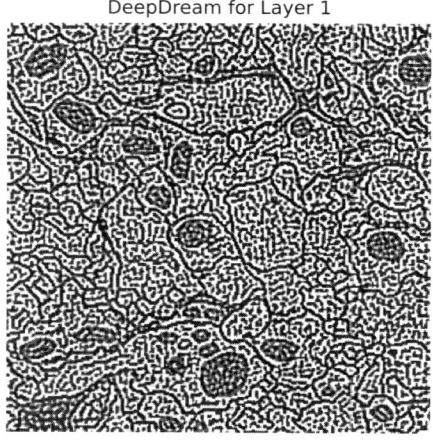

Figure 3-26: The DeepDream corresponding to the first layer

In this DeepDream corresponding to layer 1 of the neural network, the abundance of dot-like patterns and textures reflects this layer's focus on detecting basic features such as edges and simple textures in the input image.

Refactoring the DeepDreams Code as a Function

To improve the organization and reusability of your code, you can refactor the DeepDreams code into the `deepdream()` function shown in Listing 3-64.

```
def deepdream(im, layer_index, iter_num=100, eta=0.1):
    """Generate DeepDream."""
    mean = np.array([0.485, 0.456, 0.406], dtype=np.float32)
    std = np.array([0.229, 0.224, 0.225], dtype=np.float32)

    low = torch.tensor((-mean / std).reshape(1, -1, 1, 1))
    high = torch.tensor(((1 - mean) / std).reshape(1, -1, 1, 1))
```

```
im_tensor = image_to_tensor(im, mean, std)

hookdata = {}
--snip--
layer = model.features[layer_index]
for _ in range(iter_num):
    --snip--

im_deepdream = tensor_to_image(im_tensor, mean, std)

plt.imshow(im_deepdream)
plt.title(f"DeepDream for Layer {layer_index}")
plt.axis("off")
plt.show()
```

Listing 3-64: The function to generate a DeepDream (by modifying Listing 3-61 and combining it with Listings 3-59 and 3-63)

This function accepts as inputs the image (im), the index of the layer whose activation is maximized by the DeepDreams algorithm (layer_index), the iteration number (iter_num), and the step size (eta). The rest of the code is sourced from Listings 3-59, 3-61, and 3-63.

When you call this function with

```
deepdream(im, layer_index=1, iter_num=100, eta=0.1)
```

you should get the DeepDream shown in Figure 3-26.

Thanks to this refactoring of the code, next you can easily add new functionalities, as you'll do in the following sections.

Improving the DeepDreams Function with a Context Manager

You can now use a context manager for the hook. A *context manager* in Python is a special construct that provides a clean way to automatically allocate and release resources. It allows you to set up a temporary context for your code, ensuring that resources are properly managed and cleaned up after the code block is executed, typically using the with statement.

To do so, write the Fwd_Hook class, as shown in Listing 3-65.

```
class Fwd_Hook():
    """Forward hook."""

    def __init__(self, layer):
        """Initialize forward hook."""
        self.hook = layer.register_forward_hook(self.hook_func)

    def hook_func(self, layer, input, output):
        """Save activations."""
        self.activations = output
```

```
    def __enter__(self, *args):
        """Enter context management."""
❶   return self

    def __exit__(self, *args):
        """Exit context management and remove hook."""
❷   self.hook.remove()
```

Listing 3-65: The class to context-manage the hook to the activation of a layer

When the Fwd_Hook class is initialized with the __init__() method, the class registers a forward hook on the specified layer, which ensures that the designated hook_func() method is called every time the layer completes its forward pass. This hook method captures the output of the layer, storing it in the activations attribute for later use. The methods __enter__() and __exit__() define the class as a context manager. When entering the context (using a with statement), an instance of Fwd_Hook is returned ❶, and upon exiting, the context manager ensures cleanup by removing the hook ❷. This approach provides an elegant and Pythonic way to temporarily attach and safely remove hooks.

To use this context manager, you need to modify the deepdream() function as shown in Listing 3-66.

```
def deepdream(im, layer_index, iter_num=100, eta=0.1):
    --snip--
    im_tensor = image_to_tensor(im, mean, std)

    layer = model.features[layer_index]
    for _ in range(iter_num):
        with Fwd_Hook(layer) as fh:
            _ = model(im_tensor)

        loss = fh.activations.mean()
        loss.backward()
        --snip--
```

Listing 3-66: The function to generate a DeepDream with a context manager for the hook (by modifying Listing 3-64)

Verify that this updated deepdream() function still works:

```
deepdream(im, layer_index=1, iter_num=100, eta=0.1)
```

This should again generate the DeepDream in Figure 3-26.

Creating DeepDreams from Deeper Layers

Now it's time to play with your code and generate DeepDreams from deeper layers:

```
for layer_index in [1, 3, 6, 8, 11, 13, 15, 18, 20, 22, 25, 27, 29]:
    deepdream(im, layer_index, iter_num=100, eta=0.1)
```

Figure 3-27 showcases a collection of DeepDreams generated from various layers of the neural network, visualizing the complex patterns and features that each layer has learned to recognize.

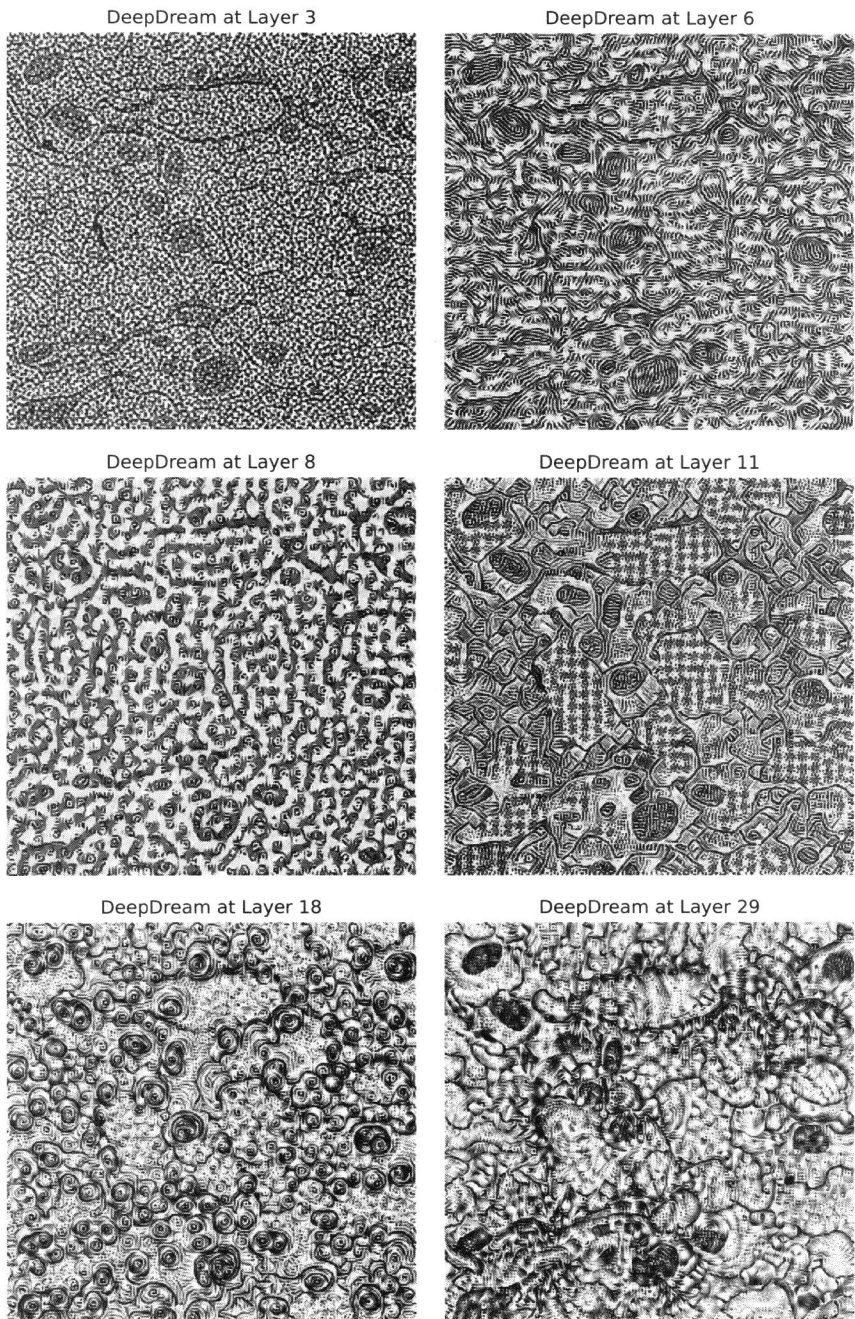

Figure 3-27: DeepDreams maximizing the activation of deeper layers

In the early layers, such as layers 3 and 6, the patterns are simple and repetitive, focusing on basic shapes and edges with vibrant colors. As you progress to intermediate layers like 8 and 11, the complexity increases, with the DeepDreams beginning to feature more-abstract motifs that suggest a transition from simple to more-complex feature recognition.

In the deeper layers, 18 and 29, the images become increasingly surreal, with elaborate, dreamlike amalgamations of shapes and textures that resemble eyes and biological forms, illustrating the network's higher-level feature detection that interprets the visual data in more-abstract ways.

Using Multiple Layers at Once

You can also generate DeepDreams by maximizing the activation of multiple layers at once. To do this, you need to capture the activations of multiple layers, which requires modifications to the context manager class, as shown in Listing 3-67.

```
class Fwd_Hooks():
    """Forward hooks."""

    def __init__(self, layers):
        """Initialize forward hooks."""
        self.hooks, self.activations_list = [], []
        for layer in layers:
            ❶ self.hooks.append(layer.register_forward_hook(self.hook_func))

    def hook_func(self, layer, input, output):
        """Save activations."""
        self.activations_list.append(output)

    --snip--

    def __exit__(self, *args):
        """Exit context management and remove hooks."""
        for hook in self.hooks:
            ❷ hook.remove()
```

Listing 3-67: The class to context-manage the hooks to the activations of multiple layers at once (by modifying Listing 3-65)

This new context manager class contains, as attributes, lists of hooks and activations, one for each layer. When the context manager is initialized, a hook function is attached to each layer ❶ and, when the context manager exits, all the functions are removed ❷.

Finally, modify the deepdream() function further to accept multiple input layers, as shown in Listing 3-68.

```
def deepdream(im, layer_indices, iter_num=100, eta=.1):
    --snip--
    layers = [model.features[layer_index] for layer_index in layer_indices]
```

```
     for _ in range(iter_num):
❶    with Fwd_Hooks(layers) as fh:
         _ = model(im_tensor)

     losses = [activations.mean() for activations in fh.activations_list]
❷    loss = torch.stack(losses).sum()
     loss.backward()
     --snip--
     plt.title(f"DeepDream for Layers {layer_indices}")
     --snip--
```

Listing 3-68: The function to generate a DeepDream from multiple layers (by modifying Listing 3-66)

This is the definitive version of the deepdream() function. It accepts as input multiple layers' indices and extracts the corresponding layers. Then it uses the context manager for hooks in multiple layers ❶. The loss is now calculated by summing up the losses for the activation of each layer ❷.

Now you can get a DeepDream that maximizes feature activations from multiple layers of VGG16 simultaneously:

```
deepdream(im, layer_indices=[1, 8, 11, 18, 25, 27, 29], iter_num=100, eta=0.1);
```

This should generate the DeepDream in Figure 3-28.

DeepDream at Layers [1, 8, 11, 18, 25, 27, 29]

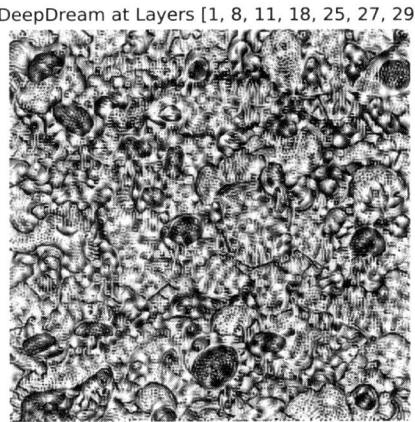

Figure 3-28: The DeepDream maximizing the activation of multiple layers at once

This multilayered approach creates a densely packed tapestry of features that vary in complexity. The image is a vibrant collage of textures and patterns, with visual elements that range from the geometric shapes found in the earliest layers to the more-complex, almost biological structures reminiscent of eyes and organic forms that emerge from the deeper layers. This visual complexity is a result of targeting a combination of layers, each contributing its own learned representations to the final image.

Code Example 3-C, "Creating DeepDreams," is available at https://github.com/ DeepTrackAI/DeepLearningCrashCourse. *Navigate to the* Ch03_CNN *folder and then* ec03_C_deepdream. *The* deepdream.ipynb *notebook provides a complete code example that loads an image and the VGG16 pretrained neural network and uses them to create DeepDreams.*

Project 3D: Transferring the Style of Images

In this last project of this chapter, you'll explore *neural style transfer*, which answers this question: How can the stylistic elements of one image be imposed onto the content of another image while preserving the original content's structure?

For example, imagine you have a photograph (content image) and a painting (style image). You want to re-create the photograph in the unique artistic style of the painting. You can achieve this by using a deep neural network trained to understand and identify various features in images. During neural style transfer, you ask the neural network to keep the large-scale structures from the photograph, but to paint them with the textures and patterns you see in the painting.

As you've seen many times by now, a deep network comprises multiple layers, each responsible for recognizing different levels of the image's details. The first layers might detect simple edges and textures typically more related to the style. The last layers capture the larger-scale complex structures that define the content. You can then instruct the computer to minimize the difference between the content of your photograph and the content recognized in a particular layer of the network, while simultaneously minimizing the difference between the style of your painting and the style recognized in other layers.

Through an iterative process of adjustments, the neural network blends the content and the style, keeping the essential elements of the photograph's structure while casting it in the colors, brush strokes, and textures of the painting, creating a hybrid image that looks like a painted version of the photograph. You'll see how this works in more detail in the rest of this project. You'll learn how to apply the texture of the Trencadís Lizard (created by Antoni Gaudí in Barcelona's Parc Güell) to a microscopic image of the neural tissue of a fruit fly larva.

Before you begin this project, you should have a solid understanding of the concepts introduced in Projects 3A and 3C, particularly regarding the use of hooks and context managers to access the activations of layers.

Loading the Content and Style Images

Start by loading the content image:

```
from PIL import Image

content = (Image.open("neuraltissue_with_colorlabels.png").convert("RGB")
        .crop((100, 170, 100 + 256, 170 + 256)))
```

This is the same image you used in Project 3C to generate DeepDreams. The only difference is that you are now cropping a square of 256×256 pixels from the image.

Then plot this crop:

```
import matplotlib.pyplot as plt

plt.imshow(content)
plt.axis("off")
plt.show()
```

The content image is shown on the left side of Figure 3-29.

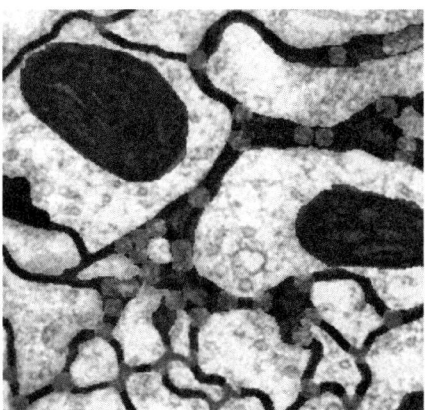

Figure 3-29: The content (left) and style (right) images for the neural style transfer

Next, load the image you'll use for the style. You'll use a photograph of a detail of Gaudí's lizard, which is in the *lizard.png* image file:

```
style = Image.open("lizard.png").convert("RGB").resize((256, 256))
```

This loads the style image, converts it to RGB, and finally resizes it to 256×256 pixels.

You can then plot the style image:

```
plt.imshow(style)
plt.axis("off")
plt.show()
```

The resulting image is shown on the right side of Figure 3-29.

Loading a Pretrained Neural Network

Now you need to import a pretrained neural network. As with the Deep-Dreams in Project 3C, you'll import the VGG16 model and freeze its weights with Listing 3-57. The printout with the architecture of the VGG16 model is in Listing 3-58. Furthermore, since this is a pretrained model, it needs normalization, which is again the same as in Project 3C (Listing 3-59).

Implementing Style Transfer

To implement style transfer, you'll reuse several tools developed already for the DeepDreams in Project 3C. In particular, you'll reuse the Fwd_Hooks class (Listing 3-67) and the image_to_tensor() and tensor_to_image() functions (Listings 3-60 and 3-62).

Start by implementing the additional gram() function to calculate the Gram matrix between all the activations of a specific layer, as shown in Listing 3-69.

```
from torch import bmm

def gram(tensor):
    """Gram matrix."""
❶  batch_size, num_channels, height, width = tensor.size()
❷  features = tensor.view(batch_size, num_channels, height * width)
    gram_matrix = bmm(features, features.transpose(1, 2)) / (height * width)
    return gram_matrix
```

Listing 3-69: The function to calculate the Gram matrix

The *Gram matrix* represents the correlations between different feature maps (or channels) of a convolutional layer's output. The gram() function unpacks the dimensions of the input tensor ❶. Then gram() reshapes the tensor into a 2D matrix ❷ (the batch_size will be equal to 1). Finally, the function computes the Gram matrix as the product of the matrix by its transpose, normalizing it by the number of elements in each feature map (height * width).

You can implement the style transfer with the style_transfer() function in Listing 3-70, which is quite similar in structure to the deepdream() function in Listing 3-68.

```
def style_transfer(image, content, style, content_layers, style_layers,
                   lr=1, iter_num=100, beta=1e3):
    """Perform style transfer."""
    mean = np.array([0.485, 0.456, 0.406], dtype=np.float32)
    std = np.array([0.229, 0.224, 0.225], dtype=np.float32)

    image_tensor = image_to_tensor(image, mean, std)

    with Fwd_Hooks(content_layers) as fh:
        _ = model(image_to_tensor(content, mean, std))
❶  con_activ_list = [activ.detach() for activ in fh.activations_list]

    with Fwd_Hooks(style_layers) as fh:
        _ = model(image_to_tensor(style, mean, std))
❷  target_gram_list = [gram(activ.detach()) for activ in fh.activations_list]
```

```
optimizer = torch.optim.LBFGS([image_tensor], lr=lr)
mse_loss = torch.nn.MSELoss(reduction="sum")

def closure():
    """Closure function for the optimizer."""
    --snip--
    return total_loss

for i in range(iter_num):
    print(f"iteration {i}")
  ❸ optimizer.step(closure)

    plt.imshow(tensor_to_image(image_tensor, mean, std))
    plt.title(f"Iteration {i}")
    plt.axis("off")
    plt.show()
```

Listing 3-70: The function for implementing style transfer

This function transforms the input image into a PyTorch tensor with the image_to_tensor() function, normalizing the image with the predefined mean and standard deviation values. Then forward hooks are used within context managers to capture content activations from specified layers when the content image is passed through the model ❶, and to calculate the Gram matrix representations of style activations when the style image is processed ❷.

As optimizer, this code uses the Limited-memory Broyden-Fletcher-Goldfarb-Shanno (L-BFGS) algorithm because of its efficiency in handling the large number of variables involved in style transfer. This optimizer is responsible for iteratively tweaking the image tensor to minimize the loss function that measures the difference between the content and style features of the current image and the desired targets. The closure() function is essential in this context because L-BFGS requires the reevaluation of the loss within each iteration to update the weights, and this function provides the mechanism to recalculate the loss and its gradients every time the optimizer takes a step, as you'll see in detail in Listing 3-71.

In each interaction, after the optimization step ❸, the current state of the image tensor is converted back to an image via the tensor_to_image() function and displayed, allowing for visually tracking the style-transfer process.

Now, add the necessary closure() function to the style_transfer() function provided in Listing 3-71.

```
def style_transfer(...):
    --snip--
    mse_loss = torch.nn.MSELoss(reduction="sum")

    def closure():
        """Closure function for the optimizer."""
      ❶ optimizer.zero_grad()
```

```
        with Fwd_Hooks(content_layers) as fh:
            _ = model(image_tensor)
        im_con_activ_list = fh.activations_list

        content_loss = 0
        for im_con_activ, con_activ in zip(im_con_activ_list, con_activ_list):
            num_feats = im_con_activ.shape[1]
          ❷ content_loss += mse_loss(im_con_activ, con_activ) / num_feats ** 2
      ❸ content_loss = content_loss / len(im_con_activ_list)

        with Fwd_Hooks(style_layers) as fh:
            _ = model(image_tensor)
      ❹ im_gram_list = [gram(activ) for activ in fh.activations_list]

        style_loss = 0
        for im_gram, target_gram in zip(im_gram_list, target_gram_list):
            num_feats = im_gram.shape[1]
          ❺ style_loss += mse_loss(im_gram, target_gram) / num_feats ** 2
      ❻ style_loss = style_loss / len(im_gram_list)

        print(f"content_loss={content_loss} style_loss={style_loss}")

      ❼ total_loss = content_loss + beta * style_loss
      ❽ total_loss.backward()
        return total_loss
    --snip--
```

Listing 3-71: The closure function for the optimizer of the style transfer (by modifying Listing 3-70)

This closure function is evaluated several times during each step of the L-BFGS optimization loop to compute the gradient of the loss function and provide it to the optimizer. This function performs the following operations:

1. Resets the optimizer's gradients to 0 ❶. This is necessary to prevent the accumulation of gradients from multiple backward passes.

2. Computes the content loss by comparing the activations from the current image tensor to those from the original content image. The function computes the MSE loss between each corresponding set of activations and then normalizes it by the number of features squared ❷. The total content loss is the average of these losses over all content layers ❸.

3. Calculates the style loss in a similar way, but instead of using the raw activations, it uses the Gram matrices of the activations to capture the style information ❹. The function calculates the MSE loss between the Gram matrix of the current image tensor and the Gram matrix of the style image, normalizes the loss by the number of elements in the Gram matrix squared ❺, and averages over all style layers ❻.

4. Combines the content loss and style loss to form the total loss ❼, with the style loss being scaled by the beta regularization factor to balance the two types of losses.

5. Calls the `backward()` method on the total loss ❽, which computes the gradient of the loss function with respect to the image tensor.

6. Returns the total loss.

Creating an Image in Gaudí's Style

You are finally ready to create a new version of the neural tissue image in Gaudí's style. You can do this with the content image as a starting point, using Listing 3-72.

```
style_transfer(
    image=content, content=content, style=style,
    content_layers=[model.features[l] for l in [14]],
    style_layers=[model.features[l] for l in [0, 2, 5, 7, 10]],
    lr=1, iter_num=50, beta=1e5,
)
```

Listing 3-72: Transforming the style of an image

This code transforms the original content image into an image that retains the content seen by the 14th VGG16 layer but features the style of the style image seen by layers 0, 2, 5, 7, and 10 of VGG16.

Figure 3-30 shows the resulting style images in the first and last iterations.

Iteration 0   Iteration 49

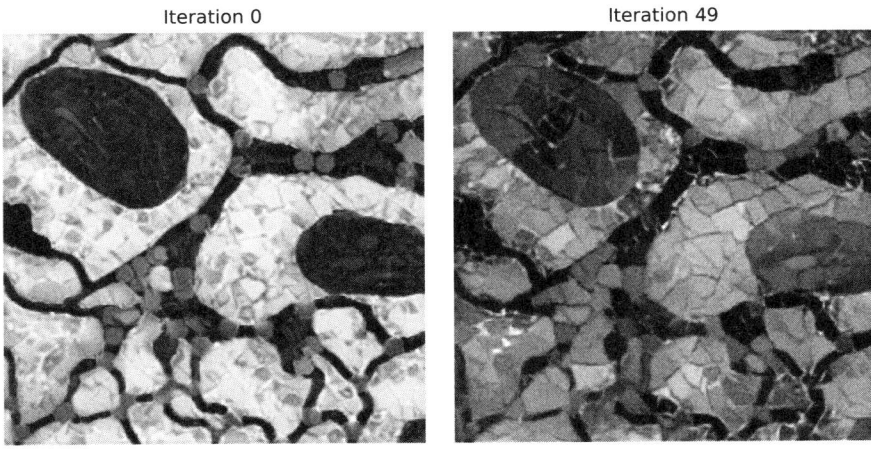

Figure 3-30: The progression of the style transfer

As the iterations proceed, the output image becomes increasingly similar in style to Gaudí's lizard.

NOTE *Code Example 3-D, "Transferring Image Styles," is available at* https://github .com/DeepTrackAI/DeepLearningCrashCourse. *Navigate to the* Ch03_CNN *folder and then* ec03_D_style_transfer. *The* style_transfer.ipynb *notebook provides a complete code example that loads the content image, the style image, and the VGG16 pretrained neural network, and uses them to transfer the style to the image.*

Summary

In this chapter, you learned to use convolutional neural networks, which are essential tools for image analysis. You began by exploring the concept of convolution and its application to both 1D and 2D data. Then you continued with the practical implementation of convolutional neural networks, using PyTorch. You gained hands-on experience in constructing convolutional layers, integrating ReLU activation functions, and mastering pooling and upsampling techniques, all crucial for processing and transforming images. The inclusion of dense layers and their role in image classification further enriched your understanding.

In Project 3A, you applied convolutional neural networks to the task of classifying malaria-infected blood smears. This project highlighted the medical application of convolutional neural networks, involving loading and preprocessing complex datasets, deploying both dense and convolutional neural networks, and visualizing the convolutional filters and layer activations to gain some understanding of the network's decision-making process.

In Project 3B, you ventured into video analysis, using convolutional neural networks to localize microscopic particles in video data. This project highlighted the critical importance of having a reliable ground truth for neural network training. To achieve this, you engaged in the demanding task of manually annotating the particle images, providing the network with ground-truth labels. You also explored the route of generating simulated particle images, offering an alternative means of creating a robust training dataset.

Project 3C introduced you to the artistic side of convolutional neural networks with the creation of DeepDreams. This project illustrated the network's ability to enhance and alter images, revealing the patterns learned by the network.

Project 3D explored the fascinating world of neural style transfer. You learned to merge the content of one image with the style of another, further showcasing the creative potential of convolutional neural networks.

Looking forward, this knowledge serves as a stepping stone to the next chapters, where you'll delve deeper into advanced neural network architectures and techniques. Your newly acquired understanding of convolutional neural networks paves the way for exploring encoder-decoders for latent space manipulation, U-Nets for image transformation, and even generative adversarial networks and diffusion models for image synthesis.

Seminal Works and Further Reading

Yann LeCun et al. introduced the LeNet-5 architecture in "Gradient-Based Learning Applied to Document Recognition," published in 1998 in *Proceedings of the IEEE* (volume 86, pages 2,278–2,324). LeNet-5 demonstrated that back-propagation could be effectively used to train convolutional neural networks, providing one of the first successful applications of convolutional neural networks for image recognition.

A significant leap came with "ImageNet Classification with Deep Convolutional Neural Networks" by Alex Krizhevsky et al., published in 2012 in *Advances in Neural Information Processing Systems* (*NeurIPS*, volume 25). This work introduced AlexNet, which won the 2012 ImageNet competition by a large margin, demonstrating the power of deeper convolutional architectures combined with GPU acceleration for training large models. AlexNet's success was a major catalyst for the deep learning revolution in computer vision.

"Very Deep Convolutional Networks for Large-Scale Image Recognition" by Karen Simonyan and Andrew Zisserman, published in 2014 on arXiv (article number 1409.1556) and presented at the 2015 International Conference on Learning Representations (ICLR), introduced the VGG network. This architecture showed that increasing the depth of convolutional neural networks by using smaller convolutional filters could yield significant improvements in image-classification accuracy.

Christian Szegedy et al. introduced the Inception architecture (also known as GoogLeNet) in 2015 in "Going Deeper with Convolutions," published in *Proceedings of the IEEE Conference on Computer Vision and Pattern Recognition* (*CVPR*, pages 1–9). Inception utilized multiple filter sizes at each layer, allowing for deeper networks while maintaining computational efficiency.

The introduction of the ResNet architecture in "Deep Residual Learning for Image Recognition" by Kaiming He et al., published in 2016 in *Proceedings of the IEEE Conference on Computer Vision and Pattern Recognition* (*CVPR*, pages 770–778), addressed the vanishing gradient problem in deep networks by using residual connections. This allowed for the successful training of very deep networks, resulting in breakthrough performance in image classification and numerous other computer vision tasks.

Project 3B is based on "Digital Video Microscopy Enhanced by Deep Learning" by Saga Helgadottir et al., published in *Optica* (volume 6, pages 506–513). This work uses convolutional neural networks to accurately measure the position of microscopic particles.

Project 3D is inspired by "Image Style Transfer Using Convolutional Neural Networks" by Leon A. Gatys et al., published in 2016 in *Proceedings of the IEEE Conference on Computer Vision and Pattern Recognition* (*CVPR*, pages 2,414–2,423). The authors introduced an artistic algorithm that was able to separate and recombine the image content and style of natural images.

CHALLENGE PROJECTS

3-1: Advanced medical image classification   Implement a convolutional neural network to classify medical images beyond the malaria-infected blood smears. Choose a medical imaging dataset from a Kaggle challenge to classify diseases or conditions (for example, the Chest CT-Scan Images dataset or the COVID-19 Chest CT Image Augmentation GAN dataset). Compare your results to those of the challenge participants.

3-2: Traffic sign recognition   Develop a convolutional neural network to recognize and classify traffic signs from real-world images. You can use the German Traffic Sign Recognition Benchmark (GTSRB) dataset. Create a model that can accurately identify various traffic signs from multiple angles, distances, and lighting conditions. Compare the performance of your model against traditional image-recognition methods.

3-3: Artistic style transfer with custom styles   Extend the neural style transfer project to explore how well your model can adapt to various styles and how it handles style transfer with complex and abstract images.

4

ENHANCING, GENERATING, AND ANALYZING DATA WITH AUTOENCODERS

In this chapter, you'll start exploring unsupervised learning with neural networks, focusing on representation learning and generative modeling. Unlike supervised learning, which requires labeled data, *unsupervised learning* trains models with unlabeled data, allowing the neural network to discover hidden patterns, structures, or relationships within the data on its own. At the heart of this exploration lies the encoder-decoder architecture.

You'll learn how the encoder network compresses data into a dense latent representation, and how the decoder network transforms this latent representation into a new form of the data. In some cases, you can even use the encoder-decoder as an *autoencoder*, which transforms the input data into itself with the ultimate goal of exploring the latent representation. As you will see in this chapter, this can be extremely powerful.

You'll apply encoder-decoders for denoising tasks, which have real-world applications such as enhancing photos taken in low-light conditions, restoring old or damaged photographs, and improving the quality of medical imaging.

You'll discover how to use these encoder-decoder networks to clean corrupted images, learning both the practical utility and the underlying principles of latent space manipulation.

Then you'll explore more-advanced applications by using autoencoders to generate more-structured latent representations. You'll generate new digits for the MNIST dataset and create smooth transitions between fashion items in the Fashion-MNIST dataset. You'll also use autoencoders to detect anomalies, distinguishing between normal and abnormal heartbeats.

Understanding Encoder-Decoders

Encoder-decoder architectures are foundational components in neural networks, widely used in many applications for their ability to transform, reconstruct, and generate data.

The *encoder-decoder* is a neural network architecture consisting of two main parts: the encoder and the decoder. The *encoder network* compresses the input data into a low-dimensional latent representation, while the *decoder network* reconstructs the output from this representation. You can use an encoder-decoder for various applications: data transformation, data reconstruction, feature extraction from the latent space, and data generation.

Figure 4-1 shows a diagram of an encoder-decoder.

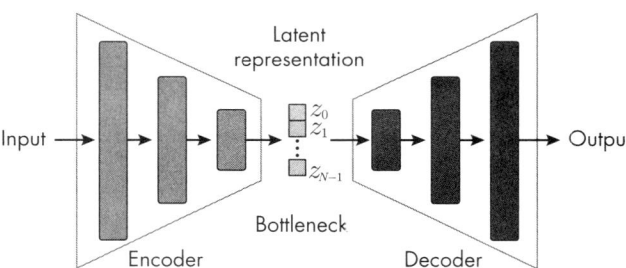

Figure 4-1: An encoder-decoder architecture

In their most common, supervised application, the encoder and decoder are trained to transform their inputs into desired outputs. You'll get a more in-depth look at this application in the first example of this chapter and in the context of U-Nets in Chapter 5. Typically, the input and output data are of the same type—for example, image-to-image or sequence-to-sequence transformations.

The target, or the desired output of the neural network, might be equal to the input itself, as in the case of autoencoders. While this practice might seem pointless, it's useful because the decoder has to rebuild the input data from scratch by using what squeezes through the bottleneck of the latent space. This is a more-compact form of the input. Essentially, the encoder squishes down the input data, and the decoder tries to bring it back to its original form. This technique is often used to filter, denoise, and compress images and audio signals.

You can also take advantage of the encoder to compress the input data into a lower-dimensional representation while preserving the most important features. This permits you to extract useful features from the input data that can be used for downstream tasks.

Additionally, the latent space itself can serve as a powerful tool to characterize the input's features, providing an understanding of the data's underlying structure. For example, in data classification tasks, the latent space can reveal distinct clusters corresponding to different classes, making it easier to identify and separate different types of data. Finally, the latent space can be harnessed through the decoder to generate new data, showcasing its versatility in both analysis and synthesis of information.

Implementing a Denoising Encoder-Decoder

In this section, you'll learn how to implement a *denoising encoder-decoder* to clean a noisy image. Along the way, you'll get a demonstration of this powerful tool's ability to enhance data quality and uncover the underlying signal amid noise.

Generating the Data

Let's start by generating a clean image of a particle observed through a microscope and then create a noisy version of the same image, which you'll eventually denoise with your encoder-decoder.

Start by defining a spherical particle with Listing 4-1.

```
import deeptrack as dt
import numpy as np

particle = dt.Sphere(
    position=np.array([0.5, 0.5]) * 64, position_unit="pixel",
    radius=500 * dt.units.nm, refractive_index=1.45 + 0.02j,
)
```

Listing 4-1: Defining a spherical particle

This code creates an object that represents a microscopic spherical particle, defining its position within the frame measured in pixels, its radius, and its complex refractive index.

Now, define the properties of the microscope used to image the particle with Listing 4-2.

```
brightfield_microscope = dt.Brightfield(
    wavelength=500 * dt.units.nm, NA=1.0, resolution=1 * dt.units.um,
    magnification=10, refractive_index_medium=1.33,
    output_region=(0, 0, 64, 64),
)
```

Listing 4-2: Defining the microscope to observe the particle

This code defines a bright-field microscope that illuminates the sample with a monochromatic light (wavelength 500 nm), with numerical aperture 1.0, resolution 1 micrometer, and 10× magnification. The code also defines the refractive index of the medium where the particle is immersed (1.33, corresponding to water), and the position and size of the camera sensor in pixels (output_region).

Next, create the image of the particle as observed through the microscope with Listing 4-3.

```
illuminated_sample = brightfield_microscope(particle)
```

Listing 4-3: Obtaining the image of the microscopic particle

This code passes particle to brightfield_microscope, generating the image as illuminated_sample.

Before creating a noisy version, generate a clean image of the particle, which will be the target of the denoising encoder-decoder, with Listing 4-4.

```
import torch

clean_particle = (illuminated_sample >> dt.NormalizeMinMax()
                  >> dt.MoveAxis(2, 0)
                  >> dt.pytorch.ToTensor(dtype=torch.float))
```

Listing 4-4: Simulating the clean image of the particle

This code takes an image of the particle, rescales it to the range from 0 to 1 with NormalizeMinMax, moves the color dimension to the first position as expected by PyTorch with MoveAxis, and transforms the image into a PyTorch tensor.

Then create the noisy version of the particle image with Listing 4-5.

```
noise = dt.Poisson(snr=lambda: 2.0 + np.random.rand())

noisy_particle = (illuminated_sample >> noise >> dt.NormalizeMinMax()
                  >> dt.MoveAxis(2, 0)
                  >> dt.pytorch.ToTensor(dtype=torch.float))
```

Listing 4-5: Simulating the noisy image of the particle (by modifying Listing 4-4)

This code introduces Poisson noise to simulate a common type of disturbance encountered in imaging, particularly in low-light conditions or with scientific instruments like microscopes and telescopes. *Poisson noise*, or *shot noise*, arises naturally when the variation in the number of detected photons follows a Poisson distribution. This noise is set to have an SNR of 2 to 3, which is a strong noise level. Then the code takes the very same image of the particle and adds the noise to it.

Finally, combine noisy_particle and clean_particle into a single pipeline, as shown in Listing 4-6.

```
pip = noisy_particle & clean_particle
```

Listing 4-6: Combining the noisy and clean particle images into a single simulation pipeline

You can then write the `plot_image()` function shown in Listing 4-7.

```
import matplotlib.pyplot as plt

def plot_image(title, image):
    """Plot a grayscale image with a title."""
    plt.imshow(image, cmap="gray")
    plt.title(title, fontsize=30)
    plt.axis("off")
    plt.show()
```

Listing 4-7: The function to plot a particle image

Use this function to plot five examples of the noisy and clean particle images, as shown in Listing 4-8.

```
for i in range(5):
    input, target = pip.update().resolve()
    plot_image(f"Input Image {i}", input.permute(1, 2, 0))
    plot_image(f"Target Image {i}", target.permute(1, 2, 0))
```

Listing 4-8: Plotting the noisy and corresponding clean particle images

The input and target images are permuted to move the color dimension to the last position, as expected by Matplotlib. This should plot images similar to those shown in Figure 4-2.

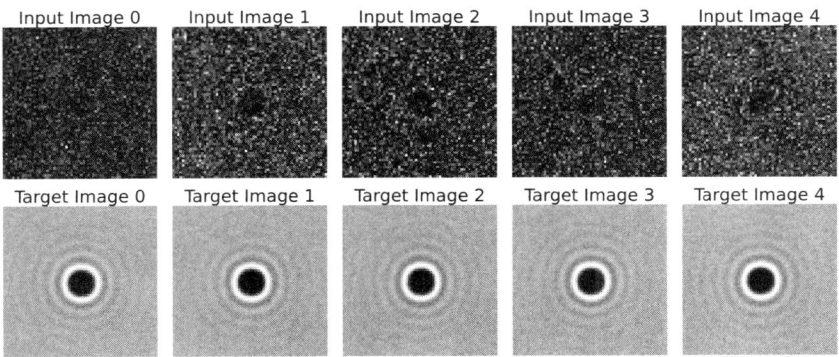

Figure 4-2: The noisy (top) and corresponding clean (bottom) simulated particle images

Note that the noisy input images in the top row are different from one another and indeed very noisy, while the corresponding clean target images in the bottom row are always the same image.

Creating a Simulated Dataset

Now you need to create a PyTorch dataset to be able to use the pipeline to generate images for the training process. You can do this by implementing the SimulatedDataset class, as shown in Listing 4-9.

```
class SimulatedDataset(torch.utils.data.Dataset):
    """Simulated dataset generating pairs of noisy and clean images."""

    def __init__(self, pip, buffer_size, replace=0):
        """Initialize the dataset."""
        self.pip, self.replace = pip, replace
        self.images = [pip.update().resolve() for _ in range(buffer_size)]

    def __len__(self):
        """Return the size of the image buffer."""
        return len(self.images)

    def __getitem__(self, idx):
        """Retrieve a noisy-clean image pair from the dataset."""
      ❶ if np.random.rand() < self.replace:
          ❷ self.images[idx] = self.pip.update().resolve()
        image_pair = self.images[idx]
        noisy_image, clean_image = image_pair[0], image_pair[1]
        return noisy_image, clean_image
```

Listing 4-9: The simulated dataset class to generate the data for training the denoising encoder-decoder

This class is instantiated with the pip pipeline to generate image pairs, a buffer size determining the number of pre-calculated images held in memory, and a replace parameter determining the probability of these images being replaced. Upon initialization, SimulatedDataset fills the buffer (self.images) with noisy-clean image pairs.

When a pair is requested, the __getitem__() method determines whether to update the image pair in the buffer ❷ stochastically with probability replace ❶. Then the method returns the noisy and clean images. Regularly updating the stored images ensures that your training data remains diverse and representative of a broad range of noise patterns, preventing overfitting.

You can now use SimulatedDataset as shown in Listing 4-10.

```
dataset = SimulatedDataset(pip, buffer_size=256, replace=0.1)
loader = torch.utils.data.DataLoader(dataset, batch_size=8, shuffle=True)
```

Listing 4-10: Creating the dataset and the data loader

This code creates the dataset, setting the replace rate to 10 percent and the data loader to a batch of 8.

Defining and Training the Encoder-Decoder

With your dataset prepared, the next step is to define and train the encoder-decoder model that will learn to denoise the images.

Start by defining the encoder-decoder, using Listing 4-11.

```
import deeplay as dl

encoderdecoder = dl.ConvolutionalEncoderDecoder2d(
    in_channels=1, encoder_channels=[16, 16], out_channels=1,
)
```

Listing 4-11: Defining the encoder-decoder

This code defines an encoder-decoder that accepts as input an image with a single color channel (in_channels=1). The encoder processes the image with two layers (encoder_channels=[16, 16]), each with 16 convolutional filters and a max pooling layer that reduces the image dimensions by a factor of 2. The decoder, designed to mirror the encoder, also consists of two stages, each with 16 convolutional filters and an upsampling layer that increases the image dimensions by a factor of 2.

Finally, the network produces an output with a single color channel (out_channels=1). This last layer has a sigmoid activation function to ensure that the output values fall from 0 to 1. You can verify the details of this encoder-decoder by using print(encoderdecoder) to print out its structure.

Now compile this encoder-decoder as shown in Listing 4-12.

```
regressor_template = dl.Regressor(
    model=encoderdecoder, loss=torch.nn.L1Loss(), optimizer=dl.Adam(),
)
ed = regressor_template.create()
```

Listing 4-12: Compiling the encoder-decoder

This code compiles the encoder-decoder as a regressor, using an L1 loss and the Adam optimizer, and then creates a concrete instance of the regressor. You can again print out the details with print(ed).

Finally, train your encoder-decoder with Listing 4-13.

```
ed_trainer = dl.Trainer(max_epochs=150, accelerator="auto")
ed_trainer.fit(ed, loader)
```

Listing 4-13: Training the encoder-decoder

This code trains the encoder-decoder for 150 epochs.

Denoising the Image

Now that you've trained your encoder-decoder, it's time to test its denoising capabilities with Listing 4-14.

```
for i in range(5):
    input, target = pip.update().resolve()
    predicted = ed(input.unsqueeze(0)).detach()

    plot_image(f"Input Image {i}", input[0, :, :])
    plot_image(f"Target Image {i}", target[0, :, :])
    plot_image(f"Predicted Image {i}", predicted[0, 0, :, :])
```

Listing 4-14: Denoising an image with the trained encoder-decoder

This code plots five example sets of input, target, and predicted images. When plotting the images, the code selects the single color channel for the input and target images, while it selects the first (and only) image in the batch and the only color channel for the predicted image.

Figure 4-3 shows examples of the resulting images.

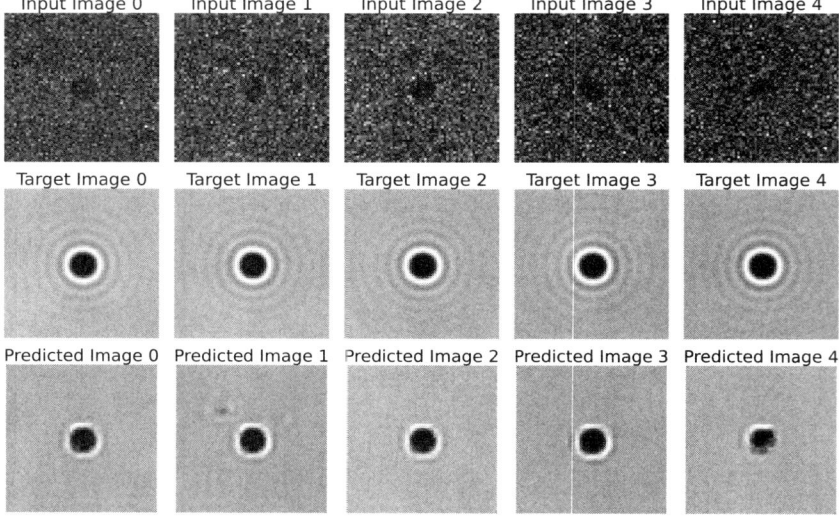

Figure 4-3: The input (top), target (middle), and predicted (bottom) particle images

The noisy input images (top row) are transformed by the encoder-decoder into images (bottom row) that closely resemble the target images (middle row).

You can assess the quality of the denoising by comparing the predicted images to the targets, as you can tell that the algorithm has effectively filtered out the noise and recovered the essential features present in the target images. However, the high-frequency diffraction rings around the target images are only partly reproduced, and some noise seems to remain in the background. This shows that while the model performs well in general, there is still room for improvement.

Checking for Absence of Mode Collapse

You may have already observed that, while the results appear good, the network might not be truly denoising the input images; it might just be generating the output while completely neglecting the input. In fact, the signal in the input image is always the same, with only the noise changing.

Such a scenario can lead to *mode collapse*: The neural network opts for a simplistic, repetitive solution instead of learning to actually perform the task. Preventing mode collapse is essential in order to ensure that the network learns to generalize and truly understand the denoising process rather than taking shortcuts to a seemingly correct output.

In this case, you can make a simple test to verify that the neural network isn't in mode collapse. Use Listing 4-15 to ask the network to denoise a blank sample containing only noise and no particle image.

```
❶ blank = brightfield_microscope(particle ^ 0)
blank_pip = (blank >> noise >> dt.NormalizeMinMax() >> dt.MoveAxis(2, 0)
             >> dt.pytorch.ToTensor(dtype=torch.float))

for i in range(5):
    blank_image = blank_pip.update().resolve()
    blank_predicted = ed(blank_image.unsqueeze(0)).detach()

    plot_image(f"Input Image {i}", blank_image[0, :, :])
    plot_image(f"Predicted Image {i}", blank_predicted[0, 0, :, :])
```

Listing 4-15: Testing the trained encoder-decoder with a blank image

This code uses particle ^ 0 ❶ to add zero particles to each image, obtaining as a result blank images that contain only noise. Figure 4-4 shows the outcome of this test.

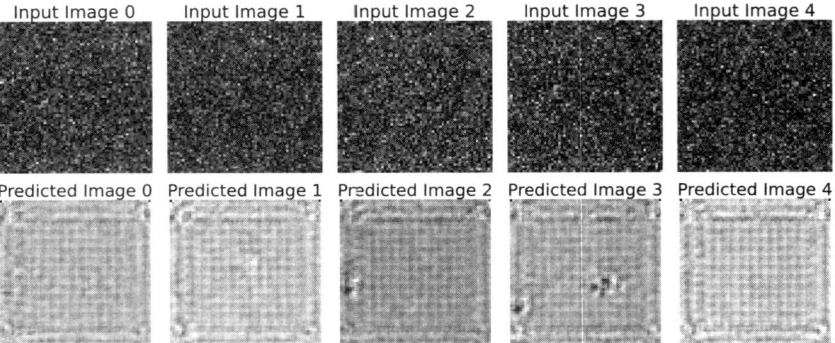

Figure 4-4: The blank input (top) and denoised (bottom) images

You can see the result (bottom row) of using the trained network to denoise blank images containing only noise (top row). The absence of a particle in the output demonstrates that the network isn't in mode collapse. Instead, it's searching for the response of the particle before re-creating its denoised version. If the network were in mode collapse, you'd see the same particle image reproduced in the output regardless of the input, indicating that the network has memorized the training data rather than learning to generalize from it.

Checking Generalization Capabilities

To understand how well the trained network is able to generalize to new images, you can check whether the encoder-decoder can denoise images of particles located at different positions and with different radii. You can do this with Listing 4-16.

```
diverse_particle = dt.Sphere(
❶ position=lambda: np.array([0.2, 0.2] + np.random.rand(2) * 0.6) * 64,
❷ radius=lambda: 500 * dt.units.nm * (1 + np.random.rand()),
    position_unit="pixel", refractive_index=1.45 + 0.02j,
)
diverse_illuminated_sample = brightfield_microscope(diverse_particle)
diverse_clean_particle = (diverse_illuminated_sample
                        >> dt.NormalizeMinMax() >> dt.MoveAxis(2, 0)
                        >> dt.pytorch.ToTensor(dtype=torch.float))
diverse_noisy_particle = (diverse_illuminated_sample >> noise
                        >> dt.NormalizeMinMax() >> dt.MoveAxis(2, 0)
                        >> dt.pytorch.ToTensor(dtype=torch.float))
diverse_pip = diverse_noisy_particle & diverse_clean_particle
```

Listing 4-16: Defining a pipeline generating images of particles with varying positions and radii (by modifying Listings 4-1, 4-3, 4-4, 4-5, and 4-6)

This code randomizes the particle position around the center of the image frame ❶, and its radius from 0.5 to 1 micrometers ❷.

You can then plot some image examples with Listing 4-17.

```
for i in range(5):
    diverse_input, diverse_target = diverse_pip.update().resolve()
    diverse_predicted = ed(diverse_input.unsqueeze(0)).detach()

    plot_image(f"Input Image {i}", diverse_input[0, :, :])
    plot_image(f"Target Image {i}", diverse_target[0, :, :])
    plot_image(f"Predicted Image {i}", diverse_predicted[0, 0, :, :])
```

Listing 4-17: Denoising images of diverse particles with the trained encoder-decoder (by modifying Listing 4-14)

This code should generate images similar to those shown in Figure 4-5.

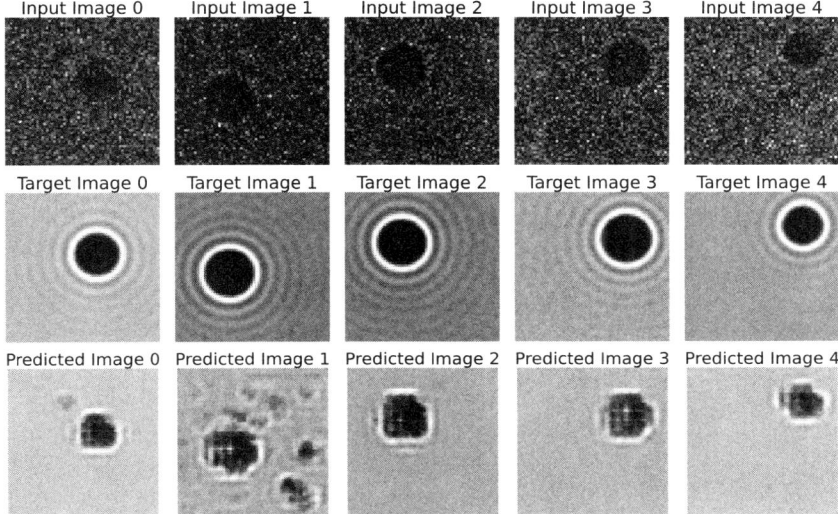

Figure 4-5: The input (top), target (middle), and predicted (bottom) images for off-center particles with different radii

Remarkably, since you've trained the encoder-decoder with only one image of a centered particle, the encoder-decoder is able to detect that the new images have something different and attempts to make a prediction. However, the encoder-decoder struggles to reproduce the denoised images since it hasn't learned to draw particles located off-center. Instead, it tends to generate clusters of particles whenever the particle is off-center or larger than the training particle.

Retraining

You can improve the generalization capabilities of the encoder-decoder by retraining it, using the diverse_pip pipeline shown in Listing 4-18.

```
diverse_dataset = SimulatedDataset(diverse_pip, buffer_size=256, replace=0.1)
diverse_loader = torch.utils.data.DataLoader(diverse_dataset, batch_size=8,
                                             shuffle=True)
```

```
diverse_ed = regressor_template.create()
diverse_ed_trainer = dl.Trainer(max_epochs=150, accelerator="auto")
diverse_ed_trainer.fit(diverse_ed, diverse_loader)
```

Listing 4-18: Training using the dataset with varying parameters (by modifying Listings 4-10, 4-12, and 4-13)

This augments the training data to include particles that are shifted off-center and with larger radii.

You can plot the resulting images with Listing 4-19.

```
for i in range(5):
    diverse_input, diverse_target = diverse_pip.update().resolve()
    diverse_predicted = diverse_ed(diverse_input.unsqueeze(0)).detach()
    --snip--
```

Listing 4-19: Plotting the images after improved training (by modifying Listing 4-17)

This code should generate images similar to those shown in Figure 4-6.

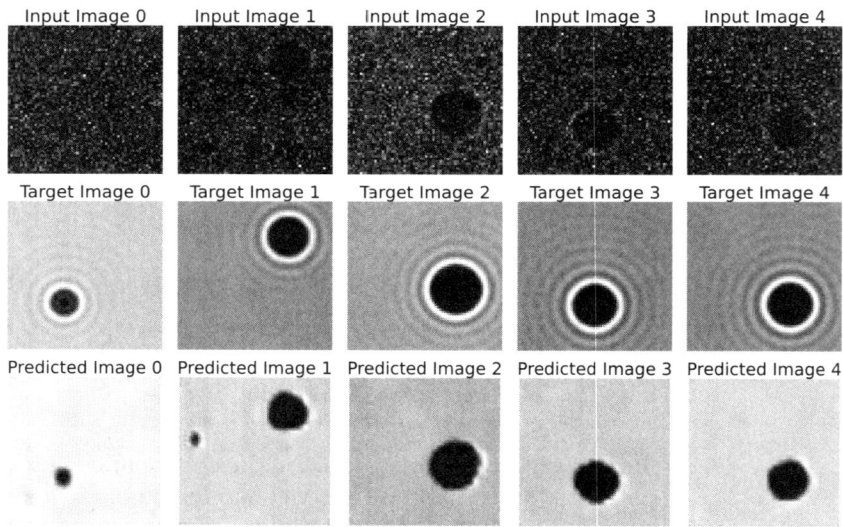

Figure 4-6: The input (top), target (middle), and predicted (bottom) images for the encoder-decoder trained on diverse particle images

Now the predicted images (bottom row) obtained from the noisy input images (top row) are much better approximations of the target images (middle row). At least, the size and location appear correct.

NOTE   *Code Example 4-1, "Denoising Images with an Encoder-Decoder," is available at https://github.com/DeepTrackAI/DeepLearningCrashCourse. Navigate to the Ch04_AE folder and then ec04_1_denoising. The denoising.ipynb notebook provides a complete code example that generates noisy bright-field microscopy images of particles, trains an encoder-decoder to denoise them, and visualizes the results.*

4-2: Increase the number of particles in the images and determine how this affects the performance of the encoder-decoder.

4-3: Alter the replacement rate and see how this affects the training.

4-4: While the size and location of the denoised particle appear correct, the high-frequency diffraction rings around it are still missing. Try to address this by increasing the number of layers and the number of filters per layer (try, for example, setting encoder_channels=[32, 64, 128]).

Project 4A: Generating Images with Variational Autoencoders

This project will introduce you to *variational autoencoders*. These powerful generative models excel in two tasks: compression and generation. First, you'll learn how this model encodes data into a compressed latent space, effectively capturing the essence of the input in a more manageable form. Then you'll explore the generative capability of variational autoencoders, using the information encoded in the latent space to generate new images that closely mirror the original dataset.

By working with the MNIST dataset of handwritten digits, you'll see firsthand how variational autoencoders can compress and reconstruct these images as well as generate entirely new digits. This capability is crucial for applications such as data augmentation, where generating new samples can help improve the performance of machine learning models, and anomaly detection, where understanding the latent space can reveal outliers.

Understanding Variational Autoencoders

Standard autoencoders work by compressing an input into a latent space representation and then reconstructing the input from this compressed form. Although this process is efficient for tasks such as dimensionality reduction and feature learning, it's strictly deterministic and leaves no room for randomness or variation in the output once trained. The encoding-decoding pathway ensures a close match between the original and reconstructed data, but it inherently lacks the ability to introduce novelty or variation beyond what is present in the training data.

In contrast, variational autoencoders introduce a probabilistic flavor to the encoding process. Figure 4-7 illustrates the architecture of a variational autoencoder; the Gaussian sampling of the latent space representation underscores the difference from standard autoencoders.

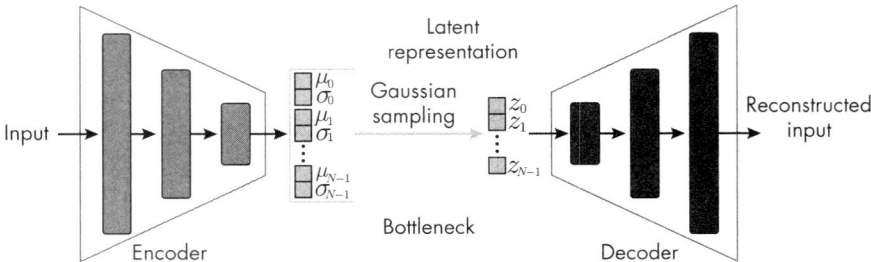

Figure 4-7: The variational autoencoder architecture

A variational autoencoder encodes each input not just as a single point in the latent space, but as a distribution characterized by a mean and a variance. Then, during the decoding phase, the variational autoencoder *samples* a point in the latent space from this distribution, leading to the generation of an output that isn't a direct replica of the input data.

By introducing an element of randomness, this sampling process ensures that the latent space is utilized more efficiently, promoting diversity and continuity among the generated images. During training, this approach encourages the variational autoencoder to learn an accurate representation of the data, while also understanding and capturing the underlying variability within the dataset. As a result, the reconstructed images retain high fidelity to the originals, and the generated images exhibit a rich variety, demonstrating the model's ability to generalize and create novel instances beyond mere reconstruction.

The training process of a variational autoencoder balances two competing objectives through its loss function. This function integrates a reconstruction term and a regularization term. The *reconstruction term* aims to enhance the model's ability to accurately reconstruct the input images. Its role is to ensure that the decoded outputs closely match the original inputs, thus preserving the detailed characteristics of the dataset. This is important because accurately reconstructing the input data ensures that the latent space representation retains its essential features.

On the other hand, the *regularization term* usually uses *Kullback–Leibler (KL) divergence*, which is a measure of how one probability distribution diverges from a second probability distribution. In the context of variational autoencoders, the regularization term encourages the distributions of latent variables to be as close as possible to the target distribution, typically a Gaussian distribution. This ensures that the latent space is well organized and continuous, which allows for smooth interpolation between points in the latent space. As a result, the variational autoencoder can generate coherent and realistic new data points by sampling from this latent space.

The interplay between these two terms in the loss function can be imagined as a repulsive force and an attractive force. The repulsive force emanates from the reconstruction loss (which spreads the data representations throughout the latent space, capturing the diverse features of the data). The attractive force is derived from the KL divergence (which acts like a magnet, pulling these representations toward a normative structure, instilling continuity and order within the latent space). This dynamic tension facilitates the training of a variational autoencoder that generates high-fidelity reconstructions (just like a standard autoencoder), while also enabling smooth and meaningful interpolation and generation of new data points (which is not guaranteed for standard autoencoders).

The relative magnitude between the two loss terms is critical for effective training. Therefore, in certain scenarios, you may have to adjust the regularization term by a scaling factor. Without proper scaling, the KL divergence can cause the network to underuse its capacity, focusing on only a few latent variables for generating new data.

Loading the MNIST Dataset

In this project, you'll use the MNIST dataset, already introduced in Project 1A. If you need a refresher, refer to that section before continuing here. Briefly, the MNIST dataset is a collection of 70,000 grayscale images of handwritten digits, ranging from 0 to 9, each with a size of 28×28 pixels and divided into a training set of 60,000 images and a test set of 10,000 images.

Similar to what you did in Project 1A, import the MNIST dataset with Listing 4-20.

```
import os
import deeptrack as dt

if not os.path.exists("MNIST_dataset"):
    os.system("git clone https://github.com/DeepTrackAI/MNIST_dataset")

data_dir = os.path.join("MNIST_dataset", "mnist")
train_files = dt.sources.ImageFolder(root=os.path.join(data_dir, "train"))
test_files = dt.sources.ImageFolder(root=os.path.join(data_dir, "test"))
files = dt.sources.Join(train_files, test_files)
```

Listing 4-20: Importing the MNIST dataset

This code downloads the MNIST digit images into the local *MNIST_dataset* folder. Then the code loads the training images (train_files) and the test images (test_files). Finally, it combines them into the files variable.

To use this data to train the neural network, create a data pipeline:

```
import torch

image_pip = (dt.LoadImage(files.path) >> dt.NormalizeMinMax()
            >> dt.MoveAxis(2, 0) >> dt.pytorch.ToTensor(dtype=torch.float))
```

This takes a digit image contained in the folders in files.path, rescales it to 0–1, moves the color dimension to the first position as expected by PyTorch, and transforms the image into a PyTorch tensor.

Training the Variational Autoencoder

You'll now define the variational autoencoder and train it to reconstruct and generate images.

Instantiation

You can easily implement a variational autoencoder as follows:

```
import deeplay as dl

vae = dl.VariationalAutoEncoder(
    latent_dim=2, channels=[32, 64],
    reconstruction_loss=torch.nn.BCELoss(reduction="sum"), beta=1,
).create()
```

This defines a variational autoencoder with a 2D latent space (latent_dim=2). For each input, the encoder will produce two means and two variances, corresponding to each dimension of the latent space. These values determine a distribution from which the model samples during the generation process. By constructing a latent space with only two dimensions, the encoder captures the essential characteristics of the input data in a highly compressed form. In terms of the MNIST digits, this compression means the model learns to represent each digit with just two variables, simplifying the complex image data while still retaining enough information to distinguish between different digits. The variances introduce an element of randomness.

The encoder comprises a sequence of convolutional layers with increasing number of filters (channels=[32, 64]), each followed by ReLU activation, with pooling layers reducing the spatial dimensions of the feature maps. This encoder compresses input images into a flattened feature vector, from which two fully connected layers output the mean and variance parameters of the latent space distributions. These parameters facilitate the sampling process that introduces randomness.

The decoder architecture mirrors the encoder, starting from a latent vector that the decoder first expands with a fully connected layer and then reshapes to match the convolutional layers' input dimensions. The decoder sequentially applies convolutional layers with ReLU activations, interspersed with transposed convolutional layers (upsampling) to gradually reconstruct the input image's spatial dimensions, ultimately producing a high-fidelity reconstruction of the original input image. The final layer uses a sigmoid activation to output the reconstructed image, ensuring that pixel values are from 0 to 1.

The model uses BCELoss, a binary cross-entropy loss for reconstruction. When dealing with images that have been scaled to the [0, 1] range as here, the decoder typically ends with a sigmoid activation. The sigmoid maps its outputs from 0 to 1, naturally interpreted as probabilities of each pixel being "on" (1) or "off" (0). Binary cross-entropy directly measures the difference between these predicted probabilities and the true binary (or near-binary) pixel values. In more technical terms, each pixel is treated as a Bernoulli random variable, facilitating a per-pixel measure of the reconstruction error that aligns with MNIST's near-binary nature; however, other losses (for example, MSE) may be preferable if your data or modeling assumptions suggest a different likelihood function.

The regularization term is scaled by the beta parameter, here set to 1. The value of 1 is a common default that balances the reconstruction loss and the regularization term equally. The model gives equal importance to accurately reconstructing the input images and maintaining a well-structured latent space. Adjusting beta can affect the trade-off between these two objectives, with higher values putting more emphasis on regularization, and lower values focusing more on reconstruction.

You can use print(vae) to see the details of this autoencoder.

Training

To train the variational autoencoder, begin by preparing the training dataset and creating a data loader to efficiently feed data into the model. You can do this as follows:

```
train_dataset = dt.pytorch.Dataset(image_pip & image_pip, inputs=train_files)
```

This creates a dataset from the MNIST images preprocessed through image_pip. Subsequently, instantiate a DataLoader object to manage batches of the dataset, enabling efficient and shuffled access to the data during training:

```
train_loader = dl.DataLoader(train_dataset, batch_size=64, shuffle=True)
```

With the data loader in place, you can start the training phase:

```
vae_trainer = dl.Trainer(max_epochs=10, accelerator="auto")
```

This configures a trainer object to manage and execute the training process. This object is set up to run for a maximum of 10 epochs, utilizing hardware acceleration if available.

Next, call the fit() method to start training, optimizing reconstruction fidelity and regularizing the latent space distributions:

```
vae_trainer.fit(vae, train_loader)
```

During training, the values of the reconstruction, regularization, and total loss are explicitly printed at each iteration and epoch, showing how the model is trained and the latent space is being regularized over time.

Generating Images with the Decoder

Now that you've completed the training of your variational autoencoder, you can finally use it to generate new digit images. These can be useful for data augmentation, enhancing the training datasets for other machine learning models, or for creative applications like generating synthetic handwritten digits. This process samples points from the latent space and uses the decoder to transform them into images, as shown in Listing 4-21.

```
import numpy as np
import matplotlib.pyplot as plt
from torch.distributions.normal import Normal

img_num, img_size = 21, 28
z0_grid = z1_grid = Normal(0, 1).icdf(torch.linspace(0.001, 0.999, img_num))

image = np.zeros((img_num * img_size, img_num * img_size))
for i0, z0 in enumerate(z0_grid):
    for i1, z1 in enumerate(z1_grid):
    ❶ z = torch.stack((z0, z1)).unsqueeze(0)
    ❷ generated_image = vae.decode(z).clone().detach()
    ❸ image[i1 * img_size : (i1 + 1) * img_size,
            i0 * img_size : (i0 + 1) * img_size] = \
        generated_image.numpy().squeeze()

plt.figure(figsize=(10, 10))
plt.imshow(image, cmap="gray")
plt.xlabel("z0", fontsize=24)
plt.xticks(np.arange(0.5 * img_size, (0.5 + img_num) * img_size, img_size),
        np.round(z0_grid.numpy(), 1))
plt.ylabel("z1", fontsize=24)
plt.yticks(np.arange(0.5 * img_size, (0.5 + img_num) * img_size, img_size),
        np.round(z1_grid.numpy(), 1))
plt.show()
```

Listing 4-21: Generating and plotting the digit images corresponding to the latent space

This code specifies the number of images (img_num) and their size (img _size). The code then generates a grid of latent variables (z0_grid and z1_grid) via icdf(), the inverse cumulative distribution function of a standard normal distribution. This approach ensures a nonuniform but representative spread of points across the latent space, facilitating the exploration of its diverse regions so that the generated images vary widely, showing the model's ability to create different digits even from slight variations in the latent space.

Next, each pair of latent space variables is combined into a single tensor, to which an additional dimension is added, preparing the tensor for the decoder network to process it as a batch with a single data point ❶. This latent-space tensor is decoded into an image of a digit and detached from the computational graph ❷, ensuring that it can be processed independently of any further gradient updates or training operations. Finally, this image is placed within a larger canvas arranging these reconstructions in a grid format ❸.

The resulting image should look similar to Figure 4-8.

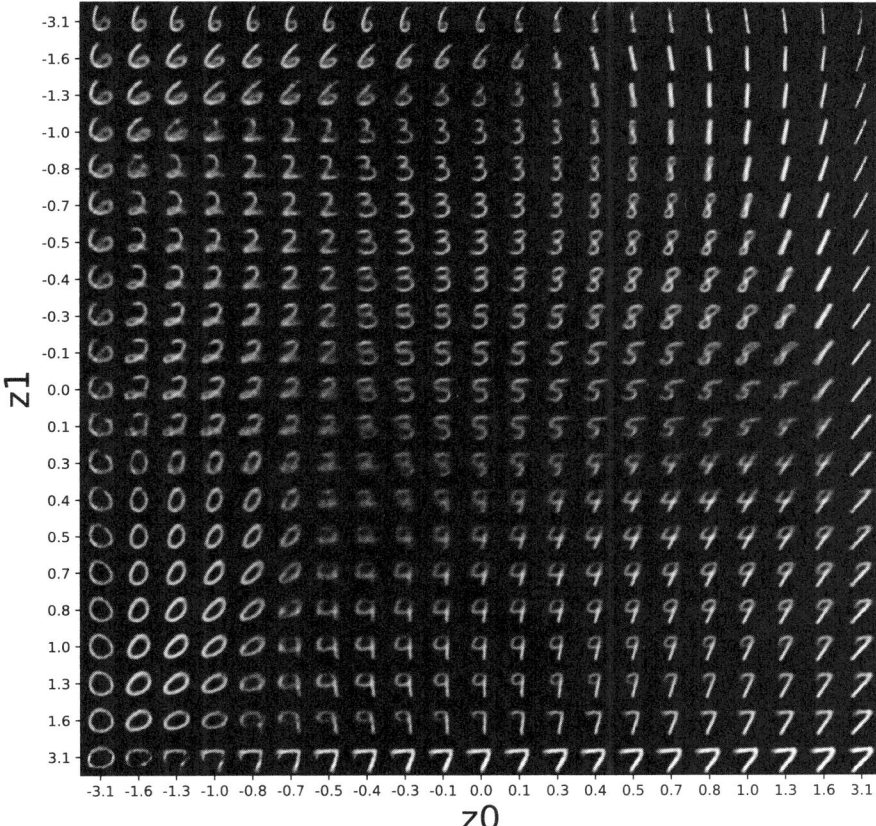

Figure 4-8: The images generated from the latent space, using the decoder

In this grid of digit images, each is synthesized by decoding distinct sample points from the latent space. The axes correspond to the two latent dimensions, where each value combination generates a different digit representation. The digits are smoothly morphing across the grid, showing the variational autoencoder's ability to learn a continuous and richly structured latent space. For example, in the top-left corner where z_0 and z_1 are both around −3.1, the generated digits resemble the number 6. As you move horizontally to the right along the z_0 axis, the digits smoothly change from 6 to 1. Moving along the diagonal from the top-left corner to the bottom-right corner, the digits transition from 6 to 2, 3, 5, 4, 9, and finally 7.

The exact layout and transition between digits you see will differ from run to run, as the latent space structure is inherently tied to the training process, which introduces variability in each training session.

Clustering Images with the Encoder

Once your variational autoencoder is trained, a fascinating application is to examine how the encoder has organized the digit images within the latent space.

To do this, you must first prepare a pipeline that aligns the test images with their corresponding digit labels, as shown in Listing 4-22.

```
label_pip = dt.Value(files.label_name[0]) >> int
test_dataset = dt.pytorch.Dataset(image_pip & label_pip, inputs=test_files)
test_loader = dl.DataLoader(test_dataset, batch_size=64, shuffle=False)
```

Listing 4-22: Defining a pipeline combining the test images and their digit values (labels)

This code defines a pipeline to pair each image with its digit label. Then the code defines a dataset for the test images and relative digit labels. Finally, a data loader is defined to provide an efficient way to iterate over this dataset, allowing for batch processing of images during the encoding step.

Next, you'll encode the images and extract the means of the latent distributions, which will serve as the coordinates for the clustering in the latent space, as in Listing 4-23.

```
mu_list, test_labels = [], []
for image, label in test_loader:
    mu, _ = vae.encode(image)
    mu_list.append(mu)
    test_labels.append(label)
mu_array = torch.cat(mu_list, dim=0).detach().numpy()
test_labels = torch.cat(test_labels, dim=0).numpy()
```

Listing 4-23: Encoding the test images in the latent space

This code iterates through test_loader to encode the images and store their mean values in the latent space (mu). Afterward, the code concatenates these mu values and labels into the mu_array and test_labels tensors, preparing them for visualization.

With the latent space coordinates and corresponding labels at hand, you can now visualize how the digit images cluster in the latent space, using Listing 4-24.

```
from matplotlib.patches import Rectangle

plt.figure(figsize=(12, 10))
plt.scatter(mu_array[:, 0], mu_array[:, 1], s=3, c=test_labels, cmap="tab10")
❶ plt.gca().add_patch(Rectangle((-3.1, -3.1), 6.2, 6.2, fc="none", ec="k", lw=1))
plt.xlabel("mu_array[:, 0]", fontsize=24)
plt.ylabel("mu_array[:, 1]", fontsize=24)
❷ plt.gca().invert_yaxis()
plt.axis("equal")
plt.colorbar()
plt.show()
```

Listing 4-24: Plotting the latent space

This code produces a scatterplot showing the clustering of the encoded test images in the latent space, with points color-coded according to their true digit labels. The inversion of the y-axis maintains consistency with the orientation of previous visualizations ❷. The rectangle delineates the boundary of the latent space shown in Figure 4-8 for comparison ❶.

Figure 4-9 shows the resulting scatterplot.

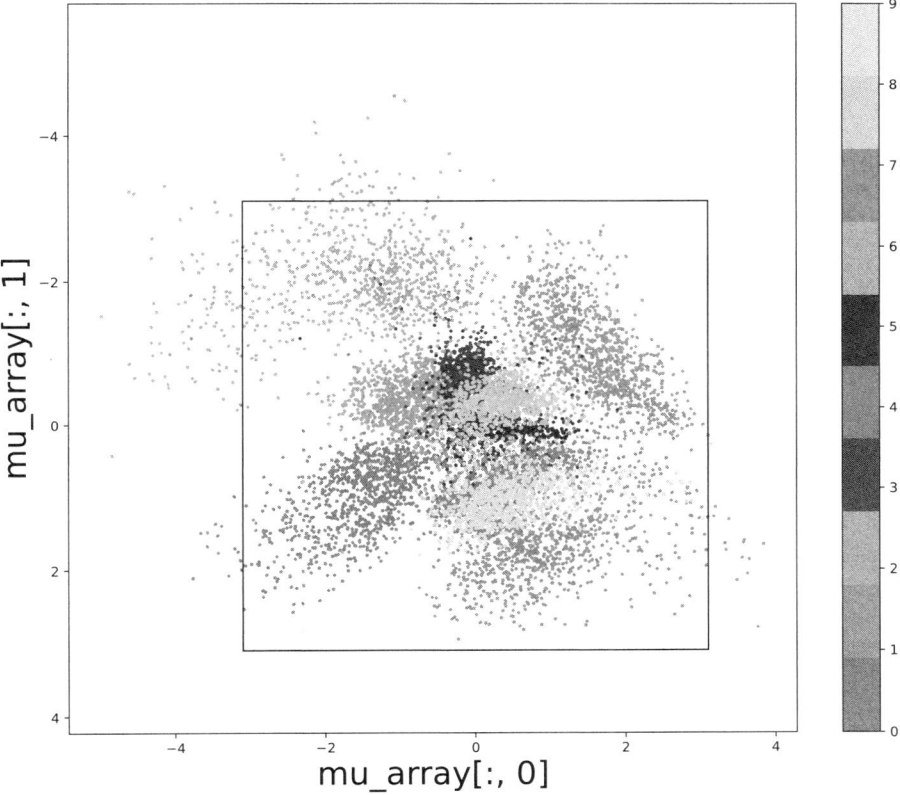

Figure 4-9: A visualization of the latent space produced by the encoder

You can see how the encoder has arranged the digit images within the latent space. Clusters of the same digits indicate that the encoder has learned to group similar images together, while the distribution of clusters across the space reveals the relationships the variational autoencoder has inferred between different digits. For example, the digits 7 and 9 are placed close to each other in the latent space, suggesting that the encoder has recognized some visual similarity between them. Your results will differ, because the randomness intrinsic in each training session influences the specific arrangement and clustering of images.

This visual representation allows you to appreciate the encoder's effectiveness in capturing the characteristics of the input data and serves as a powerful tool to interpret the model's internal representations.

NOTE *Code Example 4-A, "Generating Digit Images with a Variational Autoencoder," is available at* https://github.com/DeepTrackAI/DeepLearningCrashCourse. *Navigate to the* Ch04_AE *folder and then* ec04_A_vae_mnist. *The* vae_mnist .ipynb *notebook provides a complete code example that trains a variational autoencoder on the MNIST digits and uses it to generate new digit images and cluster the digits in the latent space.*

Project 4B: Morphing Images with Wasserstein Autoencoders

In this project, you'll use *Wasserstein autoencoders* to smoothly morph between images in the Fashion-MNIST dataset. This technique is useful in applications such as generating realistic transitions in animations and enhancing data augmentation for training machine learning models.

Wasserstein autoencoders have a structure similar to variational autoencoders: Both encode data into a latent space before reconstructing it. Wasserstein autoencoders exploit the principles of *optimal transport theory* to enhance the quality of generated samples. Optimal transport theory offers a mathematical approach to defining the most efficient way to convert one probability distribution into another. The theory does so by computing the cost of shifting mass within a given space—a cost quantified by the *Wasserstein distance*, also known as the *Earth mover's distance*. Wasserstein autoencoders use this distance to fine-tune the similarity between the distribution of the generated data and the actual data distribution.

Understanding Wasserstein Autoencoders

Autoencoders compress complex, high-dimensional data into a low-dimensional latent space. The autoencoder's expectation for the data representation in the latent space is called the *prior distribution* $p(\mathbf{z})$, where $\mathbf{z}$ is a point in the latent space. This prior distribution provides a reference for the compression process that follows.

The key distinction between variational autoencoders and Wasserstein autoencoders lies in their prior distributions—in the way they manage the data encoding in the latent space. Figure 4-10 illustrates these differences.

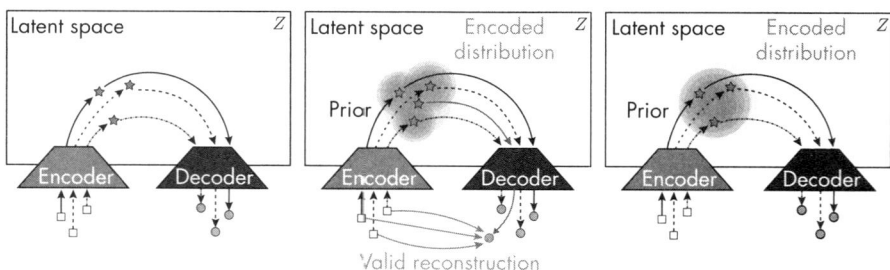

Figure 4-10: Comparing latent space management of autoencoders (left), variational autoencoders (center), and Wasserstein autoencoders (right)

Variational autoencoders approach this task by constructing a parametric distribution $q_{vae}(\mathbf{z}|\mathbf{x})$, typically a Gaussian, for each data point $\mathbf{x}$. They then utilize the KL divergence to measure the discrepancy between this constructed distribution and the prior distribution $p(\mathbf{z})$, with a value of 0 indicating a perfect match. They aim to minimize this divergence, enhancing generalization and smoothness in the latent space. However, an overemphasis on matching the prior distribution may compromise the diversity and quality of reconstructed samples.

Wasserstein autoencoders improve on this by using the Wasserstein distance to gauge the cost of transforming the learned distribution $q_{wae}(\mathbf{z}|\mathbf{x})$ into the prior distribution $p(\mathbf{z})$. This method provides a more refined perspective that allows for greater variation in the compressed representation, often resulting in reconstructions that more faithfully capture the original data's diversity.

Loading the Fashion-MNIST Dataset

The Fashion-MNIST dataset, created by the German online retailer Zalando, adds a twist to the classic MNIST digit classification task. This dataset consists of a training set of 60,000 images and a test set of 10,000 images. Each example is a 28×28 grayscale image, labeled across 10 clothing and accessory categories.

You can load Fashion-MNIST with Listing 4-25.

```
import os
import deeptrack as dt

if not os.path.exists("FashionMNIST_dataset"):
    os.system("git clone https://github.com/DeepTrackAI/FashionMNIST_dataset")

data_dir = "FashionMNIST_dataset"
train_files = dt.sources.ImageFolder(root=os.path.join(data_dir, "train"))
test_files = dt.sources.ImageFolder(root=os.path.join(data_dir, "test"))
files = dt.sources.Join(train_files, test_files)
```

Listing 4-25: Importing the Fashion-MNIST dataset

This code is similar to Listing 4-20, which loads the MNIST dataset in Project 4A. Briefly, this code downloads Fashion-MNIST, extracts the training and test files, and then combines them.

After executing the code, verify that the Fashion-MNIST dataset has been successfully downloaded and loaded by checking that there are 60,000 training files and 10,000 test files with the print(len(train_files)) and print(len(test _files)) commands, respectively.

Then create labels for the classes of the Fashion-MNIST images:

```
classes = ["T-shirt/top", "Trouser", "Pullover", "Dress", "Coat", "Sandal",
           "Shirt", "Sneaker", "Bag", "Ankle boot"]
```

This list provides a convenient reference to the 10 classes in the Fashion-MNIST dataset, which include common clothing items, footwear, and accessories.

Next, create an image-processing pipeline to prepare the images and labels for your neural network:

```
import torch

image_pip = (dt.LoadImage(files.path) >> dt.NormalizeMinMax()
             >> dt.MoveAxis(2, 0) >> dt.pytorch.ToTensor(dtype=torch.float))
label_pip = dt.Value(files.label_name[0]) >> int
```

The image_pip pipeline loads the images from the dataset, normalizes their pixel values, rearranges the axes to match PyTorch's expectations, and converts the images into PyTorch tensors. The label_pip pipeline extracts the associated labels and converts them from strings to integers.

You can now visualize some of the Fashion-MNIST images along with their labels, using Listing 4-26.

```
import matplotlib.pyplot as plt
import numpy as np

fig, axs = plt.subplots(3, 10, figsize=((10, 4)))
for ax, train_file in zip(axs.ravel(),
                          np.random.choice(train_files, axs.size)):
❶ image, label = (image_pip & label_pip)(train_file)
    ax.imshow(image.squeeze(), cmap="gray")
    ax.set_title(f"{int(label)} {classes[int(label)]}", fontsize=9)
    ax.set_axis_off()
plt.show()
```

Listing 4-26: Plotting some of the Fashion-MNIST images

This plots a random selection of images from the training set ❶ and annotates each one with its corresponding label index and class name.

The resulting plot should look similar to Figure 4-11.

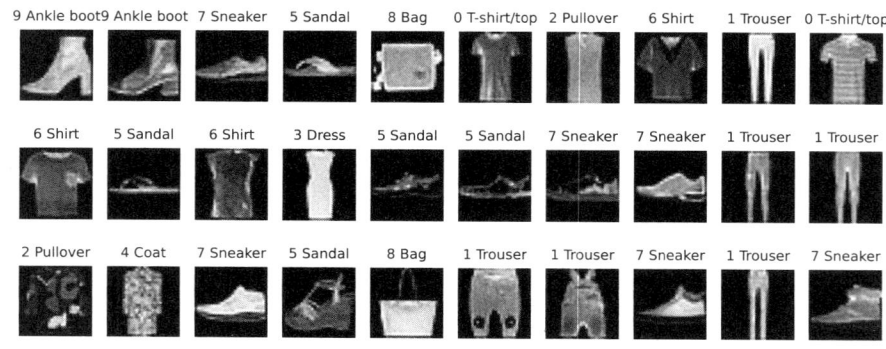

Figure 4-11: Some Fashion-MNIST images

This shows the diversity of the Fashion-MNIST dataset, with a mix of clothing and accessories.

Training the Wasserstein Autoencoder

You'll now create an instance of the Wasserstein autoencoder and train it to categorize the clothing items.

Instantiation

Create a Wasserstein autoencoder:

```
import deeplay as dl

wae = dl.WassersteinAutoEncoder(
    channels=[32, 64, 128], latent_dim=20,
    reconstruction_loss=torch.nn.MSELoss(reduction="mean"),
).create()
```

This code defines a Wasserstein autoencoder, setting the number of convolutional layers in the encoder and decoder, the latent space dimension, and the reconstruction loss. You can inspect the complete architecture and configuration of this Wasserstein autoencoder by using `print(wae)` to print the model's details.

Training

With the Wasserstein autoencoder defined, your next step is to prepare it for training. You set up a dataset to provide the Wasserstein autoencoder with training data:

```
train_dataset = dt.pytorch.Dataset(image_pip & image_pip, inputs=train_files)
```

Then use this dataset to configure a data loader:

```
train_loader = dl.DataLoader(train_dataset, batch_size=128, shuffle=True)
```

This takes the training dataset, batches it into groups of 128 images, and shuffles them to ensure that the training process exposes the Wasserstein autoencoder to a varied range of data at each step, helping the autoencoder to generalize.

Then create the trainer to manage the training process

```
wae_trainer = dl.Trainer(max_epochs=10)
```

and train your Wasserstein autoencoder:

```
wae_trainer.fit(wae, train_loader)
```

After training, be sure to set the model to evaluation mode:

```
wae.eval();
```

Switching the Wasserstein autoencoder to evaluation mode is essential because the autoencoder contains batch normalization layers. These layers operate differently during training and evaluation. During training, they adapt to the data, but for evaluation, they rely on learned parameters to provide stable outputs. Setting the model to evaluation mode freezes the weights of these layers, ensuring that the output is consistent for each input.

Reconstructing the Fashion-MNIST Images

Now that you've trained your Wasserstein autoencoder, let's observe its reconstruction capabilities with Listing 4-27.

```
fig, axs = plt.subplots(2, 10, figsize=((10, 2)))
for i, test_file in enumerate(np.random.choice(test_files, 10)):
❶ image, label = (image_pip & label_pip)(test_file)
   axs[0, i].imshow(image.squeeze(), cmap="gray")
   axs[0, i].set_title(f"{int(label)} {classes[int(label)]}", fontsize=9)
   axs[0, i].set_axis_off()

❷ reconstructed_image, _ = wae(image.unsqueeze(0))
   axs[1, i].imshow(reconstructed_image.detach().squeeze(), cmap="gray")
   axs[1, i].set_axis_off()
plt.show()
```

Listing 4-27: Plotting the input and output images

The reconstruction process selects a random image from the test set ❶ and feeds it through the Wasserstein autoencoder to generate an output that should ideally resemble the original input ❷.

The results should look similar to Figure 4-12.

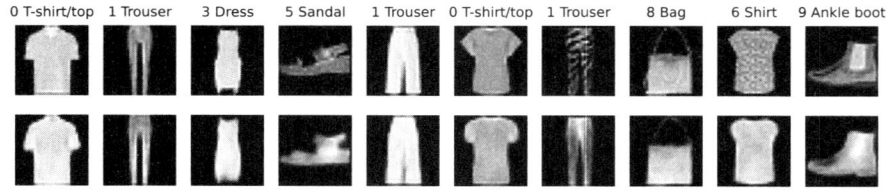

Figure 4-12: The input (top row) and reconstructed (bottom row) images

By looking at the input images in the top row and their reconstructed versions in the bottom row, you can assess the quality of the reconstructions provided by the Wasserstein autoencoder. The reconstructed images should closely match the original inputs, showing that the Wasserstein autoencoder is effectively capturing and reproducing the salient features of the dataset.

Creating New Images

Moving beyond reconstruction, Wasserstein autoencoders can generate entirely new images by sampling from the latent space. Listing 4-28 shows this creative capability in action.

```
❶ images = wae.decode(torch.randn(30, wae.latent_dim)).detach().squeeze()

fig, axs = plt.subplots(3, 10, figsize=((10, 3)))
for ax, image in zip(axs.ravel(), images):
    ax.imshow(image, cmap="gray")
    ax.set_axis_off()
plt.show()
```

Listing 4-28: Generating images with the decoder

In this snippet, the decoder generates new images by decoding 30 random latent vectors generated using `torch.randn(30, wae.latent_dim)` ❶.

This should produce images similar to those shown in Figure 4-13.

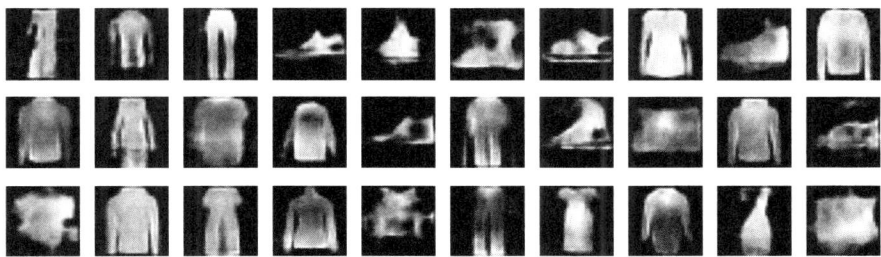

Figure 4-13: The Fashion-MNIST images generated from random points in the latent space

These images showcase a range of fashion items generated from random points within the latent space. Some images stand out with clear and recognizable features, capturing the essence of various clothing and accessory categories. Others may appear less defined or more abstract, illustrating the variability in the generation quality. This reflects the inherent randomness in sampling from the latent space; certain regions yield high-fidelity reconstructions, while others might result in less-coherent outputs.

Morphing Images

Wasserstein autoencoders also enable smooth transitions between images by interpolating points within the latent space—a process akin to morphing one image into another. This technique is useful for creating smooth animations, enhancing data augmentation, and visualizing data transformations.

Morphing one image into another via a Wasserstein autoencoder requires a smooth transition in the latent space. By interpolating between the latent vectors of two images, the Wasserstein autoencoder generates intermediate images that blend characteristics of both original images. This capability can improve the quality of the output by ensuring that the generated images maintain realistic features and smooth transitions. You can do this with Listing 4-29.

```
steps = 6

fig, axs = plt.subplots(3, steps + 2, figsize=((10, 4)))
for i, _ in enumerate(axs):
❶   test_file_0, test_file_1 = np.random.choice(test_files, 2)

    image_0, label_0 = (image_pip & label_pip)(test_file_0)
    z_0 = wae.encode(image_0.unsqueeze(0))

    image_1, label_1 = (image_pip & label_pip)(test_file_1)
    z_1 = wae.encode(image_1.unsqueeze(0))

❷   axs[i, 0].imshow(image_0.squeeze(), cmap="gray")
    axs[i, 0].set_title(f"{int(label_0)} {classes[int(label_0)]}", fontsize=9)
    axs[i, 0].set_axis_off()

    for step in range(steps):
        z_step = z_0 + (z_1 - z_0) * step / (steps - 1)
❸       image_step = wae.decode(z_step).detach()
❹       axs[i, step + 1].imshow(image_step.squeeze(), cmap="gray")
        axs[i, step + 1].set_axis_off()

❺   axs[i, -1].imshow(image_1.squeeze(), cmap="gray")
    axs[i, -1].set_title(f"{int(label_1)} {classes[int(label_1)]}", fontsize=9)
    axs[i, -1].set_axis_off()
plt.show()
```

Listing 4-29: Morphing one image into another by moving in the latent space

The number of interpolation steps defines how many images will be generated in the transition from the starting image to the target image. For each row in the output figure, two random test images are chosen ❶, and their corresponding latent space representations are computed (z_0 and z_1).

In each row, the endpoints for the morphing sequence correspond to the first image ❷ and the last image ❺. Intermediate frames are generated by linearly interpolating between the latent space representations of these two endpoints ❸. At each step, the interpolation result is decoded back into image space ❹, producing a smooth transition from one fashion item to another, visualized in a sequence that highlights the Wasserstein autoencoder's understanding of the latent structure of the dataset.

Figure 4-14 shows examples of interpolations between images.

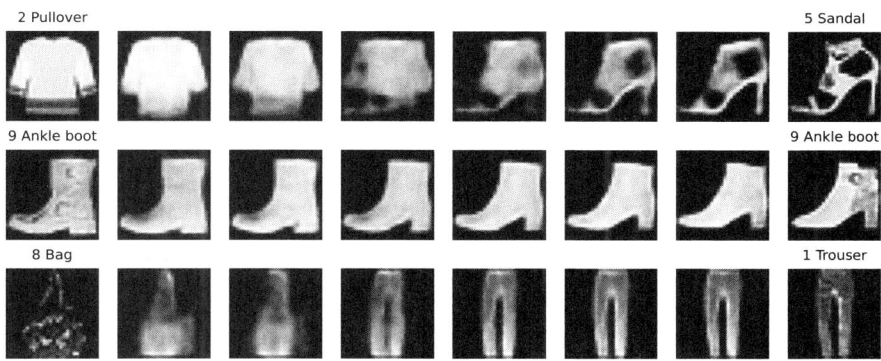

Figure 4-14: Images obtained by interpolating in latent space between the leftmost and rightmost images

The leftmost images gradually morph into the rightmost images through a series of intermediate steps. Each row begins with an original Fashion-MNIST image and ends with another, with the in-between images representing the Wasserstein autoencoder's interpretation of a continuous path in the latent space between the two endpoints. This visual progression showcases the smoothness of the latent space and the Wasserstein autoencoder's ability to generate coherent transitions between different classes of fashion items. The consistency of these transformations across each step reflects the model's capacity to understand and manipulate the underlying structure of the data it has learned.

NOTE *Code Example 4-B, "Interpolating Between Images with a Wasserstein Autoencoder," is available at* https://github.com/DeepTrackAI/DeepLearningCrashCourse. *Navigate to the* Ch04_AE *folder and then* ec04_B_wae_fashionmnist. *The* wae _fashionmnist.ipynb *notebook provides a complete code example that trains a Wasserstein autoencoder on the Fashion-MNIST images and then uses the trained autoencoder to interpolate between Fashion-MNIST images by moving in the latent space.*

Project 4C: Detecting Anomalies in ECG Data

Anomaly detection is the process of identifying observations that stand out from an established norm within a dataset. Such irregular patterns could indicate occurrences like mechanical failures or emerging trends such as changes in consumer habits. In this project, you'll use autoencoders to spot anomalies in electrocardiogram (ECG) readings—a vital task for monitoring cardiac health.

Understanding Anomaly Detection

In the context of anomaly detection, an autoencoder is trained exclusively on normal data, which teaches it to capture the typical patterns and features inherent to this data.

When a new piece of data is fed through the trained autoencoder, you can then assess the *reconstruction error*, which is the difference between the input and the output of the autoencoder. If the input data is similar to the normal examples seen during training, the reconstruction error will be low. Conversely, an anomalous input will likely result in a higher reconstruction error since the autoencoder hasn't learned the patterns associated with anomalies.

Therefore, by setting a threshold for the reconstruction error, you can flag data that exceeds this threshold as anomalous. This approach is particularly powerful when anomalies are rare or not well defined, which makes traditional supervised learning techniques ineffective. For example, if you have highly imbalanced classes, such as in rare diseases or fraud detection, training an autoencoder only on normal data can be particularly useful.

Loading the ECG Dataset

The ECG dataset is a compilation of heartbeat signals collected to support the development and evaluation of algorithms for anomaly detection in cardiac function. Each signal in the dataset corresponds to a single heartbeat, represented as a time series with 140 data points reflecting the electrical activity of the heart as it contracts and relaxes. Labels accompanying these signals categorize them as *normal* or *anomalous*, with the latter showing potential abnormalities in heart rhythm that could indicate cardiac conditions.

Start by loading the dataset with Listing 4-30.

```
import deeptrack as dt
import pandas as pd
import torch

dataframe = pd.read_csv("ecg.csv", header=None)
raw_data = dataframe.values
❶ ecgs = raw_data[:, 2:-11]
❷ labels = raw_data[:, -1].astype(bool)

sources = dt.sources.Source(ecg=ecgs, is_normal=labels)
train_sources, test_sources = dt.sources.random_split(sources, [0.7, 0.3])
❸ normal_sources = train_sources.filter(lambda ecg, is_normal: is_normal)
```

Listing 4-30: Loading the ECG dataset

This code loads the ECG dataset into the Pandas dataframe from the *ecg.csv* file. The code then extracts the raw numerical data into a NumPy array. Using the print(f"raw_data.shape = {raw_data.shape}") command, you can verify that the dataset contains 4,998 traces of length 141.

Each ECG trace has 140 data points, plus one last digit that represents the label (0 for anomalous and 1 for normal). The code separates the labels ❷ from the actual traces and cuts out the beginning and the end of the traces to reduce their size to 128 ❶, which is more suitable for the autoencoder you'll define later.

A custom Source object is created from the ECG traces and their labels to conveniently handle the data. This source is then randomly split into training and test sets with a 70:30 ratio. From the training set, another subset is created, containing only the normal ECGs ❸; this subset is crucial for training an autoencoder in an unsupervised manner to later identify anomalies by using the reconstruction error.

The training dataset contains 3,499 ECG traces, of which about 2,000 are classified as normal, as you can verify via print(f"Train ECGs = {len(train _sources)}") and print(f"Normal train ECGs = {len(normal_sources)}").

Plotting the Traces

Let's now visualize the ECG traces, using Listing 4-31.

```
import matplotlib.pyplot as plt

fig, axs = plt.subplots(1, 4, figsize=((12, 3)))
for idx, ax in enumerate(axs.ravel()):
    ecg = normal_sources[idx]["ecg"]
    ax.plot(ecg)
    ax.set_xlabel("timestep", fontsize=24)
fig.tight_layout()
plt.show()
```

Listing 4-31: Plotting some normal ECGs

This code generates Figure 4-15, which shows a series of normal ECG traces.

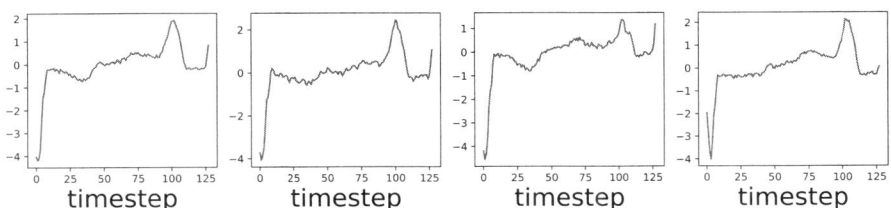

Figure 4-15: Normal ECG traces

Each trace displays the typical rhythmic patterns characteristic of a healthy heart's electrical activity. The ECGs are plotted over time, with each trace spanning the same number of time steps to demonstrate the consistency of the heartbeats.

Normalizing the Traces

Normalization is a vital preprocessing step to ensure that the model treats all data consistently and fairly, especially when the input features have varying scales. This standardization process adjusts the data to fit within a particular range, typically 0 to 1, to improve the training stability and performance.

Listing 4-32 normalizes the ECG traces.

```
import numpy as np

min_normal = np.min([source["ecg"] for source in normal_sources])
max_normal = np.max([source["ecg"] for source in normal_sources])

ecg_pip = (dt.Value(sources.ecg - min_normal) / (max_normal - min_normal)
          >> dt.Unsqueeze(axis=0) >> dt.pytorch.ToTensor(dtype=torch.float))
label_pip = dt.Value(sources.is_normal)
```

Listing 4-32: Normalizing the ECGs based on the normal range

This code calculates the minimum and maximum values across all normal ECG traces. These values establish the range within which the ECG data will be normalized. Next, the code defines the ecg_pip pipeline to perform the normalization operation for each ECG trace, ensuring that every data point is scaled in a range from 0 to 1. This pipeline also includes an operation to add a new axis to the data (dt.Unsqueeze(axis=0)), making it compatible with the expected input shape of PyTorch tensors, and finally converts the scaled data into a PyTorch tensor. Additionally, the label_pip pipeline is set up to simply pass through the normality label for each ECG.

After normalizing the ECG data, it's insightful to visualize the transformed traces to confirm that the normalization process was successful. You can do this with Listing 4-33.

```
--snip--
for idx, ax in enumerate(axs.ravel()):
    ecg = ecg_pip(normal_sources[idx])
    ax.plot(ecg.squeeze())
    ax.set_ylim([0, 1])
    --snip--
```

Listing 4-33: Plotting the normalized ECGs (by modifying Listing 4-31)

This applies ecg_pip to each selected normal ECG source to normalize the raw ECG trace. Each normalized ECG trace is then plotted on a corresponding subplot.

Figure 4-16 shows the resulting plots.

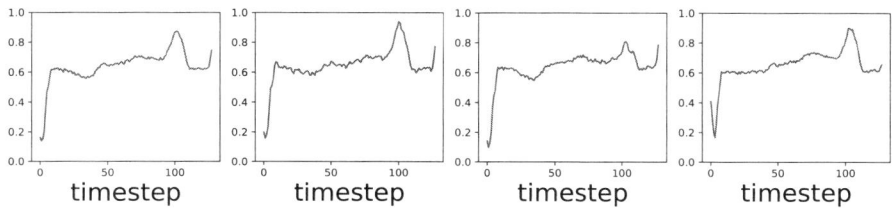

Figure 4-16: The normalized normal ECG traces

The traces have now been appropriately scaled and are ready for further processing by the autoencoder. Notice that the shapes of these normal ECG traces are all similar.

Defining and Training the Autoencoder

As usual, training an autoencoder is a two-step process. Let's start by defining the architecture and then train the model to reconstruct the input data as accurately as possible.

Define the autoencoder with Listing 4-34.

```
import deeplay as dl
import torch.nn as nn

autoencoder = dl.ConvolutionalEncoderDecoder2d(
    in_channels=1, encoder_channels=[8, 8], out_channels=1,
    out_activation=nn.Identity,
)
❶ autoencoder[..., "layer"].configure(nn.Conv1d, kernel_size=4, padding="same")
❷ autoencoder[..., "pool"].configure(nn.MaxPool1d, kernel_size=4, stride=4)
❸ autoencoder[..., "upsample"].configure(nn.ConvTranspose1d, kernel_size=4,
                                         stride=4)
```

Listing 4-34: Defining an autoencoder for 1D data

This code starts by defining an autoencoder for 2D data. However, the ECG traces are 1D data. Therefore, the code updates the convolutional layers of the encoder to use 1D convolutions ❶, its pooling layers to use 1D max-pooling layers ❷, and the deconvolutional layers of the decoder to be 1D ❸. Print the configuration via print(autoencoder) to gain insights into the details of the autoencoder's architecture.

Wrap the autoencoder into a regressor object to compile it:

```
ae = dl.Regressor( ·
    model=autoencoder, loss=nn.L1Loss(), optimizer=dl.Adam(),
).create()
```

This compiles the autoencoder model, defining the loss function and optimizer. Check the compilation with print(ae).

You can now train the autoencoder on the ECG dataset. Start by creating a data loader:

```
train_dataset = dt.pytorch.Dataset(ecg_pip & ecg_pip, inputs=normal_sources)
train_loader = dl.DataLoader(train_dataset, batch_size=16, shuffle=True)
```

Then train the autoencoder:

```
ae_trainer = dl.Trainer(max_epochs=30, accelerator="auto")
ae_trainer.fit(ae, train_loader)
```

This sets the maximum number of epochs to 30 and automatically utilizes the available hardware acceleration, such as GPU computing, to speed up the training process.

Testing with Normal and Anomalous ECGs

Now you're ready to visualize the performance of the trained autoencoder on the test dataset, which includes both normal and anomalous ECG traces. You can do this with Listing 4-35.

```
--snip--
❶ for ax, source in zip(axs.ravel(), np.random.choice(test_sources, 4)):
      test_ecg, test_label = (ecg_pip & label_pip)(source)
  ❷ pred_ecg = ae(test_ecg.float().unsqueeze(0))
  ❸ ax.plot(test_ecg.squeeze(), c="b", label="Input ECG")
  ❹ ax.plot(pred_ecg.detach().squeeze(), c="r", ls="--", label="Reconstructed")
      ax.set_title("Normal" if test_label else "Anomalous", fontsize=24)
      ax.legend()
      --snip--
```

Listing 4-35: Testing the trained autoencoder (by modifying Listing 4-31)

This code iterates over a random subset of test sources ❶, processing each through the autoencoder ❷. The original ECG is plotted with a solid line ❸, while the autoencoder's reconstruction is overlaid with a dashed line ❹. This allows you to assess how well the autoencoder has learned to reproduce the normal heartbeats and to identify anomalies.

Figure 4-17 shows the resulting plots.

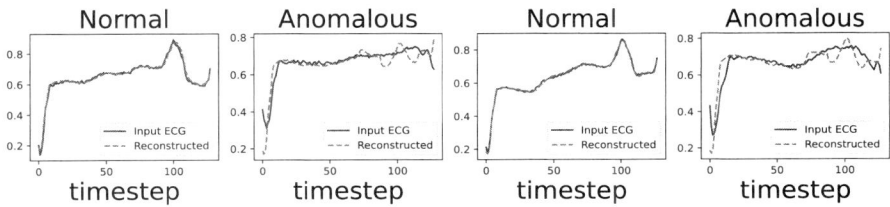

Figure 4-17: The input and reconstructed traces for normal and anomalous ECGs

Comparing the reconstructed ECG traces with the input ones, you can see that the autoencoder performs well on normal ECGs, with reconstructed traces closely mirroring the inputs. However, anomalous ECGs often result in reconstructions that are less accurate, because their characteristic patterns weren't present in the training data. As you'll learn in the following sections, this difference in reconstruction quality serves as the basis for distinguishing between normal and abnormal heart activity.

Detecting Anomalies

In this section, you'll learn two methods to identify abnormal patterns in ECG data via an autoencoder. Both methods exploit the autoencoder's ability to learn and reconstruct normal data patterns. Both also rely on setting a threshold to distinguish between normal and abnormal data, statistically analyzing the model's output on training data known to be normal. Let's go over each method in more detail.

Reconstruction Error Method

The first method focuses on exploiting the reconstruction error, which quantifies the difference between the original ECG signal and its reconstructed version. A larger error suggests an anomaly, as the model struggles to accurately reproduce data on which it hasn't been trained.

Start by using Listing 4-36 to calculate the reconstruction error on the normal ECG traces.

```
❶ normal_train_ecgs = torch.stack([ecg_pip(source) for source in normal_sources])
❷ normal_train_preds = ae(normal_train_ecgs).detach()
  normal_train_losses = [nn.functional.l1_loss(ecg, pred) for ecg, pred
                    in zip(normal_train_ecgs, normal_train_preds)]

  threshold_losses = np.quantile(normal_train_losses, 0.95)
```

Listing 4-36: Determining the normal reconstruction error

This code calculates the normal reconstruction error. The code creates a tensor containing the preprocessed ECGs from the training dataset ❶ and feeds that tensor into the autoencoder to obtain reconstructed signals ❷. Then the code calculates the L1 loss function to measure the reconstruction error for each signal, saved as normal_train_losses. By analyzing these errors, the threshold of the losses is set at the 95th percentile, which serves as a criterion to identify an ECG as anomalous.

Next, implement the hist() function shown in Listing 4-37 to plot the histogram of the reconstruction error.

```
def hist(title, xlabel, values, threshold_label, threshold):
    """Plot the error histogram highlighting the normal threshold."""
❶   plt.hist(values, bins=50, label=title)
❷   plt.axvline(x=threshold, color="k", linestyle=":", label=threshold_label)
    plt.xlabel(xlabel, fontsize=16)
    plt.ylabel("ECG Number", fontsize=16)
    plt.legend()
    plt.show()
```

Listing 4-37: The function to plot the histogram highlighting the threshold

This function plots a histogram to visualize the distribution of the values ❶, with a vertical line indicating the threshold ❷.

You can now use the hist() function with the following parameters:

```
hist("Training Dataset", "MAE", normal_train_losses, "95%", threshold_losses)
```

This should plot a histogram similar to the left side of Figure 4-18.

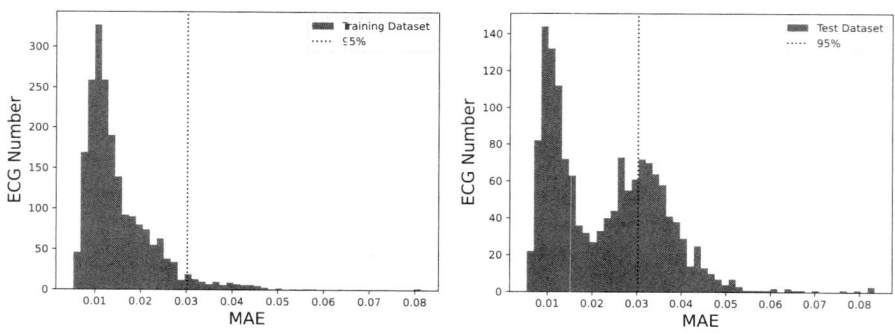

Figure 4-18: The reconstruction error in the training dataset with only normal ECGs (left) and in the test dataset (right)

The MAE is quite small, suggesting a high accuracy in reconstruction, meaning that the model is effectively capturing and reproducing the original data with minimal error. The 95th percentile, shown by the dotted vertical line, serves as the threshold beyond which ECGs are deemed anomalous.

Next, calculate and plot the reconstruction errors for the test data with Listing 4-38.

```
test_ecgs = torch.stack([ecg_pip(source) for source in test_sources])
test_preds = ae(test_ecgs).detach()
```
❶ ```
test_losses = [nn.functional.l1_loss(ecg, pred) for ecg, pred
                in zip(test_ecgs, test_preds)]
```

❷ ```
hist("Test Dataset", "MAE", test_losses, "95%", threshold_losses)
```

Listing 4-38: Calculating and plotting the reconstruction errors in the test data

This code calculates the reconstruction error for each ECG in the test dataset by comparing the original ECG signal with the signal reconstructed by the autoencoder ❶. Then the histogram is plotted to visualize the distribution of these reconstruction errors, with a vertical line representing the threshold determined from the training data ❷.

The resulting plot should resemble the right side of Figure 4-18. Now there's a second peak with a lot of data points above the threshold, suggesting that they might be abnormal heartbeats.

To quantitatively evaluate the performance of the model on the test data, you can implement the evaluate() function shown in Listing 4-39.

```
from sklearn.metrics import accuracy_score, precision_score, recall_score

def evaluate(labels, predictions):
    """Evaluate accuracy, precision, and recall of performance metric."""
    print(f"Accuracy = {accuracy_score(labels, predictions):.3f}  "
          f"Precision = {precision_score(labels, predictions):.3f}  "
          f"Recall = {recall_score(labels, predictions):.3f}")
```

Listing 4-39: The function to determine the metrics of the model

This function calculates and prints the accuracy (proportion of total predictions that are correct), precision (accuracy of positive predictions), and recall (proportion of correctly identified actual positives).

Next, use this function to evaluate the performance metrics for the anomaly detection based on the reconstruction error:

```
evaluate(labels=[label_pip(source) for source in test_sources],
         predictions=test_losses < threshold_losses)
```

This determines the performance metrics for the anomaly detection based on the reconstruction error by comparing the binary labels of the test data with the predicted labels determined by whether the reconstruction error is above the threshold.

For our run of the code, we got the following performance metrics:

```
Accuracy = 0.852  Precision = 0.823  Recall = 0.954
```

These results suggest that the model is quite effective at detecting normal ECGs as it has a high recall, but there is room to improve the precision by reducing the false positives.

Latent Space Method

The second method exploits the latent space, where data is represented in a compressed form. The assumption is that normal ECGs will cluster together in the latent space, whereas anomalous ECGs will be farther away from these clusters. By measuring the distance of each encoded ECG from its neighbors in the latent space, this approach gauges each ECG's level of normality by determining a threshold beyond which ECGs are considered anomalous.

Start by calculating the latent space of the normal ECGs:

```
latent_space_train = ae.model.encoder(normal_train_ecgs).detach()
latent_space_train = latent_space_train.view(latent_space_train.shape[0], -1)
```

This uses the trained encoder to obtain the latent representation of the normal ECG traces. The resulting `latent_space_train` tensor is then reshaped to a 2D tensor, with each row representing the latent space features of a single ECG trace.

Now you need to quantify the typicality of a point in the latent space, using Listing 4-40.

```
from sklearn.neighbors import NearestNeighbors

n_neighbors = 4   # Number of nearest neighbors

❶ neighbors = NearestNeighbors(n_neighbors=n_neighbors + 1,
                               algorithm="ball_tree").fit(latent_space_train)
❷ distances, _ = neighbors.kneighbors(latent_space_train)
  distances = distances[:, 1:]
❸ mean_distance = np.mean(distances, 1)

threshold_dist = np.quantile(mean_distance, 0.95)

hist("Training Dataset", "Mean Distance", mean_distance, "95%", threshold_dist)
```

Listing 4-40: Determining and plotting the distance between a representation in the latent space of a normal ECG and its neighbors

This code employs the *k-nearest neighbors algorithm*, a method that identifies the data points in a dataset that are nearest to a given point based on a chosen distance metric. Thus, you determine the given point's neighbors (here, with k set to 4).

By fitting the algorithm to the latent representations of the normal ECG traces ❶, the code calculates each point's distance to its k-nearest neighbors ❷ (the + 1 in n_neighbors=n_neighbors + 1 is used because the NearestNeighbors method includes the point itself as one of the closest neighbors). Since the closest neighbor of a point is the point itself, the code excludes the first column to focus on the distances to the nearest distinct neighbors. The mean distance for each point to its neighbors is computed ❸, providing insights into how tightly or loosely each ECG is embedded within the normal cluster.

The code sets a threshold at the 95th percentile of these mean distances, implying that points beyond this threshold are sufficiently far from the core cluster to be considered anomalies.

Finally, the hist() function plots the mean distances in a histogram, with the threshold indicated as a vertical dashed line. The left side of Figure 4-19 shows the corresponding plot.

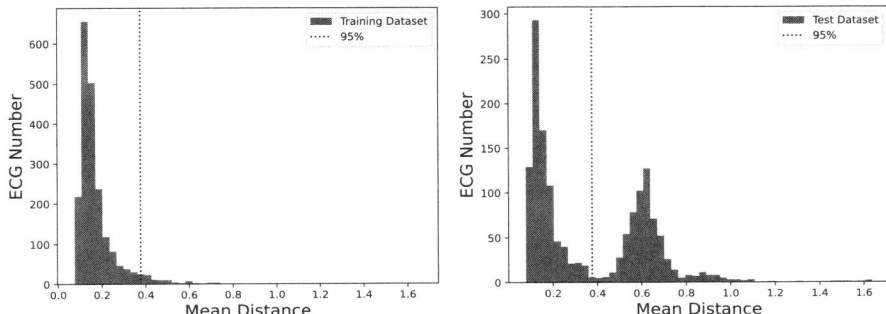

Figure 4-19: The distance from neighbors in the latent space for normal ECGs (left) and in the test dataset (right)

Like the reconstruction loss shown in Figure 4-18, this provides a clear view of the distribution of distances within the latent space and allows you to identify potential outliers.

Now calculate the latent representations for the test data:

```
latent_space_test = ae.model.encoder(test_ecgs).detach()
latent_space_test = latent_space_test.view(latent_space_test.shape[0], -1)
```

Then calculate the distances from the latent representations of the test data to their k-neighbors in the normal training data, using Listing 4-41.

```
from sklearn.metrics import pairwise_distances

❶ mean_dist_test = pairwise_distances(latent_space_test, latent_space_train)
❷ mean_dist_test = np.mean(
    np.partition(mean_dist_test, n_neighbors, axis=1)[:, :n_neighbors], 1,
)

hist("Test Dataset", "Mean Distance", mean_dist_test, "95%", threshold_dist)
```

Listing 4-41: Determining and plotting the distance between the test ECGs and the closest normal ECGs

This code begins by computing the distances between each test ECG's latent representations and those of the normal ECGs, effectively assessing how far each test ECG is from the norm. The code then finds the average distance to the nearest neighbors, which is a measure of how typical or atypical each test ECG is relative to normal patterns. Finally, the hist() function plots a histogram to visualize these mean distances across the test dataset, with a vertical line marking the threshold distance.

The results should look similar to the right side of Figure 4-19. The analysis based on the latent space identifies two clusters of ECG traces separated by the vertical threshold line. This allows you to distinguish normal from anomalous ECGs, with anything to the right of the threshold indicating anomalies and anything to the left indicating normal ECGs.

As you did previously, you can quantify this observation as follows:

```
evaluate(labels=[label_pip(source) for source in test_sources],
         predictions=mean_dist_test < threshold_dist)
```

This permits you to determine the performance metrics for the anomaly detection based on the latent space. The resulting performance metrics are shown here:

```
Accuracy = 0.976  Precision = 0.996  Recall = 0.963
```

The performance metrics using the latent space significantly surpass those obtained through reconstruction error analysis. Specifically, in our run, accuracy improved from 0.852 to 0.976, indicating a higher overall rate of correctly identified ECGs (both normal and anomalous). Precision also saw a remarkable increase from 0.823 to 0.996, showing an enhanced ability to accurately identify anomalies without as many false positives. While recall increased only slightly from 0.954 to 0.963, it still shows that the model is highly capable of identifying true anomalies.

NOTE   *Code Example 4-C, "Detecting Anomalies with an Autoencoder," is available at* https://github.com/DeepTrackAI/DeepLearningCrashCourse. *Navigate to the* Ch04_AE *folder and then* ec04_C_anomaly_detection. *The* anomaly _detection.ipynb *notebook provides a complete code example that detects anomalies in ECGs by using an autoencoder.*

Summary

In this chapter, you explored encoder-decoders, including denoising encoder-decoders, variational autoencoders, and Wasserstein autoencoders.

You started by learning how encoders and decoders work together to compress and reconstruct data, paving the way for more-complex applications. By implementing a denoising encoder-decoder, you learned the practical aspects of cleaning corrupted images, showcasing the model's ability to recover valuable data from noisy inputs.

You also learned about variational autoencoders—your first foray into the domain of generative modeling, which you'll explore in more detail in Chapters 9 and 10. Through the project with the MNIST dataset, you saw how variational autoencoders can generate new, diverse digit images that mimic the characteristics of the original dataset as well as explored the role of the latent space in controlling and understanding the generative process.

You then applied Wasserstein autoencoders to the Fashion-MNIST dataset. Here, you explored the concept of smoothly morphing between images, demonstrating the continuous nature of the latent space captured by Wasserstein autoencoders.

Finally, you applied autoencoders to detect anomalies in ECG data based on the reconstruction error and latent space features. This demonstrated the autoencoder's potential in distinguishing between normal and abnormal heartbeats, highlighting the practical significance of autoencoders in health care.

In the next chapter, you'll build on what you know about the encoder-decoder architecture to implement U-Nets, which have become a central tool for image analysis and transformation.

Seminal Works and Further Reading

The concept of autoencoders was explored in the influential 1994 work by Geoffrey E. Hinton and Richard S. Zemel, "Autoencoders, Minimum Description Length, and Helmholtz Free Energy," published in *Proceedings of the Neural Information Processing Systems* (*NeurIPS*, volume 6, pages 3–10). This work laid the foundation for using autoencoders to learn efficient representations of data by compressing and reconstructing input information, which serves as a basis for many modern architectures.

Hinton and Ruslan R. Salakhutdinov introduced the use of neural networks for unsupervised learning by training an autoencoder to generate compact representations in "Reducing the Dimensionality of Data with Neural Networks," published in 2006 in *Science* (volume 313, pages 504–507). This work paved the way for self-supervised approaches that use an inherent structure within the data to serve as a supervisory signal.

In 2015, Jonathan Long et al. introduced the use of convolutional neural networks in a fully convolutional manner to perform pixel-level image segmentation, laying the foundation for modern encoder-decoder approaches in image analysis, in "Fully Convolutional Networks for Semantic Segmentation," published in *Proceedings of the IEEE Conference on Computer Vision and Pattern Recognition* (*CVPR*, pages 3,431–3,440).

Variational autoencoders were introduced by Diederik P. Kingma and Max Welling in "Auto-Encoding Variational Bayes," published in 2013 on arXiv (article number 1312.6114) and in *Proceedings of the International Conference on Learning Representations* (*ICLR 2014*).

Ilya Tolstikhin et al. proposed the Wasserstein autoencoder by combining optimal transport theory with generative models in their 2018 article "Wasserstein Auto-Encoders," published on arXiv (article number 1711.01558) and in *Proceedings of the International Conference on Learning Representations* (*ICLR 2018*).

CHALLENGE PROJECTS

4-1: Multimodal data fusion for anomaly detection   Use sensor data from smartphones and smartwatches for anomaly detection in human activities. Use the Human Activity Recognition with Smartphones dataset available on Kaggle.

4-2: Generative models for synthetic data creation   Experiment with generative models to create synthetic images. Use the CelebFaces Attributes (CelebA) dataset for facial images, the Landscape Pictures dataset for landscapes, and the SIIM-ISIC Melanoma Classification dataset for medical images, all available on Kaggle. Assess the realism and diversity of the generated images.

4-3: Cross-domain image translation   Implement cross-domain image translation between conditions, such as day to night or summer to winter. Use the Day-Night dataset and Flickr Image dataset from Kaggle for your experiments. Evaluate the quality and authenticity of the translated images.

4-4: Advanced denoising with real-world noise patterns   Tackle the challenge of image denoising with the Darmstadt Noise dataset (DND), available on the TU Darmstadt website, and the SIDD Benchmark dataset, available on the York University website. Focus on removing real-world noise patterns from images captured under various conditions.

4-5: Anomaly detection in time-series data   Explore anomaly detection in time-series data with the Numenta Anomaly Benchmark (NAB) dataset, available on the Numenta website, and the S5–A Labeled Anomaly Detection dataset, available on Yahoo Webscope. These datasets offer real and synthetic time-series data with labeled anomalies.

5

SEGMENTING AND ANALYZING IMAGES WITH U-NETS

In this chapter, you'll learn about the U-Net, an architecture that stands at the forefront of image-transformation tasks such as image segmentation. The U-Net is a specialized form of encoder-decoder architecture, distinguished by its *skip connections*. These connections bridge the encoder and decoder at multiple scales, allowing the network to not just capture high-level features but also retain fine-grained details, which is essential for precise image transformation.

You'll start by using a U-Net for a challenging yet fascinating application: segmenting images of biological tissue to identify intracellular regions and mitochondria, which are critical for cellular functions and energy production. This practical exercise will demonstrate the capabilities of U-Nets in handling complex image-transformation tasks. Additionally, you'll use data augmentation to enhance U-Net performance, a key strategy to train robust neural network models.

In this chapter's projects, you'll apply a U-Net to find the positions of particles and to count the number of cells in an image, which are important tasks in fields such as biomedical research, drug development, and medical diagnostics.

Introducing U-Nets

Building upon the foundational principles of the encoder-decoder from Chapter 4, the U-Net architecture emerged as a sophisticated evolution designed specifically to overcome the limitations inherent in traditional encoder-decoder models.

Encoder-decoders, with their characteristic bottleneck layer, intentionally restrict the complexity of the functions they can learn, aiming to minimize noise retention at the cost of potential signal distortion or inadequate signal representation. This trade-off, while beneficial for tasks like dimensionality reduction and denoising, often falls short in applications demanding high precision and detail retention. Image segmentation, for example, requires accurately identifying and delineating boundaries within an image for tasks such as medical diagnosis, autonomous driving, and object recognition.

The U-Net architecture, illustrated in Figure 5-1, was introduced by Olaf Ronneberger and co-workers in 2015 to address these problems.

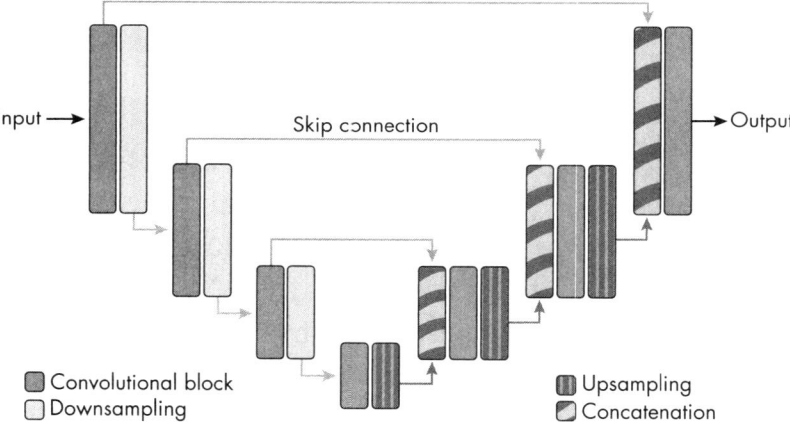

Figure 5-1: The U-Net architecture

This distinctive U-shaped architecture—hence the name "U-Net"—captures high-level features through its encoding stage while also preserving granular details during decoding. The U-Net's efficacy stems from its innovative skip connections, which link corresponding contraction and expansion convolutional layers, thus limiting the loss of detail at the bottleneck. These connections ensure that the network captures a complete picture of the input data, from the overarching global features to the minutest of details.

As in the case of an encoder-decoder, a U-Net captures complex features at different scales through a series of downsampling and upsampling operations. Downsampling reduces the spatial dimensions and increases the depth of the feature maps, while upsampling reverses this process. The skip connections bridge these two processes, concatenating feature maps of the same dimensions from the downsampling path to the upsampling path.

The inclusion of skip connections also addresses the vanishing gradient problem during backpropagation, maintaining essential signal information within the network's deeper layers. These connections essentially provide a direct pathway for gradients to flow through during training.

Understanding Semantic Segmentation with U-Nets

Semantic segmentation is the process of converting the values of each pixel in an image to another property that is more appropriate for downstream analysis.

NOTE *While semantic segmentation classifies each pixel into a category,* instance segmentation *goes a step further by distinguishing between different instances of the same class within an image. This distinction is crucial for applications requiring individual tracking or identification of objects that belong to the same category. The* panoptic segmentation *technique combines these approaches to provide comprehensive image analysis that classifies every pixel by category while also distinguishing between individual instances of these categories, effectively merging the concepts of semantic and instance segmentation for a holistic understanding of the image.*

In the context of image analysis, semantic segmentation often converts an image, which is composed of the intensity of the light received by each pixel, into a segmented image that contains the probability of each pixel to represent a specific type of, for example, cell structure.

One reason for the success of U-Nets in image segmentation is their versatile architecture, which simultaneously examines feature maps of multiple scales during upsampling and downsampling. Another important factor is the novel loss weighting introduced in the original U-Net description, which improves the accuracy of segmentation by giving more importance to certain features, such as edges and small structures.

The U-Net transforms the image-segmentation task into a pixel-wise multi-class classification problem by first applying a pixel-wise softmax function. This function converts the output values into a normalized probability distribution, which is the final feature map and is returned as the output of the network. The pixel-wise softmax is followed by the *cross-entropy loss function*, which is used to classify each pixel into one of several predefined classes.

The softmax function normalizes the final feature map into a probability distribution proportional to its exponential:

$$\sigma(z_i) = \frac{e^{z_i}}{\sum_{j=0}^{K-1} e^{z_j}} \tag{5.1}$$

Here, $z = [z_0, \ldots, z_{K-1}]$ is the feature map, and K is the number of segmentation classes. The softmax function maps this vector to a probability distribution, ensuring that each component lies in the interval $[0, 1]$ and that the components add up to 1, providing a probabilistic estimate of the class to which the input pixel belongs.

The categorical cross-entropy loss depends on the details of how the various classes are encoded. One common method is *one-hot encoding*: Each class is represented by a binary vector with all elements set to 0 except for a single element set to 1, which indicates the class. For example, if a segmentation dataset has three classes, the first one is labeled $[1, 0, 0]$, the second $[0, 1, 0]$, and the third $[0, 0, 1]$. The categorical cross-entropy loss is thereby calculated as follows:

$$L_{\text{cross-entropy}} = -\sum_{i=0}^{K-1} y_i \ln(\sigma(z_i)) \qquad (5.2)$$

Here, y_i represents the one-hot-encoded true label for each class (where i represents a specific class out of K total classes), z_i are the logits for each class produced by the model (the *logits* are the raw, unnormalized scores output by the model), and $\sigma(z_i)$ represents the softmax function applied to the logits z_i, converting them to a probability distribution over the classes. With this loss, the terms in the summation are 0 everywhere except for the correct label defined in the one-hot-encoding vector. Thus, you lose a lot of computational time computing the logarithm of values that don't change the loss value.

An alternative approach that you'll use in this chapter is *sparse categorical cross-entropy*, which can be used if the class labels are integers, as when they are one-hot encoded. This loss computes the logarithm only for the output index that corresponds to the ground truth. Therefore, the loss function is

$$L_{\text{sparse cross-entropy}} = -\ln(\sigma(z_{\text{true}})) \qquad (5.3)$$

where z_{true} is the logit for the true class. This is much more computationally efficient.

You can modify this loss function with different weightings. For example, you could weight the pixels at the borders of segmented regions to be more important than the pixels inside the segmentation to encourage the network to learn hard borders between objects. You might also consider weighting the classes differently if you have an unbalanced dataset.

Segmenting Images of Biological Tissues

In this section, you'll segment neuronal structures obtained with a high-resolution microscopy imaging technique—namely, serial-section transmission electron microscopy (ssTEM). You'll work with a database of images of the ventral nerve cord of *Drosophila melanogaster* larvae, commonly known as fruit flies. The goal is to discern and delineate the neuronal intracellular regions and mitochondria, two critical components for understanding the complex neuronal architecture of this organism, because these structures are crucial for the functioning and energy dynamics of the nerve cells.

You've already used some images from this dataset in Projects 3C and 3D when you created DeepDreams and transferred style between images.

This dataset comprises 20 high-quality ssTEM images, each with 1024×1024 pixels. These images capture minute details of the neuronal structures, offering insights into the biological makeup of the nerve cord. The ssTEM images also include corresponding segmentations, which have been manually (and painstakingly) annotated by human experts to provide a reference for the complex patterns of neuronal structures you'll now try to segment.

Loading the Segmented Tissue Images

Start by downloading the dataset with Listing 5-1.

```
import os

if not os.path.exists("tissue_images_dataset"):
    os.system("git clone https://github.com/DeepTrackAI/tissue_images_dataset")

raw_path = os.path.join("tissue_images_dataset", "stack1", "raw")
seg_path = os.path.join("tissue_images_dataset", "stack1", "labels")
```

Listing 5-1: Downloading the dataset

This code downloads the data into the *tissue_images_dataset* directory, which contains the *stack1* directory, which in turn includes two further subdirectories: *raw* for the ssTEM images and *labels* for the segmentation maps.

To manage the images and labels effectively during the training phase, you can construct some data sources, as shown in Listing 5-2.

```
import deeptrack as dt

raw_paths = dt.sources.ImageFolder(root=raw_path)
seg_paths = dt.sources.ImageFolder(root=seg_path)
❶ paths = dt.sources.Source(raw=raw_paths, label=seg_paths)
❷ train_paths, val_paths, test_paths = \
    dt.sources.random_split(paths, [0.8, 0.1, 0.1])

❸ train_srcs = train_paths.product(flip_ud=[True, False], flip_lr=[True, False])
val_srcs = val_paths.constants(flip_ud=False, flip_lr=False)
test_srcs = test_paths.constants(flip_ud=False, flip_lr=False)

sources = dt.sources.Join(train_srcs, val_srcs, test_srcs)
```

Listing 5-2: Creating the sources to manage the images during training

This code begins by loading the image paths from the dataset into two `ImageFolder` objects for the raw and segmented images. These are then combined into a single source ❶, which is subsequently divided into training, validation, and test sets with an 80:10:10 split ratio ❷. Verify that you've loaded 20 images with `len(raw_paths)` or `len(seg_paths)`, of which 16 are used for training, 2 for validation, and 2 for testing.

For the training set, data augmentation is done by generating images flipped both vertically and horizontally to enhance the model's generalization capabilities ❸. The validation set (val_srcs) and test set (test_srcs), on the other hand, are kept without augmentations.

Finally, all sources are joined together into sources, simplifying the process of iterating over different sets during training and evaluation.

Creating the Data Pipelines

These labeled segmentations aren't one-hot encoded but rather contain the class label for each pixel. The class labels represent various neuronal structures, including intracellular regions, oriented membranes, membrane junctions, mitochondria, and synapses. The class associated with each cell structure is fully described in the ssTEM dataset documentation.

For this example, you'll consider only the neuronal intracellular regions and mitochondria, to which the dataset assigns the labels 255 and 191, respectively. First, you'll extract the classes you're interested in and group the remaining class labels into a Background class. Additionally, you'll assign the class labels to be 0, 1, and 2, for background, intracellular regions, and mitochondria, respectively. This will make it easier to work with the data in the following steps.

Start by implementing the select_labels() function that selects the classes you're interested in and groups the remaining class labels into a Background class, as shown in Listing 5-3.

```
import numpy as np

def select_labels(class_labels):
    """Create a function to filter and remap labels in a segmentation map."""
    def inner(segmentation):
        seg = segmentation.copy()
        mask = seg * np.isin(seg, class_labels).astype(np.uint8)
    ❶ new_seg = (np.select([mask == c for c in class_labels],
                            np.arange(len(class_labels)) + 1)
                   .astype(np.uint8).squeeze())
    ❷ one_hot_encoded_seg = np.eye(len(class_labels) + 1)[new_seg]
        return one_hot_encoded_seg
    return inner
```

Listing 5-3: The function to filter the labels in the segmentation map

This function filters and remaps the labels in a segmentation map according to the list of labels to be selected from the segmentation map in the class_labels parameter. The select_labels() function returns the inner() function that takes a segmentation map as its input (with one color channel where the segmentations are encoded in the pixel values). This function first creates the seg copy of the input segmentation map to avoid modifying the original data. Then the function generates a mask by selecting the pixels whose values match any of those specified in class_labels. Next, the function changes the values of these selected labels to a new range, from 1 to the length of class_labels, by using the NumPy select() function, which constructs a new segmentation map replacing each of the specified labels with its new value ❶. Finally, the function returns a one-hot-encoded version of this new segmentation map (with one color channel for the background plus one color channel for each class label): Each pixel is represented as a one-hot vector indicating its class, and the vector size is one more than the number of class labels (using the 0 label to account for the background) ❷.

You can now set up pipelines that handle both images and labels, applying the necessary transformations to prepare the data, using Listing 5-4.

```
import torch

im_pip = dt.LoadImage(sources.raw.path) >> dt.NormalizeMinMax()
seg_pip = (dt.LoadImage(sources.label.path)
        ❶ >> dt.Lambda(select_labels, class_labels=[255, 191]))
pip = ((im_pip & seg_pip) >> dt.FlipLR(sources.flip_lr)
        >> dt.FlipUD(sources.flip_ud) >> dt.MoveAxis(2, 0)
        >> dt.pytorch.ToTensor(dtype=torch.float))
```

Listing 5-4: Defining the pipelines

This code creates an image pipeline (im_pip) to get the image from the file and normalize it. Then a label pipeline (seg_pip) is created to load the segmentations from the file, applying the function returned by select_labels() to filter and remap the labels ❶. Finally, the code combines these pipelines into the pip pipeline for the subsequent training process.

Now, define the training and validation datasets:

```
train_dataset = dt.pytorch.Dataset(pip, train_srcs)
val_dataset = dt.pytorch.Dataset(pip, val_srcs)
```

At this point, it's safer to double-check that the pipeline works as intended by plotting a raw image from the training dataset and the corresponding processed segmentation with Listing 5-5.

```
import matplotlib.pyplot as plt

❶ image, segmentation = train_dataset[0]

fig, axs = plt.subplots(1, 4, figsize=(10, 5))

❷ axs[0].imshow(image.permute(1, 2, 0), cmap="gray")
axs[0].set_title("Image", fontsize=16)
axs[0].set_axis_off()

for i in range(segmentation.shape[0]):
    segmentation_color = torch.ones_like(segmentation)
    for j in range(segmentation.shape[0]):
        ❸ if j != i: segmentation_color[j, ...] = 1 - segmentation[i, ...]
```

```
❹ axs[i + 1].imshow(segmentation_color.permute(1, 2, 0))
  axs[i + 1].set_title(f"Ground Truth Ch. {i}", fontsize=16)
  axs[i + 1].set_axis_off()

plt.tight_layout()
plt.show()
```

Listing 5-5: Plotting the input image and corresponding ground-truth segmentation

This code extracts the first image and relative segmentation from the dataset ❶ and then plots them. As usual, the code permutes the dimensions of the image and segmentation tensors, transforming them from the channel-first format expected by PyTorch to the channel-last format required for visualization with Matplotlib ❷ ❹. The channels of the segmentation map are manipulated to be plotted separately on a white background ❸.

Figure 5-2 shows the resulting images.

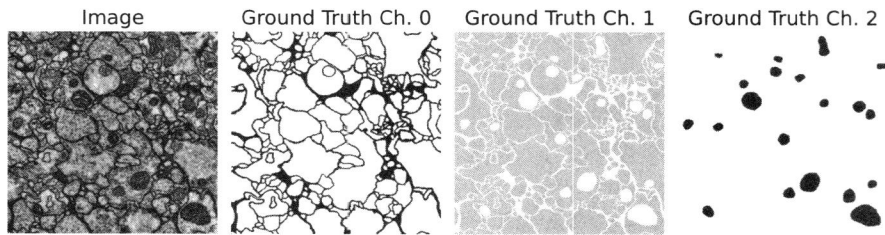

Figure 5-2: The input image (left) and the ground-truth segmentation corresponding to the background (channel 0), intracellular regions (channel 1), and mitochondria (channel 2)

On the left is an ssTEM image of the ventral nerve cord from a *Drosophila melanogaster* larva with its complex cellular textures and structures. The three panels on the right show the segmentations corresponding to background (channel 0), intracellular regions (channel 1), and mitochondria (channel 2). These segmentations show the spatial distribution and morphology of different cellular components: The background segmentation highlights the empty spaces and cell boundaries; the intracellular regions segmentation captures the dense cell interiors; and the mitochondria segmentation isolates the smaller, more sparsely distributed mitochondrial structures.

Defining and Training the U-Net

In this section, you'll train a U-Net to identify and segment the cellular components. You'll start by defining a metric to be monitored during training. Then you'll define and compile the U-Net as well as the necessary data loaders. Finally, you'll train the network.

Segmentation models, like U-Nets, require a well-thought-out strategy to evaluate their performance. The *Jaccard index*, also known as *intersection over union (IoU)*, is a common metric used to evaluate image-segmentation models. The Jaccard index measures the similarity of the predicted and true segmentations by calculating the area of overlap between the predicted segmentation and the ground-truth segmentation, divided by the area of the union of these two regions. This metric provides an intuitive way to quantify the accuracy of a segmentation model, as it directly relates to the proportion of correctly identified pixels relative to the combined area of both the prediction and the ground truth. Higher values of the Jaccard index indicate better performance, with a score of 1.0 representing a model that perfectly segments the image with no false positives or false negatives.

Predictions are typically made as probabilities for each class. A common approach to convert these probabilities to class predictions that can be used in the Jaccard index is to select the class with the maximum value by using the argmax() function. To accommodate this, you can introduce a customized metric class that extends the MulticlassJaccardIndex class to automatically apply the argmax() function to the predictions before computing the metric, as shown in Listing 5-6.

```
from torchmetrics.classification import MulticlassJaccardIndex

class ArgmaxJI(MulticlassJaccardIndex):
    """Compute Jaccard Index for multiclass predictions after argmax."""

    def update(self, preds, targets):
        """Update Jaccard Index using argmax of class predictions."""
        super().update(preds.argmax(dim=1), targets.argmax(dim=1))
```

Listing 5-6: The class to compute the Jaccard index after argmax()

The update() method updates the Jaccard index metric by comparing the predictions and targets after applying the argmax() function to both preds and targets. The argmax() function selects the index of the maximum value across the specified dimension (dim=1), effectively choosing the class with the highest predicted probability for each pixel.

Next, define the U-Net model, using Listing 5-7.

```
import deeplay as dl

ji_metric = ArgmaxJI(num_classes=3)

unet = dl.UNet2d(
    in_channels=1, channels=[16, 32, 64, 128], out_channels=3, skip=dl.Cat(),
)
unet_reg_template = dl.Regressor(
    model=unet, loss=torch.nn.CrossEntropyLoss(), metrics=[ji_metric],
    optimizer=dl.Adam(),
)
unet_reg = unet_reg_template.create()
```

Listing 5-7: Creating and compiling the U-Net

This code starts by defining the `ji_metric` metric to evaluate the model's performance, provided by the `ArgmaxJI` class defined in Listing 5-6 with three classes.

Then the code instantiates a U-Net with a single input channel, reflecting the grayscale nature of our ssTEM images (`in_channels=1`). The architecture consists of layers with increasing numbers of channels (`channels=[16, 32, 64, 128]`). The same structure is replicated in reverse for the decoder part of the U-Net. The output of the U-Net will have three channels, corresponding to the classes: background, intracellular regions, and mitochondria (`out_channels=3`). The skip connections (`skip=dl.Cat()`) simply concatenate the output of each encoder's block with the corresponding input of the decoder's block.

A regressor template is set up with the U-Net model, the `CrossEntropy Loss()` function, your custom Jaccard index metric `ji_metric`, and the Adam optimizer. Finally, the code calls the `create()` method on the regressor template to produce a U-Net regressor that is ready to be trained.

To get a better understanding of the U-Net model and its configuration, you can print the model summary with `print(unet_reg)`.

With the U-Net model defined, set up the data loaders for the training and validation datasets as shown in Listing 5-8.

```
train_loader = dl.DataLoader(train_dataset, batch_size=2, shuffle=True)
val_loader = dl.DataLoader(val_dataset, batch_size=2)
```

Listing 5-8: Defining the training and validation data loaders

These data loaders will feed batches of images and labels into the U-Net during the training process, with the batch size set to 2 and shuffling enabled for the training dataset to ensure that the model sees a diverse set of images during each epoch.

Finally, train the U-Net with Listing 5-9.

```
from lightning.pytorch.loggers import CSVLogger

logger = CSVLogger("logs", name="train_100_epochs")
trainer = dl.Trainer(max_epochs=100, accelerator="auto", logger=logger)
trainer.fit(unet_reg, train_loader, val_loader)
```

Listing 5-9: Training the U-Net for 100 epochs

This code trains the U-Net for 100 epochs. A `CSVLogger` object records the training progress, which is useful for analyzing the model's performance over time. The training and validation processes are carried out via the `train _loader` and `val_loader` data loaders, and the `fit()` method kicks off the actual training.

Plotting the Training Metrics

Monitoring the training and validation metrics throughout the training process is crucial to ensure that your model is learning effectively and to identify any potential overfitting. As you learned in Chapter 1, overfitting occurs when the model performs well on the training data but poorly on unseen data. This indicates that the model has learned the training data too closely, including its noise and outliers, rather than generalizing from the training data.

You can read the metrics logged during the training from the *metrics.csv* file as follows:

```
import pandas as pd

metrics = pd.read_csv(os.path.join(logger.log_dir, "metrics.csv")).ffill()
```

Given that the logged data may have missing values, this code uses the `.ffill()` function to apply *forward filling*, a technique used to fill missing values in a sequence by propagating the last observed non-null value forward until another non-null value is encountered, to ensure continuity in the data.

To visualize the model's learning progression and detect signs of overfitting, you can implement the `plot_training_metrics()` function in Listing 5-10.

```
def plot_training_metrics(m):
    """Plot training metrics by epoch."""
    fig, axs = plt.subplots(2, figsize=(6, 4))

    axs[0].plot(m["epoch"], m["train_loss_epoch"], label="Train Loss")
    axs[0].plot(m["epoch"], m["val_loss_epoch"], label="Validation Loss")
    axs[0].set_xlabel("Epoch")
    axs[0].set_ylabel("Loss")
    axs[0].legend()

    axs[1].plot(m["epoch"], m["trainArgmaxJI_epoch"], label="Train JI")
    axs[1].plot(m["epoch"], m["valArgmaxJI_epoch"], label="Validation JI")
```

```
axs[1].set_xlabel("Epoch")
axs[1].set_ylabel("Jaccard Index (JI)")
axs[1].legend()

plt.tight_layout()
plt.show()
```

Listing 5-10: The function to plot the training metrics

This function generates two plots: The first plot shows the loss on the training and validation datasets over each training epoch, and the second plot displays the Jaccard index for both datasets over the same epochs.

Use this function with the following:

```
plot_training_metrics(metrics)
```

The resulting plots should look like Figure 5-3.

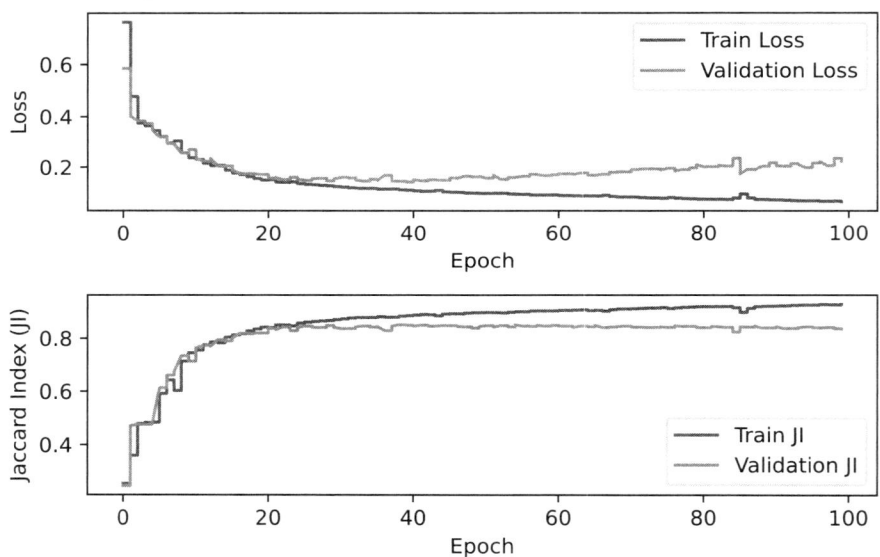

Figure 5-3: The training and validation losses and Jaccard index showing overfitting

These curves show signs of overfitting. The top graph shows the training loss decreasing steadily, while the validation loss decreases initially but then plateaus and slightly increases, indicating the model's growing discrepancy in performance on training versus unseen data. Similarly, the bottom graph depicts the Jaccard index; the training metric improves consistently, but the validation metric plateaus, highlighting a limit to the model's generalization.

Preventing Overfitting

To mitigate the overfitting in the preceding section, you can use *early stopping*, a technique that halts training when a monitored metric stops improving. Listing 5-11 sets up early stopping in the training of the U-Net.

```
from lightning.pytorch.callbacks import EarlyStopping

❶ early_stop_unet_reg = unet_reg_template.create()

early_stop = EarlyStopping(monitor="valArgmaxJI_epoch", mode="max", patience=5)
early_stop_logger = CSVLogger("logs", name="train_until_stagnation")

early_stop_trainer = dl.Trainer(max_epochs=100, logger=early_stop_logger,
                                callbacks=[early_stop])
❷ early_stop_trainer.fit(early_stop_unet_reg, train_loader, val_loader)
```

Listing 5-11: Training the U-Net with early stopping to prevent overfitting

This code first creates a new instance of the U-Net regressor ❶. Then the code specifies the EarlyStopping callback, instructing it to monitor the validation Jaccard index, maximize it, and halt training if no improvement occurs after five epochs. The code sets up a new logger called early_stop_logger to track the training process with early stopping. Finally, the code prepares a trainer with the early stopping callback and a maximum of 100 epochs and trains the new U-Net ❷.

You can then plot the training and validation metrics:

```
metrics = (pd.read_csv(os.path.join(early_stop_logger.log_dir, "metrics.csv"))
           .ffill())
plot_training_metrics(metrics)
```

This should generate plots similar to those in Figure 5-4.

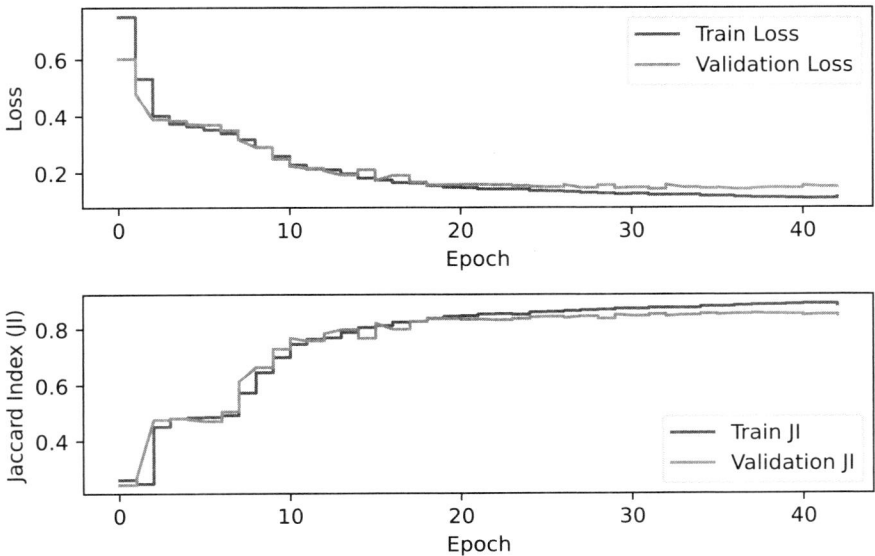

Figure 5-4: The training and validation losses and Jaccard index with early stopping to prevent overfitting

You can visually confirm that early stopping has effectively prevented the model from learning the noise and idiosyncrasies of the training data, resulting in a model that is more likely to perform well on unseen data.

Evaluating the Trained U-Net

Evaluating the performance of the trained U-Net on test data is essential to confirm that the model can effectively generalize and accurately segment unseen images.

You can calculate the predicted segmentation on the test data as shown in Listing 5-12.

```
test_dataset = dt.pytorch.Dataset(pip, test_srcs)
test_loader = dl.DataLoader(test_dataset, batch_size=2, shuffle=False)
trainer.test(early_stop_unet_reg, test_loader)
pred_seg = torch.cat(trainer.predict(early_stop_unet_reg, test_loader), dim=0)
```

Listing 5-12: Estimating the segmentations with the U-Net

This code defines test_dataset by using the previously defined pip data pipeline, ensuring consistency in the preprocessing of the images. Then a data loader called test_loader is created to manage the batch processing of the test images. Finally, the code evaluates the trained U-Net on the test dataset and aggregates the predictions for all test images into the pred_seg tensor for further analysis.

You can visually compare the predicted segmentation with the ground truth, using Listing 5-13.

```
❶ test_image, test_seg = test_dataset[0]

fig, axs = plt.subplots(1, 3, figsize=((12, 9)))

axs[0].imshow(test_image[0], cmap="gray")
axs[0].set_title("Image", fontsize=24)
axs[0].set_axis_off()

axs[1].imshow(test_seg.argmax(dim=0))
axs[1].set_title("Ground Truth", fontsize=24)
axs[1].set_axis_off()

axs[2].imshow(pred_seg[0].argmax(dim=0))
axs[2].set_title("Prediction", fontsize=24)
axs[2].set_axis_off()

plt.tight_layout()
plt.show()
```

Listing 5-13: Plotting the U-Net result against the ground-truth segmentation

This code selects the first sample image and its corresponding segmentation ❶ and then proceeds to plot the original image, the ground-truth segmentation, and the predicted segmentation.

This generates Figure 5-5.

Image   Ground Truth   Prediction

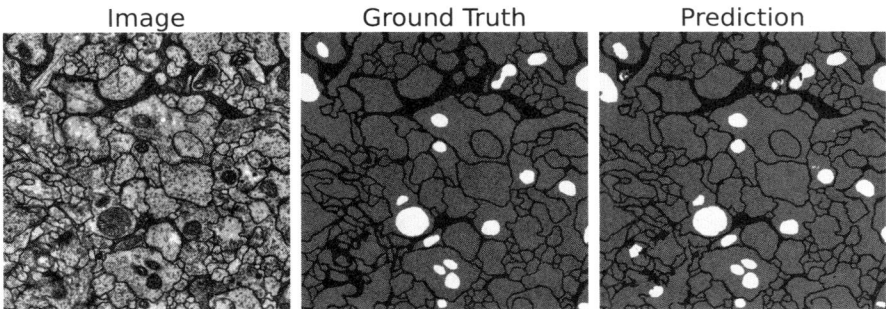

Figure 5-5: The input tissue image (left), ground-truth segmentation (middle), and segmentation generated by the U-Net (right)

Comparing the three panels reveals the U-Net's segmentation capabilities. On the left is the original ssTEM image of biological tissue, while the center image displays the ground-truth segmentation with various structures clearly outlined. The right image shows the segmentation as predicted by the U-Net, which indeed appears quite similar to the ground-truth segmentation. This similarity highlights the effectiveness of the U-Net in accurately segmenting complex biological structures.

For a more quantitative assessment, you can calculate the Jaccard index of a test image:

```
ji_metric.reset()
ji_seg = ji_metric(pred_seg[0].unsqueeze(0), test_seg.unsqueeze(0))
```

To ensure that the accuracy metric is calculated from a clean slate, this code resets the Jaccard index metric. Then the code calculates the Jaccard index for the chosen image by comparing the model's prediction with the ground-truth label.

You can then use `print(ji_seg)` to print the Jaccard index for this segmentation, which in our case is 0.861, a pretty good result. The U-Net has successfully identified and delineated the regions of interest in the tissue image.

NOTE *Code Example 5-1, "Segmenting Biological Tissue Images," is available at* https:// github.com/DeepTrackAI/DeepLearningCrashCourse. *Navigate to the* Ch05_UNet *folder and then* ec05_1_unet. *The* unet.ipynb *notebook provides a complete code example that segments the images of a biological tissue by using a U-Net employing early stopping to prevent overfitting.*

Project 5A: Detecting Quantum Dots in Fluorescence Images

You'll now solve a problem at the intersection of deep learning and nanotechnology: detecting and localizing quantum dots within fluorescence images. *Quantum dots* are nanometer-scale semiconductor particles that exhibit unique optical and electronic properties, making them invaluable in various scientific applications, from biological labeling to quantum computing.

The ability to precisely identify and locate quantum dots is critical in disciplines such as biology and materials science, where accurate spatial information is paramount. By exploiting the U-Net's exceptional capacity to capture detailed spatial data, you'll pinpoint the positions of multiple quantum dots in an image acquired with a fluorescence microscope.

Loading the Image

The first step in your quest to detect quantum dots is to load and inspect an image captured through fluorescence microscopy. This type of imaging is particularly adept at revealing the presence of quantum dots because they emit fluorescence when exposed to light of certain wavelengths.

You can load and display an image of quantum dots with Listing 5-14.

```
import matplotlib.pyplot as plt
from PIL import Image

image_of_particles = Image.open("frame_with_qdots.tif")

plt.figure(figsize=(10, 10))
plt.imshow(image_of_particles, vmin=100, vmax=200, cmap="gray")
plt.show()
```

Listing 5-14: Loading and plotting a fluorescence image of a quantum dot

This code loads the image in the *frame_with_qdots.tif* file by using the Pillow (PIL) library. The code then visualizes the image with a specific colormap and intensity range to enhance the visibility of the quantum dots against the background.

Figure 5-6 shows a plot of the fluorescence microscopy image.

Figure 5-6: A fluorescence image of quantum dots

You can see a field of quantum dots scattered across the visual plane. Each quantum dot appears as a bright, circular spot, varying slightly in size and luminosity, against the dark, homogeneous background. You'll exploit the U-Net's ability to perform pixel-wise classification to discern these luminous points from the surrounding darkness.

Simulating Quantum Dots

In this section, you'll create realistic, computer-generated images of quantum dots that mimic the experimental data. This simulation is a crucial step, because it'll allow you to generate a large dataset to train the U-Net without the need for extensive manual labeling of real images.

Image Cropping

The initial step in simulating images of quantum dots is isolating a single quantum dot to understand its characteristics. You can do this with Listing 5-15.

```
x0, y0, crop_size = 178, 271, 50
crop = image_of_particles.crop((x0, y0, x0 + crop_size, y0 + crop_size))

plt.figure(figsize=(5, 5))
plt.imshow(crop, vmin=100, vmax=200, cmap="gray")
plt.show()
```

Listing 5-15: Extracting and plotting a crop with a single quantum dot

This code extracts a small region from the larger fluorescence image to focus on a single quantum dot, specified by the top-left corner coordinates (x0 and y0) and the size of the crop (crop_size). The resulting crop is then displayed, as shown in the left panel of Figure 5-7.

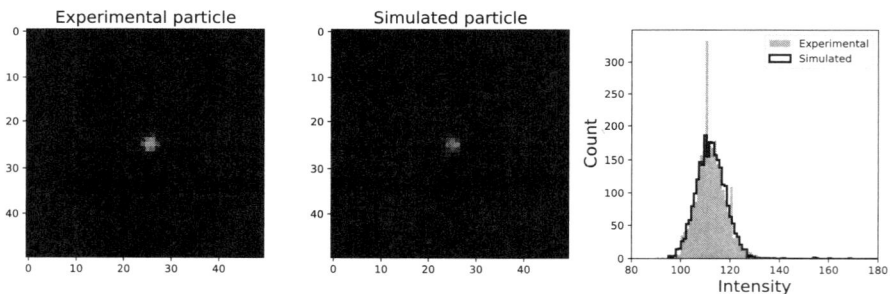

Figure 5-7: Comparing the experimental (left) and simulated (middle) quantum dot images, and their pixel-value histograms (right)

The leftmost image is a close-up view of a single quantum dot captured by fluorescence microscopy. The isolated quantum dot appears bright against the darker background, exemplifying the characteristic fluorescence of these nanometric particles when excited by light of an appropriate wavelength. This zoomed-in perspective gives you the intensity profile and size of the image of the quantum dot, which you'll use as a benchmark for the subsequent simulation process.

A Single Quantum Dot

Now let's prepare a simulation pipeline to create images of quantum dots similar to the left panel of Figure 5-7. You can do this with Listing 5-16.

```
import deeptrack as dt
import numpy as np

optics = dt.Fluorescence(
    wavelength=600 * dt.units.nm, NA=0.9, magnification=1,
    resolution=0.11 * dt.units.um, output_region=(0, 0, 50, 50),
```

```
)
particle = dt.PointParticle(position=(25, 25), intensity=1.2e4, z=0)
sim_im_pip = optics(particle) >> dt.Add(30) >> np.random.poisson >> dt.Add(82)
```

Listing 5-16: Defining the pipeline to simulate the image of a single quantum dot

This code constructs a simulation pipeline that replicates the conditions under which quantum dots emit fluorescence. The pipeline starts with the optical setting specifications of a fluorescence microscope, an instance of Fluorescence saved in the optics variable. These settings include the wavelength of the light, the numerical aperture (NA) of the lens system, the magnification factor, and the resolution of the imaging system. The output region is defined to constrain the field of view to a 50×50−pixel area, which is suitable for capturing the image of a single quantum dot.

Quantum dots have a negligible physical size with respect to the point spread function of the microscope (which determines the resolution limit, as anything smaller than the point spread function will appear as a bright spot in the microscopy image). Because of this, they can be simulated as point emitters. Therefore, a PointParticle instance saved in the particle variable is created to simulate a quantum dot with a fixed position at the center of this region and a specified intensity similar to the brightness of an actual quantum dot.

Once the optical system and quantum dot properties are established, the sim_im_pip simulation pipeline applies a sequence of operations to render the image. The fluorescence signal generated by the quantum dot is first increased by adding a constant background level. Subsequently, a Poisson noise is applied to introduce realistic signal fluctuations, followed by another increment to simulate the offset inherent in imaging detectors.

To validate the efficacy of your simulation pipeline, compare the experimental image of a single quantum dot with a simulated counterpart, using Listing 5-17.

```
❶ sim_im_pip.update()
❷ sim_im = sim_im_pip()

  plt.figure(figsize=(12, 4))

  plt.subplot(1, 3, 1)
❸ plt.imshow(crop, cmap="gray", vmin=100, vmax=250)
  plt.title("Experimental particle", fontsize=16)

  plt.subplot(1, 3, 2)
❹ plt.imshow(sim_im, cmap="gray", vmin=100, vmax=250)
  plt.title("Simulated particle", fontsize=16)

  plt.subplot(1, 3, 3)
❺ plt.hist(np.array(crop).flatten(), bins=100, label="Experimental", alpha=0.5)
❻ plt.hist(np.array(sim_im).flatten(), bins=100, label="Simulated",
           histtype="step", color="black", linewidth=2)
```

```
plt.xlabel("Intensity", fontsize=16)
plt.xlim([80, 180])
plt.ylabel("Count", fontsize=16)
plt.legend()

plt.tight_layout()
plt.show()
```

Listing 5-17: Comparing experimental and simulated images of quantum dots

This code updates the simulation pipeline ❶ and creates a new image ❷. Then the code plots the experimental image ❸, the simulated image ❹, and a comparison of their respective pixel-value histograms ❺ ❻.

The resulting plots are shown in Figure 5-7. The left panel shows the experimental image of the quantum dot you cropped with Listing 5-15. The middle image shows the simulated image generated by the pipeline in Listing 5-16. Both the experimental ❸ and simulated ❹ images are scaled to the same intensity values for an accurate comparison. The close resemblance between the experimental and simulated images shows the realism of the simulations produced by the pipeline. To assess this similarity more quantitatively, you can plot the pixel-intensity profile along the x- and y-directions at the center of both the experimental and simulated images.

The histogram on the right of Figure 5-7 compares the pixel values, highlighting the distribution of intensity values within each image. The histogram shows the frequency of pixel intensities, allowing you to evaluate whether the simulation accurately reproduces the intensity distribution of a real quantum dot.

Multiple Quantum Dots

Now you'll expand your pipeline to simulate multiple quantum dots within the same image, as shown in Listing 5-18.

```
--snip--
optics = dt.Fluorescence(..., output_region=(0, 0, 128, 128))
particle = dt.PointParticle(
    position=lambda: np.random.uniform(0, 128, size=2),
    intensity=lambda: np.random.uniform(6e3, 3e4),
    z=lambda: np.random.uniform(-1.5, 1.5) * dt.units.um,
)
```
❶ `postprocess = (dt.Add(lambda: np.random.uniform(20, 40)) >> np.random.poisson`
`            >> dt.Add(lambda: np.random.uniform(70, 90)))`
❷ `normalization = dt.AsType("float") >> dt.Subtract(110) >> dt.Divide(250)`
`particles = particle ^ (lambda: np.random.randint(10, 20))`
`sim_im_pip = optics(particles) >> postprocess >> normalization`

Listing 5-18: Updating the simulation pipeline to create images of multiple quantum dots (by modifying Listing 5-16)

This enhanced `sim_im_pip` pipeline begins by defining a larger output region, allowing for the simulation of multiple quantum dots within a 128×128–pixel frame. The pipeline then assigns random values within specified ranges to the position, intensity, and z-coordinate of the quantum dot generated by `particle`.

The simulation pipeline applies post-processing steps ❶ to introduce realistic noise and background signals into the simulated images. These steps include adding a uniform random offset to represent the baseline detector signal, applying a Poisson noise model to simulate photon shot noise, and finally adding another random offset to represent detector readout noise. The simulated images are then normalized ❷ to match the intensity range of the experimental data.

The `PointParticle` instances are created in a number that varies randomly from 10 to 20 for each simulated frame, simulating the random distribution of quantum dots. The entire simulation pipeline is then applied to these particle instances to generate the final simulated image.

After simulating the image of the quantum dots, you need to simulate the ground-truth mask, which will be the target output of the U-Net. This mask delineates the exact locations of the quantum dots, which is crucial for the subsequent training of the U-Net. Listing 5-19 shows the mask-generation pipeline.

```
sim_mask_pip = (particles
              >> dt.SampleToMasks(lambda: lambda particle: particle > 0,
                                  output_region=optics.output_region,
                                  merge_method="or")
              >> dt.AsType("int") >> dt.OneHot(num_classes=2))
```

Listing 5-19: Defining the simulation pipeline for the output mask

The pipeline to generate the ground-truth mask begins by taking the simulated `particles` and applying the `SampleToMasks` function. This function is passed a lambda function that defines the condition for a pixel to be considered part of a quantum dot, which in this case is simply whether the particle's value exceeds 0. The `SampleToMasks` function also specifies the dimensions of `output_region` to match those of the simulated image and uses a logical `"or"` operation to merge overlapping dots into a single mask. This ensures that each quantum dot, regardless of overlap, is clearly marked for the U-Net to learn.

After the binary mask is created, it's converted to an integer data type via `dt.AsType("int")`, which is suitable for one-hot encoding. The one-hot-encoding process (`dt.OneHot(num_classes=2)`) then transforms the binary mask into a categorical format that represents each pixel with a binary vector indicating its class membership. In this context, the two classes are Background and Quantum Dot, corresponding to the absence or presence of a quantum dot at each pixel location, respectively.

Finally, the simulation pipelines for the quantum dot image and the ground-truth mask are combined into a single pipeline that you'll use to train the U-Net, as shown in Listing 5-20.

```
import torch

sim_im_mask_pip = ((sim_im_pip & sim_mask_pip) >> dt.MoveAxis(2, 0)
                        >> dt.pytorch.ToTensor(dtype=torch.float))
```

Listing 5-20: Combining the pipelines for the quantum dot image and the ground-truth mask

This code merges the two pipelines into a single one, rearranges their dimensions to match the format expected by PyTorch, and converts the data into PyTorch tensors.

Plot the simulated image and corresponding ground-truth mask side by side, using Listing 5-21.

```
sim_im, sim_mask = sim_im_mask_pip.update().resolve()

plt.figure(figsize=(12, 6))

plt.subplot(1, 2, 1)
plt.imshow(sim_im.squeeze(), cmap="gray")
plt.title("Simulated image", fortsize=16)

plt.subplot(1, 2, 2)
plt.imshow(sim_mask[1], cmap="gray")
plt.title("Localization map", fcntsize=16)

plt.tight_layout()
plt.show()
```

Listing 5-21: Plotting the simulated image and corresponding ground-truth mask

The resulting figure should look similar to Figure 5-8.

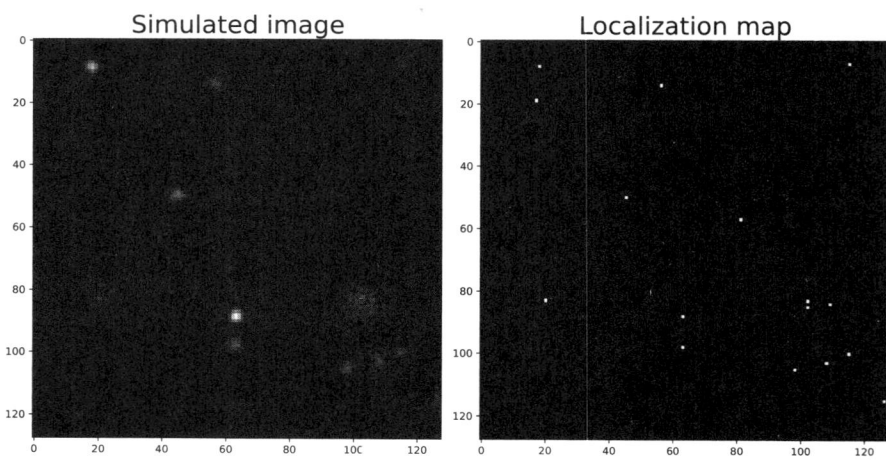

Figure 5-8: The simulated image (left) and corresponding mask (right)

This is a side-by-side comparison of a simulated fluorescence image with quantum dots (left) and the corresponding localization mask (right). In the simulated image, each quantum dot appears as a distinct, bright spot against the dark background, resembling the appearance of real fluorescence microscopy images. The localization mask, in contrast, offers a binary view; each quantum dot is marked by a white pixel on a black background. The stark contrast shown in the localization mask is desirable because it clearly delineates the quantum dots from the background, making it easier for the U-Net to learn and accurately identify these locations.

Defining and Training the U-Net

Now that you've defined the data pipelines, it's time to define and train your U-Net to detect the quantum dots. Define the U-Net as follows:

```
import deeplay as dl

unet = dl.UNet2d(in_channels=1, channels=[32, 64], out_channels=2)
```

This is a U-Net with a single input channel for grayscale images and two output channels corresponding to the predicted classes: Background and Quantum Dots. The architecture features an increasing number of channels in its layers, starting with 32 and progressing to 64, allowing for the extraction of complex features at various levels of abstraction. For a detailed overview of the U-Net structure, you can print the model summary with print(unet).

To compile the U-Net, encapsulate it within a Regressor object:

```
unet_reg = dl.Regressor(
    model=unet, loss=torch.nn.CrossEntropyLoss(weight=torch.tensor([1, 10])),
    optimizer=dl.Adam(),
).create()
```

Given that the background (represented by 0s) vastly outnumbers the quantum dot pixels, a naïve loss function could bias the network to predict only the background, ignoring the quantum dots entirely. To counteract this, this code uses a weighted CrossEntropyLoss function to assign a higher weight to the quantum dot class, thus amplifying the penalty for false negatives (cases of the network failing to identify a quantum dot) compared to false positives. This approach encourages the network to prioritize the detection of quantum dots.

NOTE *The necessity of using a weighted loss function influenced the decision to represent the output image with two channels, each dedicated to a distinct class. Dealing with a binary classification problem, a single output channel with pixel values of 0 or 1 might have sufficed (you'll see this strategy in Project 5B). However, in such a scenario, it would have been necessary to use the binary cross-entropy loss, which lacks direct control over class weights.*

You're now ready to train your U-Net with Listing 5-22.

```
train_dataset = dt.pytorch.Dataset(sim_im_mask_pip, length=320, replace=.1)
data_loader = dl.DataLoader(train_dataset, batch_size=32)
unet_trainer = dl.Trainer(max_epochs=50, accelerator="auto")
unet_trainer.fit(unet_reg, data_loader)
```

Listing 5-22: Training the U-Net

This code creates a `train_dataset` to feed batches of simulated images and masks to the model via a data loader. A `Trainer` object orchestrates the training process over 50 epochs, automatically utilizing the best available hardware, while the `fit()` method updates the model parameters to enhance the generation of a mask highlighting the positions of the quantum dots.

Evaluating the Trained U-Net

You can now apply the trained U-Net to the experimental image loaded at the beginning of this project.

To do this, you need to extract the *centroid positions*, which are the geometric centers of the segmented regions, from the predicted binary masks. You can do this with the `mask_to_positions()` function shown in Listing 5-23.

```
import skimage as sk

def mask_to_positions(mask):
    """Convert binary mask to centroid array."""
    labels = sk.measure.label(mask)
    props = sk.measure.regionprops(labels)
    return np.array([prop.centroid for prop in props])
```

Listing 5-23: The function to convert a binary mask into an array of centroid positions

This function converts a binary mask into an array of centroid positions corresponding to each labeled region within the mask. The function labels each connected region in the binary mask (`labels`), calculates the properties of these labeled regions (`props`), and returns the centroid coordinates for each region.

You can now analyze the experimental image, using Listing 5-24.

```
❶ image_of_particles_tensor = torch.from_numpy(
      (np.array(image_of_particles).astype(np.float32) - 110) / 250
  ).unsqueeze(0)

❷ pred_mask = unet_reg(image_of_particles_tensor.unsqueeze(0)).detach()
  pred_mask = torch.nn.functional.softmax(pred_mask, dim=1)
❸ positions = mask_to_positions(pred_mask[0, 1, ...] > 0.5)

  plt.figure(figsize=(10, 10))
❹ plt.imshow(image_of_particles, vmin=100, vmax=200, cmap="gray")
```

```
❺ plt.scatter(positions[:, 1], positions[:, 0], s=100, facecolors="none",
            edgecolors=(0.0039, 0.45, 0.70))
  plt.show()
```

Listing 5-24: Applying the trained U-Net to an experimental image

This code starts by preprocessing the experimental image to match the input requirements of the U-Net model, adjusting the pixel intensities to the normalized range used during training ❶. The preprocessed image is then fed into the trained U-Net model, which predicts the segmentation mask ❷. The output of the model is further processed with the softmax() function to determine the probability of each pixel representing a quantum dot.

The softmax output is converted into a binary mask by thresholding, and then into an array of centroid positions ❸. These centroids represent the localized positions of the detected quantum dots. The experimental image is subsequently displayed ❹, with the localized positions overlaid as scatter points ❺. This visualization accentuates the quantum dots that the U-Net has successfully detected, providing an intuitive and immediate assessment of the model's detection capabilities on real experimental data.

The resulting plot should look similar to Figure 5-9.

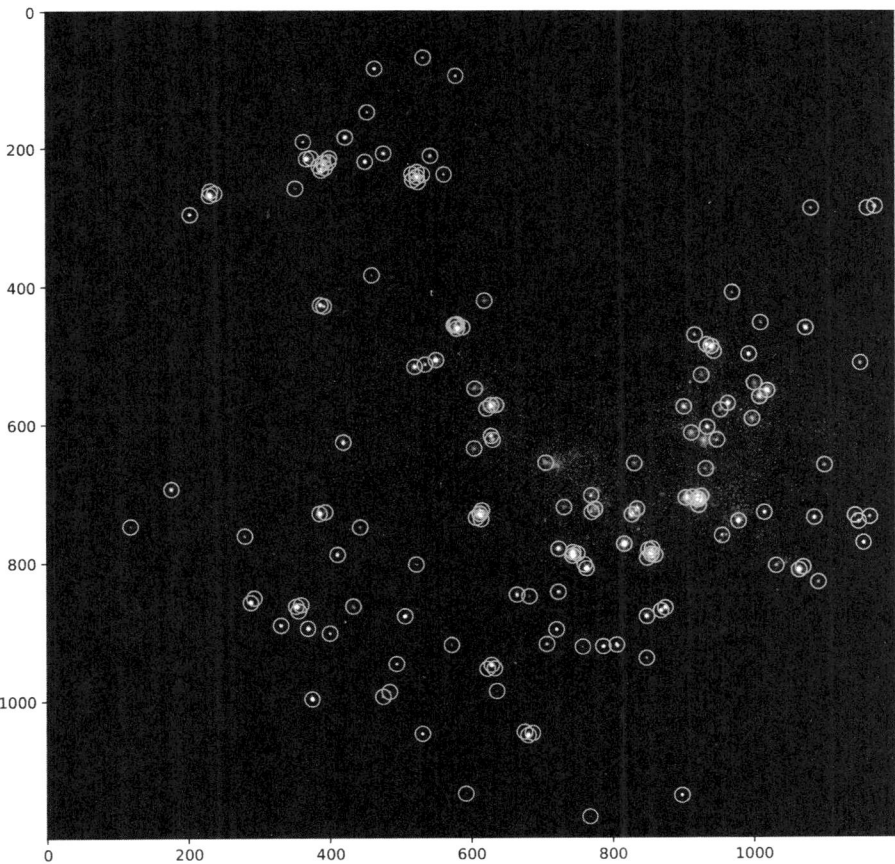

Figure 5-9: Quantum dot detections in an experimental image

Each detection is marked by a circular outline, allowing for a direct comparison of the U-Net's predicted localizations against the actual quantum dots visible in the fluorescence image. Overall, the U-Net appears to be performing pretty well on this experimental data.

NOTE   *Code Example 5-A, "Detecting Quantum Dots," is available at* https://github .com/DeepTrackAI/DeepLearningCrashCourse. *Navigate to the* Ch05_UNet *folder and then* ec05_A_qdots_localization. *The* qdots_localization.ipynb *notebook provides a complete code example that trains a U-Net to determine the positions of quantum dots in experimental images acquired with a fluorescence microscope.*

Project 5B: Counting Cells

In this project, you'll use a U-Net to count cells, an essential task in many biological and medical applications. In fact, precisely quantifying cell numbers in cellular cultures is critical for evaluating growth rates, responses to treatments, and cell behavior in various conditions. This project will show you how to automate the cell-counting process.

You'll also explore techniques to simulate realistic images of cell nuclei, going beyond the relatively simple particles you've simulated until now in previous projects. You'll see again the value of simulations for creating large, annotated datasets to train deep learning models without the labor-intensive process of manual annotation.

Loading the Dataset

For this project, you'll use the BBBC039v1 dataset, curated by Juan C. Caicedo and co-workers (2018) and made publicly available through the Broad Bioimage Benchmark Collection. This dataset consists of 200 high-resolution fields of view, capturing cell nuclei stained with Hoechst dye and imaged via fluorescence microscopy, a widely used technique for visualizing cell nuclei. Each image is carefully annotated, encompassing approximately 23,000 individual nuclei, providing a robust ground truth for segmentation and counting. Stored in *.tif* format, these images are 520×696 pixels with 16-bit depth, offering rich detail for analysis. The dataset also includes ground-truth annotations in *.png* format, encoding masks that uniquely identify each nucleus.

You can use Listing 5-25 to download the dataset and prepare the sources to access its files.

```
import os
import deeptrack as dt

if not os.path.exists("cell_counting_dataset"):
    os.system("git clone https://github.com/DeepTrackAI/cell_counting_dataset")

directory = os.path.join("cell_counting_dataset", "cell nuclei")
```

```
❶ image_paths = dt.sources.ImageFolder(root=os.path.join(directory, "images"))
❷ mask_paths = dt.sources.ImageFolder(root=os.path.join(directory, "masks"))
  sources = dt.sources.Source(image=image_paths, label=mask_paths)
```

Listing 5-25: Loading the dataset

This code begins by cloning the repository containing the dataset into the *cell_counting_dataset* folder. The code then defines the paths for loading the images ❶ and the corresponding segmentation masks ❷. Finally, these two sources are combined into a single Source, which provides a unified interface for accessing both the images and their corresponding segmentation masks. To verify that 200 images have been loaded, use the print(len(sources)) command.

Creating a Pipeline

Next, you'll implement a pipeline to load the images and the corresponding segmentation masks, as shown in Listing 5-26.

```
import deeplay as dl
import numpy as np
import torch

image_pip = (dt.LoadImage(sources.image.path) >> dt.Divide(3000)
             >> dt.Clip(0, 1) >> dt.AsType("float"))
mask_pip = dt.LoadImage(sources.label.path)[..., :1] >> dt.AsType("float")

❶ pip = ((image_pip & mask_pip) >> dt.Crop(crop=(512, 688, None), corner=(0, 0))
         >> dt.MoveAxis(2, 0) >> dt.pytorch.ToTensor(dtype=torch.float))

test_dataset = dt.pytorch.Dataset(pip, sources)
test_loader = dl.DataLoader(test_dataset, batch_size=32, shuffle=False)
```

Listing 5-26: Creating a pipeline to load the images and labels

This code constructs a data pipeline for loading and preprocessing the images and their corresponding segmentation masks.

First, the image_pip pipeline is established to load the images from the specified paths, normalize their intensity values by dividing each pixel by 3,000, clip the resulting values to the range of 0 to 1, and convert the data type to floating-point numbers. Similarly, the code defines the mask_pip pipeline to load the segmentation masks, select only the first channel, and convert them to floating-point numbers.

The code then combines image_pip and mask_pip to ensure that each image is processed alongside its corresponding segmentation mask ❶. The combined pipeline further processes the data by cropping each image and mask pair to a fixed size, rearranging the axes to match PyTorch's expected input format, and converting the data into PyTorch tensors.

Finally, the processed images and segmentation masks are wrapped into a PyTorch Dataset object, which provides a standardized interface for accessing the data. This dataset is then used to create a `DataLoader` object, enabling efficient batch processing. You'll use this data loader to test your U-Net after it's trained.

Counting the Number of Cells

To count the cells in the images, you'll use the number of connected components in the segmentation masks. This method identifies clusters of adjacent pixels that represent individual cell nuclei. By labeling these components with unique identifiers, you can easily count the total number of cells. You can do this with Listing 5-27.

```
from skimage import morphology as skmorph

image, mask = test_dataset[np.random.choice(len(test_dataset))]
labeled_mask = skmorph.label(mask)
number_of_cells = labeled_mask.nax()
```

Listing 5-27: Counting cells by using connected components

This code demonstrates how to count cells in an image by using the connected components method. The code selects a random image and its corresponding mask from the dataset, labels each unique cell nucleus within the mask with progressive integer numbers, and calculates the total number of cells as the maximum label value.

Visualizing the Data

Now let's take a closer look at the images and their segmentation masks by plotting them with Listing 5-28.

```
from matplotlib import pyplot as plt

fig, axs = plt.subplots(1, 3, figsize=(10, 3))

❶ axs[0].imshow(image.permute(1, 2, 0), vmin=0, vmax=1, cmap="gray")

❷ axs[1].imshow(mask.permute(1, 2, 0), vmin=0, vmax=1, cmap="gray")
❸ axs[1].set_title(f"Number of cells = {number_of_cells}", fontsize=16)
  axs[1].axis("off")

❹ axs[2].hist(np.array(image).flatten(), bins=200, range=(0, 1))
  axs[2].set_xlabel("Pixel Intensity", fontsize=12)
  axs[2].set_xlim([0, 1])
  axs[2].set_ylabel("Log Frequency", fontsize=12)
  axs[2].set_yscale("log")
  axs[2].set_title("Pixel Intensity Distribution", fontsize=16)

plt.tight_layout()
plt.show()
```

Listing 5-28: Visualizing the data

This code displays the original image ❶ and its segmentation mask ❷ with the cell count indicated in the title ❸. Additionally, a histogram of the image's pixel intensities is plotted to illustrate the distribution of values ❹, providing insights into the image's contrast and brightness levels. The histogram information is particularly useful for generating simulated images to train the U-Net model effectively, ensuring that the simulations are representative of the experimental conditions.

The resulting plot should look like Figure 5-10. Note that each time the code is run, it will plot the figure for a different image randomly picked from the dataset.

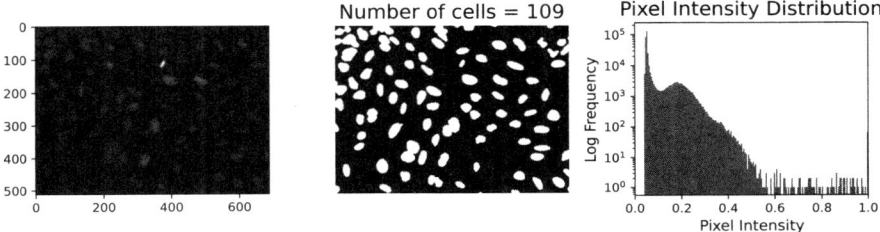

Figure 5-10: An image of cell nuclei (left), the corresponding segmentation mask (middle), and a pixel-value histogram (right)

The grayscale image on the left shows several cell nuclei, each one appearing as an individual, bright object against a dark background. The middle image shows the corresponding segmentation mask, with the outlines of each cell nucleus highlighted in white, providing a clear contrast against the background. This mask is used to identify and count the cell nuclei.

On the right is a histogram of the pixel-intensity distribution from the original cell image. The histogram, plotted on a semilogarithmic scale, shows that the majority of pixels are in the lower intensity range, which corresponds to the background, while a smaller peak represents the brighter nucleus regions. This histogram is useful for understanding the contrast within the image and setting appropriate thresholds for image segmentation and cell counting.

Simulating the Cell Images

The next essential step is to create a dataset that can be used to train your U-Net for automated cell counting. By simulating images of nuclei and their corresponding segmentation masks, you'll be able to train the U-Net to generate segmentation masks, which can then be analyzed using the connected components method you mastered in the previous section. This simulation process will allow you to generate large volumes of training data, essential for the network to learn the task of segmenting the images.

Cell Nuclei

You can start by simulating images of ellipses. In this simplistic rendition of a cell nucleus, each ellipse may vary in orientation, position, and intensity, reflecting the diversity that might be seen in a population of real cells under fluorescence imaging. The corresponding code is in Listing 5-29.

```
train_image_size = 256

def random_ellipse_axes():
    """Return the three axes of an ellipse."""
    ellipse_area = (np.random.uniform(3, 4)) ** 2
    radius_ratio = np.random.uniform(1, 1.5)
    major_axis = np.sqrt(ellipse_area) * radius_ratio
    minor_axis = np.sqrt(ellipse_area) / radius_ratio
    z_axis = np.sqrt(ellipse_area) * np.random.uniform(0.2, 0.4)
    return (major_axis, minor_axis, z_axis) * dt.units.um

ellipse = dt.Ellipsoid(
    radius=random_ellipse_axes,
❶  intensity=lambda: np.random.uniform(0.5, 1.5),
❷  position=lambda: np.random.uniform(5, train_image_size - 5, size=2),
❸  rotation=lambda: np.random.uniform(0, 2 * np.pi),
)
optics = dt.Fluorescence(
    resolution=1e-6, magnification=6, wavelength=400e-9,
    NA=lambda: np.random.uniform(0.9, 1.1),
    output_region=(0, 0, train_image_size, train_image_size),
)
sim_im_pip = optics(ellipse)

fig, axs = plt.subplots(1, 5, figsize=(10, 2))
for i, ax in enumerate(axs):
❹  sim_im_pip.update()
❺  image = sim_im_pip()
❻  ax.imshow(image, cmap="gray")
    if i != 0: ax.axis("off")
plt.tight_layout()
plt.show()
```

Listing 5-29: Simulating a single cell nucleus as an ellipse

This code starts by defining the random_ellipse_axes() function to obtain the axes of an ellipse generated from a random distribution. The code then uses this function to create an Ellipsoid object representing an ellipse with random axes, setting an intensity range ❶, and positioning it within the image ❷, while allowing for random rotation ❸. Subsequently, the code passes this Ellipsoid object through a simulated fluorescence microscope (optics). Finally, the sim_im_pip pipeline is created, representing the complete simulation process. This pipeline is iteratively updated ❹ and used to obtain an image ❺, which is then visualized ❻.

Figure 5-11 shows some examples of the obtained images.

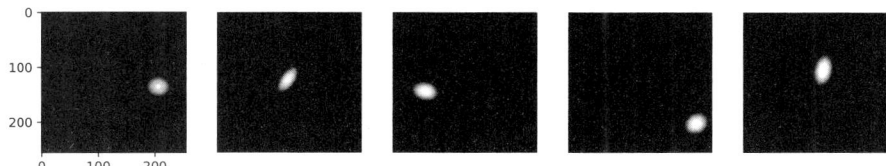

Figure 5-11: The images with a single cell nucleus simulated as an ellipse

These images, although much simplified, serve as initial approximations of the complexity of real nuclear shapes and textures found in microscopy images.

To make the images more realistic, you can make the simulated nuclei more irregular and numerous by deforming them elastically, updating the code as shown in Listing 5-30.

```
--snip--
ellipse = dt.Ellipsoid(...)
synthetic_nuclei = (
❶ (ellipse ^ (lambda: np.random.randint(5, 10)))
❷ >> dt.Pad(px=(10, 10, 10, 10), keep_size=False)
❸ >> dt.ElasticTransformation(alpha=100, sigma=10, order=1)
❹ >> dt.CropTight()
)
--snip--
sim_im_pip = optics(synthetic_nuclei)
--snip--
```

Listing 5-30: Simulating multiple nuclei as ellipses with elastic deformations (by modifying Listing 5-29)

This code enhances the realism of the previously simulated images by combining multiple ellipses representing diverse cell nuclei ❶ and by introducing elastic deformations to simulate the irregular shapes found in actual cells ❸. Padding is added to ensure that the deformations don't cause the nuclei to be cropped ❷. After the transformation, the code removes the padding, bringing the nuclei back to their original size ❹. This group of synthetic nuclei is then passed through the previously defined optical system (optics), which models the microscope's imaging process, to generate the final image.

Figure 5-12 shows examples of the resulting images.

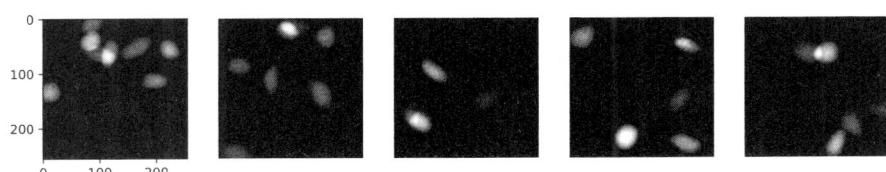

Figure 5-12: The images with multiple nuclei simulated as deformed ellipses

The irregular contours and varying sizes of the nuclei in these simulations mimic the natural heterogeneity seen in biological specimens, enhancing the authenticity of the training dataset.

To make the simulated images even more realistic, you can add noise, as shown in Listing 5-31.

```
--snip--
synthetic_nuclei = (...)
❶ synthetic_nuclei_mask = synthetic_nuclei > 0
  long_range_noise = (synthetic_nuclei >> dt.Poisson(snr=0.2)
                           >> dt.GaussianBlur(sigma=3.5))
  short_range_noise = (synthetic_nuclei >> dt.Poisson(snr=1.0)
                           >> dt.GaussianBlur(sigma=1.5))
  random_range_noise = (
      synthetic_nuclei
      >> dt.Poisson(snr=lambda: np.random.uniform(0.5, 1.5))
      >> dt.GaussianBlur(sigma=lambda: np.random.uniform(0.75, 1.5))
  )
❷ noisy_synthetic_nuclei = (
      synthetic_nuclei_mask
      * (long_range_noise + short_range_noise + random_range_noise) / 3
  )
  --snip--
❸ sim_im_pip = optics(noisy_synthetic_nuclei)
  --snip--
```

Listing 5-31: Simulating multiple nuclei as ellipses with elastic deformations and noise (by modifying Listing 5-30)

This code further enhances the realism of the simulated images by adding different types of noise to the deformed elliptical nuclei. The code begins by creating a mask of the synthetic nucleus ❶, which serves as a base for applying noise. Three kinds of noise are generated: long_range_noise, short_range_noise, and random_range_noise, each with varying SNRs and Gaussian blur parameters to mimic the texture of biological nuclei and the imperfections in imaging. These noise patterns are combined and applied to the synthetic mask ❷ to create noisy synthetic nuclei, which are then processed through the fluorescence microscope ❸ to produce the final noisy synthetic nucleus images. This process creates images that more closely resemble experimental images by including common artifacts and variations seen in actual microscopy.

Figure 5-13 shows examples of the generated images.

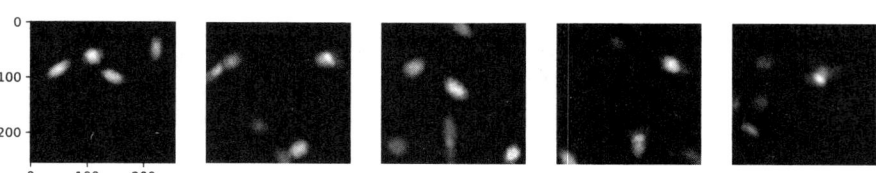

Figure 5-13: The images with multiple nuclei simulated as noisy deformed ellipses

The noise you added to the nuclei introduces variability and texture, more closely resembling the complexity found in real microscopy images. However, the background remains uniformly black, which isn't representative of actual images because the background would typically contain some level of noise or artifacts. Additionally, the nuclei are occasionally overlapping, which can be problematic for accurate cell counting as it might lead to underestimating the actual number of cells present.

In a last effort to enhance the realism of the simulated images, you can prevent overlaps between nuclei and add noise to the background, as shown in Listing 5-32.

```
--snip--
noisy_synthetic_nuclei = (...)
non_overlap_nuclei = dt.NonOverlapping(noisy_synthetic_nuclei, min_distance=-6)
--snip--
sim_im_pip = (optics(non_overlap_nuclei)
              >> dt.Gaussian(sigma=lambda: np.random.uniform(0, 0.1))
              >> dt.Divide(lambda: np.random.uniform(14, 20))
              >> dt.Add(lambda: np.random.uniform(-0.05, 0.15))
              >> dt.Clip(0, 1) >> dt.AsType("float"))
    --snip--
```

Listing 5-32: Simulating multiple nuclei as nonoverlapping ellipses with elastic deformations and noise (by modifying Listing 5-31)

This code enhances the simulation by ensuring that the synthetic nuclei don't overlap, creating a more realistic scenario for cell counting. The min_distance parameter adjusts the nuclei to maintain a specified minimum distance, which can be negative to allow slight overlaps. The sim_im_pip pipeline then adds noise to the background with a Gaussian distribution, normalizes the image intensity by dividing it, adds a random offset to the intensity, and ensures that the pixel values are clipped to the range 0 to 1. Finally, the images are converted to the floating-point type.

Figure 5-14 shows some of the results.

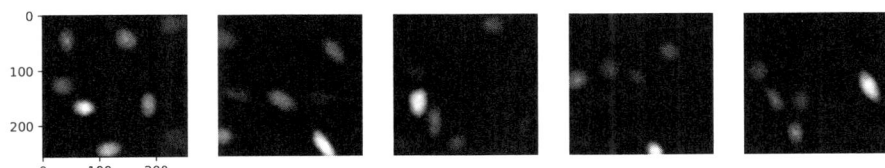

Figure 5-14: The images with multiple nuclei simulated as nonoverlapping, noisy, deformed ellipses

In these simulated images, each nucleus is distinct and separate, mostly avoiding overlaps. Noise has been added to both the nuclei and the background, which gives the images a more natural look that closely resembles real microscopy images. The shapes of the nuclei are varied and realistic, thanks to the applied elastic deformations. These improvements make the simulated images much more similar to actual images, which is helpful for training a model like the U-Net to count cells accurately.

Segmentation Masks

To complement the simulated images, you need to generate corresponding segmentation masks to serve as the target images for the U-Net. These masks will allow the U-Net to identify and count the individual cells by delineating their nuclei. You can do this with Listing 5-33.

```
def get_mask(radius):
    """Apply isotropic erosion to a binary mask."""
    def inner(mask):
      ❶ mask = np.sum(mask, -1, keepdims=True) > 0
      ❷ mask = np.pad(mask, [(1, 1), (1, 1), (0, 0)], mode="constant")
      ❸ mask = skmorph.isotropic_erosion(mask, radius=radius)
      ❹ return mask[1:-1, 1:-1]
    return inner


sim_mask_pip = (
    non_overlap_nuclei
    >> dt.SampleToMasks(get_mask, radius=6, output_region=optics.output_region,
                        merge_method="or")
    >> dt.AsType("float")
)
```

Listing 5-33: Simulating the segmentation masks

This code creates the `sim_mask_pip` pipeline to generate the segmentation masks. The custom `get_mask()` function defines the *isotropic erosion*, a procedure that shrinks the objects in the mask to separate individual nuclei. Within the nested `inner()` function, the binary mask is created ❶, padded ❷, eroded ❸, and then the padding is removed ❹, leaving a clean mask of the nuclei. Then, `sim_mask_pip` combines these steps and converts the masks to a floating-point type, preparing them for use as training targets for the U-Net model.

Combined Pipeline

The final step before training your U-Net is to combine the simulated nucleus images and their corresponding segmentation masks into a single pipeline. This will create a comprehensive dataset, pairing each image with its mask for effective supervised learning. You can do this with Listing 5-34.

```
sim_im_mask_pip = ((sim_im_pip & sim_mask_pip) >> dt.MoveAxis(2, 0)
            >> dt.pytorch.ToTensor(dtype=torch.float))
train_dataset = dt.pytorch.Dataset(sim_im_mask_pip, length=640, replace=0.01)
```

Listing 5-34: Combining the image and segmentation pipelines and creating the training dataset

This code merges the image and label pipelines and then reshapes the merged data to fit the expected input format for PyTorch models. The resulting training dataset is a collection of image-mask pairs, ready to be fed into the U-Net for training.

You can visualize the results of your simulation process with Listing 5-35.

```
❶ sim_im, sim_mask = train_dataset[np.random.choice(len(train_dataset))]

   fig, axs = plt.subplots(1, 3, figsize=(12, 4))

❷ axs[0].imshow(sim_im.permute(1, 2, 0), vmin=0, vmax=1, cmap="gray")
   axs[0].set_title("Simulated Image", fontsize=20)

❸ axs[1].imshow(sim_mask.permute(1, 2, 0), vmin=0, vmax=1, cmap="gray")
   axs[1].set_title("Simulated Mask", fontsize=20)
   axs[1].axis("off")

❹ axs[2].hist(np.array(sim_im).flatten(), bins=200, range=(0, 1))
   axs[2].set_xlabel("Pixel Intensity", fontsize=16)
   axs[2].set_xlim([0, 1])
   axs[2].set_ylabel("Log Frequency", fontsize=16)
   axs[2].set_yscale("log")
   axs[2].set_title("Pixel Intensity Distribution", fontsize=20)

   plt.tight_layout()
   plt.show()
```

Listing 5-35: Visualizing a simulated image and its corresponding segmentation mask

This code retrieves a simulated image and its mask ❶ and displays them side by side ❷ ❸. This visualization confirms that the simulated images and masks are correctly aligned. Then the code plots a histogram of the pixel intensities ❹ to assess their distribution.

Figure 5-15 shows the resulting plots.

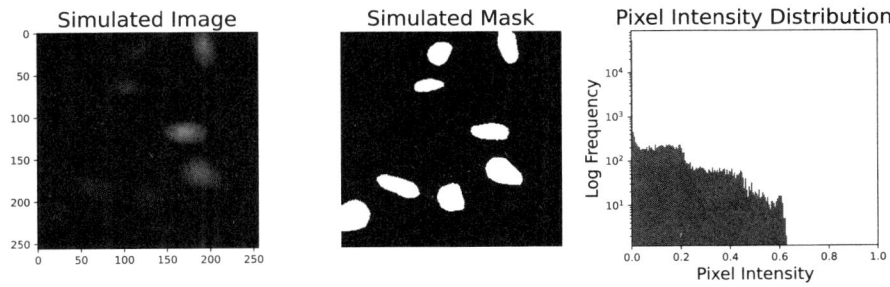

Figure 5-15: The simulated image of cells (left), its corresponding segmentation mask (middle), and a pixel-value histogram (right)

In this typical output of a simulation, you can see a side-by-side comparison of the simulated image and its corresponding segmentation mask, alongside a histogram that analyzes the pixel-intensity distribution. This histogram of the simulated images reveals a distribution of pixel intensities that mirrors those observed in experimental images, shown previously in Figure 5-10. This agreement is crucial, as it suggests that the simulated data provides a realistic approximation of the actual imaging conditions, including variability in nucleus appearance and background noise.

Implementing and Training the U-Net

Now that you've ensured that the simulated images and their intensity distributions match those of real experimental scenarios, you're ready to train a robust U-Net. Start by instantiating a U-Net:

```
unet = dl.UNet2d(in_channels=1, channels=[16, 32, 64], out_channels=1)
```

This U-Net is configured to process single-channel (grayscale) images, featuring a contracting path with a progressively increasing number of channels to capture context at various scales (the expansion path will have the same channel numbers in reverse), and designed to output a single-channel segmentation mask. By using the print(unet) command, you can examine the detailed architecture of the instantiated U-Net, including the dimensions of each layer and the total number of trainable parameters.

Now, compile the U-Net for the regression task of estimating the segmentation:

```
unet_reg = dl.Regressor(
    model=unet, loss=torch.nn.BCEWithLogitsLoss(), optimizer=dl.Adam(),
).create()
```

This code utilizes the binary cross-entropy loss provided by BCEWithLogits Loss(), a loss function suitable for binary classification tasks, such as pixel-wise segmentation that classifies each pixel as belonging to a particular segment (or not).

Finally, train your U-Net:

```
train_loader = dl.DataLoader(train_dataset, batch_size=8, shuffle=True)
unet_trainer = dl.Trainer(max_epochs=200, accelerator="auto")
unet_trainer.fit(unet_reg, train_loader)
```

The training process begins by preparing a DataLoader, which feeds the training dataset to the model in mini-batches of size 8, shuffling the data to ensure diverse mini-batch composition throughout the training epochs. A Trainer object is then configured to manage the training process, set to run for a maximum of 200 epochs and automatically select the appropriate computational accelerator (CPU or GPU) for optimized performance. Finally, the fit() method is invoked to start the training.

Testing the Trained U-Net

After training your U-Net model, it's essential to evaluate its ability to gener-alize to experimental conditions, as shown in Listing 5-36.

```
images, masks, preds = [], [], []
for image, mask in test_loader:
    images.append(image)
    masks.append(mask)
❶   pred = unet_reg(image).detach()
❷   pred = torch.nn.functional.sigmoid(pred).cpu()
    preds.append(pred)
images, masks, preds = \
    torch.cat(images, dim=0), torch.cat(masks, dim=0), torch.cat(preds, dim=0)

❸ true_count = np.array([skmorph.label(l.squeeze()).max() for l in masks])
❹ pred_count = np.array([skmorph.label(p.squeeze() > .995).max() for p in preds])

mae = abs(pred_count - true_count).mean()
mpe = (abs(pred_count[true_count > 0] - true_count[true_count > 0])
       / (true_count[true_count > 0])).mean()
```

Listing 5-36: Calculating the cell counts with the labeled and predicted segmentation masks

For all images in `test_loader`, this code collects the `images` and correspond-ing `masks`. Then it computes the predictions ❶ and processes them to saturate their values from 0 to 1 ❷. The true cell counts are determined by labeling the connected components in the true masks ❸, and the predicted cell counts by doing the same in the predicted masks ❹. The model's accuracy is then quantified via the mean absolute error (`mae`) and the mean percentage error (`mpe`), providing insight into the prediction's precision and reliability.

Using `print(f"MAE: {mae:.2f} MPE: {mpe:.2f}")`, in our run of the code, we obtain `MAE: 8.54 MPE: 0.08`. These values suggest that, on average, the U-Net predictions deviate from the true cell counts by approximately 8.5 cells, with a mean percentage error indicating that the count is generally within 8 percent of the actual value. This means the U-Net performs well on experimental data, with the predicted cell counts being close to the actual counts, typically within an 8 percent margin of error.

You can qualitatively visualize how the U-Net is performing by plotting a random experimental image, its mask, and the U-Net's prediction for a qualitative assessment with Listing 5-37.

```
❶ i = np.random.choice(len(images))

fig, axs = plt.subplots(1, 3, figsize=(10, 4))

❷ axs[0].imshow(images[i].squeeze(), vmin=0, vmax=1, cmap="gray")
axs[0].set_title("Image", fontsize=16)
```

```
❸ axs[1].imshow(masks[i].squeeze(), vmin=0, vmax=1, cmap="gray")
  axs[1].set_title(f"Label - {true_count[i]} cells", fontsize=16)
  axs[1].axis("off")

❹ axs[2].imshow(preds[i].squeeze(), cmap="gray")
  axs[2].set_title(f"Prediction - {pred_count[i]} cells", fontsize=16)
  axs[2].axis("off")

  plt.tight_layout()
  plt.show()
```

Listing 5-37: Plotting an image of cells with ground-truth and predicted segmentations

This code selects a random index ❶, then plots the original image ❷, the ground-truth mask with the true cell count ❸, and the predicted mask with the predicted cell count ❹.

Figure 5-16 shows the resulting plots.

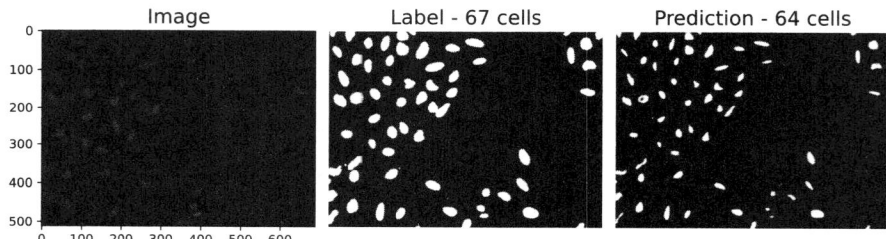

Figure 5-16: The image of cells (left) with its corresponding labeled segmentation (middle) and predicted segmentation (right)

The original image on the left shows nuclei with varying levels of brightness against a dark background. The middle image clearly delineates each nucleus with white pixels, counting 67 cells in total. The right image depicts the U-Net's attempt to replicate the segmentation, achieving a close approximation with 64 cells identified. From this visual comparison, you can validate the U-Net's capability to accurately segment cell structures from the image background (at least for this image). Keep in mind that your aim is to count the nuclei, so you need have a white region for each nucleus but don't need to exactly reproduce the ground-truth segmentation mask. By rerunning Listing 5-37, you can explore its performance on other images.

For a quantitative assessment of your U-Net's cell-counting accuracy, you can generate a scatterplot comparing the true cell counts with those predicted by the model, as illustrated in Listing 5-38.

```
  plt.figure(figsize=(8, 8))
❶ plt.scatter(true_count, pred_count, alpha=0.75)
❷ plt.axline([0, 0], [1, 1], color="black")
  plt.xlabel("True Count", fontsize=24)
  plt.xlim(0, 250)
  plt.ylabel("Predicted Count", fontsize=24)
```

```
plt.ylim(0, 250)
plt.show()
```

Listing 5-38: Plotting the predicted cell counts versus the true cell counts

This visualization plots each cell-count pair, with true counts on the x-axis and predicted counts on the y-axis ❶. The ideal performance line ❷ represents a perfect match between predicted and true counts, where each point would ideally lie.

The resulting plot should be similar to Figure 5-17.

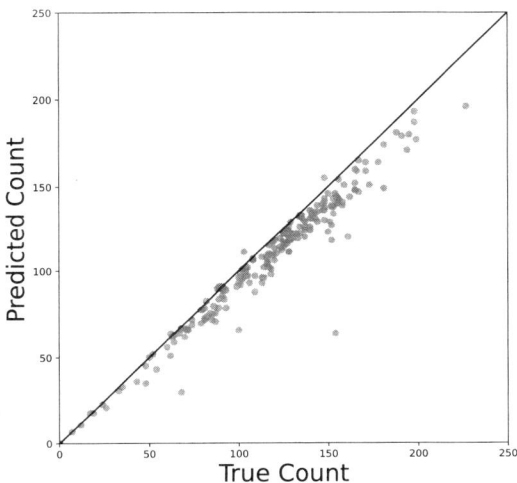

Figure 5-17: A comparison of the predicted cell counts with the true cell counts

This scatterplot compares the true cell counts and the predicted cell counts obtained from the U-Net. The dots represent individual data points. Each dot's position corresponds to the true count (x-axis) against the predicted count (y-axis). The diagonal black line serves as a reference, indicating where the points would fall if the predicted counts were exactly equal to the true counts.

The concentration of points near this line suggests a strong correlation between the U-Net's predictions and the actual cell counts, indicating the model's competence in cell-quantification tasks. The density and distribution of the points around the line provide insight into the trained U-Net's precision and any systematic bias that may exist in the cell counting (in this case, the model seems to systematically undercount the cells).

NOTE *Code Example 5-B, "Counting Cells with a U-Net," is available at* https://github .com/DeepTrackAI/DeepLearningCrashCourse. *Navigate to the* Ch05_UNet *folder and then* ec05_B_cell_counting. *The* cell_counting.ipynb *notebook provides a complete code example that uses a U-Net to count the cells in a microscopic image.*

Summary

In this chapter, you learned about the U-Net, a powerful neural network architecture designed for image transformation. Its encoder-decoder structure is enhanced with skip connections to preserve detailed information at all scales. You explored various applications of U-Nets, starting with the segmentation of intracellular regions and mitochondria in biological tissue images. This demonstrated the U-Net's prowess in handling segmentation tasks, while also emphasizing the importance of choosing the appropriate loss function and the benefits of data augmentation for improving model performance.

In the first project, you learned to detect quantum dots in fluorescence images, a critical task in biological research and nanotechnology. You learned how to apply U-Nets to localize these nanoscopic particles, showcasing the ability of U-Nets to interpret complex image data and precisely identify quantum dots.

In the second project, you explored cell counting, a critical procedure in biology and medicine. You used a U-Net to automate the counting process, accurately segmenting and counting individual nuclei within crowded microscopy images.

These projects demonstrate the utility of simulations to generate datasets with a known ground truth, enabling the efficient training of neural networks without the need for labor-intensive manual labeling.

The insights you gained about U-Nets and their applications in image transformation will pave your way toward more-advanced topics. In fact, you'll use U-Nets again in Chapters 9 and 10 to build generative adversarial networks and diffusion models to generate images.

Seminal Works and Further Reading

The U-Net architecture, which has become foundational for image-segmentation tasks in medical imaging and beyond, was introduced in 2015 by Olaf Ronneberger et al. in "U-Net: Convolutional Networks for Biomedical Image Segmentation," published in *Proceedings of the International Conference on Medical Image Computing and Computer-Assisted Intervention–MICCAI 2015* (*Lecture Notes in Computer Science*, volume 9351, pages 234–241).

In 2016, work by Özgün Çiçek et al. extended U-Nets to 3D image segmentation in "3D U-Net: Learning Dense Volumetric Segmentation from Sparse Annotation," published in *Proceedings of the International Conference on Medical Image Computing and Computer-Assisted Intervention–MICCAI 2016* (*Lecture Notes in Computer Science*, volume 9901, pages 424–432).

Further enhancing the U-Net architecture, Fabian Isensee et al. in 2020 proposed "nnU-Net: A Self-Configuring Method for Deep Learning–Based Biomedical Image Segmentation" in *Nature Methods* (volume 18, pages 203–211). The nnU-Net established a fully automated and highly adaptable pipeline for medical image segmentation. This pipeline can self-configure for a wide range of imaging datasets without manual parameter tuning.

CHALLENGE PROJECTS

5-1: Real-time video segmentation for autonomous driving Apply U-Nets to the task of real-time video segmentation in the context of autonomous driving. Use a dataset like Cityscapes, which contains urban street scenes. Your challenge is to develop a model capable of segmenting various components (for example, roads, vehicles, and pedestrians) in real time, ensuring that it's optimized for speed without sacrificing accuracy. Compare your solution's performance and efficiency against existing benchmarks in the field of autonomous driving.

5-2: Super-resolution for satellite imagery Explore the potential of U-Nets in the field of image super-resolution, specifically targeting satellite imagery. For this task, use the EuroSAT dataset, which consists of low-resolution satellite images covering various surface types. Use U-Nets to enhance the resolution of these images, aiming for improved clarity and detail that could benefit applications in mapping, urban planning, and environmental monitoring. Assess your model's effectiveness by comparing the super-resolved images against high-resolution ground-truth images.

5-3: Automated histopathology Use U-Nets to address the challenge of automating the analysis of histopathology images. Select a dataset, such as the CAMELYON16 Grand Challenge dataset, which involves the detection of cancer metastases in lymph-node sections. Design a U-Net to segment and classify regions of interest in these high-resolution images, facilitating faster and more-accurate diagnoses. Benchmark your model's performance against manual annotations provided by medical experts.

6

TRAINING NEURAL NETWORKS WITH SELF-SUPERVISED LEARNING

In this chapter, you'll learn about self-supervised learning, which you can use to train neural networks with unlabeled data, reducing reliance on costly annotation procedures.

You'll focus on the specific challenge of localizing a particle or a cell within an image obtained by a microscope. You'll exploit the symmetries inherent to this task to improve the training process. In this way, you'll reduce the need for extensive training data—from hundreds of thousands of images to just one—while also eliminating the need for prior knowledge of the object's position.

By learning the principles behind self-supervised learning in this context, you'll be able to generalize them to other problems where other symmetries can be identified, leading to more efficient and scalable machine learning solutions.

Understanding Self-Supervised Learning

You've already seen unsupervised learning while exploring autoencoders in Chapter 4. Now you'll learn about *self-supervised learning*, which differs from unsupervised learning in that it tackles tasks classically approached with supervised learning, such as classification and object detection. Sometimes self-supervised learning can completely replace supervised learning to train a model to solve a classically supervised learning task. Other times, self-supervised learning is used to provide an extensive pretraining step, which prepares a model so that a much smaller amount of labeled data can be used for training in supervised learning than typically required. Thus, pretraining is particularly beneficial when you have a large amount of unlabeled data and a limited amount of labeled data.

Self-Supervised Contrastive Learning

Self-supervised contrastive learning aims to learn useful representations from unlabeled data. This approach exploits the concept of *contrastive loss*, a type of loss function used in machine learning that measures the difference between pairs of data points, specifically by encouraging positive pairs (similar data points) to be closer together and negative pairs (dissimilar data points) to be farther apart in the representation space.

Figure 6-1 shows the general idea.

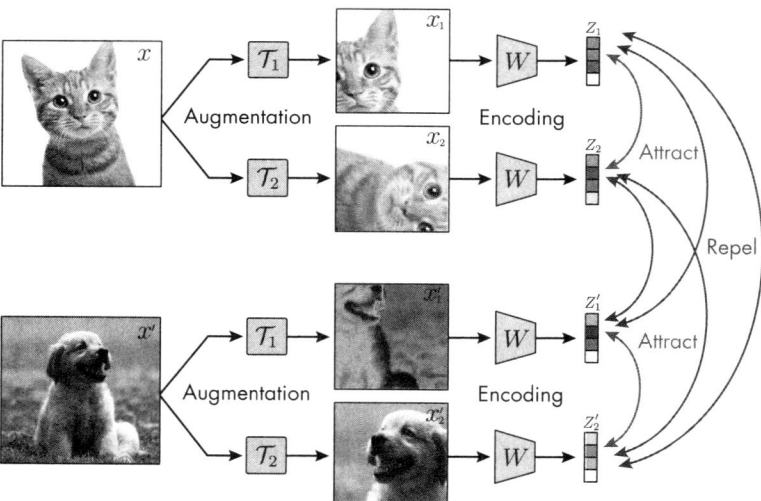

Figure 6-1: Self-supervised contrastive learning

The *positive pairs* are obtained from the same data point with different augmentations—for example, the pairs (x_1, x_2) and (x'_1, x'_2). The *negative pairs* are obtained from different data points—for example, (x_1, x'_1) and (x_2, x'_2).

The goal is to train the neural network W to learn a representation of the data points that is invariant to the augmentations, but different for different data points. This approach enables the network to capture the essential features of each data point while being robust to minor changes or distortions. This is done by minimizing the distance between the representations of the positive pairs, (Z_1, Z_2) and (Z'_1, Z'_2), while maximizing the distance between the representations of the negative pairs, (Z_1, Z'_1) and (Z_2, Z'_2).

The data points can then be classified by directly clustering their representations or by using an additional (small) neural network as a classifier. In the latter case, the advantage is that this neural network can be trained on much less data than that used in a classical supervised learning approach (like the classification of malaria-infected cells in Project 3A), because the representations have already been learned.

Self-Supervised Non-Contrastive Learning

Unlike self-supervised contrastive learning, *self-supervised non-contrastive learning* doesn't require negative pairs. Instead, the goal is simply to minimize the distance between the representations of the augmented data points. Figure 6-2 shows the working principle of this approach.

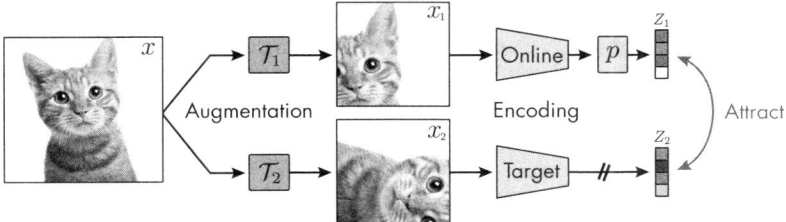

Figure 6-2: Self-supervised non-contrastive learning

In general, the algorithm takes one data point, *x*, as input and creates two augmented versions, x_1 and x_2. The neural network is trained to minimize the distance between the representations of the augmented data points, thus producing representations that are invariant to the augmentations. This is crucial for enhancing the model's robustness and generalizability, as it learns to focus on the core features of the data, improving its performance on diverse tasks and new data.

Instinctively, you might expect an algorithm that only minimizes the distance between the representations of the positive pairs to collapse to the trivial solution of always outputting the same representation, thus ending up in mode collapse. This would be problematic because it would result in a loss of diversity in the learned representations: In mode collapse, the algorithm fails to capture the distinct features of different data points, undermining its ability to discriminate between them and reducing the effectiveness of the model in tasks requiring this type of differentiation. Non-contrastive learning avoids this problem by using two neural networks: the online network and the target network.

The *target network* can be thought of as a teacher guiding the *online network*, which is often referred to as the student. The target network can be identical to the online network, or it can be constructed as a moving average of the online network. During training, only the online network is trained. The online network and the target network receive two differently augmented versions of the same image. Moreover, the online branch has an extra linear predictor, which is trained to predict the representation of the target network. This linear predictor introduces an asymmetry between the online network and the target network, which prevents the online network from collapsing to the trivial solution.

Self-supervised non-contrastive learning is especially advantageous in medical imaging and language processing, where defining negative samples is difficult. For instance, in medical imaging, such as magnetic resonance imaging (MRI) scans, identifying what constitutes a negative pair can be ambiguous and potentially misleading. Similarly, in language processing, determining negative sentence pairs can introduce biases.

Self-Supervised Geometric Learning

A subfield of self-supervised learning, *self-supervised geometric learning* focuses on learning geometric representations from unlabeled data. Generally, geometric deep learning aims to capture the underlying geometric structure, relationships, transformations, symmetries, and invariances present in the data. You'll explore the principles of geometric deep learning in the rest of this chapter. Figure 6-3 shows the general idea behind this approach.

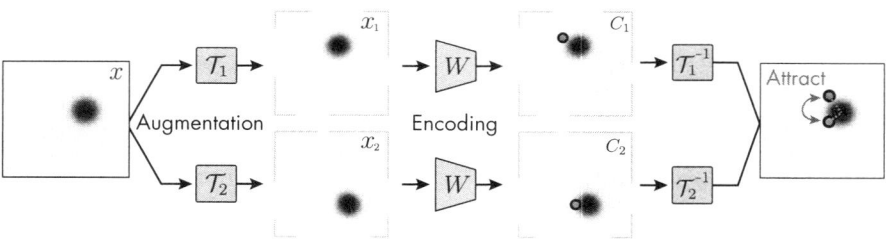

Figure 6-3: Self-supervised geometric learning

Conceptually, self-supervised geometric learning builds upon the foundation of self-supervised non-contrastive learning. Both approaches use positive pairs of images as training data. In self-supervised non-contrastive learning, the focus is primarily on achieving *invariance* to the augmentations. This means that the model's output representation should remain unchanged regardless of the specific augmentation applied.

Self-supervised geometric learning extends these principles by imposing *equivariance* to the augmentations applied to the data points. Instead of solely pursuing invariance, self-supervised geometric learning considers how the augmentations influence the output of the neural network, aiming to learn the expected changes in the output due to the specific augmentations.

To achieve this equivariance, a technique known as *detransformation* is applied. When an augmentation is applied to a data point, the network's output is transformed accordingly. However, to understand the effect of the augmentation on the output, the network applies the inverse transformation, detransforming the output by using the inverse of the augmentation. This process helps the network disentangle the effects of the augmentation from the inherent features of the data point, ensuring that the learned representation reflects the true characteristics of the data rather than the specific augmentations applied. You'll see how this works in practice in the next section.

Determining the Position of a Particle in an Image

In this section, you'll see how self-supervised geometric learning can be used to determine the position of a microscopic particle present in an image.

Specifically, you'll address the following problem: Given an image containing a single object, determine the precise x- and y-coordinates that correspond to the center of the object within that image. This problem is particularly important in microscopy and biomedical imaging, where accurately identifying the center of a cell or a microorganism is crucial for automated analysis, diagnosis, and tracking of biological specimens. Precise localization enables researchers and medical professionals to quantify properties like cell size, shape, and distribution, allowing for better understanding of biological processes and aiding in the early detection of diseases.

The approach you'll use is based on the recently developed *LodeSTAR* algorithm, published in 2022 by Benjamin Midtvedt and co-workers in *Nature Communications*. You'll then use this approach in Project 6A to localize cells.

Creating the Dataset

You'll use a simulated dataset to quantitatively evaluate the performance of your solution. This process is similar to that in Project 3B; in that project, you can find detailed explanations of the code to simulate the particle images that you'll use in this section. First, define a particle with Listing 6-1.

```
import deeptrack as dt
from numpy.random import uniform

image_size = 51

particle = dt.PointParticle(
    position=lambda: uniform(image_size / 2 - 5, image_size / 2 + 5, size=2),
)
```

Listing 6-1: Defining a particle located near the center of the image

This code defines a *point particle*, which is a very small particle, below the diffraction limit of the imaging optics. The *diffraction limit* refers to the fundamental limit on the resolution of an optical system, beyond which two points cannot be resolved as distinct. The point particle therefore appears as a diffraction-limited spot as captured by the optics—a blurred spot due to this resolution limit, representing the smallest distinguishable feature in the image.

Next, define the optical system, which is a fluorescence microscope:

```
optics = dt.Fluorescence(output_region=(0, 0, image_size, image_size))
```

Then combine the particle with the optical system, using Listing 6-2.

```
import torch

simulation = (optics(particle) >> dt.NormalizeMinMax(0, 1)
                >> dt.Gaussian(sigma=0.1) >> dt.MoveAxis(-1, 0)
                >> dt.pytorch.ToTensor(dtype=torch.float32))
```

Listing 6-2: Creating the simulation pipeline

This code creates a simulation pipeline to generate point particle images and to apply optics simulation, normalization, Gaussian noise, axis rearrangement, and conversion to a PyTorch tensor for further analysis.

Finally, create the necessary training and test datasets with Listing 6-3.

```
train_dataset = dt.pytorch.Dataset(simulation, length=100)
test_dataset = dt.pytorch.Dataset(simulation & particle.position, length=5000)
```

Listing 6-3: Creating the training and test datasets

This code creates a training dataset with 100 precalculated images and a test dataset with 5,000 images. The test dataset also contains the positions that you'll need to evaluate the performance of the trained network, while the training dataset doesn't need the positions.

You can use Listing 6-4 to plot the first five images from the test dataset.

```
import matplotlib.pyplot as plt

fig, axs = plt.subplots(1, 5, figsize=(10, 2))
for i, ax in enumerate(axs):
    image, position = test_dataset[i]
    ax.imshow(image[0], cmap="gray", origin="lower")
    ax.scatter(position[1], position[0], c="r")
    if i != 0: ax.axis("off")
plt.tight_layout()
plt.show()
```

Listing 6-4: Plotting the generated particles and their positions

This should generate images similar to those shown in Figure 6-4.

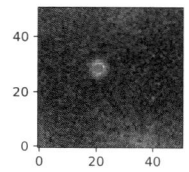

Figure 6-4: The diffraction-limited images of point particles and their centers (dots)

The particles appear as diffraction-limited bright spots against a noisy background. The ground-truth position is indicated by the dot.

Learning from Translations

Self-supervised geometric learning exploits transformations that methodically modify the neural network's input and output. Among these, *translation*, which consists of moving an object or its representation from one position to another without rotating, resizing, or otherwise altering its shape, is the most fundamental for object localization. The underlying concept is as follows: If you have an image containing a particle, even if you don't know its position, you can still be certain that translating the image by a specific amount will result in an equivalent shift in the particle's position—a concrete example of equivariance.

This principle can be used to train a neural network with the following algorithm:

1. Take a single image x as input.
2. Apply two random translations to x to create two images, x_1 and x_2.
3. Use a convolutional neural network with a dense top to predict the positions of the objects in these translated images.
4. Detransform the predicted positions by using the inverse translations to get the predicted positions in the original image frame of reference, $\mathbf{y}_1$ and $\mathbf{y}_2$.
5. Minimize the distance between $\mathbf{y}_1$ and $\mathbf{y}_2$ by using it as loss to train the neural network.

These steps constrain the neural network to be *translation equivariant*, which means that a translation of the input results in an equal translation of the output. This is the principle behind using the loss function to train the network by penalizing it for any deviation from this equivariant behavior.

Defining the Neural Network

You can use Listing 6-5 to define the neural network.

```
import deeplay as dl

❶ backbone = dl.ConvolutionalNeuralNetwork(
    in_channels=1, hidden_channels=[16, 32, 64], out_channels=128,
    pool=torch.nn.MaxPool2d(2),
)
❷ model = dl.Sequential(backbone, torch.nn.Flatten(), torch.nn.LazyLinear(2))
```

Listing 6-5: Implementing a neural network with a convolutional backbone and a dense top layer

This code defines a convolutional neural network backbone ❶. Then the code flattens the output of this backbone and analyzes it with a dense layer ❷. In order to not have to explicitly calculate a priori the output size of the convolutional backbone, which will depend on the input image size, the code uses a LazyLinear layer instead of a Linear layer. You can use print(model) to print the details of this model.

Defining the Transformations

Next, you need to define a translation transformation for the input images, as shown by the image_translation() function in Listing 6-6.

```
from kornia.geometry.transform import translate

def image_translation(batch, translation):
    """Translate a batch of images."""
    xy_flipped_translation = translation[:, [1, 0]]
    return translate(batch, xy_flipped_translation, padding_mode="reflection")
```

Listing 6-6: The function to translate the input image

This function flips the translation to match the image coordinate system and then uses the Kornia library's translate() function to perform the translation.

You can use the inverse_translation() function to implement the corresponding detransformation, as shown in Listing 6-7.

```
def inverse_translation(preds, applied_translation):
    """Invert translation of predicted positions."""
    return preds - applied_translation
```

Listing 6-7: The function to apply the inverse translation on the output positions

This function applies the inverse translation to the estimated particle positions, inverting the translation applied to the images.

Implementing LodeSTAR with Translations

You can now implement the core of the LodeSTAR algorithm trained with translations, which is given by the ParticleLocalizer class in Listing 6-8.

```
from torch import rand

class ParticleLocalizer(dl.Application):
    """LodeSTAR implementation with translations."""

    def __init__(self, model, n_transforms=8, **kwargs):
        """Initialize the ParticleLocalizer."""
        self.model, self.n_transforms = model, n_transforms
        super().__init__(**kwargs)

    def forward(self, batch):
        """Forward pass through the model."""
        return self.model(batch)
```

```
def random_arguments(self):
    """Generate random arguments for transformations."""
    return {"translation": \
        (rand(self.n_transforms, 2).float().to(self.device) * 5 - 2.5)}

def forward_transform(self, batch, translation):
    """Apply forward translation to the image."""
    return image_translation(batch, translation)

def inverse_transform(self, preds, translation):
    """Apply inverse translation to the predictions."""
    return inverse_translation(preds, translation)

def training_step(self, image, batch_idx):
    """Perform a single training step."""
❶  image, *_ = image
❷  batch = image.repeat(self.n_transforms, 1, 1, 1)

    kwargs = self.random_arguments()
❸  transformed_batch = self.forward_transform(batch, **kwargs)

❹  pred_position = self(transformed_batch)
❺  pred_position = self.inverse_transform(pred_position, **kwargs)

    average_pred_position = pred_position \
        .mean(dim=0, keepdim=True).repeat(self.n_transforms, 1)
    loss = self.loss(pred_position, average_pred_position)
    self.log("loss", loss, on_step=True, on_epoch=True, prog_bar=True)
    return loss
```

Listing 6-8: The class to implement a self-supervised particle localizer trained with translations

In this application, the most important method is training_step(). After extracting the first image from the input batch ❶, this function creates a batch of n_transforms images ❷ and applies random translation to them ❸. Then the function predicts the positions by invoking the forward() method—when self(transformed_batch) is called, it's effectively calling self.forward(transformed _batch)—and then inverts the translations to get the predicted positions in the original image ❺. Finally, training_step() then calculates the average position (repeating the average position to match the batch size), calculates the loss, and logs it. This loss is calculated as the distance between each prediction and the average prediction, so minimizing it effectively minimizes the variance of the detransformed predictions.

You can then instantiate a ParticleLocalizer:

```
localizer = ParticleLocalizer(
    model, n_transforms=8, loss=torch.nn.L1Loss(), optimizer=dl.Adam(lr=5e-4),
).create()
```

Finally, you can train the neural network model with Listing 6-9.

```
dataloader = dl.DataLoader(train_dataset, batch_size=1, shuffle=True)
trainer = dl.Trainer(max_epochs=100)
trainer.fit(localizer, dataloader)
```

Listing 6-9: Training the self-supervised particle localizer trained with translations

This code defines the data loader and the trainer and then trains the model.

Evaluating Performance

Let's evaluate the performance of your trained model, using Listing 6-10.

```
images, positions = zip(*test_dataset)
images, positions = torch.stack(images), torch.stack(positions)

predictions = localizer(images).detach().numpy()
```

Listing 6-10: Evaluating the performance of the self-supervised particle localizer trained with translations

This code unpacks the images and corresponding positions from test _dataset. Then the code stacks the list of image and position tensors for batch processing. Finally, the batch of images is passed through the localizer to get the predictions.

You can then write the plot_position_comparison() function to plot the predicted positions as a function of the real ones, as shown in Listing 6-11.

```
def plot_position_comparison(positions, predictions):
    """Plot comparison between predicted and real particle positions."""
    plt.figure(figsize=(14, 8))
    grid = plt.GridSpec(4, 7, wspace=.2, hspace=.1)

    plt.subplot(grid[1:, :3])
    plt.scatter(positions[:, 0], predictions[:, 0], alpha=.5)
    plt.axline((25, 25), slope=1, color="black")
    plt.xlabel("True Horizontal Position", fontsize=20)
    plt.ylabel("Predicted Horizontal Position", fontsize=20)
    plt.axis("equal")

    plt.subplot(grid[1:, 4:])
    plt.scatter(positions[:, 1], predictions[:, 1], alpha=.5)
    plt.axline((25, 25), slope=1, color="black")
    plt.xlabel("True Vertical Position", fontsize=20)
    plt.ylabel("Predicted Vertical Position", fontsize=20)
    plt.axis("equal")

    plt.show()
```

Listing 6-11: The function to plot the predicted positions versus the real ones

Use this function to plot the predicted versus real positions:

```
plot_position_comparison(positions, predictions)
```

Figure 6-5 shows the results.

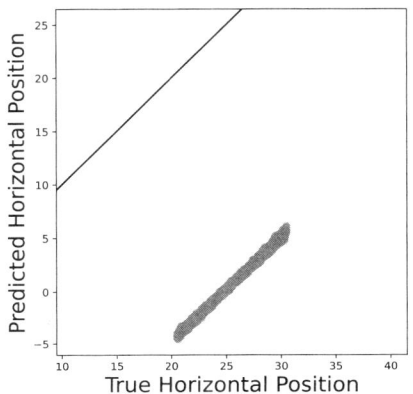 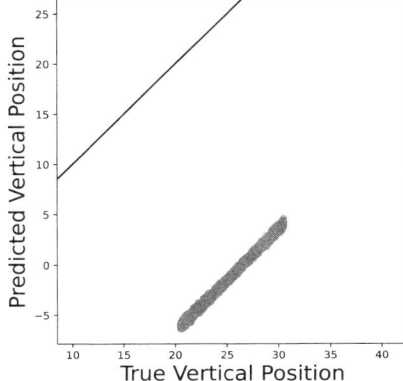

Figure 6-5: The predicted versus real positions for a self-supervised particle localizer trained with translations

You should obtain a slope of the line close to 1, but you can expect a large bias for both the vertical and horizontal position estimations, because the network is trained to correct only relative to itself. In fact, while humans often intuitively measure the position of an object relative to the corner or the center of an image, the network is currently free to choose its own reference point. For many applications, this isn't a problem. For example, to determine statistics about the dynamics of the object, the reference point isn't important, only the distance moved from one frame to the next.

However, in some scenarios, determining the absolute position of an object within an image is crucial. For example, this information might be needed to extract a specific area of the image surrounding the object. In such situations, you can use a straightforward method to adjust for any bias in the object's position.

Improving Predictions

To correct the bias, you can use a simple trick. Define the bias of the network as **b**, such that for an object centered at position **p** relative to the center of the image, the network predicts $\mathbf{y}_{\text{direct}} = \mathbf{p} + \mathbf{b}$. Now, if you flip the image about its center (this is equivalent to reflecting the image around the center both horizontally and vertically), you get a new image with the object at position $-\mathbf{p}$. The network, however, doesn't know that the image has been flipped and will still add the same bias to its prediction. Thus, the network will predict $\mathbf{y}_{\text{flipped}} = -\mathbf{p} + \mathbf{b}$. Then you have:

$$\mathbf{p} = \frac{1}{2} \left(\mathbf{y}_{\text{direct}} - \mathbf{y}_{\text{flipped}} \right)$$

You can implement this idea to correct the bias, as shown in Listing 6-12.

```
direct_preds = localizer(images).detach().numpy()

flipped_images = images.flip(dims=(2, 3))
flipped_preds = localizer(flipped_images).detach().numpy()

predictions_with_difference = ((direct_preds - flipped_preds) / 2
                               + image_size / 2 - 0.5)

plot_position_comparison(positions, predictions_with_difference)
```

Listing 6-12: Correcting the bias of a self-supervised particle localizer trained with translations

This predicts the positions for the original images (direct_preds). Then the code flips the images and predicts the positions for these flipped images (flipped_preds). Finally, these predictions are averaged (predictions_with _difference), also accounting for the image_size / 2 - 0.5 offset between the center of the image and the origin of the image coordinates (the lower-left corner in the figures plotted in this chapter).

Figure 6-6 shows the resulting plot.

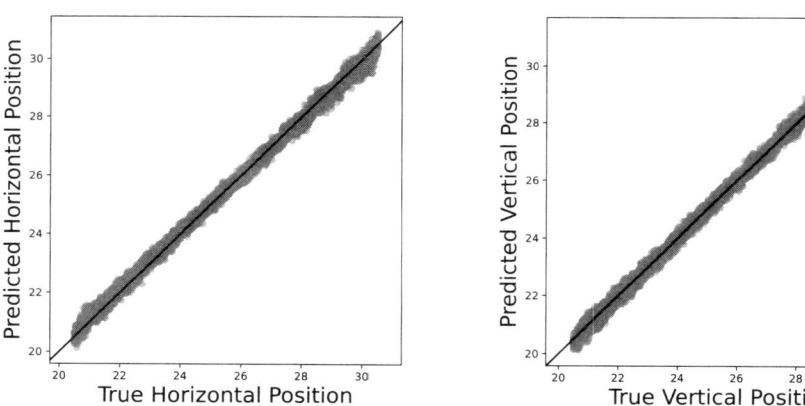

Figure 6-6: The predicted versus real positions for a self-supervised particle localizer trained with translations by using the average predicted position for the input image with and without flipping

The bias has now been corrected. While the slope of the line remains close to 1, the bias now appears to be close to 0, as shown by the points falling close to the bisectrix, the diagonal line representing the perfect prediction.

Learning from Flipping the Image

Flips, like translations, transform the image in a way that predictably changes the position of the object. As such, you can apply flips along with translations during training. By doing so, the network will learn to correct the bias automatically so that you won't need to use the flipping trick during post-processing, as you did in the preceding section.

The neural network learns to correct the bias for the same reason as in the trick described in the preceding section. The original image can be transformed in multiple ways to result in the current image, and only some of these ways include flipping. Therefore, the network cannot know whether the image has been flipped. The only way the network can be correct in all cases is to find the actual center of the object.

Start by implementing the flip_transform() function to flip the input image, as shown in Listing 6-13.

```
def flip_transform(batch, should_flip, dim):
    """Conditionally flip batch along a specified dimension."""
    should_flip = should_flip.view(-1, 1, 1, 1)
    return torch.where(should_flip, batch.flip(dims=(dim,)), batch)
```

Listing 6-13: The function to conditionally flip images along a specified dimension

This function reshapes the should_flip tensor for *broadcasting*, which is the expansion of a tensor's dimensions to make it compatible with subsequent operations. Then the function flips the images if should_flip is True.

Next, implement the inverse_flip_transform() function to invert the flip transformation on the predicted positions, as shown in Listing 6-14.

```
def inverse_flip_transform(preds, should_flip, dim):
    """Conditionally inverse flip transformation based on should_flip."""
    should_flip_mask = torch.zeros_like(preds).bool()
    should_flip_mask[should_flip, dim] = 1
    return torch.where(should_flip_mask, -preds, preds)
```

Listing 6-14: The function to conditionally inverse-flip images

This function applies the inverse flip where should_flip_mask is True.

Finally, create the ParticleLocalizerWithFlips class, inheriting from the ParticleLocalizer class, as shown in Listing 6-15.

```
class ParticleLocalizerWithFlips(ParticleLocalizer):
    """ParticleLocalizer with additional flips."""

    def forward_transform(self, batch, translation, flip_x, flip_y):
        """Apply forward translations and flips to the batch."""
        batch = image_translation(batch, translation)
        batch = flip_transform(batch, flip_x, dim=3)
        batch = flip_transform(batch, flip_y, dim=2)
        return batch
```

```
def inverse_transform(self, preds, translation, flip_x, flip_y):
    """Apply the inverse transformations to the predictions."""
    preds = inverse_flip_transform(preds, flip_x, dim=1)
    preds = inverse_flip_transform(preds, flip_y, dim=0)
    preds = inverse_translation(preds, translation)
    return preds

def random_arguments(self):
    """Generate random arguments for translation and flips."""
    return {"translation": \
        (rand(self.n_transforms, 2).float().to(self.device) * 5 - 2.5),
        "flip_x": rand(self.n_transforms).float().to(self.device) > 0.5,
        "flip_y": rand(self.n_transforms).float().to(self.device) > 0.5}
```

Listing 6-15: The class to implement a self-supervised particle localizer also trained with flips

This class adds the flip transformations around the x- and y-axes to the forward_transform(), inverse_transform(), and random_arguments() methods. All the other methods, including the one implementing the training step, are inherited from ParticleLocalizer and require no changes.

You can then instantiate this class and train it, using Listing 6-16.

```
localizer_with_flips = ParticleLocalizerWithFlips(
    model, n_transforms=8, loss=torch.nn.L1Loss(), optimizer=dl.Adam(lr=1e-3),
).create()

trainer_with_flips = dl.Trainer(max_epochs=100)
trainer_with_flips.fit(localizer_with_flips, dataloader)
```

Listing 6-16: Training a self-supervised particle localizer with flipping transformations

Plot the performance of the trained network with Listing 6-17.

```
predictions = (localizer_with_flips(images).detach().numpy()
        ❶ + image_size / 2 - 0.5)

plot_position_comparison(positions, predictions)
```

Listing 6-17: Plotting the predictions versus real positions for a self-supervised particle localizer with flips

This code plots the predictions of the trained neural network directly, just correcting for the offset between the center of the image and the origin of the image coordinates ❶.

The resulting image should look like Figure 6-7.

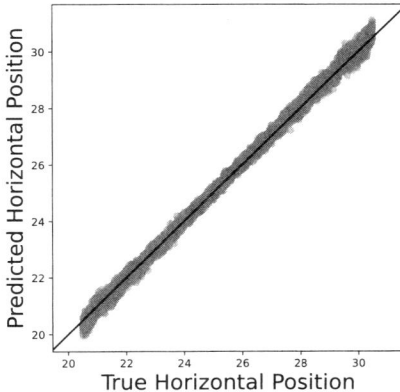 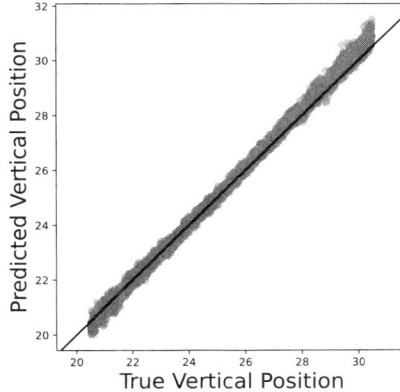

Figure 6-7: The predicted versus real positions for a self-supervised particle localizer with flipping transformations

Because the points fall close to the bisectrix, you can tell that the network has learned to automatically correct the bias during training. No additional post-processing tricks are necessary anymore.

EXERCISE

6-1: Train a neural network by using rotations instead of flips. Compare the results to those obtained using flips. Does one approach work better than the other?

Improving Performance with LodeSTAR

You can greatly improve the performance of your trained network by using a more appropriate architecture. The architecture you've used until now has consisted of a convolutional backbone followed by a dense layer, as you saw in Listing 6-5. The problem with this architecture is that it isn't equivariant to translation. In fact, while convolutional layers are equivariant to translation, dense layers are not. This means that the neural network needs to learn every possible position of the object in the image individually.

If, instead, the neural network were inherently equivariant to translation, it would only need to learn to remove the bias as you did in the previous section using flips. So, if you design a neural network without dense layers (in this case, without the dense top layer), you can shorten the training and improve performance.

To remove the dense top layer, you need to pool the spatial information produced by the convolutional layers to x- and y-coordinates. You might consider using a global average pooling layer, but this wouldn't be a good idea. The global average pooling layer isn't equivariant to translation; it's just invariant to translation. Instead, you can calculate the center of mass of the output of the convolutional layers. Ignoring edge effects (which occur when a transformation causes parts of the object to move beyond the image boundaries, leading to information loss or distortion), this operation is equivariant to translation.

This is one of the ideas behind *Localization and Detection from Symmetries, Translations, and Rotations (LodeSTAR)*, a deep learning method optimized for localization and detection of objects in images, using geometric learning.

Consider the probability ρ_i of finding a particle near the position $\mathbf{r}_i$, which is the center of the pixel i, as shown in Figure 6-8.

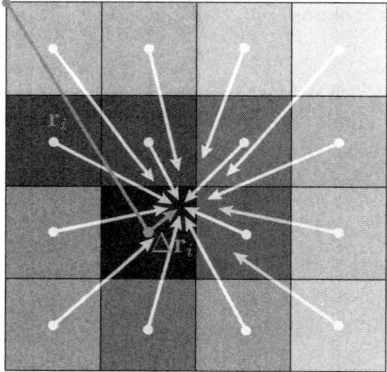

Figure 6-8: The particle position as a weighted average

The center of mass of this probability distribution gives a good statistical estimator of the position of the particle, which can be calculated as follows:

$$\mathbf{r} = \frac{\sum_i \mathbf{r}_i \rho_i}{\sum_i \rho_i} \tag{6.1}$$

LodeSTAR uses a slightly modified version of this equation, defined as

$$\mathbf{r} = \frac{\sum_i (\mathbf{r}_i + \Delta \mathbf{r}_i) \rho_i}{\sum_i \rho_i} \tag{6.2}$$

where $\Delta \mathbf{r}_i$ is the offset of the particle center from the center of pixel i (as illustrated in Figure 6-8), which is also predicted by the neural network.

In this way, LodeSTAR is trained to produce three channels: a *probability channel* for the probability ρ_i of finding a particle near the position $\mathbf{r}_i$ (the center of pixel i) and two *displacement channels* for the x- and y-offsets of the estimated particle position ($\Delta \mathbf{r}_i$), from which the particle position is then calculated.

You can train LodeSTAR with Listing 6-18.

```
dataloader_lodestar = dl.DataLoader(train_dataset, batch_size=4, shuffle=True)

lodestar = dl.LodeSTAR(optimizer=dl.Adam(lr=1e-4)).build()

trainer_lodestar = dl.Trainer(max_epochs=100)
trainer_lodestar.fit(lodestar, dataloader_lodestar)
```

Listing 6-18: Training LodeSTAR

Now let's evaluate the performance of LodeSTAR, using Listing 6-19.

```
lodestar_predictions = lodestar.pooled(images).detach().numpy()

plot_position_comparison(positions, lodestar_predictions)
```

Listing 6-19: Plotting LodeSTAR performance

This code gets the estimated particle coordinates by pooling the neural network outputs. You'll see how to get access to the values of ρ_i and $\Delta\mathbf{r}_i$ in Project 6A.

Unlike our previous neural network, LodeSTAR outputs the position of the object relative to the origin of the image coordinates and therefore doesn't need to correct for the offset between the center of the image and the origin of the image coordinates. Figure 6-9 shows the resulting plot.

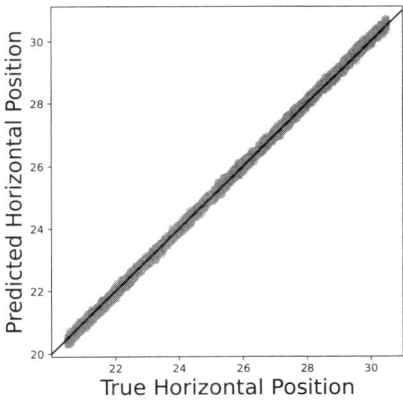 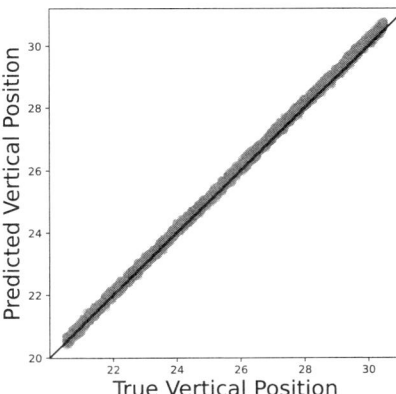

Figure 6-9: The predicted versus real positions with LodeSTAR

LodeSTAR significantly outperforms the previous networks. In fact, the predictions are very close to the bisectrix of the plane.

NOTE *Code Example 6-1, "Localizing Particles Using LodeSTAR," is available at* https://github.com/DeepTrackAI/DeepLearningCrashCourse. *Navigate to the* Ch06_SelfSupervised *folder and then* ec06_1_lodestar. *The* lodestar.ipynb *notebook provides a complete code example that demonstrates how to train and use LodeSTAR to localize particles.*

Project 6A: Localizing Mouse Stem Cells with LodeSTAR

As you learned in the preceding section, LodeSTAR uses a convolutional neural network without any dense layers to ensure translational equivariance. Beyond making the neural network equivariant to translations, the center-of-mass pooling also allows the neural network to predict on arbitrarily sized images.

In fact, as you've seen in Equation 6.2, the channel ρ_i can be thought to represent a spatial distribution of probability. When predicting on a large image with multiple objects, the neural network will produce several clusters of probability in the output. This manifests itself as several peaks in the probability channel ρ_i (and corresponding offsets in the $\Delta\mathbf{r}_i$ channels that point to the same peak). Thus, you can use LodeSTAR to detect multiple objects in an image by finding clusters of probability in the output of the neural network.

This means that you can train your neural network on small images with a single object and then use the trained network on larger images with multiple objects without any additional training. This makes the task of finding a sufficient set of training images much simpler in real-world applications.

In this project, you'll apply these principles to find the positions of mouse stem cells in images with multiple cells. To achieve this, you'll train a neural network by using a single, cropped image of a single cell. Furthermore, this approach won't require you to manually annotate the cell's exact position in the cropped image.

Using the Cell Tracking Challenge Dataset

You'll use a dataset from the Cell Tracking Challenge, which includes a series of videos of proliferating mouse hematopoietic stem cells. Even though you don't need ground-truth positions to train the neural network, you can use the annotations provided for the challenge to evaluate the detection performance of your trained network.

This dataset is available at *http://data.celltrackingchallenge.net/training -datasets/BF-C2DL-HSC.zip*. Download and extract it using Listing 6-20.

```
import os
from torchvision.datasets.utils import _extract_zip, download_url

❶ dataset_path = "cell_detection_dataset"
  if not os.path.exists(dataset_path):
      url = ("http://data.celltrackingchallenge.net/training-datasets/"
          "BF-C2DL-HSC.zip")
      download_url(url, ".")
      _extract_zip("BF-C2DL-HSC.zip", dataset_path, None)
      os.remove("BF-C2DL-HSC.zip")

❷ dir = os.path.join(dataset_path, "BF-C2DL-HSC")
```

Listing 6-20: Downloading the BF-C2DL-HSC dataset of the Cell Tracking Challenge

This script downloads and saves the dataset, unzips it into the dataset_path folder ❶, and finally removes the downloaded zipped file. The dataset is accessible in the dir folder ❷.

The dataset contains two sequences of images in the *01* and *02* folders, and their ground-truth segmentations in the *01_GT* and *02_GT* folders. Within these latter folders, the *SEG* folders contain the high-quality segmentation masks for a few images (which you won't use in this project), while the *TRA* folders contain lower-quality segmentation masks for all images (which you'll use later to determine the ground-truth cell positions to evaluate the performance of your trained network). You'll use the sequence in the *02* folder because it contains more cells than that in the *01* folder.

You can create a pipeline to dynamically load the files, including both images and the relative labels of the cell positions, with Listing 6-21.

```
import glob
import deeptrack as dt
from skimage.measure import regionprops

sources = dt.sources.Source(
    image_path=sorted(glob.glob(os.path.join(dir, "02", "*.tif"))),
    label_path=sorted(glob.glob(os.path.join(dir, "02_GT", "TRA", "*.tif"))),
)

❶ image_pip = dt.LoadImage(sources.image_path)[300:850, :300] / 256
❷ props_pip = dt.LoadImage(sources.label_path)[300:850, :300] >> regionprops

pip = image_pip & props_pip
```

Listing 6-21: Creating the pipeline to load the images and the relative ground-truth cell positions

This script uses Source to load the list of all image files from the sequence in the *02* folder and the relative ground-truth segmentations from the *02_GT/TRA* folder. The script uses the sorted() function to ensure that the images are sorted by name, because depending on the operating system and the settings, the images could be sorted by modification time instead of by name. The script crops the images to show only the part where the cells are ❶ ❷ to save computer memory and speed up the evaluation. The script also extracts the properties of the cells identified in the segmentations, using regionprops. Finally, the script creates the pip pipeline combining the images and the positions.

You can finally plot some images together with the ground-truth cell positions, using Listing 6-22.

```
import matplotlib.pyplot as plt

plt.figure(figsize=(15, 10))

for plt_index, data_index in enumerate([0, 300, 600, 900, 1200, 1500]):
    image, *props = pip(sources[data_index])

    plt.subplot(1, 6, plt_index + 1)
    plt.imshow(image, cmap="gray")
    for prop in props:
      ❶ plt.scatter(prop.centrcid[1], prop.centroid[0], s=5, color="red")
    plt.axis("off")
plt.tight_layout()
plt.show()
```

Listing 6-22: Plotting some images with the cell ground-truth positions

When plotting the positions, the ordering of the coordinates is intentionally inverted ❶ to match the image's indexing convention.

The images are shown in Figure 6-10.

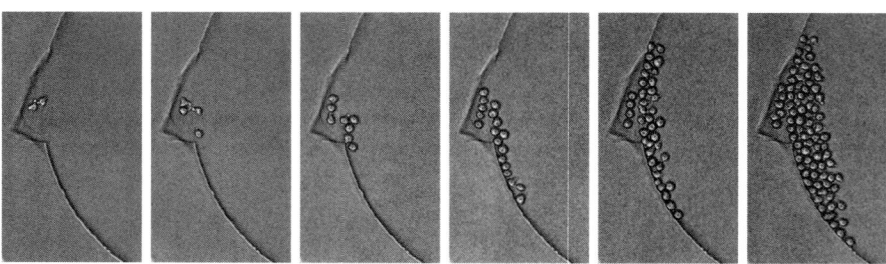

Figure 6-10: Proliferation of mouse hematopoietic stem cells with the ground-truth cell positions (dots)

You can see images from the sequence in the *02* folder of the BF-C2DL-HSC dataset demonstrating the proliferation of mouse hematopoietic stem cells. The dots represent the ground-truth cell positions obtained from the *centroid* of the cell segmentations provided by the dataset, corresponding to the geometric center point of the cell segmentation.

Preparing the Training Crop

One of the greatest advantages of LodeSTAR is that it can be trained on small crops of the images containing a single cell. In this project, you'll use a single crop of a single cell to train the neural network. To do this, you need to find a cell in the image, then crop the portion of the image around the cell. This cell doesn't need to be exactly in the center of the crop, but it should be well separated from the other cells in the image. This is to make sure that only one cell is in the crop.

You can use Listing 6-23 to select a good crop.

```
crop_frame_index, crop_size = 282, 50
crop_x0, crop_y0 = 295 - crop_size // 2, 115 - crop_size // 2

image, *props = pip(sources[crop_frame_index])
crop = image[crop_x0:crop_x0 + crop_size, crop_y0:crop_y0 + crop_size]
```

Listing 6-23: Preparing the training crop

This script extracts from one of the images a crop to be used for training. You can alter its parameters to get a crop from a different frame (crop_frame _index), with a different size (crop_size), and in a different portion of the image (crop_x0 and crop_y0).

Then plot the selected crop with Listing 6-24.

```
from matplotlib.patches import Rectangle

plt.figure(figsize=(15, 10))

plt.subplot(1, 2, 1)
❶ plt.imshow(image, cmap="gray")
❷ plt.gca().add_patch(Rectangle((crop_y0, crop_x0), crop_size, crop_size,
                                 linewidth=1, edgecolor="r", facecolor="none"))

plt.subplot(1, 2, 2)
❸ plt.imshow(crop, cmap="gray")

plt.show()
```

Listing 6-24: Plotting the selected training crop

This code plots the whole image ❶ with a square around the crop ❷ and a zoomed-in version of the crop ❸. Figure 6-11 shows the result.

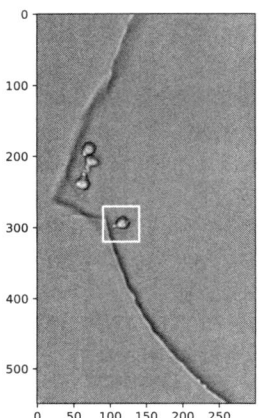 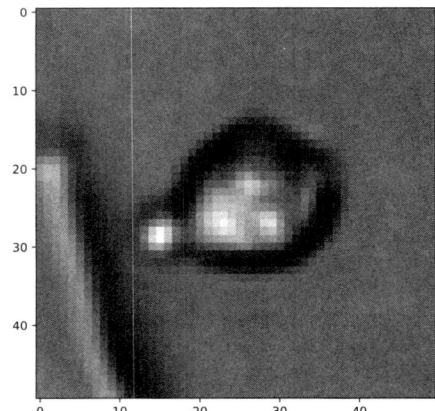

Figure 6-11: A full image (left) and a close-up (right) of the cropped portion of the image to be used for training

In the full image on the left, the area of the crop is highlighted by a square. The zoomed-in crop is shown on the right. The crop is well separated from the other cells in the image. The cell is somewhat close to the border, but this won't be a problem in this case.

Creating the Training Pipeline and Data Loader

Now you'll create a pipeline to feed this crop to the algorithm that trains the neural network; see Listing 6-25.

```
import numpy as np
import torch

train_pip = (dt.Value(crop)
❶     >> dt.Multiply(lambda: np.random.uniform(0.9, 1.1))
❷     >> dt.Add(lambda: np.random.uniform(-0.1, 0.1))
       >> dt.MoveAxis(-1, 0) >> dt.pytorch.ToTensor(dtype=torch.float32)
```

Listing 6-25: Creating the training pipeline

This code augments the training data by slightly rescaling the image by a random amount ❶ and by adding a small random offset ❷. You can, of course, experiment with different augmentations, even distorting the image slightly.

Let's use this pipeline to create a training dataset and a data loader with Listing 6-26.

```
import deeplay as dl

train_dataset = dt.pytorch.Dataset(train_pip, length=400, replace=False)
dataloader = dl.DataLoader(train_dataset, batch_size=8, shuffle=True)
```

Listing 6-26: Creating the training dataset and data loader

The dataset includes 400 augmented versions of the crop to enhance the model's ability to generalize and perform robustly on diverse and unseen data.

Training the Neural Network

You can now define and train the LodeSTAR network with Listing 6-27.

```
lodestar = dl.LodeSTAR(n_transforms=4, optimizer=dl.Adam(lr=1e-4)).build()
trainer = dl.Trainer(max_epochs=200)
trainer.fit(lodestar, dataloader)
```

Listing 6-27: Defining and training the LodeSTAR neural network

This code uses four transformations in each step of the training and trains for 200 epochs.

To gain some intuition about what the neural network does, use Listing 6-28 to plot the predictions.

```
❶ image_index = 1500
   image, *props = pip(sources[image_index])
   torch_image = torch.from_numpy(image).permute(2, 0, 1).unsqueeze(0).float()
❷ prediction = lodestar(torch_image)[0].detach().numpy()
❸ x, y, rho = prediction[0], prediction[1], prediction[-1]

   plt.figure(figsize=(15, 10))

   plt.subplot(1, 3, 1)
   plt.imshow(image, cmap="gray")
   plt.axis("off")

   plt.subplot(1, 3, 2)
   plt.imshow(rho, cmap="gray")
   plt.axis("off")

   plt.subplot(1, 3, 3)
   plt.imshow(image, cmap="gray")
❹ plt.scatter(y.flatten(), x.flatten(), alpha=rho.flatten() / rho.max(), s=5)
   plt.axis("off")
   plt.xlim(0, 299)
   plt.ylim(0, 549)
   plt.gca().invert_yaxis()

   plt.show()
```

Listing 6-28: Obtaining and plotting the predictions of the neural network

This code calculates the trained neural network prediction ❷ for the image with index 1500 ❶. The code then extracts the predictions for the x- and y-coordinates of the particles obtained from the displacement channel $\Delta \mathbf{r}_i$

summed to the pixel center $\mathbf{r}_i$ as well as for the probability channel ρ_i ❸. Note that the predicted positions are plotted with a transparency proportional to the probability by setting the alpha parameter ❹. The code then proceeds to plot them. You should obtain plots similar to Figure 6-12.

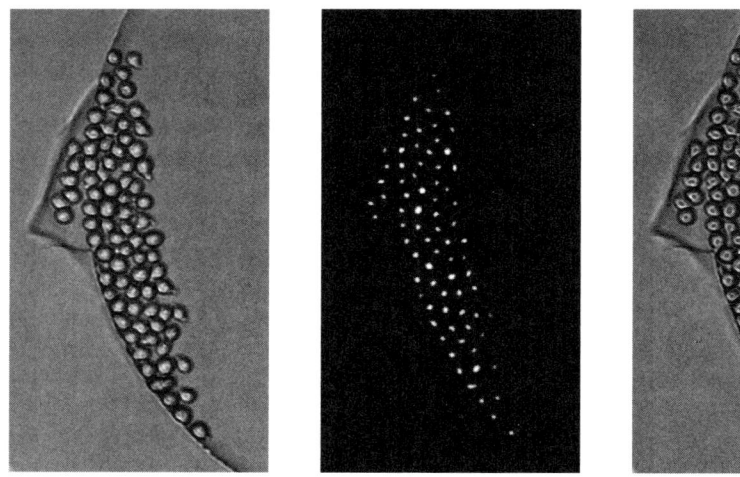

Figure 6-12: The input image (left), probability channel (middle), and displacement channel (right)

The input image is shown on the left. The middle image shows the probability channel ρ_i. The bright spots near the centers of the cells show that the neural network correctly thinks there is a high probability that a cell is in those positions. The right image shows the predicted positions, which correctly cluster near the cells, demonstrating the network's accuracy in replicating the cell positions from the input image, which is the primary goal of this task.

Evaluating Performance

You'll now evaluate the trained neural network on the images of the sequence contained in the *02* folder. LodeSTAR calculates two metrics to determine the positions of the cells in the images based on the predictions provided by the neural network.

The first metric uses a segmentation of the probability channel, thus identifying the cell positions as the centroids of the high-probability regions. The second metric uses the detection clusters in the position channel. LodeSTAR has an already-implemented method, called detect(), that combines these two metrics and provides the cell locations, which you'll soon use.

First, you need to choose the parameters to combine these metrics, which are shown in Listing 6-29.

```
alpha = 0.2
beta = 1 - alpha
cutoff = 0.2
mode = "constant"
```

Listing 6-29: Fixing the parameters to determine the positions of the cells in the images

The parameters alpha and beta weight the metrics based on the probability channel and the position channel, respectively ($\alpha + \beta = 1$). As a rule of thumb, α should be high if the objects are very different, and β should be high if the objects are very similar. The cutoff parameter determines the threshold: Higher values mean fewer objects are detected, and lower values mean more objects are detected. The mode parameter determines how the threshold is calculated. As a rule of thumb, use mode="constant" if the number of objects changes significantly between images, and use mode="quantile" if the number of objects is roughly constant between images.

Then plot the positions of the cells for some representative images, using Listing 6-30.

```
plt.figure(figsize=(15, 10))

❶ for plot_idx, frame_idx in enumerate([0, 300, 600, 900, 1200, 1500]):
    image, *props = pip(sources[frame_idx])
    torch_image = torch.from_numpy(image).permute(2, 0, 1).unsqueeze(0).float()
    ❷ detections = lodestar.detect(torch_image, alpha=alpha, beta=beta,
                        mode="constant", cutoff=cutoff)[0]

    plt.subplot(1, 6, plot_idx + 1)
    plt.imshow(image, cmap="gray")
    ❸ plt.scatter(detections[:, 1], detections[:, 0], s=5, color="red")
    plt.axis("off")
plt.tight_layout()
plt.show()
```

Listing 6-30: Determining and plotting the positions of the cells in the images

This code estimates the positions of the cells in a subset of frames ❶ by using the LodeSTAR detect() method ❷ and then plots those positions on the original images as dots ❸. Figure 6-13 shows the results.

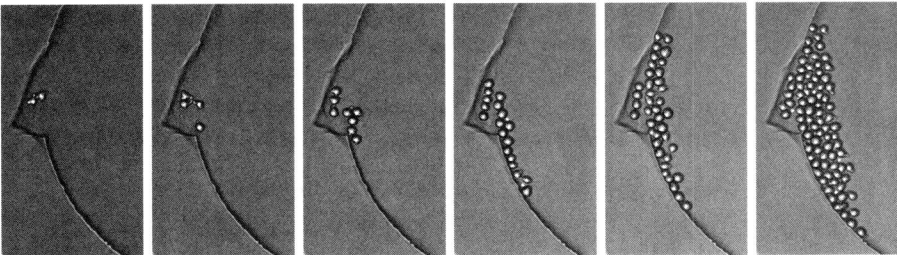

Figure 6-13: The positions of the cells detected by LodeSTAR

You should see the positions of the detected cells plotted as dots on top of the images, corresponding to proliferating mouse hematopoietic stem cells. Overall, your results should be quite good, like those shown in Figure 6-13. If needed, you can tune the parameters in Listing 6-29 to further improve the results, starting from cutoff. For example, if the model misses some cells, the cutoff parameter can be decreased. If the model detects too many cells, the cutoff parameter can be increased.

In Figure 6-13, there aren't many obvious errors. You can therefore proceed to quantitatively evaluate the model by measuring the *F1 score*. Given the true positive (TP), the false positive (FP), and the false negative (FN) detections, the F1 score is:

$$\text{F1 score} = \frac{2\text{TP}}{2\text{TP} + \text{FP} + \text{FN}}$$

This is the harmonic mean of the *precision* TP/(TP + FP) and the *recall* TP/(TP + FN). You can calculate the F1 score by using Listing 6-31.

```
import scipy, tqdm

distance_th = 10

TP, FP, FN = 0, 0, 0
❶ for source in tqdm.tqdm(sources[::10]):
    image, *props = pip(source)
    torch_image = torch.from_numpy(image).permute(2, 0, 1).unsqueeze(0).float()
    detections = lodestar.detect(torch_image, alpha=alpha, beta=beta,
                        mode="constant", cutoff=cutoff)[0]
    centroids = np.array([prop.centroid[:2] for prop in props])

    distance_matrix = scipy.spatial.distance_matrix(detections, centroids)
    row_idx, col_idx = scipy.optimize.linear_sum_assignment(distance_matrix)

    filtered_row_ind = row_idx[distance_matrix[row_idx, col_idx] < distance_th]
    filtered_col_ind = col_idx[distance_matrix[row_idx, col_idx] < distance_th]

    TP += len(filtered_row_ind)
    FP += len(detections) - len(filtered_row_ind)
    FN += len(centroids) - len(filtered_col_ind)

F1 = 2 * TP / (2 * TP + FP + FN)

print(f"TP: {TP} FP: {FP} FN: {FN} F1: {F1}")
```

Listing 6-31: Calculating the F1 score to quantify the neural network performance

Because of the similarity between the images in the dataset, you can expedite the evaluation process by analyzing only every 10th frame ❶.

When we ran the code, we got the following results: TP: 6459, FP: 339, FN: 16, and F1: 0.973. The high TP number and the F1 score close to 1 indicate that the model is highly effective in correctly identifying cell positions. The relatively low FP and FN numbers suggest that the model has both good precision and recall, making it reliable for this task. However, you may get better or worse results. In fact, because of the extremely small training set, the results may vary significantly between runs.

NOTE *Code Example 6-A, "Localizing Multiple Cells Using LodeSTAR," is available at* https://github.com/DeepTrackAI/DeepLearningCrashCourse. *Navigate to the* Ch06_SelfSupervised *folder and then* ec06_A_cell_localization. *The* cell_localization.ipynb *notebook provides a complete code example that trains a convolutional neural network to detect cells, using a single crop of a cell; the example then evaluates the performance of the trained network on all the images available in the sequence.*

Summary

In this chapter, you delved into self-supervised learning, a subfield of deep learning that's transforming the way you can use unlabeled data by exploiting hidden structures and symmetries present in the data. While exploring the mechanisms used by machines to learn from data without explicit annotations, you focused on the distinctions and potential applications of contrastive and non-contrastive learning paradigms.

Contrastive learning is particularly effective when distinguishing between similar and dissimilar data points is crucial, such as in image-recognition or clustering tasks. Non-contrastive learning excels when defining negative samples is challenging or ambiguous, such as in certain medical imaging or NLP tasks.

You also used self-supervised geometric learning to train a neural network to determine an object's position in an image by using the equivariances of translations and flips in the training process. This gave you detailed insights into the underpinning of the LodeSTAR algorithm for unsupervised particle detection. In particular, you should now understand how the equivariances of translations and flips can be used to effectively and accurately localize objects, such as particles and cells, in images. This approach demonstrates the importance of designing learning algorithms that can inherently recognize and utilize the properties of data, leading to more robust and accurate models. In the project, you used LodeSTAR to apply what you learned to localize cells.

You should now have a good understanding of self-supervised learning and its potential. From its capacity to use unlabeled data, to its ability to enhance model robustness and feature extraction by exploiting the symmetries intrinsic to the problem at hand, you now have the theoretical knowledge and practical skills necessary to navigate and innovate in this field. In the next chapter, you'll learn about tools that enable you to explore data that naturally comes as sequences, such as time series and natural speech.

Seminal Works and Further Reading

The concept of using pretext tasks to learn visual representations without labeled data was first formalized in 2015 by Carl Doersch et al. in "Unsupervised Visual Representation Learning by Context Prediction," published in *Proceedings of the IEEE International Conference on Computer Vision* (*ICCV*, pages 1,422–1,430) and on arXiv (article number 1505.05192). This work demonstrated how predicting the relative position of patches within an image could enable networks to learn meaningful features in an unsupervised manner.

A major leap forward in self-supervised learning was the introduction of contrastive learning techniques. One of the foundational works in this field is "A Simple Framework for Contrastive Learning of Visual Representations" by Ting Chen et al., published in 2020 in *Proceedings of the International Conference on Machine Learning* (pages 1,597–1,607). This work introduced a framework that relies on augmentations of the same image as positive pairs, while considering other images as negatives.

Jean-Bastien Grill et al. proposed non-contrastive learning, which focuses on learning representations without explicitly relying on negative pairs, in "Bootstrap Your Own Latent: A New Approach to Self-Supervised Learning," published in 2020 in *Advances in Neural Information Processing Systems* (*NeurIPS*, volume 33, pages 21,271–21,284).

Geometric contrastive learning was introduced in 2022 by Benjamin Midtvedt et al. in "Single-Shot Self-Supervised Object Detection in Microscopy," published in *Nature Communications* (volume 13, article number 7492). The proposed method, named LodeSTAR, applies self-supervised learning to optical microscopy, using geometric consistency to improve the localization and classification of single particles.

CHALLENGE PROJECTS

6-1: Anomaly detection in brain MRI images   Use the RSNA-MICCAI Brain Tumor Radiogenomic Classification dataset available on Kaggle to develop a self-supervised learning model for anomaly detection in brain MRI images. Employ a contrastive learning approach to train your model to differentiate between normal and abnormal brain structures without using labeled data. After training, apply your model to identify unusual patterns that could indicate the presence of tumors or other anomalies.

6-2: Self-supervised learning for predictive maintenance in aerospace
Access the NASA Turbofan Engine Degradation Simulation dataset from the Prognostics Center of Excellence dataset repository to create a self-supervised learning model for predictive maintenance of aircraft engines. Use non-contrastive learning to analyze the sensor data (temperature, pressure, vibration, and so on) and learn normal versus abnormal operational patterns. Your goal is to predict potential failures or maintenance needs before they lead to actual problems.

7

PROCESSING TIME SERIES AND LANGUAGE WITH RECURRENT NEURAL NETWORKS

In this chapter, you'll learn about recurrent neural networks, a class of neural networks particularly suited to handle sequential data, such as time series and videos.

You'll start by coding a standard recurrent neural network with PyTorch. Then you'll embed it into a Deeplay model, streamlining it for ease of use and learning how to implement your own models in Deeplay. Finally, you'll tackle real-world problems like temperature forecasting and language translation.

Understanding Recurrent Neural Networks

Unlike the neural networks you've encountered until now that treat each data sample independently, *recurrent neural networks* are designed to analyze data in a sequence, which is useful, for example, for analyzing time series and videos.

This type of network uses *recurrence relations*, mathematical operations applied to sequences in which the value of an element is determined by the preceding elements. For example, the location of an object in one frame of a movie often provides useful information about where that object will be in subsequent frames. Recurrent neural networks use a form of *memory* to utilize this past history.

Using a Comb Filter

To illustrate how recurrence relations work in practice, think about processing a numerical sequence that has as the output of one step the average of the current input and the output of the preceding step. This procedure of reintroducing the output as part of the input establishes a *feedback loop*.

In signal processing, this technique is known as a *comb filter*. Comb filters are used in various sound effects such as *reverb* (which simulates the echoes and reflections of sound within an acoustic space), *flanging* (which mixes a signal with a slightly delayed copy of itself to produce a distinctive swirling sound), and *pitch shifting* (which changes the pitch of a sound without altering its duration, allowing for adjustments in musical key or tonality).

You can implement a comb filter with the code in Listing 7-1.

```
input_series = [0, 0, 0, 0, 1, 1, 1, 1, 1, 1, 1, 1, 0, 0, 0, 0, 0, 0, 0, 0]

hidden_state, U, V = 0, 0.5, 0.5

output_series = []
for input_data in input_series:
❶   hidden_state = U * input_data + V * hidden_state
    output_data = hidden_state
    output_series.append(output_data)
```

Listing 7-1: Implementing a comb filter

This simple comb filter operates on the input_series list, which corresponds to a square wave. The hidden_state variable is initialized to 0 and, in this example, simply records the output at the preceding step. The U constant determines the weight of the current input (input_data) in the calculation, while the V constant defines the weight of the hidden_state variable. Here, these variables are set so that both input_data and hidden_state each contribute 50 percent to the final output.

This code then iteratively applies the comb filter to each value in the input series. First, the code calculates the updated average by weighing the current input and the preceding state and saves that average into the hidden_state variable ❶. Then the current output (output_data) is set to the value of the hidden _state variable. And finally, output_data is appended to the output_series list.

By printing the output series with

```
print(f"Output Series: {[f'{x:.2f}' for x in output_series]}")
```

you get this:

```
Output Series: ['0.00', '0.00', '0.00', '0.00', '0.50', '0.75', '0.88', '0.94',
'0.97', '0.98', '0.99', '1.00', '0.50', '0.25', '0.12', '0.06', '0.03', '0.02',
'0.01', '0.00']
```

When the input signal suddenly becomes equal to 1, the output series slowly starts increasing, reaching the value of 1 after some delay. A similar behavior occurs as the input changes to 0, which causes the output to decrease to 0 over multiple steps.

Understanding a Simple Recurrent Neural Network

Just as in a comb filter used to feed the preceding hidden state back as an additional input, a recurrent neural network also feeds its hidden state back in as an additional input. This feedback mechanism, as illustrated on the left side of Figure 7-1, enables the network to maintain a form of memory and effectively analyze sequential data.

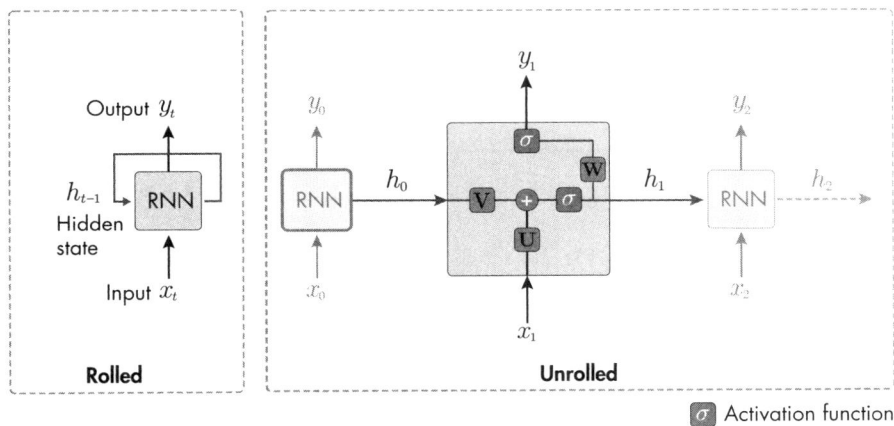

Figure 7-1: The working principle of a recurrent neural network

On the right side of Figure 7-1, the recurrent neural network is shown unfolded in time, highlighting its sequential computation process. The network receives a value of the input series as input. Next, the network transforms the input through a hidden layer, which combines the input and the previously memorized hidden state to determine the new hidden state. Then the network calculates the output through an additional layer, which is now different from the hidden state, unlike in the previous comb filter example.

You can implement this recurrent neural network by updating Listing 7-1 as shown in Listing 7-2.

```
import numpy as np

def sigmoid(x):
    """Simple implementation of sigmoid function."""
    return 1 / (1 + np.exp(-x))

input_series = [0, 0, 0, 0, 1, 1, 1, 1, 1, 1, 1, 1, 0, 0, 0, 0, 0, 0, 0, 0]

hidden_state = 0
```

```
❶ U, V, W, b = np.random.normal(size=4)

output_series = []
for input_data in input_series:
  ❷ hidden_state = sigmoid(U * input_data + V * hidden_state + b)
  ❸ output_data = sigmoid(W * hidden_state)
    output_series.append(output_data)
```

Listing 7-2: Implementing a recurrent neural network in NumPy (by modifying Listing 7-1)

In this code, the weights of the network are randomly initialized ❶. As in the previous example, hidden_state is computed by combining the input and previous hidden state, as well as by adding a bias ❷. Then the result is transformed with a sigmoid function to introduce a nonlinearity. Finally, the code computes the output as the product of the hidden state with an output weight transformed by a sigmoid function to introduce an additional nonlinearity ❸. Of course, since this simple neural network is randomly initialized, the output series will be random.

EXERCISES

7-1: Although the preceding example shows the principle behind recurrent neural networks, you can't use it to solve any concrete problem without training the weights. To do so, implement recurrent backpropagation and use it to train the recurrent neural network to perform simple operations on a time series (for example, to damp a sinusoidal wave).

7-2: Generalize this implementation of a recurrent neural network to accept multidimensional vectors as input and output. Also in this case, implement recurrent backpropagation and train the network to perform simple tasks on a time series (for example, the next set of coordinates in a 2D moving object's trajectory based on its past positions).

Predicting Temperature with Recurrent Neural Networks

In this section, you'll learn how to implement and train various recurrent neural networks to predict temperature. You'll use the Jena Climate dataset, which you'll first load and preprocess. Then you'll build and train some simple recurrent neural networks. Finally, you'll progress to more-complex architectures like gated recurrent units and long short-term memory networks.

Loading the Jena Climate Dataset

The Jena Climate dataset contains time series recorded at the Max Planck Institute for Biogeochemistry in Jena, Germany. The dataset is made up of 14 weather measurements recorded every 10 minutes over several years, from January 1, 2009, to December 31, 2016.

The dataset is contained in the *jena_climate_2009_2016.csv* file, which you can load using Listing 7-3.

```
import pandas as pd

dataframe = pd.read_csv("jena_climate_2009_2016.csv", index_col=0)
data = dataframe.values
header = dataframe.columns.tolist()
```

Listing 7-3: Loading the Jena Climate dataset

This code loads the dataset into the `data` variable, and the list of measured quantities into the `header` variable. The parameter `index_col=0` means that the first column of the *.csv* file, which contains the timestamps, is used as the index of `dataframe` instead of being included as data. You can display the header and the first few elements of the dataset with `print(dataframe.head())`.

Now visualize the time series of the Jena Climate dataset with the code in Listing 7-4.

```
import matplotlib.pyplot as plt
import numpy as np

start, days, daily_samples = 0, 14, 144
end = start + daily_samples * days

fig, axs = plt.subplots(7, 2, figsize=(16, 12), sharex=True)
for i, ax in enumerate(axs.flatten()):
❶ ax.plot(np.arange(start, end), data[start:end, i], label=header[i])
    ax.set_xlim(start, end)
    ax.tick_params(axis="both", which="major", labelsize=16)
    ax.legend(fontsize=20)

    for day in range(1, days):
      ❷ ax.axvline(x=start + daily_samples * day,
                  color="gray", linestyle="--", linewidth=0.5)
plt.tight_layout()
plt.show()
```

Listing 7-4: Visualizing the Jena Climate dataset

This code plots a portion of the time series, starting with the first sample (`start`) and over a range of 14 days (`days`); each day has 144 samples (`daily_samples`), one every 10 minutes. Then the code calculates the end of the time range to plot (`end`). Finally, the code plots the data for the chosen time range ❶ as well as vertical lines to highlight each day ❷.

Figure 7-2 shows the resulting plots.

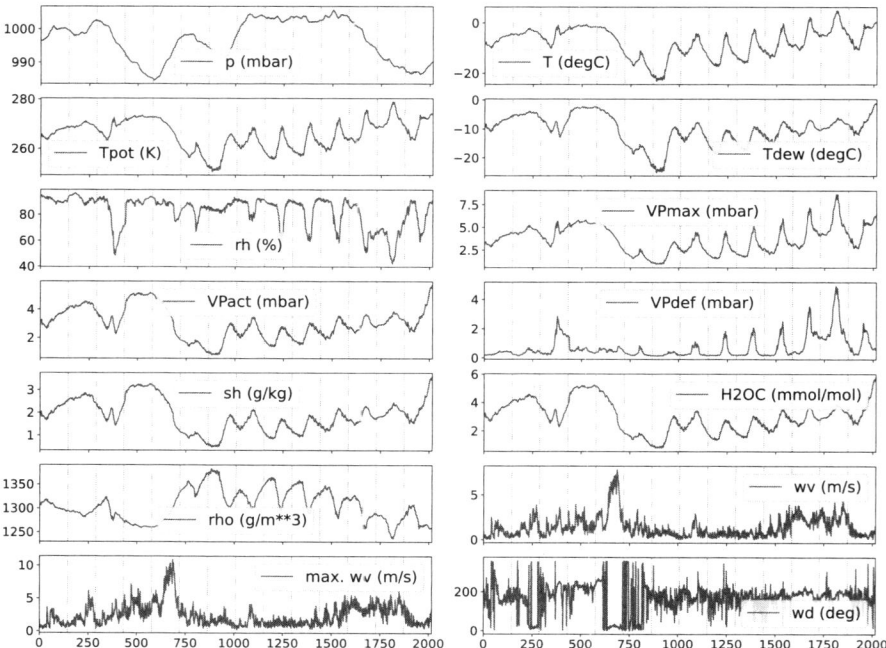

Figure 7-2: The time series of the Jena Climate dataset

The data has periodicity, such as the daily rise and fall of temperature. You can explore different ranges of data over different timescales by changing the start and days parameters in the plotting code.

EXERCISE

7-3: In the plotted dataset, several measured quantities are so highly correlated that they provide redundant information. Removing irrelevant features can help reduce overfitting, which in turn can improve the model's performance. Additionally, reducing the number of features enhances the explainability of the model by making it easier to understand and interpret.

Analyze the correlations among the quantities to identify redundant features and then select a minimal set of representative features. For example, using *correlation matrix analysis*, you could examine the correlation coefficients between pairs of features to identify those with high correlation (for example, above 0.8 or 0.9) so that you can remove one of the correlated features.

Execute the code of the following sections by using all the features and then only the minimal set to observe the difference in the trained model's performance.

Preprocessing the Data

Now that you've loaded the dataset, your objective is to train a recurrent neural network to predict the temperature at a given time of day based on the weather information collected during an earlier period—say, two days. To do this, you'll need to reformat and normalize the data.

Reformatting

First, reshape the data to fit the expected format for training the recurrent neural network to predict temperature, using the code in Listing 7-5.

```
n_samples, n_features = data.shape[0], data.shape[1]
❶ past_seq = 2 * daily_samples
❷ lag = 72
❸ temp_idx = 1   # Temperature (Celsius) index

in_sequences, targets = [], []
for i in range(past_seq, n_samples - lag, daily_samples):
    in_sequences.append(data[i - past_seq:i, :])
    targets.append(data[i + lag:i + lag + 1, temp_idx])
in_sequences, targets = np.asarray(in_sequences), np.asarray(targets)
```

Listing 7-5: Reshaping the data for the recurrent neural network

This code extracts the total number of samples (n_samples) and the number of features (n_features, the 14 types of weather data). Then it defines the length of the sequences to be fed to the recurrent neural network as inputs ❶ (calculated as the number of days times the number of samples per day); the prediction lag ❷ (how many time steps ahead in time the recurrent neural network should predict temperature—72, providing the temperature at 12:00 PM of the following day); and the index of the target time series to be the temperature in degrees Celsius ❸. In the for loop, the code fills the input sequences with the time series, and the targets with the temperature values at the prediction time. Finally, the code converts the input sequences and targets into NumPy arrays.

Check the shape of the inputs via print(in_sequences.shape), which prints (2918, 288, 14), and check the shape of the targets via print(targets.shape), which prints (2918, 1). This means that you have 2,918 sequences for training and validating your neural network.

Now you'll need to determine which sequences to use for training and which to use for validation, using Listing 7-6.

```
import deeptrack as dt

sources = dt.sources.Source(inputs=in_sequences, targets=targets)
train_sources, val_sources = dt.sources.random_split(sources, [0.8, 0.2])
```

Listing 7-6: Splitting the data into training and validation datasets

This code defines the dataset sources and splits them into training and validation datasets in the proportions 80 percent and 20 percent.

Normalizing

Reviewing Figure 7-2, you can see that the data spans a broad range of values with features on considerably different scales, which isn't ideal for neural network training. In these conditions, some weights may update faster than others because the feature values influence the magnitude of the gradients used by the backpropagation algorithm. This can lead to slower convergence or even divergence of the learning algorithm.

To mitigate these issues, you can rescale all the features to a mean of 0 and a standard deviation of 1. This step simplifies the network's training. However, be careful not to inadvertently discard crucial information when normalizing your data. For example, temperature trends over months or years might show gradual shifts. Normalizing the data without considering these long-term trends can obscure meaningful patterns. A better approach might be detrending the data before applying normalization.

Listing 7-7 normalizes the data by subtracting the mean and dividing by the standard deviation of the training set, using DeepTrack2 pipelines.

```
import torch

train_mean = np.mean([src["inputs"] for src in train_sources], axis=(0, 1))
train_std = np.std([src["inputs"] for src in train_sources], axis=(0, 1))

inputs_pipeline = (dt.Value(sources.inputs - train_mean) / train_std
                   >> dt.pytorch.ToTensor(dtype=torch.float))
targets_pipeline = (dt.Value(sources.targets - train_mean[temp_idx])
                   / train_std[temp_idx])
```

Listing 7-7: Normalizing the data

This code calculates the mean and the standard deviation of the training dataset and defines pipelines to normalize the inputs and targets.

Preparing the Training and Validation Data Loaders

Finally, prepare the training and validation data loaders with Listing 7-8.

```
from torch.utils.data import DataLoader

train_dataset = dt.pytorch.Dataset(inputs_pipeline & targets_pipeline,
                                   inputs=train_sources)
val_dataset = dt.pytorch.Dataset(inputs_pipeline & targets_pipeline,
                                 inputs=val_sources)

train_loader = DataLoader(train_dataset, batch_size=32, shuffle=True)
val_loader = DataLoader(val_dataset, batch_size=32, shuffle=False)
```

Listing 7-8: Defining the data loaders for the training and validation datasets

This code creates the training and validation datasets and data loaders, which you'll use in the next sections to train and validate the neural networks.

Implementing a Commonsense Benchmark

You can now introduce a *commonsense benchmark*, which allows you to compare your network's results to a simple standard or "commonsense" method as a reference. This is good practice in machine learning in general because it provides a baseline to evaluate the performance of your model. Without such a benchmark, determining whether your model is genuinely effective can be difficult.

For temperature forecasting, a simple benchmark is to assume that the next day's temperature will be equal to the previous day's temperature at the same time. You can do this with Listing 7-9.

```
  temperature = data[:, temp_idx]
❶ benchmark_celsius = np.mean(
      np.abs(
          temperature[daily_samples + lag::daily_samples]
          - temperature[lag:-(daily_samples - lag):daily_samples]
      )
  )
❷ benchmark = benchmark_celsius / train_std[temp_idx]
```

Listing 7-9: Defining a commonsense benchmark

This code extracts the `temperature` time series. Then the code calculates the benchmark as the MAE between each day's temperatures at midday and the preceding day's temperatures at the same time ❶. Finally, the code normalizes the benchmark by the standard deviation of the training set ❷.

You can use `print(f"Benchmark Celsius: {benchmark_celsius}")` to print out the value of the benchmark, which is $2.67°C$. Then you can print out the value of the normalized benchmark with `print(f"Normalized Benchmark: {benchmark}")`, which is 0.32. You'll use the latter value to check whether your trained network outperforms this commonsense benchmark.

Now you can implement a recurrent neural network and use it to predict the temperature. In the following sections, you'll implement various recurrent neural networks and compare them with the commonsense benchmark you just defined. Before doing that, you need to choose an appropriate device for the computations.

Determining the Computational Device

Training recurrent neural networks is computationally expensive, making it important to select an appropriate device that ensures efficiency and speed. Usually, packages like PyTorch, Lightning, or Deeplay handle this selection automatically. However, understanding how to manually set the device can help you optimize the computation, especially when writing models from scratch, as you're doing in this chapter.

You can select the device via the `get_device()` function in Listing 7-10.

```
def get_device():
    """Select device where to perform the computations."""
    if torch.cuda.is_available():
     ❶ return torch.device("cuda:0")
    elif torch.backends.mps.is_available():
     ❷ return torch.device("mps")
    else:
     ❸ return torch.device("cpu")
```

Listing 7-10: The function to determine the device to be used for computations

This function selects a GPU if it's available ❶ ❷. If not, the function selects the CPU ❸. The cuda:0 statement selects the first GPU if multiple GPUs are available and is equivalent to just cuda in most cases. The mps statement selects the Apple Silicon GPU device on macOS, if available.

You can use this function with the code shown in Listing 7-11.

```
device = get_device()
```

Listing 7-11: Selecting the device to be used to perform the computations

You can now use print(device) to see which device has been selected, which will depend on your hardware.

NOTE
Unlike the Compute Unified Device Architecture (CUDA) *backend for PyTorch (which is highly stable and well tested for GPU computations), the integration of Apple's* Metal Performance Shaders (MPS) *backend is relatively recent. Therefore, you may encounter bugs or instabilities, especially when working with large tensors. These instabilities often manifest as inconsistent loss values or erratic gradients during training. If you experience such issues, you can try to reduce the model size (smaller models might reduce the load on the MPS backend and mitigate instability) or the batch size (decreasing the data batch size can help manage memory constraints and improve stability). If the issues persist, you can fall back to running the code on the CPU, which is more stable but significantly slower. Additionally, to ensure that training is proceeding as expected, consider comparing results between shorter training runs on the CPU and MPS. This comparison can help identify whether the instabilities are affecting the convergence of the model.*

Predicting with a Simple Recurrent Neural Network

You can now implement a simple recurrent neural network in PyTorch, as shown in Listing 7-12.

```
import torch.nn as nn

rnn = nn.RNN(input_size=in_sequences.shape[2], hidden_size=2, batch_first=True)
fc = nn.Linear(in_features=2, out_features=1)
❶ rnn.to(device); fc.to(device);
```

Listing 7-12: Defining a recurrent neural network in PyTorch

This code defines a simple recurrent neural network with two hidden units (rnn), which will transform the input time series into a sequence of hidden states. The code also separately defines a linear (fully connected) dense layer (fc), which will take the last hidden state of the network and use it to estimate the expected temperature. Finally, the computations are moved to the selected device ❶.

Training

Listing 7-13 provides a script for training this neural network. This is also a good example of a training loop written in PyTorch from scratch.

```
criterion = nn.L1Loss()  # MAE Loss
❶ parameter_list = list(rnn.parameters()) + list(fc.parameters())
optimizer = torch.optim.Adam(parameter_list, lr=0.001)

epochs = 100
for epoch in range(epochs):
    for in_sequences, targets in train_loader:
        ❷ optimizer.zero_grad()

        ❸ in_sequences, targets = in_sequences.to(device), targets.to(device)
        ❹ hidden_sequences, _ = rnn(in_sequences)  # RNN layer
        ❺ last_hidden_states = hidden_sequences[:, -1, :]  # Last hidden states
        ❻ predictions = fc(last_hidden_states)  # Linear layer

        loss = criterion(predictions, targets)
        ❼ loss.backward()
        ❽ optimizer.step()
    print(f"Epoch {epoch}")
```

Listing 7-13: Training the PyTorch recurrent neural network

This code defines the criterion used to calculate the loss. Then the parameters (weights and biases) of the recurrent neural network and the linear layer are combined into one list ❶, which is then passed to the optimizer to update during training. Next, the code trains the neural network for the set number of epochs.

In each epoch, the code iterates over the batches of data provided by train_loader. The loop first resets the gradients of the model parameters to 0 to prevent accumulation from previous iterations ❷. Then the code transfers the in_sequences and targets tensors to the device ❸, feeds the input sequences through the recurrent layer ❹, and selects the last hidden states of hidden_sequences returned by the recurrent layer ❺. These last hidden states are then passed through the linear layer ❻ to obtain the final output predictions of the next day's temperatures. The criterion computes the loss between the model's predictions and the actual targets, which is then used to calculate the gradients of the model parameters ❼. Finally, these gradients are used to update the model's weights during the optimization step ❽.

Monitoring the Training Loss

To gain more insights into the training process and ensure that the model is learning effectively, you can update Listing 7-13 to print the loss in each epoch, as shown in Listing 7-14. Monitoring the training loss helps you detect issues such as overfitting, underfitting, or convergence problems, allowing you to make necessary adjustments to the training parameters or model architecture.

```
--snip--
train_losses = []
for epoch in range(epochs):
    train_loss = 0.0
    for in_sequences, targets in train_loader:
        --snip--
      ❶ train_loss += loss.item()
    train_losses.append(train_loss / len(train_loader))
    print(f"Epoch {epoch} Training Loss: {train_losses[-1]:.4f}")
```

Listing 7-14: Printing the training loss for each epoch (by modifying Listing 7-13)

This updated code allows you to observe the training's progress. At the beginning of each training epoch, the code initializes the train_loss variable to track the loss accumulated over the epoch. Then the loss for each batch is added to the running total for the epoch ❶. Finally, the code saves the loss in the train_losses list and prints it.

Monitoring the Validation Loss

You can also monitor the evolution of the validation loss during training, using Listing 7-15.

```
--snip--
train_losses, val_losses = [], []
for epoch in range(epochs):
    --snip--
    val_loss = 0.0
  ❶ with torch.no_grad():
        for in_sequences, targets in val_loader:
            in_sequences, targets = in_sequences.to(device), targets.to(device)
            hidden_sequences, _ = rnn(in_sequences)
            last_hidden_states = hidden_sequences[:, -1, :]
            predictions = fc(last_hidden_states)

            loss = criterion(predictions, targets)
            val_loss += loss.item()
        val_losses.append(val_loss / len(val_loader))
        print(f"Epoch {epoch} Validation Loss: {val_losses[-1]:.4f}")
```

Listing 7-15: Monitoring the evolution of the validation loss (by modifying Listing 7-14)

This code calculates, saves, and prints the loss for the validation set. The calculations are similar to those of the training code in Listing 7-13, except that there is no backpropagation step, so the code is executed without calculating the gradients ❶.

Plotting the Training and Validation Losses

Visualizing the evolution of the training and validation losses can help you identify trends and potential issues during training, such as overfitting or underfitting. To plot the losses during training, you can implement the plot_training() function shown in Listing 7-16.

```
def plot_training(epochs, train_losses, val_losses, benchmark):
    """Plot the training and validation losses."""
    plt.plot(range(epochs), train_losses, label="Training Loss")
    plt.plot(range(epochs), val_losses, "--", label="Validation Loss")
    plt.plot([0, epochs - 1], [benchmark, benchmark], ":k", label="Benchmark")
    plt.xlabel("Epoch")
    plt.xlim([0, epochs - 1])
    plt.ylabel("Loss")
    plt.legend()
    plt.show()
```

Listing 7-16: The function to plot the training and validation losses

Then use plot_training() with this command:

```
plot_training(epochs, train_losses, val_losses, benchmark)
```

This should plot something similar to Figure 7-3.

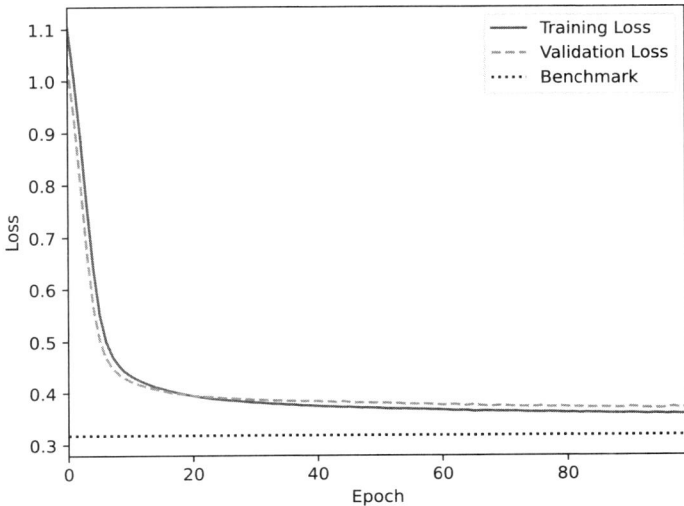

Figure 7-3: Training and validation losses for the simple recurrent neural network

The training and validation losses both decrease during training, reaching an MAE of about 0.36 for the training loss and 0.38 for the validation loss. Even though these results might appear good, they are worse than the 0.32 MAE obtained with the commonsense benchmark (represented by the dotted line). Therefore, this network has less predictive power than saying that the temperature will be the same as that of the preceding day. You'll see how to improve on this in the following sections.

Implementing the Network in Deeplay

Before proceeding, you can reimplement the preceding recurrent neural network in a more compact form by using Deeplay, as shown in Listing 7-17.

```
import deeplay as dl

rnn_dl = dl.RecurrentModel(
    in_features=n_features,
    hidden_features=[2],
    out_features=1,
  ❶ rnn_type="RNN",
)
❷ rnn_simple = dl.Regressor(rnn_dl, optimizer=dl.Adam(lr=0.001)).create()
```

Listing 7-17: Defining a recurrent neural network in Deeplay

Besides the number of input, hidden, and output features, you can further specify the type of network ❶, which here is set to RNN (the default value). You can visualize the model architecture via print(rnn_dl).

The code then compiles the neural network as a regression application that uses the Adam optimizer ❷. You can print out the details of this compiled application with print(rnn_simple).

You can train this recurrent neural network and display the learning curves with Listing 7-18.

```
trainer = dl.Trainer(max_epochs=epochs, accelerator="auto")
trainer.fit(rnn_simple, train_loader, val_loader)

train_losses = trainer.history.history["train_loss_epoch"]["value"]
val_losses = trainer.history.history["val_loss_epoch"]["value"][1:]
plot_training(epochs, train_losses, val_losses, benchmark)
```

Listing 7-18: Training the Deeplay recurrent neural network

This code creates a trainer that automatically checks the availability of an accelerating device (eliminating the need to use get_device() from Listing 7-10). The code then proceeds to the training via the fit() method of the trainer.

The losses calculated during training and validation are automatically logged in the history field of the trainer, where you can retrieve them. The plot of the training and validation losses should be similar to Figure 7-3, which you obtained by using the explicit PyTorch implementation in Listings 7-13, 7-14, and 7-15.

Stacking Multiple Recurrent Layers

To enhance the performance of your recurrent neural network, one straightforward strategy is to increase the number of recurrent layers and hidden-state features. In fact, stacking multiple recurrent layers can help the network capture more-complex patterns and dependencies in the time-series data.

You can think of *stacked recurrent neural networks* as individual recurrent modules linked together, with the output of one module acting as input to the next. Unlike the output layer, where only the final element of the output time series is returned, each layer of a stacked recurrent neural network forwards the entire time series it computes to the next layer. This permits each layer to process the entire time-dependent sequence, allowing the network to discover and understand the temporal patterns in the input data.

Similar to the deep convolutional neural networks you encountered in Chapter 3, the first layers tend to learn basic and generic features, while deeper layers can learn task-specific features. In this way, each subsequent layer can build a more sophisticated understanding of the sequential data, recognizing complex patterns based on the simpler patterns recognized by the previous layers.

With more parameters to adjust, stacked recurrent neural networks have a greater learning capacity, allowing them to analyze more-complex time series. These networks can remember information over longer sequences, which is beneficial for tasks that require understanding context over long time intervals.

However, stacking recurrent layers has potential downsides. As the number of layers increases, training the network becomes more difficult because the gradient can become too small (the vanishing gradient problem) or too large (exploding gradients) to propagate useful learning signals through all the layers. In addition, deeper networks have more parameters and are therefore more prone to overfitting, especially if the training data is limited.

You can implement a stacked recurrent neural network as shown in Listing 7-19.

```
rnn_dl = dl.RecurrentModel(
    in_features=n_features,
❶ hidden_features=[16, 16, 16],
    out_features=1,
    rnn_type="RNN",
)
❷ rnn_stacked = dl.Regressor(rnn_dl, optimizer=dl.Adam(lr=0.0001)).create()

trainer = dl.Trainer(max_epochs=epochs)
trainer.fit(rnn_stacked, train_loader, val_loader)
--snip--
```

Listing 7-19: Defining and training a stacked recurrent neural network (by modifying Listings 7-17 and 7-18)

This code updates the recurrent neural network to have three hidden layers, each with 16 features ❶. A lower learning rate ❷ helps smooth out the noise in the loss curve, ensuring more-stable convergence during training.

This stacked recurrent neural network has about 1,600 trainable parameters, whereas the simple architecture you used before (Listing 7-17) had only 39. Thanks to this increased number of trainable parameters, the stacked recurrent neural network achieves a better performance than the simple one, but it still only reaches an MAE similar to the commonsense benchmark. This indicates that while stacking layers enhances the model's capacity to learn, further improvement is still necessary. You'll now explore more-advanced architectures that achieve better predictive performance.

Using Gated Recurrent Units

Let's now introduce a different type of recurrent neural network, known as the *gated recurrent unit (GRU)*, shown in Figure 7-4.

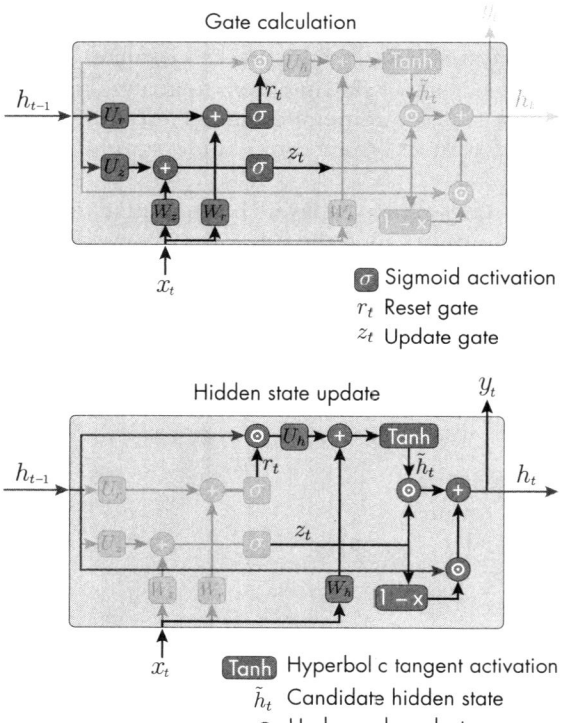

Figure 7-4: A gated recurrent unit (GRU)

As the name suggests, the GRU is characterized by the use of *gates*, a key feature in modern neural networks inspired by the gating functions found in biological neural systems. Gates play a crucial role in regulating the flow of information. They're designed to selectively retain or forget information depending on its relevance to the task at hand. They're typically implemented using activation functions that output values ranging from 0 to 1, acting as switches that can either block information or allow it to pass.

GRUs use two types of gates: the update gate and the reset gate. The *update gate* helps the model determine how much of the information from previous time steps needs to be passed along. This gate controls the extent to which the previous state influences the current state, balancing between old information and new inputs.

The *reset gate* is responsible for deciding how much of the past information should be forgotten as the network processes new inputs. This gate allows the GRU to discard information from the past that is deemed unnecessary for the current context or future predictions. A reset-gate value close to 0 allows the network to nearly forget the previous hidden state, treating the new input as the start of a new sequence. This capability is particularly useful when the sequence contains distinct segments of information that don't benefit from being combined with prior data. In contrast, a reset-gate value close to 1 retains the previous hidden state, indicating that the new input should be combined with the existing memory to inform the current state.

Since gating introduces additional parameters into the network, you can integrate dropout into the training process to reduce the risk of overfitting. *Dropout* randomly deactivates a subset of neurons during each training iteration, temporarily preventing them from contributing to the data processing. When these neurons are deactivated, other neurons are forced to learn to use the information formerly handled by the deactivated ones. Consequently, various neurons are forced to learn and adapt to the information, ensuring that no single neuron becomes overly specialized to specific traits of the training data.

A probability value determines the *dropout rate*, or the likelihood that any given neuron will be turned off at each step. This technique enhances the model's ability to generalize to new, unseen data—for example, to predict tomorrow's temperature. Importantly, dropout is used only during training; all neurons are fully active when the network makes predictions, such as during validation or testing.

Update the network architecture to incorporate a GRU and dropout as shown in Listing 7-20.

```
gru_dl = dl.RecurrentModel(
    in_features=n_features,
    hidden_features=[8, 8, 8],
    out_features=1,
    rnn_type="GRU",
    dropout=0.2,
)
gru_stacked = dl.Regressor(gru_dl, optimizer=dl.Adam(lr=0.001)).create()
--snip--
trainer.fit(gru_stacked, train_loader, val_loader)
--snip--
```

Listing 7-20: Defining and training a stacked GRU network (by modifying Listing 7-19)

This code sets the network type to GRU and introduces dropout with probability 0.2. The dropout is automatically applied to all the layers except the last one.

Figure 7-5 shows the resulting learning curves.

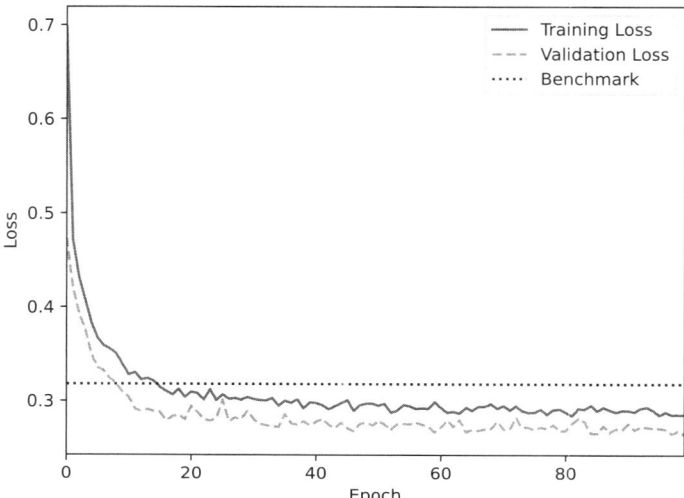

Figure 7-5: The training and validation losses for the recurrent neural network implemented with GRUs

The learning curves show a noticeable improvement over the simple recurrent neural network shown in Figure 7-3, achieving a validation loss of 0.27—substantially lower than the commonsense benchmark. Interestingly, the validation loss is consistently lower than the training loss throughout the training process thanks to the use of dropout, which randomly deactivates a subset of neurons during each training iteration. During validation, all neurons are active, allowing the model to use the full capacity of its learned features. In simpler terms, dropout helps the network learn better during training by preventing overfitting, and the model performs even better when all its neurons are used during validation.

Using Long Short-Term Memory Networks

A *long short-term memory (LSTM)* network is an alternative architecture that offers a more sophisticated gating mechanism than GRUs. LSTMs are particularly suited for tasks requiring the capture of long-term dependencies, such as language translation, speech recognition, and time-series forecasting—all cases where the influence of earlier data points is significant. Figure 7-6 shows the structure of an LSTM network.

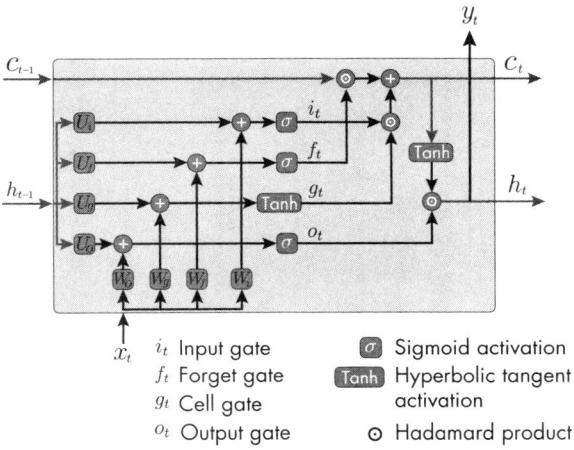

Figure 7-6: A long short-term memory (LSTM) unit

LSTMs incorporate four gates: the input gate, the forget gate, the cell gate, and the output gate. Together, these gates selectively preserve or eliminate information over various time intervals. Specifically, the *input gate* evaluates incoming data to identify crucial information used to update the state; the *forget gate* determines how much information from the previous state should be retained or discarded; the *cell gate*, also called the *candidate gate*, generates new candidate values for updating the cell state; and the *output gate* decides the composition of the next hidden state, influencing the network's subsequent outputs. More gating mechanisms generally result in a higher number of parameters for LSTMs compared to GRUs. This enhances the LSTMs' ability to model complex patterns while also increasing their risk of overfitting.

You can incorporate an LSTM as shown in Listing 7-21.

```
lstm_dl = dl.RecurrentModel(
    --snip--
    rnn_type="LSTM",
    dropout=0.3,
)
lstm_stacked = dl.Regressor(lstm_dl, optimizer=dl.Adam(lr=0.001)).create()
--snip--
trainer.fit(lstm_stacked, train_loader, val_loader)
--snip--
```

Listing 7-21: Defining and training a stacked LSTM network (by modifying Listing 7-20)

As in the GRU case, this code requires only changing the network type to LSTM. Furthermore, because the LSTM has more learnable parameters than the GRU, the code increases the dropout rate to 0.3.

Figure 7-7 shows the resulting learning curves.

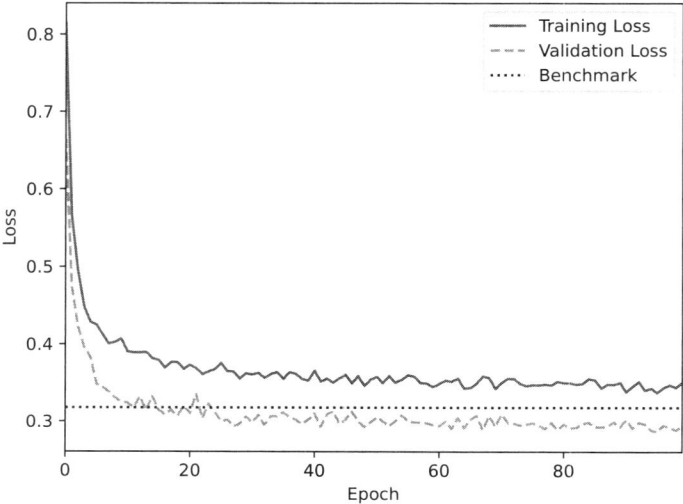

Figure 7-7: The training and validation losses for the recurrent neural network implemented with LSTM units

The behavior of the learning curves is qualitatively similar to that observed for the GRU in Figure 7-5, achieving a similar validation loss of about 0.27, well below the commonsense benchmark. However, although these LSTM units achieve results similar to GRUs, LSTMs generally are likely to outperform GRUs in more-complex tasks involving crucial long-term dependencies, such as in language modeling, speech recognition, and financial time-series forecasting.

As in the GRU case, the validation loss remains consistently lower than the training loss because of the use of dropout. This difference is accentuated by the higher dropout rate of 0.3 used in the LSTM units, compared to 0.2 in the GRUs.

NOTE *Code Example 7-1: "Predicting Temperatures Using Recurrent Neural Networks," is available at* https://github.com/DeepTrackAI/DeepLearningCrashCourse. *Navigate to the* Ch07_RNN *folder and then* ec07_1_rnn. *The* rnn.ipynb *notebook provides a complete code example that uses various kinds of recurrent neural networks to predict the temperature in the Jena Climate dataset.*

EXERCISE

7-4: Construct a network that combines a stacked LSTM with a preliminary dense network layer for preprocessing. This dense layer provides a trainable embedding layer. After training this composite model, evaluate its performance against that of the stand-alone stacked LSTM.

Project 7A: Translating with Recurrent Neural Networks

Recurrent neural networks excel at processing sequences performing *sequence-to-sequence* (*seq2seq*) transformations. Because natural language sentences are essentially sequences of words, recurrent neural networks are ideal for *natural language processing (NLP)* tasks such as translation, summarization, and question answering. In general, NLP involves the interaction between computers and humans via natural language, with applications ranging from machine translation and sentiment analysis to chatbots.

To understand how this works, consider the task of translation. In a *seq2seq model*, an encoder recurrent neural network reads and processes a source language sentence word by word, capturing the meaning of the entire sentence into its internal hidden state. This state, often called the *context vector*, is then passed to the decoder. The decoder generates the output sentence. Starting with the context vector from the encoder, the decoder begins generating the sentence in the target language word by word. Each generated word becomes part of the input for the next step in the sequence, along with the updated internal state of the decoder's recurrent neural network. By learning to transform the source language sentence (input sequence) into a target language sentence (output sequence), the model effectively learns to map patterns from one language to another.

In this project, you'll use recurrent neural networks to implement a seq2seq model to translate sentences from English to Spanish. For example, given the English sentence "The cat sits on the mat," your encoder will process each word, compressing this information into a context vector. Your decoder will then use this vector to produce the Spanish sentence "El gato se sienta en la alfombra" one word at a time. Using this ability to transform sequences of words, you'll also learn to develop neural networks to handle other NLP tasks.

Preparing the Bilingual Dataset

To train the seq2seq model, you'll use data from the ManyThings.org website at *https://www.manythings.org/anki/*. This platform hosts numerous datasets, referred to as *Anki decks*, which consist of flash cards with bilingual sentence pairs across various language combinations. Each dataset is downloadable in a simple text format, typically as a *.txt* file with the naming convention *language_1-language_2.txt*. This file is known as a *corpus file* and contains thousands of sentence pairs; each pair consists of a sentence in one language and its translation into another. This structure is ideally suited for training translation models.

You'll use the *eng-spa.txt* file with English-to-Spanish translations. Here are some excerpts from this file:

```
Go. Ve. CC-BY 2.0 ...
Go. Vete. CC-BY 2.0 ...
Go. Vaya. CC-BY 2.0 ...
Go. Váyase. CC-BY 2.0 ...
```

```
Hi. Hola. CC-BY 2.0 ...
--snip--
Cheer up! ¡Anímate! CC-BY 2.0 ...
Cheer up! Anímate. CC-BY 2.0 ...
Cheer up. Venga. CC-BY 2.0 ...
--snip--
```

Each line consists of a sentence in English followed by its Spanish translation, with some metadata at the end, separated by tab characters.

Before using this data to train and test the translation model, some preprocessing is necessary. This includes loading the raw text data, tokenizing it, building vocabularies, and preprocessing the data for the model. You'll finally construct data loaders to facilitate efficient batching during training and testing.

Tokenizing the Sentences

The first preprocessing step is *tokenization*, which breaks sentences into individual words, or *tokens*. Listing 7-22 defines a tokenize() function that splits the input text into tokens based on punctuation and whitespaces.

```
import spacy

❶ tokenizers = {"eng": spacy.blank("en"), "spa": spacy.blank("es")}

def tokenize(text, lang="eng"):
    """Tokenize text."""
    tokens = tokenizers[lang](text)
    return tokens
```

Listing 7-22: The function to tokenize a sentence

This code first initializes the English and Spanish tokenizers by using spaCy models ❶. Since loading spaCy models can be time-consuming because it requires loading large model files into memory and initializing various components, the code executes this initialization outside the tokenize() function to run it only once and minimize the initialization overhead.

The output of this function is a spaCy Doc object, which contains a sequence of Token objects representing the individual words and symbols extracted from the input text. Each token in this Doc object can be accessed by using a loop or by converting the Doc object into a list of strings. For example, you can tokenize a sentence by using

```
print([token.text for token in tokenize("This is a simple example!")])
```

which results in:

```
['This', 'is', 'a', 'simple', 'example', '!']
```

You can see that each word and punctuation mark has been separated.

Handling Contractions

Basic tokenization may not be sufficient for complex sentences, especially those containing contractions. While contractions are commonly used in English, language models can struggle with them because they can represent the same idea in multiple forms, leading to inconsistencies in understanding. Listing 7-23 enhances the tokenize() function by expanding English contractions into their full forms.

```
import contractions, spacy
--snip--
def tokenize(text, lang="eng"):
    """Tokenize text."""
    text = contractions.fix(text) if lang == "eng" else text
    tokens = tokenizers[lang](text)
    return tokens
```

Listing 7-23: The function to tokenize a sentence while expanding contractions (by modifying Listing 7-22)

Once you've finished, use this updated function with

```
print([token.text for token in tokenize("This isn't the same example!")])
```

which results in:

```
['This', 'is', 'not', 'the', 'same', 'example', '!']
```

Note that "isn't" is handled correctly.

Removing Noise

Text data often contains elements that are irrelevant to the task, such as some punctuation and nonalphabetic characters. These elements are treated as noise in the context of NLP. Listing 7-24 further refines the tokenize() function by removing such noise.

```
import contractions, re, spacy, unicodedata
--snip--
regular_expression = r"^[a-zA-Z0-9áéíóúüñÁÉÍÓÚÜÑ.,!?¡¿/:()]+$"
pattern = re.compile(unicodedata.normalize("NFC", regular_expression))

def tokenize(text, lang="eng"):
    """Tokenize text."""
❶  swaps = {"'": "'", "'": "'", """: '"', """: '"', "´": "'", "´´": "'"}
    for old, new in swaps.items():
        text = text.replace(old, new)
    text = contractions.fix(text) if lang == "eng" else text
    tokens = tokenizers[lang](text)
❷  return [token.text for token in tokens if pattern.match(token.text)]
```

Listing 7-24: The function to tokenize a sentence while dealing with contractions and removing noise (by modifying Listing 7-23)

This function replaces various types of quotation marks and apostrophes with their ASCII equivalents ❶. Tokens are then filtered to retain only those matching a regular expression (pattern) that consist of alphanumeric characters (a-zA-Z0-9) or some punctuation marks (.,!?¡¿/:()). Note that now the returned tokens are already strings of text and not Token objects contained in a Doc object ❷.

For example, you can use this function with

```
print([token for token in tokenize("Double-check your code!")])
```

which results in:

```
['Double', 'check', 'your', 'code', '!']
```

The code has correctly separated the compound word Double-check.

NOTE *In Unicode, the widely adopted text-encoding standard, some characters can be encoded in different ways. Characters with accent marks (used in some languages, such as Spanish and French), like the letter é, can be represented as either a single precomposed character (é), known as Normalization Form C (NFC), or the base letter e followed by a combining accent mark (´), known as Normalization Form D (NFD). Having different representations of the same character exist in the text could lead to mismatches during tokenization and filtering. The unicode.normalize() function normalizes the text to NFC to ensure consistency in the way characters are represented. Applying NFC standardizes these characters into their precomposed form, ensuring that all instances of the same character are handled uniformly throughout the processing pipeline. This reduces the risk of errors and ensures that pattern matching works reliably. When working exclusively with non-accented languages like English, normalization might not have a significant impact. In addition, characters like ´, `, ´´, and `` can have different representations that might cause similar issues if not handled properly.*

Implementing a Corpus Iterator

Next, you need the corpus_iterator() function in Listing 7-25 to apply this tokenization to all the sentences contained in the datafile.

```
def corpus_iterator(filename, lang, lang_position):
    """Read and tokenize texts by iterating through a corpus file."""
    with open(filename, "r", encoding="utf-8") as file:
        for line in file:
            sentences = line.strip().split("\t")
            sentence = unicodedata.normalize("NFC", sentences[lang_position])
            yield tokenize(sentence, lang)
```

Listing 7-25: The function to read and tokenize sentences by iterating through a corpus file

This function opens the specified file in read mode with UTF-8 encoding to ensure compatibility with various languages and special characters. The function reads the file line by line. Each line contains a sentence in the source language and its translation in the target language, separated by a tab character. The function strips any extraneous whitespace from the line and splits it into components based on the tab character. The function then selects either the first (English) or second (Spanish) element (identified by lang_position) of the split line as the sentence to be tokenized and normalizes it to NFC. Finally, the function tokenizes the selected text via the tokenize() function and yields the tokenized sentence for further processing.

Building a Vocabulary

Once the text has been tokenized and cleaned, the next step is to convert these tokens into numerical representations. This involves building a *vocabulary* that maps each unique token to an integer.

Start by implementing the Vocab class in Listing 7-26.

```
class Vocab:
    """Vocabulary as callable dictionary."""

    def __init__(self, vocab_dict, unk_token="<unk>"):
        """Initialize vocabulary."""
        self.vocab_dict, self.unk_token = vocab_dict, unk_token
        self.default_index = vocab_dict.get(unk_token, -1)
        self.index_to_token = {idx: token for token, idx in vocab_dict.items()}

    def __call__(self, token_or_tokens):
        """Return the index(es) for given token or list of tokens."""
        if not isinstance(token_or_tokens, list):
            return self.vocab_dict.get(token_or_tokens, self.default_index)
        else:
            return [self.vocab_dict.get(token, self.default_index)
                    for token in token_or_tokens]

    def set_default_index(self, index):
        """Set default index for unknown tokens."""
        self.default_index = index

    def lookup_token(self, index_or_indices):
        """Retrieve token corresponding to given index or list of indices."""
        if not isinstance(index_or_indices, list):
            return self.index_to_token.get(int(index_or_indices),
                                           self.unk_token)
        else:
            return [self.index_to_token.get(int(index), self.unk_token)
                    for index in index_or_indices]

    def get_tokens(self):
        """Return a list of tokens ordered by their index."""
        tokens = [None] * len(self.index_to_token)
        for index, token in self.index_to_token.items():
            tokens[index] = token
        return tokens
```

```
    def __iter__(self):
        """Iterate over the tokens in the vocabulary."""
        return iter(self.vocab_dict)

    def __len__(self):
        """Return the number of tokens in the vocabulary."""
        return len(self.vocab_dict)

    def __contains__(self, token):
        """Check if a token is in the vocabulary."""
        return token in self.vocab_dict
```

Listing 7-26: The class to represent a vocabulary

This class is a wrapper around a dictionary that can be used as a vocabulary. The class allows for a quick lookup of the index corresponding to a given token (or list of tokens), or the reverse operation of retrieving the token for a given index (or list of indices).

For example, if you have a vocabulary dictionary like

```
vocab_dict = {"hello": 0, "world": 1, "<unk>": 2}
```

you can instantiate a Vocab object using:

```
vocab = Vocab(vocab_dict)
```

With this object, you can look up the index of a token: vocab("hello") will return 0, and vocab("unknown") will return 2 (the index for <unk>). Similarly, you can retrieve the token corresponding to an index: vocab.lookup_token(1) will return "world" and vocab.lookup_token(5) will return "<unk>".

To automatically construct a vocabulary from a collection of tokenized sentences, you can use the build_vocab_from_iterator() function, as defined in Listing 7-27.

```
from collections import Counter

def build_vocab_from_iterator(iterator, specials=None, min_freq=1):
    """Build vocabulary from an iterator over tokenized sentences."""
    token_freq = Counter(token for tokens in iterator for token in tokens)
    vocab, index = {}, 0
    if specials:
        for token in specials:
            vocab[token] = index
            index += 1
    for token, freq in token_freq.items():
        if freq >= min_freq:
            vocab[token] = index
            index += 1
    return vocab
```

Listing 7-27: The function to build a vocabulary from an iterator

This function constructs a vocabulary from an iterator over tokenized sentences. The iterator could be a list of lists, with each inner list containing the tokens from a particular sentence. The function counts the frequency of each token via the Counter class from Python's collections module, allowing you to filter out infrequent tokens by specifying a minimum frequency (min_freq). Additionally, the function supports the inclusion of special tokens such as "<unk>" (unknown) or "<pad>" (padding). These special tokens can be passed through the specials argument, and they will be added to the vocabulary before the other tokens, ensuring that they have reserved indices.

For example, you can use this function to build a vocabulary from a list of tokenized sentences:

```
tokenized_sentences = [["this", "is", "an", "example"],
                       ["another", "example", "sentence"]
                       ["this", "is", "a", "test"]]
vocab_dict = build_vocab_from_iterator(
    tokenized_sentences, specials=["<unk>", "<pad>"], min_freq=1,
)
```

Using print(vocab_dict), you should get the following:

```
{ "<unk>": 0, "<pad>": 1, "this": 2, "is": 3, "an": 4, "example": 5,
"another": 6, "sentence": 7, "a": 8, "test": 9 }
```

In this example, each unique token that appears at least once is assigned a unique index, starting with the special tokens "<unk>" and "<pad>" at indices 0 and 1, respectively. Tokens like "this", "is", and "example" follow in the order of their appearance.

You can now implement the build_vocab() function to build the vocabulary, as shown in Listing 7-28.

```
def build_vocab(filename, lang, lang_position, specials=["<unk>"], min_freq=5):
    """Build vocabulary."""
    vocab_dict = build_vocab_from_iterator(
        corpus_iterator(filename, lang, lang_position), specials, min_freq,
    )
    vocab = Vocab(vocab_dict, unk_token=specials[0])
❶ vocab.set_default_index(vocab(specials[0]))
    return vocab
```

Listing 7-28: The function to build a vocabulary from a corpus file

This function uses the build_vocab_from_iterator() function from Listing 7-27 to construct the vocabulary with the iterator returned by the corpus_iterator() function from Listing 7-25. The min_freq parameter sets the minimum frequency a word must have to be included in the vocabulary, and the specials parameter sets the special tokens to be included. These special tokens, such as "<unk>" (unknown), "<pad>" (padding), "<sos>" (start of sentence), and "<eos>" (end of sentence), are crucial for handling common NLP tasks like padding sequences to a given length or marking sentence boundaries. Finally, the default index for the vocabulary is set to the index of the first special token ❶. If no special tokens are indicated, this will be set by default to the string "<unk>".

Use this function to create the input and output vocabularies, as shown in Listing 7-29.

```
in_lang, out_lang, filename = "eng", "spa", "eng-spa.txt"
specials = ["<pad>", "<sos>", "<eos>", "<unk>"]

in_vocab = build_vocab(filename, in_lang, lang_position=0, specials=specials)
out_vocab = build_vocab(filename, out_lang, lang_position=1, specials=specials)
```

Listing 7-29: Building the vocabularies

This code defines the input language (in_lang) and the output language (out_lang) as well as the filename containing the list of translated sentences. The list of special tokens that need to be included in the vocabularies is then defined: "<pad>" for padding, "<sos>" for start of a sequence, "<eos>" for end of a sequence, and "<unk>" for unknown words. Finally, the code builds the vocabularies for the input language (in_vocab) and for the target language (out_vocab).

Preparing the Datasets and Data Loaders

When using a corpus to train a network for translation tasks, sentences must be tokenized, validated against a vocabulary, padded to ensure that all sequences are of a consistent length, and transformed into a format suitable for machine learning models.

You'll need the all_words_in_vocab() function in Listing 7-30 to check whether all words in a sentence are present in a vocabulary.

```
def all_words_in_vocab(sentence, vocab):
    """Check whether all words in a sentence are present in a vocabulary"""
    return all(word in vocab for word in sentence)
```

Listing 7-30: The function to check whether all words in a sentence are present in a vocabulary

Then you'll need the pad() function in Listing 7-31 to pad a sequence of tokens to a predefined length.

```
def pad(tokens, max_length=10):
    """Pad sequence of tokens."""
    padding_length = max_length - len(tokens)
    return ["<sos>"] + tokens + ["<eos>"] + ["<pad>"] * padding_length
```

Listing 7-31: The function to pad a sequence of tokens

This function takes a sequence of words, adds the special tokens for the start of the sentence ("<sos>") and for the end of the sentence ("<eos>"), and pads the sentence to a designated maximum length with a padding token

("<pad>"). In calculating the length of the token sequence, the "<sos>" and "<eos>" special tokens are ignored.

Finally, you'll need the process() function in Listing 7-32 to process the entire corpus file.

```python
import numpy as np

def process(filename, in_lang, out_lang, in_vocab, out_vocab, max_length=10):
    """Process language corpus."""
    in_sequences, out_sequences = [], []
    with open(filename, "r", encoding="utf-8") as file:
        for line in file:
          ❶ sentences = line.strip().split("\t")
            in_tokens = tokenize(unicodedata.normalize("NFC", sentences[0]),
                                 in_lang)
            out_tokens = tokenize(unicodedata.normalize("NFC", sentences[1]),
                                  out_lang)

            if (all_words_in_vocab(in_tokens, in_vocab)
                and len(in_tokens) <= max_length
                and all_words_in_vocab(out_tokens, out_vocab)
                and len(out_tokens) <= max_length):

                padded_in_tokens = pad(in_tokens)
                in_sequence = in_vocab(padded_in_tokens)
                in_sequences.append(in_sequence)

                padded_out_tokens = pad(out_tokens)
                out_sequence = out_vocab(padded_out_tokens)
                out_sequences.append(out_sequence)
    return np.array(in_sequences), np.array(out_sequences)
```

Listing 7-32: The function to process the language corpus

This function reads each line and splits it into input and output sentences based on the tab delimiter ❶. Then the function normalizes the sentences to NFC and tokenizes them (in_tokens and out_tokens). If in_tokens and out_tokens meet a set of criteria (all words are in the respective vocabularies and don't exceed the maximum length), the function pads them, transforms them into numerical sequences according to the word indices defined in the vocabularies, and appends them to the in_sequences and out_sequences lists. Finally, the function converts the output lists into NumPy arrays and returns them.

You can now use the process() function to preprocess the text corpus and the preprocessed data as a source to build the data loaders, as shown in Listing 7-33.

```python
import deeplay as dl
import deeptrack as dt
import torch
```

```
in_sequences, out_sequences = \
    process(filename, in_lang, out_lang, in_vocab, out_vocab)

sources = dt.sources.Source(inputs=in_sequences, targets=out_sequences)
train_sources, test_sources = dt.sources.random_split(sources, [0.85, 0.15])

inputs_pip = dt.Value(sources.inputs) >> dt.pytorch.ToTensor(dtype=torch.int)
outputs_pip = dt.Value(sources.targets) >> dt.pytorch.ToTensor(dtype=torch.int)

train_dataset = \
    dt.pytorch.Dataset(inputs_pip & outputs_pip, inputs=train_sources)
test_dataset = \
    dt.pytorch.Dataset(inputs_pip & outputs_pip, inputs=test_sources)

train_loader = dl.DataLoader(train_dataset, batch_size=256, shuffle=True)
test_loader = dl.DataLoader(test_dataset, batch_size=256, shuffle=False)
```

Listing 7-33: Building the datasets and data loaders

This code begins by processing the corpus file with the process() function. Then the code creates the sources object to house both the input and
output sequences. The sources object is split into training and test sets according to the proportions 85 percent and 15 percent, respectively. Next,
DeepTrack2 pipelines are created for both inputs (inputs_pip) and targets
(outputs_pip) to transform the data into PyTorch tensors. The train_dataset
and test_dataset objects are created to associate inputs and targets with their
respective sources. Finally, the code creates the train_loader and test_loader
data loaders to handle data batching.

Defining the Sequence-to-Sequence Application

A typical seq2seq model consists of two main components: an encoder and
a decoder. The encoder focuses on reading and understanding the input
sequence, such as a sentence in English, and compressing it into a rich context vector. This context vector is like a mental snapshot of what the input
sequence represents—for example, a summary that captures the meaning of
the entire input sentence. The decoder then takes this context vector and
transforms it into a meaningful output sequence, such as the translation into
a Spanish sentence.

Implementing the Encoder

The encoder reads the input sequence representing a sentence and converts
each index representing a word into an *embedding*, which is a vector representation that captures the semantic meaning of the word that the neural
network can more easily process. Each word's embedding is then fed into a
recurrent neural network. As each word is processed, the recurrent neural

network updates its internal state contained in its context vector. After processing the last word, the context vector provides a compact representation of the meaning of the entire input sentence.

Listing 7-34 shows the `Seq2SeqEncoder` class that implements this encoder logic.

```
class Seq2SeqEncoder(dl.DeeplayModule):
    """Sequence-to-sequence encoder."""

    def __init__(self, vocab_size, in_feats=300, hidden_feats=128,
                 hidden_layers=1, dropout=0.0):
        """Initialize sequence-to-sequence encoder."""
        super().__init__()
        self.hidden_feats, self.hidden_layers = hidden_feats, hidden_layers

  ❶     self.embedding = dl.Layer(torch.nn.Embedding, vocab_size, in_feats)
  ❷     self.rnn = dl.Layer(torch.nn.GRU, input_size=in_feats,
                            hidden_size=hidden_feats, num_layers=hidden_layers,
                            dropout=(0 if hidden_layers == 1 else dropout),
                            bidirectional=True, batch_first=True)

    def forward(self, in_sequences, contexts=None):
        """Calculate the encoded sequences and contexts."""
        in_embeddings = self.embedding(in_sequences)
  ❸     encoded_sequences, contexts = self.rnn(in_embeddings, contexts)
  ❹     encoded_sequences = (encoded_sequences[:, :, :self.hidden_feats]
                             + encoded_sequences[:, :, self.hidden_feats:])
  ❺     contexts = contexts[:self.hidden_layers]
        return encoded_sequences, contexts
```

Listing 7-34: The class implementing the encoder network

The encoder has two components: the embedding layer ❶ and the recurrent neural network layer ❷. The *embedding layer* converts token indices into vectors of a fixed size (`in_feats`), which are the embeddings corresponding to the words in the input vocabulary of size `vocab_size`. The *recurrent neural network layer* processes the sequence of embeddings and provides two outputs ❸: `encoded_sequences` and `contexts`. Both outputs correspond to hidden states of the recurrent neural network: `encoded_sequences` contains the hidden state of the last layer for every token, whereas `contexts` contains the hidden state of the last step for every layer.

The `forward()` method defines how the input sequences are transformed as they pass through the network layers. It takes a batch of input sequences and context vectors (set to `None` by default). The input sequences first pass through the embedding layer. The recurrent neural network layer then processes the embedded sequences, returning some encoded sequences (`encoded_sequences`, which won't be used by the decoder) and new context vectors (which will serve to initialize the decoder's context vectors).

The recurrent neural network of the encoder is set to be bidirectional via bidirectional=True ❷ because this allows the network to capture both past and future context within the input sequence, providing a more comprehensive understanding of each word's meaning in relation to the entire sentence. Therefore, the code of the forward pass sums the encoded sequences from both directions to combine the forward and backward contextual information ❹, and discards the context vectors from the backward pass, retaining only the context vectors from the forward pass (which corresponds to the first half of the bidirectional context vector) ❺.

Implementing the Decoder

The decoder's role is to generate an output sequence from the encoded data. The decoder translates the context vector obtained by the encoder into a new sequence, thus translating the input sentence into the target language. Listing 7-35 shows the Seq2SeqDecoder class that implements the decoder network by taking the context vector from the encoder and generating the target sequence word by word.

```
class Seq2SeqDecoder(dl.DeeplayModule):
    """Sequence-to-sequence decoder."""

    def __init__(self, vocab_size, in_feats=300, hidden_feats=128,
                 hidden_layers=1, dropout=0.0):
        """Initialize sequence-to-sequence decoder."""
        super().__init__()

        self.embedding = dl.Layer(torch.nn.Embedding, vocab_size, in_feats)
        self.rnn = dl.Layer(torch.nn.GRU, input_size=in_feats,
                            hidden_size=hidden_feats, num_layers=hidden_layers,
                      ❶ bidirectional=False, batch_first=True,
                            dropout=(0 if hidden_layers == 1 else dropout))
        self.dense = dl.Layer(torch.nn.Linear, hidden_feats, vocab_size)
        self.softmax = dl.Layer(torch.nn.Softmax, dim=-1)

    def forward(self, decoder_in_values, contexts):
        """Calculate the decoder outputs and contexts."""
        out_embeddings = self.embedding(decoder_in_values)
        decoder_outputs, contexts = self.rnn(out_embeddings, contexts)
        decoder_outputs = self.dense(decoder_outputs)
        decoder_outputs = self.softmax(decoder_outputs)
        return decoder_outputs, contexts
```

Listing 7-35: The class implementing the decoder network

The decoder has a similar structure as the encoder. However, the decoder is typically unidirectional ❶ because it generates the output sequence in the forward direction, building on the values of the output sequence it's generating step-by-step.

The `forward()` method of the decoder is more complex than that of the encoder because it needs to generate coherent and contextually appropriate outputs. The code operates on `decoder_in_values`, a tensor containing the index values of a single word for each sequence of the batch, and transforms them into embeddings. Next, the recurrent neural network processes `out_embeddings` along with the previous `contexts` to produce the decoder outputs and new context vectors. These outputs are transformed by the dense layer and converted into probability distributions across the vocabulary by the softmax function. Finally, `forward()` returns the softmax probabilities (which can be interpreted as the probabilistic predictions of the next tokens' indexes in the decoder output sequences) and the new context vectors.

Instead of directly predicting the next value of the output sequence, the decoder generates a probability distribution over the entire vocabulary. Then it selects the most likely word index from this distribution and adds the corresponding word to the output sequence. This process is repeated for each subsequent word index in the output sequence until the full output is generated, enabling the model to produce a coherent translation.

Combining the Encoder and the Decoder

Now that you've implemented both the encoder and the decoder, you can combine them into the full seq2seq model to translate text sequences from one language to another. Figure 7-8 shows the overall architecture as well as the data flow.

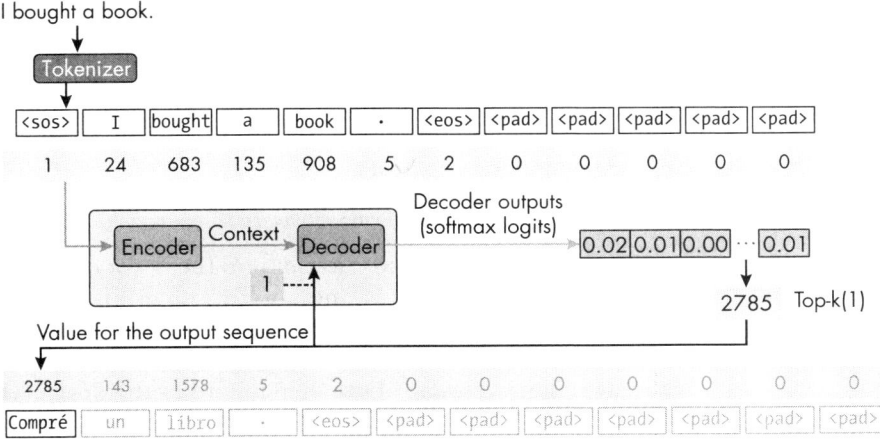

Figure 7-8: The seq2seq architecture for translation

Listing 7-36 shows the resulting model.

```
class Seq2SeqModel(dl.DeeplayModule):
    """Sequence-to-sequence model."""

    def __init__(self, in_vocab_size=None, out_vocab_size=None, embed_dim=300,
            hidden_feats=128, hidden_layers=1, dropout=0.0):
        """Initialize the sequence-to-sequence model."""
```

```
        super().__init__()
        self.in_vocab_size, self.out_vocab_size = in_vocab_size, out_vocab_size

        self.encoder = Seq2SeqEncoder(in_vocab_size, embed_dim, hidden_feats,
                                      hidden_layers, dropout)
        self.decoder = Seq2SeqDecoder(out_vocab_size, embed_dim, hidden_feats,
                                      hidden_layers, dropout)

    def forward(self, batch):
        """Calculate the decoder output vectors for the input sequences."""
        in_sequences, out_sequences = batch
        num_sequences, sequence_length = in_sequences.size()
❶   device = next(self.encoder.parameters()).device

❷   _, contexts = self.encoder(in_sequences)

        decoder_outputs_vec = torch.zeros(num_sequences, sequence_length,
                                          self.out_vocab_size).to(device)
❸   decoder_in_values = torch.full(size=(num_sequences, 1),
                                   fill_value=1, device=device)  # <sos>
        for t in range(sequence_length):
            decoder_outputs, contexts = \
                self.decoder(decoder_in_values, contexts)
          ❹ decoder_outputs_vec[:, t, :] = decoder_outputs.squeeze(1)

          ❺ _, top_decoder_outputs = decoder_outputs.topk(1)
          ❻ decoder_in_values = \
                top_decoder_outputs.squeeze(-1).detach().to(device)

        return decoder_outputs_vec
```

Listing 7-36: The class implementing the full seq2seq model

This class combines the encoder and the decoder to create the complete
seq2seq model. The forward() method first determines the computational
device used by the model ❶. Here, self.encoder.parameters() retrieves the
parameters (weights and biases) of the encoder, and next() extracts the first
parameter. The device attribute then identifies the device where this parameter is stored. This device will be used to ensure that all tensors and operations are placed on the appropriate device, whether it's a CPU or GPU.

Then the forward() method passes the input sequences through the encoder. The encoder generates a set of encoded outputs (which will be ignored by the decoder and therefore are not returned) and context vectors
that capture the contextual information of the input sequences ❷.

Next, it's the turn of the decoder, which constructs the decoder outputs
word by word in a for loop that saves the decoder outputs for each iteration
in the decoder_outputs_vec PyTorch tensor ❹. Each step's output depends
on the preceding steps' outputs, making the process inherently sequential

and dependent on prior results. In its first iteration, the decoder receives initial input sequences initialized to the indexes corresponding to the "<sos>" special token ❸ and the context vectors generated by the encoder ❷. In the subsequent interactions, the code selects the most-likely-word index from the probability distribution returned by the decoder in the preceding iteration ❺. Then it uses this word index to define the input to pass to the decoder ❻, while using the context vectors generated by the decoder in the preceding iteration. In this way, the decoder generates the next word indices step-by-step.

You can improve the training of this model by using *teacher forcing*. In this training strategy, the actual target-word indices (corresponding to the correct translations from the ground truth) are used as the next input to the decoder with a certain probability, while otherwise the model's prediction from the preceding time step is used. This training technique is implemented in Listing 7-37.

```
class Seq2SeqModel(dl.DeeplayModule):
    """"Sequence-to-sequence model.""

    def __init__(..., teacher_prob=1.0):
        --snip--
        self.teacher_prob = teacher_prob

    def forward(self, batch):
        --snip--
        for t in range(sequence_length):
            --snip--

            if (np.random.rand() < self.teacher_prob
                and t < sequence_length - 1):  # Teacher forcing
                decoder_in_values = \
                    out_sequences[:, t + 1].unsqueeze(-1).to(device)
            else:  # Model prediction
                _, top_decoder_outputs = decoder_outputs.topk(1)
                decoder_in_values = \
                    top_decoder_outputs.squeeze(-1).detach().to(device)

        return decoder_outputs_vec
```

Listing 7-37: The class implementing the full seq2seq model with teacher forcing (by modifying Listing 7-36)

Now the actual target-word indices are used as the next input to the decoder with probability teacher_prob, while otherwise the model's prediction from the preceding time step is used. Setting teacher_prob to different levels has various effects: A high probability (closer to 1) helps the model learn more quickly and accurately when the correct sequences are provided but may cause the model to struggle during inference without the ground truth; a low probability (closer to 0) makes the model more robust to errors and improves performance during inference, though it may slow training and make convergence less stable. Finding the right balance is key to effective training and often requires experimentation. When training recurrent neural networks, this strategy speeds up training and often leads to more stable convergence. However, this approach can also lead to the model becoming overly reliant on the ground truth during training and not learning to recover from its own mistakes—a phenomenon called *exposure bias*.

To evaluate the model on unseen data, the `Seq2SeqModel` class needs an `evaluate()` method that uses a similar approach to the `forward()` method but without teacher forcing. In fact, during evaluation, you need to perform the inference without access to the ground truth for the next value in the sequence of word indices. You can implement this method with Listing 7-38.

```python
class Seq2SeqModel(dl.DeeplayModule):
    """Sequence-to-sequence model with evaluation method."""
    --snip--

    def evaluate(self, in_sequences):
        """Evaluate model."""
        num_sequences, sequence_length = in_sequences.size()
        device = next(self.encoder.parameters()).device

        with torch.no_grad():
            _, contexts = self.encoder(in_sequences)

        pred_sequences = torch.zeros(num_sequences, sequence_length).to(device)
        decoder_in_values = torch.full(size=(num_sequences, 1),
                                       fill_value=1, device=device)  # <sos>
        for t in range(sequence_length):
            with torch.no_grad():
                decoder_outputs, contexts = \
                    self.decoder(decoder_in_values, contexts)
            _, top_decoder_outputs = decoder_outputs.topk(1)
            pred_sequences[:, t] = top_decoder_outputs.squeeze()

            decoder_in_values = top_decoder_outputs.squeeze(-1).detach()

        return pred_sequences
```

Listing 7-38: The class implementing the full seq2seq model with an evaluation method (by modifying Listing 7-37)

This method is similar to `forward()`. The main differences are that during evaluation, teacher forcing is not applied, meaning the decoder must rely on its own predictions from the previous time steps to generate the next token. Additionally, gradient computations are disabled via `torch.no_grad()` to save memory and speed up the evaluation process. Instead of using the ground truth to guide the sequence generation, the decoder's predicted output at each step is fed back as input for the next step, allowing the model to generate the entire output sequence independently. The decoder also returns `pred_sequences`, which contains the final predicted sequence of token indices, instead of `decoder_outputs_vec`, which holds the intermediate softmax probabilities over the vocabulary. This allows the evaluation method to directly provide the predicted output sequence without the need for further processing.

Defining the Loss Function

For the loss function, you'll use the *negative log-likelihood loss*, which measures the performance of a classification model whose output is a probability value ranging from 0 to 1. Importantly, values corresponding to padding tokens should be ignored for the loss function calculation so that the model's training process focuses solely on the meaningful part of the sequence. The `maskedNLL()` function in Listing 7-39 is an efficient way to calculate a masked version of the negative log-likelihood for batched data.

```
def maskedNLL(decoder_outputs, out_sequences, padding=0):
    """Calculate the masked negative log-likelihood (NLL) loss."""
    flat_pred_sequences = decoder_outputs.view(-1, decoder_outputs.shape[-1])
    flat_target_sequences = out_sequences.view(-1, 1)
    pred_probs = torch.gather(flat_pred_sequences, 1, flat_target_sequences)

    nll = - torch.log(pred_probs)

    mask = out_sequences != padding
    masked_nll = nll.masked_select(mask.view(-1, 1))

    return masked_nll.mean()  # Loss
```

Listing 7-39: The function to calculate the masked negative log-likelihood loss

This function measures how well the model's predicted probability distributions (contained in `decoder_outputs`, representing softmax probability distributions for each token in the vocabulary at every position in the sequence) match the actual target sequences (stored in `out_sequences`, representing the integer indices of the actual tokens). First, the function flattens both the predicted and target sequences into 2D arrays and uses `torch.gather()` to extract the predicted probabilities for the correct target tokens. The function calculates the negative log of these probabilities as the loss. Then the function applies a mask to ignore the padding tokens, ensuring that the loss focuses on only meaningful parts of the sequences. Finally, the function returns the mean loss over all non-padded tokens.

Implementing the Sequence-to-Sequence Application

Finally, you're ready to define the `Seq2Seq()` class by extending the `Application` class of Deeplay, as shown in Listing 7-40.

```
class Seq2Seq(dl.Application):
    """Application for the sequence-to-sequence model."""
```

```
    def __init__(self, in_vocab, out_vocab, teacher_prob=1.0):
        """Initialize the application."""
        super().__init__(loss=maskedNLL, optimizer=dl.Adam(lr=1e-3))
❶       self.model = Seq2SeqModel(in_vocab_size=len(in_vocab),
                                  out_vocab_size=len(out_vocab),
                                  teacher_prob=teacher_prob)

    def train_preprocess(self, batch):
        """Adjust the target sequence by shifting it one position backward."""
        in_sequences, out_sequences = batch
        shifted_out_sequences = \
            torch.cat((out_sequences[:, 1:], out_sequences[:, -1:]), dim=1)
        return (in_sequences, out_sequences), shifted_out_sequences

    def forward(self, batch):
        """Perform forward pass."""
        return self.model(batch)
```

Listing 7-40: The class implementing the application to train the seq2seq model

This class creates a default model from the Seq2SeqModel class from
Listing 7-36 ❶. The class uses both the maskedNLL() function defined in
Listing 7-39 as the loss function and the Adam optimizer.

The application implements train_preprocess(). This preprocessing
method adjusts the target sequence to calculate the loss by shifting the sequence one position backward and repeating the last element, which is a
padding or an end-of-sequence element. This adjustment is crucial for accurately computing the loss function, as the predicted sequences lack the
initial start-of-sequence token. In fact, during training, you need to train the
model to predict the next token in the sequence, excluding the initial token
that typically serves as a signal for the start of a new sequence. Shifting the
target sequence ensures that the model is evaluated correctly against the
ground-truth tokens for each step in the sequence.

Loading Pretrained Embeddings

Embeddings represent words (and their semantic and syntactic properties)
in a dense, continuous vector space. Although training embeddings within a
machine translation model has benefits, using fixed, pretrained embeddings
can be more efficient and effective.

Here, you'll take advantage of the extensive pretrained embeddings in
the Global Vectors for Word Representation (GloVe) model, which is widely
used to derive dense word embeddings from a text corpus. This approach
ensures that the translation model benefits from a deep, nuanced understanding of language semantics and syntax from the start, without having to
learn it from the data.

Start by downloading the GloVe embeddings with Listing 7-41.

```
import os
from torchvision.datasets.utils import download_url, extract_archive

glove_folder = ".glove_cache"
if not os.path.exists(glove_folder):
    os.makedirs(glove_folder, exist_ok=True)
    url = "https://nlp.stanford.edu/data/glove.42B.300d.zip"
    download_url(url, glove_folder)
    zip_filepath = os.path.join(glove_folder, "glove.42B.300d.zip")
    extract_archive(zip_filepath, glove_folder)
    os.remove(zip_filepath)
```

Listing 7-41: Downloading the GloVe embeddings

This code downloads and extracts the GloVe embeddings into a directory named *.glove_cache* in the current working directory. (If this directory doesn't exist, the script creates it.) The GloVe embeddings are downloaded as a ZIP file from the Stanford Natural Language Processing Group website, and after extraction, the script removes the ZIP file to save disk space.

Now implement the load_glove_embeddings() function in Listing 7-42.

```
def load_glove_embeddings(glove_file):
    """Load GloVe embeddings."""
    glove_embeddings = {}
    with open(glove_file, "r", encoding="utf-8") as file:
        for line in file:
            values = line.split()
            word = values[0]
            glove_embeddings[word] = np.round(
                np.asarray(values[1:], dtype="float32"), decimals=6,
            )
    return glove_embeddings
```

Listing 7-42: The function to load the GloVe embeddings

This function loads the GloVe embeddings from the specified file. Next, implement the get_glove_embeddings() function in Listing 7-43.

```
def get_glove_embeddings(vocab, glove_embeddings, embed_dim):
    """Get GloVe embeddings for a vocabulary."""
    embeddings = torch.zeros((len(vocab), embed_dim), dtype=torch.float32)
    for i, token in enumerate(vocab):
        embedding = glove_embeddings.get(token)
        if embedding is None:
            embedding = glove_embeddings.get(token.lower())
        if embedding is not None:
            embeddings[i] = torch.tensor(embedding, dtype=torch.float32)
    return embeddings
```

Listing 7-43: The function to get GloVe embeddings for a vocabulary

This function constructs an embeddings matrix for the given vocabulary by mapping each token to its corresponding GloVe embedding. For each token in the vocabulary, the function attempts to retrieve its embedding from the glove_embeddings dictionary. If the exact token is not found, the function tries the lowercase version. If an embedding is found, the function replaces the corresponding row in the embeddings matrix with the GloVe embedding. Tokens without a matching GloVe embedding remain as zero vectors in the matrix. The resulting embeddings matrix ensures that each token's index in the vocabulary aligns with the same index in the embeddings matrix.

You can finally load the GloVe embeddings with Listing 7-44.

```
glove_file = os.path.join(glove_folder, "glove.42B.300d.txt")
glove_embeddings, glove_dim = load_glove_embeddings(glove_file), 300

embeddings_in = get_glove_embeddings(in_vocab.get_tokens(),
                                     glove_embeddings, glove_dim)
embeddings_out = get_glove_embeddings(out_vocab.get_tokens(),
                                      glove_embeddings, glove_dim)

num_specials = len(specials)
❶ embeddings_in[1:num_specials] = torch.rand(num_specials - 1, glove_dim) * 0.01
❷ embeddings_out[1:num_specials] = torch.rand(num_specials - 1, glove_dim) * 0.01
```

Listing 7-44: Loading the pretrained embeddings

This code loads the pretrained GloVe embeddings and integrates them with the model's vocabularies. Using the load_glove_embeddings() function from Listing 7-42, the code loads the GloVe embeddings with 300 dimensions (glove_dim) into a dictionary (glove_embeddings). Then the get_glove _embeddings() function from Listing 7-43 is used to create embedding matrices for the input and output vocabularies by mapping each token to its corresponding GloVe embedding.

The special tokens defined in Listing 7-28 don't have predefined GloVe embeddings, so they are assigned 0 by default. You'll keep this initialization for padding tokens (corresponding to the index 0). Since these padding tokens don't carry semantic information, assigning the zero vector ensures that they don't influence the model's outputs or gradients during training. However, the non-padding special tokens serve specific semantic roles. Thus, the code assigns small random numbers to their embeddings ❶ ❷ so that the model learns how to handle them during training.

Training the Sequence-to-Sequence Application

Now you're ready to create the seq2seq model as shown in Listing 7-45.

```
seq2seq = Seq2Seq(in_vocab=in_vocab, out_vocab=out_vocab, teacher_prob=0.85)
seq2seq = seq2seq.create()

❶ seq2seq.model.encoder.embedding.weight.data = embeddings_in
```

```
❷ seq2seq.model.encoder.embedding.weight.requires_grad = False
❸ seq2seq.model.decoder.embedding.weight.data = embeddings_out
❹ seq2seq.model.decoder.embedding.weight.requires_grad = False
```

Listing 7-45: Creating the seq2seq model

All the model parameters are set to their default values except the teacher-forcing probability, which is set to 0.85. This rather high value is useful in early training when the model's predictions are likely inaccurate. The value ensures that the model sees a lot of correct sequences and learns the basic structure of the target language. During later training, you could gradually decrease the teacher-forcing probability to help the model transition from learning to reproduce correct sequences to generating them autonomously.

The GloVe embeddings are integrated into the model by being assigned to the embedding layer of the encoder ❶ and decoder ❸. Gradient computations are disabled to freeze these weights ❷ ❹, preventing them from being distorted by gradients derived from potentially much smaller task-specific datasets, and simplifying the training process.

Train this model as follows:

```
trainer = dl.Trainer(max_epochs=25, accelerator="auto")
trainer.fit(seq2seq, train_loader)
```

This configures a training environment and executes the training process. You can then visualize the training history with `trainer.history.plot()`. During the 25 epochs, the loss should decay from about 9 to about 1.2.

Testing the Model Performance

Before quantifying the model's performance over the test set, let's test its capabilities by translating some sentences.

First, you need to define the `unprocess()` function in Listing 7-46, which converts the processed sequences into readable text.

```
def unprocess(sequences, vocab, specials):
    """Convert numeric sequences to sentences."""
    sentences = []
    for sequence in sequences:
    ❶  idxs = sequence[sequence > len(specials) - 1]
        words = [vocab.lookup_token(idx) for idx in idxs]
        sentences.append(" ".join(words))
    return sentences
```

Listing 7-46: The function to convert numerical sequences into their corresponding text

The inputs for this function are the sequences list of lists and the vocab vocabulary object. In sequences, each inner list contains integer indices corresponding to words as per the given vocabulary. The vocab object returns the word associated with a given index through the `lookup_token()` method.

The function filters indices that are less than or equal to the number of special tokens minus one, to exclude the special tokens "<pad>", "<sos>", and "<eos>" ❶, because these special tokens are used to manage padding, the start of a sequence, and the end of a sequence, respectively, and thus are not part of the actual sentence content (instead, the special token "<unk>" will be kept in the sentence as it can be considered meaningful). The output provides a list of reconstructed sentences.

Now implement the `translate()` function in Listing 7-47 to apply the trained model to the translation of sentences provided by the user.

```
def translate(in_sentence, model, in_lang, in_vocab, out_vocab, specials):
    """Translate a sentence."""
    in_sentence = unicodedata.normalize("NFC", in_sentence)
    in_tokens = pad(tokenize(in_sentence, in_lang))
    in_sequence = (torch.tensor(in_vocab(in_tokens), dtype=torch.int)
                    .unsqueeze(0).to(next(model.parameters()).device))
    pred_sequence = model.evaluate(in_sequence)
    pred_sentence = unprocess(pred_sequence, out_vocab, specials)
    print(f"Predicted Translation: {pred_sentence[0]}\n")
```

Listing 7-47: The function to translate user-defined sentences

This function begins by normalizing to NFC, tokenizing, and padding the input text via the `unicodedata.normalize()`, `tokenize()`, and `pad()` functions, respectively. The resulting token sequence is then converted into a numerical sequence using the input vocabulary and transformed into a PyTorch tensor. This tensor is unsqueezed to add a batch dimension, which is necessary because PyTorch models expect input data to include a batch dimension, even if the batch size is 1. The tensor is then moved to the same device as the model's parameters. The model's `evaluate()` method is called to generate the predicted sequence, which is then converted back into readable text via the `unprocess()` function. Finally, the code prints out the translated text.

Now let's try using `translate()` on a simple sentence:

```
in_sentence = "I bought a book.'
translate(in_sentence, seq2seq.model, in_lang, in_vocab, out_vocab, specials)
```

This should generate a faithful translation:

```
Predicted Translation: Compré un libro .
```

Note the space before the period; this occurs because the tokenizer treats punctuation as a separate token, resulting in a space when the tokens are rejoined into a sentence.

Try another simple sentence:

```
in_sentence = "This book is very interesting."
translate(in_sentence, seq2seq.model, in_lang, in_vocab, out_vocab, specials)
```

This should also produce a correct translation:

```
Predicted Translation: Este libro es muy interesante .
```

However, on more difficult translations, the model runs into problems. For example, the following combines the previous two sentences into a single sentence with a main clause and a relative clause:

```
in_sentence = "The book that I bought is very interesting."
translate(in_sentence, seq2seq.model, in_lang, in_vocab, out_vocab, specials)
```

This results in the following translation (in our run of the code):

```
Predicted Translation: El libro es muy interesante que compré .
```

The model struggles to handle the more complex sentence structure, showing its limitations.

In Chapter 8, you'll learn how to improve the translation by using an attention mechanism to provide more contextual information to the decoder.

Evaluating the Model with the BLEU Score

To develop and refine models, it's crucial to accurately assess the quality of the translated text. One of the most prominent metrics used to do this is the *BiLingual Evaluation Understudy (BLEU) score*, designed to quantify a machine translation's closeness to human translations.

The BLEU score calculates the match of n-grams between the machine translation and the reference translations. An *n-gram* is a contiguous sequence of *n* items (such as words or characters) from a given sample of text. The BLEU score counts the number of n-grams that are in both the machine translation and in any of the reference translations, then divides this number by the total number of n-grams in the machine translation. The BLEU score considers n-grams with lengths up to 4 because this length typically encompasses the range from single words to short phrases, capturing both lexical choice and local coherence of translations.

The BLEU score has been instrumental in the development of machine translation systems thanks to its simplicity and effectiveness in comparing translated texts across languages. However, the BLEU score is not without its limitations. It focuses on the surface form of the language and may not fully capture the semantic accuracy or the stylistic appropriateness of the translation. Its effectiveness is also dependent on the quality of the references.

The script in Listing 7-48 evaluates the model on the test dataset, calculating the BLEU score for the model's translations, and printing examples of translations.

```
from torchmetrics.text import BLEUScore

bleu_score = BLEUScore()

device = next(seq2seq.model.parameters()).device
```

```
for batch_index, (in_sequences, out_sequences) in enumerate(test_loader):
    in_sentences = unprocess(in_sequences.to(device), in_vocab, specials)
    pred_sequences = seq2seq.model.evaluate(in_sequences.to(device))
    pred_sentences = unprocess(pred_sequences, out_vocab, specials)
    out_sentences = unprocess(out_sequences.to(device), out_vocab, specials)

❶ bleu_score.update(pred_sentences, [[s] for s in out_sentences])

    print(f"Input Sentence: {in_sentences[0]}\n"
        + f"Predicted Translation: {pred_sentences[0]}\n"
        + f"Actual Translation: {out_sentences[0]}\n")
final_bleu = bleu_score.compute()
print(f"Validation BLEU Score: {final_bleu:.3f}")
```

Listing 7-48: Testing the model and calculating the BLEU score

This code initializes an instance of the BLEUScore class. It gets the device on which the model is running and then loops through each batch in the test loader, moving the input and target data to the same device as the model and using the model's evaluate() method to get predictions.

The unprocess() function is used to convert indices to words, using the proper vocabulary for inputs, predictions, and targets. The code reformats the targets into a list-of-lists format, which is required by the BLEU score metric for proper evaluation, and it accumulates the results for BLEU score calculation over all the batches ❶.

For each batch, the code displays a translation example, printing the original input sentence, the model's predicted translation, and the actual human translation for comparison. After processing all batches, the code calculates and prints the final BLEU score for the entire test dataset. For this example, you should get a BLEU score of around 0.26. In Project 8A, you'll learn how to improve this score.

NOTE   *Code Example 7-A, "Translating with a Recurrent Neural Network," is available at* https://github.com/DeepTrackAI/DeepLearningCrashCourse. *Navigate to the* Ch07_RNN *folder and then* ec07_A_nlp_rnn. *The nlp_rnn.ipynb notebook provides a complete code example that uses recurrent neural networks to implement a seq2seq model for machine translation.*

Summary

In this chapter, you learned how to use recurrent neural networks in time-series analysis, focusing on their unique ability to handle sequential data and capture temporal dependencies.

You started with the comb filter example, showcasing how recurrent neural networks use feedback loops and memory to process sequences. You then used the PyTorch and Deeplay frameworks to analyze the Jena Climate dataset, and you used recurrent neural networks to predict future temperatures based on past weather data. Beginning with a straightforward implementation of a basic recurrent neural network, you went on to refine the model by stacking layers, including dropout techniques to combat overfitting, and incorporating more-advanced structures like GRUs and LSTM networks.

In the project, you applied recurrent neural networks to implement a seq2seq model for machine translation in Deeplay. This project gave you a firsthand look at natural language processing, deepening your understanding of neural network architectures specifically designed for handling sequential data. You saw how encoder-decoder models exploit the context of entire sentences rather than individual words, to produce more-coherent and contextually appropriate translations.

In the next chapter, you'll explore transformers, a powerful alternative to recurrent neural networks that can process entire sequences in parallel and capture long-range dependencies more effectively.

Seminal Works and Further Reading

The application of recurrent neural networks to temporal sequences began in 1990 with Jeffrey L. Elman's "Finding Structure in Time," published in *Cognitive Science* (volume 14, pages 179–211). This work demonstrated how recurrent neural networks can effectively model time dependencies, making it a foundational reference for the use of recurrent neural networks in processing sequential data.

Building on the early advancements in recurrent neural networks, Sepp Hochreiter and Jürgen Schmidhuber introduced the LSTM network in "Long Short-Term Memory," published in 1997 in *Neural Computation* (volume 9, pages 1,735–1,780). LSTMs were designed to overcome the vanishing gradient problem commonly encountered in training standard recurrent neural networks.

The exploration of sequence modeling took another step forward with the introduction of the recurrent encoder-decoder framework in 2014 by Kyunghyun Cho et al. in "Learning Phrase Representations Using RNN Encoder-Decoder for Statistical Machine Translation," published on arXiv (article number 1406.1078). This framework laid the groundwork for subsequent advancements, particularly in models incorporating attention mechanisms.

Ilya Sutskever et al. expanded the use of recurrent neural networks to sequence-to-sequence tasks in "Sequence to Sequence Learning with Neural Networks," published in 2014 in *Advances in Neural Information Processing Systems* (NeurIPS, volume 27). This work established the seq2seq framework, which mapped input sequences to output sequences in various domains, such as translating sentences between languages, and became a key architecture for many NLP tasks.

CHALLENGE PROJECTS

7-1: Predict stock market prices   Use a recurrent neural network to predict the future prices of a particular stock based on its historical price data. You can start by using the daily closing prices from the Yahoo! Finance website's historical market data and then attempt to include more features such as opening prices, highs and lows, and volume traded.

7-2: Predict disease spread   Use a recurrent neural network to predict the future spread of a disease (for example, COVID-19) based on past infection rates and possibly other features like mobility data or vaccination rates. Use the COVID-19 Data Repository by the Center for Systems Science and Engineering (CSSE) at Johns Hopkins University for infection rates and additional data sources for mobility and vaccination rates.

7-3: Analyze sentiment of movie reviews   Implement a recurrent neural network to classify the sentiment of movie reviews as positive or negative. Using the Large Movie Reviews Dataset provided by Stanford University, preprocess the textual data into a suitable format and then train your recurrent neural network to learn the sentiment expressed in the reviews.

7-4: Music genre classification   Develop a recurrent neural network that classifies short clips of music into genres. Use the GTZAN Music Genre Classification dataset, which consists of audio files categorized by genre. This task will require preprocessing audio data into a suitable format for recurrent neural network training.

7-5: Create a chatbot   Build a chatbot that is based on a recurrent neural network and is capable of engaging in basic conversations. Use the Cornell Movie-Dialogs Corpus to train your chatbot. This dataset contains a large collection of movie character dialogue that can be used to teach your model how to handle a conversation and generate appropriate responses. Focus on preprocessing the text data, designing a suitable recurrent neural network architecture, and implementing a mechanism to handle context and conversation flow.

8

PROCESSING LANGUAGE AND CLASSIFYING IMAGES WITH ATTENTION AND TRANSFORMERS

In this chapter, you'll learn about *attention*, a mechanism that enables models making predictions to focus on specific parts of the input data, based on their relevance. Attention was first introduced in encoder-decoder architectures to improve machine translation by allowing models to selectively focus on the most relevant parts of a sentence. This approach addressed the difficulty of capturing dependencies between faraway words.

The concept of attention has since become fundamental for *transformers*, a revolutionary neural network architecture that has changed the handling of sequence data such as sentences and time series. Transformers' self-attention mechanism allows them to capture long-range dependencies, which leads to improved performance compared to older models like the recurrent neural networks you met in Chapter 7.

Since Google introduced the transformer architecture in 2017, transformers have become the go-to model for many language-processing tasks, including translating text (machine translation), creating a short summary of a long document (text summarization), and determining whether a piece of text has a positive or negative tone (sentiment analysis). Transformers have also been used to predict protein structure from genetic sequences (AlphaFold), analyze images (vision transformers, or ViTs), and link language and images by learning visual concepts from natural language supervision (Contrastive Language-Image Pre-training, or CLIP).

In this chapter, you'll begin by implementing a machine translation network that uses attention, which outperforms the recurrent neural network you used in Project 7A. Next, you'll explore sentiment analysis, applying transformers to determine the emotional tone of a text (namely, whether a movie review is positive or negative). Finally, you'll apply transformer principles to image analysis via ViT, a groundbreaking architecture that outperforms traditional convolutional neural networks. By this chapter's end, your understanding of the attention mechanism and transformers will allow you to apply them to your own projects.

Understanding Attention

Before diving into concrete applications, let's use a simple example to illustrate how the attention mechanism operates. Consider this sentence: "The teacher praised a student because she improved." For humans, deriving semantic information from this sentence is straightforward. You can immediately answer questions like "Does *improved* refer to the teacher or the student?"

However, this task poses serious challenges for an algorithm because it lacks the inherent ability to understand context and resolve ambiguous references as humans do. Determining whether *improved* refers to *teacher* or *student* requires analyzing the relationships and dependencies between words in the sentence. Traditional models struggle with this because of their limitations in capturing long-range dependencies and nuanced semantic information.

The attention mechanism allows models to evaluate the importance of each word in a sentence relative to other words, either within the same sentence (*self-attention*) or across different sentences (*cross-attention*). In self-attention, a sentence attends to itself to capture internal dependencies, whereas in cross-attention, one sentence attends to another to capture intersentence relationships. For simplicity, we will focus on cross-attention in the following example.

Implementing Dot-Product Attention

Let's see the cross-attention mechanism in action. Start by defining two sentences:

```
query_sentence = "The teacher praised a student because she improved"
key_sentence = "A student asked the teacher to help her improve"
```

As you'll see in the rest of this section, the attention mechanism allows the neural network to focus on relevant parts of the key sentence when processing the query sentence, thus enhancing its understanding of important relationships between the two sentences.

Because neural networks cannot directly process raw text, you need to tokenize the sentences and convert each word into an embedding vector. An *embedding* is a numerical representation of a word in a continuous vector space, capturing its semantic meaning and relationships to other words. By employing the attention mechanism, you'll be able to compute attention weights that highlight the relevance of each word in the key sentence to each word in the query sentence. These attention weights are stored in an *attention matrix*, representing the extent to which each word in the query sentence attends to every word in the key sentence.

Then you'll update the embeddings of the query sentence by using the attention weights to compute a weighted sum of the key sentence embeddings. The updated embeddings, known as *attention outputs*, provide enriched representations of the query tokens that incorporate relevant contextual information from the key sentence. This process allows the model to focus on important relationships between the two sentences.

Tokenization and Conversion to Embeddings

You'll first need to tokenize the sentence and convert the words into embedding vectors; you've already seen this process in Project 7A.

Tokenize the sentences to separate the individual words they contain. You can do this as follows:

```
query_tokens = query_sentence.split()
key_tokens = key_sentence.split()
```

Then print the resulting lists of tokens with print(query_tokens) and print(key _tokens):

```
['The', 'teacher', 'praised', 'a', 'student', 'because', 'she', 'improved']
['A', 'student', 'asked', 'the', 'teacher', 'to', 'help', 'her', 'improve']
```

Note that both sentences contain pronouns like *she* and *her*, which can be ambiguous without context. The attention mechanism can help the model resolve such ambiguities by focusing on relevant words in the key sentence.

Next, you need to convert these lists of tokens into embeddings. Each word will become a vector of numbers, and each sentence will become a matrix, as shown in Figure 8-1.

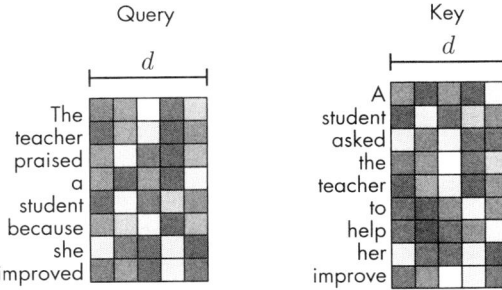

Figure 8-1: A matrix representation of the query and key sentences

These matrices represent the embedded query and key sentences; each row corresponds to a word in the sentence, and each column represents the features of the embedding. Formally, these matrices belong to the vector space $\mathbb{R}^{n \times d}$, where n is the sequence length and d is the embedding dimension.

To obtain meaningful embeddings that capture the semantic relationships between words, you'll use GloVe, the popular pretrained embedding model that you used in Project 7A. To recap briefly, GloVe embeddings are learned from a large corpus of text and encode both semantic and syntactic information by capturing global word co-occurrence statistics. Using pretrained embeddings like GloVe allows your model to obtain rich linguistic information without the need to train embeddings from scratch.

You downloaded the GloVe embeddings previously with Listing 7-41, so now you can obtain the GloVe embeddings of the sentences as shown in Listing 8-1.

```
import numpy as np
import torch

glove_file = os.path.join(glove_folder, "glove.42B.300d.txt")
glove_embed, embed_dim = load_glove_embeddings(glove_file), 300

query_embeddings = get_glove_embeddings(query_tokens, glove_embed, embed_dim)
key_embeddings = get_glove_embeddings(key_tokens, glove_embed, embed_dim)
```

Listing 8-1: Calculating the embeddings of the query and key sentences

Using the load_glove_embeddings() function (Listing 7-42), this code loads the 300-dimensional embeddings into the glove_embed dictionary, which maps each word to its corresponding 300-dimensional embedding vector. Then this code employs the get_glove_embeddings() function (Listing 7-43) to transform the tokenized sentences (query_tokens and key_tokens) into embedding matrices (query_embeddings and key_embeddings).

Each row in these matrices represents a word's embedding in a 300-dimensional space. These embeddings effectively transform your tokenized sentences into numerical formats that the attention mechanism can process, enabling the model to capture the semantic relationships between words in your query and key sentences.

Attention Mechanism

A simple way to compute the attention matrix is by calculating the *dot product* between the matrices containing the query and key embeddings. This means calculating the similarity between each word in the query sentence and each word in the key sentence by performing a dot product of their respective embedding vectors.

This operation results in an attention matrix with each element representing the degree of relevance, or similarity, between a query word and a key word. The higher the dot product value, the more similar the words in terms of their embeddings. This attention matrix effectively quantifies how much each word in the query sentence "attends to" (or focuses on) each word in the key sentence, enabling the model to prioritize the most relevant information when updating the query embeddings with contextual information from the key sentence.

NOTE *In this matrix representation of the sentences, each word corresponds to a row, which can be interpreted as a vector. You can think of vectors as arrows, and the dot product as an alignment score: You're essentially determining how much one vector points in the direction of another. If they have exactly the same direction, the dot product is maximum and corresponds to the product of their lengths. If the vectors are at a 90-degree angle to each other, the dot product is 0.*

After calculating the dot product between the query and key embeddings, you usually divide the attention matrix by the square root of the embedding dimension (d) to help stabilize the gradients when working with high-dimensional vectors. This division is what gives the operation the name *scaled dot product*. Finally, you need to normalize the scores into weights by applying the softmax function.

The whole dot-attention process is shown in the top row of Figure 8-2.

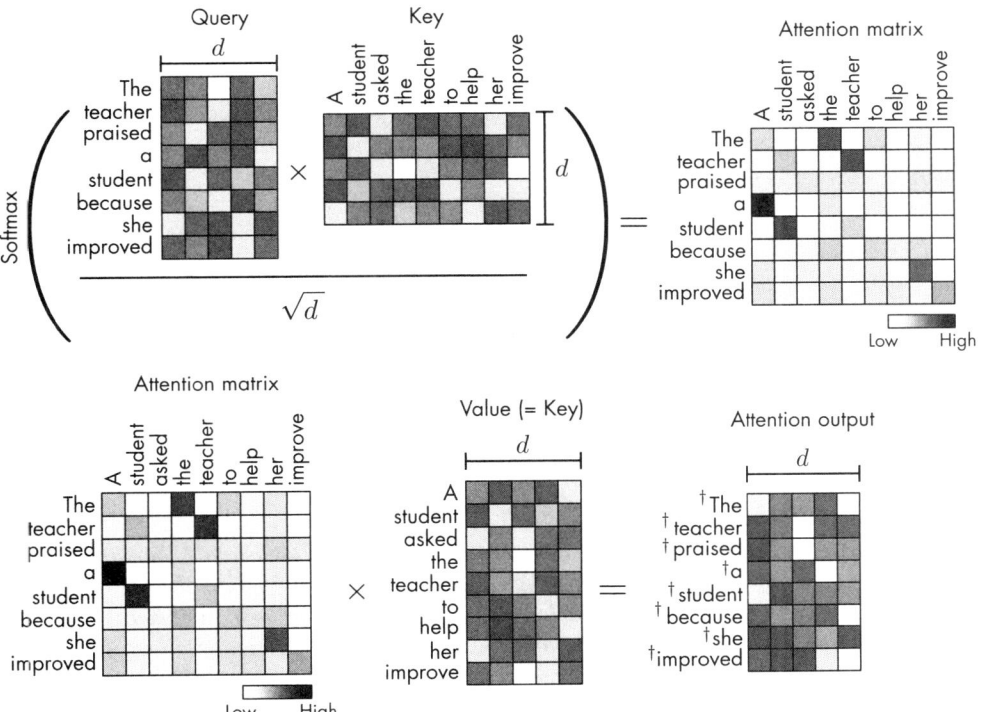

Figure 8-2: Calculating the attention matrix and attention output

To calculate the attention output, you need to multiply the attention matrix by the *value embeddings*, resulting in an updated representation of the query sentence. In this case, you'll also use the key embeddings as the value embeddings so that the values are the same as the keys. This operation effectively aggregates the value embeddings, weighted by the attention scores, to produce new embeddings for the query words that incorporate relevant information from the key sentence. The attention output provides enriched embeddings for the query tokens that reflect the contextual relationships captured by the attention mechanism, as illustrated in the bottom row of Figure 8-2.

You can implement the dot-product attention with the DotProductAttention class shown in Listing 8-2.

```
import deeplay as dl

class DotProductAttention(dl.DeeplayModule):
    """Dot-product attention."""'

    def __init__(self):
        """Initialize dot-product attention."""
        super().__init__()

    def forward(self, queries, keys, values):
        """Calculate dot-product attention."""
        attn_scores = (torch.matmul(queries, keys.transpose(-2, -1))
                       / (keys.size(-1) ** 0.5))
        attn_matrix = torch.nn.functional.softmax(attn_scores, dim=-1)
        attn_output = torch.matmul(attn_matrix, values)
        return attn_output, attn_matrix
```

Listing 8-2: The class implementing the dot-product attention

The forward() method calculates the attention scores (attn_scores) by performing a scaled dot product between the queries and the transposed keys. The method then normalizes the attention scores via the softmax function to obtain the attention matrix (attn_matrix), which represents the normalized relevance of each key to each query. Finally, the method computes the attention output (attn_output) by multiplying the attention matrix with the values, resulting in updated query embeddings that incorporate information from the key sentence.

NOTE   *The dot-product attention mechanism is analogous to a hash table lookup, where queries are like search terms, keys are the entries, and values are the returned data. The mechanism compares each query to the keys to find the most relevant match, with higher similarity scores (dot products) indicating more-relevant values. This explains the terminology: Like looking up a query in a key-value store, the attention process retrieves information (values) based on the relevance of keys to the query.*

You can finally calculate the attention matrix and outputs:

```
attention = DotProductAttention()
attn_output, attn_matrix = attention(
    queries=query_embeddings, keys=key_embeddings, values=key_embeddings,
)
```

With the attention outputs and matrix calculated, you have now fully implemented the dot-product attention mechanism, enabling your model to effectively capture and utilize the contextual relationships between the query and key sentences.

Visualizing Attention

You can now use the function in Listing 8-3 to visualize the attention matrix.

```
from matplotlib import pyplot as plt
from matplotlib.ticker import FixedLocator

def plot_attention(query_tokens, key_tokens, attn_matrix):
    """Plot attention."""
    fig, ax = plt.subplots()
    cax = ax.matshow(attn_matrix, cmap="Greens")
    fig.colorbar(cax)
    ax.xaxis.set_major_locator(FixedLocator(range(len(key_tokens))))
    ax.yaxis.set_major_locator(FixedLocator(range(len(query_tokens))))
    ax.set_xticklabels(key_tokens, rotation=90)
    ax.set_yticklabels(query_tokens)
    plt.show()
```

Listing 8-3: The function to plot an attention matrix

This function generates a heatmap that provides insight into how much focus the model places on each word in the key sentence when processing the query sentence. The function accepts three arguments: query_tokens, key_tokens, and attn_matrix. The query_tokens and key_tokens arguments represent the words in the query and key sentences, respectively, while attn_matrix is the attention matrix that the model has generated.

You can then use this function with

```
plot_attention(query_tokens, key_tokens, attn_matrix.detach().squeeze())
```

which should generate Figure 8-3.

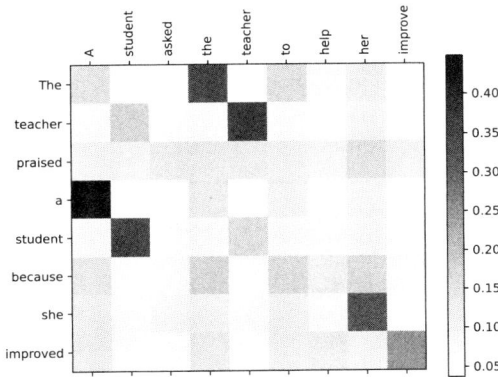

Figure 8-3: The attention matrix heatmap

The rows represent the tokens of the query sentence, while the columns represent the tokens of the key sentence. The heatmap displays the attention weights, with darker areas indicating higher attention scores.

Upon closely examining the heatmap, it does indeed illustrate a case of cross-attention using GloVe embeddings, where not only direct correspondences are highlighted but also cross-attention between semantically related words. The most noticeable pattern is the attention between corresponding words in the query and key, indicating that words like *teacher* in the query sentence align well with *teacher* in the key sentence, and *student* aligns well with *student*—but also, less meaningful words such as *a* and *the* align. These direct correspondences are expected, given that both words appear in both sentences.

However, what is particularly interesting in this cross-attention example is the way the model highlights semantically related but nonidentical words. For example, there's attention between *she* in the query and *her* in the key sentence. This suggests that the attention mechanism is capable of recognizing that these words are related, even though they are not exact matches. This demonstrates the strength of cross-attention with pretrained embeddings like GloVe, as semantically related words that don't necessarily match exactly can still share attention.

It's important to note that, in this example, there are no learnable weights, either in the words' encodings or in the attention mechanism itself. Therefore, the results simply reflect the basic relationships between embedding vectors. These embeddings have been pretrained on a large corpus and capture semantic similarities between words based on their co-occurrence statistics in that corpus. As a result, the attention mechanism here is using these fixed relationships, with words that are semantically related or frequently co-occurring (such as *she* and *her*) receiving higher attention weights. However, because the embeddings and the attention mechanism are not fine-tuned to the specific task or dataset, the model's performance is limited by the general relationships encoded in GloVe, rather than being adapted to optimize for this particular example (for example, returning a low attention between *her* and *student*).

While this is reasonable for exact matching tasks, the true strength of attention comes with models that can learn to assign higher attention weights to words that are relevant to the query based on context. In these situations, attention helps the model focus on the most relevant information, improving its ability to understand and process data. You'll see this in Project 8A, where the dot-product attention will improve the translation ability of the seq2seq model you implemented in Project 7A.

EXERCISES

8-1: Use the sentence "Gardens and zoos are full of plants and animals" to compute a self-attention matrix, obtained using the same sentence as both query and key. Analyze the self-attention matrix to see how the model attends to different words. Identify which words pay more attention to each other, and explain how this reflects the semantic relationships between them. Visualize the matrix as a heatmap to assist in interpreting the attention patterns.

8-2: Replace the pretrained GloVe embeddings in the attention mechanism with randomly initialized embeddings. Use these random embeddings to compute the attention matrix for the sentence "Gardens and zoos are full of plants and animals." Compare the resulting attention patterns to those obtained with GloVe embeddings, and discuss how the absence of semantic information in the random embeddings impacts the attention mechanism's performance. Notice and explain the prominence of the diagonal elements.

Making the Attention Mechanism Trainable

The dot-product attention introduced earlier is a form of multiplicative attention: The queries and keys are multiplied directly. More-complex forms of multiplicative attention can include learnable weights or transformations that allow the model to adjust its focus dynamically based on the input data, offering more flexibility in capturing relevant information from different parts of the sequence.

A notable example is *standard scaled dot-product attention*, in which queries, keys, and values are transformed by applying a learned linear transformation with learnable weights. This enables the model to learn more-sophisticated interactions between the queries and keys by modifying their representations, as shown in Figure 8-4.

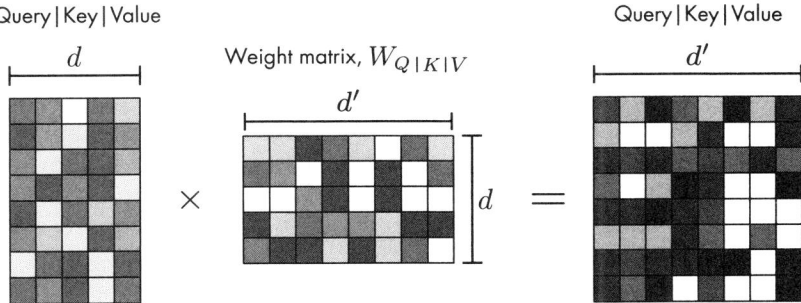

Figure 8-4: Trainable dot-product attention

The learnable linear transformations that generate the query, key, and value matrices in this form of attention permit the model to be trained to optimize the attention mechanism for a specific task. This enables the model to capture more-nuanced and task-relevant relationships between the queries and keys.

This form of attention is implemented by the `TrainableAttention` class in Listing 8-4.

```
--snip--
class TrainableAttention(dl.DeeplayModule):
    """Trainable dot-product attention."""

    def __init__(self, num_in_features=300, num_out_features=256):
        """Initialize trainable dot-product attention."""
        super().__init__()
        self.Wq = torch.nn.Linear(num_in_features, num_out_features)
        self.Wk = torch.nn.Linear(num_in_features, num_out_features)
        self.Wv = torch.nn.Linear(num_in_features, num_out_features)

    def forward(self, queries, keys, values):
        """Calculate dot-product attention with linear transformations."""
        Q, K, V = self.Wq(queries), self.Wk(keys), self.Wv(values)
        attn_scores = (torch.matmul(Q, K.transpose(-2, -1))
                        / (K.shape[-1] ** 0.5))
        attn_matrix = torch.nn.functional.softm.softmax(attn_scores, dim=-1)
        attn_output = torch.matmul(attn_weights, V)
        return attn_output, attr_matrix
```

Listing 8-4: The class implementing trainable dot-product attention (by modifying Listing 8-2)

In this case, the weight matrices (Wq, Wk, and Wv) are initialized randomly, and the training process will later determine their final values.

In the forward() method, the input query, key, and value matrices are first transformed by applying the learnable linear transformations Wq, Wk, and Wv. These transformations adjust the original representations of the queries, keys, and values, allowing the model to learn task-specific representations. The num_in_features parameter represents the dimensionality of the input embeddings (typically, the size of the pretrained word embeddings or other input features), while num_out_features refers to the dimensionality of the transformed query, key, and value matrices. By adjusting num_out_features, you can control the size of the latent space where the attention mechanism operates, increasing or decreasing the model's capacity to capture complex relationships.

The dot-product attention scores are then computed by taking the scaled dot product between the transformed query and key matrices. As in the preceding case, the attention scores are normalized by using the softmax function to produce attention weights, which represent the relative importance of each key in relation to the query. Finally, the attention output is computed by applying these weights to the value matrix.

This approach adds significant flexibility, as the model can learn the optimal way to represent and relate queries, keys, and values for the task at hand. For example, in a machine translation task, the model may learn that certain transformations of the query (such as focusing more on specific syntactic structures) improve translation accuracy, or that certain key representations should be downplayed in favor of others.

This trainable dot-product attention forms the backbone of the self-attention mechanism in modern transformers, as it allows the model to dynamically focus on different parts of the input sequence during both training and inference.

Implementing Other Attention Mechanisms

Beyond simple dot-product attention, several other mechanisms may better capture relationships between the input and output sequences, depending on the task. These include translation, summarization, and question answering.

Historically, the first attention mechanism used for translation tasks was *additive attention*, which differs from dot-product attention in that it combines the transformed queries and keys by computing a weighted sum of their elements, followed by a nonlinear activation function. This method allows the attention mechanism to capture more-complex relationships but is computationally more intensive. An implementation of this method can be seen in Listing 8-5.

```
--snip--
class AdditiveAttention(dl.DeeplayModule):
    """Additive attention."""

    def __init__(self, num_in_features=300, num_out_features=256):
        """Initialize additive attention."""
        super().__init__()
        self.Wq = torch.nn.Linear(num_in_features, num_out_features)
        self.Wk = torch.nn.Linear(num_in_features, num_out_features)
        self.Ws = torch.nn.Linear(num_out_features, 1)

    def forward(self, queries, keys, values):
        """Calculate additive attention."""
        Q, K = self.Wq(queries), self.Wk(keys)
        attn_scores = self.Ws(
            torch.tanh(Q.unsqueeze(-2) + K.unsqueeze(-3))
        ).squeeze(-1)
```

```
attn_matrix = torch.nn.functional.softmax(attn_scores, dim=-1)
attn_output = torch.matmul(attn_matrix, values)
return attn_output, attn_matrix
```

Listing 8-5: The class implementing additive attention (by modifying Listing 8-4)

Instead of using a dot product between the query and key matrices, this class first combines the transformed queries and keys by summing them element-wise. Then the class passes this sum through a nonlinear activation function (torch.tanh()) to introduce nonlinearity, allowing the model to capture more-complex relationships between queries and keys. Afterward, the attention scores are transformed through an additional linear layer (Ws), reducing the dimensionality to a single score per key-query pair. Finally, the scores are normalized via softmax to form the attention matrix.

While dot-product attention (and other types of multiplicative attention) is computationally efficient and well suited to high-dimensional vectors, it may struggle to capture complex relationships when working with lower-dimensional data. As you'll see in Project 8B, this makes it a popular choice for large-scale models like transformers, where computational speed is critical.

On the other hand, additive attention is more expressive and better equipped to capture complex relationships between queries and keys. This makes it suitable when understanding subtle interactions between elements is important. However, this approach comes with higher computational costs and slower processing. The choice between these mechanisms should be guided by the model architecture, the complexity of the data, and the desired balance between performance and computational efficiency.

NOTE *Code Example 8-1, "Understanding Attention," is available at* https://github .com/DeepTrackAI/DeepLearningCrashCourse. *Navigate to the* Ch08 _Attention *folder and then* ec08_1_attention. *The* attention.ipynb *notebook provides a complete code example to create the attention classes, apply them to the example sentences, and visualize the attention heatmaps.*

Project 8A: Using Attention to Improve Language Translation

In complex sequence-to-sequence tasks like machine translation, relationships between words and phrases often span long sequences. In Project 7A, for example, you might remember that "This book is very interesting." was correctly translated as "Este libro es muy interesante ." However, the output was often less accurate with longer and more complex sentences like "The book that I bought is very interesting."

In the basic seq2seq model from Project 7A, the decoder generates each word sequentially, relying heavily on the encoder's final hidden state for context. This final hidden state, which condenses the entire input sequence into a single vector, must capture all relevant information. With longer sequences, this leads to significant information loss, limiting the decoder's ability to produce accurate translations.

The attention mechanism addresses this limitation by allowing the model to focus on different parts of the input sequence for each word being generated, improving its ability to capture and handle long-range dependencies dynamically.

Incorporating Attention

Here, you'll enhance the seq2seq model by incorporating attention into the translation process. You'll also analyze why attention improves translation performance over the basic recurrent neural network from Project 7A by visualizing the attention mechanism with heatmaps. To do this, you'll start from the *nlp_rnn.ipynb* notebook from Project 7A and alter it.

Modifying the Decoder

In seq2seq tasks such as translation, the model uses the encoder's hidden state to store information about the source sentence. The decoder then generates the translated words one at a time, relying on a context vector that is updated iteratively.

However, not all words in the source sentence are equally relevant to the current word being translated. To address this, you can apply dot-product cross-attention. This mechanism uses the decoder's hidden state at each step as the queries, and the encoder's hidden states as the keys. This allows the model to focus on the most relevant parts of the source sentence as needed, improving translation accuracy.

To include the attention mechanism defined by the DotProductAttention class (Listing 8-2) in the seq2seq model, you'll first need to modify Seq2Seq Decoder(), described in Listing 7-35. The changes to the decoder are shown in Listing 8-6.

```
class Seq2SeqDecoder(dl.DeeplayModule):
    """Sequence-to-sequence decoder with dot-product attention."""

    def __init__(...):
        --snip--
        self.softmax = dl.Layer(torch.nn.Softmax, dim=-1)
        self.attn = DotProductAttention()

    def forward(self, decoder_in_values, contexts, encoded_sequences):
        --snip--
        decoder_outputs, contexts = self.rnn(out_embeddings, contexts)
        attn_contexts, attn_weights = self.attn(queries=decoder_outputs,
                                                 keys=encoded_sequences,
                                                 values=encoded_sequences)
        decoder_outputs = decoder_outputs + attn_contexts
        decoder_outputs = self.dense(decoder_outputs)
        --snip--
        return decoder_outputs, contexts, attn_weights
```

Listing 8-6: The class implementing a decoder with attention (by modifying Listing 7-35)

In this updated code, the `DotProductAttention` module is added as the attention mechanism, allowing the decoder to focus on specific parts of the input sequence. The signature of the `forward()` method now includes `encoded_sequences`, which is necessary for the attention mechanism to function. The decoder uses the dot product to compute the attentional context vectors stored in `attn_contexts` from the decoder's hidden states (queries) and the encoder's hidden states (keys). Since the value matrix is given by `encoded_sequences`, the attentional context vectors in `attn_contexts` are a weighted average of the encoder hidden states, with weights determined by the attention scores.

The resulting attentional context vectors are combined with the decoder's outputs by simply summing them. This approach helps limit the number of weights in the model, simplifying the architecture and reducing the computational load. However, alternative strategies, such as concatenating the context vectors with the decoder's outputs, may provide more-expressive representations. While concatenation typically requires additional adjustments, such as increasing the input size of subsequent layers, it can offer improved performance by allowing the model to make use of more-complex interactions.

The combination of attentional context vectors and the decoder's outputs provides additional contextual information from the encoder. This enhances the decoder's ability to generate accurate translations. The `forward()` method also returns the attention weights (`attn_weights`), which can be used to visualize which words in the input sequence were most influential for each translated word.

Modifying the Seq2Seq Model

Next, you'll modify `Seq2SeqModel`, described in Listing 7-36, as highlighted in Listing 8-7.

```
class Seq2SeqModel(dl.DeeplayModule):
    """Sequence-to-sequence model with attention."
        --snip--

    def forward(self, batch):
        --snip--
        encoder_outputs, contexts = self.encoder(in_sequences)
        --snip--
        for t in range(sequence_length):
            decoder_outputs, contexts, _ = \
                self.decoder(decoder_in_values, contexts, encoder_outputs)
        --snip--

    def evaluate(self, in_sequences):
        --snip--
        with torch.no_grad():
            encoder_outputs, contexts = self.encoder(in_sequences)
        --snip--
```

```
attn_matrices = torch.zeros(
    num_sequences, sequence_length, sequence_length
).to(device)
for t in range(sequence_length):
    --snip--
    with torch.no_grad():
        decoder_outputs, contexts, attn_weights = \
            self.decoder(decoder_inputs, contexts, encoder_outputs)
        attn_matrices[:, t, :] = attn_weights.squeeze(1)
    --snip--
return pred_sequences, attn_matrices
```

Listing 8-7: The class implementing a seq2seq model with attention (by modifying Listing 7-36)

Integrating the attention mechanism into the model requires modifying the forward() and evaluate() methods to obtain the encoder outputs in encoder_outputs from the encoder and use them as input in the call to the decoder. These encoder outputs allow the decoder to focus on relevant parts of the input sequence at each decoding step.

In the forward() method, you'll use a placeholder (_) to ignore the attention weights, as they aren't needed as an output of the model during training. However, in the evaluate() method, you'll store the attention weights in a tensor (attn_matrices) to return them alongside the predicted sequences. This will allow you to later visualize and interpret the attention patterns used by the model during translation.

Training and Testing the Seq2Seq Model with Attention

You're now ready to perform all the steps described in Project 7A to train the seq2seq model with dot-product attention. Although using dot-product attention doesn't increase the network's trainable parameters, it significantly enhances performance. When trained under the same conditions as the basic seq2seq model from Project 7A, the final loss consistently reaches values around 0.5. Additionally, evaluating the translation quality on the test dataset yields a BLEU score of 0.43.

To assess performance, you need to slightly modify the code from Listing 7-48 by adding a placeholder to ignore the attention matrix returned by the evaluate() method, as shown in Listing 8-8.

```
--snip--
for batch_index, (in_sequences, out_sequences) in enumerate(test_loader):
    in_sentences = unprocess(in_sequences.to(device), in_vocab, specials)
    pred_sequences, _ = seq2seq.model.evaluate(in_sequences.to(device))
--snip--
```

Listing 8-8: Testing the model and calculating the BLEU score (by modifying Listing 7-48)

Beyond improving model performance, attention weights provide insights into how different parts of the source sequence influence the output.

This makes the translation process more interpretable. Since the `evaluate()` method now returns both the predicted sequence and the attention weights, you can modify the `translate()` function (Listing 7-47) to also return the attention matrix alongside the word tokens, as shown in Listing 8-9.

```
def translate(...:
    --snip--
    pred_sequence, attn_matrix = model.evaluate(in_sequence)
    --snip--
    print(f"Predicted Translation: {pred_sentence[0]}\n")
    pred_tokens = [out_vocab.lookup_token(idx) for idx in pred_sequence[0]]
    return in_tokens, pred_tokens, attn_matrix.squeeze()
```

Listing 8-9: Translating user-defined sentences (by modifying Listing 7-47)

The updated `translate()` function now returns the tokenized words of the input and predicted sentences, along with the attention matrix. These outputs can be jointly used to visualize attention with a heatmap.

Interpreting the Attention Matrix

Let's examine the behavior of the dot-product attention model when applied to the same sentence that yielded poor results for the basic model in Project 7A:

```
in_sentence = "The book that I bought is very interesting."
in_tokens, pred_tokens, attn_matrix = translate(
    in_sentence, seq2seq.model, in_lang, in_vocab, out_vocab, specials,
)
```

The improved translation now reads as follows:

```
Predicted Translation: El libro que compré es muy interesante .
```

You can now use the `plot_attention()` function (Listing 8-3) to plot the attention matrix as shown in Listing 8-10.

```
in_tokens = [token for token in in_tokens if token not in specials]
pred_tokens = [token for token in pred_tokens if token not in specials]
attn_matrix = attn_matrix[:len(pred_tokens), 1:len(in_tokens) + 1]
plot_attention(pred_tokens, in_tokens, attn_matrix)
```

Listing 8-10: Plotting the translation attention matrix

This code removes the special tokens from the input token sequence (`in_tokens`) and the translated token sequence (`pred_tokens`). Then the code extracts the semantically meaningful part of the attention matrix by removing the portions of the attention matrix relative to the special tokens. The left panel of Figure 8-5 shows the resulting attention heatmap.

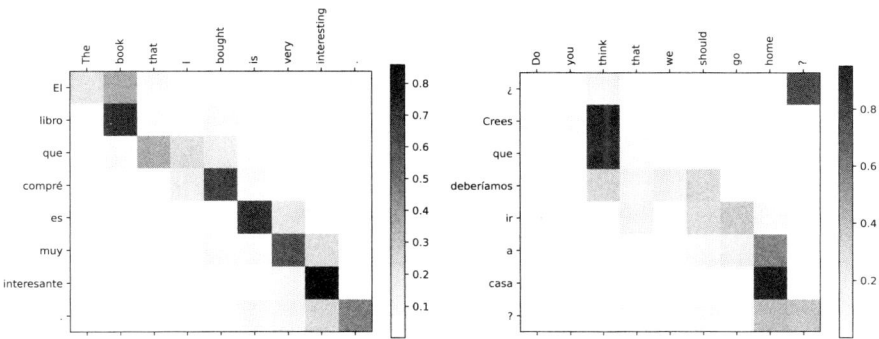

Figure 8-5: The translation attention heatmaps

The x-axis represents the tokens of the source sentence in English, while the y-axis represents the tokens of the translated sentence in Spanish. The heatmap displays the attention weights, with darker areas indicating higher attention scores. This helps us identify which parts of the input sequence the model focuses on during translation.

With attention, the model now provides an accurate translation. The first part of the phrase, "The book that I bought," is translated as "El libro que compré," with the model correctly attending to the corresponding parts of each sequence. The pronoun *I* is not explicitly translated into Spanish, as it's implicitly understood in the verb *compré* (which means *I bought*). The phrase "is very interesting" is directly translated as "es muy interesante," maintaining the proper sequence and context.

This translation, along with the corresponding attention heatmap in the left panel of Figure 8-5, illustrates the concept of soft alignment. Specifically, *compré* aligns with both *I* and *bought*, capturing the meaning conveyed by both words. Similarly, the word *El*, used to translate *The*, attends to both *The* and *book* in the source sentence, as Spanish articles change to reflect the gender of the noun. This alignment demonstrates how the model correctly associates multiple parts of a phrase, even when grammatical structures differ between languages, producing a more coherent and contextually accurate translation compared to the basic model in Project 7A.

Let's now challenge the model with an interrogative sentence:

```
in_sentence = "Do you think that we should go home?"
in_tokens, pred_tokens, attn_matrix = translate(
    in_sentence, seq2seq.model, in_lang, in_vocab, out_vocab, specials,
)
```

Here's the result:

```
Predicted Translation: ¿ Crees que deberíamos ir a casa ?
```

The model again provides an accurate translation. You can use Listing 8-10 to plot the attention map. The result should be similar to the right panel of Figure 8-5 and should highlight the parts of the input sequence that the model focuses on when generating each word in the output.

In this example, because of the interrogative form, the word order differs in the source and target sentences, so the heatmap doesn't follow a diagonal pattern. The initial inverted question mark in Spanish, ¿, which has no equivalent in English, shows strong attention to the final question mark in the source sentence, indicating the interrogative nature. Similarly, the preposition *a*, which has no direct translation in the English sentence, has high attention weights for *home*, as it establishes the correct grammatical structure in Spanish.

NOTE   *Code Example 8-A, "Translating with Attention," is available at* https://github.com/DeepTrackAI/DeepLearningCrashCourse. *Navigate to the* Ch08_Attention *folder and then* ec08_A_nlp_attn. *The* nlp_attn.ipynb *notebook provides a complete code example demonstrating how to implement a seq2seq model for machine translation that uses recurrent neural networks and the dot-product attention mechanism.*

Project 8B: Performing Sentiment Analysis with a Transformer

The power of self-attention to capture long-range dependencies between words or tokens in a sentence is fully exploited by transformers. *Transformers*, unlike earlier models such as recurrent neural networks, don't rely on sequential processing to manage dependencies within a sentence. Instead, they use a multi-head attention mechanism to focus on different parts of a sentence simultaneously while processing the sequence in parallel. This makes transformers highly efficient and effective for NLP tasks.

This parallel attention enables transformers to amplify important tokens, such as key sentiment words, while reducing the influence of less relevant ones. This dynamic focus adjustment across the input sequence enhances the model's understanding and representation of text, particularly in complex tasks like sentiment analysis, which may tie sentiment to specific phrases or words within a longer sentence. Additionally, the parallel processing capabilities of transformers make them more scalable, allowing them to handle longer texts more efficiently and perform better than models based on recurrent neural networks.

To see these concepts in action, you'll implement a transformer encoder to perform sentiment analysis, a common NLP task that categorizes text based on its positive or negative tone.

Breaking Down Multi-Head Attention

The ability of transformers to process input data in parallel is made possible by *multi-head attention*, a mechanism that enhances the expressiveness of the attention layers without significantly increasing the parameter count. The structure of multi-head attention is shown in Figure 8-6.

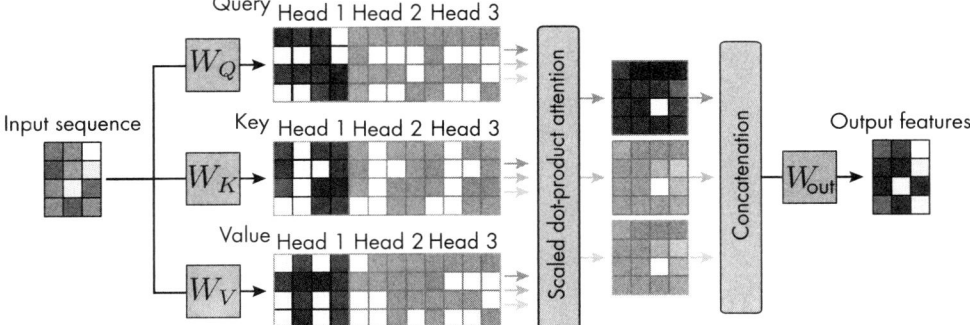

Figure 8-6: Multi-head attention

Multi-head attention employs a divide-and-conquer approach by splitting the attention process into multiple *attention heads*. Each head independently attends to different parts of the input sequence, extracting distinct features. These individual outputs are then concatenated and passed through a linear transformation to produce the final attention output. This multifaceted approach enables the model to gain a deeper and more comprehensive understanding of the input sequence.

This process is often likened to a team of experts analyzing multiple facets of a complex problem and combining their insights to reach a conclusion. Similarly, multi-head attention allows each head to focus on different parts of the input, making the overall model more robust in its interpretation.

You can implement multi-head self-attention as shown in Listing 8-11.

```
import deeplay as dl
import torch

class MultiHeadAttentionLayer(dl.DeeplayModule):
    """Multi-head attention layer."""

    def __init__(self, num_features, num_heads):
        """Initialize multi-head attention."""
        super().__init__()
        self.num_features, self.num_heads = num_features, num_heads
        self.head_dim = num_features // num_heads  # Must be integer

        self.Wq = dl.Layer(torch.nn.Linear, num_features, num_features)
        self.Wk = dl.Layer(torch.nn.Linear, num_features, num_features)
        self.Wv = dl.Layer(torch.nn.Linear, num_features, num_features)
        self.Wout = dl.Layer(torch.nn.Linear, num_features, num_features)

    def forward(self, in_sequence):
        """Apply the multi-head attention mechanism to the input sequence."""
        seq_len, embed_dim = in_sequence.shape
```

```
        Q = self.Wq(in_sequence)
        Q = Q.view(seq_len, self.num_heads, self.head_dim).permute(1, 0, 2)
        K = self.Wk(in_sequence)
        K = K.view(seq_len, self.num_heads, self.head_dim).permute(1, 0, 2)
        V = self.Wv(in_sequence)
        V = V.view(seq_len, self.num_heads, self.head_dim).permute(1, 0, 2)

        attn_scores = (torch.matmul(Q, K.transpose(-2, -1))
                        / (self.head_dim ** 0.5))
        attn_weights = torch.nn.functional.softmax(attn_scores, dim=-1)
        attn_output = torch.matmul(attn_weights, V)
❶     attn_output = attn_output.permute(1, 0, 2).contiguous()
❷     attn_output = attn_output.view(seq_len, self.num_features)
        return self.Wout(attn_output)
```

Listing 8-11: The class to implement multi-head attention

This implementation is an advanced variation of the standard scaled dot-product attention shown previously in Listing 8-4. The class takes as arguments num_features, which defines the dimensionality of the input, and num_heads, which specifies the number of attention heads (num_features must be divisible by num_heads, as each attention head processes a subset of the features).

In the forward() method, the input sequences are transformed using linear layers (Wq, Wk, and Wv). After the query, key, and value matrices are computed, the code reshapes the tensors to accommodate multiple attention heads via the view() method, which splits the input into num_heads parts, each with head_dim dimensions. The subsequent permute(1, 0, 2) method rearranges the tensor dimensions by swapping the sequence length and the number of heads, allowing each attention head to process its portion of the sequence independently and in parallel.

After the heads are split, the dot products and attention weights are computed just as in the standard scaled dot-product attention mechanism. After processing, the individual head outputs are concatenated back together ❶ and reshaped into their original sequence length and dimension ❷. A final linear transformation via Wout is applied to combine the outputs from all heads, producing the final result.

Understanding the Transformer Structure

Transformers consist of a stack of layers, each containing a multi-head attention mechanism followed by a feed-forward neural network. These layers are further enhanced with layer normalization and residual connections to ensure stability during training and to facilitate effective gradient flow.

The classical transformer architecture is an encoder-decoder model. Similar to the seq2seq architecture, the encoder processes the input sequence to generate contextual representations, while the decoder uses these representations to produce the output sequence; producing the output may involve translating the input into another language or transforming it into a different form. The decoder mirrors the encoder's structure but includes an additional cross-attention layer, enabling the decoder to focus on relevant parts of the encoded input while generating the output sequence.

However, the transformer architecture is highly flexible: Beyond the classical encoder-decoder model, it can also be designed as an *encoder-only* or *decoder-only* variant. Each variation serves distinct learning objectives depending on the task requirements. For example, encoder-only transformers are well suited for tasks like classification, which focus on understanding and representing the input. On the other hand, decoder-only transformers are often employed in tasks involving generative modeling, such as text generation.

In this section, you'll implement an encoder-only transformer, as illustrated in Figure 8-7.

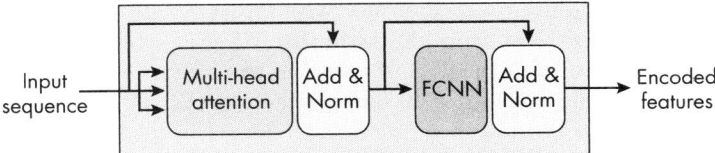

Figure 8-7: An encoder-only transformer including a multi-head attention layer and a fully connected neural network (FCNN) layer

The encoder alone is sufficient for tasks such as classification and sequence embedding, where the primary objective is to comprehend and represent the input sequence rather than generate a new output sequence.

Loading the IMDb Dataset

You'll start by downloading the IMDb Large Movie Review dataset at *https://huggingface.co/datasets/imdb*. It contains 50,000 movie reviews, labeled as positive or negative. The dataset is divided into 25,000 reviews for training and 25,000 reviews for testing. You can download it with Listing 8-12 (you'll need to install the Hugging Face Datasets library with `pip install datasets`).

```
from datasets import load_dataset

dataset = load_dataset("imdb")
```

Listing 8-12: Downloading the IMDb dataset

This code downloads the dataset dictionary that contains the "train" and "test" sets. Each set is also a dictionary with two keys: "text", which contains movie reviews, and "label", which contains the sentiment of the review; 0 denotes a negative sentiment, and 1 denotes a positive sentiment.

Before proceeding, you'll split the training set into training and validation datasets, as shown in Listing 8-13.

```
split = dataset["train"].train_test_split(test_size=0.2,
                                           stratify_by_column="label", seed=42)
train_dataset, val_dataset = split["train"], split["test"]
```

Listing 8-13: Splitting the training and validation datasets

This code splits the "train" portion of the dataset into a training dataset (80 percent) and a validation dataset (20 percent). To retain the same distribution of labels in both datasets as in the original, the code uses stratify_by _column="label". This maintains a balanced representation of classes, meaning that both the training and validation sets will have the same proportion of positive and negative examples as the original dataset. Finally, seeding the random-number generator with seed=42 ensures reproducibility of the split. In this way, every time you run the code, you'll get the same split into training and validation sets, allowing you to consistently reproduce your results and debug your code more effectively. (Instead of 42, you could use any other seed.)

You can now print some example reviews with Listing 8-14.

```
import numpy as np
import pandas as pd

❶ samples = train_dataset.select(np.random.randint(0, len(train_dataset), 3))
texts, labels = samples["text"], samples["label"]

df = pd.DataFrame({"Text": texts, "Label": labels})
styled_df = df.style.set_properties(**{"text-align": "left"}).set_table_styles(
    [{"selector": "th", "props": [("text-align", "center")]}]
)
with pd.option_context("display.max_colwidth", None):
    display(styled_df)
```

Listing 8-14: Printing some example reviews from the training set

This code selects three samples from the training dataset ❶, creates a Pandas dataframe, styles it, and displays it. The resulting display should resemble Figure 8-8.

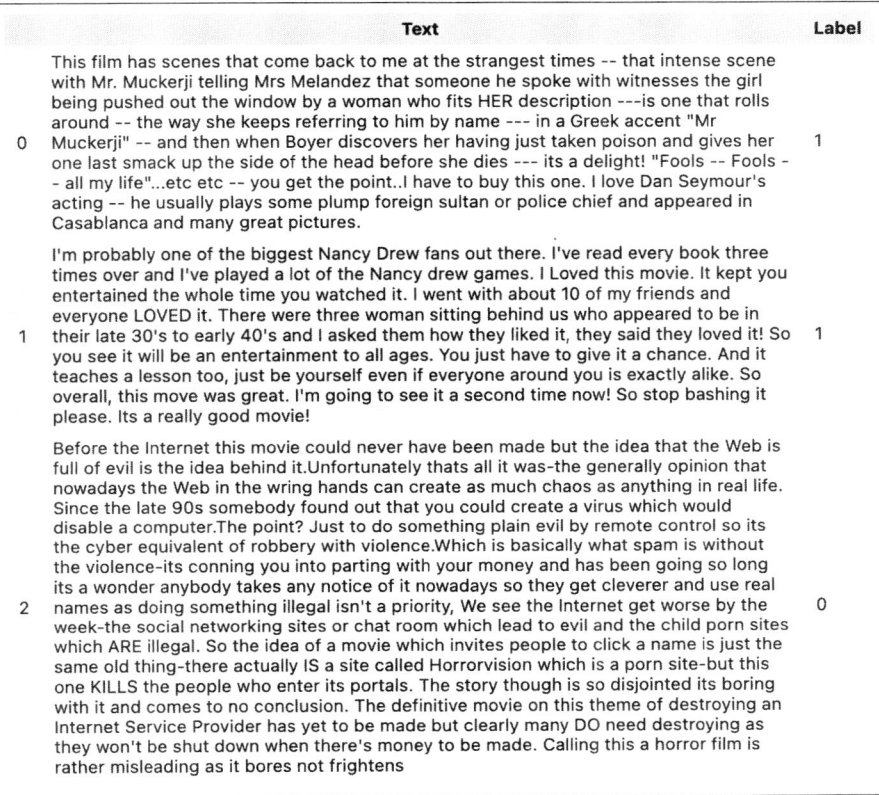

	Text	Label
0	This film has scenes that come back to me at the strangest times -- that intense scene with Mr. Muckerji telling Mrs Melandez that someone he spoke with witnesses the girl being pushed out the window by a woman who fits HER description ---is one that rolls around -- the way she keeps referring to him by name --- in a Greek accent "Mr Muckerji" -- and then when Boyer discovers her having just taken poison and gives her one last smack up the side of the head before she dies --- its a delight! "Fools -- Fools -- all my life"...etc etc -- you get the point..I have to buy this one. I love Dan Seymour's acting -- he usually plays some plump foreign sultan or police chief and appeared in Casablanca and many great pictures.	1
1	I'm probably one of the biggest Nancy Drew fans out there. I've read every book three times over and I've played a lot of the Nancy drew games. I Loved this movie. It kept you entertained the whole time you watched it. I went with about 10 of my friends and everyone LOVED it. There were three woman sitting behind us who appeared to be in their late 30's to early 40's and I asked them how they liked it, they said they loved it! So you see it will be an entertainment to all ages. You just have to give it a chance. And it teaches a lesson too, just be yourself even if everyone around you is exactly alike. So overall, this move was great. I'm going to see it a second time now! So stop bashing it please. Its a really good movie!	1
2	Before the Internet this movie could never have been made but the idea that the Web is full of evil is the idea behind it.Unfortunately thats all it was-the generally opinion that nowadays the Web in the wring hands can create as much chaos as anything in real life. Since the late 90s somebody found out that you could create a virus which would disable a computer.The point? Just to do something plain evil by remote control so its the cyber equivalent of robbery with violence.Which is basically what spam is without the violence-its conning you into parting with your money and has been going so long its a wonder anybody takes any notice of it nowadays so they get cleverer and use real names as doing something illegal isn't a priority, We see the Internet get worse by the week-the social networking sites or chat room which lead to evil and the child porn sites which ARE illegal. So the idea of a movie which invites people to click a name is just the same old thing-there actually IS a site called Horrorvision which is a porn site-but this one KILLS the people who enter its portals. The story though is so disjointed its boring with it and comes to no conclusion. The definitive movie on this theme of destroying an Internet Service Provider has yet to be made but clearly many DO need destroying as they won't be shut down when there's money to be made. Calling this a horror film is rather misleading as it bores not frightens	0

Figure 8-8: Example reviews

In this case, the first two reviews are positive, while the third is negative.

Preprocessing the Reviews

Before performing sentiment analysis, you must preprocess the reviews to convert them into a format suitable for the model. As you've seen in Project 7A, this requires several steps including cleaning the text, tokenizing the reviews, building a vocabulary, and transforming the tokens into numerical representations that the model can interpret. To do this, you'll need the tokenize() function from Listing 7-24, which divides each review into individual words or tokens; the Vocab class from Listing 7-26, which creates a mapping from these tokens to unique indices to build the vocabulary; and the build_vocab_from_iterator() function from Listing 7-27, which constructs the vocabulary by iterating over the tokenized reviews.

Building a Vocabulary

Once the text has been tokenized and cleaned, the next step is to convert these tokens into numerical representations. You'll build a *vocabulary* that maps each unique token into an integer. Listing 8-15 shows how to create the vocabulary.

```
def imdb_iterator(dataset):
    """Iterate over the IMDB dataset."""
    for sample in dataset:
        yield tokenize(sample["text"])


vocab_dict = build_vocab_from_iterator(
    imdb_iterator(train_dataset), specials=["<unk>"], min_freq=10,
)
vocab = Vocab(vocab_dict, unk_token="<unk>")
vocab.set_default_index(vocab(vocab.unk_token))
```

Listing 8-15: Creating the vocabulary

The vocab object acts as a lookup table, assigning a unique integer to each token. The vocabulary dictionary is built with the imdb_iterator() function, which tokenizes each sample in the dataset and is then used to create vocab. The specials argument adds a special token ("<unk>") to handle out-of-vocabulary words, ensuring that the model can manage unseen words effectively.

Preprocessing the Datasets

With the vocabulary ready, the next step is to preprocess the datasets by standardizing, cleaning, tokenizing, and converting tokens into numerical indices. This is done using the preprocessing() function in Listing 8-16.

```
def preprocessing(sample):
    """Preprocess a movie review."""
    sentence = sample["text"]
    tokens = tokenize(unicodedata.normalize("NFC", sentence))
    sequence_of_indices = vocab(tokens)
    sample.update({"sequences": sequence_of_indices})
    return sample


train_dataset = train_dataset.map(preprocessing)
val_dataset = val_dataset.map(preprocessing)
test_dataset = dataset["test"].map(preprocessing)
```

Listing 8-16: Preprocessing the datasets

The preprocessing() function first tokenizes and cleans the text defined by the key "text" from the sample dictionary and then maps the tokens to their corresponding numerical indices in the vocabulary. The resulting indices are added back to the sample as the new key "sequences". The function is then applied to all elements in the training, validation, and test datasets.

Defining the Data Loaders

Before training the model, data loaders must be defined to supply the training, validation, and test data during both training and evaluation.

An important consideration is that the input consists of sentences of varying lengths. In the seq2seq model, you used padding to make the sequence lengths consistent. In this example, however, the sequences in a batch will be concatenated into a single, long sequence instead of being padded. This approach requires the generation of *batch indices* that specify which parts of the concatenated sequence correspond to each individual sequence in the batch. During the attention mechanism, these batch indices are used to create a *mask*, ensuring that tokens from one sequence don't attend to tokens from another. This allows each sequence to be processed independently while maintaining the efficiency of batch processing.

Listing 8-17 provides the implementation.

```
from torch.utils.data import DataLoader
from torch_geometric.data import Data

def collate(batch_of_sequences):
    """Prepare a batch of sequences for the model to process."""
    sequences, labels, batch_indices = [], [], []
    for batch_index, sample in enumerate(batch_of_sequences):
        sequence = torch.tensor(sample["sequences"])
        sequences.append(sequence)
        batch_indices.append(torch.ones_like(sequence, dtype=torch.long)
                        * batch_index)
        label = torch.tensor(sample["label"])
        labels.append(label)
    return Data(sequences=torch.cat(sequences),
                batch_indices=torch.cat(batch_indices),
                y=torch.tensor(labels).float())

train_dataloader = \
    DataLoader(train_dataset, batch_size=8, shuffle=True, collate_fn=collate)
val_dataloader = \
    DataLoader(val_dataset, batch_size=8, shuffle=False, collate_fn=collate)
test_dataloader = \
    DataLoader(test_dataset, batch_size=8, shuffle=False, collate_fn=collate)
```

Listing 8-17: Creating the data loaders

The code first defines the `collate()` function, which preprocesses batches of sequences. Its input is a list of dictionaries, each containing an input sequence (`sample["sequences"]`) and a label (`sample["label"]`). The function converts each sequence and label to a tensor and appends them to the sequences and labels lists.

The `batch_indices` list is created to indicate which tokens belong to which sequence by assigning a batch index to each token. This is achieved by multiplying a tensor of 1s, which matches the shape of `sequence`, by the current batch index. The function then concatenates the sequences, batch indices, and labels into a single `Data` object and returns it.

Finally, the data loaders for the training, validation, and test datasets are created by passing the `collate()` function to the `collate_fn` argument of PyTorch's `DataLoader` class, which specifies how the data points in a batch should be combined for processing.

Building an Encoder-Only Transformer

You'll now implement an encoder-only transformer, building each element step-by-step and assembling them into a model class.

Adding Masking to the Multi-Head Attention Layer

As a starting point for the multi-head attention layer, you'll use the code implemented in Listing 8-11. Since the data loader is collating sequences in the same batch, you'll first modify the data loader to also accept batch indices as inputs and use them for masking.

Listing 8-18 extends the implementation of the `MultiHeadAttention` class in Listing 8-11 to include masking functionality.

```
--snip--
class MultiHeadAttentionLayer(dl.DeeplayModule):
    """Multi-head attention layer with masking."""
    --snip--

    def forward(self, in_sequence, batch_indices):
        --snip--
        attn_scores = (torch.matmul(Q, K.transpose(-2, -1))
                        / (self.head_dim ** 0.5))

        attn_mask = torch.eq(batch_indices.unsqueeze(1),
                                batch_indices.unsqueeze(0))
❶       attn_mask = attn_mask.unsqueeze(0)
        attn_scores = attn_scores.masked_fill(attn_mask == False,
                                                float("-inf"))

        attn_weights = torch.nn.functional.soft.softmax(attn_scores, dim=-1)
        --snip--
```

Listing 8-18: The class to add masking to the multi-head attention layer (by modifying Listing 8-11)

This updated `MultiHeadAttentionLayer()` class introduces masking to ensure that tokens from different sequences don't influence one another. In the `forward()` method, an additional tensor (`batch_indices`) is used to determine which tokens belong to the same sequence.

The mask is generated using torch.eq(), which produces a square matrix indicating valid attention positions based on the sequence assignments. The mask is expanded to include a batch dimension ❶, giving it the shape (1, len(in_sequence), len(in_sequence)), matching the attention scores. The mask is used to set attn_scores for unrelated tokens to negative infinity (float("-inf")), ensuring that they receive zero attention after applying softmax().

This prevents unintended information flow between different sequences in the batch and ensures that each sequence is processed independently, preserving context and maintaining the integrity of attention operations.

Implementing a Transformer Encoder Layer

Next, you'll combine the multi-head attention layer with a feed-forward neural network to construct the transformer encoder layer.

The multi-head attention layer processes the input sequence by enabling each token to attend to others, capturing relationships across the sequence. A residual connection is then applied to add features from the original input to the attention output, followed by layer normalization to ensure stability.

The feed-forward network further refines the representation by applying linear transformations and activation functions, followed by another residual connection and normalization. This process enriches each token representation with meaningful contextual information.

Now implement the transformer encoder layer as shown in Listing 8-19.

```
from torch_geometric.nn.norm import LayerNorm

class TransformerEncoderLayer(dl.DeeplayModule):
    """Transformer encoder layer."""

    def __init__(self, num_features, num_heads, feedforward_dim, dropout=0.0):
        """Initialize transformer encoder layer."""
        super().__init__()

        self.self_attn = MultiHeadAttentionLayer(num_features, num_heads)
        self.attn_dropout = dl.Layer(torch.nn.Dropout, dropout)
        self.attn_skip = dl.Add()
        self.attn_norm = dl.Layer(LayerNorm, num_features, eps=1e-6)

        self.feedforward = dl.Sequential(
            dl.Layer(torch.nn.Linear, num_features, feedforward_dim),
            dl.Layer(torch.nn.ReLU),
            dl.Layer(torch.nn.Linear, feedforward_dim, num_features),
        )
        self.feedforward_dropout = dl.Layer(torch.nn.Dropout, dropout)
        self.feedforward_skip = dl.Add()
        self.feedforward_norm = dl.Layer(LayerNorm, num_features, eps=1e-6)
```

```
def forward(self, in_sequence, batch_indices):
    """Refine sequence via attention and feedforward layers."""
❶   attns = self.self_attn(in_sequence, batch_indices)
❷   attns = self.attn_dropout(attns)
❸   attns = self.attn_skip(in_sequence, attns)
❹   attns = self.attn_norm(attns, batch_indices)

❺   out_sequence = self.feedforward(attns)
❻   out_sequence = self.feedforward_dropout(out_sequence)
❼   out_sequence = self.feedforward_skip(attns, out_sequence)
❽   out_sequence = self.feedforward_norm(out_sequence, batch_indices)

    return out_sequence
```

Listing 8-19: The class to implement a transformer encoder layer

The `forward()` method of this class first applies multi-head attention on the input sequences, `in_sequence` ❶. The method applies dropout to the attention output ❷, which randomly deactivates a fraction of neurons during training to prevent overfitting and help the model generalize better. The method adds the original input, `in_sequence`, to the dropout-adjusted attention output, implementing a residual connection ❸. The method normalizes the output of the residual connection with layer normalization ❹.

Next, `forward()` passes the normalized attention output through the feed-forward network ❺. Dropout is applied to the feedforward network's output ❻. The feed-forward output is added to the original attention output, creating another residual connection ❼. Finally, the final output is normalized with layer normalization ❽.

The final output, `out_sequence`, is a set of sequences obtained by enriching the input sequences with contextual information, producing a comprehensive representation that is crucial for the subsequent tasks.

Building a Transformer Encoder Model

As in a seq2seq model, the input is processed by an embedding layer that converts the sparse categorical data of the input sequences into a dense numerical format, making it more suitable for neural network processing.

Unlike traditional sequence models, such as recurrent neural networks, which inherently understand sequence order, transformers treat inputs as unordered sets. To address this, transformers use *positional encodings*, which assign each token a unique positional marker. This allows the model to incorporate the order of tokens, which is crucial for understanding their relationships and the overall meaning of a sequence.

Positional encodings *are generated using a combination of sine and cosine functions of different frequencies. For each position* i *in the sequence and each dimension* j *of the positional encoding vector, the encoding is defined as*

$$PE_{i,2j} = \sin\left(\frac{i}{10000^{2j/d_m}}\right)$$

$$PE_{i,2j+1} = \cos\left(\frac{i}{10000^{2j/d_m}}\right)$$

where d_m *is the dimension of the positional encoding vector. The oscillatory patterns created by the sine and cosine functions permit the encoding values to change across positions for individual dimensions.*

The encoded input is thus passed to a stack of transformer encoder layers with a dense top.

You can implement the transformer encoder model with the class shown in Listing 8-20.

```
class TransformerEncoderModel(dl.DeeplayModule):
    """Transformer encoder model."""

    def __init__(self, vocab_size, num_features, num_heads, feedforward_dim,
                 num_layers, out_dim, dropout=0.0):
        """Initialize transformer encoder model."""
        super().__init__()
        self.num_features = num_features

        self.embedding = dl.Layer(torch.nn.Embedding, vocab_size, num_features)

        self.pos_encoder = dl.IndexedPositionalEmbedding(num_features)
        self.pos_encoder.dropout.configure(p=dropout)

        self.transformer_block = dl.LayerList()
        for _ in range(num_layers):
            self.transformer_block.append(TransformerEncoderLayer(
                num_features, num_heads, feedforward_dim, dropout=dropout,
            ))

        self.out_block = dl.Sequential(
            dl.Layer(torch.nn.Dropout, dropout),
            dl.Layer(torch.nn.Linear, num_features, num_features // 2),
            dl.Layer(torch.nn.ReLU),
            dl.Layer(torch.nn.Linear, num_features // 2, out_dim),
            dl.Layer(torch.nn.Sigmoid),
        )
```

```
def forward(self, dict):
    """Predict sentiment of movie reviews."""
    in_sequence, batch_indices = dict["sequences"], dict["batch_indices"]

❶  embeddings = self.embedding(in_sequence) * self.num_features ** 0.5
❷  pos_embeddings = self.pos_encoder(embeddings, batch_indices)

    out_sequence = pos_embeddings
    for transformer_layer in self.transformer_block:
❸      out_sequence = transformer_layer(out_sequence, batch_indices)

    batch_size = torch.max(batch_indices) + 1
    aggregates = torch.zeros(batch_size, self.num_features,
                             device=out_sequence.device)
❹  for batch_index in torch.unique(batch_indices):
        mask = batch_indices == batch_index
        aggregates[batch_index] = out_sequence[mask].mean(dim=0)

❺  pred_sentiment = self.out_block(aggregates).squeeze()
    return pred_sentiment
```

Listing 8-20: The class to implement a transformer encoder model

This class takes input sequences and batch indices, applies embedding and positional encoding, processes them through multiple transformer layers, and then aggregates each sequence's information to predict the sentiment of the reviews.

The forward() method of this class accepts a dictionary as input, which includes two key components: dict["sequences"] containing the input sequences, and dict["batch_indices"] containing the corresponding batch indices.

Initially, the embedding layer maps each token's numerical value to a unique vector in a high-dimensional space ❶ defined by the specified embedding dimension (num_features). The model then applies positional encoding ❷ to incorporate information about the order of tokens within each sequence (see the note on page 353). This process adds a unique vector to each token embedding based on its position in the sequence, ensuring that the model captures the sequential nature of the data. The core of the model comprises a stack of transformer encoder layers that process the sequence in several iterations ❸. Each layer takes the output of the previous layer, allowing the attention mechanisms and feed-forward neural networks to identify complex relationships between tokens.

Then the model computes an aggregate representation for each sequence in the batch ❹. This is achieved by averaging the output vectors across the sequence length, thereby condensing each sequence into a single vector that captures the essence of the entire sequence.

Finally, the aggregated sequence representations are passed through a series of dense layers with nonlinear activations and dropouts ❺, which transform the enriched representations into a final prediction. This prediction indicates whether the input movie reviews are positive or negative, thus completing the sentiment analysis.

You're finally ready to instantiate your transformer encoder model with Listing 8-21.

```
model = TransformerEncoderModel(
    vocab_size=len(vocab), num_features=300, num_heads=12, feedforward_dim=512,
    num_layers=4, out_dim=1, dropout=0.1,
).create()
```

Listing 8-21: Instantiating the transformer encoder model

You can print out the details of this model with print(model).

Although the model is ready for training, incorporating pretrained embeddings can significantly enhance its performance. *Pretrained embeddings* are rich word representations derived from large text corpora. Often used to initialize the embedding layer, these pretrained embeddings help the model start with a better understanding of the input, which then leads to faster convergence and improved generalization. As you've already seen in Project 7A and in the first section of this chapter, GloVe provides some of the most popular pretrained embeddings. You downloaded them previously with Listing 7-41, and now you can use them to initialize the model's embedding layer with Listing 8-22.

```
glove_file = os.path.join(glove_folder, "glove.42B.300d.txt")
glove_embed, embed_dim = load_glove_embeddings(glove_file), 300

❶ model.embedding.weight.data = \
    get_glove_embeddings(vocab.get_tokens(), glove_embed, embed_dim)
model.embedding.weight.requires_grad = False
```

Listing 8-22: Adding the pretrained embeddings

This code uses the load_glove_embeddings() function (Listing 7-42) to load the 300-dimensional GloVe embeddings into the glove_embed dictionary. Next, the code initializes the model's embedding layer with these pretrained embeddings by calling the get_glove_embeddings() function (Listing 7-43), which creates an embedding matrix corresponding to the vocabulary tokens retrieved using vocab.get_tokens(). The code then replaces the random initial weights with the GloVe embeddings ❶. Finally, the code freezes the embedding layer during training, preventing the pretrained embeddings from being updated and ensuring that the model uses these rich word representations without altering them.

Training the Model

You can now compile the model as shown in Listing 8-23.

```
classifier = dl.BinaryClassifier(
    model=model, optimizer=dl.AdamW(lr=1e-4),
).create()
```

Listing 8-23: Compiling the model

This code compiles the model with the AdamW optimizer and the default binary cross-entropy loss function.

Next, you'll create a trainer and train the model, using Listing 8-24.

```
trainer = dl.Trainer(max_epochs=5)
trainer.fit(classifier, train_dataloader, val_dataloader)
```

Listing 8-24: Training the model

This code trains the model for five epochs.

Evaluating the Trained Model

After training, you can evaluate the model on the test set with Listing 8-25.

```
test_results = trainer.test(classifier, test_dataloader)
```

Listing 8-25: Evaluating the model

The model should achieve around 87 percent accuracy on the test set, demonstrating the effectiveness of transformers for NLP tasks.

You can also display the model's predictions for a few test reviews, using Listing 8-26.

```
import random

classifier.model.eval()

texts, labels, predictions = [], [], []
for idx in random.sample(range(len(test_dataset)), 3):
    sample = test_dataset[idx]
    input_sequence = torch.tensor(vocab(tokenize(sample["text"]))).long()
    test_input = {
        "sequences": input_sequence,
        "batch_indices": torch.zeros_like(input_sequence, dtype=torch.long),
    }
    probability = classifier.model(test_input)
    prediction = probability > 0.5

    texts.append(sample["text"])
    labels.append(sample["label"])
    predictions.append(prediction.item() * 1)
```

```
df = pd.DataFrame({"text": texts, "label": labels, "prediction": predictions})
styled_df = df.style.set_properties(**{"text-align": "left"}).set_table_styles(
    [{"selector": "th", "props": [("text-align", "center")]}]
)
with pd.option_context("display.max_colwidth", None):
    display(styled_df)
```

Listing 8-26: Displaying the model's predictions on some reviews

The output should be similar to Figure 8-9.

	text	label	prediction
0	OK, the show was a little uneven, but I still loved it. I found the main two bunnies annoying, but Hamton & Plucky were always amusing. I really want the Baby Plucky episodes on DVD (or even VHS). Please release those! Specifically the "Potty years" episode aired on 11/22/91; the "Going up" episode aired on 9/17/92 and the "Minister golf" episode in 11/92. They are the funniest bits of the whole series and even over a decade later we still reference these bits! (I have nothing more to say, please reduce the minimum to something like 5 lines and rewards us for brevity!)	1	1
1	I watched the 1st scarecrow movie and didn't bag out that one, though i knew it was b grade it actually had some decent gore and the guy playing the scarecrow was an awesome acrobat and had some good skills going. The effects were better and the costume looked heaps better then this movie. I borrowed this one with an open mind, i am also a fan of ken shamrock (former ufc superfight champ) and was hoping it was a decent movie. Boy was i wrong, the movie sucked, the monster was pathetic in both appearance and in actually being scary, the storyline was SO predictable it was like watching the movie in preview mode, as i already would guess what will happen, the music was so bad, with a horrible lip sync song that made me wanna punch the screen. Overall avoid this crappy movie. Save some money.	0	0
2	Without a doubt, the WORST movie I have ever seen in my life. There was nothing entertaining about this film. I know it was supposed to be a comedy, but it actually made me cry at the thought of losing the $4.75 admission price.	0	0

Figure 8-9: The example reviews with model predictions

The model's performance can be further improved by fine-tuning its hyperparameters, increasing training epochs, or applying advanced techniques like learning rate schedules, gradient clipping, and early stopping.

NOTE *Code Example 8-B, "Predicting Sentiment Using a Transformer," is available at https://github.com/DeepTrackAI/DeepLearningCrashCourse. Navigate to the Ch08_Attention folder and then ec08_B_transformer. The transformer .ipynb notebook provides a complete code example that uses an encoder-only transformer to predict the sentiment of movie reviews.*

Project 8C: Classifying Images with a Vision Transformer

Historically, convolutional neural networks, introduced in Chapter 3, have dominated image-analysis tasks. However, inspired by the success of transformers in NLP, Google Research developed the *vision transformer (ViT)* in 2020, marking a breakthrough in image interpretation. ViT demonstrated that a model originally designed for text could excel in visual domains as well. In fact, it has outperformed traditional convolutional methods in various image-classification benchmarks, showcasing exceptional scalability and generalization.

The success of ViT has led to its adoption in cutting-edge applications such as *image segmentation* (dividing an image into meaningful regions for easier analysis) and *multimodal learning* (integrating and processing information from multiple sources like text, images, and audio).

This project introduces the ViT model, explains its architecture, and demonstrates its use in image-classification tasks. You'll begin by exploring the CIFAR-10 dataset, which contains images categorized into classes like Cats and Cars. You'll learn how to preprocess these images, build the ViT model, and train it. After noting the unimpressive results of training ViT on small datasets, you'll apply CutMix augmentation to enhance performance. Finally, you'll observe how powerful ViT can be when pretrained on larger datasets.

Using the CIFAR-10 Dataset

The CIFAR-10 dataset will serve as the primary playground for experimenting with ViT. CIFAR-10 contains 60,000 full-color images, each 32×32 pixels, divided across 10 distinct classes, with each class containing 6,000 images. The dataset is split into a training set of 50,000 images and a test set of 10,000 images.

Use Listing 8-27 to download and prepare the data.

```
from torchvision import datasets

train_val_dataset = datasets.CIFAR10(root="./data", train=True, download=True)
test_dataset = datasets.CIFAR10(root="./data", train=False, download=True)
```

Listing 8-27: Preparing the CIFAR-10 datasets

This script initializes the CIFAR-10 training and test datasets via PyTorch's datasets.CIFAR10 class. The train parameter specifies whether to load the training or test dataset, and the download option ensures that the data is downloaded if not already present.

You can visualize some images from the CIFAR-10 dataset by using the plot_class_examples() function in Listing 8-28.

```
import matplotlib.pyplot as plt

def plot_class_examples(dataset, n_images):
    """Plot the first images for each class in the dataset."""
    classes = dataset.classes
```

```
class_img_dict = {c: [] for c in range(len(classes))}
for i, (_, label) in enumerate(dataset):
    if all(len(v) == n_images for v in class_img_dict.values()):
      ❶ break
    if len(class_img_dict[label]) < n_images:
      ❷ class_img_dict[label].append(i)

fig, axs = plt.subplots(n_images, len(classes), figsize=(len(classes), 3))
for class_idx, img_indices in class_img_dict.items():
    for j, img_index in enumerate(img_indices):
        img = dataset[img_index][0]
        axs[j, class_idx].imshow(img)
        axs[j, class_idx].set(xticks=[], yticks=[])
        if j == 0:
            axs[j, class_idx].set_title(classes[class_idx], size="medium")
plt.show()
```

Listing 8-28: Visualizing the first CIFAR-10 images for each class

This function displays the first n_images examples for each CIFAR-10 class in the dataset. The function starts by extracting the classes from the dataset and initializing a dictionary to store image indices for each class. The function then iterates over the dataset, collecting indices until it has enough examples for each class ❶. If a class still needs more images, the function adds the current index to its dictionary of indices ❷. Once enough images are collected, the function retrieves and formats the images, plotting them in the appropriate subplots.

You can run the function and visualize three images per class as follows:

```
plot_class_examples(train_val_dataset, n_images=3)
```

Figure 8-10 shows the result.

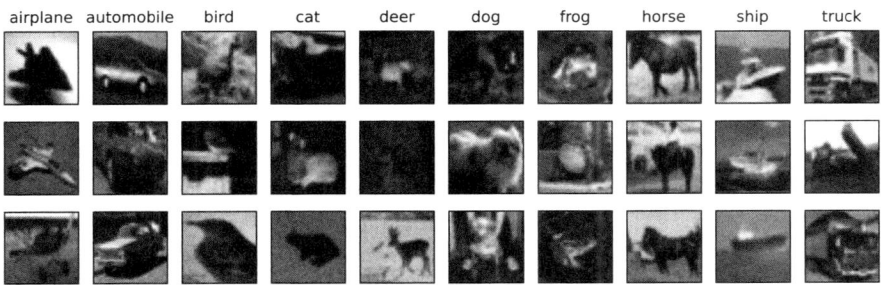

Figure 8-10: The example images from the CIFAR-10 dataset

The visualization showcases the diversity of categories in the CIFAR-10 dataset, ranging from vehicles like trucks and ships to animals such as horses, frogs, and dogs. This diversity, along with variations in color, orientation, and context, highlights the challenge of classifying these images.

Data Preprocessing

To ensure effective training and good generalization to unseen data, you need to partition the CIFAR-10 training dataset into training and validation subsets, since it originally lacks a separate validation set. You can do this with Listing 8-29.

```
import copy, torch
from torch.utils.data import Subset

❶ indices = torch.randperm(len(train_val_dataset)).tolist()
split = int(len(train_val_dataset) * 0.20)
train_indices, val_indices = indices[split:], indices[:split]
train_dataset = Subset(copy.deepcopy(train_val_dataset), train_indices)
val_dataset = Subset(copy.deepcopy(train_val_dataset), val_indices)
```

Listing 8-29: Splitting the training and validation datasets

This code shuffles the dataset indices ❶, uses a validation ratio of 20 percent to split them, and creates the training and validation subsets via PyTorch's Subset class. The copy.deepcopy() function ensures that the two subsets are independent.

To help the model generalize better and prevent overfitting, you'll apply data augmentation techniques to the training dataset, as shown in Listing 8-30.

```
from torchvision import transforms

train_transform = transforms.Compose([
❶ transforms.RandomCrop(32, padding=4),
❷ transforms.RandomHorizontalFlip(), transforms.ToTensor(),
❸ transforms.Normalize(mean=[0.49139968, 0.48215841, 0.44653091],
                        std=[0.24703223, 0.24348513, 0.26158784]),
])
train_dataset.dataset.transform = train_transform
```

Listing 8-30: Preprocessing the training dataset

This transformation augments the training data by random cropping with padding ❶ and horizontal flipping ❷. The code then converts the data to tensors and normalizes them by using the mean and standard deviation values for each channel of the training set ❸.

For the validation dataset, only tensor conversion and normalization are performed to ensure evaluation accuracy, as shown in Listing 8-31.

```
val_transform = transforms.Compose([
    transforms.ToTensor(),
    transforms.Normalize(mean=[0.49139968, 0.48215841, 0.44653091],
                         std=[0.24703223, 0.24348513, 0.26158784]),
])
val_dataset.dataset.transform = val_transform
```

Listing 8-31: Preprocessing the validation dataset

Finally, define the data loaders to feed the training and validation data to the model, as detailed in Listing 8-32.

```
import deeplay as dl

train_loader = dl.DataLoader(train_dataset, batch_size=128, shuffle=True)
val_loader = dl.DataLoader(val_dataset, batch_size=128, shuffle=False)
```

Listing 8-32: Defining the data loaders

The batch size is set to 128 for both data loaders, while shuffling is applied only to the training data.

Building the ViT Model

With the data prepared, you can define the ViT model. Figure 8-11 illustrates the ViT architecture.

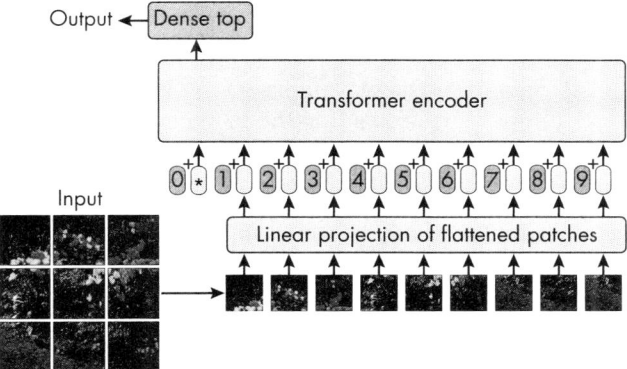

Figure 8-11: The ViT architecture

The ViT architecture consists of four components that work together to process and classify images.

First, *image patch embeddings* divide the input image into smaller, fixed-size, nonoverlapping patches from which the model can learn local features. Each patch is then flattened and passed through a linear transformation (see the following note). To capture global information about the image, the ViT appends a learnable class token to the patch embeddings. This token doesn't directly correspond to any individual patch; instead, it symbolizes the collective image and its relationships with the embeddings, providing a comprehensive view during classification.

Second, *positional encodings* are added to the patch embeddings to provide spatial context, ensuring that the model understands the layout and position of each patch. These positional encodings are randomly initialized and learned during training.

Third, the *transformer encoder* serves as the core of the model. It consists of multiple layers of transformer blocks, each with a multi-head self-attention mechanism and a feed-forward neural network. The multi-head attention allows the model to attend to different parts of the image simultaneously, capturing both local and global information. This contrasts with convolutional neural networks, which have a fixed receptive field and may struggle with capturing long-range dependencies.

Fourth, the *classification head* takes the output class token from the transformer encoder and passes it through a *dense top* neural network to predict the image class.

You can instantiate the ViT model with Listing 8-33.

```
vit = dl.ViT(in_channels=3, image_size=32, patch_size=4,
             hidden_features=[384,] * 7, out_features=10, num_heads=12)
```

Listing 8-33: Instantiating the ViT model

The ViT class from Deeplay manages the ViT architecture, initializing the model components, including the patch embeddings, positional encodings, transformer encoder, and classification head. The key parameters are as follows: in_channels, the number of input channels in the image, which is three (RGB) for the CIFAR-10 dataset; image_size, the size of the input image, which is 32×32 pixels for the CIFAR-10 dataset; patch_size, the size of the image patches, which is set to 4, resulting in a total of 64 patches of size 4×4; hidden_features, the number and size of the hidden layers in the transformer encoder (here, seven transformer layers, each with a hidden size of 384 channels); out_features, the number of classes in the dataset, which is 10 for CIFAR-10; and num_heads, the number of attention heads in the multi-head self-attention mechanism, here set to 12.

You can visualize the ViT architecture by executing print(vit).

NOTE *When visualizing the ViT architecture, you'll notice that the* patch embedder *uses a convolutional layer with a kernel size and stride equal to the patch size. This is a more efficient alternative to explicitly extracting patches, flattening them, and applying a linear transformation. By using this approach, the convolutional layer directly captures and embeds patches as it slides over the image. The kernel size defines the patch size, while the stride ensures that the patches are nonoverlapping.*

After applying the convolution, the resulting feature map is equivalent to the output produced by manually extracting and linearly embedding patches. This method improves computational efficiency, while also adding flexibility, allowing the model to easily adapt to different image resolutions and patch configurations.

Training and Evaluating the ViT Model

With the images preprocessed and the ViT model initialized, you can begin training. Listing 8-34 sets up a classifier, specifies the optimizer, and creates a trainer object.

```
classifier = dl.Classifier(
    model=vit, num_classes=10,
    optimizer=dl.Adam(lr=1e-3, weight_decay=5e-5, betas=(0.9, 0.999)),
).build()
```

Listing 8-34: Defining the classifier

The classifier uses the Adam optimizer with a learning rate of 10^{-3} and a weight decay of 5×10^{-5} for regularization. The betas parameter sets the coefficients for computing running averages of the gradient and its square. By default, the loss function used is CrossEntropyLoss.

Now you can train the model and visualize the training and validation loss and accuracy:

```
trainer = dl.Trainer(max_epochs=100)
trainer.fit(classifier, train_loader, val_loader)
trainer.history.plot();
```

Figure 8-12 shows the resulting plot.

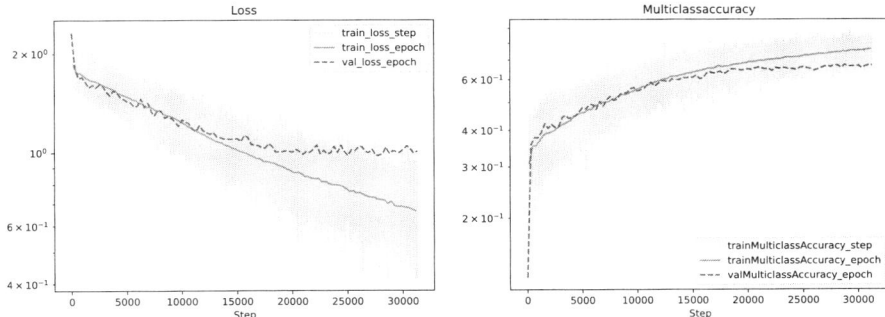

Figure 8-12: The training and validation loss and multiclass accuracy

The ViT model achieves a validation accuracy of approximately 70 percent, where it hits a ceiling.

To evaluate the model on the test dataset, you'll first define the test data loader, as shown in Listing 8-35.

```
test_dataset.transform = val_transform
test_loader = dl.DataLoader(test_dataset, batch_size=128, shuffle=False)
```

Listing 8-35: Defining the test data loader

The test data uses the same preprocessing as the validation set. You can now apply the trained model to the test data:

```
trainer.test(classifier, test_loader)
```

Running the classifier on the test dataset should yield an accuracy similar to that of the validation set. While this performance is reasonable, it's still below that of state-of-the-art convolutional neural networks. In the next section, you'll see how to fine-tune the ViT model to improve its performance.

Improving the ViT Model with CutMix

Compared to convolutional neural networks, ViT models lack strong inductive biases. *Inductive biases*, which are the assumptions a model makes about the structure of the data, help the model generalize effectively. Convolutional neural networks inherently assume spatial relationships in images, recognizing that nearby pixels are more related than distant ones. Then, early layers detect local patterns like edges and textures, while deeper layers combine these features into higher-order structures, as you've seen in Chapter 3.

Without these built-in inductive biases, ViTs need a substantial amount of data to learn effectively. Unlike convolutional neural networks, which are designed to capture spatial locality and translation invariance from the start, ViTs must learn these relationships from scratch by interpreting images as sequences of patches. Therefore, ViTs generally require much larger datasets to achieve strong performance. The CIFAR-10 dataset, with only 60,000 images, is quite small compared to larger datasets like ImageNet, which contains over 14 million images and is often used to train ViTs to state-of-the-art performance.

To address this challenge and help ViTs learn spatial relationships more effectively from smaller datasets, researchers have developed techniques such as CutMix, which you'll implement next.

Implementing CutMix

CutMix is a data augmentation technique that helps the model learn and integrate local features within images, enhancing its ability to generalize and handle variations in input data. Inspired by the concept of *Mixup*, which blends two images by averaging their pixels, CutMix combines patches from two different images rather than blending their entire content.

In a typical CutMix augmentation, a random patch from one image is cut and pasted onto another image, while the labels are mixed proportionally to the area of the patches. This creates a composite training example containing features from both images, with a mixed label that reflects this composition. The primary advantage of this approach is to force the model to focus on less dominant features, promoting a deeper and more robust understanding of spatial relationships. Furthermore, this increases resiliency to variations in the data, such as occlusions or changes in background. Listing 8-36 implements the CutMix class.

```
import numpy as np

class CutMix():
    """CutMix."""

    def __init__(self, size, beta):
        """Initialize CutMix."""
        self.size, self.beta = size, beta

    def __call__(self, batch):
        """Execute CutMix."""
        imgs, labels = batch
        rand_idx = torch.randperm(imgs.size(0))
        rand_imgs, rand_labels = imgs[rand_idx], labels[rand_idx]
❶     augmented_imgs = imgs.clone()

        r_x = np.random.uniform(0, self.size)
        r_y = np.random.uniform(0, self.size)

❷     initial_mix_ratio = np.random.beta(self.beta, self.beta)
        r_w = self.size * np.sqrt(1 - initial_mix_ratio)
        r_h = self.size * np.sqrt(1 - initial_mix_ratio)

        x1 = np.clip(int(r_x - r_w // 2), a_min=0, a_max=self.size)
        x2 = np.clip(int(r_x + r_w // 2), a_min=0, a_max=self.size)
        y1 = np.clip(int(r_y - r_h // 2), a_min=0, a_max=self.size)
        y2 = np.clip(int(r_y + r_h // 2), a_min=0, a_max=self.size)

❸     augmented_imgs[:, :, y1:y2, x1:x2] = rand_imgs[:, :, y1:y2, x1:x2]
❹     final_mix_ratio = 1 - ((x2 - x1) * (y2 - y1) / (self.size ** 2))
        return augmented_imgs, labels, rand_labels, final_mix_ratio
```

Listing 8-36: The class implementing CutMix

The CutMix class is initialized with two parameters: size, specifying the dimensions of the images, and beta, a hyperparameter for the Beta distribution that determines the mixing coefficient (see the note on page 366). The mixing coefficient determines the proportion of the area from the source image that will be mixed into the target image.

The __call__() method takes a batch of images and labels as input and shuffles them, creating rand_imgs and rand_labels. The method also creates a cloned copy of the original images to preserve the original batch ❶. Next, the method samples some random coordinates (r_x, r_y) from a uniform distribution, and an initial mixing coefficient (initial_mix_ratio) from a Beta distribution ❷, to determine the patch dimensions (r_w, r_h). Then the method clips the coordinates for the patch boundaries (x1, x2, y1, y2) to ensure that they stay within the image dimensions. Finally, the method modifies the cloned images by replacing the corresponding patch with a patch from the shuffled images ❸, and recalculates the mixing coefficients based on the patch area to reflect the proportion of the image that was replaced ❹. The method returns the augmented images, original labels, shuffled labels, and adjusted mixing coefficient (final_mix_ratio).

NOTE *The* Beta distribution, *a probability distribution defined on the interval [0, 1], is commonly used to model the behavior of random variables constrained within a fixed range, like proportions or probabilities. The Beta distribution's shape can be left-skewed, right-skewed, or symmetric, depending on the value of its two shape parameters, making it highly flexible for various modeling scenarios.*

Listing 8-37 visualizes the CutMix augmentation applied to a random pair of images from the training dataset.

```
import random
from itertools import chain

def create_batch(samples):
    """Create batch."""
    images, labels = zip(*samples)
    return torch.stack(images), torch.tensor(labels)

def normalize_image(image):
    """Normalize image."""
    mean = torch.tensor([0.49139968, 0.48215841, 0.44653091]).view(3, 1, 1)
    std = torch.tensor([0.24703223, 0.24348513, 0.26158784]).view(3, 1, 1)
    return image * std + mean

❶ samples = random.choices(train_dataset, k=2)
batch = create_batch(samples)

augmented_imgs, *_, mix_ratio = CutMix(size=32, beta=1.0)(batch)

fig, axs = plt.subplots(1, 4, figsize=(12, 3))
for i, img in enumerate(chain(batch[0], augmented_imgs)):
    axs[i].imshow(normalize_image(img).permute(1, 2, 0))
    axs[i].set_title("Original" if i < 2 else f"CutMix {mix_ratio:.2f}")
    axs[i].axis("off")
plt.show()
```

Listing 8-37: Displaying an example of CutMix augmentation

This code selects two random images from the training dataset ❶. The create_batch() function creates a batch of images and labels from the selection, and the CutMix() class is applied to generate the augmented images and labels. The original and augmented images are displayed side by side for comparison. The resulting image should be similar to Figure 8-13.

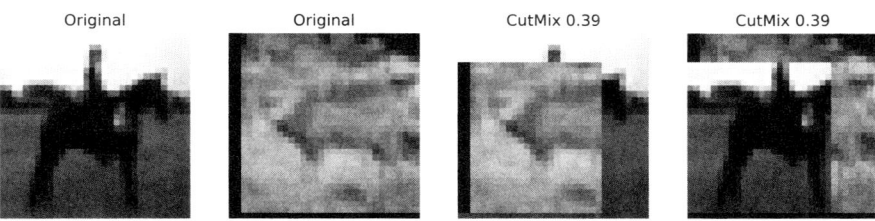

Figure 8-13: The original and CutMix-augmented images

The first two images are the originals from the CIFAR-10 dataset, while the next two show the result of CutMix, with patches exchanged between the two images. The CutMix value shows the proportion of each image in the mix. The figure illustrates how CutMix enriches the dataset, making the model more robust against variations and mixed information.

Note that since the shuffle operation may place a batch of images in its original order, the mixed images might sometimes appear identical to the original ones. If this occurs, rerun Listing 8-37.

Training with CutMix

To train the model with CutMix, you need to define the CutMixClassifier() class, which extends the functionality of Classifier() from Listing 8-34 to incorporate the CutMix augmentation, as shown in Listing 8-38.

```
from torch.optim.lr_scheduler import CosineAnnealingLR
from warmup_scheduler import GradualWarmupScheduler as GradualWarmup

class CutMixClassifier(dl.Classifier):
    """Classifier with CutMix."""

    def __init__(self, model, size=32, beta=1.0, **kwargs):
        """Initialize classifier with CutMix."""
        super().__init__(model, **kwargs)
        self.cutmix = CutMix(size=size, beta=beta)

    def training_step(self, batch, batch_idx):
        """Perform one training step."""
        ❶ augmented_imgs, labels, rand_labels, mix_ratio = self.cutmix(batch)
        ❷ pred_labels = self.model(augmented_imgs)
        ❸ loss = (mix_ratio * self.loss(pred_labels, labels)
                + (1 - mix_ratio) * self.loss(pred_labels, rand_labels))
```

```
                self.log("train_loss", loss, on_step=True, on_epoch=True,
                        prog_bar=True, logger=True)
                self.log_metrics("train", pred_labels, labels, on_step=True,
                            on_epoch=True, prog_bar=True, logger=True)
                return loss

        def configure_optimizers(self):
            """Configure optimizers."""
            optimizer = super().configure_optimizers()
    ❹      base_scheduler = CosineAnnealingLR(optimizer, T_max=200, eta_min=1e-5)
    ❺      scheduler = GradualWarmup(optimizer, multiplier=1.0, total_epoch=5,
                                        after_scheduler=base_scheduler)
            return {"optimizer": optimizer,
                    "lr_scheduler": {"scheduler": scheduler, "interval": "epoch"}}
```

Listing 8-38: The class implementing a classifier with CutMix

During training, the classifier applies CutMix augmentation to the input batch, generating augmented images, original labels, shuffled labels, and a mixing coefficient (mix_ratio) ❶. The model processes the augmented images ❷, and the loss is calculated as a weighted sum of the losses from the original and shuffled labels, with weights mix_ratio and 1 - mix_ratio proportional to the area of each image in the augmented mix ❸.

To enhance training performance, the code implements an annealing schedule that adjusts the learning rate during training, promoting smooth convergence while avoiding overshooting. In this implementation, the base scheduler is CosineAnnealingLR, which progressively decreases the learning rate following a cosine curve ❹. Before applying the cosine schedule, a warm-up phase using GradualWarmupScheduler gradually increases the learning rate from a low initial value over the first five epochs ❺. This combination helps stabilize the training process in the initial stages and then adaptively reduce the learning rate, effectively balancing exploration and convergence for optimal training results.

Now you'll proceed to train the model via the CutMixClassifier class, using Listing 8-39.

```
vit_cutmix = dl.ViT(in_channels=3, image_size=32, patch_size=4,
                    hidden_features=[384,] * 7, out_features=10, num_heads=12)
❶ vit_cutmix[..., "attention#-1"].log_output("attention_output")

classifier_cutmix = CutMixClassifier(
    model=vit_cutmix, num_classes=10,
    optimizer=dl.Adam(lr=1e-3, weight_decay=5e-5, betas=(0.9, 0.999)),
).build()
trainer_cutmix = dl.Trainer(max_epochs=700)
trainer_cutmix.fit(classifier_cutmix, train_loader, val_loader)
```

Listing 8-39: Training the ViT model with CutMix

The model is trained for 700 epochs, giving it sufficient time to learn from the augmented data and improve its performance. The log_output() method logs the output of the attention layer in the last transformer block ❶, allowing you to visualize and interpret the attention maps generated by the model.

You can now apply the trained model to the test data:

```
trainer_cutmix.test(classifier_cutmix, test_loader)
```

With the trained CutMix-augmented model, you should observe a validation accuracy of approximately 90 percent, significantly higher than the previous 70 percent.

Visualizing Attention Maps

Attention maps provide valuable insights into which regions of the image the model focuses on while making predictions, helping you understand the model's decision-making process and the areas that most contribute to its predictions.

Use Listing 8-40 for plotting test images and attention maps, together with ground-truth and predicted labels.

```
from skimage.transform import resize

samples = random.choices(test_dataset, k=4)
imgs, labels = create_batch(samples)

classifier_cutmix.model.eval()
output = classifier_cutmix(imgs)
preds = torch.argmax(output, dim=1)

attn_maps = \
    classifier_cutmix.logs["attention_output"][1][:, 0, 1:].reshape(4, 8, 8)

fig, axs = plt.subplots(2, 4, figsize=(12, 6))
for i, (img, label, pred, attn_map) in enumerate(
    zip(imgs, labels, preds, attn_maps)
):
    img = normalize_image(img).detach().permute(1, 2, 0)

    axs[0, i].imshow(img)
    axs[0, i].set_title(f"Label: {test_dataset.classes[label]}\n"
                        + f"Prediction: {test_dataset.classes[pred]}")
    axs[0, i].axis("off")

    resized_attn_map = resize(attn_map.detach().numpy(), (32, 32),
                            anti_aliasing=True)
    axs[1, i].imshow(img)
    axs[1, i].imshow(resized_attn_map, cmap="hot", alpha=0.5)
```

```
        axs[1, i].set_title("Attention Map")
        axs[1, i].axis("off")
plt.show()
```

Listing 8-40: Visualizing the attention maps

The resulting images should look similar to Figure 8-14.

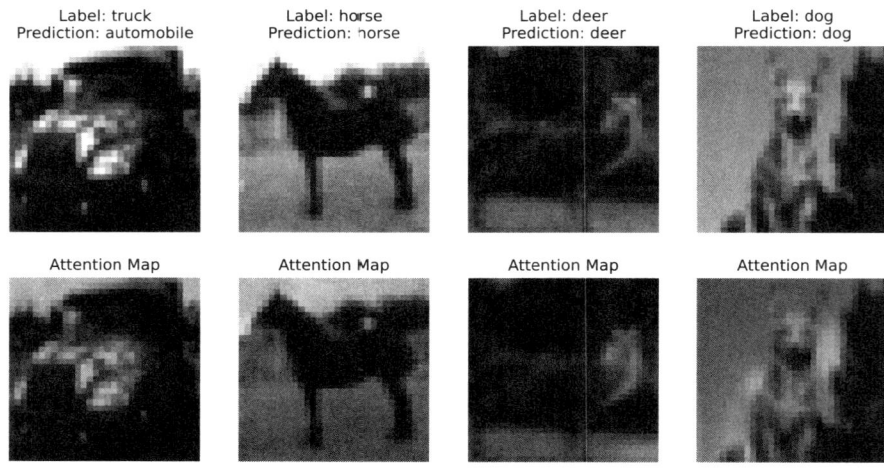

Figure 8-14: The CIFAR-10 images (top) and the attention maps from the model trained with CutMix (bottom)

The top row shows the original images along with their ground-truth and predicted labels. The bottom row displays the same images with their respective attention maps overlaid, highlighting the regions that the model focused on. Brighter regions in the attention map indicate higher attention scores, providing insights into the most influential features in the model's decision.

Using a Pretrained ViT Model

The ViT model trained from scratch achieved a 90 percent accuracy, comparable to convolutional neural networks on CIFAR-10. However, ViT models truly excel when trained on large-scale datasets like ImageNet, which contains millions of images. Such vast datasets unlock the model's full capacity to learn and generalize, often outperforming convolutional neural networks.

To demonstrate this, you'll use a ViT model pretrained on the ImageNet dataset. Listing 8-41 shows how to load the pretrained ViT model from the Hugging Face Model Hub and append a *classification head* that maps the features extracted by the ViT to the output classes, similar to the dense layer used in convolutional models for classification in Project 3A.

```
from transformers import ViTModel

class PretrainedViTModel(torch.nr.Module):
    """Pretrained ViT model."""
```

```
    def __init__(self, pretrained_model, output_channels):
        """Initialize pretrained ViT model."""
        super().__init__()
    ❶ self.backbone = ViTModel.from_pretrained(pretrained_model)
    ❷ hidden_features = self.backbone.config.hidden_size
    ❸ self.classifier = torch.nn.Linear(hidden_features, output_channels)

    def forward(self, imgs):
        """Perform forward step."""
        features = self.backbone(imgs).last_hidden_state[:, 0]
        return self.classifier(features)
```

Listing 8-41: The class to use a pretrained ViT model

When this class is initialized, it downloads and loads the pretrained ViT model weights via `ViTModel.from_pretrained()` ❶. Then the class retrieves the hidden size of the model ❷, which serves as the input size for the fully connected layer that maps the hidden features to the output classes ❸.

Next, you'll use Listing 8-42 to configure the preprocessing and augmentation pipelines to make the training, validation, and testing datasets compatible with the pretrained ViT model.

```
from transformers import ViTImageProcessor

pretrained_model = "google/vit-base-patch16-224-in21k"
processor = ViTImageProcessor.from_pretrained(pretrained_model)

image_mean, image_std = processor.image_mean, processor.image_std
size = processor.size["height"]

train_transform_pt = transforms.Compose([
    transforms.Resize((size, size)), transforms.RandomCrop(size, padding=4),
    transforms.RandomHorizontalFlip(), transforms.ToTensor(),
    transforms.Normalize(image_mean, image_std),
])
val_transform_pt = transforms.Compose([
    transforms.Resize((size, size)), transforms.ToTensor(),
    transforms.Normalize(image_mean, image_std),
])

train_dataset_pt = copy.deepcopy(train_dataset)
train_dataset_pt.dataset.transform = train_transform_pt
val_dataset_pt = copy.deepcopy(val_dataset)
val_dataset_pt.dataset.transform = val_transform_pt
test_dataset_pt = copy.deepcopy(test_dataset)
test_dataset_pt.transform = val_transform_pt
```

Listing 8-42: Implementing the preprocessing and augmentation pipelines

Using `ViTImageProcessor` from the Hugging Face library, the images are resized, augmented, and normalized to meet the requirements of the pretrained model. Similar transformations are applied to the validation and test sets, but without augmentations, to ensure consistent evaluation.

With Listing 8-43, you'll redefine the data loaders to handle the resized and normalized images.

```
train_loader_pt = dl.DataLoader(train_dataset_pt, batch_size=32, shuffle=True)
val_loader_pt = dl.DataLoader(val_dataset_pt, batch_size=32, shuffle=False)
test_loader_pt = dl.DataLoader(test_dataset_pt, batch_size=32, shuffle=False)
```

Listing 8-43: Redefining the data loaders

Running the code in Listing 8-44, you'll set up and train the classifier using the pretrained ViT model.

```
classifier_pt = dl.Classifier(
    model=PretrainedViTModel(pretrained_model, output_channels=10),
    num_classes=10, optimizer=dl.Adam(lr=2e-5),
).build()
trainer_pt = dl.Trainer(max_epochs=2)
trainer_pt.fit(classifier_pt, train_loader_pt, val_loader_pt)
```

Listing 8-44: Setting up and training the classifier

The `Classifier()` class is used to initialize the classifier with the pretrained model and an Adam optimizer. The learning rate is set to the unusually small value of 2×10^{-5}, which permits fine-tuning without overwriting the learned features from the pretrained ViT model. The classifier is set to handle the 10 output classes of the CIFAR-10 dataset. Once the classifier is created, the code instantiates a `Trainer` object with a maximum of two epochs. Then the code calls the `fit()` method of `Trainer` to start the training process.

You can test the performance as follows:

```
trainer_pt.test(classifier_pt, test_loader_pt)
```

After only two epochs, the pretrained ViT model achieves an accuracy of approximately 98 percent on the CIFAR-10 dataset, significantly outperforming the version trained from scratch.

NOTE   *Code Example 8-C, "Classifying Images with a Vision Transformer," is available at https://github.com/DeepTrackAI/DeepLearningCrashCourse. Navigate to the Ch08_Attention folder and then ec08_C_vit. The vit.ipynb notebook provides a complete code example that demonstrates how to use a ViT to classify images.*

Summary

In this chapter, you explored the impact of attention mechanisms and transformer models on sequence processing and image classification. To do so, you built attention modules from scratch and applied them to explore the relationships between words in a sentence.

The first project on machine translation showed how incorporating multiplicative and additive attention mechanisms significantly enhances the model's ability to identify and exploit complex dependencies in sequential data. Through attention maps, you visualized the attention mechanism's ability to dynamically focus on relevant parts of the input sequence, providing insights into the translation model's decision-making process.

The second project presented the architecture of transformers, which use multi-head attention to understand complex relationships within input data. You saw the attention mechanism in action through applications like sentiment analysis and language translation, which demonstrate how transformers outperform traditional recurrent neural network–based models by capturing long-term dependencies and contextual information more effectively.

The third project introduced ViT, a pioneering model that uses the transformer architecture for image processing. By breaking images into patches and applying self-attention, ViT remarkably outperforms convolutional neural networks in image classification, challenging their dominance. This project demonstrated the ViT model's effectiveness on the CIFAR-10 dataset. In particular, the pretrained models achieved high accuracy even with limited training epochs.

Programmers are finding more and more applications for the attention concept in many areas of deep learning. By understanding and using these powerful techniques, you'll be well equipped to tackle a wide range of advanced machine learning tasks.

Seminal Works and Further Reading

The concept of attention in neural networks was introduced by Dzmitry Bahdanau et al. in "Neural Machine Translation by Jointly Learning to Align and Translate," published in 2014 on arXiv (article number 1409.0473) and later presented at the 2015 International Conference on Learning Representations (ICLR). They developed a dynamic attention model that enabled neural networks to focus on specific parts of an input sequence.

Building on this foundational work, Minh-Thang Luong et al. in 2015 explored various attention mechanisms in "Effective Approaches to Attention-Based Neural Machine Translation," published on arXiv (article number 1508.04025) and presented at the 2015 Conference on Empirical Methods in Natural Language Processing (EMNLP). They systematically examined various attention techniques, such as dot-product, general, and concatenative attention.

A significant breakthrough came in 2017 with the introduction of the transformer architecture by Ashish Vaswani et al. in "Attention Is All You Need," presented at the 31st Conference on Neural Information Processing Systems (NeurIPS 2017) and published in *Advances in Neural Information Processing Systems* (volume 30). This work discarded traditional recurrent and convolutional structures in favor of self-attention mechanisms for seq2seq tasks. The transformer architecture paved the way for the development of models like BERT and GPT, which have become dominant in NLP thanks to their ability to handle long-range dependencies and parallelize computations.

The adaptability of transformers was further demonstrated in 2020 by Alexey Dosovitskiy et al. in "An Image Is Worth 16×16 Words: Transformers for Image Recognition at Scale," published on arXiv (article number 2010.11929) and presented at the 2021 ICLR. This research introduced the vision transformer (ViT), showing that self-attention mechanisms could be effectively applied to image-classification tasks.

CHALLENGE PROJECTS

8-1: Transformer for time-series forecasting Implement a transformer model for time-series forecasting on the Jena Climate dataset and compare its performance with more-traditional methods, such as the recurrent neural networks you implemented in Chapter 7.

8-2: Language translation Develop a transformer model capable of translating multiple languages. Use the well-known TED Talks Open Translation Project dataset available from the AI4Bharat IndicNLP Catalog, which offers parallel collections of texts for several language pairs. Construct and train a transformer with both encoder and decoder components to handle translation. Assess the quality of translations by using BLEU scores, and compare your results with baseline models provided within the dataset.

8-3: Multimodal learning with ViT and text transformers Build a multimodal learning system that combines visual data from a ViT model and textual data from a transformer model to perform a classification task. Use the Twitter Sentiment Analysis dataset or the Hateful Memes dataset to create a system that classifies social media posts based on both their image and text content. Preprocess the image and text data, train the multimodal model, and evaluate its performance. Analyze how the integration of visual and textual information improves classification accuracy and provides richer context for decision-making.

8-4: Create a chatbot Build an attention-based chatbot capable of engaging in basic conversations. Use the Cornell Movie-Dialogs Corpus to train your chatbot. This dataset contains a large collection of movie character dialogues that can teach your model how to handle conversational context and generate appropriate responses. Focus on preprocessing the text data, designing a suitable recurrent neural network architecture, and implementing a mechanism to handle context and conversation flow. Compare the performance of this chatbot with that of a chatbot implemented using a recurrent neural network.

9

CREATING AND TRANSFORMING IMAGES WITH GENERATIVE ADVERSARIAL NETWORKS

In this chapter, you'll learn about *generative adversarial networks*, or GANs, a groundbreaking innovation in generative deep learning that has reshaped image synthesis. Emerging as a powerful successor to models like the variational autoencoders in Chapter 4, GANs have excelled in applications ranging from artistic image generation to style transfer and image inpainting.

GANs have far-reaching applications in various fields. In the entertainment industry, GANs are revolutionizing video game design by creating lifelike characters and environments, as well as enhancing content creation in films and virtual reality by generating high-quality textures, backgrounds, and even entire scenes. In security, they're employed for data synthesis and anomaly detection, helping to identify unusual patterns that could signal threats or fraud. In biomedical and pharmaceutical research, GANs are revolutionizing the study of cellular and subcellular structures by offering a noninvasive alternative to traditional chemical staining methods, which often involve toxic substances that can alter the cells' natural state and behavior.

Additionally, in health care, GANs aid in generating synthetic medical images, which can be used for training diagnostic models, ultimately improving disease detection and treatment planning.

You'll begin by discovering the adversarial learning approach that powers GANs. This architecture consists of a dual-network system: the generator, which creates new, unseen data; and the discriminator, which evaluates the authenticity of this generated data. Crucially, both networks are trained to compete with each other. This adversarial relationship results in the generator producing increasingly realistic data, while the discriminator becomes more adept at distinguishing real from fake data.

To understand these concepts, you'll implement a basic GAN architecture generating MNIST digits. Afterward, you'll progress to the more advanced task of coding a GAN to perform virtual stainings. Finally, you'll create a CycleGAN for cross-modality microscopy.

Understanding GANs

This section will guide you through the fundamental concepts behind GANs, including their architecture, the mathematical principles governing their operation, and the training process that allows them to produce high-quality synthetic data.

When attempting to generate a new, unseen sample that convincingly resembles those in a given dataset, a neural network first needs to understand the underlying data distribution. This means the network must learn the statistical properties and patterns that define the dataset, ensuring that the generated sample fits the same set of criteria that characterizes the original data. Essentially, the generated sample should be indistinguishable from the real samples, making it a plausible member of the dataset.

Different generative models get this information in different ways. As you saw in Chapter 4, autoencoders learn the underlying data distribution by mapping the input data to a latent space. They achieve this by compressing the images through an encoder network into the latent space, then reconstructing the original data from the latent space through a decoder network. In a more refined approach, variational and Wasserstein autoencoders grasp the distribution of the data by assuming a prior distribution of the latent space. Subsequently, they learn the distribution's parameters through a variational inference approach. GANs improve upon these strategies by implementing a separate neural network to define and update the loss function.

GANs are composed of two neural networks, the generator and the discriminator, as illustrated in Figure 9-1.

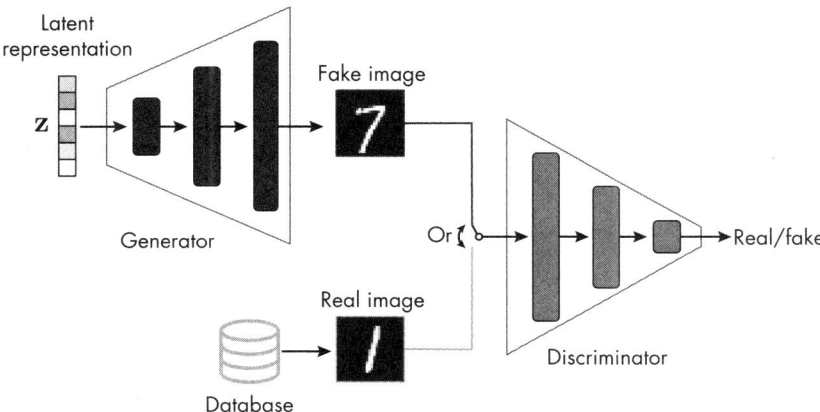

Figure 9-1: The GAN architecture

As the name suggests, the *generator* generates new data from pure noise by sampling points in a latent space, much like a decoder in an autoencoder. However, unlike an autoencoder, the generator in a GAN doesn't have a predefined loss function to minimize the difference between the generated images and the original images. Instead, the loss function is dynamically defined by the discriminator.

The *discriminator* differentiates real data from fake data produced by the generator. In turn, the generator tries to fool the discriminator by generating fake data that is indistinguishable from the real data.

This adversarial setup gives rise to a *dynamically learned loss function*; the loss function is not fixed but is learned in the training process. In the following subsection, you'll explore the math behind this process—specifically, the principal equation of GANs and their training loop.

Discriminating Between Real and Fake Data

If the discriminator's job is to distinguish between real and fake data, then in essence, it performs a binary classification task. The discriminator classifies the provided data into one of two classes, Real or Fake, similar to the way you classified the dataset containing images of uninfected and parasitized malaria stains in Project 3A. The difference here is that one of the classes, the one containing the fake images, is constantly changing as the generator becomes better at its job.

The output of the discriminator is a single value ranging from 0 to 1 that predicts the probability of the image belonging to the Real (1) or Fake (0) class. As you've seen in several projects, a common loss function used for binary classification tasks is the binary cross-entropy loss. This can be written as

$$\mathcal{L}_{BCE} = -y \log \hat{y} - (1 - y) \log(1 - \hat{y}) \tag{9.1}$$

where y is the ground-truth label (either 0 or 1), and $\hat{y}$ is the predicted label, which can acquire continuous values from 0 to 1.

Let's define $\mathbf{x}$ as some real data belonging to a dataset, such as an image of a handwritten digit from the MNIST dataset. If we represent the discriminator as D, the output of the discriminator is $D(\mathbf{x})$—a value that can be interpreted as the estimated probability of the image $\mathbf{x}$ being real. By setting the ground-truth label $y = 1$ in Equation 9.1, you get this:

$$\mathcal{L}_{\text{real}} = -\log \hat{y} \qquad (9.2)$$
$$= -\log(D(\mathbf{x}))$$

Similarly, let $\mathbf{z}$ be the noise vector input into the generator. Representing the generator as G, the output of the generator is $G(\mathbf{z})$—the fake image generated from the noise vector $\mathbf{z}$. After setting the ground-truth label $y = 0$ in Equation 9.1, when the discriminator takes this fake image as input, you get the following:

$$\mathcal{L}_{\text{fake}} = -\log(1 - \hat{y}) \qquad (9.3)$$
$$= -\log(1 - D(G(\mathbf{z})))$$

The loss function for the discriminator is defined as the average of the loss functions for the real and fake images, which can be written as follows:

$$\mathcal{L}_{\text{D}} = \frac{1}{2}\mathcal{L}_{\text{real}} + \frac{1}{2}\mathcal{L}_{\text{fake}} \qquad (9.4)$$

During the training process, the discriminator optimizes its parameters to minimize this loss function.

Generating Realistic Fake Data

The generator aims to produce fake images that the discriminator can't tell apart from the real ones. This means that the generator tries to create images that cause the discriminator to output a probability value of 1 that the data belongs to the real class. Accordingly, to calculate the generator's loss function, setting the ground-truth label $y = 1$ in Equation 9.1, you get the following:

$$\mathcal{L}_{\text{G}} = -\log \hat{y} \qquad (9.5)$$
$$= -\log(D(G(\mathbf{z})))$$

During the training process, the generator optimizes its parameters to minimize this loss function; to do so, it needs to produce fake images from noise vectors, denoted as $G(\mathbf{z})$, that the discriminator is more likely to classify as real. This means that the generator seeks to minimize the loss function $\mathcal{L}_{\text{G}}$ (Equation 9.5) to increase the probability that the discriminator will assign a label of 1 to the generated image.

In other words, the generator tries to maximize, $\mathcal{L}_{\text{fake}} = -\log(1 - D(G(\mathbf{z})))$, the second term in the loss function of the discriminator (Equation 9.4).

With this interpretation, you now should understand the adversarial dynamics underlying the training of GANs. The generator and discriminator continuously adapt to each other, with the generator trying to produce realistic data, and the discriminator striving to distinguish between real and fake data. This interplay forms the basis of the adversarial objective, originally defined in the 2014 seminal paper "Generative Adversarial Networks" by Ian Goodfellow and co-workers.

Training a GAN

The following steps describe the training loop for a GAN:

1. Sample a real data point $\mathbf{x}$ from the dataset (such as an image of a handwritten digit from the MNIST dataset).

2. Pass the real data point through the discriminator to get the discriminator prediction for the real data point, $D(\mathbf{x})$.

3. Use binary cross-entropy loss to calculate the first part of the discriminator loss ($\mathcal{L}_{real}$) for the real image by setting the ground-truth label $y = 1$ (Equation 9.2).

4. Sample a noise vector $\mathbf{z}$ from a normal distribution $\mathcal{N}(0, 1)$.

5. Generate a fake data point by passing the noise vector $\mathbf{z}$ through the generator, $G(\mathbf{z})$.

6. Pass $G(\mathbf{z})$ through the discriminator to get the discriminator prediction for the fake data point, $D(G(\mathbf{z}))$.

7. Use binary cross-entropy loss to calculate the second part of the discriminator loss ($\mathcal{L}_{fake}$) for the fake image by setting the ground-truth label $y = 0$ (Equation 9.3).

8. Calculate the total discriminator loss ($\mathcal{L}_D$) as the average of the two losses (Equation 9.4).

9. Train the discriminator by backpropagating $\mathcal{L}_D$.

10. Calculate the generator loss by setting the ground-truth label for the fake image as $y = 1$ in the binary cross-entropy loss function $\mathcal{L}_G$ (Equation 9.5).

11. Train the generator by backpropagating $\mathcal{L}_G$.

12. Repeat these steps until the generator and the discriminator loss curves reach equilibrium, or until the generator produces realistic data.

Unlike conventional training algorithms that minimize the loss, GANs aim to achieve an equilibrium between the generator and the discriminator. This balance ensures that while the generator produces realistic outputs, the discriminator becomes proficient at distinguishing real from generated data. In the next section, you'll implement this training loop from scratch.

Generating Digits with a GAN

Now that you understand the underlying math of GANs, you'll build a deep convolutional GAN to generate images of handwritten digits from the MNIST dataset. To do so, after preprocessing the dataset, you'll define the generator and discriminator. Afterward, you'll train the GAN and analyze its results by visualizing the images and loss functions output by the generator and discriminator.

Loading the MNIST Dataset with PyTorch

You've already encountered the MNIST dataset several times, starting with Project 1A. It consists of grayscale images of handwritten digits from 0 to 9, each 28×28 pixels. There are 60,000 training images and 10,000 test images. For this example, you'll load the MNIST dataset by using the TorchVision package provided by PyTorch.

Before downloading the dataset, you'll define some transformations to convert it into a usable form with Listing 9-1.

```
from torchvision.transforms import import Compose, Normalize, Resize, ToTensor

transform = Compose([Resize((64, 64)), ToTensor(),
                    Normalize(mean=[0.5], std=[0.5], inplace=True)])
```

Listing 9-1: Implementing the digit transformations

Since the GAN that you'll define later expects images of 64×64 pixels, this code defines a transformation that resizes the images to the expected size and converts them into PyTorch tensors. The Normalize transformation then normalizes their pixel values to lie from −1 to 1 and subtracts mean from the images and subsequently divides them by std. This normalization is standard practice when training GANs because it helps stabilize and speed up the training process by ensuring that the input data has a consistent scale, reducing the risk of vanishing or exploding gradients. However, normalizing is not strictly required.

You can now import and transform the MNIST digits with Listing 9-2.

```
from torchvision.datasets import MNIST

trainset = MNIST(root="data", train=True, transform=transform, download=True)
```

Listing 9-2: Importing the MNIST digits

This code downloads the MNIST training data, applies the transformations defined by transform to each image, and saves it to the *data* folder.

You can now visualize some transformed MNIST digits with Listing 9-3.

```
import torch
import matplotlib.pyplot as plt

fig, axs = plt.subplots(1, 8, figsize=(15, 3))
for ax in axs.ravel():
❶ img, label = trainset[torch.randint(0, len(trainset), (1,)).squeeze()]
❷ ax.imshow(img.squeeze(), cmap="gray")
    ax.set_title(f"Label: {label}", fontsize=16)
    ax.axis("off")
```

```
plt.tight_layout()
plt.show()
```

Listing 9-3: Plotting some of the transformed MNIST digits

This code randomly selects some images from the training set ❶ and plots them ❷, as shown in Figure 9-2.

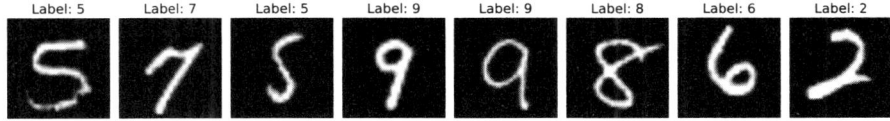

Figure 9-2: Examples of transformed MNIST digits

These are typical MNIST digits like those you've encountered in previous examples and projects, but with a slightly higher resolution.

Defining the Generator and Discriminator

After converting the dataset into a usable format, you'll define the generator and discriminator networks.

Computation Device

Start by defining the device you'll use for training:

```
device = get_device()
```

This uses the get_device() function (Listing 7-10). Because of their complex architecture and adversarial training method, GANs are computationally demanding. Using a GPU will allow you to train them within practical time frames—typically, minutes per epoch. In contrast, relying on a CPU might require several hours for each training epoch.

Generator

To produce fake digits, your generator will take a latent vector (noise vector) of size 100 as input and transform it into a 64×64–pixel image. Use the DCGANGenerator class to define the deep convolutional network that will serve as your generator, as shown in Listing 9-4.

```
import deeplay as dl

latent_dim = 100

gen = dl.DCGANGenerator(
    latent_dim=latent_dim, features_dim=64, output_channels=1,
).build().to(device)
```

Listing 9-4: Instantiating the generator

This code defines the parameters for the generator, builds it, and moves it to the device. The generator consists of four upsampling layers (convolutional transpose layers), each followed by a batch normalization layer and a ReLU activation. The last layer is followed by a hyperbolic tangent activation.

In this example, the number of input latent-space dimensions in the `latent_dim` parameter is set to 100. The number of convolutional filters in each upsampling layer is defined by `features_dim`, which is set to 64. This results in `features_dim * 16`, `features_dim * 8`, `features_dim * 4`, and `features_dim * 2` filters in the first, second, third, and fourth layers, respectively. Since the MNIST dataset consists of grayscale images, the number of output channels is set to 1.

You can print the details of the generator's structure with `print(gen)`.

Discriminator

Finally, you'll create a discriminator that takes a 64×64–pixel image as input and outputs a value of 0 to 1, which predicts the probability that the input image is real. Use the `DCGANDiscriminator` class to define the deep convolutional network that will serve as your discriminator, as shown in Listing 9-5.

```
disc = dl.DCGANDiscriminator(
    input_channels=1, features_dim=64,
).build().to(device)
```

Listing 9-5: Instantiating the discriminator

This code defines the parameters for the discriminator, builds it, and moves it to the device. The discriminator network consists of four convolutional layers, each followed by a batch normalization layer and a leaky ReLU activation layer.

Since the MNIST dataset consists of grayscale images, the number of input channels is set to 1. The number of convolutional filters in each layer is defined by the `features_dim` parameter, which is set to 64. This results in `features_dim`, `features_dim * 2`, `features_dim * 4`, and `features_dim * 8` filters in the first, second, third, and fourth layers, respectively.

By default, both the generator and the discriminator are initialized with starting weights sampled from a normal distribution with a mean of 0, a standard deviation of 0.02, and biases sampled from a uniform random distribution of −1 to 1. This initialization makes the model more stable and reproducible, preventing mode collapse.

You can use `print(disc)` to print the details of the discriminator architecture.

Training the GAN

Now that you've defined your generator and discriminator, you can implement the code to train the GAN.

Loading the Data

You'll first create a data loader that splits the training data into mini-batches, as shown in Listing 9-6.

```
loader = dl.DataLoader(trainset, batch_size=128, shuffle=True)
```

Listing 9-6: Defining the data loader

This code initializes a data loader that shuffles the dataset before creating batches with a batch size of 128.

Next, you'll introduce a loss function, as shown in Listing 9-7.

```
loss = torch.nn.BCELoss()
```

Listing 9-7: Defining the loss function

This code defines a binary cross–entropy loss that will be used for both the discriminator and generator.

Finally, set up the optimizers, as shown in Listing 9-8.

```
optim_gen = torch.optim.Adam(gen.parameters(), lr=0.0002, betas=(0.5, 0.999))
optim_disc = torch.optim.Adam(disc.parameters(), lr=0.0002, betas=(0.5, 0.999))
```

Listing 9-8: Defining the optimizers

This code uses the Adam optimizer for both the generator and discriminator. The `lr` parameter controls the learning rate, the rate at which the model weights are updated to minimize the loss. Adjusting the individual learning rates of the generator and discriminator can help maintain the balance between them, ensuring that neither network becomes too dominant during training, which is crucial for stable and effective GAN training.

The `betas` parameters, often referred to as β_1 and β_2, determine how the optimizers compute the moving averages of the gradient and its square. β_1 controls the decay rate for the moving average of the gradients, affecting how quickly the optimizer incorporates new gradient information. Here, the value is 0.5, meaning that the model adapts relatively quickly to recent gradients (to slow the adaptation, you would increase β_1; to speed it up, you would decrease β_1). β_2 regulates the decay rate for the moving average of the squared gradients, influencing the adaptive learning rate's stability and responsiveness. Here, the value is 0.999, causing the model to use a stable estimate of gradient variance over time (to make the estimate more responsive to recent changes, you would decrease β_2; to make it even more stable, you would increase β_2).

The values in this example were chosen to balance the trade-off between responsiveness to gradient changes and stability in learning rate adaptation. Striking this balance is crucial to maintain the necessary equilibrium between the generator and discriminator when training a GAN.

Implementing the Adversarial Training

You'll now implement the training loop shown in Listing 9-9 to teach the GAN to generate MNIST digits from noise.

```
epochs = 20

for epoch in range(epochs):
    for batch_idx, (real_images, class_labels) in enumerate(loader, start=0):
        real_images = real_images.to(device)

❶       noise = torch.randn(loader.batch_size, latent_dim, 1, 1).to(device)
        fake_images = gen(noise)

        # 1. Discriminator training: minimize - log(D(x)) - log(1 - D(G(z)))
        real_output = disc(real_images).reshape(-1)
        fake_output = disc(fake_images).reshape(-1)

        real_loss = loss(real_output, torch.ones_like(real_output))
        fake_loss = loss(fake_output, torch.zeros_like(fake_output))

        disc_loss = (real_loss + fake_loss) / 2

        optim_disc.zero_grad()
❷       disc_loss.backward(retain_graph=True)
❸       optim_disc.step()

        # 2. Generator training: minimize - log(D(G(z)))
        fake_output = disc(fake_images).reshape(-1)
        gen_loss = loss(fake_output, torch.ones_like(fake_output))

        optim_gen.zero_grad()
        gen_loss.backward()
        optim_gen.step()
```

Listing 9-9: Implementing the training cycle

This code trains the GAN. The loop runs for 20 epochs, iterating over batches of real images and corresponding class labels from the data loader. For each batch, the loop transfers the real images to the designated computing device, while producing a noise vector ❶ and feeding it into the generator to create fake images.

First, the discriminator is trained to distinguish between real and fake images. It calculates individual losses for both real and generated images, then averages them to get the total disc_loss. The discriminator's parameters are then updated. To do so, the code sets the gradient buffers of the optimizer to 0. Then the code backpropagates the loss through the discriminator's network, which calculates the gradients of the loss with respect to each parameter ❷. Finally, the optimizer updates the parameters in the direction that minimizes the loss ❸. Importantly, during backpropagation for the discriminator, the parameter retain_graph=True preserves the computational graph. This preservation is necessary because the fake images output by the generator will be used again in the generator's training step. This retention is critical because it allows the gradients to flow back from the discriminator's output to the generator's parameters, enabling the generator to learn from the way the discriminator distinguishes between real and fake images.

Subsequently, the generator is trained to maximize the probability of the discriminator misclassifying the generated images as real. To do so, gen_loss is computed, followed by an optimization process that updates the generator's parameters.

Adding Timing and Notifications

To get real-time feedback, you can include timing and notifications within your training loop. This allows you to monitor the training duration and understand the model's learning trend. Listing 9-10 sets up these functions.

```python
import time
from datetime import timedelta
--snip--
num_batches = len(loader)
gen_losses_avg, disc_losses_avg = [], []
for epoch in range(epochs):
    print("\n" + f"Epoch {epoch + 1}/{epochs}" + "\n" + "-" * 10)
❶ start_time = time.time()

    running_gen_loss, running_disc_loss = 0.0, 0.0
    for batch_idx, (real_images, class_labels) in enumerate(loader, start=0):
        --snip--
        if batch_idx % 100 == 0:
          ❷ print(f"Batch {batch_idx + 1}/{num_batches}: "
                    f"Generator Loss: {gen_loss.item():.4f}, "
                    f"Discriminator Loss: {disc_loss.item():.4f}")

        running_gen_loss += gen_loss.item()
        running_disc_loss += disc_loss.item()

    gen_losses_avg.append(running_gen_loss / num_batches)
    disc_losses_avg.append(running_disc_loss / num_batches)
❸ end_time = time.time()

    print("-" * 10 + "\n" + f"Epoch {epoch + 1}/{epochs}: "
            f"Generator Loss: {gen_losses_avg[-1]:.4f}, "
            f"Discriminator Loss: {disc_losses_avg[-1]:.4f}, "
          ❹ + f"Time taken: {timedelta(seconds=end_time - start_time)}")
```

Listing 9-10: Timing the training and notifying the user (by modifying Listing 9-9)

This code adds timing and logging functionalities within the training loop to monitor and evaluate training progress.

The current time is recorded at the beginning ❶ and end ❸ of each epoch. To determine the total duration of the epoch, the code calculates the difference between the two timestamps. The timedelta() function then converts the total time delta into a human-readable format and prints it ❹. Note that the training time per epoch will vary greatly depending on the computational device employed, from a few seconds on an A100 GPU to hours on a standard CPU.

To track the losses throughout its runtime, this code initializes the gen _losses_avg and disc_losses_avg lists to store the average losses for the generator and discriminator across epochs. To track how losses accumulate *within* each epoch, the code initializes the running_gen_loss and running_disc_loss variables and sets them to 0 at the beginning of each main loop. Within the inner loop, after each batch is processed, the losses are printed every 100 batches ❷, offering real-time insight into the model's performance at regular intervals. Then the running loss for both the generator and the discriminator is updated with the loss from the current batch. At each epoch's conclusion, the average losses are computed, added to their respective lists, and printed, allowing you to compare the model's loss across different epochs and assess its learning trajectory and stability over time.

You can use this feedback to diagnose issues such as overfitting or underfitting and to make decisions about potential adjustments to the model or training regimen. For instance, if you notice overfitting, you might increase regularization or reduce the complexity of the generator or discriminator. Conversely, underfitting could be addressed by increasing the model's capacity or training for more epochs.

Plotting the Intermediate Results

You can gain further insights into how the generator evolves and improves during training by visualizing the images it generates at the end of each epoch, demonstrated by Listing 9-11.

```
--snip--
fix_latent_vector = torch.randn(30, latent_dim, 1, 1).to(device)
for epoch in range(epochs):
    gen.train(), disc.train()
    --snip--
    gen.eval(), disc.eval()
❶  fake_images = gen(fix_latent_vector).detach().cpu().numpy()

    fig, axs = plt.subplots(3, 10, figsize=(20, 6))
    for i, ax in enumerate(axs.ravel()):
        ax.imshow(fake_images[i][0], cmap="gray")
        ax.axis("off")
    plt.tight_layout()
    plt.show()
❷  plt.close(fig)
```

Listing 9-11: Plotting some sample images after each epoch (by modifying Listing 9-10)

At the beginning of the training, this code creates `fix_latent_vector` to serve as a constant input to the generator, permitting you to observe how the output images evolve as the generator learns.

To begin each epoch, both the generator and discriminator are set to training mode, the correct state for learning. After processing all batches for a given epoch, the generator and discriminator are switched to evaluation mode. This mode change is crucial for generating images because it disables certain layers and behaviors that are relevant only during training, such as dropout. Then, the fixed latent vector is passed through the generator to produce a set of images ❶. These images are detached from the computation graph and transferred back to the CPU for plotting. Finally, at the end of each training epoch, the figure is closed to prevent memory leaks ❷.

Figure 9-3 presents the images generated after the first training epoch.

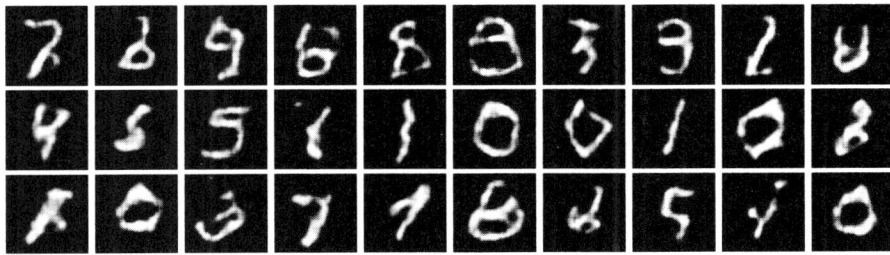

Figure 9-3: Generated images after one training epoch

These images lack structure and hardly resemble handwritten digits, reflecting the generator's initial randomness.

In contrast, Figure 9-4 shows the images generated after the full training course of 20 epochs.

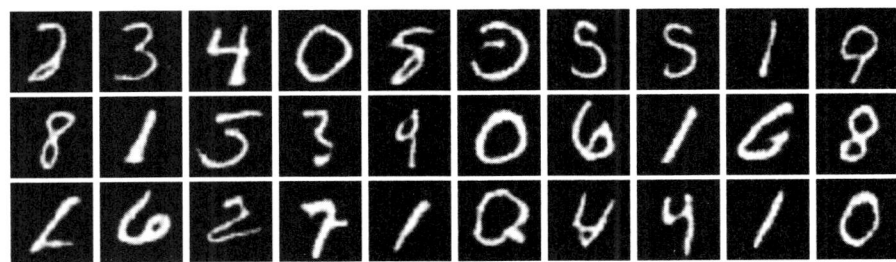

Figure 9-4: Generated images at the end of the 20-epoch training

As the generator and discriminator improve iteratively through the adversarial training process, the images become more defined and closely resemble actual MNIST digits. This improvement displays the generator's ability to learn from the discriminator's feedback, fine-tuning its parameters to create images that are increasingly difficult for the discriminator to distinguish from real data. Even so, some images still don't represent well-defined digits. Even though there are no sure recipes to improve this, you might explore what happens when you modify the power of the generator and discriminator, the learning rates defined in the optimizers, and the number of epochs.

Plotting the Training Losses

By analyzing the training losses of the generator and discriminator, you can investigate the dynamics of the adversarial training process. Listing 9-12 plots these losses over time.

```
import numpy as np

plt.plot(np.arange(len(gen_losses_avg)), gen_losses_avg, "g--o",
        label="Generator Loss")
plt.plot(np.arange(len(disc_losses_avg)), disc_losses_avg, "r-o",
        label="Discriminator Loss")
plt.xlabel("Epoch", fontsize=16)
plt.ylabel("Loss", fontsize=16)
plt.legend()
plt.show()
```

Listing 9-12: Plotting the generator and discriminator losses

The resulting Figure 9-5 displays the generator and discriminator losses over the course of the training.

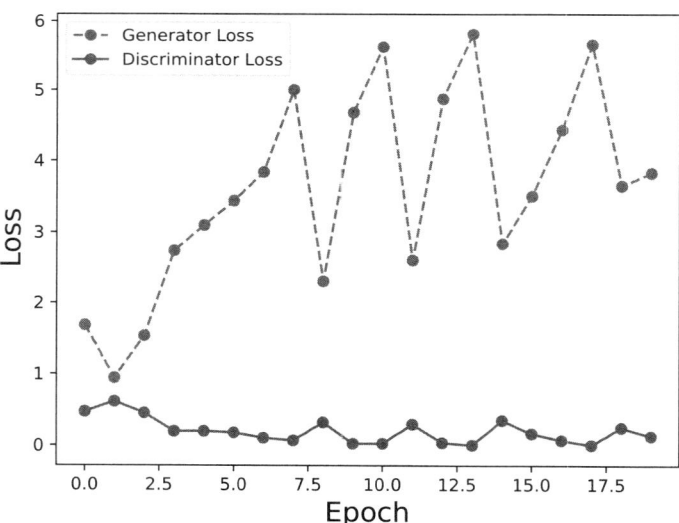

Figure 9-5: The generator (dashed line) and discriminator (solid line) losses

In general, the discriminator loss tends to decrease over time, reflecting its growing ability to distinguish between real and fake images. On the other hand, the generator loss tends to be more volatile. It can either decrease, indicating that its ability to fool the discriminator is improving, or increase, suggesting that the discriminator is performing well.

These losses illustrate that the adversarial training process in GANs results in a tension between the generator and discriminator. The generator aims to produce increasingly realistic images, while the discriminator strives to become better at detecting the fakes. Ideally, these networks reach a point where the generator produces perfect forgeries, and the discriminator must guess at random with a 50 percent chance of correctly identifying real versus fake, achieving a corresponding loss value of about 0.5. However, this equilibrium is challenging to achieve in practice.

The fluctuating losses depicted in the graph are typical in GAN training and reflect the ongoing battle between the two networks. This dynamic can sometimes lead to training instability as the losses oscillate or diverge—a form of mode collapse. In such a case, the generator produces a limited diversity of outputs, independent of the input. To address mode collapse, you might introduce techniques like adding noise to the labels or adjusting the learning rates to stabilize training.

NOTE *Code Example 9-1, "Generating New MNIST Digits with a GAN," is available at* https://github.com/DeepTrackAI/DeepLearningCrashCourse. *Navigate to the* Ch09_GAN *folder and then* ec09_1_gan_mnist. *The* gan_mnist.ipynb *notebook provides a complete code example to generate MNIST digits with a GAN.*

EXERCISES

9-1: The quality of generated images in GANs depends on the interplay between the generator and discriminator during the training process. To optimize quality, you must ensure that the networks are in equilibrium as long as possible without one overpowering the other. By observing the loss curves, adjust the learning rates of the generator and discriminator to maximize the time they remain in balance. If the discriminator is learning more quickly, reduce its learning rates, and vice versa. Plot the generated images and loss curves for three different choices of learning rates for the discriminator and for a fixed learning rate for the generator.

9-2: Modify the generator and discriminator architectures by changing the features_dim parameters during model instantiation. For the optimal learning rates discovered in the previous exercise, find out what value of the features_dim parameter further optimizes image quality. Plot the loss curves and observe how they relate to the quality of the generated digits.

Project 9A: Generating Digits with a Conditional GAN

In the previous section, you learned how to use GANs to generate random MNIST digits that closely resemble those in the original dataset. Yet, this process doesn't control the specific digits produced. You can't directly request a particular digit, such as a 4 or a 2. To address this limitation, you can use a *conditional GAN*, which incorporates class labels into the process, permitting you to condition the image generation.

In this section, you'll train a conditional GAN to create specific MNIST digits on demand. You'll start by exploring the fundamental concept behind conditional GANs and how they differ from traditional GANs. You'll then move on to preparing the data, building the conditional GAN architecture, and training the model. Finally, you'll generate specific digits and evaluate the model's performance.

Since you'll closely follow the code you've implemented in the preceding section, you'll use the *gan_mnist.ipynb* notebook as a starting point.

Defining the Conditional Generator and Discriminator

After you've loaded the MNIST data and chosen the device to use for training, you can instantiate the generator and discriminator.

Conditional Generator

In contrast to the traditional setup that bases output solely on a noise vector, the generator of conditional GANs produces images based on provided class labels. You can achieve this using an *embedding layer*. This layer transforms each class label into a vector of a specified *embedding dimension*. The addition of this embedding layer to the GAN architecture is shown in Figure 9-6.

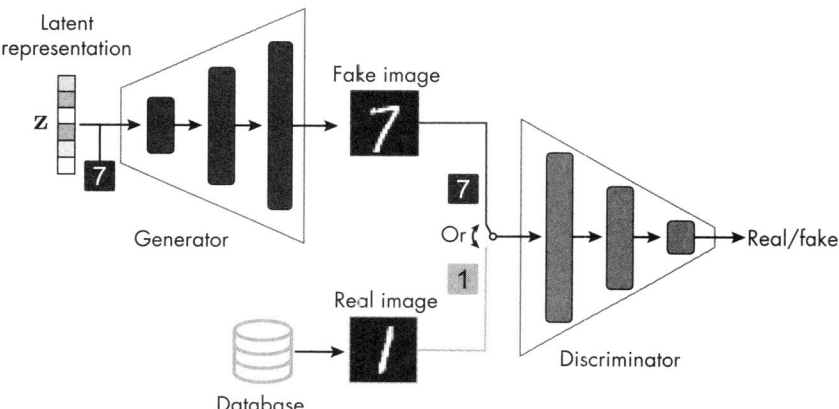

Figure 9-6: The conditional GAN architecture

The embedding layer is a learnable component of the network, meaning that the model adjusts the embeddings during the training process to better suit the specific requirements of the generation of class-conditioned images. To do so, the network optimizes these embeddings to capture the most relevant features to distinguish classes, thereby enhancing the quality and accuracy of the generated images.

The noise vector and the class embedding are then concatenated to form an extended latent vector, combining both the random-noise input and the class-specific information. Finally, this extended vector is fed into the generator network, enabling it to generate images that are diverse because of the random noise, but also tailored to the specified class label provided as input.

You can easily do this by adapting Listing 9-4 as shown in Listing 9-13.

```
--snip--
gen = dl.DCGANGenerator(
    latent_dim=latent_dim, features_dim=64, output_channels=1,
    class_conditioned_model=True, embedding_dim=100, num_classes=10,
).build().to(device)
```

Listing 9-13: Instantiating the conditional generator (by modifying Listing 9-4)

This code initializes the DCGANGenerator object you'll use as a conditional GAN (class_conditioned_model=True). To generate learnable class embedding vectors for each class, the class labels are passed through an embedding layer. This code sets the parameter embedding_dim to 100 dimensions.

Together, the parameters for the number of classes and embedding dimensions define the embedding layer, which functions like a learnable matrix with dimensions corresponding to the number of classes by the number of embedding dimensions. As a result, the embedding layer ensures a proper mapping between the single-value class label and the vector class embedding. The remaining parameters are the same as the non-conditional GAN model.

Conditional Discriminator

In a conditional GAN, the discriminator is also modified to process additional class label inputs. Similar to the changes to the generator, this is done by adding a trainable embedding layer, also shown in Figure 9-6.

This layer takes the class labels and transforms them into embedding vectors of a specified embedding dimension. Each vector is then passed through a dense layer followed by a leaky ReLU activation function, which extends the vector's dimensions to match the spatial dimensions of the input images. In the example, a vector of embedding dimension 100 is transformed into a vector of size 4,096, the product of the dimensions of the input images (64×64). The resulting output vector is then reshaped back into an image of size equal to the input image (64×64). Essentially, this process translates the class label information into image form by concatenating the information about the label to the input image as an additional channel. This results in an augmented input that includes both image and class information.

The adapted discriminator processes this augmented input, using the additional class label information to differentiate between real and fake images of a given class. However, to accommodate the extra channel from the concatenated class embeddings, you must adjust the discriminator's architecture. The rest of the discriminator network processes this combined input similarly to an unconditional GAN, outputting a prediction of whether the input image is real or fake.

You can implement this with Listing 9-14.

```
disc = dl.DCGANDiscriminator(
    input_channels=1, features_dim=64, class_conditioned_model=True,
    embedding_dim=100, num_classes=10,
).build().to(device)
```

Listing 9-14: Instantiating the conditional discriminator (by modifying Listing 9-5)

This code sets the discriminator network to conditional with class _conditioned_model=True. Then it specifies the embedding dimension (embedding _dim=100) and the number of classes (num_classes=10).

As with the unconditional GAN, the weights of the generator and discriminator models are initialized with starting values sampled from a normal distribution with a mean of 0 and a standard deviation of 0.02 by default.

Training the Conditional GAN

You can now train the conditional GAN. Start by defining the data loader with Listing 9-6, the loss function with Listing 9-7, and the optimizers with Listing 9-8.

The adversarial training resembles the one for the standard GAN in Listing 9-10. The differences are shown in Listing 9-15.

```
epochs = 10
--snip--
fix_latent_vector = torch.randn(30, latent_dim, 1, 1).to(device)
fix_class_labels = torch.arange(0, 10).repeat(3).to(device)
for epoch in range(epochs):
    --snip--
    for batch_idx, (real_images, class_labels) in enumerate(loader, start=0):
        real_images = real_images.to(device)
        class_labels = class_labels.to(device)

      ❶ noise = torch.randn(real_images.shape[0],
                        latent_dim, 1, 1).to(device)
        fake_images = gen(noise, class_labels)

        # 1. Discriminator training: minimize -log(D(x)) - log(1 - D(G(z)))
        real_output = disc(real_images, class_labels).reshape(-1)
        fake_output = disc(fake_images, class_labels).reshape(-1)
        --snip--

        # 2. Generator training: minimize - log(D(G(z)))
        fake_output = disc(fake_images, class_labels).reshape(-1)
        --snip--

    gen.eval(), disc.eval()
```

```
❷ fake_images = gen(fix_latent_vector,
                 fix_class_labels).detach().cpu().numpy()
  --snip--
```

Listing 9-15: Training a conditional GAN (by modifying Listing 9-11)

First, the number of epochs is changed to 10, since with the additional class label information, the networks will learn more quickly. Increasing the number of epochs makes the networks susceptible to mode collapse, which would result in the generated images for different noise vectors becoming indistinguishable.

Second, to evaluate the model performance, this code now creates fixed class labels in addition to the fixed latent vectors, and both are passed through the generator during the evaluation phase ❷. Similarly, in the training process, the new code passes the class labels to the device and inputs them to the generator and discriminator.

Finally, the number of noise vectors generated is modified from the nominal batch size to the number of real images ❶ in every batch. This ensures that the networks receive the same number of noise vectors as class labels in every batch. Without this step, if there are fewer class labels than the number of elements in the last batch, there would be more noise vectors than class labels, which would result in an error.

Since your GAN's performance depends on the dynamic balance between the generator and discriminator, you'll want to inspect the plots of the generated images during training as well as the losses to determine whether you need to adjust your parameters.

Plotting the Generated Digits

Figure 9-7 presents the images generated by the trained GAN.

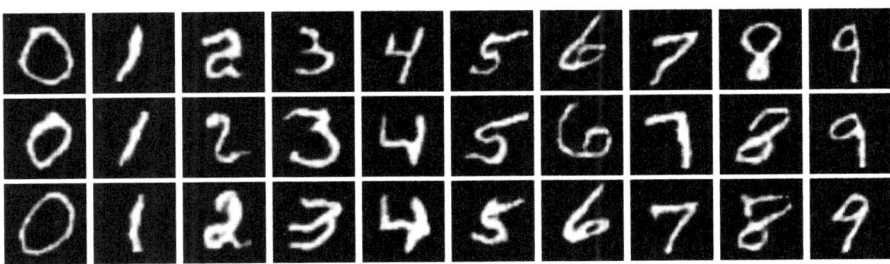

Figure 9-7: Generated images at the end of the 10-epoch training

Upon completing 10 training epochs, the generator produces specific digits corresponding to the conditioned class labels it receives. Beyond these training epochs, you must be vigilant to prevent mode collapse. You might observe that despite providing varied class labels, the generator starts producing similar or identical images across these classes. This phenomenon indicates that the network is no longer using the class-specific information effectively.

You can plot the losses as you train the conditional GAN to understand the networks' dynamic interplay and balance. Typically, the generator's loss starts higher during its initial struggles to create convincing images, but decreases over time as it learns to synthesize more-realistic outputs conditioned on class labels. Conversely, the discriminator's loss usually starts lower because of its initial effectiveness in distinguishing real from fake images. However, if the discriminator's loss remains too low, the generator likely isn't providing a sufficient challenge, potentially leading to mode collapse.

Monitoring these losses is essential to ensure equilibrium. Ideally, they converge to a point where the generator produces high-quality images and the discriminator has a 50 percent success rate in identifying them correctly. Significant divergence in these losses necessitates adjustments such as altering learning rates or modifying network architectures to maintain a balance that ensures the generation of diverse, high-quality images.

NOTE *Code Example 9-A, "Generating MNIST Digits On Demand with a Conditional GAN," is available at* https://github.com/DeepTrackAI/DeepLearning CrashCourse. *Navigate to the* Ch09_GAN *folder and then* ec09_A_cgan_mnist. *The* cgan_mnist.ipynb *notebook provides a complete code example to generate specific MNIST digits on demand with a conditional GAN.*

Project 9B: Virtually Staining a Biological Tissue

Biomedical and pharmaceutical research relies on the study of cellular and subcellular structures. This task traditionally requires chemically staining cells and their compartments to enhance their visibility under a fluorescence microscope. Unfortunately, these staining procedures are invasive and often involve toxic substances, potentially altering the cells' natural state and behavior.

In this project, you'll use a conditional GAN to circumvent this procedure by transforming bright-field microscopy images of human motor neurons to mimic fluorescence staining. Known as *virtual staining*, this technique allows researchers to generate fluorescence images without the need for actual chemical staining, preserving the cells' integrity while enhancing the visibility of cellular structures of interest.

To accomplish this task, you'll train a conditional GAN with pairs of bright-field and fluorescence images, allowing the model to learn the mapping between the two modalities. Finally, you'll evaluate the model's performance by generating virtual fluorescence images from new bright-field images and by comparing them to the real fluorescence-stained images to assess accuracy and quality.

Downloading the Human Motor Neurons Dataset

To train your GAN, you'll use part of a dataset that was originally published in 2018 in "*In Silico* Labeling: Predicting Fluorescent Labels in Unlabeled Images" by Eric M. Christiansen and co-workers. This paper helped pioneer the use of deep learning for virtual staining. Specifically, you'll download the paper's human motor neurons dataset designated as Condition A.

This dataset comprises 22 pairs of bright-field images and their corresponding fluorescence images. These images are *spatially coregistered*, meaning that the bright-field and fluorescence images are matched pixel by pixel so that corresponding features appear in the same locations in both. The images depict two fluorescent channels: an anti-TuJ1 stain, which stains neurons green, and a Hoechst stain, which stains nuclei blue. Notably, the bright-field images consist of a z-stack of 13 images across different focal planes, offering a comprehensive view of the cellular structures.

The full dataset is available in a public Google Cloud Storage bucket. A replicate containing only data used in this project can be downloaded from GitHub, as illustrated in Listing 9-16.

```
import os

if not os.path.exists("vs_dataset"):
    os.system("git clone https://github.com/DeepTrackAI/vs_dataset")
```

Listing 9-16: Importing the virtual staining dataset

The dataset is about 20GB and will take at least a few minutes to download (or longer, depending on your internet connection).

Creating a Dataset

Once the download is complete, you'll create a custom dataset class to load the dataset and preprocess the images, as shown in Listing 9-17.

```
import glob
import numpy as np
from PIL import Image
import torch
from tqdm import tqdm

class VirtualStainingDataset(torch.utils.data.Dataset):
    """Dataset containing the bright-field and fluorescence images."""

    _cache = {}  # Class variable to cache loaded images

    def __init__(self, dir, transforms=None, preload=False):
        """Initialize dataset."""
        self.dir, self.transforms, self.preload = dir, transforms, preload
    ❶ self.images = []

        pattern = ("lab-Rubin,condition-scott_1_0,acquisition_date,"
            ❷ "year-2016,month-2,day-6,well-r0*c0*,depth_computation,"
                "value-MAXPROJECT,is_mask-false,kind,value-ORIGINAL.png")
    ❸ self.image_list = glob.glob(os.path.join(self.dir, pattern))
```

```
    if self.preload:
        if dir in VirtualStainingDataset._cache:
        ❹ self.images = VirtualStainingDataset._cache[dir]
        else:
            for image_path in tqdm(self.image_list,
                                   total=len(self.image_list),
                                   desc="Preloading images ..."):
            ❺ self.images.append(self.load_image(image_path))
            ❻ VirtualStainingDataset._cache[dir] = self.images

def load_image(self, image_path):
    """Load input-target image couple."""
    input_image = []
    for i in range(13):
        image_path_i = (
            image_path.replace("MAXPROJECT", "BRIGHTFIELD")
            .replace("depth_computation", f"z_depth-{i},channel")
        )
        input_image.append(np.array(Image.open(image_path_i).convert("L")))
    input_image = np.stack(input_image, axis=-1)

    target_image = np.array(Image.open(image_path))

    return input_image, target_image
--snip--
```

Listing 9-17: The dataset class with the initialization method

This class, derived from the PyTorch Dataset class, manages the data during the training and testing processes. After initialization, it loads a dataset and then applies custom transformations and normalizations to the images for you to specify later.

The code starts by creating the _cache class variable to ensure that the dataset isn't loaded multiple times into memory when you run more than one instance of the class.

The __init__() method takes three input parameters: dir, which contains the path to the dataset; transforms, which contains a list of two transformations to be applied to the bright-field images and the fluorescence images, respectively; and preload, which specifies whether to load the dataset into memory before training (True) or during training (False). The method then initiates an empty list ❶ to store the images.

Next, the pattern variable specifies the common string in the target image filenames of the dataset. These files are differentiated by their well numbers ❷, with the asterisks acting as placeholders for the variable parts of the filenames.

Afterward, the glob.glob() function gathers a list of all the files that match this pattern; this list comprises the target fluorescence images ❸.

Later, the code will use this list to load the target fluorescence images and, after minor modification, the input bright-field images.

If preload is set to True, the load_image() function loads the input and target images into the self.images list ❺. At the method's end, the _cache dictionary is updated with the list of images as values and dir as cache keys ❻.

To prevent the dataset from being loaded multiple times, the code uses the if condition to check for the dir cache key in the _cache variable. If the key already exists, the images will be directly loaded from the cache ❹.

Finally, the load_image() method loads the images in a structured manner based on the image path. The method first loads all 13 channels in the input bright-field image by modifying the filenames indicating the target images in a loop. The method then appends these channels to an empty list and converts them to a stack. Subsequently, the target fluorescence image is loaded via the image path. Finally, the method returns the input and target images as outputs.

To specify the dataset length and ensure consistent transformations across the images you load, implement the remaining methods in the class, as shown in Listing 9-18.

```
--snip--
class VirtualStainingDataset(torch.utils.data.Dataset):
    --snip--

    def __len__(self):
        """Return number of images."""
        return len(self.image_list)

    def __getitem__(self, i):
        """Get input-target image couple."""
        if self.preload:
            input_image, target_image = self.images[i]
        else:
            input_image, target_image = self.load_image(self.image_list[i])

        if self.transforms:
          ❶ seed = np.random.randint(1_000_000_000)
          ❷ torch.manual_seed(seed)
            input_image = self.transforms[0](input_image)
          ❸ torch.manual_seed(seed)
            target_image = self.transforms[1](target_image)

        return input_image, target_image
```

Listing 9-18: The dataset class with all the methods (by modifying Listing 9-17)

The __len__() method specifies the length of the dataset. Here, __len__() returns the length of the image list gathered by glob.glob() in Listing 9-17.

The __getitem__() method returns an input-target image pair. If preload is True, the images are loaded directly from the images list that already contains the images. If preload is False, the images are loaded into memory on demand when each batch is needed during training. Then, if the transforms parameter is set so that some transformations are to be applied to the images, the code creates a random-number generator ❶. The random-number generator is seeded before the corresponding transformations are applied to both the input ❷ and target ❸ images. This ensures that the same transformation is applied to both sets of images if the transformation is randomly sampled. However, the order of any randomized transformations needs to be consistent across both the input and target images. If the transformations are applied in an order different from that of the input and target images, the resulting pairs would no longer be aligned, leading to incorrect training.

Preprocessing the Images

Define the transformations and normalizations to be applied to the images, as shown in Listing 9-19.

```
from torchvision import transforms

trans_bright = transforms.Compose([
    transforms.ToTensor(), transforms.RandomCrop((256, 256)),
    transforms.RandomHorizontalFlip(p=.5), transforms.RandomVerticalFlip(p=.5),
    transforms.Normalize(mean=[0.5] * 13, std=[0.5] * 13),
])
trans_fluorescent = transforms.Compose([
    transforms.ToTensor(), transforms.RandomCrop((256, 256)),
    transforms.RandomHorizontalFlip(p=.5), transforms.RandomVerticalFlip(p=.5),
    transforms.Normalize(mean=[0.5] * 3, std=[0.5] * 3),
])
```

Listing 9-19: Defining the image transformations and normalizations

These transformations crop the images to 256×256 pixels and randomly flip them horizontally and vertically. The code also normalizes the values within the images to fall from −1 to 1 (by subtracting mean from the images and dividing them by std). Since the bright-field images have 13 channels, the means and standard deviations are given as lists of 13 values. The means and standard deviations of the fluorescence images, which have three channels, are given as lists of three values.

Creating the Training and Testing Datasets

Now that your code is ready to manage and preprocess the data, create the training and testing datasets as shown in Listing 9-20.

```
train_set = VirtualStainingDataset(
    dir=os.path.join("vs_dataset", "train"),
    transforms=[trans_bright, trans_fluorescent], preload=True,
)
```

```
test_set = VirtualStainingDataset(
    dir=os.path.join("vs_dataset", "test"),
    transforms=[trans_bright, trans_fluorescent], preload=True,
)
```

Listing 9-20: Creating the training and testing datasets

By setting the `preload` argument to `True`, this code preloads the entire dataset into memory to speed up the training. If you don't have enough memory, you can set this argument to `False` at the cost of a longer computing time, as the images will be loaded each time they're needed. The `transforms` argument consists of the list of transformations you defined earlier for the bright-field and fluorescence images.

Visualizing Some Images

Using the datasets you've constructed, visualize some bright-field and corresponding fluorescence images, using Listing 9-21.

```
import matplotlib.pyplot as plt

input_image, target_image = train_set[np.random.randint(0, len(train_set))]

def denormalize(image):
    """Denormalize image for visualization."""
    return (image + 1) / 2

plt.subplot(1, 3, 1)
plt.imshow(input_image.mean(axis=0), cmap="gray")
plt.title("Brightfield Image")
plt.axis("off")

plt.subplot(1, 3, 2)
plt.imshow(denormalize(target_image[1, :, :].numpy()), cmap="Greens")
plt.title("Stained Neurons")
plt.axis("off")

plt.subplot(1, 3, 3)
plt.imshow(denormalize(target_image[2, :, :].numpy()), cmap="Blues")
plt.title("Stained Nuclei")
plt.axis("off")

plt.tight_layout()
plt.show()
```

Listing 9-21: Visualizing the bright-field and corresponding fluorescence images

This code plots the bright-field image averaged over all the focal planes and its corresponding fluorescence images channel by channel: the green channel (anti-TuJ1 stain) representing motor neurons, and the blue channel

(Hoechst stain) representing nuclei. The red channel is empty since these fluorescence images don't contain any information in that channel.

Since the images are normalized to the [−1, 1] range, this code implements the denormalize() function to denormalize the images back to a range of [0, 1] for visualization.

This results in Figure 9-8.

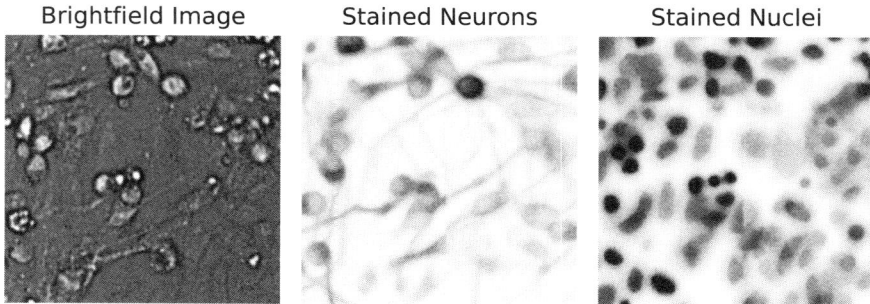

Figure 9-8: The bright-field image (left) and the corresponding fluorescence stained images

You can see the bright-field image of human motor neurons on the left and the corresponding fluorescence images staining the neurons (middle) and nuclei (right).

Instantiating the Generator and Discriminator

Now specify the computing device for training:

```
device = get_device()
```

This uses the get_device() function (Listing 7-10). Next, you'll initialize the generator and discriminator models.

Generator

Define the generator as a slightly modified U-Net, as shown in Listing 9-22.

```
import deeplay as dl
from torch.nn import InstanceNcrm2d, LeakyReLU, Tanh

gen = dl.UNet2d(
    in_channels=13, channels=[32, 64, 128, 256, 512], out_channels=3,
)
❶ gen["encoder", ..., "activation"].configure(LeakyReLU, negative_slope=0.2)
❷ gen["decoder", ..., "activation#:-1"].configure(LeakyReLU, negative_slope=0.2)
❸ gen["decoder", ..., "activation#-1"].configure(Tanh)
❹ gen["decoder", "blocks", :-1].all.normalized(InstanceNorm2d)
❺ gen[..., "blocks"].configure(order=["layer", "normalization", "activation"])
gen.build().to(device);
```

Listing 9-22: Defining the generator

This code uses the Deeplay `UNet2d` class to define the generator network with 13 input channels corresponding to the number of bright-field planes, 5 convolutional layers, and 3 output channels corresponding to the 3 channels of the fluorescence image. (You can omit the fifth convolutional layer for computational efficiency and still obtain good results.)

Next, the code modifies the hidden layers' activations to use leaky ReLU in both the encoder ❶ and the decoder ❷, except for the decoder output layer activation that is modified to a hyperbolic tangent ❸ to ensure that the output values are bounded from −1 to 1. Likewise, instead of the default `BatchNorm2d`, the code uses `InstanceNorm2d` in the decoder ❹ to increase performance in image-to-image translation tasks. Finally, the order of the normalization and activation in both the encoder and the decoder is changed ❺; this ensures that the normalization is applied before the activation function, which leads to more-stable training and better convergence by maintaining consistent data distributions across the network.

Once these steps are complete, the code builds the model and transfers it to the selected device. You can use `print(gen)` to print out the details of this architecture.

Discriminator

Now that you've instantiated the generator, let's set up the discriminator. The discriminator takes a fluorescence image (either a real one or one output by the generator) and a bright-field image as inputs; then it outputs a smaller image, with each pixel representing the probability that a given patch in the fluorescence image is a real patch. This process of evaluating an image patch by patch, known as the *PatchGAN approach*, helps the discriminator better judge the local features and structures in the original image.

Define the discriminator as illustrated in Listing 9-23.

```
from torch.nn import Sigmoid

disc = dl.ConvolutionalNeuralNetwork(
    in_channels=16, hidden_channels=[8, 16, 32, 64], out_channels=1,
)
disc["blocks", ..., "layer"].configure(kernel_size=4, stride=2, padding=1)
```
❶ `disc["blocks", ..., "activation#-1"].configure(LeakyReLU, negative_slope=0.2)`
❷ `disc["blocks", 1:-1].all.normalized(InstanceNorm2d)`
❸ `disc["blocks", ..., "activation#-1"].configure(Sigmoid)`
❹ `disc["blocks"].configure(order=["layer", "normalization", "activation"])`
```
disc.build().to(device);
```

Listing 9-23: Defining the discriminator

This code uses the Deeplay `ConvolutionalNeuralNetwork` class with 16 input channels, 4 hidden layers, and a single output. The 16 input channels represent the 13 channels in the bright-field image plus the 3 channels in the fluorescence image. You can further strengthen the discriminator by increasing the number of features in the hidden layers.

Next, the code alters the parameters of the hidden layers by switching their activations to leaky ReLU ❶ (to help prevent the vanishing gradient problem) and their normalizations to `InstanceNorm2d` ❷ (which provides better performance by normalizing the activations across each channel independently). Then the code changes the activation of the output layer to sigmoid ❸ to ensure that the output values are scaled to a range from 0 to 1, which is appropriate for tasks involving pixel intensity. Finally, the code rearranges the order of the layers, activations, and normalizations ❹.

After applying these modifications, the code builds the model and transfers it to the selected device. You can use `print(disc)` to print its architecture.

Compiling the Conditional GAN

Now that you've set up the generator and discriminator, you can implement the conditional GAN. To do this, you'll define the loss functions, optimizers, and data loaders.

First, you need to define the loss functions as shown in Listing 9-24.

```
from torchmetrics.image.lpip import LearnedPerceptualImagePatchSimilarity

loss_disc = torch.nn.MSELoss()
loss_recon = torch.nn.L1Loss()
loss_percep = LearnedPerceptualImagePatchSimilarity(net_type="vgg").to(device)
```

Listing 9-24: Defining the losses

This code defines three losses. The adversarial loss for the discriminator (`loss_disc`) is calculated using the MSE loss function. The reconstruction loss for the generator (`loss_recon`) is calculated using an L1 loss function, which directly compares the generated fluorescence image with the target image via the MAE loss function. Finally, the perceptual loss (`loss_percep`) is calculated using the *learned perceptual image patch similarity (LPIPS)* metric to ensure that the generated fluorescence image is perceptually similar to the actual fluorescence image.

To capture texture and detail discrepancies that might not be evident through direct pixel comparison, the LPIPS metric uses a pretrained VGG16 network—the same one you used for the DeepDreams in Project 3C and for the neural style transfer in Project 3D. This network computes the loss by measuring the difference between the feature maps of the generated and real images at various layers of the network. Doing so allows the LPIPS metric to capture many perceptual differences that the human visual system would also notice. This approach enables the model to output images that perceptually resemble the actual fluorescence images.

After specifying the loss functions, implement the optimizers with Listing 9-25.

```
optim_gen = torch.optim.Adam(gen.parameters(), lr=.0002, betas=(.5, .999))
optim_disc = torch.optim.Adam(disc.parameters(), lr=.00005, betas=(.5, .999))
```

Listing 9-25: Defining the optimizers

This code uses the Adam optimizer for both generator and discriminator, but with different learning rates. You can adjust these rates to balance the performance of the generator and discriminator so that neither dominates during training.

Now instantiate the data loaders, using Listing 9-26.

```
train_loader = dl.DataLoader(train_set, batch_size=2, shuffle=True)
test_loader = dl.DataLoader(test_set, batch_size=2, shuffle=False)
```

Listing 9-26: Defining the data loaders

This code defines the data loaders with a batch size of 2.

Training the Conditional GAN

You're now ready to implement the training procedure for the conditional GAN. You'll first define functions to train the discriminator, train the generator, and evaluate the model in each training epoch. Then you'll define the loop where these functions train the model.

Training the Discriminator

Define the train_disc() function shown in Listing 9-27.

```
def train_disc(inputs, targets, optim_disc, loss_disc):
    """Train the discriminator."""
    optim_disc.zero_grad()

    # Compute real loss
    disc_outputs_real = disc(torch.cat([inputs, targets], dim=1))
    labels_real = torch.ones_like(disc_outputs_real)
    disc_loss_real = loss_disc(disc_outputs_real, labels_real)

    # Compute fake loss
    gen_outputs = gen(inputs)
    disc_outputs_fake = disc(torch.cat([inputs, gen_outputs], dim=1))
    labels_fake = torch.zeros_like(disc_outputs_fake)
    disc_loss_fake = loss_disc(disc_outputs_fake, labels_fake)

    disc_loss = (disc_loss_real + disc_loss_fake) / 2
    disc_loss.backward()
    optim_disc.step()

    return disc_loss
```

Listing 9-27: The function to train the discriminator

This function takes bright-field images and their corresponding fluorescence images as inputs, and outputs the loss of the discriminator network. The function starts by zeroing the discriminator gradients. Next, it computes the real loss and the fake loss before averaging them to calculate the total loss. Finally, the function backpropagates the loss and updates the discriminator weights, similar to the steps in Listing 9-9.

Training the Generator

Now define the train_gen() function shown in Listing 9-28.

```
def train_gen(inputs, targets, optim_gen, loss_disc, loss_recon, loss_percep,
              recon_coef=100, percep_coef=10):
    """Train the generator."""
    optim_gen.zero_grad()

    gen_outputs = gen(inputs)
    disc_outputs = disc(torch.cat([inputs, gen_outputs], dim=1))

    labels = torch.ones_like(disc_outputs)
    adv_loss = loss_disc(disc_outputs, labels)
    recon_loss = loss_recon(gen_outputs, targets)
    percep_loss = loss_percep(gen_outputs, targets)

    gen_loss = adv_loss + recon_coef * recon_loss + percep_coef * percep_loss
    gen_loss.backward()
    optim_gen.step()

    return gen_loss, adv_loss, recon_loss, percep_loss
```

Listing 9-28: The function to train the generator

This function takes bright-field images and their corresponding fluorescence images as inputs, and outputs the loss used by the generator network. This loss is a combination of three losses (adversarial loss, reconstruction loss, and perceptual loss), which are also returned.

After setting the optimizer gradients to 0, the generator takes the input bright-field images to generate the fluorescence images. Then the discriminator processes the input images and generated images, and outputs the predictions of whether the generated images are real or fake (patch by patch) based on the provided input images.

Next, the function calculates the adversarial loss: A label value of 1 indicates that the generated images are real (adv_loss). Additionally, the function directly compares the input and generated images through the reconstruction loss to ensure pixel-wise similarity (recon_loss) as well as the perceptual loss to ensure perceptual similarity (percep_loss).

Finally, this function calculates the total generator loss (gen_loss) with the recon_coef parameter as the weight for the reconstruction loss and percep_coef as the weight for the perceptual loss, backpropagates the total loss, updates the generator weights, and returns the different losses.

Evaluating the Model

Define the `evaluate_model()` function in Listing 9-29 to evaluate the model on the test dataset.

```
def evaluate_model(input, target):
    """Evaluate model on test data."""
    gen.eval()
    with torch.no_grad():
        prediction = gen(input.to(device))
    gen.train()

    fig, ax = plt.subplots(2, 3, figsize=(10, 7))

    ax[0, 0].imshow(
        denormalize(input[0].permute(1, 2, 0).cpu().numpy().mean(axis=-1)),
        cmap="gray",
    )
    ax[0, 0].set_title("Input Image")
    ax[0, 0].axis("off")

    ax[0, 1].imshow(
        denormalize(prediction[0].permute(1, 2, 0).cpu().numpy())[:, :, 1],
        cmap="Greens",
    )
    ax[0, 1].set_title("Prediction - Neurons")
    ax[0, 1].axis("off")

    ax[1, 1].imshow(
        denormalize(target[0].permute(1, 2, 0).cpu().numpy())[:, :, 1],
        cmap="Greens",
    )
    ax[1, 1].set_title("Ground Truth - Neurons")
    ax[1, 1].axis("off")

    ax[0, 2].imshow(
        denormalize(prediction[0].permute(1, 2, 0).cpu().numpy())[:, :, 2],
        cmap="Blues",
    )
    ax[0, 2].set_title("Prediction - Nuclei")
    ax[0, 2].axis("off")

    ax[1, 2].imshow(
        denormalize(target[0].permute(1, 2, 0).cpu().numpy())[:, :, 2],
        cmap="Blues",
    )
    ax[1, 2].set_title("Ground Truth - Nuclei")
    ax[1, 2].axis("off")
```

```
        ax[1, 0].axis("off")  # Leave the [1, 0] subplot empty

    plt.tight_layout()
    plt.show()
    plt.close(fig)
```

Listing 9-29: The function to evaluate the model on the test dataset

This function takes an input image, processes it through the generator, and renders a figure containing the input image, the generated fluorescence image, and the label. The function starts by setting the generator to evaluation mode, generating the fluorescence image, passing the input image to the generator, and setting the generator back to training mode.

The function then creates a figure with different subplots to show the input image, the generated image, and label fluorescence images. The input bright-field image is plotted first, then both the generated and the label fluorescence images are plotted channel-wise. The green-channel image (neurons) is created using a color map of Greens. Subsequently, the blue-channel image (nuclei) is produced with a color map of Blues.

Implementing the Training Cycle

Now use the functions you just implemented to define the training loop, as shown in Listing 9-30.

```
epochs = 500

for epoch in range (epochs):
    for i, (inputs, targets) in enumerate(train_loader, 0):
        inputs, targets = inputs.to(device), targets.to(device)

        # 1. Train the discriminator
        disc_loss = train_disc(inputs, targets, optim_disc, loss_disc)

        # 2. Train the generator
    ❶ for _ in range(2):
            gen_loss, adv_loss, recon_loss, percep_loss = train_gen(
                inputs, targets, optim_gen, loss_disc, loss_recon, loss_percep,
            )

    if epoch % 50 == 0 or epoch + 1 == epochs:
        for i, (test_input, test_target) in enumerate(test_loader, 0):
            evaluate_model(test_input, test_target)
            break
```

Listing 9-30: Implementing the training cycle

The training loop iterates over 500 epochs. In each epoch, the loop processes the full training dataset in batches of two samples as defined by train_loader from Listing 9-26. In each batch, the inputs (bright-field images) and the labels (fluorescence images) are transferred to the designated device.

The discriminator is trained first using the train_disc() function defined in Listing 9-27. The discriminator takes the bright-field images, the labels, the discriminator optimizer, and the discriminator loss function as inputs and returns the discriminator loss for the current batch. For each discriminator training, the generator is trained twice ❶ via the train_gen() function defined in Listing 9-28. You can adjust the ratio of generator versus discriminator training steps after you've empirically observed the results. The function to train the generator returns the total generator loss (gen_loss) as well as the three partial losses—namely, the adversarial loss (adv_loss), the reconstruction loss (recon_loss), and the perceptual loss (percep_loss).

Once every 50 epochs, the code evaluates the quality of generated images with the evaluate_model() function defined in Listing 9-29. This function renders a figure to observe the generated fluorescence images against the label images.

Adding Timing and Notifications

Similarly to Listing 9-10, you can add timing and notification features within the training loop to monitor the training duration and loss trends. Listing 9-31 implements these functionalities.

```
import time
from datetime import timedelta
--snip--
disc_losses, gen_losses, recon_losses, percep_losses = [], [], [], []
for epoch in range(epochs + 1):
❶   start_time = time.time()
    print("\n" + f"Epoch {epoch + 1}/{epochs}" + "\n" + "-" * 10)

    disc_loss_epoch, gen_loss_epoch, recon_loss_epoch, percep_loss_epoch = \
        [], [], [], []
    for i, data in enumerate(train_loader, 0):
        --snip--
        if i % 5 == 0:
            print(f"Batch {i + 1}/{len(train_loader)} : "
                    f"Total Generator Loss: {gen_loss.item():.4f}, "
                    f"Discriminator Loss: {disc_loss.item():.4f}")

        disc_loss_epoch.append(disc_loss.item())
        gen_loss_epoch.append(gen_loss.item())
        recon_loss_epoch.append(recon_loss.item())
        percep_loss_epoch.append(percep_loss.item())

❷   end_time = time.time()

    disc_losses.append(np.mean(disc_loss_epoch))
    gen_losses.append(np.mean(gen_loss_epoch))
    recon_losses.append(np.mean(recon_loss_epoch))
    percep_losses.append(np.mean(percep_loss_epoch))
```

```
print(f"-" * 10 + "\n" + f'Epoch {epoch + 1}/{epochs} : "
    f"Discriminator Loss: {disc_losses[-1]:.4f}, "
    f"Total Generator Loss: {gen_losses[-1]:.4f}, "
    f"Reconstrucntion Loss: {recon_losses[-1]:.4f}, "
    f"Perceptual Loss: {percep_losses[-1]:.4f}" + "\n"
    f"Time taken: {timedelta(seconds=end_time - start_time)}")
--snip--
```

Listing 9-31: Timing the training and notifying the user (by modifying Listing 9-30)

The changes to the code are very similar to those made in Listing 9-10. This code records the time before ❶ and after each epoch ❷, then calculates the time elapsed between the two.

To track the losses, the code initializes four empty lists to store the average loss for each loss type at the end of every epoch as well as a second set of empty lists inside the first for loop to track the losses for each batch within an epoch.

Throughout the code, statements are printed to track the losses as the training progresses, similar to those in Listing 9-10.

Evaluating the Trained Conditional GAN

Figure 9-9 shows the results after training for 500 epochs.

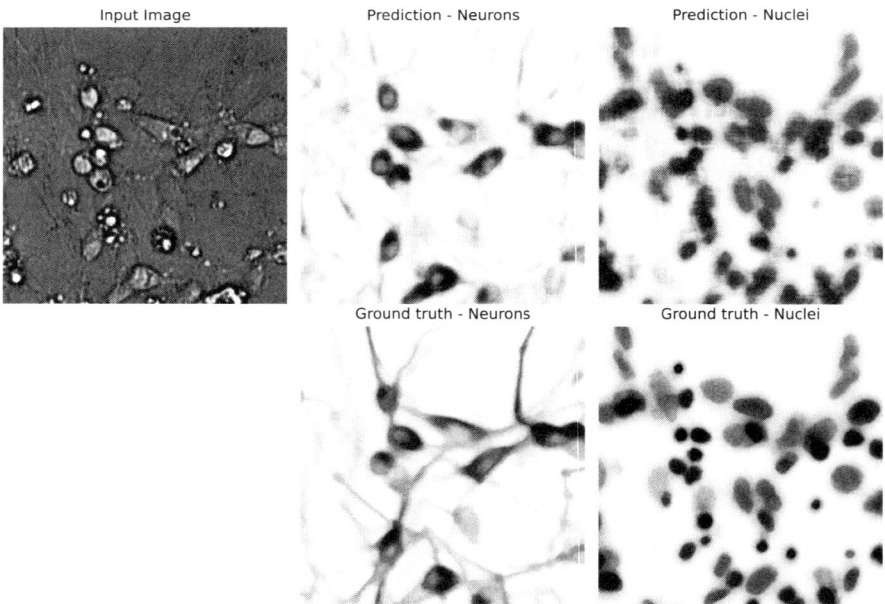

Figure 9-9: The bright-field image (left) and its corresponding ground-truth (middle and right, top row) and virtually stained fluorescence images (bottom row)

The input image on the left shows an averaged bright-field image from the test dataset, corresponding to the images that the generator uses to generate the fluorescence image. The top row shows the green and blue channels of the generated fluorescence image, with the corresponding fluorescence ground-truth targets shown below. The generated and target images closely resemble each other. The two fluorescence stains, green and blue (representing motor neurons and nuclei, respectively), are added by the network in similar regions to those of the chemically stained image. This indicates that the generator is able to correctly grasp the biological information in the bright-field image and to virtually stain the images. The quality of the generated images can be improved by more training and by tuning the network and training hyperparameters.

NOTE *Code Example 9-B, "Virtually Straining a Biological Tissue with a Conditional GAN," is available at* https://github.com/DeepTrackAI/DeepLearning CrashCourse. *Navigate to the* Ch09_GAN *folder and then* ec09_B_virtual _staining. *The* virtual_staining.ipynb *notebook provides a complete code example to virtually stain a biological tissue with a conditional GAN.*

Project 9C: Converting Between Holographic and Bright-Field Microscopy Images

In this project, you'll use CycleGANs to bridge the gap between two fundamentally different microscopy techniques: holography and bright-field microscopy. *Holographic microscopy* captures 3D information about microscopic entities by measuring a single hologram of the object under observation. In contrast, *bright-field microscopy* provides a higher-quality image of the sample but can't capture 3D information without taking multiple images and repeatedly adjusting the microscope stage—a far slower process.

One of the significant challenges in the application of advanced image-transformation techniques is the need for precisely coregistered images of each type, as you had for the virtual staining in the preceding project. This requirement often necessitates capturing the same sample with two different microscopes before the sample can change or degrade, a practical impossibility for many microscopy studies that deal with dynamic biological samples.

Herein lies the challenge: transforming unpaired images between these microscopy modalities without having perfectly coregistered image pairs. CycleGANs offer a powerful solution by enabling the transformation of images between holographic and bright-field modalities (or between other imaging modalities) without the need for coregistration.

This project will first introduce you to the fundamental principle behind CycleGANS: cycle consistency. Afterward, you'll prepare the holographic and bright-field microscopy datasets for the CycleGAN training. You'll then implement the generators and discriminators as well as a training loop. This loop will allow the CycleGAN to convert images between holographic and bright-field representations.

Understanding CycleGANs

CycleGANs represent a breakthrough for cross-modality transformation between two datasets that lack coregistered pairs. The concept at the heart of CycleGANs is the principle of *cycle consistency*, a loss function ensuring that a transformation from one domain to another can be mapped back to the original domain, preserving the essence of the initial input. Figure 9-10 illustrates this concept.

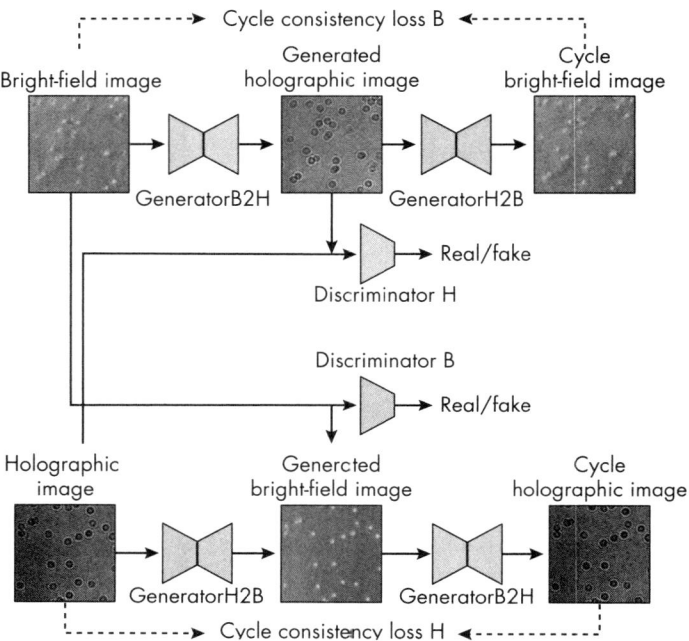

Figure 9-10: The concept of cycle consistency

To grasp this concept more concretely, imagine you possess two distinct generator networks: GeneratorH2B, tasked with converting images from the holographic domain (H) to the bright-field domain (B), and GeneratorB2H, tasked with performing the inverse transformation.

Let's say that an image from the H domain undergoes transformation through GeneratorH2B into the B domain. If the result were then processed by GeneratorB2H, you would expect to recover the original H domain image. Likewise, the same cycle consistency applies when an image starts in the B domain, moves to H, and then is returned to B. This cyclical process ensures that despite the lack of direct pairing, the transformation maintains a logical and consistent link between the two modalities.

To achieve this transformation and maintain cycle consistency, CycleGANs employ two discriminator networks: DiscriminatorH and DiscriminatorB. These networks are trained in tandem with the generators, sharpening their ability to differentiate between genuine and synthetically transformed images within their respective domains.

Using the Holo2Bright Dataset

The Holo2Bright dataset consists of holographic and bright-field microscopy images of marine microplankton. It is divided into 4,500 holographic and 880 bright-field images for training and 4,500 holographic and 244 bright-field images for testing. The size of all images is 256×256 pixels. You can download this dataset from a GitHub repository as shown in Listing 9-32.

```
import os

if not os.path.exists("holo2bright_dataset"):
    os.system("git clone https://github.com/DeepTrackAI/holo2bright_dataset")
```

Listing 9-32: Downloading the Holo2Bright dataset

This code checks whether the dataset directory already exists. If not, the code downloads the dataset from GitHub.

Implementing the Dataset

Once your download is complete, you need to prepare the data you'll use to train the CycleGAN. To do so, use Listing 9-33 to implement a custom dataset class to load the images from the dataset folder, apply the required transformations, and return the images and their corresponding labels in a consistent manner.

```
import numpy as np
import torch
from PIL import Image

class Holo2BrightDataset(torch.utils.data.Dataset):
    """Dataset containing the unpaired holographic and bright-field images."""

    def __init__(self, directory, transforms=None):
        """Initialize dataset."""
        self.transforms = transforms
        self.holo_dir = os.path.join(directory, "holography")
        self.holo_images = os.listdir(self.holo_dir)
        self.bright_dir = os.path.join(directory, "brightfield")
        self.bright_images = os.listdir(self.bright_dir)

    def __len__(self):
        """Return number of images."""
    ❶ return min(len(self.holo_images), len(self.bright_images))

    def __getitem__(self, index):
        """Get unpaired holographic and brightfield images."""
        holo_index = np.random.randint(len(self.holo_images))
        holo_image = Image.open(
            os.path.join(self.holo_dir, self.holo_images[holo_index])
        )
```

```
        bright_index = np.random.randint(len(self.bright_images))
        bright_image = Image.open(
            os.path.join(self.bright_dir, self.bright_images[bright_index])
        )

        if self.transforms:
            seed = np.random.randint(1_000_000_000)
            torch.manual_seed(seed)
            holo_image = self.transforms[0](holo_image)
            torch.manual_seed(seed)
            bright_image = self.transforms[1](bright_image)

        return holo_image, bright_image
```

Listing 9-33: The class to manage the dataset images

This class loads the images in small batches without having to load the entire dataset into memory before training. The class is initialized with two input parameters: `directory`, which sets the dataset directory path, and `transform`, which contains a list of two transformations. The first is applied to the holographic images, and the second to the bright-field images. Finally, the initialization method saves a list of available holographic images and a list of their corresponding bright-field images.

Since the dataset has more holographic than bright-field images, the length of the dataset is set to the smaller number ❶. This length will be used to calculate the batch size and number of steps in each epoch.

The _getitem_() method samples random holographic and bright-field images. This ensures that all the images are sampled in both sets, irrespective of their sizes, ensuring a more thorough training. The method then applies the transformations you'll define. Finally, it returns the individual holographic and bright-field images.

Preprocessing the Dataset

Next, define the necessary augmentations, transformations, and normalizations you'll apply to preprocess the dataset, as demonstrated in Listing 9-34.

```
from torchvision import transforms as trans

trans_holo = trans.Compose([
    trans.RandomHorizontalFlip(p=.5), trans.RandomVerticalFlip(p=.5),
    trans.ToTensor(), trans.Normalize(mean=[.5], std=[.5]),
])
trans_bright = trans.Compose([
    trans.RandomHorizontalFlip(p=.5), trans.RandomVerticalFlip(p=.5),
    trans.ToTensor(), trans.Normalize(mean=[.5, .5, .5], std=[.5, .5, .5]),
])
```

Listing 9-34: Implementing the necessary augmentations, transformations, and normalizations

This code defines two sets of transformations for holographic and bright-field images. It augments the images by flipping them vertically and horizontally with a probability of 0.5. Finally, the code normalizes the pixel values of the images to lie from −1 to 1 for the single channel in the grayscale holographic image and for all three channels in the color bright-field images.

Creating the Training and Testing Datasets

After preprocessing, you're ready to create the training and testing datasets as shown in Listing 9-35.

```
train_dataset = Holo2BrightDataset(
    directory=os.path.join("holo2bright_dataset", "holo2bright", "train"),
    transforms=[trans_holo, trans_bright],
)
test_dataset = Holo2BrightDataset(
    directory=os.path.join("holo2bright_dataset", "holo2bright", "test"),
    transforms=[trans_holo, trans_bright],
)
```

Listing 9-35: Creating the datasets

As required by the class you initialized previously, the transformations are provided as a list.

Visualizing Holographic and Bright-Field Images

Finally, you're ready to visualize some example images, using Listing 9-36.

```
import matplotlib.pyplot as plt

fig, axs = plt.subplots(1, 4, figsize=(8, 2))
for i in range(4):
    axs[i].imshow(train_dataset[i][0][0], cmap="gray")
    axs[i].axis("off")
fig.suptitle("Holography")
plt.show()

fig, axs = plt.subplots(1, 4, figsize=(8, 2))
for i in range(4):
    img = train_dataset[i][1].permute(1, 2, 0).numpy()
  ❶ img = (((img * 0.5) + 0.5) * 255.0).astype(np.uint8)
    axs[i].imshow(img)
    axs[i].axis("off")
fig.suptitle("Brightfield")
plt.show()
```

Listing 9-36: Plotting some holographic and bright-field images

This code plots four holographic images and four bright-field images from the training dataset. Since the bright-field images are normalized to fall within the [−1, 1] range, they're first denormalized to the [0, 1] range for visualization ❶. The results should be similar to Figure 9-11.

Holography

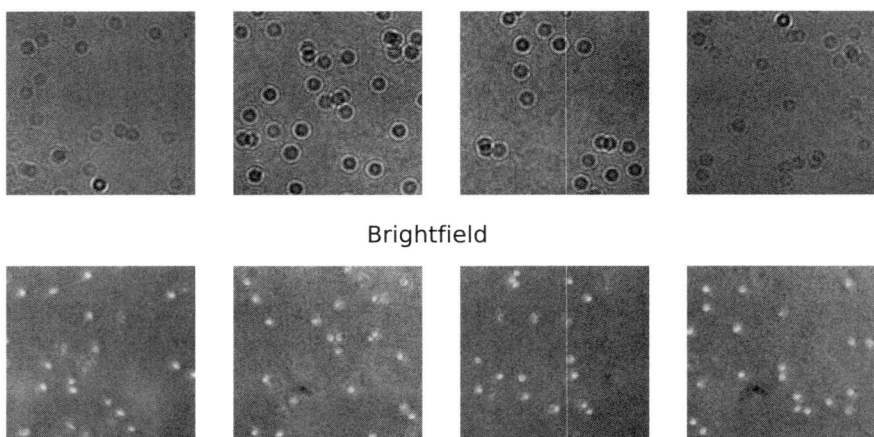

Brightfield

Figure 9-11: The holographic (top) and bright-field (bottom) images of marine microplankton

By looking at their different features, you can clearly see that the holographic and bright-field images aren't coregistered. This means that you can't apply traditional deep learning architectures or even conditional GANs to transform one microscopy technique into another.

Instantiating the CycleGAN Generators and Discriminators

Once you've determined the computing device using

```
device = get_device()
```

which uses the get_device() function (Listing 7-10), you're ready to initialize both the generators and the discriminators.

Generators

You'll use the Deeplay CycleGANResnetGenerator class to define the CycleGAN generators, as shown in Listing 9-37.

```
import deeplay as dl

gen_H2B = dl.CycleGANResnetGenerator(in_channels=1, out_channels=3).build()
gen_B2H = dl.CycleGANResnetGenerator(in_channels=3, out_channels=1).build()
gen_H2B.to(device), gen_B2H.to(device);
```

Listing 9-37: Defining the generators

This code instantiates the two generators to transform monochromatic holographic images to color bright-field images, and vice versa. Then it passes the generators to the selected computational device. You can print their architecture with print(gen_H2B) and print(gen_B2H).

These generators are U-Nets, which consist of a convolutional backbone with residual connections, as you've seen in Chapter 5. The generators begin with an initial convolutional block, enhancing feature extraction by expanding the input's channel depth. Subsequently, the input data proceeds through a series of convolutional blocks, progressively doubling the channels while halving the spatial dimensions to capture a rich, hierarchical representation of the input. At the core of the architecture lies a sequence of nine residual blocks. The blocks refine the features they receive in input without altering their spatial dimensions, ensuring that essential information is preserved and enhanced through the network.

Afterward, the architecture transitions into the upsampling phase, utilizing convolutional transpose blocks to gradually restore the spatial dimensions while reducing the depth of the feature maps, the inverse of the U-Net's expansive path. This process effectively reconstructs the image from the encoded feature representation, with the final convolutional layer consolidating the features into the output image. Instance normalizations and ReLU activations ensure that the model dynamically adapts to the data, promoting stability and efficiency in learning.

Discriminators

Now that you've created the generators, use the Deeplay `CycleGANDiscriminator` class to define the discriminators, as shown in Listing 9-38.

```
disc_H = dl.CycleGANDiscriminator(in_channels=1).build()
disc_B = dl.CycleGANDiscriminator(in_channels=3).build()
disc_H.to(device), disc_B.to(device);
```

Listing 9-38: Defining the discriminators

This code instantiates two discriminators: one for the holographic images, and one for the bright-field images. Then the code passes the discriminators to the selected computational device. You can print their structure with `print(disc_H)` and `print(disc_B)`.

Your CycleGAN will use PatchGAN discriminators, designed to classify small patches of an image as real or fake by focusing on high-frequency details. Their architecture starts with convolutional layers that progressively decrease the image size while increasing channel depth, using leaky ReLU for nonlinearity and instance normalization for stability. Instead of classifying the entire image at once, the discriminator evaluates smaller patches, with each patch receiving a scalar value through a sigmoid function that indicates that patch's probability of being real. The final output is a grid of these scalar values, reflecting the estimated authenticity of each patch.

Loss Functions, Optimizers, and Data Loaders

At this point, you're ready to define two different loss functions for the generators and discriminators, as shown in Listing 9-39.

```
loss_gen = torch.nn.L1Loss()
loss_disc = torch.nn.MSELoss()
```

Listing 9-39: Defining the losses

This code sets the loss_gen generator loss function as MAE, also called L1 loss. Then it sets the loss_disc discriminator loss as MSE, also called L2 loss.

After specifying the loss functions, create the optimizers for the generators and discriminators, as shown in Listing 9-40.

```
optim_gen = torch.optim.Adam(
    list(gen_H2B.parameters()) + list(gen_B2H.parameters()),
    lr=0.0002, betas=(0.5, 0.999),
)
optim_disc = torch.optim.Adam(
    list(disc_H.parameters()) + list(disc_B.parameters()),
    lr=0.0002, betas=(0.5, 0.999),
)
```

Listing 9-40: Defining the optimizers

This code defines two optimizers: optim_gen for both generators, and optim_disc for both discriminators. As a result, during the backpropagation step, both generators will be trained together, and both discriminators will be trained together.

Next, create the data loaders as shown in Listing 9-41.

```
train_loader = dl.DataLoader(train_dataset, batch_size=8, shuffle=True)
test_loader = dl.DataLoader(test_dataset, batch_size=1, shuffle=False)
```

Listing 9-41: Defining the data loaders

This code sets the batch size to 8 for the training dataset (as usual, larger batches improve the training but require more memory) and 1 for the testing dataset. These parameters can be changed according to the available computational resources.

Training the CycleGAN

Now that you've prepared your data and instantiated the generators and discriminators, you'll implement the training procedure for the CycleGAN. First, you'll specify the functions for training and evaluation. Then you'll create a training loop to use these functions.

Defining the Training Function

To begin, implement the train_model() function shown in Listing 9-42. You'll use this function during every epoch of the training loop.

```
def train_model(input_images_H, input_images_B, optim_disc, optim_gen,
                loss_disc, loss_gen, cycle_coef_H=10, cycle_coef_B=5):
    """Train CycleGAN for one batch."""
    # 1. Training discriminators
    optim_disc.zero_grad()

    # Use discriminator B (as a part of the transformation H -> B)
    fake_images_B = gen_H2B(input_images_H)
```

```
disc_B_fakes = disc_B(fake_images_B.detach())
disc_B_reals = disc_B(input_images_B)

# Compute discriminator B losses
disc_B_loss_fake = loss_disc(disc_B_fakes, torch.zeros_like(disc_B_fakes))
disc_B_loss_real = loss_disc(disc_B_reals, torch.ones_like(disc_B_reals))
disc_B_loss = disc_B_loss_fake + disc_B_loss_real

# Use discriminator H (as a part of the transformation B -> H)
fake_images_H = gen_B2H(input_images_B)
disc_H_fakes = disc_H(fake_images_H.detach())
disc_H_reals = disc_H(input_images_H)

# Compute discriminator H losses
disc_H_loss_fake = loss_disc(disc_H_fakes, torch.zeros_like(disc_H_fakes))
disc_H_loss_real = loss_disc(disc_H_reals, torch.ones_like(disc_H_reals))
disc_H_loss = disc_H_loss_fake + disc_H_loss_real

# Total discriminator loss, backpropagation, and weight update
disc_loss = (disc_B_loss + disc_H_loss) / 2
disc_loss.backward()
optim_disc.step()

# 2. Training generators
optim_gen.zero_grad()

# Adversarial loss (from generators perspective)
disc_H_fakes = disc_H(fake_images_H)
disc_B_fakes = disc_B(fake_images_B)
gen_H2B_loss = loss_disc(disc_B_fakes, torch.ones_like(disc_B_fakes))
gen_B2H_loss = loss_disc(disc_H_fakes, torch.ones_like(disc_H_fakes))

# 3. Cycle consistency loss
cycle_images_H = gen_B2H(fake_images_B)
cycle_images_B = gen_H2B(fake_images_H)
cycle_H_loss = loss_gen(input_images_H, cycle_images_H)
cycle_B_loss = loss_gen(input_images_B, cycle_images_B)

# Total generator loss, backpropagation, and weight update
gen_loss = (gen_H2B_loss + gen_B2H_loss
            + cycle_coef_H * cycle_H_loss + cycle_coef_B * cycle_B_loss)
gen_loss.backward()
optim_gen.step()

return disc_loss, gen_loss
```

Listing 9-42: The function to train the CycleGAN

This function inputs the images of both domains as arguments along with the optimizers and the `cycle_coef_H` and `cycle_coef_B` loss coefficients. It returns the losses computed for the discriminators and generators.

Before training the discriminators, this code zeroes their optimizer gradients. Next, to train the bright-field discriminator to detect when holographic images have been transformed to bright-field, a set of fake bright-field images generated by `gen_H2B` is passed through `disc_B`, which generates an output for the fake image. Then a set of real bright-field images from the dataset is passed through the discriminator to generate another output for the real image. Afterward, the losses of both outputs are computed using the discriminator loss (`loss_disc`) by setting the label to 0 for the fake output and 1 for the real output. The combined loss for the bright-field discriminator is calculated by summing both losses. The code follows a similar procedure to get the loss of the holography discriminator. Finally, the losses for both discriminators are averaged to get a total discriminator loss, which is then used for backpropagation and for updating the weights of both discriminators.

Subsequently, the code trains the generators. Similar to the preceding process, it starts by getting the discriminator outputs for fake images of both domains. Afterward, the adversarial losses are calculated by setting the labels to 1 in the discriminator loss for the fake outputs.

Finally, the code calculates a cycle consistency loss. For both generators, the code passes the fake images that mimic a transformation from one domain into the other through the complementary generator of the original domain, which outputs an image belonging to the original domain. In this case, a fake bright-field image is passed through `gen_B2H` to generate a holographic image, while a fake holographic image is passed through `gen_H2B` to generate the bright-field image. A pixel-wise loss is then calculated between both these images.

The code then sums the adversarial losses and cycle consistency losses for both generators to get a total generator loss. The cycle consistency losses are weighted through the coefficients `cycle_coef_H` and `cycle_coef_B` to control the balance between the pixel-wise error and the adversarial loss. Afterward, the total loss is backpropagated through the generators, and the weights for both generators are updated.

In the end, the function returns the generator and discriminator losses. This process will be repeated for every batch.

Defining the Evaluation Function

For the second stage of the training procedure, implement the `evaluate _model()` function shown in Listing 9-43. You'll use this function during every epoch of the training loop to visualize the generated images.

```
def evaluate_model(image_H, image_B):
    """Evaluate CycleGAN on unpaired holographic and bright-field images."""
    # Generate fake images
    gen_H2B.eval(), gen_B2H.eval()
    fake_image_B, fake_image_H = gen_H2B(image_H), gen_B2H(image_B)
    gen_H2B.train(), gen_B2H.train()

    fig, axs = plt.subplots(2, 2, figsize=(5, 5))

    img_B_in = image_B[0].permute(1, 2, 0).cpu().detach().numpy()
    img_B_in = (((img_B_in * 0.5) + 0.5) * 255.0).astype(np.uint8)
    axs[0, 0].imshow(img_B_in)
    axs[0, 0].set_title("Input: Brightfield", fontsize=8)
    axs[0, 0].axis("off")

    img_H_out = fake_image_H[0].permute(1, 2, 0).cpu().detach().numpy()
    axs[0, 1].imshow(img_H_out, cmap="gray")
    axs[0, 1].set_title("Output: Holography", fontsize=8)
    axs[0, 1].axis("off")

    img_H_in = image_H[0].permute(1, 2, 0).cpu().detach().numpy()
    axs[1, 0].imshow(img_H_in, cmap="gray")
    axs[1, 0].set_title("Input: Holography", fontsize=8)
    axs[1, 0].axis("off")

    img_B_out = fake_image_B[0].permute(1, 2, 0).cpu().detach().numpy()
    img_B_out = (((img_B_out * 0.5) + 0.5) * 255.0).astype(np.uint8)
    axs[1, 1].imshow(img_B_out)
    axs[1, 1].set_title("Output: Brightfield", fontsize=8)
    axs[1, 1].axis("off")

    plt.show()
    plt.close(fig)
```

Listing 9-43: The function to evaluate the CycleGAN

This function takes the input images belonging to both domains, image_H and image_B, as arguments. The code then sets the generators to evaluation mode, generates images of the other domain, sets the generators back to training mode, and finally plots the input and generated images of both domains in a grid.

Implementing the Training Cycle

Using the `train_model()` and `evaluate_model()` functions you just defined, you'll create a training loop, as shown in Listing 9-44.

```
epochs = 100

for epoch in range(epochs):
    for i, (inputs_H, inputs_B) in enumerate(train_loader, 0):
        inputs_H, inputs_B = inputs_H.to(device), inputs_B.to(device)
        disc_loss, gen_loss = train_model(
            inputs_H, inputs_B, optim_disc, optim_gen, loss_disc, loss_gen,
        )

    for test_inputs_H, test_inputs_B in test_loader:
        break
    evaluate_model(test_inputs_H.to(device), test_inputs_B.to(device))
```

Listing 9-44: Defining the training cycle

This code trains the model for 100 epochs. In each epoch, the training dataset is processed through the generators and discriminators in batches. In each batch, the input images belonging to both domains are extracted and sent to the designated device.

The input images are then fed into the `train_model()` function for the CycleGAN training, along with the optimizers, loss functions, and coefficients for cycle consistency loss. The function then outputs the total discriminator and generator losses for the processed batch. Finally, the code processes the images from the test dataset through the `evaluate_model()` function to generate and plot output images of the opposite domains.

Adding Timing and Notifications

You can log the losses for every epoch and add timing and notification features within the training loop for troubleshooting. This is shown in Listing 9-45.

```
import time
from datetime import timedelta
--snip--
gen_losses, disc_losses = [], []
for epoch in range(epochs):
    start_time = time.time()
    print("\n" + f"Epoch {epoch + 1}/{epochs}" + "\n" + "-" * 10)

    gen_losses_epoch, disc_losses_epoch = [], []
    for i, data in enumerate(train_loader, 0):
        --snip--
```

```
                    if i % 20 == 0:
                        print(f"Batch {i + 1}/{len(train_loader)} : "
                              f"Generators Loss: {gen_loss.item():.4f}, "
                              f"Discriminators Loss: {disc_loss.item():.4f}")

                    gen_losses_epoch.append(gen_loss.item())
                    disc_losses_epoch.append(disc_loss.item())

                end_time = time.time()

                gen_losses.append(np.mean(gen_losses_epoch))
                disc_losses.append(np.mean(disc_losses_epoch))

                print("-" * 10 + "\n" + f"Epoch {epoch + 1}/{epochs} : "
                      f"Generators Loss: {gen_losses[-1]:.4f}, "
                      f"Discriminators Loss: {disc_losses[-1]:.4f}"
                      "\n" + f"Time taken: {timedelta(seconds=end_time - start_time)}")
                --snip--
```

Listing 9-45: Timing the training and notifying the user

The timing and notification features resemble those in Listings 9-10 and 9-31. For logging the losses, this code creates two empty lists for the generator and discriminator losses outside the training loop to store the average losses calculated in every epoch. Within every epoch, the code creates two more empty lists to store the loss values of each batch. At the end of each epoch, the average values of the second set of lists are appended to the first set.

You can plot the losses of the generator and discriminator during training to visualize their dynamic interplay. The generator's loss typically starts higher and decreases as the generator learns, while the discriminator's loss usually starts lower, indicating the discriminator's initial effectiveness.

Significant shifts in the loss curves can indicate improvements in image quality for one of the domains. For example, downward shifts in the generator's loss curve, along with upward shifts in the discriminator's loss, suggest that the generator is improving and producing more-realistic images. By monitoring and comparing these losses with the generated image quality, you can adjust the training parameters to achieve better results. For instance, if the generator's loss stagnates while the discriminator's loss decreases too rapidly, you might lower the discriminator's learning rate to avoid overpowering the generator.

Evaluating the Trained CycleGAN

Figure 9-12 shows the results after training for 100 epochs.

Input: Brightfield   Output: Holography

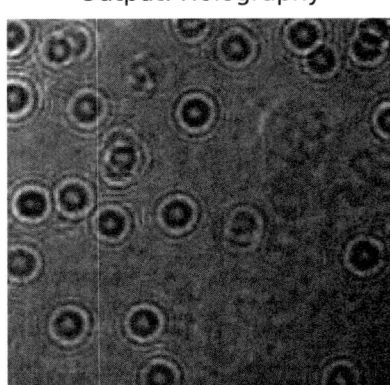

Input: Holography   Output: Brightfield

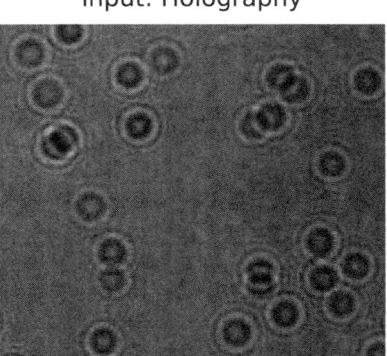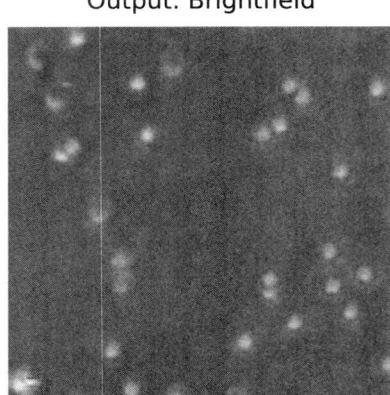

Figure 9-12: The CycleGAN in action: from holographic to bright-field images (top) and vice versa (bottom)

You can see that the bright-field generator successfully transforms the holographic image into a bright-field image (top row), while the holography generator successfully transforms the bright-field image into a holographic image (bottom row). You can see that the real positions of the objects are preserved in each image pair, which illustrates the power of CycleGANs since the dataset didn't contain paired images of both domains. Further training can improve the similarity between real and fake images.

NOTE *Code Example 9-C, "Converting Microscopy Images with a CycleGAN," is available at* https://github.com/DeepTrackAI/DeepLearningCrashCourse. *Navigate to the* Ch09_GAN *folder and then* ec09_C_cyclegan. *The* cyclegan.ipynb *notebook provides a complete code example that uses a CycleGAN to convert between holographic and bright-field images.*

Summary

In this chapter, you discovered the power of GANs to create and transform images. Starting with the foundational principles of their operation, you witnessed how GANs pit a generator against a discriminator: The generator tries to create data indistinguishable from real data, while the discriminator attempts to accurately classify data as real or generated. This adversarial setup forms the heart of GAN technology, driving both networks to improve continuously so that the model can generate increasingly realistic data.

Through hands-on projects, you learned to harness the capabilities of GANs for a variety of tasks. You started by generating digit images with a basic GAN model, which demonstrated how GANs shape noise into recognizable forms. Upon advancing to conditional GANs, you gained the ability to guide the generation process with specific conditions, enabling targeted image synthesis.

You then applied these principles to virtual staining to transform bright-field microscopy images into their fluorescent counterparts without actual staining, demonstrating the potential of GANs in biomedical imaging.

Finally, you used CycleGANs to tackle the challenge of unpaired image transformation, converting images between holographic and bright-field microscopy techniques. This foray into unpaired image translation highlighted how GANs can adapt to bridge the gap between imaging modalities, combining their advantages to advance scientific exploration as well as the practical applications of GANs. Ultimately, this journey has illustrated the versatility of GANs while equipping you with the skills to adapt GAN architectures for your unique applications.

In the next chapter, you'll build on the foundation laid by GANs to investigate another groundbreaking generative approach: diffusion models.

Seminal Works and Further Reading

The concept of GANs was first introduced in 2014 by Ian J. Goodfellow et al. in "Generative Adversarial Networks," published on arXiv (article number 1406.2661) and presented at Advances in Neural Information Processing Systems (NeurIPS). This groundbreaking work introduced the adversarial training framework, where generator and discriminator networks compete against each other, leading to impressive improvements in the generation of realistic images.

To improve the quality of generated images and make them perceptually closer to the real data, Justin Johnson et al. introduced perceptual loss in 2016 in "Perceptual Losses for Real-Time Style Transfer and Super-Resolution," published in *Proceedings of the European Conference on Computer Vision–ECCV 2016* (*Lecture Notes in Computer Science*, volume 9906, pages 694–711). Perceptual loss uses feature representations from pretrained convolutional networks to capture perceptual differences, which significantly improves the quality of generated images in tasks like style transfer and super-resolution.

Further advancements in GANs were made in 2017 by Jun-Yan Zhu et al. in "Unpaired Image-to-Image Translation Using Cycle-Consistent Adversarial Networks," published in *2017 IEEE International Conference on Computer Vision* (*ICCV 2017*, pages 2242–2251). This work introduced CycleGANs.

CHALLENGE PROJECTS

9-1: Advanced denoising with real-world noise patterns   Tackle the challenge of image denoising with the Darmstadt Noise dataset (DND), available through the TU Darmstadt website, and the SIDD Benchmark dataset, available through the York University website. Focus on removing real-world noise patterns from images captured under various conditions.

9-2: Cross-domain image translation   Implement cross-domain image translation between different conditions, such as day to night or summer to winter. Use the Day-Night dataset and the Flickr Image dataset from Kaggle for your experiments. Evaluate the quality and authenticity of the translated images.

10

IMPLEMENTING GENERATIVE AI WITH DIFFUSION MODELS

In this chapter, you'll explore diffusion models, the latest torchbearers in generative AI. Alongside variational autoencoders and generative adversarial networks (GANs), which you've seen in Chapters 4 and 9, *diffusion models* have quickly gained acclaim for their exceptional ability to generate high-quality, lifelike images.

Famous diffusion models include the CompVis Latent Diffusion models, the OpenAI DALL-E series, Google Imagen, and the community-driven Stable Diffusion. However, the applications of diffusion models extend far beyond mere image generation. These models excel in tasks like image denoising, inpainting, and super-resolution, often outperforming even the most advanced GANs. Moreover, diffusion models have significant real-world applications. For instance, image denoising can improve the clarity of medical images, aiding in more-accurate diagnostics. Inpainting can be used to restore damaged historical photographs or artwork, preserving cultural heritage. Super-resolution techniques can enhance satellite imagery, allowing for better environmental monitoring and urban planning.

To prepare you to apply these tools, this chapter will teach you the core principles of diffusion models and their connection to diffusion in physics and mathematics. You'll then learn how to implement denoising diffusion probabilistic models (DDPMs) to generate images from noise. Later, you'll progress to more-advanced applications of DDPMs, such as conditional models that turn text prompts into images. Finally, you'll see how DDPMs can be used to transform low-resolution images into high-resolution ones.

Understanding Diffusion

Diffusion is a fundamental concept in physics and mathematics that describes how particles in a solution spread from regions of higher concentration to regions of lower concentration. Figure 10-1 illustrates this process.

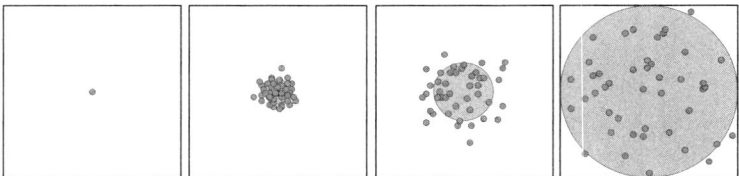

Figure 10-1: Physical diffusion

This figure depicts an ensemble of microscopic particles in a hypothetical solution. At the beginning (left), all particles share the same position. In subsequent panels, these particles spread out over time as they collide with the molecules of the surrounding solution. As a result, the system of particles goes from a highly dense peaked distribution to a homogeneous distribution. Each particle will take a random-looking trajectory in position space.

Famously, Robert Brown first observed this phenomenon while studying the motion of microscopic particles within pollen grains (hence the name *Brownian motion*). Later, Albert Einstein explained this process. Everyday examples of diffusion include perfume spreading in a room without airflow and tea seeping from a bag into hot water, but the equations derived from studying this process have applications beyond physics. In the mid-20th century, mathematicians used the concept of diffusion to develop *stochastic differential equations* and *diffusion equations* to describe the behavior of complex systems such as ecosystems and markets.

Diffusion has also found analogies in deep learning. For example, given an image, it's possible to gradually add noise to it in multiple steps. This process is like blurring a picture little by little until it's entirely unrecognizable, similar to the way particles spread out randomly in a fluid in their Brownian motion. In this context, the image is moving through the space of all possible (noisy) versions of itself, and this process eventually transforms the initial sharp image into a completely noisy one, as illustrated in Figure 10-2.

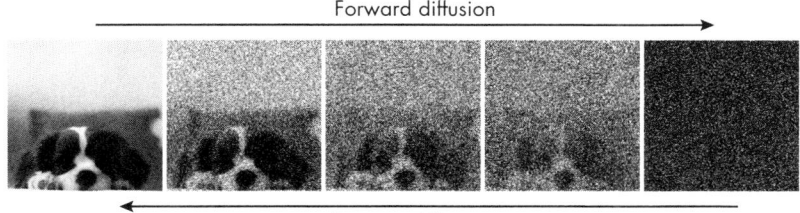

Figure 10-2: The forward and reverse diffusion processes for an image

The *forward diffusion process* involves the sequential addition of noise to an image until it's completely corrupted, as illustrated in Figure 10-2 when going from left to right. Conversely, the *reverse diffusion process* successively removes noise from an image to generate a clean version, as illustrated here when going from right to left. Clearly, this is a much more challenging process, but as you'll see in this chapter, you can train a neural network to gradually denoise images in this way.

The processes of forward and reverse diffusion are fundamental to understanding diffusion models, especially denoising diffusion probabilistic models, the foundation of more-advanced diffusion models. In the next section, you'll learn the details of both processes within the context of machine learning and their application in image generation.

Breaking Down Denoising Diffusion Probabilistic Models

Denoising diffusion probabilistic models, or *DDPMs*, learn the underlying probabilistic distribution of an image dataset by understanding the patterns, features, and variations that are common across all images in the dataset. This means that they can generate images with the same statistical properties.

Ideally, these generated images will be new and plausible, meaning that they aren't present in the original dataset, and a viewer shouldn't be able to notice that they are generated images. The ultimate goal is to create images that are entirely new yet look realistic and fit well within the style and content of the original dataset.

DDPMs achieve this by modeling both the *forward process* of adding noise to images in the dataset until they gradually turn into pure noise, as well as the *reverse process*, which gradually generates a clean image starting from pure noise.

The forward process is a Markov process in the space of all images, which is the entire set of possible images that can be created by adding different amounts of noise to an original image. In the context of image transformation, a *Markov process* is one that generates the features and structure of the next image by using only information contained in the current one. The resulting image is independent of the previous images. You can see this in the forward process shown in Figure 10-2, where the next image is just the current image plus some noise, and the new image doesn't explicitly depend on the previous images. This is easy to generate.

Unfortunately, implementing the reverse process is more complex, requiring the sequential application of neural networks.

In the next sections, you'll see the forward and reverse diffusion processes in their mathematical and Pythonic forms. You'll then use them to train a diffusion model to generate MNIST digits.

Modeling the Forward Diffusion Process

In the forward diffusion process, you iteratively add a small amount of Gaussian noise to an image until it's completely corrupted, as shown in Figure 10-2.

Start with one image from a dataset—for example, the image of a dog or one of the MNIST digits. Let's say that the matrix $\mathbf{x}_0$ contains the pixels of the image. The subindex 0 denotes the time $t = 0$, corresponding to the original image before noise is added over multiple time steps.

Each iteration in the forward diffusion process makes the image slightly noisier by adding Gaussian noise. This can be represented as follows:

$$\mathbf{x}_t \longrightarrow \mathbf{x}_{t+1} = \underbrace{\sqrt{1 - \beta_t}\,\mathbf{x}_t}_{\text{rescaled image}} + \underbrace{\sqrt{\beta_t}\,\mathbf{n}_t}_{\text{noise}} \qquad (10.1)$$

Here, $t = 0, 1, \ldots, T$ is the timestep; β_t is a time-dependent parameter known as the *variance schedule* that controls the amount of noise added at each step; and $\mathbf{n}_t$ is a matrix of noise containing a random number for each pixel of the image, whose values are obtained from a Gaussian distribution with a mean of 0 and identity covariance. The subindex t in $\mathbf{n}_t$ shows that its values are different at each time step, even though the noise is always sampled from the same normal distribution. This process generates images that correspond to the probability of a multivariate Gaussian random variable (a generalization of the Gaussian distribution to higher dimensions), which is key to the model's ability to reverse this process and generate realistic images later.

The β_t variable determines how much noise from the $\mathbf{n}_t$ matrix is added to the image at step t. The higher the β_t value, the more noise is added. The inventors of the DDPM used a linear schedule for β_t that ranges from 0.0001 to 0.02, but other choices are also possible and work equally well.

You can also understand Equation 10.1 as describing the forward diffusion in a probabilistic sense with the help of Gaussian distributions, a useful perspective when working with diffusion models. In fact, you can view the process of going from $\mathbf{x}_t \to \mathbf{x}_{t+1}$ as a sampling process, which samples the noisier image, $\mathbf{x}_{t+1}$, from a Gaussian distribution whose mean and variance depend on the previous image, $\mathbf{x}_t$. As you might have already noticed from Equation 10.1, the mean of this Gaussian distribution is given by $\sqrt{1 - \beta_t}\mathbf{x}_t$ and its variance is given by $\beta_t\mathbf{I}$, where $\mathbf{I}$ is the identity matrix. To arrive at Equation 10.1 from this distribution, you need to use an important property of Gaussian distributions known as reparameterization. This trick allows you to write a Gaussian distribution with any mean and variance in terms of the standard normal distribution, a Gaussian distribution with mean 0 and variance 1. In mathematical terms, you can write a random variable $x \in \mathcal{N}(\mu, \sigma^2)$, in which $\mathcal{N}(\mu, \sigma^2)$ is a Gaussian distribution with mean μ and variance σ^2, as $x = \mu + \sigma\epsilon$, where $\epsilon \in \mathcal{N}(0, 1)$.

Using Equation 10.1, you can generate the noisy version of the image at time $t + 1$, given the image at time t. For example, for an MNIST digit $\mathbf{x}_0$, you can generate its first noisy version $\mathbf{x}_1$, then iteratively use $\mathbf{x}_1$ to generate $\mathbf{x}_2$, then $\mathbf{x}_2$ to generate $\mathbf{x}_3$, and so on until $\mathbf{x}_T$. You can repeat this process so that from a single initial image, you can get multiple different images that have diffused in image space, similar to the way the particles in Figure 10-1 diffuse in position space.

Deriving the Fast Forward Process

Now that you understand the mathematical model for the forward process, you can exploit its Markovian nature and the noise's Gaussian structure to simplify the computation of the noisy images. This is crucial because when training the neural network to model the reverse process, you need many examples of the forward process at different times.

However, since DDPMs require large T values (often on the order of 1,000), generating all the intermediate noisy images to reach a noisy image of a specific time step becomes computationally prohibitive. Luckily, you can use the mathematical properties of the stochastic process described by Equation 10.1 to jump directly from the initial image to the image at time t without generating all the intermediate images. This is known as the *fast forward process*, represented by this equation:

$$\mathbf{x}_0 \quad \longrightarrow \quad \mathbf{x}_t = \sqrt{\bar{\alpha}_t}\, \mathbf{x}_0 + \sqrt{1 - \bar{\alpha}_t}\, \mathbf{n} \tag{10.2}$$

Here, $\bar{\alpha}_t = \prod_{s=1}^{t} \alpha_s$, $\alpha_t = 1 - \beta_t$, and $\mathbf{n}$ is still a random variable sampled from a standard normal distribution with mean 0 and variance 1.

In the rest of this section, you'll derive Equation 10.2 for the fast forward process, starting from Equation 10.1. You can safely skip this part if you aren't mathematically inclined.

From Equation 10.1, you have this:

$$\mathbf{x}_t = \sqrt{1 - \beta_t}\, \mathbf{x}_{t-1} + \sqrt{\beta_t}\, \mathbf{n}_{t-1} \tag{10.3}$$

Rewriting the previous equation in terms of $\alpha_t = 1 - \beta_t$, you get this:

$$\mathbf{x}_t = \sqrt{\alpha_t}\, \mathbf{x}_{t-1} + \sqrt{1 - \alpha_t}\, \mathbf{n}_{t-1} \tag{10.4}$$

Now rewrite this equation by expanding $\mathbf{x}_{t-1}$ in terms of $\mathbf{x}_{t-2}$:

$$\begin{aligned} \mathbf{x}_t &= \sqrt{\alpha_t}\left(\sqrt{\alpha_{t-1}}\, \mathbf{x}_{t-2} + \sqrt{1 - \alpha_{t-1}}\, \mathbf{n}_{t-2}\right) + \sqrt{1 - \alpha_t}\, \mathbf{n}_{t-1} \\ &= \sqrt{\alpha_t \alpha_{t-1}}\, \mathbf{x}_{t-2} + \sqrt{\alpha_t(1 - \alpha_{t-1})}\, \mathbf{n}_{t-2} + \sqrt{1 - \alpha_t}\, \mathbf{n}_{t-1} \end{aligned} \tag{10.5}$$

In Equation 10.5, you can think of the last two terms as random variables sampled from two different Gaussian distributions with mean 0, and variances $\alpha_t(1 - \alpha_{t-1})$ for the first term and $1 - \alpha_t$ for the second term, respectively.

From the properties of Gaussian distributions, the sum of two independent Gaussian random variables is also a Gaussian random variable. Its mean equals the sum of the means of the two random variables, while its variance is equal to the sum of the variances of the two random variables. Combining these two properties, you can merge the last two terms into a single random variable sampled from a combined Gaussian distribution with mean 0 and variance $\alpha_t(1 - \alpha_{t-1}) + 1 - \alpha_t = 1 - \alpha_{t-1}\alpha_t$. This gives you the next equation:

$$\mathbf{x}_t = \sqrt{\alpha_t \alpha_{t-1}}\, \mathbf{x}_{t-2} + \sqrt{1 - \alpha_{t-1}\alpha_t}\, \mathbf{n} \qquad (10.6)$$

If you repeat this process recursively, you'll get Equation 10.2.

Modeling the Reverse Diffusion Process

The reverse diffusion process is the opposite of the forward diffusion process. The idea is to slightly reduce the amount of noise in an image in each time step so that an initial pure noise image becomes a sharp, clean image, as in Figure 10-2.

Since the forward process (Equation 10.1) is a Gaussian process, you can safely assume that the reverse process will have the same structure. Accordingly, you can use a similar probabilistic intuition as in the forward process, where you treat the noisier version of the image as sampled from a Gaussian distribution whose mean and variance depend on the previous image. In the reverse process, you do the opposite. Specifically, you treat the cleaner version of the image as sampled from a Gaussian distribution whose parameters are dependent on the previous noisy image. With this intuition in mind, the reverse diffusion process can be written as follows:

$$\mathbf{x}_{t+1} \rightarrow \mathbf{x}_t = \underbrace{\mathbf{m}(\mathbf{x}_{t+1}, t)}_{\text{average image}} + \underbrace{\mathbf{r}(\mathbf{x}_{t+1}, t)}_{\text{reverse-process noise}} \qquad (10.7)$$

Here, $\mathbf{m}(\mathbf{x}_{t+1}, t)$ and $\mathbf{r}(\mathbf{x}_{t+1}, t)$ are the mean and variance (respectively) of the sampled image, which depend on the image at time $t + 1$ and on the time step. Note that this equation uses the reparameterization trick as in the forward process, where the *average image* becomes the mean of the Gaussian distribution, and the *reverse-process noise* becomes the square root of the variance (or standard deviation) of this assumed Gaussian distribution. The challenge of the reverse diffusion process is how to determine the underlying Gaussian distribution. There are plenty of ways to do so; for example, you can train a neural network to provide them.

Let's start by simplifying the problem and fixing the noise term so that the neural network needs to learn only the mean of the distribution of images. You can therefore rewrite Equation 10.7 as follows:

$$\mathbf{x}_{t+1} \longrightarrow \mathbf{x}_t = \mathbf{m}(\mathbf{x}_{t+1}, t) + \sigma_t\, \mathbf{r}_t \qquad (10.8)$$

Here, the parameter σ_t represents the variance of the noise, and $\mathbf{r}_t$ represents a matrix of Gaussian random noise. You'll set the value of the noise to $\sigma_t = \sqrt{\beta_t}$, even though other choices are possible. For example, the inventors of DDPM experimented with setting this value to $\sigma_t = \sqrt{\tilde{\beta}_t}$, where

$\tilde{\beta}_t = \left[(1 - \bar{\alpha}_{t-1})/(1 - \bar{\alpha}_t)\right] \beta_t$, obtaining similar results. By setting $\sigma_t = \sqrt{\tilde{\beta}_t}$, you get this:

$$\mathbf{x}_{t+1} \quad \longrightarrow \quad \mathbf{x}_t = \mathbf{m}(\mathbf{x}_{t+1}, t) + \sqrt{\tilde{\beta}_t}\,\mathbf{r}_t \tag{10.9}$$

You now just need to find a way to determine the mean. While this chapter doesn't include the details, the inventors of DDPM arrive at the following expression for the optimal mean value:

$$\mathbf{x}_{t+1} \quad \longrightarrow \quad \mathbf{x}_t = \frac{1}{\sqrt{\alpha_t}}\left(\mathbf{x}_{t+1} - \frac{\beta_t}{\sqrt{1 - \bar{\alpha}_t}}\,\mathbf{n}_t\right) + \sqrt{\tilde{\beta}_t}\,\mathbf{r}_t \tag{10.10}$$

Here, $\mathbf{n}_t$ is the noise used to generate the noisier image $\mathbf{x}_{t+1}$ from $\mathbf{x}_t$.

EXERCISE

10-1: The derivation of Equation 10.10 is nontrivial and uses advanced probability concepts that are beyond the scope of this chapter. Reproduce the detailed derivation, which you can find in the appendix of the original article, "Denoising Diffusion Probabilistic Models" by Jonathan Ho et al., published in 2020 in *Advances in Neural Information Processing Systems* (volume 33, pages 6,480–6,851).

You can substitute $\beta_t = 1 - \alpha_t$ to get an expression in terms of α_t:

$$\mathbf{x}_{t+1} \quad \longrightarrow \quad \mathbf{x}_t = \frac{1}{\sqrt{\alpha_t}}\left(\mathbf{x}_{t+1} - \frac{1 - \alpha_t}{\sqrt{1 - \bar{\alpha}_t}}\,\mathbf{n}_t\right) + \sqrt{1 - \alpha_t}\,\mathbf{r}_t \tag{10.11}$$

With this equation, you can make the neural network predict the noise $\mathbf{n}_t$, taking the noisy image $\mathbf{x}_{t+1}$ and the corresponding time step t as inputs. As it turns out, this is a simpler task than asking the neural network to predict the slightly less noisy image itself $\mathbf{x}_t$. If $\tilde{\mathbf{n}}(\mathbf{x}_t, t)$ is the noise predicted by the neural network, the MSE loss is given by this equation:

$$E = \left\|\mathbf{n}_t - \tilde{\mathbf{n}}(\mathbf{x}_t, t)\right\|^2 = \left\|\mathbf{n}_t - \tilde{\mathbf{n}}(\sqrt{\bar{\alpha}_t}\,\mathbf{x}_0 + \sqrt{1 - \bar{\alpha}_t}\,\mathbf{n}, t)\right\|^2 \tag{10.12}$$

This uses the fast forward process in Equation 10.2 to get a more computationally efficient loss function that can be calculated using the initial image ($\mathbf{x}_0$) instead of the image at time t ($\mathbf{x}_t$).

In addition, for the reverse diffusion process, the series of denoised images will have some randomness. This randomness comes from the term $\mathbf{r}_t$, which is drawn from a random distribution and is therefore different for each sampling. Through the example in the following section, you'll see how this randomness in the reverse diffusion process leads to the creation of different generated images, even when you start from the same initial noisy one.

For the moment, think about how the network learns the forward diffusion process and about the data itself. Remember that all the network takes as inputs are the noisy image and the time step corresponding to the noise level of the image. Beyond that, the network has information about the noise used to generate the noisy image from the loss function. Now, keep in mind that every time the network sees the same image, it sees a different noisy version of the image, since a different noise matrix is added to the noisy image at each time step.

This leads you to the central concept of *diffusion trajectory*. After encountering the same image with a different added noise, the network comes to understand the forward diffusion trajectory of the image for any randomly sampled noise, thereby learning the reverse diffusion process. In essence, the network implicitly learns the data distribution by looking at the data through the lens of noise, much as the GANs in Chapter 9 learn through a competitive process.

However, the generation process based on a diffusion trajectory differs from other generative models, like the variational autoencoders from Chapter 4, which map data to a condensed latent space. This difference is the main strength of diffusion models. Their power lies in their exceptional ability to implicitly create an expansive and varied latent space in a higher-dimensional manifold—a mathematical space where the data lives, but with many more dimensions than just the pixel values of the images. In simpler terms, instead of compressing the data into a smaller, simplified representation (as in autoencoders), diffusion models operate in a much larger space where subtle variations in the data can be preserved.

Generating Digits with a Diffusion Model

Now that you understand the equations for forward and reverse diffusion, you're ready to build a DDPM to generate handwritten digits based on the MNIST dataset.

Loading the MNIST Dataset

You've encountered the MNIST dataset several times. It consists of grayscale images of handwritten digits from 0 to 9. Each image is 28×28 pixels, and there are 60,000 training images and 10,000 test images. Here, you'll load the MNIST dataset via the TorchVision package of PyTorch.

Before downloading it, you'll define the transformations and normalization to apply to the dataset, as shown in Listing 10-1.

```
from torchvision.transforms import Compose, Normalize, ToTensor

trans = Compose([ToTensor(), Normalize(mean=[0.5], std=[0.5], inplace=True)])
```

Listing 10-1: Normalizing the MNIST digits

This code converts the images to PyTorch tensors, then normalizes their pixel values to lie from −1 to 1 (Normalize subtracts mean from the images and then divides them by std). This is standard practice when training DDPM models.

You can now import and transform the MNIST digits with Listing 10-2.

```
from torchvision.datasets import MNIST

trainset = MNIST(root="data", train=True, transform=trans, download=True)
```

Listing 10-2: Importing the MNIST digits

This code downloads the training set of MNIST data into the *data* folder while taking the transformations you'll apply to the images as an input parameter. The transformations will be executed during the training process. Afterward, you can visualize the MNIST digits via Listing 9-3.

Before proceeding, define the computational device:

```
device = get_device()
```

This code uses the get_device() function (Listing 7-10). You can see the selected device with print(device). Also see the note on page 288 about the use of MPS.

Implementing the Forward Diffusion Process

Next, create a custom Diffusion class that implements the forward diffusion process for generating noisy versions of MNIST digits, as shown in Listing 10-3.

```
class Diffusion:
    """Denoising diffusion probabilistic model (DDPM)."""

    def __init__(self, steps=1000, beta_start=1e-4, beta_end=0.02,
                 device=device):
        """Initialize the diffusion model."""
        self.steps, self.device = steps, device
        self.beta = torch.linspace(beta_start, beta_end, steps).to(device)
        self.alpha = 1.0 - self.beta
        self.alpha_bar = torch.cumprod(self.alpha, dim=0)

    def forward_diffusion(self, x, t):
        """Implement the forward diffusion process."""
        sqrt_alpha_bar = torch.sqrt(self.alpha_bar[t])[:, None, None, None]
        sqrt_one_minus_alpha_bar = \
            torch.sqrt(1 - self.alpha_bar[t])[:, None, None, None]
        noise = torch.randn_like(x)
        return sqrt_alpha_bar * x + sqrt_one_minus_alpha_bar * noise, noise
```

Listing 10-3: Implementing the forward diffusion process

This class uses Equation 10.2 to execute the forward diffusion process. The __init__() method takes as inputs the number of noise steps (steps), the parameters to define a noise schedule (beta_start and beta_end), and the device for the computations (device). Next, the method prepares a linear noise schedule (beta). The beta value is then used to calculate the alpha and alpha_bar values, essential terms in the fast forward process represented in Equation 10.2.

The `forward_diffusion()` method takes the input image, x, and the time step, t, to return the noisy version of the image you get by applying the noise through the fast forward process.

After creating your custom `Diffusion` class, instantiate it to generate some noisy versions of a clean image, as shown in Listing 10-4.

```
diffusion = Diffusion(steps=401, beta_start=0.0001, beta_end=0.02)

❶ clean_image, label = trainset[torch.randint(0, len(trainset), (1,)).squeeze()]

steps, noisy_images = [0, 100, 200, 300, 400], []
for t in steps:
❷ noisy_image, noise = diffusion.forward_diffusion(
        x=clean_image[None, ...].to(device), t=torch.tensor([t]).to(device),
    )
    noisy_images.append(noisy_image)
```

Listing 10-4: Sampling images in the forward diffusion process

This code creates the diffusion class with 401 noise steps and beta values that start at 0.0001 and end at 0.02. Then the code randomly samples a clean image from the dataset to generate a noisy image ❶. Four noisy images are generated at intervals of 100 time steps via the `forward_diffusion()` method of the `Diffusion` class ❷. The noisy images are stored in the noisy _images list.

You can visualize the forward diffusion process in action by plotting the noisy images with Listing 10-5.

```
fig, axs = plt.subplots(1, len(steps))
for i, ax in enumerate(axs.flatten()):
    ax.imshow(noisy_images[i].cpu().numpy().squeeze(), cmap="gray")
    ax.set_title(f"t = {steps[i]}", fontsize=10)
    ax.axis("off")
plt.tight_layout()
plt.show()
```

Listing 10-5: Visualizing the noisy digits generated in the forward diffusion process

This code gets the noisy images generated in Listing 10-4 and plots them in a sequence. The resulting plot should be similar to Figure 10-3.

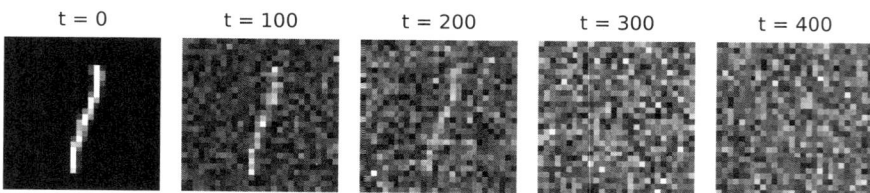

Figure 10-3: A sequence of images from the forward diffusion process

In the forward diffusion process, the clean image on the left at $t = 0$ is progressively corrupted, resulting in the pure noise image on the right at $t = 400$.

Applying the Reverse Diffusion Process

Now that you've finished setting up the forward diffusion process, you're ready to implement the reverse diffusion process, as described earlier in Equation 10.11. You'll do so by adding a new method to the Diffusion class, as shown in Listing 10-6.

```
from tqdm import tqdm

class Diffusion:
    """Denoising diffusion probabilistic model (DDPM)."""

    def __init__(..., img_size=28, device=device):
        """Initialize the diffusion model."""
        self.steps, self.img_size, self.device = steps, img_size, device
        --snip--

    def reverse_diffusion(self, model, n_images, n_channels, pos_enc_dim,
                          pos_enc_func, save_time_steps=None):
        """Reverse diffusion process."""
        with torch.no_grad():
        ❶ x = torch.randn(
               (n_images, n_channels, self.img_size, self.img_size)
            ).to(self.device)

            denoised_images = []
            for i in tqdm(reversed(range(0, self.steps)),
                          desc="U-Net inference", total=self.steps):
            ❷ t = (torch.ones(n_images) * i).long()
                t_pos_enc = (pos_enc_func(t.unsqueeze(1), pos_enc_dim)
                             .to(self.device))
                pred_noise = model(x=x, t=t_pos_enc)
                alpha = self.alpha[t][:, None, None, None]
                alpha_bar = self.alpha_bar[t][:, None, None, None]
                noise = torch.randn_like(x) if i > 0 else torch.zeros_like(x)
            ❸ x = (1 / torch.sqrt(alpha)
                    * (x - ((1 - alpha) / torch.sqrt(1 - alpha_bar))
                       * pred_noise)
                    + torch.sqrt(1 - alpha) * noise)
            ❹ if i in save_time_steps: denoised_images.append(x)

            denoised_images = torch.stack(denoised_images).swapaxes(0, 1)
            return denoised_images
```

Listing 10-6: Implementing the reverse diffusion process (by modifying Listing 10-3)

The Diffusion class is now initialized with the additional img_size parameter, which controls the image size in the reverse diffusion process. The value is set to 28 pixels, the same as the MNIST digit images.

The new reverse_diffusion() method applies the reverse diffusion process. It starts by creating pure noise images by sampling them from a Gaussian distribution ❶.

The code then iteratively denoises the image through a for loop, which runs from steps to 0. The for loop is wrapped with the tqdm function to track the reverse diffusion process with a progress bar.

Within each iteration, the code creates a time-step value for that iteration and sets it equal to the loop variable (i). This value is repeated n_images times to account for sampling n_images ❷.

The code then passes the time-step information through a positional encoding function given by the pos_enc_func parameter. The purpose of this is to map the time-step value to an encoded vector of a specified dimension, given by the pos_enc_dim parameter to capture the temporal information in a way that the network can better understand and use the time-step data during training. You'll see the positional_encoding() function in detail in Listing 10-7.

Next, the code passes the noisy image and the encoded time step through a U-Net (model) that predicts the noise applied to the image. You'll see the architecture and functioning of this model in Listing 10-10. Using the predicted noise output by the U-Net, the noisy image is then cleaned via the reverse diffusion process ❸ defined by Equation 10.11. Notice the similarity between the code and the mathematical forms of the equation.

This process repeats over all time steps, after which the noisy image is fully denoised. To monitor the noisy image at different steps in the denoising process, the code stores the intermediate denoised images at the time steps defined by the save_time_steps parameter into the denoised_images list ❹, which the method finally returns.

Defining the Positional Encoding Function

You'll now specify the positional encoding function that converts the time step from its single-value representation to a vector of specified dimensions. This new representation helps the model grasp the time-step information in a more nuanced way. You'll use a sinusoidal position function, shown in Listing 10-7.

```
def positional_encoding(t, enc_dim):
    """Encode position information with a sinusoid."""
    scaled_positions = torch.arange(0, enc_dim, 2).float() / enc_dim
    frequency = 10_000 ** scaled_positions
    inverse_frequency = (1.0 / frequency).to(t.device)
    angle = t.repeat(1, enc_dim // 2) * inverse_frequency
    pos_enc_sin, pos_enc_cos = torch.sin(angle), torch.cos(angle)
    pos_enc = torch.cat([pos_enc_sin, pos_enc_cos], dim=-1)
    return pos_enc
```

Listing 10-7: The function to implement the positional encoding

This function implements the sinusoidal positional encoding. The function takes the time step, t, and the dimension of the encoded vector, enc_dim, as inputs and then outputs a vector providing a unique signature corresponding to each time step.

First, this code creates a sequence of positions that are scaled by the encoding dimension, scaled_positions. To do so, the code creates an array with the even numbers from 0 to the encoding dimension and then divides this array by the encoding dimension. This results in a sequence with a length equal to half the encoding dimension.

Second, the code creates an array of frequencies, frequency, by raising the base value of 10,000 to the power of each value in the scaled_positions array. This exponential operation generates a series of frequencies that decrease progressively.

Third, the code creates an array of inverse frequencies, inverse_frequency, by dividing 1.0 by each frequency value in frequency. Finally, the resulting array is moved to the same device as the input tensor t. This array of inverse frequencies is essential for the sinusoidal positional encoding, as it defines the periodicity of the sine and cosine functions applied later in the process.

Fourth, the code creates the angle tensor by element-wise multiplying a tensor containing enc_dim // 2 (half the encoding dimension) copies of t by the inverse_frequency array, effectively scaling each repeated time-step value by the corresponding inverse frequency.

Fifth, the code applies the sine and cosine functions to the angle tensor, creating two separate tensors: pos_enc_sin and pos_enc_cos. These two tensors represent different aspects of the positional encoding, with each encoding half of the total dimension.

Finally, the code concatenates pos_enc_sin and pos_enc_cos along the last dimension (dim=-1) to form a complete positional encoding vector. This final vector, pos_enc, combines the sine and cosine encodings to uniquely represent the time step in a way that helps the model capture temporal dependencies in the data. The resulting vector is then returned as the output of the function.

With this function, you can generate the positional encodings of different time steps, using Listing 10-8.

```
pos_enc_dim = 256

pos_encs = []
for i in range(0, 100):
    t = torch.tensor([i])
❶ pos_enc = positional_encoding(t, pos_enc_dim)
    pos_encs.append(pos_enc.squeeze())
pos_encs = torch.stack(pos_encs)
```

Listing 10-8: Generating the sinusoidal positional encodings for different time steps

This code starts by setting the dimension of the encoded vector to 256. From there, it generates positional encodings for time steps starting from 0 to 100 in a for loop ❶. The code then stores the encodings in a list and stacks them into a torch tensor.

You can visualize the positional encodings with Listing 10-9.

```
plt.imshow(pos_encs.cpu().numpy())
plt.xlabel("Encoding dimension")
plt.ylabel("Time step (t)")
plt.show()
```

Listing 10-9: Visualizing the positional encodings

Figure 10-4 shows the resulting image.

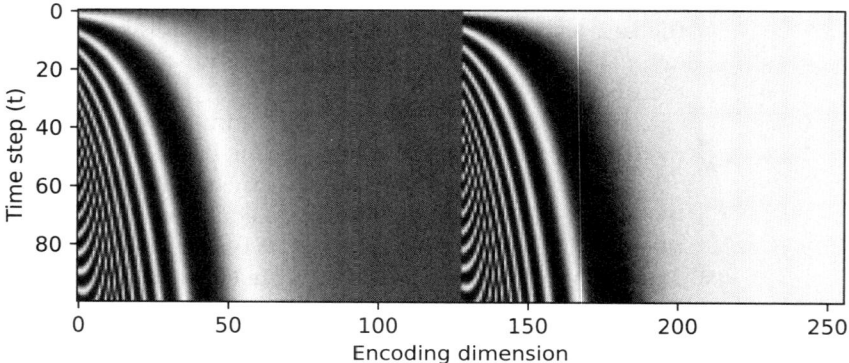

Figure 10-4: The sinusoidal positional encodings for time steps 0 to 100

Each row in the image corresponds to the positional encoding of a specific time step. The alternating patterns of the sine and cosine functions within each vector give a unique signature to each step, plotted here on the left and right sides of the image, respectively.

Instantiating the Attention U-Net

After you've finished generating the positional encodings, you'll instantiate a U-Net architecture that will be used to train the diffusion model. This will be structurally similar to the traditional U-Net in Chapter 5. The main difference is that the feature maps are now wrapped with attention layers to integrate the time-step information. Figure 10-5 illustrates the attention U-Net architecture.

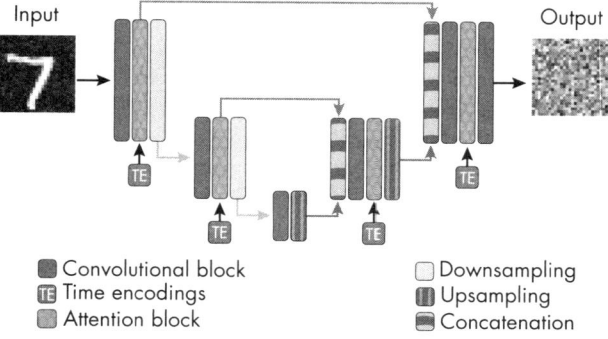

Figure 10-5: The attention U-Net architecture

This attention U-Net takes the noisy image and the corresponding time-step encoding as inputs. Then the attention U-Net outputs an estimation of the noise applied to the image, which is then used in the reverse diffusion process, as described previously.

Use the attention U-Net model from the Deeplay package as shown in Listing 10-10.

```
import deeplay as dl

unet = dl.AttentionUNet(
    in_channels=1, channels=[32, 64, 128], base_channels=[256, 256],
    channel_attention=[True, True, True], out_channels=1,
  ❶ position_embedding_dim=pos_enc_dim,
).build().to(device)
```

Listing 10-10: Defining the attention U-Net model

This code instantiates AttentionUNet, builds it, and moves it to the device. You can print the details of the model with print(unet).

The code sets the number of input channels and output channels to 1, since the images are grayscale. It then instantiates the model with three convolutional layers that have 32, 64, and 128 filters, respectively. This code also automatically creates the same number of filters for the upsampling layers. At the bottleneck, the code initializes the U-Net with two additional convolutional layers, each with 256 filters (base_channels=[256, 256]). You can reduce the number of filters in downsampling, upsampling, and bottleneck layers if your computational resources are insufficient.

Unlike the traditional U-Net, the attention U-Net in diffusion models also takes the time-step positional encodings as an input. The code integrates time-step encodings into the model at different sections, as shown in Figure 10-5. First, the code reshapes the encodings to the dimensions of the feature maps through dense layers. Then it adds them directly to the feature maps at different levels. To facilitate these operations, the model also takes the dimension of the positional encoding vector as input ❶, which in this case is set to 256.

Afterward, the code applies a self-attention mechanism to the resulting feature map to help the model interpret the relationship between the noisy image and the corresponding time step. Since the attention mechanism can be computationally heavy, the channel_attention parameter is used to control the attention mechanism applied at different levels. The Boolean values (True or False) switch the attention on or off at the channels defined in the channels parameter. Here, all the channel attentions are set to True.

Training the Diffusion Model

With your dataset, forward process, reverse process, and positional encodings in place, you can proceed to implement the code to train the diffusion model.

Instantiating the Data Loader, Loss Function, Optimizer, and Diffusion Class

First, create the data loader as shown in Listing 10-11.

```
loader = dl.DataLoader(dataset=trainset, batch_size=128, shuffle=True)
```

Listing 10-11: Defining the data loader

This code defines a data loader using a batch size of 128 and shuffles the data before creating batches.

Next, define a loss function, as shown in Listing 10-12.

```
criterion = torch.nn.MSELoss()
```

Listing 10-12: Defining the loss function

This code specifies an MSE loss between the noise predicted by the model and the actual noise sampled.

Now instantiate the optimizer, as shown in Listing 10-13.

```
optimizer = torch.optim.AdamW(unet.parameters(), lr=1e-4)
```

Listing 10-13: Defining the optimizer

This code sets up the Adam optimizer.

Finally, initialize the diffusion class for the actual training of the model, as shown in Listing 10-14.

```
diffusion = Diffusion(steps=1000, beta_start=1e-4, beta_end=0.02, img_size=28)
```

Listing 10-14: Instantiating the diffusion class for training

This code constructs a diffusion class with 1,000 noise steps, with the image size set to 28×28 pixels, and with noise values ranging from 0.0001 to 0.02.

Implementing the Training Loop

Before implementing the loop, create the `prepare_data()` helper function that takes a clean image from the dataset and returns the noisy version of the image, the time-step encoding, and the noise, which together constitute the input-output pairs for training the model. This function is shown in Listing 10-15.

```
def prepare_data(image, steps=1000, device=device):
    """Prepare data."""
    batch_size = image.shape[0]
❶  t = torch.randint(low=0, high=steps, size=(batch_size,)).to(device)
    image = image.to(device)
    x_t, noise = diffusion.forward_diffusion(image, t)
❷  t_pos_enc = positional_encoding(t.unsqueeze(1), pos_enc_dim)
    return x_t.to(device), t_pos_enc.to(device), noise.to(device)
```

Listing 10-15: The function to prepare the data

This function creates a batch of random time-step values that fall from 0 to steps ❶. Then it sends the clean images and the time steps to the `forward_diffusion()` method, which returns the noisy versions of the images and the corresponding noises. The time steps are then sent to the `positional_encoding` function to get the time-step encodings ❷. Finally, the noisy images, noises, and time-step encodings are sent to the device and returned as outputs of the function.

Once you've set up the helper function, implement the training loop to teach the U-Net to predict the noise in noisy images, as shown in Listing 10-16.

```
epochs = 20

for epoch in range(epochs):
    for batch_idx, (images, class_labels) in enumerate(loader, start=0):
        x_t, t_pos_enc, noise = prepare_data(images)

  ❶ outputs = unet(x=x_t, t=t_pos_enc)

        optimizer.zero_grad()
        loss = criterion(outputs, noise)
        loss.backward()
        optimizer.step()
```

Listing 10-16: Implementing the training cycle

This code trains the attention U-Net to predict the noise present in the noisy images. The loop runs for 20 epochs, iterating over batches of clean images and corresponding class labels from the data loader. For each batch, the clean images are transferred to the `prepare_data()` function to generate the noisy image (`x_t`), the time-step encoding (`t_pos_enc`), and the noise (`noise`) batches.

The model then takes the noisy images and time-step encoding as inputs and returns an estimate of the noise present in the images ❶.

The training begins by setting the gradient buffers of the optimizer to 0. The code calculates the loss between the predicted noise and the actual noise via the `criterion` function. The loss is then backpropagated through the attention U-Net to calculate its gradients with respect to each internal parameter of the network. Finally, the optimizer updates the parameters in the direction that minimizes the loss.

Adding Timing and Notifications

Similar to the GANs in Listing 9-10, you can get real-time feedback on training progress by including timing and notifications within your loop, using Listing 10-17.

```
import time
from datetime import timedelta
--snip--
train_loss = []
for epoch in range(epochs):
  ❶ start_time = time.time()
```

```
        print("\n" + f"Epoch {epoch + 1}/{epochs}" + "\n" + "_" * 10)

        running_loss = 0.0
        for batch_idx, (image, class_labels) in enumerate(loader, start=0):
            --snip--
            if batch_idx % 100 == 0:
                print(f"Batch {batch_idx + 1}/{len(loader)}: "
                      f"Train loss: {loss.item():.4f}")
            running_loss += loss.item()

        train_loss.append(running_loss / len(loader))
    ❷   end_time = time.time()

        print("-" * 10 + "\n" + f"Epoch {epoch + 1}/{epochs} : "
              f"Train loss: {train_loss[-1]:.4f}, "
              f"Time taken: {timedelta(seconds=end_time - start_time)}")
```

Listing 10-17: Timing the training and notifying the user (by modifying Listing 10-16)

The changes to the code are similar to those you made in Listing 9-10.
This code records the time before ❶ and after each epoch ❷, calculating
the time elapsed between the two. To track the loss, the code initializes the
train_loss list to store the average loss in every epoch. The average loss is
computed by updating the running loss for every batch and dividing by the
total number of batches. Throughout the code, print statements are added
to keep track of the loss as the training progresses.

Plotting the Intermediate Training Results

You can further assess the quality of the images generated by the diffusion
model during training by visualizing the images at the end of each epoch.
Listing 10-18 adds this functionality.

```
--snip--
n_images, steps = 5, [999, 900, 800, 700, 600, 500, 400, 300, 200, 100, 0]
train_loss = []
for epoch in range(epochs):
  ❶ unet.train()
    --snip--
  ❷ unet.eval()
    generated_images = diffusion.reverse_diffusion(
        model=unet, n_images=n_images, n_channels=1, pos_enc_dim=pos_enc_dim,
        pos_enc_func=positional_encoding, save_time_steps=steps,
    )

    fig = plt.figure(figsize=(len(steps), n_images))
    for idx in range(n_images):
        image_reverse_diff_traj = generated_images[idx]
        for j in range(len(steps)):
            plt.subplot(n_images, len(steps), idx * len(steps) + j + 1)
```

```
❸ plt.imshow(image_reverse_diff_traj[j]
            .permute(1, 2, 0).cpu().numpy(), cmap="gray")
    plt.axis("off")
    if idx == 0: plt.title(f"t={steps[j]}", fontsize=10)
plt.show()
plt.close()
```

Listing 10-18: Plotting sample images after each epoch (by modifying Listing 10-17)

At the end of every epoch, this code sets the model to evaluation mode ❷, while returning it to training mode at the beginning of each epoch ❶. The code then generates n_images images from pure noise through the reverse diffusion process implemented in the reverse_diffusion() method.

Additionally, the save_time_steps parameter specifies the time steps at which the images are returned. Next, the code processes the generated image to get the reverse diffusion trajectory. Then the code plots the trajectory ❸.

Figure 10-6 displays an image generated after the full training course of 20 epochs.

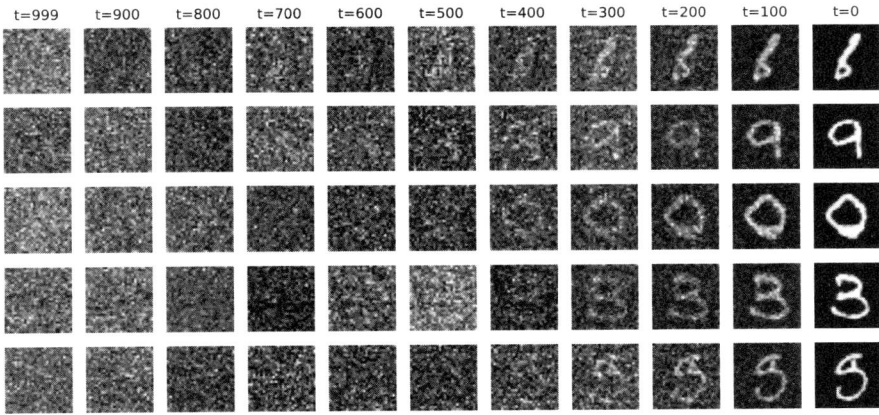

Figure 10-6: The generated images at the end of training

As the model learns to grasp the dataset distribution, the generated images resemble the actual MNIST digits. The image quality can be improved by tweaking the noise range in the forward diffusion process via the beta values and by adjusting the model architecture, learning rates, and epoch number. Setting the beta values higher increases the noise added in each step, which can make it harder for the model to denoise the image effectively, potentially leading to blurry outputs. Conversely, lower beta values might result in less noise, allowing the model to generate sharper images but risking overfitting to the training data.

If the images remain blurry or the loss stagnates after plotting, the beta values could be too high, or the learning rate too low. On the other hand, if the model quickly produces sharp images but fails to generalize to new data, this could indicate the need for more epochs or a more complex model architecture.

Common failure modes include mode collapse, where the model generates a limited variety of images, and excessive blurring or noise in the generated images. These issues can often be addressed by carefully tuning the beta values in the noise scheduler to control the noise levels, adjusting the learning rates to ensure stable training, and increasing the number of training epochs to allow the model to learn more-robust patterns.

Sampling Images from Fixed Noise

Since the model has been trained, you can now take a fixed noise image and run the reverse diffusion process several times to observe the different images it generates. For that, you'll add a new parameter, fix_noise, to the reverse_diffusion() method, as shown in Listing 10-19.

```
class Diffusion:
    --snip--

    def reverse_diffusion(..., fix_noise=None, save_time_steps=None):
        """Reverse diffusion process"""
        with torch.no_grad():
            if fix_noise is not None:
                x = fix_noise.to(self.device)
            else:
                x = torch.randn(
                    (n_images, n_channels, self.img_size, self.img_size)
                ).to(self.device)
            --snip--
```

Listing 10-19: The class to perform reverse diffusion with fixed noise (by modifying Listing 10-6)

This code adds the new fix_noise parameter to enable passing fixed noise to the method instead of randomly sampled noise.

Next, you'll use Listing 10-20 to run the reverse diffusion process on a fixed noisy image multiple times to see the generated images.

```
unet.eval()

fix_noise = torch.randn((1, 1, 28, 28))
n_images_fix_noise = 2

fig = plt.figure(figsize=(len(steps), n_images_fix_noise))
for idx in range(n_images_fix_noise):
    generated_images = diffusion.reverse_diffusion(
        model=unet, n_images=1, n_channels=1, fix_noise=fix_noise,
        pos_enc_dim=pos_enc_dim, pos_enc_func=positional_encoding,
        save_time_steps=steps,
    )

    image_reverse_diff_traj = generated_images[0]
    for j in range(len(steps)):
```

```
        plt.subplot(n_images_fix_noise, len(steps), idx * len(steps) + j + 1)
        plt.imshow(image_reverse_diff_traj[j]
                    .permute(1, 2, 0).cpu().numpy(), cmap="gray")
        plt.axis("off")
        if idx == 0: plt.title(f"t={steps[j]}", fontsize=10)
plt.show()
```

Listing 10-20: Obtaining the images from the fixed noise

This code begins by setting the model to evaluation mode. Next, the code generates a fixed noise image and sets a list of time steps at which the images should be stored in the reverse diffusion process. Then the code generates two images in a for loop by running the reverse_diffusion() method. This method takes the fixed noise and the list of time steps to save images as inputs, in addition to the rest of the parameters from Listing 10-18. Finally, it plots the reverse diffusion trajectories of the images generated in each run.

Figure 10-7 shows the results.

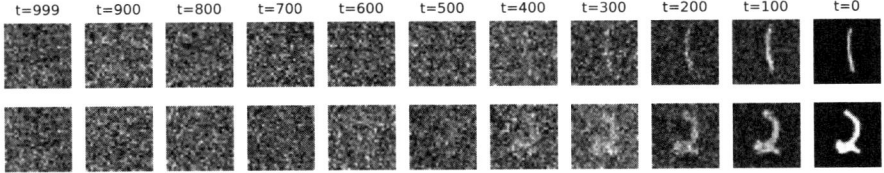

Figure 10-7: The images generated from the same fixed noise

Although the starting noise images in the leftmost column are the same, the resulting images after the reverse diffusion process are different (rightmost column). This is due to the randomness in the reverse diffusion process, as indicated in Equation 10.11.

NOTE *Code Example 10-1, "Generating Digits with a Diffusion Model," is available at* https://github.com/DeepTrackAI/DeepLearningCrashCourse. *Navigate to the* Ch10_Diffusion *folder and then* ec10_1_ddpm_mnist. *The* ddpm_mnist .ipynb *notebook provides a complete code example to generate MNIST digits with a diffusion model.*

EXERCISES

10-2: Modify the attention U-Net architecture by changing the channels, base_channels, and channel_attention parameters. Switch off the attention at certain channels and then check the model's performance.

10-3: Try a different noise range by changing the beta_start and beta _end parameters in the Diffusion class and then verify the model performance. Also, modify the noise scheduler to a nonlinear function and observe how this affects the model's performance.

In the preceding section, you learned how to use a diffusion model to generate random digits resembling those in the MNIST dataset. However, you might have noticed that this process lacks control over the digits being produced. There is no direct way to request a particular digit, such as a 4 or a 2. To address this limitation, you can use a *conditional diffusion model*, which conditions the generation process with class labels.

In this project, you'll implement a conditional diffusion model to generate specific digits on demand by incorporating class labels into the generation process. First, you'll modify the diffusion model to accept class labels as input alongside the noise and time step, allowing the model to learn to generate specific digits. Next, you'll train the model on the MNIST dataset, ensuring that it learns to generate the correct digits. Finally, you'll test the model, observing how well it can produce bespoke digits.

You'll start from the *ddpm_mnist.ipynb* notebook you implemented in the first part of this chapter.

Guiding the Diffusion Model

Let's recall how you trained the conditional GAN in Project 9A to generate bespoke digits. To accomplish this, you provided the class labels as additional inputs to the generator and the discriminator. The generator produced images from noise while accounting for the class label information, and the discriminator used this information when classifying the generated images as real or fake. Therefore, the discriminator learned not only to classify the input image as real or fake but also to check whether it belonged to the labeled class.

In contrast, diffusion models don't have this built-in guidance mechanism, since they have only a single network and no adversarial loss. One solution would be to train an external classifier to learn the dataset's class label information and pass it to the diffusion model. At each step in the reverse diffusion process, the code could then combine the gradients of the trained classifier model with the noise images predicted by the diffusion model. This strategy, known as *classifier guidance*, resembles the approach used for conditional GANs. Although this process works well, it complicates the training process because it requires training two independent networks.

You can avoid this complication by using a *classifier-free guidance* approach. In this technique, a single network, the U-Net, is trained both conditionally and unconditionally by randomly inputting the class labels into the network at sporadic intervals, effectively providing guidance without an external classifier.

For the generation process in the reverse diffusion, the model returns the denoised image at every time step as a linear combination of two outputs generated by the U-Net: one with class labels and the other without. An additional weighting factor called *guidance strength* controls their relative weight. In this way, the classifier-free guidance approach preserves the generative power of the diffusion model while eliminating the need for a separate classifier, making the process less computationally intensive and more streamlined.

Now that you understand the advantages of this strategy, you're ready to implement the classifier-free guidance approach. Starting with your code from Listing 10-19, integrate classifier-free guidance into the reverse diffusion process, as shown in Listing 10-21.

```
class Diffusion:
    --snip--
    def reverse_diffusion(..., class_labels=None, guidance_strength=None):
        --snip--
            for i in tqdm(reversed(range(0, self.steps)),
                        desc="UNet inference", total=self.steps):
                --snip--
                if class_labels is None:
                    pred_noise = model(x=x, t=t_pos_enc)
                else:
                    conditional_pred = model(x=x, t=t_pos_enc, y=class_labels)
                    unconditional_pred = model(x=x, t=t_pos_enc, y=None)
                    pred_noise = torch.lerp(unconditional_pred,
                                            conditional_pred,
                                            guidance_strength)
                --snip--
```

Listing 10-21: Implementing classifier-free guidance (by modifying Listing 10-19)

This code adds the class_labels and guidance_strength parameters to the reverse diffusion method, enabling the reverse diffusion process to operate in classifier-free guidance mode. This mode activates when the class labels are given as input. The U-Net model returns two outputs. First, the model generates the conditional output where the class labels are passed as input. Then the model generates the unconditional output where the class labels are set to None. Finally, the code gets a combined noise image by linearly interpolating the unconditional and conditional outputs through the torch.lerp() function, with weights given by the guidance strength.

Defining the Conditional Attention U-Net

The conditional attention U-Net works similarly to its unconditional variant from Figure 10-5, except it takes class labels as additional inputs. When provided, the class labels are passed through an embedding layer, which transforms them into a vector of a specific dimension, much like the way you included the class labels in the conditional GANs. Here, the embedding dimension is set equal to the positional encoding dimension for the time step to ensure that they can be combined.

Finally, these class embeddings are added to the time-step positional encodings, and the resulting output is integrated into the U-Net akin to the time-step encodings in an unconditional attention U-Net.

You can set up the conditional attention U-Net by modifying Listing 10-10 as shown in Listing 10-22.

```
--snip--
unet = dl.AttentionUNet(..., num_classes=10)
--snip--
```

Listing 10-22: Instantiating the conditional attention U-Net (by modifying Listing 10-10)

When the num_classes parameter is given as input, AttentionUNet will automatically operate in a conditional mode. Here, the number of classes is set to 10, corresponding to the number of digits in the MNIST dataset.

Training the Conditional Diffusion Model

After modifying your U-Net, you can train the conditional diffusion model.

The training loop is very similar to that of the unconditional diffusion model in Listing 10-16. The modifications are highlighted in Listing 10-23.

```
import numpy as np
--snip--
for epoch in range(epochs):
    for batch_idx, (images, class_labels) in enumerate(loader, start=0):
        x_t, t_pos_enc, noise = prepare_data(images)
        class_labels = class_labels.to(device)
    ❶ if np.random.rand() < 0.1: class_labels = None

    ❷ outputs = unet(x_t, t=t_pos_enc, y=class_labels)
        --snip--
```

Listing 10-23: Training a conditional diffusion model (by modifying Listing 10-16)

This code trains the attention U-Net with the classifier-free guidance approach, which trains the model both conditionally and unconditionally by randomly dropping the class labels in 10 percent of the cases ❶. The class labels are now given as an additional input to the model ❷.

Plotting the Intermediate Training Results

You can visualize the images generated for a given class at the end of each epoch by tweaking your code from Listing 10-18 as shown in Listing 10-24.

```
--snip--
n_images, steps = 10, [999, 900, 800, 700, 600, 500, 400, 300, 200, 100, 0]
--snip--
for epoch in range(epochs):
    --snip--
    unet.eval()
    class_labels = torch.arange(0, 10).long().to(device)
```

```
generated_images = diffusion.reverse_diffusion(
    ..., class_labels=class_labels, guidance_strength=3,
)
--snip--
```

Listing 10-24: Plotting the sample images after each epoch (by modifying Listing 10-18)

This code sets the class labels for the digits from 0 to 9 and plots the generated digits as the training progresses. The code then passes the class label to the reverse_diffusion() method and sets the classifier-free guidance strength to 3.

Figure 10-8 shows the images generated after 20 epochs.

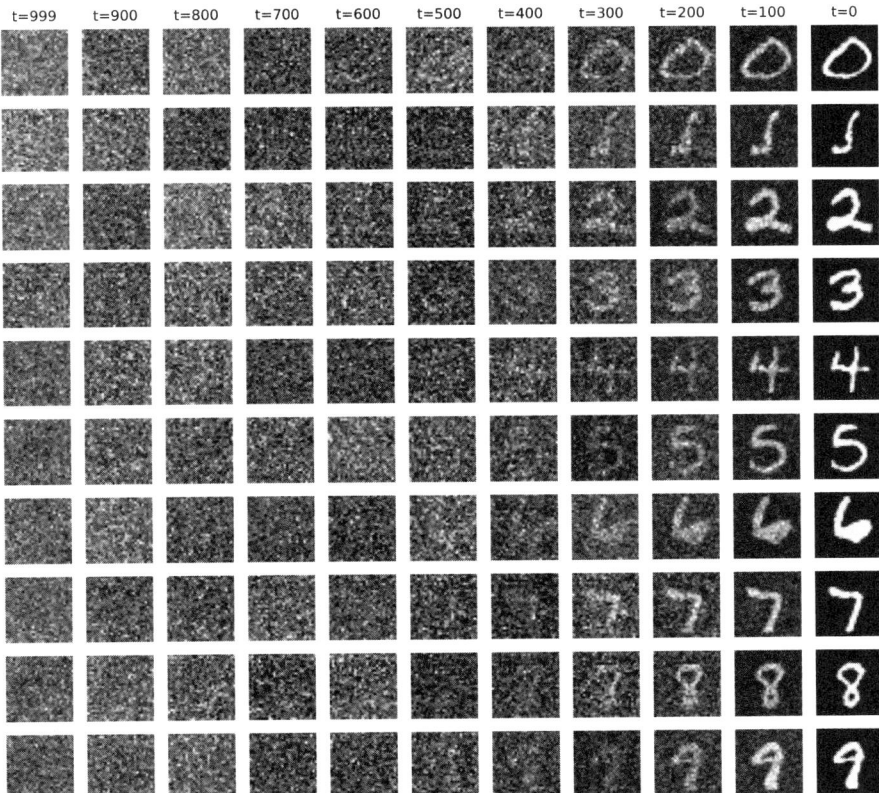

Figure 10-8: The generated images at the end of the training

As you can see, the model can now generate specific MNIST digits on demand.

NOTE *Code Example 10-A, "Generating Bespoke Digits with a Conditional Diffusion Model," is available at* github.com/DeepTrackAI/DeepLearningCrashCourse. *Navigate to the* Ch10_Diffusion *folder and then* ec10_A_cddpm_mnist. *The* cddpm_mnist.ipynb *notebook provides a complete code example to generate bespoke MNIST digits with a conditional diffusion model.*

Project 10B: Generating Images from Text Prompts

At the core of popular text-to-image models like DALL-E 3 and Stable Diffusion lie diffusion models similar to those from the previous sections. These models take text as a conditional input to generate images from descriptions, just as you used a class label as a condition in Project 10A to generate bespoke images of digits. While developing a state-of-the-art text-to-image diffusion model requires a huge corpus of text and image data as well as immense computational power, you can grasp the underlying concepts by combining the diffusion models from the previous sections of this chapter and the transformer models from Chapter 8.

In this project, you'll build your own small-scale text-to-image model that can generate MNIST handwritten digits in response to textual prompts. First, you'll prepare text prompts and implement a custom text encoder to convert these prompts into embeddings. Next, you'll integrate these embeddings into a conditional diffusion model, modifying the U-Net architecture to process both text and image information. Finally, you'll train the model by using classifier-free guidance and generate MNIST digit images based on the provided text prompts. You'll start from the *cddpm_mnist.ipynb* notebook you implemented in the preceding project.

Providing a Conditional Text Input

In the preceding project, you provided the model with class labels as a condition in the form of class embeddings and then trained the diffusion model through the classifier-free guidance approach.

Here, you'll use *textual prompts* such as "Generate an image of the digit one" as conditional inputs. Then you'll train the model by using the classifier-free guidance approach, similar to Project 10A. However, unlike the class labels, which are already in a numeric format and can be easily converted into class embeddings, the textual prompts are sequences of words. Consequently, you'll need to use a *text encoder* to convert the text into vector form and generate *text embeddings* that are meaningful to the model.

A well-known text encoder used in recent text-to-image diffusion models is the *Contrastive Language-Image Pre-training (CLIP)* model trained by OpenAI. CLIP is a transformer-based model that connects text and images. It's trained on a huge corpus of 400 million images and their corresponding captions scraped from all over the internet. At its core, CLIP has two encoders: a text encoder that converts the text into a vectorial representation (the text embedding), and an image encoder that converts the image to a different vectorial representation called the *image embedding*. During training, these embeddings are compared, using cosine similarity to determine semantic relations between text and image. This process, known as *contrastive learning*, ensures that the text and image embeddings are closely related after the model is trained.

In this project, you'll first build your own text encoder by using a small-scale transformer to generate text embeddings. You'll then use these embeddings to train a conditional diffusion model through the classifier-free guidance approach. Later, you'll see how to use the CLIP text encoder instead of your own homemade encoder.

Importing the Dataset with Sentences and Corresponding Images

To begin, clone the repository with the MNIST digits:

```
import os

if not os.path.exists("MNIST_dataset"):
    os.system("git clone https://github.com/DeepTrackAI/MNIST_dataset")
MNIST_path = os.path.join("MNIST_dataset", "mnist", "train")
MNIST_images_files = sorted(os.listdir(MNIST_path))
```

This code downloads the dataset with MNIST digits in the *data* folder and then creates the variables containing the path to the 60,000 training digits (MNIST_path) and the list of all filenames ordered alphabetically (MNIST_images _files).

Load the sentences corresponding to each digit from the *mnist_sentences .json* file:

```
import json

with open("mnist_sentences.json", "r") as file:
    filenames_sentences = json.load(file)
```

This creates the filenames_sentences dictionary, with a sentence corresponding to each MNIST digit file.

You can print some of these sentences as follows:

```
import random

for filename, sentence in random.sample(filenames_sentences.items(), 100):
    print(f"{filename} : {sentence}")
```

As you'll see, the file contains text prompts with varying levels of difficulty to challenge the model to grasp the text's meaning. The simplest sentences are direct requests for a specific digit, like

```
0_000015.png : Produce the handwritten digit 0.
```

while more-difficult sentences look like this:

```
3_002277.png : In the zoological garden, there are five elephants and three
lions. How many felines are there?
```

This sentence contains multiple numbers (five elephants and three lions) and a question asking for a specific digit (How many felines are there?). Note that the subject in the statement (lions) and the subject of the question (felines) are synonymous but not the same word, to further challenge your model. Also, note that the numbers can be written both as words and as digits.

Finally, you can create the training dataset by modifying Listing 10-2 as shown in Listing 10-25.

```
import matplotlib.pyplot as plt

images, digits, sentences = [], [], []
for filename in MNIST_images_files:
    image = plt.imread(os.path.join(MNIST_path, filename))
    images.append(trans(image))

    digit = int(filename[0])
    digits.append(digit)

    sentence = filenames_sentences.get(filename, "")
    sentences.append(sentence)

trainset = list(zip(images, digits, sentences))
```

Listing 10-25: Creating the training dataset with digit images and corresponding sentences (by modifying Listing 10-2)

This code reads the MNIST images along with their digit labels and corresponding sentences to create the training dataset. The code first initializes empty lists for images, digits, and sentences. Then it loops over each filename in the MNIST image files, reads the image, applies the trans transformation, and appends it to images. The code extracts the digit label from the filename (as the first character represents the digit) and adds that label to digits. The code retrieves the associated sentence from the filenames_sentences dictionary, using filename as the key (and defaulting to an empty string if not found), and appends the retrieved sentence to sentences. Finally, the code combines these three lists into trainset via the zip() function, resulting in a list of tuples that each contain an image, its digit label, and the corresponding sentence—ready to be used for training the text-to-image diffusion model.

Adding a Context Parameter to the Reverse Diffusion

Now you'll modify the Diffusion class to add an additional parameter into the reverse_diffusion() method that can take the text information as input when implementing classifier-free guidance. Listing 10-26 shows the modifications.

```
class Diffusion:
    --snip--
    def reverse_diffusion(
        ..., save_time_steps=None, context=None, guidance_strength=None,
    ):
        --snip--
            for i in tqdm(reversed(range(0, self.steps)),
                         desc="UNet inference", total=self.steps):
                --snip--
```

```
        if context is None:
            pred_noise = model(x, t_pos_enc)
        else:
            conditional_pred = model(x, t_pos_enc, context=context)
            unconditional_pred = model(x, t_pos_enc, context=None)
    --snip--
```

Listing 10-26: Adding a context parameter to the reverse diffusion class (by modifying Listing 10-21)

This code substitutes the class label with the context parameter to incorporate the text information into the model. When the context is passed to the method, the reverse diffusion process operates in classifier-free guidance mode, generating two outputs from the U-Net model: a conditional output with the text information and an unconditional output without the text information.

Defining a Custom Tokenizer and Text Encoder

Once you've prepared the text prompts, the next step is to transform them into a representation that your model can interpret. You're already familiar with tokenization and text encoding from Project 7A. You'll follow the same approach here. To begin, you'll tokenize the text by splitting the sentences into words and assigning numeric indices for each word from a custom vocabulary. Then you'll pass the tokenized sentence to a trainable text encoder to generate the text embeddings. From there, you'll pass the text embeddings to the U-Net as a conditional input, similar to the class embeddings in the preceding project.

To tokenize the text, you'll use the same tokenize() function that you implemented in Listing 7-24. This function breaks the sentences into individual words while taking care of contractions and punctuation. In the next section, you'll use all the words that occur in the training and test text prompts to build your own vocabulary.

Building a Vocabulary

You can build a custom vocabulary by assigning a numerical value to each word that occurs in the data. This is shown in Listing 10-27.

```
with open("test_sentences.txt", "r") as file:
❶ test_sentences = [line.strip() for line in file.readlines()]

def sentence_iterator(list_of_sentences):
    """Iterate over a list of sentences to tokenize them."""
    for sentence in list_of_sentences:
        yield tokenize(sentence)

vocab_dict = build_vocab_from_iterator(
    sentence_iterator(sentences + test_sentences),
    specials=["<sos>", "<eos>", "<pad>", "<unk>"], min_freq=1,
)
```

```
vocab = Vocab(vocab_dict, unk_token="<unk>")
vocab.set_default_index(vocab(vocab.unk_token))
```

Listing 10-27: Building a custom vocabulary

This code first extracts the test sentences from the *test_sentences.txt* file ❶.
Then the code defines the sentence_iterator() function that iterates over the
text prompts and generates tokens via the tokenize() function (Listing 7-24).
Next, the vocabulary is built with the build_vocab_from_iterator() function
from Listing 7-27 (you'll also need the Vocab class from Listing 7-26). This
function takes the sentence iterator as its first input, which iterates over all
the text data that will be used for training and testing. The function also
takes the specials parameter, which is the list of special tokens included in
the vocabulary. In this listing, the list contains four special tokens: "<sos>"
for start of sequence, "<eos>" for end of sequence, "<pad>" for padding, and
"<unk>" for unknown words. Finally, the code sets the default index (that is,
the index of an unknown word) to the index of the special token "<unk>".

You can now check the string-to-number mapping:

```
for word, index in vocab_dict.items(): print(f"{word}: {index}")
```

This prints a dictionary that maps each word in the vocabulary to its corresponding numerical index. The output begins with the special tokens "<sos>",
"<eos>", "<pad>", and "<unk>", which are assigned indices from 0 to 3. Following
this, the vocabulary words are listed along with their indices; for example,
"zero" is mapped to 4, "squirrels" to 5, "are" to 6, and so on, up to words like
"seminar" at index 668.

You can now implement the pad_and_process() function in Listing 10-28.

```
def pad_and_process(texts, vocab=vocab, max_token_length=77):
    """Pad and process text."""
    batch_tokens = []
    for text_prompt in texts:
        tokens = ([vocab("<sos>")]
                  + [vocab(toker) for token in tokenize(text_prompt)]
                  + [vocab("<eos>")])

        if len(tokens) > max_token_length:
            tokens = tokens[:max_token_length]
        else:
            tokens += [vocab("<pad>")] * (max_token_length - len(tokens))

        tokens = torch.tensor(tokens, dtype=torch.long)
        batch_tokens.append(tokens)
    return torch.stack(batch_tokens)
```

Listing 10-28: The function to pad and process text

This function processes each text prompt in the input list by tokenizing it,
adding special start-of-sequence "<sos>" and end-of-sequence "<eos>" tokens.
The function then adjusts the sequence length to a fixed max_token_length by

either truncating excess tokens or padding shorter sequences with "<pad>" tokens. Finally, it converts each sequence into a PyTorch tensor and stacks all tensors into a single batch tensor.

Using this function, you can observe a tokenized version of an example text prompt by using the following code:

```
_, _, example_sentence = random.choice(trainset)
tokens = pad_and_process([example_sentence])
print(example_sentence), print(tokens);
```

This code will generate a random text prompt from the training set and will print something similar to this:

```
In the forest, there are four squirrels and one owls. How many birds are there?
tensor([[   0,   42,    9,  450,   11,   22,    6,  199,    5,   26,   88,  451,   15,   16,
          17,  455,    6,   22,   19,    1,    2,    2,    2,    2,    2,    2,    2,    2,
           2,    2,    2,    2,    2,    2,    2,    2,    2,    2,    2,    2,    2,    2,
           2,    2,    2,    2,    2,    2,    2,    2,    2,    2,    2,    2,    2,    2,
           2,    2,    2,    2,    2,    2,    2,    2,    2,    2,    2,    2,    2,    2,
           2,    2,    2,    2,    2,    2,    2]])
```

The tokenized version of the text prompt starts with the starting index (0), followed by word indices and the end index (1). The sequence is then padded with the pad index (2) up to the maximum length (77 tokens).

Implementing a Custom Text Encoder

Having generated the tokenized text, you can implement a simple text encoder based on the transformer architecture in Chapter 8. Text encoders use the self-attention mechanism to understand the relationship between words in a text and their underlying meaning. Listing 10-29 defines a text encoder.

```
class TextEncoder(torch.nn.Module):
    """Text encoder."""

    def __init__(self, max_token_length, vocab_size, embedding_dim, num_heads):
        """Initialize the text encoder module."""
        super(TextEncoder, self).__init__()

❶      self.token_embedding = torch.nn.Embedding(vocab_size, embedding_dim)
❷      self.position_encoding = positional_encoding(
            torch.arange(0, max_token_length).unsqueeze(1), embedding_dim,
        )

❸      self.self_attention = torch.nn.MultiheadAttention(
            embedding_dim, num_heads=num_heads, batch_first=True,
        )
        self.layer_norm1 = torch.nn.LayerNorm(embedding_dim)
        self.layer_norm2 = torch.nn.LayerNorm(embedding_dim)
```

```
❹ self.feed_forward = torch.nn.Sequential(
        torch.nn.Linear(embedding_dim, embedding_dim), torch.nn.GELU(),
        torch.nn.Linear(embedding_dim, embedding_dim),
    )

def forward(self, tokens):
    """Forward pass of text encoder module."""
❺ token_embeddings = self.token_embedding(tokens)
❻ position_encodings = (self.position_encoding
                        .repeat(tokens.size(0), 1, 1).to(tokens.device))

❼ token_embeddings_with_pos = token_embeddings + position_encodings

    normalized_embeddings = self.layer_norm1(token_embeddings_with_pos)
❽
    attention_output, _ = self.self_attention(query=normalized_embeddings,
                                              key=normalized_embeddings,
                                              value=normalized_embeddings)
    attention_output = attention_output + normalized_embeddings

    residual_input = attention_output
    normalized_attention_output = self.layer_norm2(attention_output)
❾ feed_forward_output = self.feed_forward(normalized_attention_output)
    residual_output = feed_forward_output + residual_input

    return residual_output
```

Listing 10-29: The class implementing a custom text encoder

The TextEncoder class is initialized by implementing the token embedding layer ❶. As training progresses, this layer maps all the indices in the vocabulary to a higher-dimensional vector, given by the embedding_dim parameter. Because transformer architectures lack an inherent notion of token order, this class also creates the positional encodings of numbers ranging from 0 to the max token length, using the sinusoidal positional encoding function that you defined in Listing 10-7 ❷. The class then sets up a multi-head attention layer ❸ and a feed-forward network ❹. Together, these constitute the basic units of a transformer, as you saw in Chapter 8.

In the forward() method, the token embeddings are generated via the token embedding layer ❺, and the positional encodings ❻ are added together to get a new embedding. This embedding contains the token information in higher dimensions while also preserving the token order ❼. Subsequently, this output is processed through the basic transformer action, first by applying the self-attention mechanism ❽, then by passing the output through the feed-forward network ❾ to generate the final text embedding.

Once you've defined it, you can instantiate the custom text encoder with Listing 10-30.

```
custom_text_encoder = TextEncoder(
    max_token_length=77, vocab_size=len(vocab), embedding_dim=768, num_heads=4,
).to(device)
```

Listing 10-30: Instantiating a custom text encoder

This code instantiates the text encoder by setting `max_token_length` to 77, `vocab_size` to the length of the vocabulary from Listing 10-27, the embedding dimension to 768, and the number of heads in the multi-head attention to 4. The model is then sent to the selected computational device.

You can check the shape of example text prompts as follows:

```
_, _, example_sentence = random.choice(trainset)
tokens = pad_and_process([example_sentence])
text_embedding = custom_text_encoder(tokens.to(device))

print(f"tokens shape: {tokens.shape}")
print(f"text embeddings shape: {text_embedding.shape}")
```

This code samples a text prompt from the training set, passes it through the tokenizer, and finally processes it with the text encoder. Here's the output:

```
tokens shape: torch.Size([1, 77])
text embeddings shape: torch.Size([1, 77, 768])
```

The first dimension indicates the batch size (the number of sampled texts). The second dimension indicates the token length (set to 77). The third dimension in the text embedding shape indicates the size of the embedding, which projects each of the 77 tokens into a vector of 768 dimensions.

With this machinery to properly process the text data, you'll instantiate a conditional attention U-Net that takes this text information as an input.

Defining the Conditional Attention U-Net

The conditional attention U-Net for the text-to-image model works similarly to the network that you defined for class-conditioned image generation in Project 10A. The difference now is that the text prompts are given as conditional inputs.

Recall that in the preceding project, the time steps and class labels were merged into the attention U-Net. Here, the text prompts, provided in the form of text embeddings, are also integrated into the attention U-Net at various sections through its feature maps, as shown in Figure 10-5. In this process, the text embeddings are first projected onto the dimensions of each feature map. Afterward, a cross-attention mechanism is applied between the feature maps and the projected text embedding. In other words, the attention mechanism gets queries from the feature maps, and the keys and values from the text embedding. The current project requires the time-step positional encodings and class embeddings to be directly added to the feature maps and then the self-attention. In contrast, for text embeddings, a cross-attention mechanism is computed directly between the feature maps and the text embeddings.

These projects require different approaches because in the preceding project, the time step and class labels contained fixed and direct information. Conversely, text embeddings contain rich, detailed, and context-specific information. In turn, the cross-attention mechanism allows for a more sophisticated and selective merging of text and image features, ensuring that the textual information effectively guides the image generation.

You can implement the conditional attention U-Net for text-to-image generation by adapting Listing 10-10 as shown in Listing 10-31.

```
--snip--
unet_template = dl.AttentionUNet(..., context_embedding_dim=768)
unet = unet_template.create().to(device)
```

Listing 10-31: Instantiating the conditional attention U-Net (by modifying Listing 10-10)

This code creates a template for the attention U-Net (unet_template) and then uses it to create a concrete instance of the U-Net (unet). Later you'll reuse the template to create a second U-Net when training it with the CLIP tokenizer. With the context_embedding_dim parameter given as input, AttentionUNet takes the text information as input and operates as a conditional model. Here, the context embedding dimension is set to 768, the same value used to instantiate the text encoder in Listing 10-30.

Training the Conditional Diffusion Model

Once you've set up the U-Net, you can train the text-to-image diffusion model. Start by defining the data loaders with Listing 10-11 and the loss function with Listing 10-12, then instantiate the Diffusion class from Listing 10-14.

Next, you'll need to modify the optimizer from Listing 10-13. Since you'll be training the text encoder in addition to the attention U-Net, you must add its parameters to the optimizer, as shown in Listing 10-32.

```
optimizer = torch.optim.AdamW(
    list(unet.parameters()) + list(custom_text_encoder.parameters()), lr=1e-4,
)
```

Listing 10-32: Defining the optimizer (by modifying Listing 10-13)

This code provides the list of parameters for the text encoder to be updated during training, along with the existing parameters for the attention U-Net.

The training loop shown in Listing 10-33 resembles that of the conditional diffusion model from Listing 10-23, which generated bespoke MNIST digits using classifier-free guidance.

```
--snip--
n_images, steps = 5, [999, 900, 800, 700, 600, 500, 400, 300, 200, 100, 0]
--snip--
```

```
for epoch in range(epochs):
    for batch_idx, (images, _, sentences) in enumerate(loader, start=0):
        x_t, t_pos_enc, noise = prepare_data(images)

❶      tokens = pad_and_process(sentences)
❷      text_embeddings = custom_text_encoder(tokens.to(device))
        context = None if np.random.rand() < 0.1 else text_embeddings

        outputs = unet(x_t, t_pos_enc, context=context)
        --snip--
```

Listing 10-33: Training a conditional diffusion model (by modifying Listing 10-23)

This code tokenizes the text prompts ❶ and passes them through the custom text encoder to generate the text embeddings ❷. The text embeddings are stored in the context variable and are input to the model through the context parameter. The code trains the attention U-Net through the classifier-free guidance approach, training the model both conditionally and unconditionally by randomly dropping the text embeddings in 10 percent of cases.

Plotting the Intermediate Training Results

Now that you've implemented the training loop, you can use Listing 10-34 to visualize images generated for the example text prompts at the end of each epoch.

```
--snip--
❶ example_sentences = random.sample(test_sentences, n_images)
for epoch in range(epochs):
    unet.train(), custom_text_encoder.train()
    --snip--
    unet.eval(), custom_text_encoder.eval()
❷   tokens = pad_and_process(example_sentences)
❸   text_embeddings = custom_text_encoder(tokens.to(device))
    generated_images = diffusion.reverse_diffusion(
        ..., save_time_steps=save_time_steps,
        context=text_embeddings, guidance_strength=3,
    )
    --snip--
    fig = plt.figure(figsize=(len(save_time_steps), 1.2 * n_images))
    for idx in range(n_images):
        image_reverse_diff_traj = generated_images[idx]
        for j in range(len(steps)):
            --snip--
            if j == 5: plt.title(example_sentences[idx], fontsize=10)
--snip--
```

Listing 10-34: Plotting the sample images from the text prompt after each epoch (by modifying Listing 10-24)

This code starts by extracting five random validation text prompts that the model will use to create images ❶. When the code enters the training cycle, it first sets the attention U-Net and the custom_text_encoder to evaluation mode, similar to previous projects. Next, the code tokenizes the text prompts ❷ and generates the corresponding text embeddings by passing the tokens through the text encoder ❸. Afterward, the code initiates the reverse diffusion function by setting the number of images to the number of text prompts, the context parameter to take the text embeddings, and the classifier-free guidance strength to 3. Finally, this code plots the reverse diffusion trajectory of each of the 10 generated images, setting the image titles to their corresponding text prompts.

Figure 10-9 shows the generated images after 20 epochs.

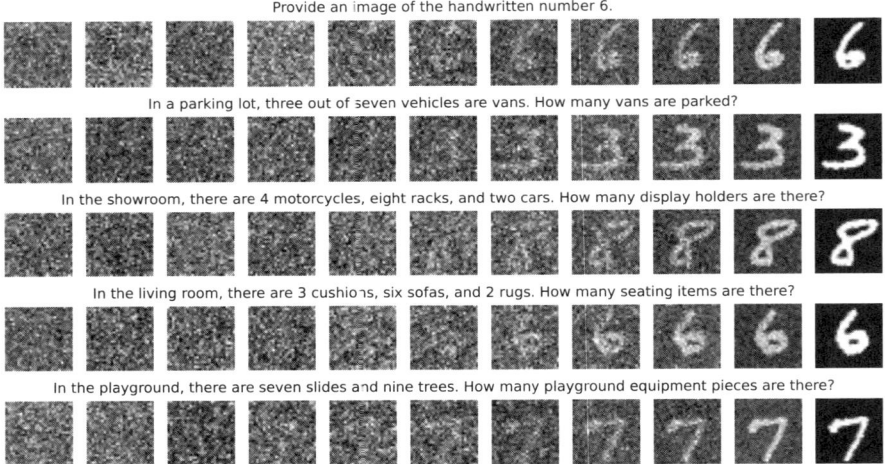

Figure 10-9: The generated images at the end of the training after 20 epochs

The digits not only are clearly visible against the black background but also correspond to the correct numbers in the text prompts, meaning that the model grasps the contextual meaning of the prompt as it generates each image. The model produces the requested number even when the text includes multiple numbers.

Training with the CLIP Tokenizer and CLIP Text Encoder

As an alternative to implementing your own tokenizer and text encoder, you can use pretrained tokenizers and text encoders trained on large corpora of image-caption data. Pretrained tokenizers and text encoders are particularly advantageous when textual descriptions and their corresponding images are more complex.

First, create another concrete instance of the attention U-Net:

```
unet_clip = unet_template.create().to(device)
```

Then remove the custom_text_encoder parameters from the optimizer in Listing 10-32, creating the following:

```
optimizer_clip = torch.optim.AdamW(unet_clip.parameters(), lr=1e-4)
```

Next, import the pretrained CLIP tokenizer and CLIP text encoder from the transformers package, as shown in Listing 10-35.

```
from transformers import CLIPTextModel, CLIPTokenizer

CLIP_tokenizer = CLIPTokenizer.from_pretrained(
    "openai/clip-vit-large-patch14", torch_dtype=torch.float32,
)
CLIP_text_encoder = CLIPTextModel.from_pretrained(
    "openai/clip-vit-large-patch14", torch_dtype=torch.float32,
).to(device)
```

Listing 10-35: Importing the CLIP tokenizer and CLIP text encoder

This code loads the pretrained CLIP text model and tokenizer.

You can now check the tokens and the text embeddings of an example text prompt generated by CLIP with the following commands:

```
example_sentence = random.choice(test_sentences)
tokens = CLIP_tokenizer(example_sentence, padding="max_length",
                  ❶ max_length=CLIP_tokenizer.model_max_length,
                     truncation=True, return_tensors="pt")
text_embedding = CLIP_text_encoder(tokens.input_ids.to(device))[0]
print(example_sentence), print(tokens.input_ids)
print(f"tokens shape: {tokens.input_ids.shape}")
print(f"text embeddings: {text_embedding.shape}")
```

This code samples an example text prompt and passes it through the CLIP tokenizer to generate tokens. The maximum length is again set to 77, the maximum token length the CLIP model can offer ❶. Finally, the code generates the text embeddings by passing the tokens through the CLIP text encoder.

The print statements at the end of the code produce the following outputs:

```
In the forest, there are four squirrels and one owls. How many birds are there?
tensor([[49406,   530,   518,  4167,   267,   997,   631,  2721, 26623,   537,
           637, 18247,   269,   829,  1346,  4337,   631,   997,   286, 49407,
         49407, 49407, 49407, 49407, 49407, 49407, 49407, 49407, 49407, 49407,
         49407, 49407, 49407, 49407, 49407, 49407, 49407, 49407, 49407, 49407,
         49407, 49407, 49407, 49407, 49407, 49407, 49407, 49407, 49407, 49407,
         49407, 49407, 49407, 49407, 49407, 49407, 49407, 49407, 49407, 49407,
         49407, 49407, 49407, 49407, 49407, 49407, 49407, 49407, 49407, 49407,
         49407, 49407, 49407, 49407, 49407, 49407, 49407]])
tokens shape: torch.Size([1, 77])
text embeddings: torch.Size([1, 77, 768])
```

CLIP assigns 49406 for the sentence start and 49407 for the sentence end and padding. The text embedding shape is the same as that of your custom text encoder.

By making minor changes to your existing training loop, you can retrain the text-to-image diffusion model with a CLIP tokenizer and text encoder. First, since the CLIP text encoder is already pretrained, you should set the gradients of the CLIP text encoder to False, freezing its weights as follows:

```
for param in CLIP_text_encoder.parameters():
    param.requires_grad = False
```

This code loops through the parameters for the CLIP text encoder and disables the gradient computation, ensuring that the weights are frozen.

Next, alter the training loop from Listing 10-33 to pass the text inputs through the CLIP tokenizer and CLIP text encoder instead of your custom tokenizer and text encoder, as shown in Listing 10-36.

```
--snip--
for epoch in range(epochs):
    for batch_idx, (images, class_labels) in enumerate(loader, start=0):
        unet_clip.train()
        --snip--
        tokens = CLIP_tokenizer(
            sentences, padding="max_length",
            max_length=CLIP_tokenizer.model_max_length, truncation=True,
            return_tensors="pt",
        )
        text_embeddings = CLIP_text_encoder(tokens.input_ids.to(device))[0]
        --snip--
        outputs = unet_clip(x=x_t, t=t_pos_enc, context=context)

        optimizer_clip.zero_grad()
        loss = criterion(outputs, noise)
        loss.backward()
        optimizer_clip.step()
        --snip--
    unet_clip.eval()
    --snip--
    tokens = CLIP_tokenizer(
        example_sentences, padding="max_length",
        max_length=CLIP_tokenizer.model_max_length, truncation=True,
        return_tensors="pt",
    )
    text_embeddings = CLIP_text_encoder(tokens.input_ids.to(device))[0]

    generated_images = diffusion.reverse_diffusion(model=unet_clip, ...)
    --snip--
```

Listing 10-36: Training with CLIP (by modifying Listing 10-34)

This code passes the generated text prompts in each batch through the CLIP tokenizer. Then the resulting tokens are fed into the CLIP text encoder to generate the text embeddings.

The results will be similar to those of the custom tokenizer and text encoder. In general, you should determine whether to use CLIP or a custom implementation based on the complexity of your specific task and your need for custom modifications and control. Keep in mind that text-to-image performance is highly contingent on the input text data. With a greater number and variety of text prompts, the quality and relevance of the generated images can improve significantly.

NOTE   *Code Example 10-B, "Generating Images of Digits from Text Prompts," is available at* https://github.com/DeepTrackAI/DeepLearningCrashCourse. *Navigate to the* Ch10_Diffusion *folder and then* ec10_B_text2image. *The* text2image.ipynb *notebook provides a complete code example to generate MNIST digits from text prompts. The* mnist_sentences.json *and* test_sentences.txt *files provide the text data used for training and testing.*

Project 10C: Generating Super-Resolution Images

Over a century ago, the microscopist Ernst Abbe devised an equation showing that the resolution of an optical microscope is limited by the wavelength of the light used to illuminate the sample. In practice, this limit, known as *Abbe's diffraction limit*, means that it isn't possible to distinguish details separated by less than 200 nm with an optical microscope. For scale, the diameter of a DNA molecule is about 2 nm, approximately 100 times smaller than this limit. Since then, the quest to surpass this limit and develop techniques for high-resolution imaging of cellular and subcellular structures has driven significant advances in biomedical research, leading to the advent of *super-resolution microscopy*. Unfortunately, this breakthrough technique is expensive, requires complex instrumentation, and is not readily accessible.

In this project, you'll explore a possible solution to this challenge. You'll use a conditional diffusion model to transform a low-resolution microscopic image of a biological structure into its high-resolution counterpart without the need for advanced and costly microscopes. Importantly, this approach is not limited to optical microscopy but can be applied to various types of low-resolution images, such as photographs, to achieve exceptional resolution and detail.

Downloading the BioSR Dataset

For this project, you'll use images of microtubules from the BioSR dataset originally published in 2021 by Chang Qiao and co-workers in *Nature Methods* (volume 18, pages 194–202). Because the original images need to be reformatted and preprocessed, we've uploaded the processed images to a GitHub repository. This processed dataset contains 40,320 image pairs for training and 2,080 image pairs for testing. Each image is 128×128 pixels. You can download this dataset from the GitHub repository with Listing 10-37.

```
import os

if not os.path.exists("biosr_dataset"):
    os.system("git clone https://github.com/DeepTrackAI/biosr_dataset")
```

Listing 10-37: Downloading the BioSR dataset of microtubules

This code checks whether the dataset directory already exists. If not, the dataset is downloaded from the GitHub repository.

Managing the Dataset

Once you've downloaded the dataset, you can create a custom dataset class to load the images, apply the required transformations, and return the images and their corresponding labels. This is shown in Listing 10-38.

```
import torch
from tifffile import tifffile as tiff

class BioSRDataset(torch.utils.data.Dataset):
    """Dataset class to load the BioSR dataset."""

    def __init__(self, lr_dir, hr_dir, transform):
        """Initialize dataset."""
        self.lr_dir, self.hr_dir, self.transform = lr_dir, hr_dir, transform
    ❶ self.files = [file for file in os.listdir(self.lr_dir)
                         if file.endswith(".tif")]

    def __len__(self):
        """Return the number of image pairs."""
    ❷ return len(self.files)

    def __getitem__(self, index):
        """Get a low-resolution--high-resolution image pair."""
        lr_image = tiff.imread(os.path.join(self.lr_dir, self.files[index]))
        hr_image = tiff.imread(os.path.join(self.hr_dir, self.files[index]))
        if self.transform:
            lr_image = self.transform(lr_image)
            hr_image = self.transform(hr_image)
        return lr_image, hr_image
```

Listing 10-38: The dataset class to manage the images

This class permits you to load the images in small batches without having to load the entire dataset into memory before training. The class takes three input parameters: lr_dir sets the directory for the low-resolution images, hr_dir sets the directory for the high-resolution images, and transform contains the transformations to be applied to the images. The initialization method concludes by saving a list of available *.tiff* files in the low-resolution image folder ❶. The dataset length is the length of the file list ❷.

The __getitem__() method loads the low- and high-resolution images corresponding to index, applies the transformations, and returns them.

Preprocessing the Images

Next, you'll define the necessary transformations and normalization to apply to the dataset, as shown in Listing 10-39.

```
from torchvision.transforms import Compose, Normalize, ToTensor

transform = Compose([ToTensor(), Normalize(mean=(0.5,), std=(0.5,))])
```

Listing 10-39: Implementing the necessary transformations and normalizations

This code defines the transformation for the low-resolution and high-resolution images, which transforms the images to PyTorch tensors and then normalizes them so that their pixel values range from −1 to 1.

Creating the Training and Test Datasets

Now that you've preprocessed the images, create the training and test datasets with Listing 10-40.

```
root = os.path.join("biosr_dataset", "BioSR", "Microtubules")
train_set = BioSRDataset(lr_dir=os.path.join(root, "training_wf"),
                         hr_dir=os.path.join(root, "training_gt"),
                         transform=transform)
test_set = BioSRDataset(lr_dir=os.path.join(root, "test_wf", "level_09"),
                        hr_dir=os.path.join(root, "test_gt"),
                        transform=transform)
```

Listing 10-40: Creating the datasets

You can now visualize some example images, using Listing 10-41.

```
import matplotlib.pyplot as plt
import numpy as np

lr_image, hr_image = train_set[np.random.randint(0, len(train_set))]

plt.subplot(1, 2, 1)
plt.imshow(lr_image.permute(1, 2, 0), cmap="gray")
plt.title("Low-resolution image")

plt.subplot(1, 2, 2)
plt.imshow(hr_image.permute(1, 2, 0), cmap="gray")
plt.title("High-resolution image")
```

```
plt.tight_layout()
plt.show()
```

Listing 10-41: Plotting a low-resolution and high-resolution image pair

This code samples a random low- and high-resolution image pair from the training dataset and plots them side by side. Figure 10-10 shows an example.

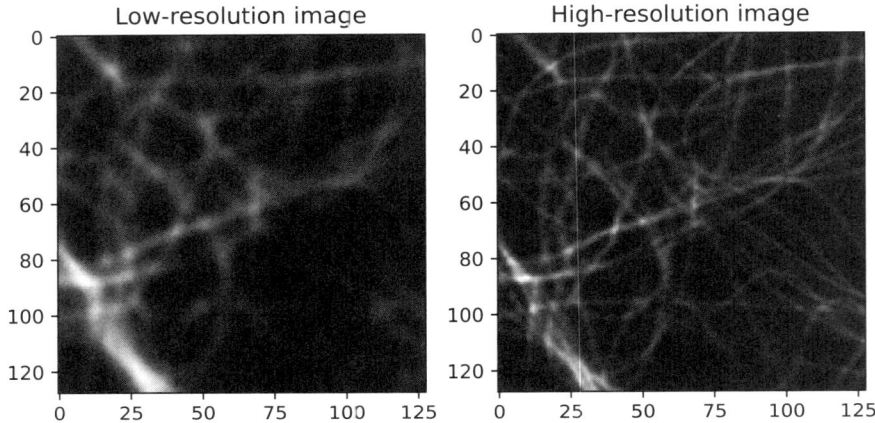

Figure 10-10: Low-resolution (left) and high-resolution (right) images of microtubules

The low-resolution image is significantly blurred in comparison to its high-resolution counterpart, which has details of the microtubules that are more clearly visible.

Adapting the Diffusion Process for Super-Resolution

In the previous projects of this chapter, you generated MNIST digits from noise and various conditional inputs. You applied the forward diffusion process to MNIST images to add noise, while in the reverse diffusion process you generated images from pure noise by using an attention U-Net. You provided conditional inputs like class labels and text as parameters to the model.

In the super-resolution task, the difference lies in the conditional input and target. Both are in image format: one low resolution and one high resolution. For this project, you'll apply the forward diffusion process to the high-resolution image. You'll then concatenate the low-resolution image with the noisy image to provide as input to the attention U-Net. This adaptation allows the diffusion model to learn the underlying probabilistic distribution of the high-resolution images based on the corresponding low-resolution images.

Define the computational device with

```
device = get_device()
```

which uses the get_device() function defined in Listing 7-10 (also see the note on page 288 about the use of MPS). Then you can easily make the change to the reverse diffusion process by modifying Listing 10-19 as shown in Listing 10-42.

```
class Diffusion:
    """Denoising diffusion probabilistic model (DDPM)."""
    --snip--

    def reverse_diffusion(--snip--, input_image, fix_noise=None, ...):
        """Reverse diffusion process"""
        --snip--
            for i in tqdm(reversed(range(0, self.steps)),
                        desc="UNet inference", total=self.steps):
                --snip--
                pred_noise = model(
                    torch.cat((input_image.to(self.device), x), dim=1),
                    t_pos_enc,
                )
        --snip--
```

Listing 10-42: Implementing reverse diffusion for super-resolution (by modifying Listing 10-19)

This code adds the input_image parameter to the reverse diffusion process, enabling it to perform image-to-image translation tasks. In this case, the low-resolution image given as an input is concatenated to the noisy image before being fed through the attention U-Net.

Defining the Conditional Attention U-Net

Similarly to the way you modified the reverse diffusion method, you can adapt the conditional attention U-Net from Listing 10-10 for this super-resolution task, with Listing 10-43.

```
--snip--
pos_enc_dim = 256

model = dl.AttentionUNet(
    in_channels=2, ...,
    channel_attention=[False, False, False], ...,
).build().to(device)
```

Listing 10-43: Instantiating the conditional attention U-Net (by modifying Listing 10-10)

This code sets the number of input channels to 2 to account for the noise image and low-resolution image that have been concatenated and passed as a conditional input. To conserve memory and speed up the training, the code turns off the attention mechanism by setting the channel attentions of the feature maps to False.

Training the Conditional Diffusion Model

After completing these modifications, you can train the conditional diffusion model for super-resolution.

Defining the Data Loaders, Diffusion Class, and Loss Function

To begin, you'll define two data loaders for the training and test datasets, as shown in Listing 10-44.

```
train_loader = dl.DataLoader(train_set, batch_size=64, shuffle=True)
test_loader = dl.DataLoader(test_set, batch_size=64, shuffle=False)
```

Listing 10-44: Defining the data loaders

This code defines training and test data loaders with a batch size of 64. The training loader shuffles the data before creating batches. You can adjust the batch size depending on your computational resources.

Next, instantiate the diffusion class:

```
diffusion = Diffusion(steps=2000, img_size=128, beta_start=1e-6, beta_end=0.01)
```

This code instantiates a diffusion class with 2,000 noise steps, an image size of 128, and noise values ranging from 0.000001 to 0.01.

Now specify the loss function:

```
criterion = torch.nn.L1Loss()
```

This code calculates an L1 loss between the noise predicted by the model and the actual noise sampled, in contrast to the L2 loss in previous projects.

Once you've modified the loss function, you can define the positional encoding function from Listing 10-7 and the optimizer from Listing 10-13.

Finally, before implementing the training loop, you'll need to alter the prepare_data() helper function from Listing 10-15 to take both the low-resolution and high-resolution images as inputs and return the concatenated noisy image, the time-step encoding, and the noise applied during the forward diffusion process. Listing 10-45 shows these modifications.

```
def prepare_data(input_image, target_image, steps=2000, device=device):
    """Prepare data."""
    batch_size = input_image.shape[0]
    t = torch.randint(low=0, high=steps, size=(batch_size,)).to(device)
    input_image, target_image = input_image.to(device), target_image.to(device)
❶  x_t, noise = diffusion.forward_diffusion(target_image, t)
❷  x_t = torch.cat((input_image, x_t), dim=1)
    t_pos_enc = positional_encoding(t.unsqueeze(1), pos_enc_dim)
    return x_t.to(device), t_pos_enc.to(device), noise.to(device)
```

Listing 10-45: The function to prepare the super-resolution data (by modifying Listing 10-15)

This function takes two images as inputs, the low-resolution input image and the high-resolution target image. The function processes the target image by the forward diffusion process ❶ and concatenates the input image with the noisy image ❷. The function then returns the concatenated noisy image (which includes both the low-resolution and noisy high-resolution components), the time-step encoding, and the noise applied during the forward diffusion process.

Implementing the Training Loop

Now you're ready to implement the training loop to teach the diffusion model to generate high-resolution images from low-resolution images. The training loop is similar to Listing 10-17, with some minor modifications shown in Listing 10-46.

```
epochs = 30

for epoch in range(epochs):
    --snip--
    for batch_idx, (input_images, target_images) in enumerate(train_loader):
        x_t, t_pos_enc, noise = prepare_data(input_images, target_images)
        --snip--
        if batch_idx % 100 == 0:
            print(f"Batch {batch_idx + 1}/{len(train_loader)}: "
                  f"Train loss: {loss.item():.4f}")
        --snip--
    train_loss.append(running_loss / len(train_loader))
```

Listing 10-46: Training a conditional diffusion model for the super-resolution task (by modifying Listing 10-17)

This code trains the attention U-Net for the super-resolution task, increasing the number of epochs to 30. The images are passed through the updated prepare_data() function, which outputs the noisy image, the time step, and the noise step. The rest of the training loop is the same as in Listing 10-17.

Plotting the Intermediate Training Results

You can now modify the working training loop to visualize the high-resolution images generated from a set of low-resolution images at the end of each epoch, as shown in Listing 10-47.

```
--snip--
for epoch in range(epochs):
    unet.train()
    --snip--
    unet.eval()
    for test_input_images, test_target_images in test_loader:
        generated_images = diffusion.reverse_diffusion(
            model=unet, n_images=1, n_channels=1,
            pos_enc_dim=pos_enc_dim, pos_enc_func=positional_encoding,
            input_image=test_input_images[:1], save_time_steps=[0],
        )
        break
```

```
lr_image = test_input_images[0]
image_diff_traj = generated_images[0]
hr_generated_image = image_diff_traj[-1]
target_image = test_target_images[0]

fig = plt.figure(figsize=(7, 3))

plt.subplot(1, 3, 1)
plt.imshow(lr_image.permute(1, 2, 0), cmap="gray")
plt.title("Input")
plt.axis("off")

plt.subplot(1, 3, 2)
plt.imshow(hr_generated_image.permute(1, 2, 0).cpu().numpy(), cmap="gray")
plt.title("Output")
plt.axis("off")

plt.subplot(1, 3, 3)
plt.imshow(target_image.permute(1, 2, 0), cmap="gray")
plt.title("Target")
plt.axis("off")

plt.tight_layout()
plt.show()
plt.close()
```

Listing 10-47: Plotting images after each epoch (by modifying Listing 10-46)

This code extracts the test low-resolution and high-resolution images from the test loader, passes the low-resolution images to the reverse diffusion process, and extracts the generated high-resolution image by setting the save_time_steps parameter to the last time step, which is 0. Then the code plots the input low-resolution image, the generated high-resolution image, and the target high-resolution image side by side for visualization and comparison.

Figure 10-11 shows the generated images after 30 epochs.

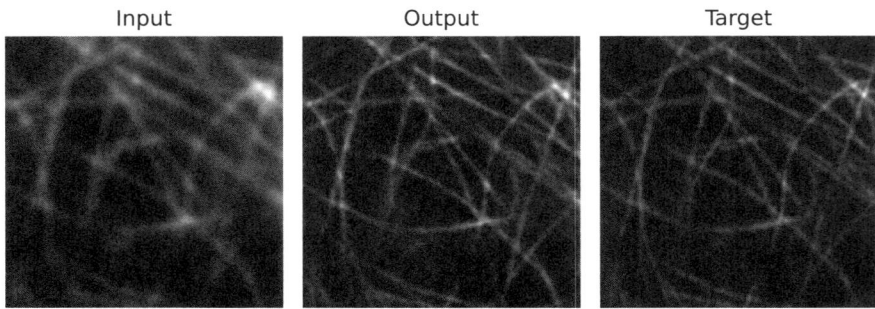

Figure 10-11: The low-resolution input image (left), generated high-resolution image (center), and target high-resolution image (right) after 30 epochs

The generated high-resolution image (center) is very similar to the target high-resolution image (right).

NOTE *Code Example 10-C, "Generating Super-Resolution Images," is available at* https://github.com/DeepTrackAI/DeepLearningCrashCourse. *Navigate to the* Ch10_Diffusion *folder and then* ec10_C_superresolution. *The* superresolution.ipynb *notebook provides a complete code example to increase the resolution of microscopy images by using a diffusion model.*

Summary

In this chapter, you learned about diffusion models and how they can be applied to generate and transform images. You began by discovering the underlying concepts and equations behind diffusion models. You then explored how diffusion models can be trained to generate random MNIST digits and how to plot intermediate results to ensure the model's progress.

The first project involved generating bespoke digits by using a conditional diffusion model. You learned to guide the generation process by conditioning the model on specific inputs.

Building on this foundation, the second project introduced you to the concept of generating images from text prompts. This section taught you how to provide text inputs as conditions to the diffusion model.

The final project tackled the challenge of generating super-resolution images. Using the BioSR dataset, this project demonstrated how to adapt the diffusion process for super-resolution tasks, culminating in the generation of high-resolution images from low-resolution counterparts.

Since diffusion models are among the most innovative tools in deep learning, you're now ideally positioned to take advantage of their potential in a wide array of applications. As these models evolve, their versatility and power will open up new possibilities and advancements in various fields over the coming years. For instance, in health care, diffusion models could revolutionize medical imaging by enhancing the resolution of scans, enabling earlier and more-accurate diagnoses. In creative industries, these models could generate high-quality, photorealistic images for use in films, video games, and virtual reality, pushing the boundaries of what's visually possible. Additionally, in scientific research, diffusion models might assist in simulating complex physical systems or generating detailed molecular structures, accelerating discoveries in areas like drug development and materials science.

Seminal Works and Further Reading

The concept of diffusion models was first introduced in 2015 by Jascha Sohl-Dickstein et al. in "Deep Unsupervised Learning Using Nonequilibrium Thermodynamics," published in *Proceedings of the 32nd International Conference on Machine Learning* (*ICML 2015*, volume 37, pages 2,256–2,265). This work established the theoretical basis for diffusion models.

A key advancement came in 2020 with Jonathan Ho et al. in "Denoising Diffusion Probabilistic Models," published in *34th Conference on Neural Information Processing Systems* (*NeurIPS 2020*, volume 33, pages 6,840–6,851). This work introduced DDPMs, which generate data by progressively adding noise during training and learning to reverse the process.

In 2021, Prafulla Dhariwal and Alexander Nichol further improved diffusion models in "Diffusion Models Beat GANs on Image Synthesis," published in *NeurIPS 2021* (volume 34, pages 8,780–8,794). Their work demonstrated that diffusion models could outperform GANs on key image synthesis benchmarks, offering higher-quality image generation.

The application of diffusion models was extended in 2022 by Chitwan Saharia et al. in "Image Super-Resolution via Iterative Refinement," published in *IEEE Transactions on Pattern Analysis and Machine Intelligence* (volume 45, pages 4,713–4,726). They presented SR3, a method that applied diffusion models to image super-resolution, using iterative refinement to upscale low-resolution images, demonstrating the versatility of diffusion models beyond traditional generation tasks.

Another significant contribution came from Robin Rombach et al. in 2022 in "High-Resolution Image Synthesis with Latent Diffusion Models," published in *Proceedings of the IEEE Conference on Computer Vision and Pattern Recognition* (CVPR, pages 10,674–10,685). This work introduced latent diffusion models, which diffuse in a lower-dimensional latent space, making the process more computationally efficient while still generating high-quality, high-resolution images.

An extended version of the super-resolution example was published in 2025 by Harshith Bachimanchi and Giovanni Volpe in "Diffusion Models for Super-Resolution Microscopy: A Tutorial," published in *Journal of Physics: Photonics* (volume 7, article 013001). Their tutorial provided practical insights into using diffusion models to improve spatial resolution in microscopy images, reinforcing the versatility of diffusion models in microscopy applications.

CHALLENGE PROJECTS

10-1: Super-resolution on natural images   Apply a diffusion model to enhance the resolution of natural images such as landscapes or portraits. Use a publicly available dataset like the DIV2K dataset, which contains high-quality images and their lower-resolution counterparts.

10-2: Text-to-image generation with a custom dataset   Create a text-to-image generation model using a custom dataset of your choice. Collect a dataset of image-caption pairs from sources such as Flickr 8k or Common Objects in Context (COCO). Preprocess the text and images, train a conditional diffusion model, and test its ability to generate images based on the provided text prompts. Analyze the coherence and quality of the generated images.

10-3: Enhancement of medical imaging data   Utilize a diffusion model to improve the resolution of medical images, such as MRI or CT scans. Access a publicly available medical imaging dataset, like the MICCAI BRATS dataset. Train your model to enhance the resolution of these images and assess the improvements in visual clarity and diagnostic utility.

10-4: Domain-specific image generation   Implement a diffusion model to generate images in a specific domain, such as fashion, architecture, or food. Gather a dataset relevant to your chosen domain. For example, for fashion, use the DeepFashion dataset. For architecture, use the CMP Facade Database. For food, use the Food-101 dataset. Preprocess the images and train the model to generate new, high-quality images. Evaluate the model's performance by examining the creativity and relevance of the generated images.

10-5: Multimodal image enhancement   Develop a multimodal diffusion model that can enhance images by incorporating additional modalities, such as depth information or thermal imaging. Use datasets like the NYU Depth V2 dataset, which provides RGB and depth images, or the FLIR ADAS dataset, which includes RGB and thermal images. Preprocess the data and train your model. Evaluate the model's ability to improve image quality by integrating information from the additional modalities.

11

MODELING MOLECULES AND COMPLEX SYSTEMS WITH GRAPH NEURAL NETWORKS

In this chapter, you'll explore graph neural networks, a family of deep learning models tailored to analyze graph-structured data. Because they can grasp relationships within the structures of graphs, graph neural networks are ideal for uncovering complex patterns within data.

As they've grown popular in recent years, these networks have been applied to a wide range of problems. The main reason for their success is that graph neural networks exploit the way graphs represent connections and interactions among objects. For example, in molecular property prediction, graph neural networks can predict how a molecule might behave based on the connections between its atoms. In protein structure determination, these networks help predict the 3D structure of proteins by analyzing the relationships between amino acids. In algorithmic reasoning, these networks might tackle complex tasks like sorting or finding the shortest path by representing these tasks as graph problems. In particle tracking, graph neural networks can analyze the trajectories of particles in physics experiments by understanding the connections between their movements.

You'll first learn the basic concepts behind graph neural networks by using them to estimate the properties of molecules. You'll discover how to improve a basic graph neural network's predictive accuracy by adding message passing. You'll then apply these tools to two projects: simulating complex physical phenomena and tracking the motion of cells.

Understanding Graph Convolutions

A *graph* is a fundamental mathematical structure that models the way things are connected or related to one another. A graph is composed of *nodes* (also known as *vertices*) and *edges* (sometimes referred to as *links* or *connections*). Edges, which represent the relationships or interactions between nodes, are crucial as they often carry valuable information about the nature of these connections, such as the strength of a bond in a molecule or the frequency of communication between individuals in a social network. This simple yet powerful concept allows you to map networks of all kinds, from the web of social interactions connecting individuals to the routes that form transportation networks. In this way, graphs provide a universal language to describe and analyze the patterns and connections of various domains, such as biology, computer science, social science, and more.

Graph neural networks are ideally suited to analyze graphs. They apply *graph convolutions*. These are analogous to the image convolutions used in image analysis by the convolutional neural networks in Chapter 3. Image convolutions use filters that take advantage of the uniform grid of pixels that make up most images. However, graphs are irregular structures of nodes and edges without a fixed pattern. This irregularity requires redefining convolutions to fit graphs. This is done by aggregating and weighing information from a node's connected neighbors. In this process, graph convolutions use the graph structure to direct information flow during data processing. For example, in social network analysis, a graph convolution could be used to predict a person's preferences by considering the preferences of their friends (connected nodes). The model thus aggregates and weighs the information from these connections, using the structure of the social network graph to inform its predictions.

For example, consider a simple cycle graph like the one on the left side of Figure 11-1. This graph consists of five nodes connected by directed edges in a cycle.

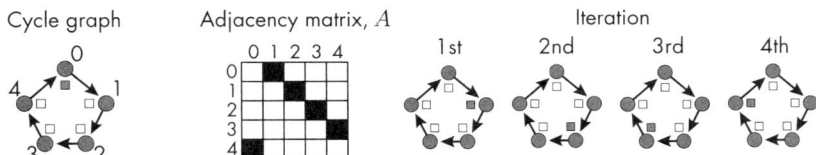

Figure 11-1: A cycle graph (left), its adjacency matrix (middle), and the evolution of its node attributes as a graph convolution is applied multiple times (right)

The middle of Figure 11-1 shows the *adjacency matrix*, *A*, which numerically represents this graph. Its rows and columns correspond to the nodes, while a nonzero entry indicates an edge, marked here with a black square. Each entry A_{ij} is set to 1 if there is a link going from node *i* to node *j*. Otherwise, the entry remains 0. This matrix representation of the graph is particularly useful for computational analyses.

You can get this adjacency matrix with Listing 11-1.

```
import numpy as np

node_num = 5

A = np.zeros((node_num, node_num))
for i in range(node_num):
    for j in range(node_num):
        if j % node_num == (i + 1) % node_num:
❶           A[i, j] = 1
```

Listing 11-1: Calculating the adjacency matrix of a simple cycle graph

This code defines the adjacency matrix A of the graph shown in Figure 11-1. The code starts by creating an empty matrix corresponding to a graph without edges. Then the code iterates through all possible edges, going from node *i* to node *j*. If there is an edge in the graph, the code changes the matrix element from 0 to 1 to represent the connection between this node and the next one with a (directed) edge ❶.

You can print the resulting adjacency matrix with print(f"A: {A}"), which returns the following:

```
A: [[0. 1. 0. 0. 0.]
 [0. 0. 1. 0. 0.]
 [0. 0. 0. 1. 0.]
 [0. 0. 0. 0. 1.]
 [1. 0. 0. 0. 0.]]
```

Here, you can notice the edges going from nodes 0 to 1, 1 to 2, 2 to 3, 3 to 4, and, closing the cycle, 4 to 0.

NOTE *The adjacency matrix A can represent both directed and undirected graphs. In a directed graph, an entry $A_{ij} = 1$ indicates a directed edge from node i to node j, corresponding to the direction of information flow. Instead, in an undirected graph, both A_{ij} and A_{ji} must have the same value. This reflects the bidirectional edges allowing information to flow in both directions, resulting in a symmetric adjacency matrix.*

You can now introduce *node attributes* (also known as *node features*). These are properties assigned to the nodes that help describe their characteristics or roles within the graph. For example, in the graph of a social network, node attributes could include a person's age, location, or interests. In a molecular graph, node attributes might represent an atom's type, charge, or bond structure. You can use Listing 11-2 to assign a single attribute to each node in the cycle graph.

```
node_attributes = np.zeros(node_num)
node_attributes[0] = 1
```

Listing 11-2: Assigning node attributes

After creating the node_attributes vector, this code assigns a value of 1 to the first node. You can print these node attributes with print(f{"node_attributes:{node_attributes}"), which returns the following:

```
node_attributes: [1. 0. 0. 0. 0.]
```

In Figure 11-1, these properties are shown as boxes next to each node in the graph, with the filled box representing the node with attribute 1.

A graph convolution transforms the node attributes by using the adjacency matrix for guidance. You can implement the graph_convolution() function with Listing 11-3.

```
def graph_convolution(A, node_attributes):
    """Calculate graph convolution."""
    conv = np.zeros(node_num)
    for i in range(node_num):
        for j in range(node_num):
            ❶ conv[j] = conv[j] + A[i, j] * node_attributes[i]
    return conv
```

Listing 11-3: The function to implement a graph convolution

This function starts by initializing the conv vector to contain the graph-convolved node attributes. Then, for each edge going from node i to node j, the function multiplies the original attribute value of node i by the edge from node i to node j, then adds the result to the graph-convolved node attribute corresponding to node j ❶.

Next, you can iteratively apply the graph convolution to get new node attributes, using Listing 11-4.

```
for c in range(5):
    node_attributes = graph_convolution(A, node_attributes)
    print(f"Convolution {c + 1}: {node_attributes}")
```

Listing 11-4: Applying the graph convolution

This loop runs for five steps, but you can use a different number. During each iteration, the vector containing the node attributes is updated through a graph convolution operation and then printed. The resulting graph convolutions are shown here:

```
Convolution 1: [0. 1. 0. 0. 0.]
Convolution 2: [0. 0. 1. 0. 0.]
Convolution 3: [0. 0. 0. 1. 0.]
Convolution 4: [0. 0. 0. 0. 1.]
Convolution 5: [1. 0. 0. 0. 0.]
```

Reflecting this graph's cyclic nature, each convolution step propagates each node's attributes to its immediate neighbor based on the structure stored in the adjacency matrix. As illustrated in the right panel of Figure 11-1, the output shows how the attribute initially set at the first node (indexed at 0) travels along the directed edges of the graph. After each iteration, the attribute moves to the next node in the sequence. This sequential updating of attributes across the graph continues until the attribute with value 1 completes a cycle and returns to the first node, demonstrating how graph convolutions facilitate the flow and transformation of information across a network's structure.

EXERCISES

11-1: Enlarge your cycle graph to include more nodes, and initiate several nodes with nonzero attributes. Apply graph convolutions iteratively. Observe how the distribution of node attributes over the graph evolves. What patterns emerge from different initial attribute configurations?

11-2: Convert your cycle graph into an undirected graph by making each connection reciprocal. Reapply the graph convolution operations and observe the resulting explosion of node attributes, a phenomenon of attribute values escalating quickly over iterations. To counteract this effect, implement a normalization step that divides each node attribute by its degree (the number of edges connected to the node). Analyze how this normalization influences the distribution of attributes after several convolutions.

11-3: Construct a noncyclical graph by designing a more complex adjacency matrix where at least some nodes aren't part of a loop. Introduce node attributes and apply graph convolution operations. Observe the spread of attributes across the noncyclical graph. Consider how the absence of cycles affects the propagation of attributes and what it implies about how information can spread in noncyclical structures.

Predicting Molecular Properties with Graph Convolutions

Now that you understand the basic concept behind graph convolutions, you can use them to predict molecular properties. Scientists often need to predict properties such as a molecule's solubility, toxicity, or binding affinity to specific proteins. Traditional methods, like molecular dynamics simulations, have been used for these predictions, but they can be computationally intensive and may not capture complex interactions effectively. Graph neural networks are particularly well suited to this task because they can naturally represent molecules as graphs, with atoms as nodes and chemical bonds as edges, allowing the model to consider the complex relationships among these elements.

To see this in action, you'll implement a *graph convolution layer* and apply it to predict the solubility of a molecule in fat from a graph representation of its structure. First, you'll define the graph convolution layer and apply it to a simple molecular graph. Next, you'll extend this implementation to more-complex molecules, using the ZINC dataset. Finally, you'll evaluate the model's performance in predicting the solubility of the molecules. Note that unlike the directed graph example from the preceding section, this task will involve undirected graphs.

Implementing a Graph Convolution Layer

Implementing a graph convolution layer typically involves three sequential operations:

1. *Transform* the attributes of each node through a learnable function. This transformation prepares the node attributes for further processing, allowing the graph convolution layer to learn complex representations of the nodes' attributes.

2. *Propagate* the information across the graph. During this step, each node receives the transformed attributes from its neighbors, thus aggregating information from its local neighborhood.

3. *Update* each node's aggregated attributes based on the information collected during the propagation step. This typically involves applying another learnable function or a nonlinear activation function to the aggregated attributes.

You can implement a simple graph convolution by using Listing 11-5.

```
import torch

class GraphConvolution(torch.nn.Module):
    """Graph convolution."""

    def forward(self, A, node_attr):
        """Compute the graph convolution."""
    ❶ return torch.matmul(A, node_attr)
```

Listing 11-5: The class to define a graph convolution

This class implements a simple graph convolution for an undirected graph. The forward pass is implemented by multiplying the adjacency matrix by the node attribute vector ❶.

Once you've defined a simple convolution, you can create a graph convolution layer with Listing 11-6.

```
import deeplay as dl

class GCL(dl.DeeplayModule):
    """Graph convolution layer."""

    def __init__(self, in_feats, out_feats):
        """Initialize graph convolution layer."""
        super().__init__()
        self.transform = dl.Layer(torch.nn.Linear, in_feats, out_feats)
        self.propagate = dl.Layer(GraphConvolution)
        self.update = dl.Layer(torch.nn.ReLU)

    def forward(self, A, node_attr):
        """Transform, propagate, and update the node attributes."""
        transformed_node_attr = self.transform(node_attr)
        propagated_node_attr = self.propagate(A, transformed_node_attr)
        updated_node_attr = self.update(propagated_node_attr)
        return updated_node_attr
```

Listing 11-6: The class to define a graph convolution layer

This class instantiates a simple graph convolution layer containing the transform, propagate, and update operations. The transform operation uses a linear layer to transform the original node attributes with in_feats dimensions into a new attribute space with out_feats dimensions. The propagate operation shares the transformed attributes with other nodes via the GraphConvolution class. Finally, after the transformed attributes are propagated across the graph, the update operation applies a nonlinear activation function to the aggregated attributes to produce the final node attributes.

You can now further improve the graph convolution layer in Listing 11-6. In fact, it has two major limitations that hinder its real-world effectiveness. First, while it aggregates attributes from neighboring nodes, it doesn't consider the node's own attributes. However, a node's intrinsic attributes often play an important role in the convolution operation, influencing the outcome and effectiveness of the model. This issue can be solved by adding edges that represent self-loops, which lie on the adjacency matrix's diagonal.

The second major limitation is that A has not been normalized. Without normalization, nodes with a higher degree (a greater number of neighbors) will possess larger aggregated attribute values than those with fewer neighbors. This discrepancy can lead to pronounced variance in the aggregated attributes, potentially skewing the model's performance and its ability to generalize across the graph.

Listing 11-7 introduces self-loops and normalization into the class representing the graph convolution.

```
--snip--
class GCL(dl.DeeplayModule):
    --snip--
    def add_self_loops(self, A):
        """Add diagonal self-loops to adjacency matrix."""
    ❶ return A + torch.eye(A.size(0)).to(A.device)

    def normalize(self, A):
        """Normalize adjacency matrix."""
    ❷ node_degrees = torch.sum(A, dim=1)
    ❸ inv_sqrt_node_degrees = node_degrees.pow(-0.5)
    ❹ inv_sqrt_node_degrees[inv_sqrt_node_degrees == float("inf")] = 0
    ❺ diag_matrix = torch.diag(inv_sqrt_node_degrees)
    ❻ return torch.matmul(torch.matmul(diag_matrix, A), diag_matrix)

    def forward(self, A, node_attr):
        """Transform, propagate, and update the node attributes."""
        A = self.normalize(self.add_self_loops(A))
        --snip--
```

Listing 11-7: The class to improve the graph convolution (by modifying Listing 11-6)

This code adds the add_self_loops() and normalize() methods to the GCL class. The add_self_loops() method adds self-loops to the adjacency matrix by adding the identity matrix ❶.

The normalize() method normalizes the adjacency matrix. This method calculates the degree of each node as the sum of its connections ❷. Then the method scales each degree by its reciprocal square root ❸ and replaces infinite values with 0 ❹, ensuring stable computation. Afterward, the method constructs a diagonal degree matrix with the reciprocal square roots of the degrees ❺. Finally, it applies symmetric normalization to the adjacency matrix by multiplying it by the degree matrix on both sides ❻, balancing the influence of each node's attributes during the aggregation step.

The forward pass applies the add_self_loops() and normalize() methods to the adjacency matrix before propagating the transformed attributes.

Representing a Molecule as a Graph

In the rest of this section, you'll apply the graph convolution layer you've implemented to predict properties of molecules based on their structure.

Before doing this, you need to represent the arrangement of atoms in a molecule as a graph. Figure 11-2 demonstrates how to do so.

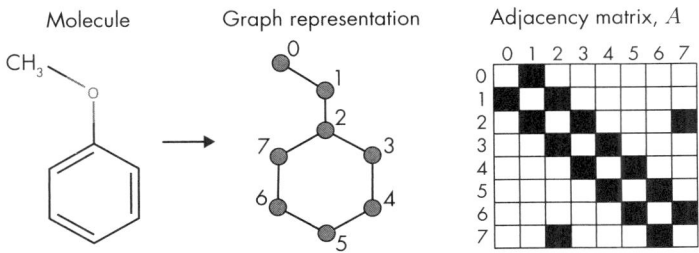

Figure 11-2: A molecule (left), its corresponding graph (middle), and its adjacency matrix (right)

The diagram on the left represents the chemical structure of the molecule toluene with an added methoxy group, a methyl group (CH_3) attached to an oxygen atom. The presence of this methoxy group makes this compound a methoxybenzene, commonly known as an *anisole*. This organic compound has a sweet smell and is often found in natural and artificial fragrances.

The middle diagram abstracts the molecular structure into a graph representation, with the nodes representing the atoms and the edges representing the chemical bonds between them. The diagram on the right converts this graph into an adjacency matrix, A, where each entry A_{ij} is set to 1 if a link exists between nodes i and j, and 0 otherwise.

Using the ZINC Dataset

The ZINC dataset is a collection of molecular graphs. The dataset provides a crucial resource for computational chemistry, especially in fields like drug discovery. Your goal with this dataset will be to predict a molecule's *penalized water-octanol partition coefficient*, commonly abbreviated as *logP*. The logP value measures a molecule's lipophilicity, which indicates the solubility of the molecule in fat as compared to water.

This coefficient is important in drug discovery since it impacts a drug's absorption, distribution, metabolic interactions, and excretion properties. Compounds with optimal logP values are more likely to pass through cell membranes, making them potentially effective as pharmaceuticals. Therefore, accurately predicting this measure can streamline the process of identifying new drug candidates by highlighting molecules with desirable logP values.

Downloading the ZINC Dataset

Start by downloading the dataset, using Listing 11-8.

```
from torch_geometric.datasets import ZINC

train_set = ZINC(root="ZINC_dataset/", subset=True, split="train")
```

```
val_set = ZINC(root="ZINC_dataset/", subset=True, split="val")
test_set = ZINC(root="ZINC_dataset/", subset=True, split="test")
```

Listing 11-8: Downloading the ZINC dataset

This code automatically downloads and prepares the data by splitting it into groups for training (10,000 molecules), validation (1,000 molecules), and testing (1,000 molecules).

Visualizing the ZINC Dataset

In the ZINC dataset, each molecule is represented as a graph, with nodes and edges describing atoms and chemical bonds, respectively. The plot_molecule() function in Listing 11-9 displays a molecule's structure by visualizing its adjacency matrix.

```
import matplotlib.pyplot as plt
from matplotlib import colormaps
from torch_geometric.utils import to_dense_adj

def plot_molecule(molecule):
    """Plot adjacency matrix of a molecule."""
❶  node_attr = molecule["x"].numpy().squeeze()  # Atom type numbers
❷  A = to_dense_adj(molecule["edge_index"]).numpy().squeeze(0)
❸  logP = molecule["y"].item()

❹  plt.matshow(A, cmap=colormaps["gray"].reversed())
    plt.title(f"LogP={np.round(logP, 2)}", fontsize=24)
    plt.xlabel("Atom type", fontsize=16)
    plt.xticks(np.arange(len(node_attr)), node_attr, fontsize=12)
    plt.ylabel("Atom type", fontsize=16)
    plt.yticks(np.arange(len(node_attr)), node_attr, fontsize=12)
    ax = plt.gca()
    ax.xaxis.set_ticks_position("bottom")
    plt.show()
```

Listing 11-9: The function to plot the adjacency matrix of a molecule

This function takes the graph representation of a molecule as input, which contains node attributes as a list of numbers corresponding to the atom types (molecule["x"]), edge connectivity as a list of paired indices corresponding to the nodes connected by an edge (molecule["edge_index"]), and a target property (molecule["y"]), which in this case is a scalar with the logP. Within this function, the list of atoms is converted into a NumPy array ❶. The adjacency matrix A is computed from the edge connectivity tensor ❷. Finally, the logP is taken from the target property ❸.

Next, the function plots the adjacency matrix ❹. The presence of an edge is colored in black, while the other cells are left white. The atom type number is displayed in every row and column.

You can visualize the structure of three example molecules from the training dataset:

```
for molecule_index in [2, 1235, 9887]:
    plot_molecule(molecule=train_set[molecule_index])
```

Figure 11-3 shows the resulting plots.

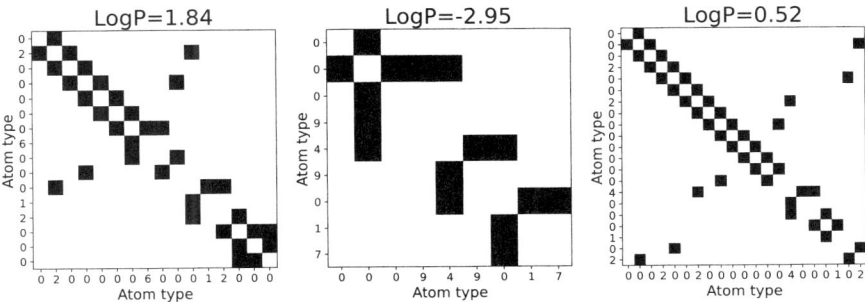

Figure 11-3: Examples of adjacency matrices representing molecules in the ZINC dataset

These adjacency matrices represent three molecules in the ZINC dataset; the numbers correspond to the atom types making up each molecule. The ZINC dataset has 28 atom types, numbered from 0 to 27 (see Table 11-1).

Table 11-1: Atom Types and Corresponding Numbers

Number	Atom type
0	Carbon (C)
1	Oxygen (O)
2	Nitrogen (N)
3	Fluorine (F)
4	Carbon atom with a single hydrogen (CH_1)
5	Sulfur (S)
6	Chlorine (Cl)
7	Oxygen atom with a negative charge (O^-)
8	Nitrogen atom with a single hydrogen and a positive charge (NH_1^+)
9	Bromine (Br)
10	Nitrogen atom with three hydrogens and a positive charge (NH_3^+)
11	Nitrogen atom with two hydrogens and a positive charge (NH_2^+)
12	Positively charged nitrogen (N^+)
13	Negatively charged nitrogen (N^-)
14	Negatively charged sulfur (S^-)
15	Iodine (I)
16	Phosphorus (P)
17	Oxygen atom with a single hydrogen and a positive charge (OH_1^+)
18	Nitrogen atom with a single hydrogen and a negative charge (NH_1^-)
19	Positively charged oxygen (O^+)

(continued)

Table 11-1: Atom Types and Corresponding Numbers *(continued)*

Number	Atom type
20	Positively charged sulfur (S^+)
21	Phosphorus with a single hydrogen (PH_1)
22	Phosphorus with two hydrogens (PH_2)
23	Carbon atom with two hydrogens and a negative charge (CH_2^-)
24	Positively charged phosphorus (P^+)
25	Sulfur with a single hydrogen and a positive charge (SH_1^+)
26	Carbon atom with a single hydrogen and a negative charge (CH_1^-)
27	Phosphorus with a single hydrogen and a positive charge (PH_1^+)

Notice that the graphs in Figure 11-3 have different numbers of nodes because the molecules they represent have different numbers of atoms.

Applying a Graph Convolutional Network

In its simplest form, a graph convolutional network consists of a series of graph convolution layers. You can implement this network with the GCN class in Listing 11-10.

```
class GCN(dl.DeeplayModule):
    """Graph convolutional network."""
    def __init__(self, in_feats, hidden_feats, out_feats):
        """Initialize graph convolutional network."""
        super().__init__()
        self.blocks = dl.LayerList()
        for f_in, f_out in zip([in_feats, *hidden_feats],
                               [*hidden_feats, out_feats]):
        ❶ self.blocks.append(GCL(in_feats=f_in, out_feats=f_out))

    def forward(self, G):
        """Apply graph convolution layers to update node attributes."""
        for block in self.blocks:
        ❷ G["node_attr"] = block(G["A"], G["node_attr"])
        return G["node_attr"]
```

Listing 11-10: The class to implement a graph convolutional network

This class defines the model architecture as a stack of graph convolution layers ❶. Its forward() method takes a graph, G, as input. This graph's node attributes are passed through each graph convolution layer in the list, where the output of each layer serves as the input to the next ❷. Finally, the method returns the node attributes calculated by the last layer.

Getting Properties from Node Attributes

This simple graph convolutional network needs three additional components to be able to predict molecular properties. First, in the ZINC dataset, nodes representing atom types are encoded as categorical attributes (integers).

To process such attributes, you need to use an embedding layer, which acts as a lookup table that converts each atom type into a continuous vector representation.

Second, while the current model outputs attributes for each node, the ultimate goal is to predict a global property for the entire molecule (the logP value). To accomplish this, you need to combine the attributes of all nodes into a single representation of the entire graph. This can be done using *global average pooling*, which involves computing the mean of all node attributes.

Third, to perform the regression task, a dense top should be added to map the graph-level representation to a single output value, the predicted logP.

You can add these components to the model with Listing 11-11.

```
class GCN(dl.DeeplayModule):
    --snip--
    def __init__(self, num_atoms, embed_dim, hidden_feats, out_feats):
        """Initialize graph convolutional network."""
        super().__init__()
      ❶ self.node_embed = dl.Layer(torch.nn.Embedding, num_atoms, embed_dim)
        self.blocks = LayerList()
        for f_in, f_out in zip([embed_dim, *hidden_feats[:-1]],
                               hidden_feats):
            self.blocks.append(GCL(in_feats=f_in, out_feats=f_out))
      ❷ self.dense_top = dl.Sequential(
            dl.Layer(torch.nn.Linear, hidden_feats[-1], hidden_feats[-1] // 4),
            dl.Layer(torch.nn.ReLU),
            dl.Layer(torch.nn.Linear, hidden_feats[-1] // 4, out_feats),
        )

    def forward(self, G):
        """Predict graph properties."""
      ❸ G["node_attr"] = self.node_embed(G["node_attr"])
        for block in self.blocks:
            G["node_attr"] = block(G["A"], G["node_attr"])
      ❹ pooled_graph_attr = torch.mean(G["node_attr"], dim=0)
      ❺ return self.dense_top(pooled_graph_attr).squeeze()  # LogP
```

Listing 11-11: The class to implement a graph convolutional network including an embedding layer, global average pooling, and dense top (by modifying Listing 11-10)

This code modifies the GCN class to include an embedding layer, a global average pooling, and a dense top. The initialization method includes two new parameters: the number of atom types (num_atoms) and the number of embedding dimensions (embed_dim). These parameters are used to initialize the embedding layer ❶, which is applied to the list of atoms before passing the node attributes through the graph convolution layers ❸.

The global average pooling operation is added to the forward method to aggregate the node attributes into a single graph-level representation ❹.

This is achieved by computing the mean of the node attributes across the graph.

The dense top is defined as a sequential model comprising two linear layers with a ReLU activation function between them ❷. The first linear layer maps the graph-level representation to a hidden layer, while the second linear layer maps the hidden layer to the output value. This dense top takes the pooled node attributes as input to predict the output ❺, which in this case will be the logP.

Adding Batch Processing

You can now complete the model by enabling batch processing to improve the efficiency and scalability of the training process. To do this, modify the GCN class, as shown in Listing 11-12.

```
class GCN(dl.DeeplayModule):
    --snip--
    def forward(self, G):
        --snip--
        for block in self.blocks:
            G["node_attr"] = block(G["A"], G["node_attr"])

        num_graphs = torch.max(G["graph_ids"]) + 1
❶      pooled_graph_attr = torch.zeros(
            num_graphs, G["node_attr"].shape[1], device=G["node_attr"].device,
        )
❷      pooled_graph_attr = pooled_graph_attr.scatter_add(
            0, G["graph_ids"][:, None].expand_as(G["node_attr"]),
            G["node_attr"],
        )
        node_counts = torch.bincount(G["graph_ids"])
❸      pooled_graph_attr = pooled_graph_attr / node_counts[:, None]

        return self.dense_top(pcoled_graph_attr).squeeze()  # LogP
```

Listing 11-12: The class to implement a graph convolutional network with batch processing (by modifying Listing 11-11)

This code updates the forward() method to accept a batched graph G as input. Since different graphs can have different numbers of nodes, G["node_attr"] stores the node attributes of all graphs in a single tensor of a shape equal to the total number of nodes by the number of node attributes. Similarly, G["A"] stores all the adjacency matrices of the graphs as a block-diagonal matrix with a shape equal to the total number of nodes squared, with each block corresponding to the adjacency matrix of a single graph in the batch. Finally, G["graph_ids"] is a tensor of a shape equal to the total number of nodes that stores the graph indices of each node.

In the forward() method, the entire batch is passed into the embedding layer, graph convolution layers, global average pooling, and dense top. These operations are exactly the same as before. However, after the batch is fed through the graph convolution layers, the node attributes are aggregated to form a graph-level representation for each graph rather than the whole batch.

To achieve this, the updated method replaces the global average pooling with a new approach. First, the code initializes the pooled_graph_attr tensor to hold the aggregated node attributes for each graph with a shape equal to the number of graphs by the number of node features ❶. Then the code sums the node attributes belonging to the same graph to get aggregated attributes for each graph ❷, applying the scatter_add() function along the batch dimension, using the graph indices. Next, the code normalizes the aggregated attributes by the number of nodes in each graph to compute the mean node attributes per graph ❸, by dividing the aggregated node features by the node counts for each graph. Finally, the code returns the predicted logP values by passing the aggregated node features through the dense-top layers.

Instantiating the Graph Convolutional Network Model

Now that you've added batch processing, you can instantiate the model with Listing 11-13.

```
gcn_model = GCN(
    num_atoms=28, embed_dim=64, hidden_feats=[64,] * 4, out_feats=1,
).create()
```

Listing 11-13: Instantiating the graph convolutional network

This code creates a graph convolutional network. The number of node embeddings is set to 28, corresponding to the number of atom types in the ZINC dataset. You can print the model with print(gcn_model) to check the details of its architecture.

Training the Graph Convolutional Network

After instantiating the model, you'll define the data loaders, compile the graph convolutional network, and train it.

First, specify the data loaders with Listing 11-14.

```
from torch_geometric.loader import DataLoader

train_loader = DataLoader(dataset=train_set, batch_size=32, shuffle=True)
val_loader = DataLoader(dataset=val_set, batch_size=32, shuffle=False)
test_loader = DataLoader(dataset=test_set, batch_size=32, shuffle=False)
```

Listing 11-14: Defining the data loaders

This code initializes the data loaders to train, validate, and test the neural network by defining how the dataset is split into manageable batches. The training loader shuffles the batches to ensure that the model sees the data in a different order each epoch, promoting better generalization. In contrast, the validation and test loaders don't shuffle, maintaining a consistent order to accurately evaluate performance.

Next, implement the `MolecularRegressor` class that will train and evaluate the model, as shown in Listing 11-15.

```
class MolecularRegressor(dl.Regressor):
    """Regressor model for molecular property prediction."""

    def __init__(self, model, **kwargs):
        """Initialize molecular regressor."""
        super().__init__(model, **kwargs)

    def batch_preprocess(self, G):
        """Preprocess the graph batch for model input."""
        G["node_attr"] = G["x"].squeeze()
        G["A"] = to_dense_adj(G["edge_index"]).squeeze(0)
        G["graph_ids"] = G["batch"]
        return G.to(self.device)

    def forward(self, G):
        """Calculate model output for input graph batch."""
        return self.model(self.batch_preprocess(G))
```

Listing 11-15: The class to compile, train, and evaluate the graph convolutional network

This class handles the batch processing, training, and evaluation loops. The `batch_preprocess()` method prepares the input to the model. The method receives a batch of graphs as inputs (G). It saves the node attributes as G["node _attr"] after squeezing the G("x") tensor to eliminate any singleton dimensions, ensuring that its shape matches the model requirements. Then the method calculates and saves the adjacency matrix (G["A"]) from the edge index (G["edge_index"]). Finally, the method assigns the graph indices to G["graph_ids"] via G["batch"], which indicates the graph that each node belongs to in the batch.

Next, create this class and train the model with Listing 11-16.

```
import os
from lightning.pytorch.callbacks import ModelCheckpoint

gcn = MolecularRegressor(
    gcn_model, loss=torch.nn.L1Loss(), optimizer=dl.Adam(lr=1e-3),
).create()
❶ checkpoint_callback = ModelCheckpoint(
    monitor="val_loss", dirpath=os.path.join("models", "gcn"),
    filename="ZINC-{epoch:02d}-{val_loss:.2f}", auto_insert_metric_name=False,
)
trainer = dl.Trainer(max_epochs=400, callbacks=[checkpoint_callback])
trainer.fit(gcn, train_loader, val_loader)
```

Listing 11-16: Training the graph convolutional network

This code initializes the model with an MAE loss function and Adam optimizer. Then the code instantiates the trainer and starts training.

In addition, the code creates a checkpoint callback to save the best model during training ❶. This callback monitors the validation loss and saves the model with the lowest loss in the `dirpath` directory. The filename includes the epoch and the validation loss for ease of identification.

Evaluating the Graph Convolutional Network

After you've trained the model and saved its weights, you can evaluate it on the test set by loading the best model with Listing 11-17.

```
import glob

model_paths = glob.glob(os.path.join("models", "gcn", "ZINC-*.ckpt"))
best_model_path = sorted(model_paths, key=os.path.getmtime)[-1]
gcn_best = MolecularRegressor.load_from_checkpoint(best_model_path,
                                                   model=gcn_model)

test_results = trainer.test(gcn_best, test_loader)
```

Listing 11-17: Evaluating the performance of the trained graph convolutional network

This code first identifies the best model checkpoint in the directory by searching for files that match the pattern `"ZINC-*.ckpt"` and sorting them by their modification time to find the latest one. The code then loads the model into a new instance of the `MolecularRegressor` class (`gcn_best`), using the same MAE loss function employed during training. Finally, the code evaluates the model's performance on the test set and returns the MAE.

You should expect an MAE of around 0.46 on the test data. While this is a strong result for the model as currently configured, you could improve it by tweaking parameters such as the learning rate or the number of epochs, or by experimenting with different model architectures.

EXERCISE

11-5: Use your trained model to predict the logP values on the test set and plot those values against the actual ones by using a heatmap. What does the resulting plot indicate about your model's performance?

Predicting Molecular Properties with Message Passing

When dealing with graphs, valuable information is found not only in the nodes but also in the edges. This information, known as *edge attributes* (or *edge features*), is crucial for capturing relationships between nodes in the graph. For example, in molecular graphs, edge attributes can represent the type of chemical bond between atoms. This information is essential for understanding the molecule's structure and properties. In the ZINC dataset, the edge attributes correspond to the number of bonds between atoms. These attributes are encoded as categorical attributes, which can be single, double, or triple. Unsurprisingly, the number of bonds is represented by the value 1, 2, or 3.

Unfortunately, the graph convolution layers in the previous sections can't process edge attributes. To learn from both node and edge attributes, you need a model that uses message-passing layers, which you'll explore in this section.

Implementing a Message-Passing Layer

Like graph convolution layers, *message-passing layers* consist of three main steps: transform, propagate, and update. Indeed, graph convolution layers can be viewed as a special case of message-passing layers. Message-passing layers tailor these three steps to incorporate edge attributes, equipping the model to integrate insights from both nodes and edges.

Importantly, the message-passing layers you'll use in this section will store edge information in the form of an edge index instead of an adjacency matrix. An *edge index* is a tensor that consists of two rows. The first row contains the source nodes of each edge, and the second row contains the target nodes of each edge. Accordingly, each column represents an edge, and the total number of columns equals the number of edges in the graph. For example, the graph in Figure 11-1 would have the following edge index:

```
[[0, 1, 2, 3, 4],
 [1, 2, 3, 4, 0]]
```

Although edge indices and adjacency matrices represent the same information, the edge-based representation is best for message-passing layers because it makes accessing graph edges more intuitive.

Transforming Attributes into Messages

As the first major operation in the layer, the transform step merges the node and edge attributes into a single, unified attribute vector called a *message*. A *message* is a representation that encodes information about the interaction between two connected nodes. This representation contains the attributes of the source node where the message originates, the attributes of the target node that receives the source node's message, and the attributes of the edge that transmits the message from the source to a target.

You can implement this via the TransformLayer class in Listing 11-18.

```
class TransformLayer(torch.nn.Module):
    """Transform layer."""

    def __init__(self, hidden_feats):
        """Initialize the transform layer."""
        super().__init__()
        self.linear = torch.nn.LazyLinear(hidden_feats)
        self.activation = torch.nn.ReLU()
```

```
def forward(self, G):
    """Compute messages by transforming node and edge attributes."""
    src_node_attr = G["node_attr"][G["edge_index"][0]]
    tgt_node_attr = G["node_attr"][G["edge_index"][1]]
    edge_attr = G["edge_attr"]

    msg = torch.cat([src_node_attr, tgt_node_attr, edge_attr], dim=-1)
 ❶  G["msg"] = self.activation(self.linear(msg))
    return G
```

Listing 11-18: The class to implement a layer to perform the transform step

The forward() method computes the messages by concatenating the source and target nodes' attributes with the connecting edge attributes and passing the result through a learnable function. In this case, the concatenated vector is fed into a linear layer, followed by a nonlinear activation function ❶.

Instead of an adjacency matrix, the code uses G["edge_index"] to represent graph connectivity.

Propagating Messages

After you compute the messages, the PropagateLayer class transmits them across the graph by aggregating the messages from neighboring nodes, as shown in Listing 11-19.

```
class PropagateLayer(torch.nn.Module):
    """Propagate layer."""

    def __init__(self, hidden_feats):
        """Initialize propagate layer."""
        super().__init__()
        self.hidden_feats = hidden_feats

    def forward(self, G):
        """Aggregate messages from neighboring nodes."""
        num_nodes = G["node_attr"].size(0)
 ❶      aggregated_msg = torch.zeros(num_nodes, self.hidden_feats,
                                     dtype=G["node_attr"].dtype,
                                     device=G["node_attr"].device)
 ❷      tgt_node_idxs = G["edge_index"][1].unsqueeze(1).expand_as(G["msg"])
 ❸      aggregated_msg = aggregated_msg.scatter_add(0, tgt_node_idxs, G["msg"])
        G["aggregated_msg"] = aggregated_msg
        return G
```

Listing 11-19: The class to implement a layer to perform the propagate step

This code creates the PropagateLayer class, which aggregates messages from neighboring nodes. The forward() method of this class starts by initializing a tensor to store the aggregated messages, adjusted to match the data type and device of the node attributes tensor ❶ to ensure that the tensor is compatible with the computation settings of the input graph data.

Next, the code prepares the target node indices within the edge index for each message ❷. This is done by unsqueezing and expanding the target node indices (G["edge_index"][1]) to match the shape of the messages (G["msg"]). This process positions the target node indices so that each aligns with its corresponding message, facilitating the directed aggregation of messages to their designated receivers in the graph.

Finally, the aggregation is performed via a scatter_add() operation, which adds the prepared messages to the initialized tensor at the positions specified by the expanded indices tensor ❸. This operation sums all messages directed to each node, updating the aggregate tensor with the aggregated message information from neighboring nodes.

Updating the Node Attributes

In the final update step, the aggregated messages are used to update the node attributes. Implement this with the UpdateLayer class in Listing 11-20.

```
class UpdateLayer(torch.nn.Module):
    """Update layer."""

    def __init__(self, hidden_feats):
        """Initialize update layer."""
        super().__init__()
        self.linear = torch.nn.LazyLinear(hidden_feats)
        self.activation = torch.nn.ReLU()

    def forward(self, G):
        """Update node attributes combining them with aggregated messages."""
        attr = torch.cat([G["node_attr"], G["aggregated_msg"]], dim=-1)
    ❶  G["node_attr"] = self.activation(self.linear(attr))
    ❷  G["edge_attr"] = G["msg"]
        return G
```

Listing 11-20: The class to implement a layer to perform the update step

This code concatenates the node attributes and aggregated messages. Then the code applies a linear layer and a nonlinear activation function to produce the final updated node attributes ❶.

The code also updates the edge attributes by using the messages as the edge attributes for the next iteration of message passing ❷.

Creating a Message-Passing Layer

Now that you've finished setting up these three main operations, you can create a simple message-passing layer with Listing 11-21.

```
mpl = dl.Sequential(
    dl.Layer(TransformLayer, hidden_feats=64),
    dl.Layer(PropagateLayer, hidden_feats=64),
    dl.Layer(UpdateLayer, hidden_feats=64),
).create()
```

Listing 11-21: Defining the message-passing layer

This layer is defined as a sequential layer that consists of the transform, propagate, and update operations. You can use `print(mpl)` to print out the details of its architecture.

Implementing a Message-Passing Network

Now that you've specified your message-passing layer, you'll construct a *message-passing network* by combining the classes from the previous sections. Then you'll train it to predict the logP values of molecules in the ZINC dataset.

The architecture of the message-passing network is similar to that of the graph convolutional network, except it is modified to incorporate edge attributes. You can implement the network as shown in Listing 11-22.

```
class MPN(dl.DeeplayModule):
    """Message-passing network."""

    def __init__(self, num_atoms, num_edge_embed, embed_dim, hidden_feats,
                 out_feats):
        """Initialize message-passing network."""
        super().__init__()
        self.node_embed = dl.Layer(torch.nn.Embedding, num_atoms, embed_dim)
    ❶   self.edge_embed = \
            dl.Layer(torch.nn.Embedding, num_edge_embed, embed_dim)
        self.blocks = dl.LayerList()
        for f_out in hidden_feats:
    ❷       mpl = dl.Sequential(
                dl.Layer(TransformLayer, hidden_feats=f_out),
                dl.Layer(PropagateLayer, hidden_feats=f_out),
                dl.Layer(UpdateLayer, hidden_feats=f_out),
            )
            self.blocks.append(mpl)
        --snip--

    def forward(self, G):
        """Predict graph properties."""
        G["node_attr"] = self.node_embed(G["node_attr"])
        G["edge_attr"] = self.edge_embed(G["edge_attr"])
        for block in self.blocks:
            G = block(G)
        --snip--
```

Listing 11-22: The class to implement a message-passing network (by modifying Listing 11-12)

This class uses an additional edge embedding layer to process the edge attributes ❶, converting each bond type into a continuous vector representation. Furthermore, the class uses message-passing layers instead of graph convolution layers to enable the model to learn from both node and edge attributes ❷. The network refines the node attributes by repeatedly aggregating information from neighboring nodes and edges, ultimately summarizing the entire graph's structure in a final graph-level representation. This representation is then passed through a dense top layer to produce the predicted logP value.

You can now instantiate this model with Listing 11-23.

```
mpn_model = MPN(
    num_atoms=28, num_edge_embed=4, embed_dim=64, hidden_feats=[64,] * 4,
    out_feats=1,
).create()
```

Listing 11-23: Instantiating the message-passing network

The number of node embeddings is set to the number of unique atom types in the ZINC dataset, and the number of edge embeddings is set to the various types of chemical bonds between atoms (absent, single, double, triple). You can use print(mpn_model) to see all details of this model.

Training and Evaluating the Message-Passing Network

Now use the MolecularRegressor class to train and evaluate the model for the message-passing network, as shown in Listing 11-24.

```
--snip--
mpn = MolecularRegressor(
    mpn_model, loss=torch.nn.L1Loss(), optimizer=dl.Adam(lr=1e-3),
).create()
checkpoint_callback = ModelCheckpoint(
    monitor="val_loss", dirpath=os.path.join("models", "mpn"), ...
)
trainer = dl.Trainer(max_epochs=400, callbacks=[checkpoint_callback])
trainer.fit(mpn, train_loader, val_loader)
```

Listing 11-24: Training the message-passing network (by modifying Listing 11-16)

After training, you can evaluate the best model via Listing 11-25.

```
model_paths = glob.glob(os.path.join("models", "mpn", "ZINC-*.ckpt"))
best_model_path = sorted(model_paths, key=os.path.getmtime)[-1]
mpn_best = MolecularRegressor.load_from_checkpoint(best_model_path,
                                                   model=mpn_model)
test_results = trainer.test(mpn_best, test_loader)
```

Listing 11-25: Evaluating the performance of the trained message-passing network (by modifying Listing 11-17)

You should expect an MAE of around 0.22. This result significantly improves that of the graph convolutional network, demonstrating the effectiveness of message-passing networks in capturing the structure of molecular graphs.

NOTE *Code Example 11-1, "Predicting Molecular Properties with Graph Neural Networks," is available at* https://github.com/DeepTrackAI/DeepLearningCrashCourse. *Navigate to the* Ch11_GNN *folder and then* ec11_1_gnn. *The* gnn.ipynb *notebook provides a complete code example to predict the properties of small molecules by using graph convolution layers with message passing.*

Project 11A: Simulating Complex Physical Phenomena

Realistic simulations of complex systems are crucial for science and engineering. Traditional approaches, such as molecular dynamics simulations, often attempt to brute-force calculate the interactions between every atom or particle in a system. Yet, these models typically come with high computational requirements, making them impractical for simulating large-scale systems or processes over long periods.

In this project, you'll implement a *graph network–based simulator,* a machine-learning framework designed to simulate complex systems learning from observations of the system dynamics. You'll work with the SAND dataset, which contains simulations of granular systems. You'll implement a graph neural network that uses message passing to update particle states and train the model to predict future particle positions and velocities. Finally, you'll simulate the system by using the trained model and visualize the results to see how well the model replicates complex physical phenomena.

Working with the SAND Dataset

You'll use the SAND dataset, which contains simulations of granular systems mimicking the complex frictional characteristics of sand. The dataset provides time-series data capturing the positions of particles over multiple time steps as they interact with one another within a simulated environment. Each simulation in the dataset represents a sequence of particle positions, with each particle's location recorded at discrete time intervals.

The SAND dataset is divided into three subsets: a training set consisting of 1,000 simulations, a validation set of 30 simulations, and a test set of 30 simulations. Each simulation is stored as a separate dataset entry, with the particle positions at each time step represented as a 3D array. The first two dimensions correspond to the number of particles and the number of time steps, respectively, while the third dimension represents the spatial coordinates $\mathbf{r} = (x, y)$ of each particle. This data structure allows you to track the movement and interactions of particles over time. These subsets are stored as *.npz* files.

You can use Listing 11-26 to load the data.

```
import os
from huggingface_hub import snapshot_download

if not os.path.exists("sand_dataset"):
    snapshot_download(repo_id="DeepTrackAI/Sand", local_dir="sand_dataset",
                      allow_patterns=["*.npz", "*.json"], repo_type="dataset")
```

Listing 11-26: Downloading the SAND data

This code downloads the SAND data into the *sand_dataset* local folder. Now load the training, validation, and test data with Listing 11-27.

```
import numpy as np

def load_npz_data(path):
    """Load NPZ data."""
    with np.load(path, allow_pickle=True) as data_file:
        data = [item for _, item in data_file.items()]
    return data

train_data = load_npz_data("sand_dataset/train.npz")
val_data = load_npz_data("sand_dataset/valid.npz")
test_data = load_npz_data("sand_dataset/test.npz")
```

Listing 11-27: Loading the SAND data

This code defines the load_npz_data() function to load the SAND datasets; then the function loads the training, validation, and testing sets.

Accompanying the dataset, the *metadata.json* file contains metadata extracted from the simulations. This includes information such as simulation durations and statistics like the average velocities and accelerations. These will serve as normalization parameters later in the project. Use Listing 11-28 to load the metadata.

```
import json

with open("sand_dataset/metadata.json", "r") as data_file:
    metadata = json.load(data_file)
```

Listing 11-28: Loading the SAND metadata

You can use print(json.dumps(metadata, indent=4)) to print the metadata.

After you've downloaded the dataset, you can visualize one of the simulations via Listing 11-29.

```
import matplotlib.pyplot as plt
from IPython.display import HTML
from matplotlib.animation import FuncAnimation

sample_id = np.random.randint(0, len(train_data))
r = train_data[sample_id][0]  # Particle positions

fig, ax = plt.subplots(figsize=(6, 6))
scatter = ax.scatter([], [], s=50, c="y", edgecolors="k", linewidth=0.5)
ax.set_xlim(0, 1); ax.set_xticks([]); ax.set_ylim(0, 1); ax.set_yticks([])

def update(frame):
    """Update frame."""
    scatter.set_offsets(r[frame])
    return [scatter]

ani = FuncAnimation(fig, update, frames=len(r), interval=10, blit=True)
video = HTML(ani.to_jshtml())
plt.close()
```

Listing 11-29: Visualizing a SAND simulation

This code animates the simulation. The code randomly selects sample_id within the range of train_data and gets the corresponding positions data (r). Then the code creates a scatterplot canvas with no data points plotted, setting the x-axis and y-axis to range from 0 to 1 and removing the ticks from both.

To create each frame of the animation, the code defines the update() function. It takes a frame parameter representing the frame number, updates the scatterplot based on the data for the current frame, and returns a list containing the scatterplot object.

The animation is created using the FuncAnimation class. This class takes the figure, the update function, the number of frames, and the interval between frames as input parameters. Setting blit=True improves rendering performance. The animation is then converted into JavaScript by the HTML class. You can display the animation by typing video.

Figure 11-4 shows some frames from this animation.

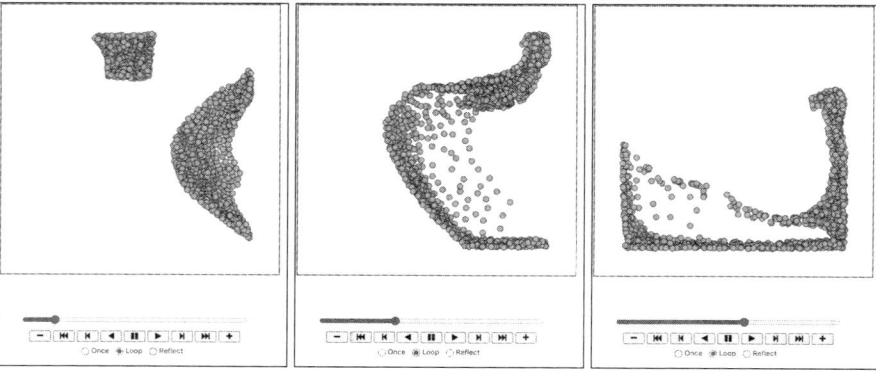

Figure 11-4: The SAND simulation illustrating the dynamics of granular particles over time

These frames illustrate the simulation's progression. The particles represent a granular material. The particles' positions change over time under the action of gravity, interaction forces, and boundaries.

Building a Graph Network–Based Simulator

A graph network–based simulator models physical phenomena through three steps. First, the model predicts the future accelerations of all particles. Next, it uses these predictions to update the velocities and positions of the particles through an *Euler integration scheme*, which is a simple numerical method for approximating the solutions of differential equations. Specifically, the model updates the position of each particle, incrementing it by its current velocity multiplied by the time step. Similarly, the model updates the velocity by adding the acceleration multiplied by the time step. Finally, the model uses the updated positions as input for the next prediction step, allowing the simulation to evolve over time.

This iterative process enables the graph network–based simulator to model complex systems accurately. Unlike traditional force-field simulations, which require calculating every interaction and frictional force between particles (a process that is computationally expensive), the graph network–based simulator approximates these dynamics by using learned relationships between particles, significantly reducing the computational burden while still capturing the essential system behavior.

Predicting Physical States from Graphs

To accomplish this goal, the graph network–based simulator uses a graph neural network to model and simulate the physical states of a system by representing it as an interconnected graph of particles. In this graph, nodes represent particles, and edges describe the interactions between particles within a specified distance threshold.

The simulator makes its predictions via three main steps:

1. *Constructing the graph* to represent the physical system
2. *Passing messages* between nodes, through the edges, to update the particles' states and then aggregating and propagating messages through multiple layers of the graph network
3. *Getting dynamics information* of the system by using the updated states from the final layer of the graph network to provide insights into the system's evolution over time

Defining the Message-Passing Model

The graph network–based simulator updates the graph representation through message passing. You can define a message-passing model with Listing 11-30.

```
import deeplay as dl

model = dl.GraphToNodeMPM(hidden_features=[64,] * 9, out_features=2)
```

Listing 11-30: Implementing the message-passing model

This code instantiates a model with an encoder, a message-passing backbone processor, and a decoder. Consisting of two dense neural networks, the encoder initially transforms the node and edge attributes to high-level representations. Next, the message-passing backbone iteratively updates these attributes, employing nine message-passing layers, each with a latent dimension of 64. Finally, the decoder uses the updated node attributes to predict the system's dynamic attributes—namely, the 2D accelerations for each particle.

Additionally, the graph network–based simulator will modify the standard message-passing approach by incorporating skip connections between the input and updated attributes so that the input attributes skip some of the layers in the network and are fed into later layers. This modification helps the model retain input attribute information, facilitating deeper and more stable information propagation. You can implement this with Listing 11-31.

```
import torch

rmp_backbone = dl.ResidualMessagePassingNeuralNetwork(
    hidden_features=model.backbone.hidden_features,
    out_features=model.backbone.out_features, out_activation=torch.nn.ReLU,
)
model.replace("backbone", rmp_backbone)
model.build()
```

Listing 11-31: Incorporating skip connections in the message-passing layer

This code creates a residual message-passing backbone (rmp_backbone) by configuring it with parameters inherited from model. In particular, the hidden and output attributes as well as the ReLU activation function for the output layer should all match their counterparts in model. With these specifications in place, the code replaces the existing backbone of model with rmp_backbone and creates the model.

You can now print and verify the model summary with print(model).

Building the Dataset

To effectively train the graph network–based simulator, you must construct a dataset that captures the temporal dynamics of the system. The SAND simulation dataset records the positions of particles at different time steps. You'll use this sequential data to calculate ground-truth values for key physical properties such as velocity and acceleration.

Creating the Graph

First, you need to create the graph to represent this system, defining the attributes of its nodes, the edge index describing the adjacency matrix, and the attributes of the edges. The node attributes include a sequence of some of the particles' previous velocities and their relative distances to the simulation boundaries. The edge index includes the edges between particles within a specified distance threshold. The edge attributes capture the relative positional displacement between connected particles and the magnitude of these displacements.

First, implement the compute_node_attr() function to compute the node attributes, as shown in Listing 11-32.

```
def compute_node_attr(r_next, r, n_std, metadata=metadata):
    """Compute node attributes."""
    v = np.diff(r, axis=1)  # Velocities
    v_mean = np.array(metadata["vel_mean"])
    v_std = np.array(metadata["vel_std"])
    v = (v - v_mean) / (v_std ** 2 + n_std ** 2) ** 0.5
    v = v.reshape(r_next.shape[0], -1)

    boundaries = np.array(metadata["bounds"])
    distance_to_lower_bound = r_next - boundaries[:, 0][None]
    distance_to_upper_bound = boundaries[:, 1][None] - r_next
    distance_to_bounds = np.concatenate(
        [distance_to_lower_bound, distance_to_upper_bound], axis=-1,
    )
    norm_distance_to_bounds = np.clip(
        distance_to_bounds / metadata["default_connectivity_radius"], -1, 1,
    )

    return np.concatenate([v, norm_distance_to_bounds], axis=-1)
```

Listing 11-32: The function to compute the node attributes

This function generates the attributes for each node in the graph. The function starts by calculating the velocities between consecutive frames. Then it normalizes the velocities by subtracting the mean velocity and dividing the result by the velocity standard deviation from the metadata plus the noise standard deviation. Next, the function reshapes the normalized velocities into a single attribute vector for each particle.

Additionally, the function computes the distance of each particle to the simulation boundaries and normalizes these distances relative to the connectivity radius so that they fall within a range of −1 to 1. Ultimately, the function returns a concatenation of the normalized velocities and the normalized distances to the boundaries in the form of node attributes, comprehensively representing each particle's state and environment.

Next, you'll create the compute_connectivity() function to compute the edge index and edge attributes, shown in Listing 11-33.

```
def compute_connectivity(r, metadata=metadata):
    """Compute graph connectivity from particle positions and radii."""
    Dr = r[:, None, :] - r[None, :, :]  # Displacements
    D = np.linalg.norm(Dr, axis=-1)  # Distance matrix
    radius = metadata["default_connectivity_radius"]
    mask = D < radius
    np.fill_diagonal(mask, False)  # Eliminate self-connections
    edge_index = np.argwhere(mask).T
    edge_attr = np.concatenate([Dr[mask], D[mask][:, None]], axis=-1) / radius
    return edge_index, edge_attr
```

Listing 11-33: The function to compute graph connectivity and edge attributes

This function determines the connectivity between particles based on their positions and a radius specified in the metadata. The function computes the displacement vectors between all pairs of particles (Dr) and then calculates their Euclidean distance matrix (D). Next, the function creates a Boolean mask to identify pairs of connected particles within the specified radius before excluding self-connections by setting the diagonal to False. Finally, the function returns the edge index of the connected particle pairs (edge_index) and a concatenated array of their corresponding attributes (edge_attr), including the normalized displacement vectors and distances. These operations define the edges in the graph, indicating which particles influence each other.

Finally, you can implement the compute_graph() function, as shown in Listing 11-34.

```
def compute_graph(r, n_std):
    """Compute the graph representation for the positions."""
    r_next = r[:, -1]
    node_attr = compute_node_attr(r_next, r, n_std)
    edge_index, edge_attr = compute_connectivity(r_next)
    return node_attr, edge_index, edge_attr
```

Listing 11-34: The function to compute the graph representation for the windowed positions

This function constructs the graph representation from a window of particle positions. The function begins by getting the current positions of the particles from the last frame of the position window (r_next). Using r_next, the function determines which particles have edges between them based on their proximity and then creates an edge index through the compute _connectivity() function (Listing 11-33). The function computes the node attributes from the noisy windowed positions via the compute_node_attr() function (Listing 11-32)—specifically, the normalized particle velocities and distances to the boundaries. Finally, the function returns the node attributes (node_attr), the connectivity information (edge_index), and the edge attributes (edge_attr) necessary to construct the graph network.

Setting Up the Dataset Class

To begin, use Listing 11-35 to create a dataset class that will prepare the inputs and outputs required during training.

```
class ParticleDataset(torch.utils.data.Dataset):
    """Dataset for particle simulations."""

    def __init__(self, data, metadata, Dt, n_std):
        """Initialize dataset."""
        super().__init__()
        self.data, self.metadata, self.Dt, self.n_std, self.traj_length = \
            data, metadata, Dt, n_std, len(data[0][0])
```

Listing 11-35: The class to manage the dataset with particle simulations including only its constructor

The class constructor initializes the dataset with the provided data and metadata, the size of the time window for cropping trajectory sections (Dt), and the standard deviation of the noise for data augmentation (n_std). The class then extracts the trajectory length (traj_length), which is 320 for all trajectories in the SAND dataset.

You'll now add the necessary supporting methods one by one, starting with the get_r() method shown in Listing 11-36.

```
class ParticleDataset(torch.utils.data.Dataset):
    --snip--
    def get_r(self, i):
        """Get a position window."""
        sample_id, r_start = divmod(i, self.traj_length - self.Dt)
        r = self.data[sample_id][0].copy()
        r_window = np.transpose(r[r_start:r_start + self.Dt], (1, 0, 2))
        r_next = r[r_start + self.Dt]
        return r_window, r_next
```

Listing 11-36: The method to get the windowed positions (by modifying Listing 11-35)

For a given index i, the get_r() method gets a sequential segment of particle positions within a specified time window (called *windowed positions*), along with a label containing their subsequent positions from the dataset. The method first identifies the sample (`sample_id`) and starting position (`r_start`) corresponding to i. Next, the method gets an array of particle positions for this window before transposing it so that the data is in the correct shape for future steps (`r_window`). Finally, the method gets the subsequent particle positions (`r_next`) to serve as the ground truth for the next time step in the simulation.

Next, add the `noise()` method as shown in Listing 11-37.

```
class ParticleDataset(torch.utils.data.Dataset):
    --snip--
    def noise(self, r_window, n_std):
        """Generate random walk noise to be added to a position window."""
        v = np.diff(r_window, axis=1)
        v_noise = (np.random.randn(*list(v.shape)) * n_std / v.shape[1] ** 0.5)
❶       noise = np.concatenate([
            np.zeros_like(v_noise[:, 0:1]), np.cumsum(v_noise, axis=1),
        ], axis=1)
        return noise
```

Listing 11-37: The method to generate random walk noise (by modifying Listing 11-36)

This method generates random walk noise to simulate more-realistic particle trajectories during training. The method starts by calculating the velocities (v) from the differences between consecutive windowed positions. These velocities represent the movement of particles between time steps. Next, the method generates noise for each velocity (v_noise) by multiplying random numbers by the noise standard deviation over the inverse square root of the number of velocity segments. This scaling ensures that the noise magnitude is inversely proportional to the length of the time window, keeping the overall noise level consistent across windows of varying lengths.

Finally, the method concatenates this velocity noise with an initial 0 value ❶. This value ensures that the first position in the sequence remains unchanged, meaning that no displacement occurs at the start of the window. The cumulative sum of the noise is then calculated, which results in the random walk pattern. By simulating the natural stochastic movements in particle systems, this approach makes the model more robust to noisy inputs and better suited for real-world variability.

You can now complete the `ParticleDataset` by adding the required `__len__()` and `__getitem__()` methods, as shown in Listing 11-38.

```
from torch_geometric.data import Data

class ParticleDataset(torch.utils.data.Dataset):
    --snip--
    def __len__(self):
        """Return the total number of position windows in the dataset."""
        return len(self.data) * (self.traj_length - self.Dt)
```

```
        def __getitem__(self, i):
            """Get a position window from the dataset."""
            r_window, r_next = self.get_r(i)

            noise = self.noise(r_window, self.n_std)
    ❶     r_window, r_next = r_window + noise, r_next + noise[:, -1]

            v_current = r_window[:, -1] - r_window[:, -2]
            v_next = r_next - r_window[:, -1]

    ❷     a = v_next - v_current    # Acceleration
            a_mean = np.array(self.metadata["acc_mean"])
            a_std = np.array(self.metadata["acc_std"])
            a = (a - a_mean) / (a_std ** 2 + self.n_std ** 2) ** 0.5

            node_attr, edge_index, edge_attr = compute_graph(r_window, self.n_std)

            return Data(x=torch.tensor(node_attr, dtype=torch.float32),
                        edge_index=torch.tensor(edge_index, dtype=torch.long),
                        edge_attr=torch.tensor(edge_attr, dtype=torch.float32),
                        y=torch.tensor(a, dtype=torch.float32))
```

Listing 11-38: The complete class for managing the SAND dataset (by modifying Listing 11-37)

This completes the class for managing the SAND dataset. The __len__() method returns the length of the dataset—that is, the total number of position windows, given by the number of simulations (len(self.data) multiplied by the length of each trajectory (traj_length) minus the length of the cropping window (Dt). For the training dataset, this corresponds to 1,000 times 314 position windows when the window length is 6.

The __get_item__() method starts by cropping a trajectory section of the specified time window size via the get_r() method (Listing 11-36). This cropping ensures that each sample represents a sequential segment of the trajectory, which is crucial for learning temporal patterns. By focusing on short trajectories, the model can more easily identify immediate cause-and-effect relationships between particle positions, velocities, and accelerations. Additionally, the get_r() method provides the target particle positions of the next time step after the window (r_next) so that you can compute ground-truth accelerations.

To minimize the accumulation of errors during prediction, especially when iteratively forecasting future particle positions, the code makes the model robust to noisy inputs. The noise() method (Listing 11-37) generated the random-walk noise to corrupt the input velocities. After calling this method, the __getitem__() method adds this noise to the positions in the trajectory section and to the next position ❶.

Next, the method calculates the current velocity (v_current) and the next velocity (v_next). Then the method computes target accelerations of particles by calculating the difference between next and current velocities ❷. For training stability, the target accelerations are normalized by using average acceleration statistics from the metadata and the noise standard deviation.

Finally, the method constructs the input graph from the noisy cropped trajectory via the `compute_graph()` function (Listing 11-34). The method returns a dictionary containing the node attributes (`node_attr`), edge information (`edge_index`), edge attributes (`edge_attr`), and target accelerations (`a`).

Initializing the Datasets

Now that you've created the `ParticleDataset` class, use it to initialize the dataset, as shown in Listing 11-39.

```
Dt, n_std = 6, 3e-4

train_set = ParticleDataset(train_data, metadata, Dt, n_std)
val_set = ParticleDataset(val_data, metadata, Dt, n_std)
test_set = ParticleDataset(test_data, metadata, Dt, n_std)
```

Listing 11-39: Initializing the training, validation, and test datasets

This code sets the window size to 6 to include the current time step and the preceding five time steps and sets the noise standard deviation to 3e-4. The choice of these parameters can affect the type and precision of the dynamics that can be learned. In particular, the window size determines how far back in time the model sees the system's state, which can be critical for capturing longer-range temporal dependencies. Similarly, the noise standard deviation sets the magnitude of the data augmentation noise added to the states.

The datasets are initialized with the training, validation, and test data, along with the metadata.

Configuring the Data Loaders

Define the data loaders by using Listing 11-40.

```
from torch_geometric.loader import DataLoader

train_loader, val_loader, test_loader = \
    DataLoader(train_set, batch_size=4, shuffle=True, pin_memory=True), \
    DataLoader(val_set, batch_size=4, shuffle=False, pin_memory=True), \
    DataLoader(test_set, batch_size=4, shuffle=False, pin_memory=True)
```

Listing 11-40: Defining the data loaders

These data loaders will feed the data to the model during training and evaluation.

Training the Model

Once you've finished building the dataset, you can train the model with Listing 11-41.

```
from lightning.pytorch.callbacks import ModelCheckpoint

regressor = dl.Regressor(
    model, loss=torch.nn.MSELoss(), optimizer=dl.Adam(lr=1e-4),
).create()

checkpoint_callback = ModelCheckpoint(
    monitor="val_loss", dirpath="models",
    filename="SAND-GNS-model{epoch:02d}-val_loss{val_loss:.2f}",
    auto_insert_metric_name=False,
)
trainer = dl.Trainer(max_epochs=5, callbacks=[checkpoint_callback])
trainer.fit(regressor, train_loader, val_loader)
```

Listing 11-41: Training the model

The training process optimizes the model by using an MSE loss function and the Adam optimizer. The model is trained for five epochs by default, with the validation loss being monitored to save the best-performing model, which produces good results.

For better performance, you can increase the number of epochs, but this will result in longer training times of up to several weeks, depending on the number of epochs and the available hardware. However, once trained, the graph network–based simulator can perform simulations much faster than traditional force-field methods. While a single force-field simulation might be quicker for one-off calculations, the trained network can be reused for any number of simulations, offering significant time savings over repeated traditional simulations.

Alternatively, you can bypass the training process and download a pretrained model. To do so, you need to determine the optimal device to make the computations via the get_device() function (Listing 7-10):

```
device = get_device()
```

Then load the pretrained model with Listing 11-42.

```
best_model_path = os.path.join("models", "SAND-GNS-model.ckpt")
best_model = torch.load(best_model_path, map_location=torch.device(device))
regressor.load_state_dict(best_model["state_dict"]);
```

Listing 11-42: Loading a pretrained model

This code loads a model that has been pretrained for 30 epochs (it took several days on a computer equipped with an A100 GPU) and saved in the *SAND-GNS-model.ckpt* file.

Testing the Model

Now that you have either trained a new model or loaded the pretrained model, you can evaluate its performance on the test set:

```
trainer.test(regressor, test_loader)
```

Using the pretrained model, you should expect an MAE of around 0.05 for the test set, displaying the model's ability to accurately predict particle accelerations despite the presence of noise.

Simulating the System

With your trained model, you can simulate a system of particles. This process involves iteratively predicting future accelerations and updating particle positions based on these predictions.

Performing the Simulation

Start by defining the simulate() function to perform a simulation with the trained model, as shown in Listing 11-43.

```
def simulate(model, r, metadata, Dt, n_std):
    """Simulate the system."""
    model.eval()

    T = r.shape[0]  # Total time steps
❶ r_sim = np.transpose(r[:Dt].copy(), (1, 0, 2))  # Simulated positions
    for _ in range(T - Dt):
        with torch.no_grad():
            node_attr, edge_index, edge_attr = \
                compute_graph(r_sim[:, -Dt:, :], n_std)
            graph = Data(
                x=torch.tensor(node_attr, dtype=torch.float32),
                edge_index=torch.tensor(edge_index, dtype=torch.long),
                edge_attr=torch.tensor(edge_attr, dtype=torch.float32),
            )
            graph = graph.to(model.device)

        ❷ a = model(graph)  # Acceleration
            a_mean = np.array(metadata["acc_mean"])
            a_std = np.array(metadata["acc_std"])
            a = a.cpu().numpy() * (a_std ** 2 + n_std ** 2) ** 0.5 + a_mean

            v = r_sim[:, -1] - r_sim[:, -2]  # Velocity
            v_next = v + a  # Next velocity

            r_next = r_sim[:, -1] + v_next  # Next position
        ❸ r_sim = np.concatenate([r_sim, r_next[:, None]], axis=1)
    return r_sim
```

Listing 11-43: The function to simulate the system

This code iteratively uses the last particle positions to compute the predicted accelerations and the next particle positions to simulate their movement. The code starts with the first Dt cropped from the ground-truth data as initial positions for the simulation ❶.

A for loop iterates through the time steps. Within each iteration, the code calls the compute_graph() function to generate the graph representation of the current window of positions. Next, the code creates a Data object to store the graph with its node attributes (node_attr), edge index (edge_index), and edge attributes (edge_attr).

Subsequently, the model predicts accelerations from the provided graph representation ❷ and scales the predicted accelerations to match the data distribution.

Then, based on the predicted accelerations, the function calculates the next positions of the particles by using an Euler integration scheme to calculate the next velocity (v_next) and next position (r_next) from the current velocity (v) and current position (r_sim[:, -1]).

Finally, the next positions are concatenated with the current positions to update the simulation window for the next iteration ❸.

Visualizing the Simulation

After you've implemented the simulation function, visualize the simulation by using the animate() function in Listing 11-44.

```
def animate(sample_id, regressor, data, metadata, Dt, n_std):
    """Animate simulation."""
    r = data[sample_id][0]  # Ground-truth positions
    r_sim = np.transpose(simulate(regressor, r, metadata, Dt, n_std),
                         (1, 0, 2))  # Simulated positions

    fig, axs = plt.subplots(1, 2, figsize=(12, 6))
    scatters = [
        axs[0].scatter([], [], s=50, c="y", edgecolors="k", linewidth=0.5),
        axs[1].scatter([], [], s=50, c="y", edgecolors="k", linewidth=0.5),
    ]
    axs[0].set_title("Ground Truth"); axs[1].set_title("Simulated")
    axs[0].set_xlim(0, 1); axs[0].set_xticks([])
    axs[0].set_ylim(0, 1); axs[0].set_yticks([])
    axs[1].set_xlim(0, 1); axs[1].set_xticks([])
    axs[1].set_ylim(0, 1); axs[1].set_yticks([])

    def update(frame):
        """Update frame."""
        scatters[0].set_offsets(r[frame])
        scatters[1].set_offsets(r_sim[frame])
        return scatters

    ani = FuncAnimation(fig, update, frames=len(r), interval=10, blit=True)
    video = HTML(ani.to_jshtml())
```

```
plt.close()
return video
```

Listing 11-44: The function to animate a simulation

This function is very similar to the code in Listing 11-29.

You can now try this simulation with various samples from the test set by setting the sample_id parameter from 0 to 29. For example, set it to 23 as follows:

```
animate(23, regressor, test_data, metadata, Dt, n_std)
```

You should get the simulation shown in Figure 11-5.

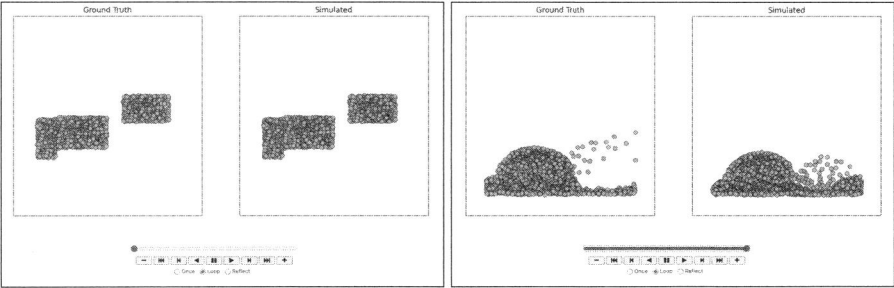

Figure 11-5: The first (left) and last (right) frames

Figure 11-5 displays the first and last frames of both the ground-truth and the simulated data from sample 23. The ground-truth frames are shown on the left, while the simulated frames are illustrated on the right. This comparison demonstrates the effectiveness of the pretrained model in replicating the dynamics of the granular system.

NOTE *Code Example 11-A, "Simulating Complex Physical Phenomena," is available at* https://github.com/DeepTrackAI/DeepLearningCrashCourse. *Navigate to the* Ch11_GNN *folder and then* ec11_A_dynamics. *The* dynamics.ipynb *notebook provides a complete code example that uses graph neural networks to simulate complex systems of interacting particles.*

Project 11B: Identifying Cell Trajectories

Tracking the movement of cells is a common task in biological image analysis. This process usually has two steps: detecting and segmenting cells in each frame and then linking them across frames to form trajectories. In previous chapters, you learned various methods for detecting and segmenting cells. For this project, you'll focus on linking the cells you detect across frames of segmented images to create trajectories via MAGIK, an algorithm based on graph neural networks that was published in 2023 by Jesús Pineda and co-workers in *Nature Machine Intelligence*.

You'll start by loading and visualizing some segmented images from the cell-tracking dataset. Next, you'll create a graph from these segmented images to model cell motion and build a dataset for training a graph neural network. After setting up the data, you'll train the MAGIK model to predict connections between cells across frames. Finally, you'll evaluate the model's performance, compute cell trajectories from the model's output, and visualize these trajectories over the original video frames.

Exploring the Cell-Tracking Data

You'll use the DIC-C2DH-HeLa dataset from the Cell Tracking Challenge. The dataset consists of two videos showing proliferating HeLa cells, a commonly used line of metastatic cells.

Download and extract this dataset with Listing 11-45.

```
import os
from torchvision.datasets.utils import _extract_zip, download_url

dataset_name = "DIC-C2DH-HeLa"
dataset_path = os.path.join(".", "cell_detection_dataset")
if not os.path.exists(dataset_path):
    url = ("http://data.celltrackingchallenge.net/training-datasets/"
           f"{dataset_name}.zip")
    download_url(url, ".")
    _extract_zip(f"{dataset_name}.zip", dataset_path, None)
    os.remove(f"{dataset_name}.zip")
```

Listing 11-45: Downloading the dataset

This script downloads the dataset, unzips it into the dataset_path directory, and removes the downloaded ZIP file.

The data consists of two sets of image sequences stored in the *01* and *02* folders. Each set includes segmentation masks in two quality levels: gold standard and silver standard. The gold-standard corpus contains man-made reference annotations as the gold truth (GT). The silver-standard corpus contains computer-generated reference annotations as the silver truth (ST). Furthermore, each *GT* folder has an additional *TRA* folder containing ground-truth cell trajectories in the form of both text files and images.

You'll use sequence 02 for training and sequence 01 for testing. In both cases, you'll use the silver-standard segmentation masks to simulate real-world scenarios with imperfect segmentation masks.

Loading the Images

Load the data with Listing 11-46.

```
import cv2, glob

def load_images(path):
    """Load images."""
```

```
    images = []
❶ for file in sorted(glob.glob(path + "/*.tif")):
        image = cv2.imread(file, cv2.IMREAD_UNCHANGED)
        images.append(image)
    return images

train_image_path = os.path.join(dataset_path, "DIC-C2DH-HeLa", "02")
train_images = load_images(train_image_path)

train_seg_path = os.path.join(dataset_path, "DIC-C2DH-HeLa", "02_ST", "SEG")
train_segs = load_images(train_seg_path)
```

Listing 11-46: Loading the images

This function iterates over each file in the specified directory path containing a *.tif* extension ❶. The function reads the corresponding image via the OpenCV cv2.imread() function with the cv2.IMREAD_UNCHANGED flag to indicate that the image should be loaded without any modification or conversion. Finally, the function appends the loaded image to the images list. The code uses the load_images() function to load the training images (train_images) and the corresponding segmentations (train_segs).

Visualizing Some Images

Now that you've loaded the images, you can visualize some frames from the training image sequence, along with their corresponding segmentation masks, via Listing 11-47.

```
import matplotlib.pyplot as plt

❶ frames_to_plot = [i for i in range(0, len(train_segs), len(train_segs) // 5)]

fig, axs = plt.subplots(2, len(frames_to_plot), figsize=(20, 6))
fig.patch.set_facecolor("white")
for i, frame in enumerate(frames_to_plot):
    axs[0, i].imshow(train_images[frame], cmap="gray")
    axs[0, i].set_title(f"Frame {frame}", fontsize=16)
    axs[0, i].tick_params(axis="both", which="both", bottom=False, top=False,
                          left=False, right=False, labelleft=False,
                          labelbottom=False)
    if i == 0: axs[0, i].set_ylabel("Intensity image", fontsize=16)

    axs[1, i].imshow(train_segs[frame], cmap="tab20b")
    axs[1, i].tick_params(axis="both", which="both", bottom=False, top=False,
                          left=False, right=False, labelleft=False,
                          labelbottom=False)
    if i == 0: axs[1, i].set_ylabel("Segmentation", fontsize=16)
plt.subplots_adjust(wspace=0.02, hspace=0.02)
plt.show()
```

Listing 11-47: Visualizing some of the images and corresponding segmentations

This code plots six frames, distributed evenly over the training-image sequence ❶. Figure 11-6 shows the resulting plot.

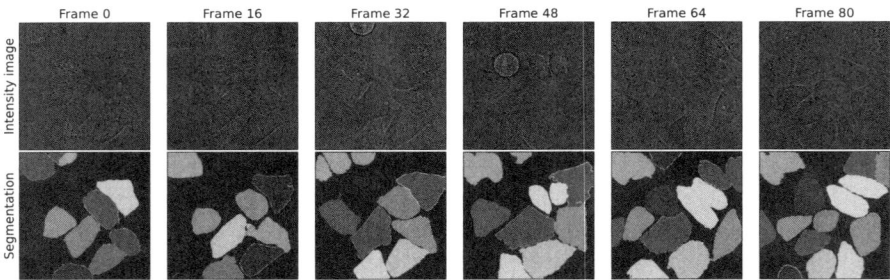

Figure 11-6: The cell images and corresponding segmentations

The top row shows the cell images, while the bottom row displays the corresponding (silver-standard) ground-truth segmentations. Each cell is assigned an integer number that's kept across frames, while the background is assigned a value of 0.

Creating a Graph from Segmented Images

To use MAGIK on the image dataset, you need to model cell motion and interactions as a directed graph. In this graph, nodes represent segmented cells, and edges represent connections between spatially close cells within and across frames.

Obtaining the Graph

You'll implement the GraphFromSegmentations class to convert segmented video frames of cells into a graph. In this graph, each node represents a detected cell in the video, while edges represent potential connections between cells, both within the same frame and across consecutive frames. This class will take into account spatial proximity (through a connectivity radius) and temporal proximity (maximum frame distance) to determine which nodes should be connected by edges. Additionally, the class will calculate ground-truth connections between cells based on known parent-child relationships, allowing the resulting graph to be used for training and for evaluating cell-tracking algorithms like MAGIK.

Start implementing this class as shown in Listing 11-48.

```
class GraphFromSegmentations:
    """Graph representation of the motion of cells."""

    def __init__(self, connectivity_radius, max_frame_distance):
        """Initialize graph."""
        self.connectivity_radius = connectivity_radius
        self.max_frame_distance = max_frame_distance
```

Listing 11-48: The class for constructing a graph from segmentations

This code initializes the class with the parameters `connectivity_radius` and `max_frame_distance`, which set the thresholds for determining whether two nodes are connected within the graph structure.

You'll now progressively add the necessary auxiliary methods to construct the graph, the node attributes, and the ground-truth connectivity. Then you'll use those methods in the `__call__()` method of the class. You'll start by adding the get_node_attr() method, as shown in Listing 11-49.

```python
import numpy as np
from skimage import measure

class GraphFromSegmentations:
    --snip--
    def get_node_attr(self, segmentation):
        """Compute node attributes."""
❶      labels = np.unique(segmentation)[1:]  # Labels without background
        node_attr = []
        for label in labels:
            mask = segmentation == label
            props = measure.regionprops(mask.astype(np.int32))[0]
            centroid = props.centroid / np.array(segmentation.shape)
            eccentricity = props.eccentricity
            node_attr.append([*centroid, eccentricity])
        return node_attr, labels
```

Listing 11-49: The method for computing the node attributes (by modifying Listing 11-48)

This method identifies separate objects in each frame of the segmented video data by using their integer labels, excluding the background with label 0 ❶. For every cell in the frame, the method calculates the relevant attributes (namely, the normalized centroid and eccentricity of the cell) and stores them in node_attr. Finally, the method returns a collection of node attributes (node_attr) and labels (labels).

Next, add the get_connectivity() method, as shown in Listing 11-50.

```python
--snip--
class GraphFromSegmentations:
    --snip--
    def get_connectivity(self, node_attr, frames):
        """Compute connectivity."""
        xy = node_attr[:, :2]  # Extracted centroids
        distances = np.linalg.norm(xy[:, None] - xy, axis=-1)
        frame_diff = (frames[:, None] - frames) * -1
        mask = ((distances < self.connectivity_radius)
                & (frame_diff <= self.max_frame_distance) & (frame_diff > 0))
        edge_index, edge_attr = np.argwhere(mask), distances[mask]
        return edge_index, edge_attr
```

Listing 11-50: The method for computing the connectivity (by modifying Listing 11-49)

This method calculates pairwise distances between the cell centroids and the corresponding time difference between frames. Then, based on the thresholds specified by connectivity_radius and max_frame_distance, the method identifies nodes that are both spatially and temporally close. From these nodes, the method returns a set of edge indices (edge_index) and corresponding distances (edge_attr) representing their connectivity.

Now add the get_gt_connectivity() method, as shown in Listing 11-51.

```
--snip--
class GraphFromSegmentations:
    --snip--
  def get_gt_connectivity(self, labels, edge_index, relation):
      """Compute ground-truth connectivity."""
      src_cell = labels[edge_index[:, 0]]
      tgt_cell = labels[edge_index[:, 1]]
    ❶ self_connections_mask = src_cell == tgt_cell

      relation_labels = relation[:, [-1, 0]]
      relation_labels = relation_labels[relation_labels[:, 0] != 0]
      relation_mask = np.zeros(len(edge_index), dtype=bool)
      for i, (s, t) in enumerate(zip(src_cell, tgt_cell)):
          if np.any((relation_labels == [s, t]).all(1)):
              relation_mask[i] = True

      gt_connectivity = self_connections_mask | relation_mask
      return gt_connectivity
```

Listing 11-51: The method for computing the ground-truth connectivity (by modifying Listing 11-50)

This method computes the ground-truth edges. The graph generated by get_connectivity() includes redundant edges that exceed the actual parent-child relationship between cells. Since MAGIK aims to prune redundant edges while retaining true connections, the ground truth for each edge is a binary value indicating whether an edge should connect two detected cells. Therefore, the method identifies self-connections where sender and receiver nodes have the same cell labels ❶, indicating that they are the same cell that changed positions as time has passed.

Next, the method iterates over the parent-child relationships to find relational connections such as cell divisions. Finally, the method returns the ground-truth connectivity obtained from the combination of self-connections and relational connections.

You're now finally ready to add the __call__() method, which uses the methods you've implemented to construct the graph from the segmentations, as shown in Listing 11-52.

```
import torch
from torch_geometric.data import Data
--snip--
class GraphFromSegmentations:
```

```
--snip--
def __call__(self, segmentations, relation):
    """Compute graph."""
    node_attr, node_labels, frames = [], [], []
    for frame, segmentation in enumerate(segmentations):
        features, labels = self.get_node_attr(segmentation)
        node_attr.append(features), node_labels.append(labels)
        frames.append([frame] * len(features))
    node_attr = np.concatenate(node_attr)
    node_labels = np.concatenate(node_labels)
    frames = np.concatenate(frames)

    edge_index, edge_attr = self.get_connectivity(node_attr, frames)
    edge_gt = self.get_gt_connectivity(node_labels, edge_index, relation)

    graph = Data(
        x=torch.tensor(node_attr, dtype=torch.float),
        edge_index=torch.tensor(edge_index.T, dtype=torch.long),
        edge_attr=torch.tensor(edge_attr[:, None], dtype=torch.float),
        distance=torch.tensor(edge_attr[:, None], dtype=torch.float),
        frames=torch.tensor(frames, dtype=torch.float),
        y=torch.tensor(edge_gt[:, None], dtype=torch.float),
    )
    return graph
```

Listing 11-52: The class with the call method for obtaining the graph (by modifying Listing 11-50)

The __call__() method takes two inputs: the segmented video frames (segmentations) and the parent-child relationships between cells (relation). First, it uses the get_node_attr() method (Listing 11-49) to identify the cells in each frame of the segmented video data based on their labels. Then the get_connectivity() method (Listing 11-50) is called to calculate pairwise distances between the cell centroids and the time differences between frames. After getting the nodes and edges, the get_gt_connectivity() method is called (Listing 11-51) to compute the ground-truth edges. Finally, it constructs a PyTorch Data object by using node attributes, edge indices, attributes, distances, frames, and ground-truth connectivity. This object encapsulates all necessary information for training and testing.

You can now instantiate the GraphFromSegmentations class with a connectivity radius of 0.2 (20 percent of the image size) and a maximum frame distance of 2 to reconnect cells not detected in consecutive frames:

```
graph_constructor = GraphFromSegmentations(connectivity_radius=0.2,
                                           max_frame_distance=2)
```

Then use graph_constructor to construct the training graph:

```
train_file = os.path.join(dataset_path, "DIC-C2DH-HeLa", "02_GT", "TRA",
                          "man_track.txt")
```

```
train_graph = graph_constructor(segmentations=train_segs,
                          relation=np.loadtxt(train_file, dtype=int))
```

This code constructs the graph by using the training segmentations and parent-child relationships between cells contained in the *man_track.txt* file.

Visualizing the Graph Data Structure

After constructing the graph, let's visualize its properties. Start by identifying the number of nodes and edges with print("Number of nodes:", len(train_graph.x)) and print("Number of edges:", len(train_graph.edge_index[0])), which print Number of nodes: 988 and Number of edges: 3036, respectively.

You can also plot the structure of the graph with Listing 11-53.

```
plt.figure(figsize=(8, 8))
for i, j in train_graph.edge_index.T:
    plt.plot([train_graph.x[i, 1], train_graph.x[j, 1]],
              [train_graph.x[i, 0], train_graph.x[j, 0]], c="black", alpha=0.5)
plt.scatter(train_graph.x[:, 1], train_graph.x[:, 0],
            c=train_graph.frames, cmap="viridis", zorder=10)
cb = plt.colorbar()
cb.ax.set_title("Frame", fontsize=14)
plt.xlabel("x", fontsize=14)
plt.ylabel("y", fontsize=14)
plt.show()
```

Listing 11-53: Plotting the graph

This code produces the graph in Figure 11-7.

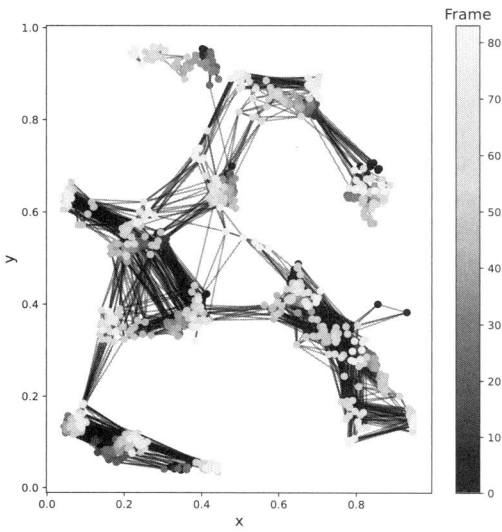

Figure 11-7: The graph representing the cells and their relations

This scatterplot depicts a graph with nodes represented as dots. The x- and y-coordinates represent the normalized node centroids. The color of each dot corresponds to the frame number, as shown by the color bar. The black lines on the plot illustrate the edges. Even though it's quite crowded, this graph allows you to visualize how cells move and divide over time. For example, a single node connected to multiple nodes in subsequent frames may indicate a cell division, while the patterns of edges can reveal how cells interact spatially and temporally across the video sequence.

Building a Training Dataset

The training dataset consists of a single graph derived from the training video sequence. Although this data may appear too limited, it's sufficient to train the MAGIK model. To address the scarcity of data, you can augment the training graph by splitting it into smaller subgraphs obtained from a limited range of frames. The CellTracingDataset class in Listing 11-54 implements this augmentation strategy.

```python
class CellTracingDataset(torch.utils.data.Dataset):
    """Class to prepare the graph dataset."""

    def __init__(self, graph, Dt, dataset_size, transform=None):
        """Initialize the graph dataset."""
        self.graph, self.Dt, self.dataset_size, self.transform = \
            graph, Dt, dataset_size, transform

    def __len__(self):
        """Obtain length of dataset."""
        return self.dataset_size

    def __getitem__(self, idx):
        """Return a graph from the dataset."""
        frames, edge_index = self.graph.frames, self.graph.edge_index
❶       select_frame = np.random.randint(self.Dt, frames.max() + 1)

        start_frame = select_frame - self.Dt
        node_mask = (frames >= start_frame) & (frames < select_frame)
        node_attr = self.graph.x[node_mask]

        frame_pairs = torch.stack([frames[edge_index[0, :]],
                                   frames[edge_index[1, :]]], axis=1)
        edge_mask = (frame_pairs >= start_frame) & (frame_pairs < select_frame)
        edge_mask = edge_mask.all(axis=1)
        edge_index = edge_index[:, edge_mask] - edge_index[:, edge_mask].min()

        graph = Data(
            x=node_attr,
            edge_index=edge_index,
```

```
        edge_attr=self.graph.edge_attr[edge_mask],
        distance=self.graph.edge_attr[edge_mask],
        y=self.graph.y[edge_mask],  # Ground-truth edges
    )
    if self.transform: graph = self.transform(graph)
    return graph
```

Listing 11-54: The class for preparing the graph dataset

This code constructs a class to divide the training graph into smaller temporal subgraphs. The `Dt` parameter determines the number of frames in each subgraph. The `dataset_size` parameter determines the number of subgraphs to be generated in each training epoch. The `__getitem__()` method generates subgraphs from the dataset by randomly selecting a starting frame ❶ and then constructing the subgraph by getting nodes and edges within a `Dt` window from that frame. Finally, the class returns the subgraph as a PyTorch `Data` object.

To further enhance the training dataset, you can apply additional augmentations to the subgraphs. The `CellTracingDataset` class provides the flexibility to include custom augmentations by inputting them into the `transform` parameter. For example, Listing 11-55 defines two augmentations.

```
from math import cos, pi, sin

class RandomRotation:
    """Random rotation."""

    def __call__(self, graph):
        """Perform the random rotation."""
        graph = graph.clone()
        node_attr = graph.x[:, :2] - 0.5  # Centered positions
        angle = np.random.rand() * 2 * pi
        R = torch.tensor([[cos(angle), -sin(angle)], [sin(angle), cos(angle)]])
        rotated_node_attr = torch.matmul(node_attr, R)
        graph.x[:, :2] = rotated_node_attr + 0.5  # Restored positions
        return graph

class RandomFlip:
    """Random flip."""

    def __call__(self, graph):
        """Perform the random flip."""
        graph = graph.clone()
        node_attr = graph.x[:, :2] - 0.5  # Centered positions
        if np.random.randint(2): node_attr[:, 0] *= -1
        if np.random.randint(2): node_attr[:, 1] *= -1
        graph.x[:, :2] = node_attr + 0.5  # Restored positions
        return graph
```

Listing 11-55: The classes for defining the random rotation and random flip

This code defines the `RandomRotation` class to randomly rotate the positional attributes of the nodes within the subgraph and the `RandomFlip` class to randomly flip the positional attributes of the nodes along the x- or y-axis.

You can finally create the training dataset with Listing 11-56.

```
from torchvision.transforms import Compose

train_set = CellTracingDataset(
    train_graph, Dt=5, dataset_size=512,
    transform=Compose([RandomRotation(), RandomFlip()]),
)
```

Listing 11-56: Creating the training dataset

This code creates the training dataset with a time window size of 5. In each epoch, the code generates 512 subgraphs from the training graph by using the augmentations defined in Listing 11-55.

From here, you can define the data loaders with Listing 11-57.

```
from torch_geometric.loader import DataLoader

train_loader = DataLoader(train_set, batch_size=8, shuffle=True)
```

Listing 11-57: Defining the data loaders

This code defines the data loaders with a batch size of 8.

Making MAGIK

Now that you've prepared the dataset, you're ready to train MAGIK. This algorithm is similar to the message-passing neural networks from previous examples. The main difference is that MAGIK implements a local attention mechanism that allows the model to concentrate on specific nodes and edges during message passing.

This mechanism comes into play when aggregating messages. Each message's contribution has a weight that depends on the distance between the connected nodes. A function with learnable parameters defines a learnable local receptive field. When deciding how to update the information for a particular cell, the model doesn't treat all connections equally. Instead, it gives more importance, or weight, to connections with nearby cells. The model learns how much importance to give based on the distance between the cells, helping it better understand and predict the way cells are likely to move and interact over time.

With this mechanism, MAGIK can focus on relevant, distance-based attributes during message passing. This approach is crucial for cell-tracking tasks because it enables the model to accurately identify which connections between cells in different frames represent true movements and interactions, while filtering out redundant or irrelevant edges.

Instantiating MAGIK

You can instantiate the MAGIK model with Listing 11-58.

```
import deeplay as dl

model = dl.GraphToEdgeMAGIK([96,] * 4, 1, out_activation=torch.nn.Sigmoid)
model.encoder[0].configure(hidden_features=[32, 64], out_features=96,
                           out_activation=torch.nn.ReLU)
model.encoder[1].configure(hidden_features=[32, 64], out_features=96,
                           out_activation=torch.nn.ReLU)
model.head.configure(hidden_features=[64, 32])
```

Listing 11-58: Defining the MAGIK model

This code sets up the GraphToEdgeMAGIK simplified version of MAGIK. The model has four layers, each containing 96 hidden attributes. Along with the message-passing layers, the model also includes a node encoder, an edge encoder, and a classification head.

The node and edge encoders are configured with three layers, each with 32, 64, and 96 hidden attributes. The classification head consists of two hidden layers with 64 and 32 hidden attributes and a final output layer with a single output and a sigmoid activation function by default.

You can use print(model) to print a detailed model summary.

Training MAGIK

After instantiating MAGIK, you can use Listing 11-59 to train the model.

```
classifier = dl.BinaryClassifier(model=model, optimizer=dl.Adam(lr=1e-3))
classifier = classifier.create()

trainer = dl.Trainer(max_epochs=10)
trainer.fit(classifier, train_loader)
```

Listing 11-59: Training the MAGIK model

This code compiles the MAGIK model as a binary classifier and trains it for 10 epochs.

Evaluating Performance

Once you've trained the model, you can evaluate its performance on the test dataset. Start by loading the test data with Listing 11-60.

```
test_image_path = os.path.join(dataset_path, "DIC-C2DH-HeLa", "01")
test_seg_path = os.path.join(dataset_path, "DIC-C2DH-HeLa", "01_ST", "SEG")

test_images = load_images(test_image_path)
test_segs = load_images(test_seg_path)
```

Listing 11-60: Loading the test data

Next, construct the test graph with Listing 11-61.

```
test_file = os.path.join(dataset_path, "DIC-C2DH-HeLa", "01_GT", "TRA",
                         "man_track.txt")
test_graph = graph_constructor(segmentations=test_segs,
                               relation=np.loadtxt(test_file, dtype=int))
```

Listing 11-61: Constructing the test graph

This code uses the parent-child relationships from the test data *TRA* file.

Calculating the F1 Score

After creating the test graph, you can assess the model's performance by calculating the F1 score of the predicted and ground-truth edge classifications, as shown in Listing 11-62.

```
from sklearn.metrics import f1_score

classifier.eval()
pred = classifier(test_graph)
predictions = pred.detach().numpy() > 0.5

ground_truth = test_graph.y

score = f1_score(ground_truth, predictions)
print(f"Test F1 score: {score}")
```

Listing 11-62: Assessing the model performance with the F1 score

You can expect an F1 score of approximately 0.99 on the test graph, exhibiting the model's ability to accurately predict cell temporal associations.

Getting the Cell Trajectories

Unfortunately, MAGIK doesn't output cell trajectories. It outputs only a graph structure that shows potential connections between cells across frames and can include both same-cell connections and parent-child relations. MAGIK provides each potential connection with a weight factor that can be interpreted as a probability. To generate cell trajectories, you need to apply a post-processing algorithm to the predicted graph structure.

The ComputeTrajectories class in Listing 11-63 implements a simple post-processing algorithm to compute cell trajectories from MAGIK predictions.

```
import networkx as nx

class ComputeTrajectories:
    """Computation of trajectories."""

    def __call__(self, graph, predictions):
        """Compute trajectories."""
        pruned_edges = self.prune_edges(graph, predictions)
```

```
        pruned_graph = nx.Graph()
        pruned_graph.add_edges_from(pruned_edges)
        trajectories = list(nx.connected_components(pruned_graph))
        return trajectories

    def prune_edges(self, graph, predictions):
        """Prune edges."""
        pruned_edges = []
        frame_pairs = np.stack([graph.frames[graph.edge_index[0]],
                                graph.frames[graph.edge_index[1]]], axis=1)
        for src_cell in np.unique(graph.edge_index[0]):
    ❶     src_cell_mask = graph.edge_index[0] == src_cell
    ❷     tgt_cell_candidates = predictions[src_cell_mask] == True
            if np.any(tgt_cell_candidates):
                frame_diff = (frame_pairs[src_cell_mask, 1]
                              - frame_pairs[src_cell_mask, 0])
                min_frame_diff = frame_diff[tgt_cell_candidates].min()
                tgt_cell_mask = (tgt_cell_candidates
                                 & (frame_diff == min_frame_diff))
        ❸   edge = graph.edge_index[:, src_cell_mask][:, tgt_cell_mask]
            edge = edge.reshape(-1, 2)
        ❹   if len(edge) == 1:
                pruned_edges.append(tuple(*edge.numpy()))
        return pruned_edges
```

Listing 11-63: The class to compute trajectories from MAGIK results

This code generates a set of trajectories from the linked edges labeled by MAGIK. The algorithm starts by selecting a node in the first frame (at time $t = 0$) ❶, then links it to other nodes in the following frames, using only edges labeled as "linked" by MAGIK ❷. If there are no "linked" edges connecting the sender node at time t to any receiver nodes at time $t + 1$, the algorithm checks future frames up to a maximum time delay ❸. If no "linked" edges are found within this time frame, the trajectory ends. When a sender node has two "linked" edges connecting it to two receiver nodes in a later frame, it's identified as a cell division. In this case, the algorithm creates two new trajectories ❹. This process repeats until all "linked" edges are dealt with.

You can now compute the trajectories with the following commands:

```
compute_trajectories = ComputeTrajectories()
trajectories = compute_trajectories(test_graph, predictions.squeeze())
```

Here, the code instantiates the class to compute the trajectories and applies it to the test graph output by MAGIK.

Visualizing the Cell Trajectories

Now that you've computed the trajectories, you can visualize them on top of the segmented video frames, using Listing 11-64.

```
from IPython.display import HTML
from matplotlib.animation import FuncAnimation

fig, ax = plt.subplots(figsize=(8, 8))
list_of_colors = plt.get_cmap("tab20b", len(trajectories))

def update(frame):
    """Update frame."""
    ax.clear()
    ax.imshow(test_images[frame], cmap="gray")

    segmentation = test_segs[frame]
    for label in np.unique(segmentation)[1:]:
        contour = measure.find_contours(segmentation == label, 0.5)[0]
        ax.fill(contour[:, 1], contour[:, 0], color=list_of_colors(label),
                alpha=0.5, linewidth=2)
    ax.text(0, -5, f"Frame: {frame}", fontsize=16, c="k")

    for i, t in enumerate(trajectories):
        frames = test_graph.frames[list(t)]
        xy_all = test_graph.x[list(t)] * 512
        xy_frame = xy_all[frames == frame]
        if len(xy_frame) != 0:
            ax.scatter(xy_frame[:, 1], xy_frame[:, 0])
            ax.text(xy_frame[0, 1], xy_frame[0, 0], str(i), fontsize=16, c="w")

            xy_previous = xy_all[(frames <= frame) & (frames >= frame - 10)]
            ax.plot(xy_previous[:, 1], xy_previous[:, 0], c="w")

            ax.plot(xy_frame[max(0, frame - 10):frame, 1],
                    xy_frame[max(0, frame - 10):frame, 0], c="r")
    return ax

animation = FuncAnimation(fig, update, frames=len(test_segs))
video = HTML(animation.to_jshtml())
plt.close()
```

Listing 11-64: Visualizing the cell trajectories as a video

This code produces a video showing the linked cell trajectories. You can view this video by typing video. Figure 11-8 shows a frame.

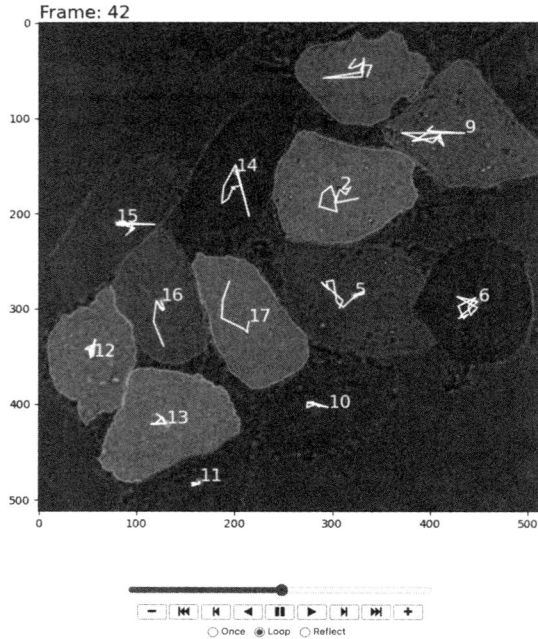

Figure 11-8: A frame from the reconstructed video, with the cell trajectories

When you watch the video, you should see that the cell trajectories are mostly correctly reconstructed, even when a cell divides.

NOTE *Code Example 11-B, "Identifying Trajectories with MAGIK," is available at* https:// github.com/DeepTrackAI/DeepLearningCrashCourse. *Navigate to the* Ch11 _GNN *folder and then* ec11_B_magik. *The* magik.ipynb *notebook provides a complete code example to track the motion of cells by using a simplified version of MAGIK.*

Summary

In this chapter, you explored the theory, implementation, and applications of graph neural networks, focusing on how they capture the relationships inherent in graphs to analyze complex patterns in graph-structured data.

The chapter started by explaining the basics of graph convolutions, comparing them to the image convolutions used by the convolutional neural networks from Chapter 3. You learned how to represent graphs by using adjacency matrices and how to implement graph convolutions to transform node attributes based on their edges. Through practical examples, you grasped the process of applying graph convolutions to different types of graphs, including cycle graphs and undirected graphs.

You moved on to more advanced problems such as predicting molecular properties via graph neural networks. For this task, you implemented a graph convolution layer, improved it with self-loops and normalization, and applied it to the ZINC dataset for molecular property prediction. You also enhanced your graph convolutional network with embedding layers, global average pooling, and a dense top for regression tasks.

To help you increase the network's accuracy, this chapter taught you about message-passing neural networks, highlighting their ability to incorporate edge attributes into the graph representation. You learned to implement a message-passing layer and apply it to predict molecular properties, which improved your model's performance over simple graph convolutional networks.

You also worked on two extensive projects: simulating complex physical phenomena and identifying cell trajectories. In the first project, you built a graph network–based simulator to model granular systems with the SAND dataset. You mastered the process of constructing graphs, passing messages, and simulating system dynamics. In the second project, you implemented MAGIK, a graph neural network–based algorithm for tracking cell motion in biological images. This required creating graphs from segmented images, training the model, and evaluating its performance in identifying cell trajectories.

As graph neural networks evolve, their potential applications are bound to expand. From advancements in drug discovery and personalized medicine to breakthroughs in social network analysis and artificial intelligence, graph neural networks are set to revolutionize various fields by leveraging the interconnected nature of data. By mastering these innovative tools, you're ideally positioned to exploit their potential in a whole new series of applications.

Seminal Works and Further Reading

The foundation of graph neural networks was laid by Franco Scarselli et al. in 2009 in "The Graph Neural Network Model," published in *IEEE Transactions on Neural Networks* (volume 20, pages 61–80). This work proposed a framework for processing data represented as graphs, enabling the learning of representations directly from graph structures.

In 2014, Joan Bruna et al. presented "Spectral Networks and Locally Connected Networks on Graphs" at the International Conference on Learning Representations (ICLR) and also published it on arXiv (article number 1312.6203), extending the idea of convolution to graphs.

In 2017, Justin Gilmer et al. introduced the message-passing neural network framework in "Neural Message Passing for Quantum Chemistry," presented at the 34th International Conference on Machine Learning (ICML) and published in its proceedings (*PMLR*, volume 70, pages 1,263–1,272). This framework unified various graph neural network architectures under a single message-passing paradigm, where nodes iteratively exchange messages with neighbors to update their state representation. The message-passing mechanism became a cornerstone for graph neural networks, underlying many later models, such as graph convolutional networks and graph attention networks.

Graph convolutional networks were introduced in 2016 by Thomas N. Kipf and Max Welling in "Semi-Supervised Classification with Graph Convolutional Networks," published on arXiv (article number 1609.02907) and presented in 2017 at ICLR.

Graph attention networks were introduced in 2017 by Petar Velickovic et al. in "Graph Attention Networks," published on arXiv (article number 1710.10903) and presented in 2018 at ICLR. Graph attention networks incorporated an attention mechanism into the graph learning process, allowing the network to assign varying levels of importance to different nodes in the neighborhood and enhancing the model's ability to capture complex relationships in graph data.

Another notable application of graph-based deep learning is the MAGIK algorithm, published in 2023 by Jesús Pineda et al. in "Geometric Deep Learning Reveals the Spatiotemporal Features of Microscopic Motion," published in *Nature Machine Intelligence* (volume 5, pages 71–82). You used MAGIK in Project 11B to track and analyze the motion of cells.

A landmark application of graph-based neural networks in biological sciences was demonstrated in 2021 by John Jumper et al. in "Highly Accurate Protein Structure Prediction with AlphaFold," published in *Nature* (volume 596, pages 583–589). AlphaFold achieved unprecedented success in predicting protein structures using advanced graph neural networks and attention mechanisms, treating the protein structure prediction problem as a spatial graph learning challenge. The profound impact of AlphaFold on the scientific community has been recognized with the award of a share of the 2024 Nobel Prize in Chemistry to two of its creators, Demis Hassabis and John Jumper.

CHALLENGE PROJECTS

11-1: Node classification on citation networks   Implement a graph convolutional network to classify scientific publications into predefined categories. Use the Cora dataset, which contains 2,708 nodes (papers) with 1,433 dimensional attribute vectors and 5,429 edges (citations). Train your model to predict the class of each paper and evaluate its performance by using metrics such as accuracy and F1 score. Compare your results with a baseline model, such as a simple multilayer perceptron.

11-2: Link prediction in biomedical literature   Develop a graph convolutional network model to predict missing links in a citation network. Use the PubMed Diabetes dataset, which includes 19,717 scientific publications with 500 dimensional attribute vectors and 44,338 edges. Train your model to identify potential new citations and assess its performance by using AUROC and precision-recall metrics. Compare your model's performance with methods that are not based on graph neural networks, like common neighbors or Jaccard similarity.

11-3: Graph classification for chemical compounds   Construct a graph convolutional network to classify chemical compounds based on their mutagenicity. Use the MUTAG dataset, consisting of 188 graphs with nodes representing atoms and edges representing chemical bonds. Each graph is labeled as mutagenic or non-mutagenic. Train your model to perform graph classification and then evaluate its performance by using accuracy and F1 score. Compare your results with traditional machine learning methods, such as random forests or support vector machines, applied to graph kernel attributes.

12

CONTINUOUSLY IMPROVING PERFORMANCE WITH ACTIVE LEARNING

Not all data is created equal. In many cases, the cost of labeling data is high, and the amount of labeled data is limited. In this chapter, you'll explore *active learning*, a semi-supervised learning method that aims to reduce the cost of labeling data by selecting the most informative data points to label.

Active learning is an advanced approach in the field of machine learning that emphasizes continuous, iterative learning. It stands out because of its dynamic nature—specifically, the way the learning algorithm actively selects the most informative and relevant data points to learn from. This approach makes the learning process more efficient, addressing a major challenge in traditional machine learning by significantly reducing the amount of labeled data required.

To begin, you'll discover the principles and strategies of active learning, particularly how it differs from standard learning paradigms and its practical advantages. This chapter will guide you through the application of active learning to binary and multiclass classification tasks, culminating in a project that applies active learning strategies to classify MNIST digits by using a neural network.

By the end of this chapter, you'll have a solid understanding of how active learning operates so that you can implement it in your own projects to make your models more responsive and efficient.

Understanding Active Learning

In traditional supervised learning, models depend heavily on extensive labeled datasets. Acquiring these labels often involves considerable time and cost, especially in specialized fields requiring expert annotations. Active learning mitigates this issue by selecting only the most informative samples for labeling. In doing so, it reduces the required amount of labeled data, making the learning process more efficient. Through iterative querying and labeling, active learning enables models to achieve higher accuracy with fewer labeled samples.

A core component of active learning is the *query strategy*. This strategy determines the way the active learning algorithm selects data points to label. Common query strategies include *uncertainty sampling*, where the model queries samples it's least confident about, and *query-by-committee*, where a committee of models selects the most contentious samples for labeling. The underlying idea is that samples with high uncertainty or disagreement between models are often the most informative, because they represent areas where the models' understanding is weakest and can benefit most from additional labeled data.

The *unlabeled pool* is another essential element in active learning. It consists of a large set of unlabeled data from which the active learning algorithm selects samples to query as potential candidates for labeling. The diversity and size of the unlabeled pool directly impact the effectiveness of the active learning strategy.

The *labeling oracle* supplies the final crucial part of the active learning loop. This is the source of ground-truth labels for the queried samples. Depending on the application, the labeling oracle could be a human annotator, an expert in the field, or an automated labeling system. The oracle's accuracy and efficiency in providing labels are critical for the active learning process.

Besides its efficiency and cost-effectiveness, another key advantage of active learning is its adaptability. In a rapidly changing environment, it's crucial for machine learning models to continuously adapt to new data and evolving patterns. Active learning facilitates this by enabling continuous learning. The iterative querying and labeling process allows the model to update its knowledge base in response to new information. This adaptability ensures that the model remains relevant and accurate over time, even as the underlying data distribution changes.

Performing Binary Classification

To begin developing an intuition for how active learning works, you'll classify a simple dataset composed of two distinct groups of data points. You'll start by generating and visualizing the dataset, which will help you understand the fundamental concepts of binary classification. Then you'll implement a logistic regression model to classify these data points. Finally, you'll explore how active learning can improve the model's performance by selectively querying the most informative samples.

Creating a Dataset with Two Groups of Data Points

Start by creating two groups of data points with Listing 12-1.

```
import numpy as np

gr0 = np.random.normal(loc=(-2, 0), scale=(1, 1), size=(100, 2))
gr1 = np.random.normal(loc=(2, 0), scale=(1, 1), size=(100, 2))

❶ x = np.vstack((gr0, gr1))
❷ y = np.hstack((np.zeros(len(gr0)), np.ones(len(gr1))))
```

Listing 12-1: Creating a dataset with two groups of data

This code generates two groups of data points (gr0 and gr1), each containing 100 samples. It centers the gr0 group on the point $(-2, 0)$ with a standard deviation of 1 for both coordinates, and the gr1 group on $(2, 0)$ with the same standard deviation. The code then combines the data points from both groups into a single NumPy array ❶ and combines their labels corresponding to which dataset they belong to into another NumPy array ❷.

Now plot the dataset using Listing 12-2.

```
import matplotlib.pyplot as plt

plt.scatter(gr0[:, 0], gr0[:, 1], marker="o", s=5, c="C0")
plt.scatter(gr1[:, 0], gr1[:, 1], marker="^", s=5, c="C1")
plt.xlim(-5, 5)
plt.ylim(-3, 3)
plt.show()
```

Listing 12-2: Plotting the dataset with two groups of data

Figure 12-1 shows the resulting plot.

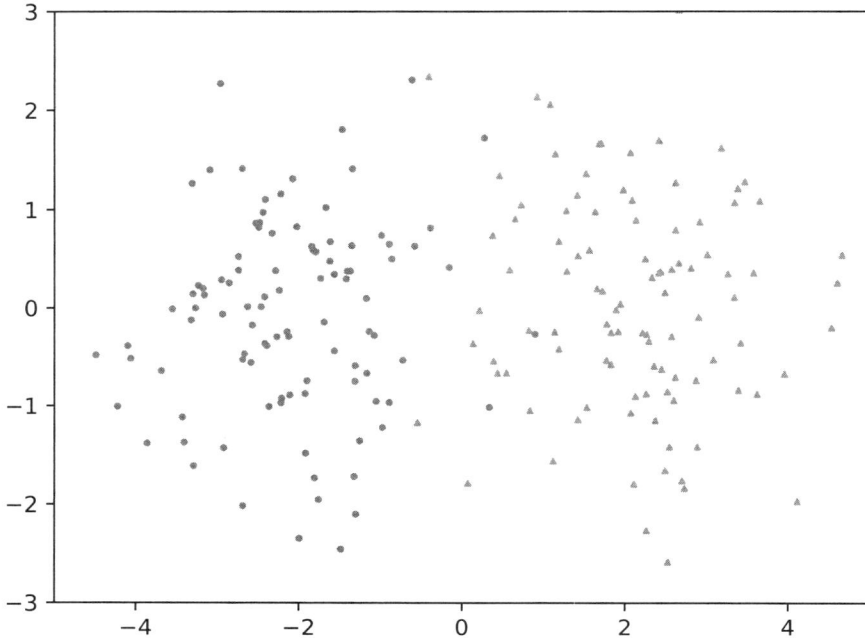

Figure 12-1: Data for binary classification with two groups

You can see the two groups of data points that are generated. The circles represent gr0, centered on the point $(-2, 0)$, while the triangles represent gr1, centered on $(2, 0)$. These two groups will serve as the basis for the binary classification task.

Classifying the Data Points with a Logistic Regression

To classify the data points, let's use a simple logistic regression model instead of a neural network to keep the focus on the active learning process. Listing 12-3 shows the code for training and testing the model.

```
from sklearn.linear_model import LogisticRegression

def train_model(x_train, y_train, x_test, y_test):
    """Find optimal decision boundary using a logistic regression."""
    model = LogisticRegression()
    model.fit(x_train, y_train)
    accuracy = model.score(x_test, y_test)
    return model, accuracy
```

Listing 12-3: The function to train and test the model with a logistic regression

This function trains a logistic regression model by fitting it to the training data; then the function evaluates the model's accuracy on the test data. Once you've defined the function, train the model on the entire dataset:

```
model, full_accuracy = train_model(x, y, x, y)
```

Here, you use the same data for training and testing. You can print the accuracy of the trained model with print(full_accuracy), which in our run was 0.97. Such a high accuracy means that the logistic regression model is capable of effectively distinguishing between the two groups of data points.

In the next sections, you'll use the active learning process to iteratively select the most informative data points to label, train the model on these selected points, and observe how the model's performance evolves as you increase the labeled samples. This approach aims to achieve similar or even better accuracy with significantly less labeled data.

Implementing the Active Learning Process

Now that you've set up the logistic regression model, you'll define a function for the active learning process, as shown in Listing 12-4.

```
def train_active_learning(x, y, budget, query):
    """Train binary classifier with active learning."""
❶  annotated_idxs = [np.random.choice(np.where(y == i)[0]) for i in [0, 1]]
    unannotated_idxs = np.setdiff1d(np.arange(x.shape[0]), annotated_idxs)

    accuracy_history = []
    for _ in range(budget):
❷      annotated_x, annotations = x[annotated_idxs], y[annotated_idxs]
        unannotated_x = x[unannotated_idxs]

❸      model, accuracy = train_model(annotated_x, annotations, x, y)
        accuracy_history.append(accuracy)

❹      idx_to_annotate = query(model, unannotated_x)
❺      annotated_idxs = np.append(annotated_idxs,
                                   unannotated_idxs[idx_to_annotate])
        unannotated_idxs = np.delete(unannotated_idxs, idx_to_annotate)

    return accuracy_history, model, annotated_idxs
```

Listing 12-4: The function to perform the active learning for binary classification

This code implements the core loop of the active learning process. To begin, it annotates a small seed dataset by picking one random data point from each class ❶. In a real-world scenario, this is usually a small, randomly selected subset of the full dataset.

In each loop of the active learning cycle, the function extracts the annotated data ❷, trains the model on the annotated dataset ❸, and stores the model's accuracy calculated on the test data. Then the function selects a new data point to annotate, using a query strategy that aims to select the most informative data point from the unannotated dataset ❹, and adds this data point to the list of annotated data ❺. The function repeats these steps until it exhausts the budget for labeling data. By iteratively selecting and annotating the most informative data points, the model becomes increasingly accurate with each cycle.

Random Sampling

As you learned at the beginning of the chapter, active learning uses a query strategy to select the most informative samples for labeling. In turn, it's crucial to familiarize yourself with multiple query strategies so that you can choose the one most suited to your particular task. For the binary classification example, you can first test what happens if you use a random query strategy. To do so, implement the query_random() function with Listing 12-5.

```
def query_random(model, unannotated_x):
    """Randomly select data point to annotate."""
    return np.random.randint(len(unannotated_x))
```

Listing 12-5: The function to select a data point at random

This function extracts a point at random to add to the annotated dataset. Now perform active learning with a random query strategy:

```
accuracy_history_random, model_random, annotated_idxs_random = \
    train_active_learning(x, y, budget=25, query=query_random)
```

In our run of the code, this strategy resulted in an accuracy of around 0.95, which is slightly worse than the accuracy the model achieved when using the whole dataset.

To understand the model's decision-making and assess the effectiveness of the active learning process, it's useful to visualize which data has been annotated as well as the model's final decision boundary. You can do this via the plot_model() function in Listing 12-6.

```
def plot_model(model, gr0, gr1, annotated_x, annotations):
    """Plot model decision boundary and annotated data."""
    plt.scatter(gr0[:, 0], gr0[:, 1], marker="o", s=0.5, c="C0")
    plt.scatter(gr1[:, 0], gr1[:, 1], marker="^", s=0.5, c="C1")
```

```
    plt.scatter(annotated_x[~annotations, 0], annotated_x[~annotations, 1],
             marker="o", s=100, c="C0", label="Selected Group 1")
    plt.scatter(annotated_x[annotations, 0], annotated_x[annotations, 1],
             marker="^", s=100, c="C1", label="Selected Group 2")

    beta_1, beta_2 = model.coef_[0]
    intercept = model.intercept_
❶  boundary_x = np.linspace(-5, 5, 100)
❷  boundary_y = (- intercept - beta_1 * boundary_x) / beta_2
    plt.plot(boundary_x, boundary_y, c="black", label="Decision Boundary")

    plt.xlim(-5, 5)
    plt.ylim(-3, 3)
    plt.legend()
    plt.show()
```

Listing 12-6: The function to plot the model, the annotated data, and its decision boundary

This function plots the points in the two classes of the dataset as small circles and small triangles. It then highlights the selected points from each class with larger markers.

In addition to the data points, the function calculates and plots the decision boundary of the logistic regression model. First, the function extracts the coefficients β_1 and β_2 from the trained model, which represent the weights of the features in the decision function. The function also retrieves the intercept term of the model, y_0, the bias added to the weighted sum of the features. Then the function generates a range of x-values to cover the span of the data ❶ and computes the corresponding y-values by using the equation of the line $y = (-y_0 + \beta_1 x)/\beta_2$, which forms the decision boundary ❷. Finally, the function plots this decision boundary as a black line on the graph, illustrating where the model separated the two groups based on its learned parameters.

You can now use this function with the following:

```
plot_model(model_random, gr0, gr1,
        annotated_x=x[annotated_idxs_random],
        annotations=y[annotated_idxs_random].astype(bool))
```

This should generate a scatterplot similar to Figure 12-2.

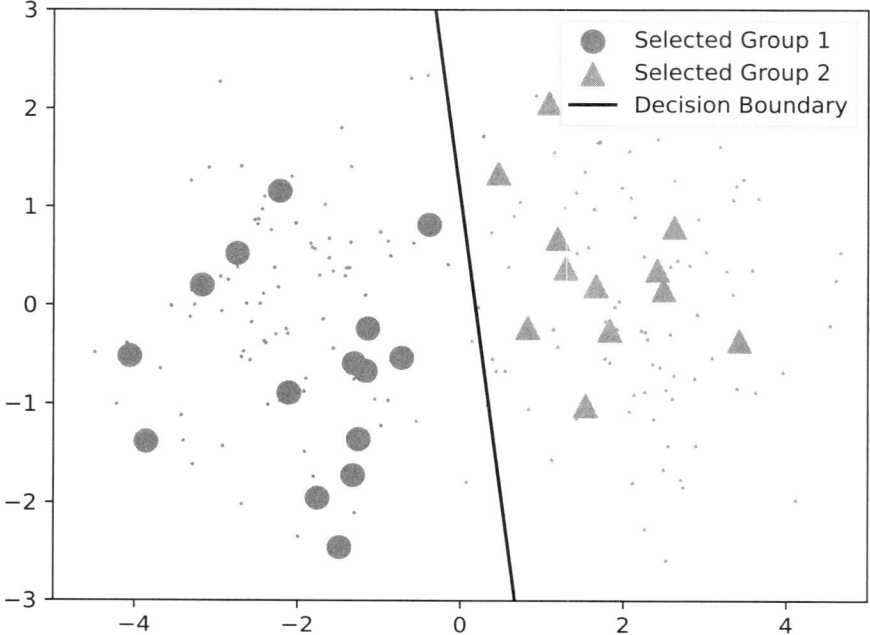

Figure 12-2: The decision boundary (line) and annotated data (large symbols) with random sampling

The small markers represent the entire dataset, while the large markers indicate the points selected for annotation during the active learning process. The black line indicates the decision boundary of the logistic regression model. The plot reveals that the model sampled most points from the center of the groups, which isn't ideal for estimating the decision boundary and, consequently, reduces accuracy.

Uncertainty Sampling

Having established a baseline query strategy with the random sampling, you can now use a more informative query strategy known as *uncertainty sampling*. As its name indicates, this approach selects the data points for which the model's predictions have the most uncertainty. In other words, these are the points from which you can extract the greatest amount of new information. You can implement this strategy with the query_uncertainty function in Listing 12-7.

```
def query_uncertainty(model, unannotated_x):
    """Select data point to annotate randomly with uncertainty sampling."""
    probabilities = model.predict_proba(unannotated_x)
    return np.argmin(np.max(probabilities, axis=1))
```

Listing 12-7: The function to select data with uncertainty sampling

This function implements uncertainty sampling by selecting the data point about which the model is least confident, based on the predicted probabilities. Initially, the function uses the `predict_proba()` method from the `LogisticRegression` object to return an array where each row corresponds to a sample and each column corresponds to a class. The values in the array represent the probability that a given sample belongs to a given class. For a binary classification problem, the output will be an array with shape (`n_samples`, `2`). For a multiclass classification problem, the output will have shape (`n_samples`, `n_classes`).

The function then identifies the data point whose prediction poses the highest uncertainty for the model by finding the sample with the smallest maximum probability across all classes. By selecting this sample, the model can gain the most information from having it labeled.

Perform the active learning with uncertainty sampling:

```
accuracy_history_uncertainty, model_uncertainty, annotated_idxs_uncertainty = \
    train_active_learning(x, y, budget=25, query=query_uncertainty)
```

In our run of the code, the uncertainty sampling resulted in an accuracy of 0.965.

You can then plot the decision boundary and sampled annotations:

```
plot_model(model_uncertainty, gr0, gr1,
           annotated_x=x[annotated_idxs_uncertainty],
           annotations=y[annotated_idxs_uncertainty].astype(bool))
```

This should produce a scatterplot similar to Figure 12-3.

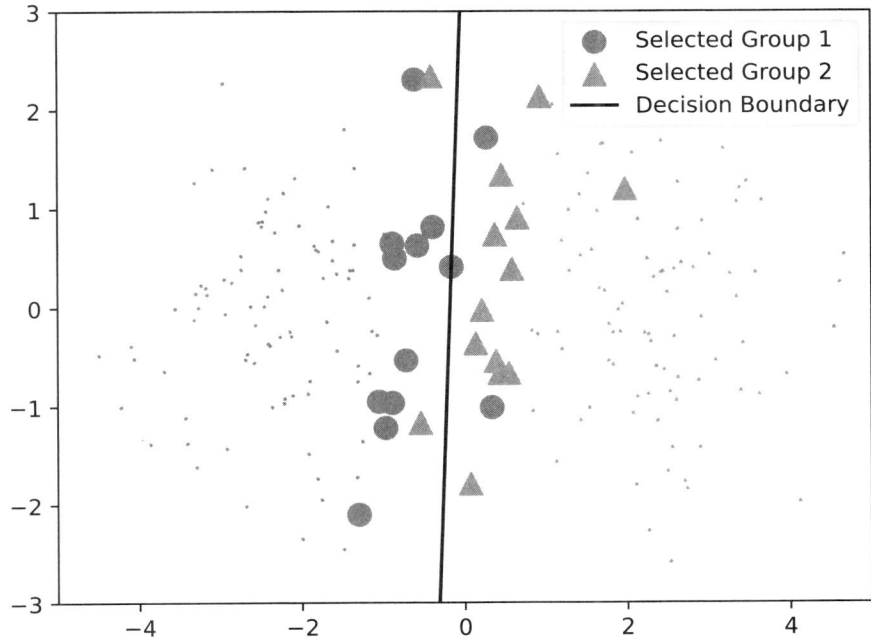

Figure 12-3: The decision boundary (line) and annotated data (large symbols) with uncertainty sampling

You can see that these data points, unlike those in Figure 12-2, are sampled near the decision boundary. This line represents where the model is most uncertain and can gain the most information from additional labels.

Comparing Random and Uncertainty Sampling Strategies

Because of the stochastic nature of random sampling, your results may vary. To compare the two strategies, you should average them over multiple runs. Using Listing 12-8, conduct multiple experiments for each query strategy, enabling you to compare the mean result.

```
trials = 50

accuracy_histories_random, accuracy_histories_uncertainty = [], []
for _ in range(trials):
    accuracy_history_random, *_ = \
        train_active_learning(x, y, budget=25, query=query_random)
    accuracy_histories_random.append(accuracy_history_random)

    accuracy_history_uncertainty, *_ = \
        train_active_learning(x, y, budget=25, query=query_uncertainty)
    accuracy_histories_uncertainty.append(accuracy_history_uncertainty)
```

Listing 12-8: Calculating the average accuracy as a function of annotations

This code conducts 50 experiments for each query strategy and logs the resulting accuracy as a function of the number of annotations into NumPy arrays.

You can then plot the average accuracy as a function of the number of annotations, using Listing 12-9.

```
plt.plot(np.mean(accuracy_histories_random, axis=0), "^:", label="Random")
plt.plot(np.mean(accuracy_histories_uncertainty, axis=0), "v--",
        label="Uncertainty Sampling")
plt.xlabel("Number of Annotations", fontsize=16)
plt.ylabel("Accuracy", fontsize=16)
plt.legend()
plt.show()
```

Listing 12-9: Plotting the average accuracy as a function of annotations

This code should produce a plot similar to Figure 12-4.

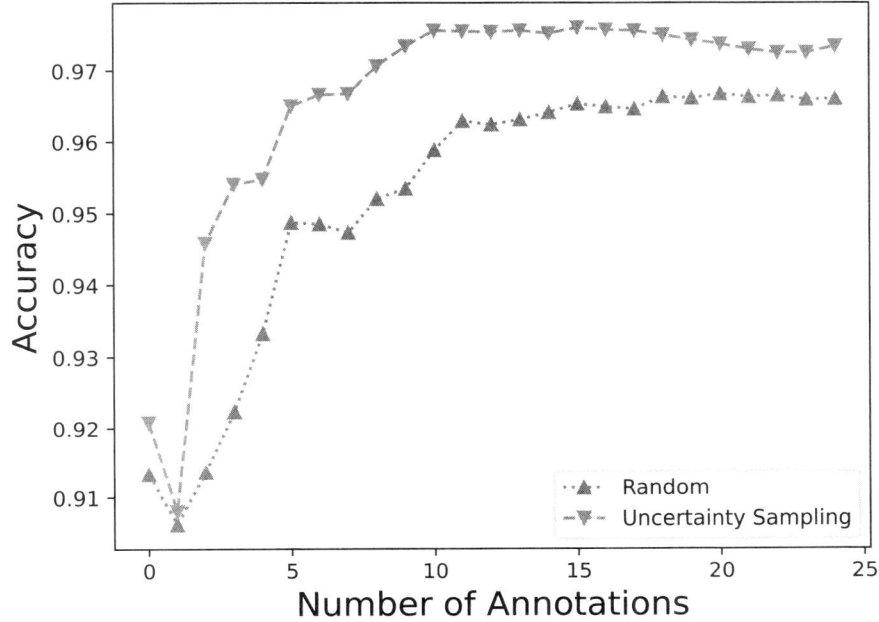

Figure 12-4: The average accuracy as a function of annotations over multiple trials

The uncertainty sampling strategy converges more quickly and achieves better average performance than the random sampling strategy.

NOTE   *Code Example 12-1, "Training a Binary Classifier with Active Learning," is available at* https://github.com/DeepTrackAI/DeepLearningCrashCourse. *Navigate to the* Ch12_AL *folder and then* ec12_1_active2. *The* active2.ipynb *notebook provides a complete code example that uses active learning to classify points in a plane into two classes.*

Performing Multiclass Classification

When transitioning to multiclass classification, the concept of uncertainty becomes more complex. In binary classification, uncertainty can be represented as a single value, but in multiclass classification, uncertainty becomes a vector of values. You can measure uncertainty in several ways in this context, and your choice will significantly impact the performance of the active learning algorithm. You'll see the most common options in this section.

Creating a Dataset with Three Groups of Data Points

To illustrate the complexities of multiclass classification, use Listing 12-10 to create a dataset consisting of three distinct groups of data points, with each group representing a different class.

```
--snip--
gr0 = np.random.normal(loc=(-2.2, 0), scale=(1, 1), size=(150, 2))
gr1 = np.random.normal(loc=(2.2, 0), scale=(1, 1), size=(150, 2))
gr2 = np.random.normal(loc=(0, 2.5), scale=(1, 1), size=(150, 2))

x = np.vstack((gr0, gr1, gr2))
y = np.hstack((np.zeros(len(gr0)), np.ones(len(gr1)), 2 * np.ones(len(gr2))))
```

Listing 12-10: Creating a dataset with three groups of data (by modifying Listing 12-1)

This code generates three groups of data points, each containing 150 samples. The first group is centered on the point $(-2.2, 0)$, the second group on $(2.2, 0)$, and the third group on $(0, 2.5)$, all with a standard deviation of 1 for both coordinates. The data points from all groups are combined into a single NumPy array, and their corresponding labels are combined into another NumPy array.

Next, use Listing 12-11 to plot the dataset in order to visualize the three groups.

```
--snip--
plt.scatter(gr0[:, 0], gr0[:, 1], marker="o", s=5, c="C0")
plt.scatter(gr1[:, 0], gr1[:, 1], marker="^", s=5, c="C1")
plt.scatter(gr2[:, 0], gr2[:, 1], marker="s", s=5, c="C2")
--snip--
```

Listing 12-11: Plotting the dataset with three groups of data (by modifying Listing 12-2)

This code uses different markers to distinguish the three groups: circles for gr0, triangles for gr1, and squares for gr2. Figure 12-5 shows the resulting plot.

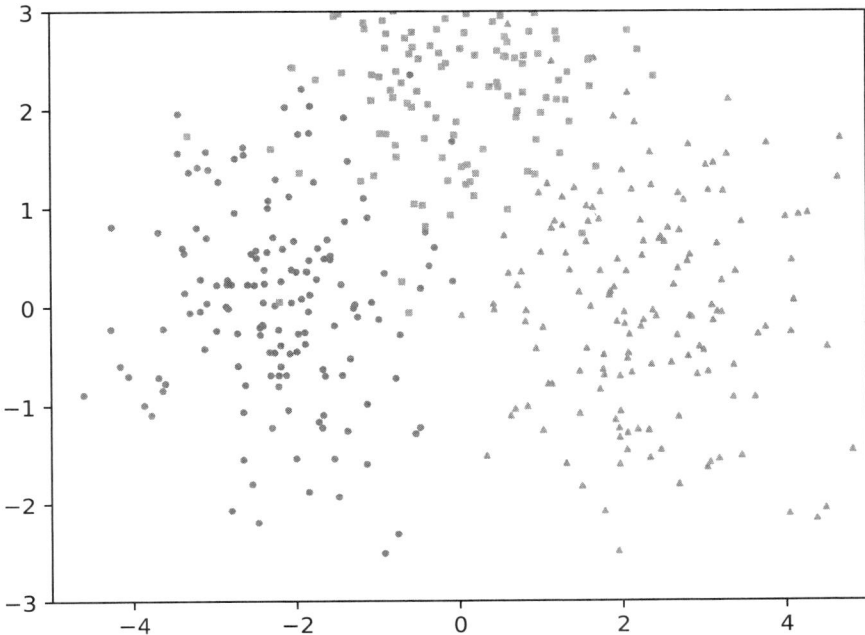

Figure 12-5: The data for the multiclass classification of three groups

The three groups of data points are clearly separated, but they have some overlap, making the multiclass classification task nontrivial.

Implementing the Active Learning Process with Multiple Classes

Now update the train_active_learning() function from Listing 12-4 to allow for any number of classes, as shown in Listing 12-12.

```
def train_active_learning(x, y, budget, query):
    """Train multiclass classifier with active learning.."""
    annotated_idxs = [np.random.choice(np.where(y == i)[0])
                      for i in range(int(y.max()) + 1)]
    --snip--
```

Listing 12-12: The function to perform the active learning for the multiclass classification (by modifying Listing 12-4)

This function initializes the annotated indices by selecting one random data point from each class, ensuring that the initial training set contains all classes. The function does so by iterating through each class index from 0 to the maximum. For each index, the function uses `np.random.choice()` to randomly pick one sample from the corresponding class. Next, in the active learning cycle, the function trains the model via the `train_model()` function (Listing 12-3) on gradually increasing annotated datasets; this part is identical to the function in Listing 12-4.

You'll also need to upgrade `plot_model()` from Listing 12-6 to plot three classes, as shown in Listing 12-13.

```
def plot_model3(model, gr0, gr1, gr2, annotated_x, annotated_y):
    """Plot model decision boundary and annotated data with 3 classes."""
    plt.scatter(gr0[:, 0], gr0[:, 1], marker="o", s=0.5, c="C0")
    plt.scatter(gr1[:, 0], gr1[:, 1], marker="^", s=0.5, c="C1")
    plt.scatter(gr2[:, 0], gr2[:, 1], marker="s", s=0.5, c="C2")

    is0, is1, is2 = annotations == 0, annotations == 1, annotations == 2
    plt.scatter(annotated_x[is0, 0], annotated_x[is0, 1],
                marker="o", s=50, c="C0", label="Selected Group 1")
    plt.scatter(annotated_x[is1, 0], annotated_x[is1, 1],
                marker="^", s=50, c="C1", label="Selected Group 2")
    plt.scatter(annotated_x[is2, 0], annotated_x[is2, 1],
                marker="s", s=50, c="C2", label="Selected Group 3")

❶ xx, yy = np.meshgrid(np.linspace(-5, 5, 1000), np.linspace(-3, 3, 1000))
❷ z = model.predict(np.c_[xx.ravel(), yy.ravel()])
    z = z.reshape(xx.shape)
    plt.contour(xx, yy, z, levels=[0.5, 1.5], colors="black")
    plt.xlim(-5, 5)
    --snip--
```

Listing 12-13: The function for plotting the multiclass classification (by modifying Listing 12-6)

This function initializes the scatterplots for the three groups of data points. Then it separately plots the selected data points for each group.

Afterward, the function calculates and plots the decision boundaries by generating a mesh grid and using the model's predictions to draw contour lines separating the classes. To do so, the code first generates a mesh grid covering the entire plot area ❶. The code then predicts the class for each point in the mesh grid and reshapes the predicted classes to match the shape of the mesh grid ❷. Finally, the function plots contour lines that represent the decision boundaries between the classes. The contour levels are set to 0.5 and 1.5, which effectively separates the three classes by drawing lines where the predicted class probabilities are equal.

Random Sampling

To see how the model performs with random sampling for three classes, you can use the following:

```
accuracy_random, model_random, idxs_random = \
    train_active_learning(x, y, budget=30, query=query_random)
plot_model3(model_random, gr0, gr1, gr2, x[idxs_random], y[idxs_random])
```

This code uses the random sampling strategy implemented by query_random() in Listing 12-5. In our run of this code, the resulting accuracy is 0.91.

Figure 12-6 shows the decision boundary and annotated data points.

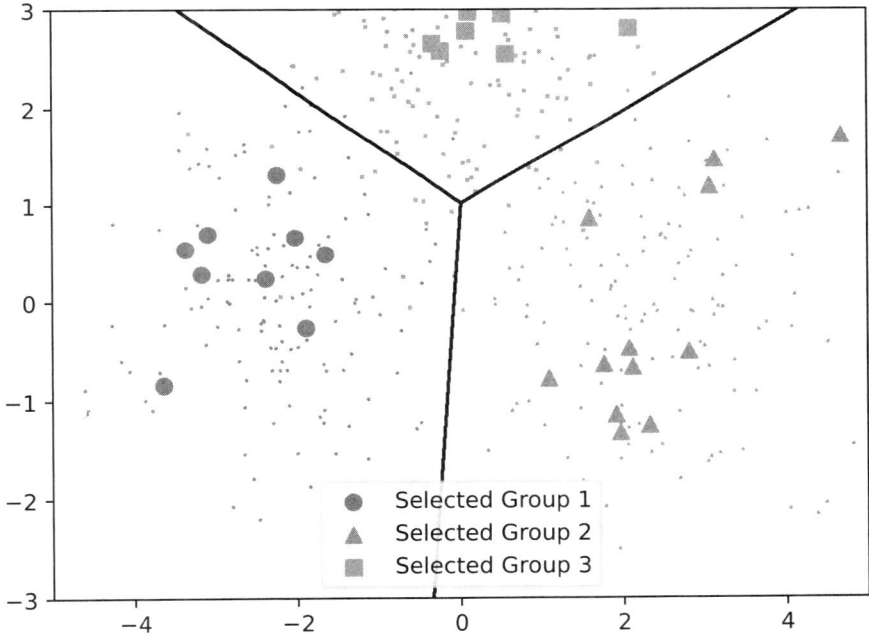

Figure 12-6: The decision boundary (lines) and annotated data (large symbols) with random sampling and three classes

The decision boundaries between the three classes are shown as contour lines, and the annotated data points are highlighted as larger symbols. Similar to the binary classification case shown in Figure 12-2, the function mostly samples points from the center of the distributions. This central sampling pattern indicates that with random sampling, the model tends to select data points in densely populated areas of each class, which aren't the most informative for refining the decision boundaries.

Uncertainty Sampling

Now that we've established some baseline results with random sampling, let's see how uncertainty sampling performs with three classes. As you've seen, this method selects the data points for which the model has the most uncertain predictions, potentially providing more-informative samples for training. Implement the active learning with uncertainty sampling as shown here:

```
accuracy_uncertainty, model_uncertainty, idxs_uncertainty = \
    train_active_learning(x, y, budget=30, query=query_uncertainty)
plot_model3(model_uncertainty, gr0, gr1, gr2,
            x[idxs_uncertainty], y[idxs_uncertainty])
```

This code uses the uncertainty sampling strategy implemented by the query _uncertainty() function in Listing 12-7. Our run gave an accuracy of 0.951, indicating that uncertainty sampling leads to a better model performance by focusing on the most informative samples, as we anticipated. Figure 12-7 shows the corresponding decision boundary and selected samples.

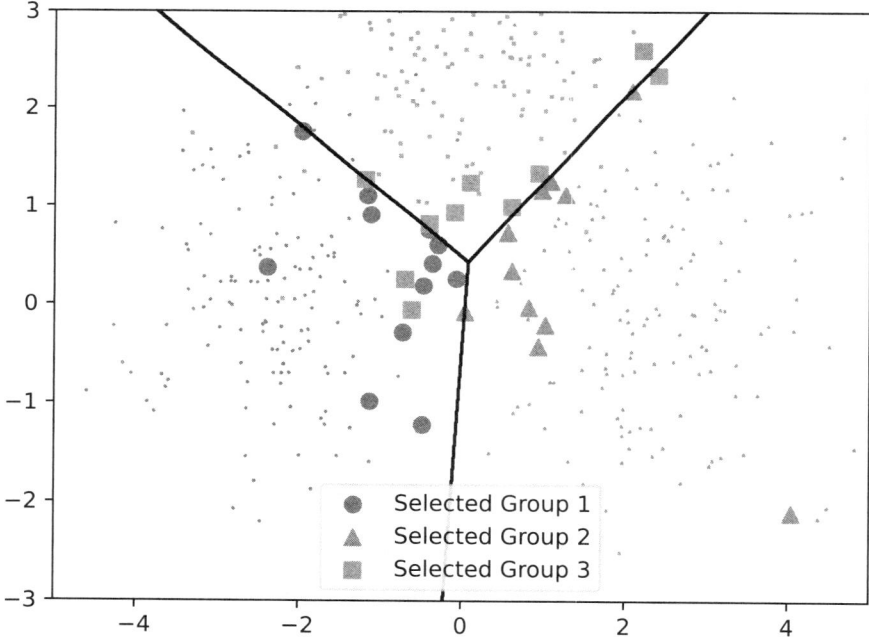

Figure 12-7: The decision boundary (lines) and annotated data (large symbols) with uncertainty sampling and three classes

Unlike random sampling, the points selected by uncertainty sampling are primarily located near the decision boundaries between the classes. This sampling strategy helps the model refine its decision boundaries more effectively by learning from the points where the model is least certain.

Comparing Sampling Strategies

After implementing various sampling strategies, comparing their performance is insightful. To do so, you can calculate the average accuracy as a function of the number of annotations over multiple trials for each sampling strategy, as shown in Listing 12-14.

```
trials = 100
--snip--
for _ in range(trials):
    accuracy_history_random, *_ = \
        train_active_learning(x, y, budget=30, query=query_random)
    --snip--
    accuracy_history_uncertainty, *_ = \
        train_active_learning(x, y, budget=30, query=query_uncertainty)
    --snip--
```

Listing 12-14: Calculating the average accuracy for multiclass classification (by modifying Listing 12-8)

The code performs 100 trials of active learning for each sampling strategy and records the accuracy at each step. For each trial, the function applies the random sampling strategy and the uncertainty sampling strategy.

You can then plot the average accuracy as a function of the number of annotations, using Listing 12-9. Figure 12-8 shows the resulting plot.

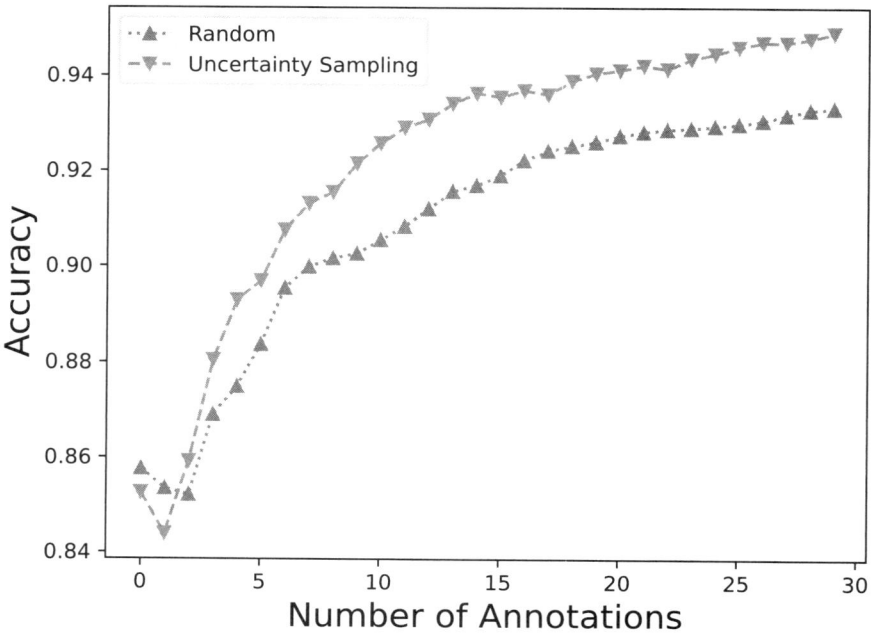

Figure 12-8: The average accuracy for multiclass classification

The uncertainty sampling strategy achieves higher accuracy with fewer annotated samples compared to random sampling. This highlights the efficiency of the uncertainty sampling strategy in selecting the most informative samples for annotation, thereby improving the model's performance more quickly than random sampling. The results demonstrate that active learning strategies focusing on sample informativeness can significantly enhance model training efficiency.

NOTE *Code Example 12-2, "Training a Three-Class Classifier with Active Learning," is available at* https://github.com/DeepTrackAI/DeepLearningCrashCourse. *Navigate to the* Ch12_AL *folder and then* ec12_2_active3. *The* active3.ipynb *notebook provides a complete code example that uses active learning to classify points in a plane into three classes.*

EXERCISE

12-4: Compare the performance of the following active learning strategies: random sampling, uncertainty sampling, small margin sampling, large margin sampling, and entropy sampling. Implement each strategy, perform active learning on a common dataset, and plot the average accuracy as a function of the number of annotated samples. Evaluate which strategy achieves the highest accuracy with the fewest annotations and discuss the strengths and weaknesses of each approach. Note that small margin sampling is often more stable because it finds points close to a boundary between two classes, not necessarily near the intersection of multiple classes.

Project 12A: Classifying MNIST Digits with Active Learning

In this project, you'll use active learning strategies to classify handwritten digits from the MNIST dataset. You've already encountered the MNIST dataset several times. In brief, it consists of 60,000 training images and 10,000 testing images. Each image is a 28×28−pixel grayscale representation of a handwritten digit from 0 to 9.

Unlike the previous examples in this chapter that employed a logistic regression, you'll use a convolutional neural network as the classifier, similar to what you employed in Project 3A to classify malaria-infected blood stains. Furthermore, you'll compare active learning strategies to determine which yields the best performance with the fewest labeled samples—namely, random sampling, uncertainty sampling, and an adversarial approach.

Training a Baseline Model

To appreciate the effectiveness of active learning, you'll first calculate the model's accuracy when trained on the full dataset. To begin, load the MNIST dataset and prepare the training and testing data loaders with Listing 12-15.

```
import deeplay as dl
from torchvision import datasets, transforms

train_data = datasets.MNIST(root="data", train=True, download=True,
                            transform=transforms.ToTensor())
test_data = datasets.MNIST(root="data", train=False, download=True,
                           transform=transforms.ToTensor())

train_dataloader = dl.DataLoader(train_data, batch_size=128, shuffle=True)
test_dataloader = dl.DataLoader(test_data, batch_size=1024, shuffle=False)
```

Listing 12-15: Loading the MNIST digits

This code loads the train and test MNIST datasets, then prepares the corresponding data loaders.

Next, define the classifier neural network. This network consists of a convolutional backbone followed by a simple multilayer perceptron head for classification, as shown in Listing 12-16.

```
import torch

backbone = dl.ConvolutionalNeuralNetwork(1, [64] * 4, 128)
backbone.blocks[1:].pool.configure(torch.nn.MaxPool2d, kernel_size=2)
❶ backbone.blocks[-1].append(dl.Layer(torch.nn.AdaptiveAvgPool2d, output_size=1))
❷ backbone.blocks[-1].append(dl.Layer(torch.nn.Flatten, output_size=1))

head = dl.MultiLayerPerceptron(128, [], 10)

classifier_template = dl.Sequential(backbone, head)
```

Listing 12-16: Defining the classifier neural network

This code initializes the backbone with one input channel to match the grayscale MNIST images, four convolutional layers with 64 filters each, and an output convolutional layer with 128 filters. Then the code adds an adaptive averaging filter that transforms each output feature map into a feature map with only 1 pixel ❶ and a flattening layer ❷. The classification head is a multilayer perceptron that takes the 128-dimensional output from the convolutional backbone and maps it onto 10 output classes. Finally, the code combines these components into a sequential model, where the backbone extracts features from the input images and the head performs the classification task. As usual, you can use `print(classifier_template)` to see details of the model.

After defining the network architecture, compile the classifier and train it on the entire dataset as a baseline, as shown in Listing 12-17.

```
from torchmetrics import Accuracy

classifier = dl.CategoricalClassifier(
    classifier_template.new(), optimizer=dl.Adam(lr=1e-3), num_classes=10,
    metrics=[Accuracy(task="multiclass", num_classes=10)],
).build()

trainer = dl.Trainer(max_epochs=10)
trainer.fit(classifier, train_dataloader)

full_results = trainer.test(classifier, test_dataloader)
```

Listing 12-17: Defining, training, and testing the classifier with all data

This code builds the classifier with a categorical classification head, an Adam optimizer, and accuracy as the evaluation metric, tailored for classification tasks with 10 distinct classes, corresponding to the number of MNIST digits. A `Trainer` object configured to run for 10 epochs manages the training process. After training, the code evaluates the model on the test set to determine its performance.

Printing the results with `print(full_results[0])`, you should observe a test loss of around 0.03 and an accuracy of around 99 percent, indicating that this model performs very well on the MNIST dataset when trained on the full dataset. You can use this as a reference point for evaluating the efficiency and effectiveness of various active learning strategies in the subsequent sections.

Implementing Multiple Active Learning Strategies

Now that you've established this baseline accuracy, you'll evaluate three distinct active learning strategies by using the same model trained on small subsets of the MNIST dataset: uniform random sampling, which selects samples randomly from the unlabeled pool; uncertainty sampling, which selects samples the model is least confident about based on the smallest difference between the highest and second-highest predicted class probabilities; and adversarial sampling, which uses an adversarial approach to select the most informative samples.

To ensure the reliability and statistical significance of your findings, you'll repeat each experiment five times (you can change this number depending on your availability of computational power). Afterward, you'll compare the performance of the models on the test set, focusing on the number of labeled samples required to achieve a specified level of accuracy.

Implementing a Common Configuration for All Samplings

To ensure the same conditions for testing each active learning strategy, configure the experiments with Listing 12-18.

```
trials, budget_per_iteration, max_budget = 5, 120, 1800
rounds = max_budget // budget_per_iteration - 1  # Number of rounds per trial
```

Listing 12-18: Configuring the general parameters

This code defines the key parameters for each experiment. The number of trials is set to 5, ensuring statistical significance by repeating each experiment multiple times. The budget_per_iteration is defined as 120 samples, specifying the number of new samples to annotate and add to the training set in each round of active learning. This contrasts with the previous examples, where only one annotation was added per iteration, making this approach more time efficient by processing multiple annotations at once. The code sets the maximum budget (max_budget) to 1800 samples, indicating the total number of samples available for annotation during the entire active learning process. Finally, the code calculates the number of rounds per trial by dividing the maximum budget by the budget per iteration and subtracting 1 to account for the random samples selected in the first iteration.

Next, define a reusable active learning loop, as shown in Listing 12-19. You'll use this loop to test the three strategies.

```
def al_loop(strategy, epochs):
    """Perform active learning loop."""
    trainer = dl.Trainer(max_epochs=epochs, enable_checkpointing=False,
                         enable_model_summary=False)
    trainer.fit(strategy)

    test_results = trainer.test(strategy, test_dataloader)
    accuracy = test_results[0]["testMulticlassAccuracy"]

    strategy.query_and_update(budget_per_iteration)
    strategy.reset_model()  # Reset the model to the initial state
    return accuracy
```

Listing 12-19: The function to perform an active training loop

First, this function trains the model on the current training set. Next, the function evaluates the model on the test set, calculating the accuracy to return. Then the function uses the active learning strategy to select the next samples. Finally, the function resets the model to the starting state so that each round of active learning starts training from scratch.

If the model is computationally expensive, you can omit the fourth step and continue training from the previous model state. Continuing from the previous state may result in the model becoming more specialized to the earlier samples, potentially leading to overfitting and less generalization. On the other hand, resetting the model to the starting state allows each round of active learning to begin with a fresh perspective, ensuring that the model remains adaptable to new data.

Uniform Random Sampling

As your first query strategy, you'll execute uniform random sampling with Listing 12-20.

```
import deeplay.activelearning as al
import numpy as np

uniform_acc = np.empty((trials, rounds))
for t in range(trials):
    uniform_train_pool = al.ActiveLearningDataset(train_data)
❶   uniform_train_pool.annotate_random(budget_per_iteration)
❷   uniform_strategy = al.UniformStrategy(
        classifier_template.new(), train_pool=uniform_train_pool,
        test=test_data, batch_size=128,
        test_metrics=[Accuracy(task="multiclass", num_classes=10)],
    ).build()

    for r in range(rounds):
        print(f"Trial {t + 1}/{trials} Round {r + 1}/{rounds}", flush=True)
        uniform_acc[t, r] = al_loop(uniform_strategy, epochs=10)
```

Listing 12-20: Training with uniform random sampling

This code first wraps the training data with an ActiveLearningDataset object. This object keeps track of which samples are annotated and unannotated. It also provides a method to query the next samples to annotate. At the start, the object assumes that all data is unannotated. Then the code initializes the training dataset by randomly annotating a small subset of the data ❶. This is required for all three active learning strategies you'll test.

Next, the code creates a UniformStrategy object, which contains the query strategy ❷. This object takes a model as input, together with the training data pool, the test set, a batch size, and a list of metrics. Finally, the active learning loop is run for rounds iterations. For each round, training lasts 10 epochs. The resulting accuracies are saved for each trial and round in the uniform_acc NumPy array, reaching an accuracy of around 92 percent.

Uncertainty Sampling

Once you've performed random sampling, you can similarly test uncertainty sampling with Listing 12-21.

```
--snip--
uncertainty_acc = np.empty((trials, rounds))
for t in range(trials):
    uncertainty_train_pool = al.ActiveLearningDataset(train_data)
    uncertainty_train_pool.annotate_random(budget_per_iteration)
❶ uncertainty_strategy = al.UncertaintyStrategy(
        classifier_template.new(), train_pool=uncertainty_train_pool,
        criterion=al.Margin(), test=test_data, batch_size=128,
        test_metrics=[Accuracy(task="multiclass", num_classes=10)],
    ).build()

    for r in range(rounds):
        print(f"Trial {t + 1}/{trials} Round {r + 1}/{rounds}", flush=True)
        uncertainty_acc[t, r] = al_loop(uncertainty_strategy, epochs=10)
```

Listing 12-21: Training with uncertainty sampling (by modifying Listing 12-20)

This code implements the uncertainty sampling strategy. For each trial, the training data is wrapped with an `ActiveLearningDataset` object, similarly to the random sampling strategy.

Then the code defines the uncertainty strategy by using the Uncertainty Strategy class ❶, which includes a model, the training data pool, the test set, a batch size, and a list of metrics. The criterion parameter is set to `al.Margin()`, specifying that the model should measure uncertainty by the smallest margin between the two highest class probabilities.

The code iterates through the active learning loop for the specified number of rounds, training the model for 10 epochs each round. The resulting accuracies are stored in the `uncertainty_acc` array.

Uncertainty sampling does indeed work better than random sampling, reaching an accuracy of around 95 percent. However, the gap between the baseline accuracy of 99 percent and the accuracy achieved through uncertainty sampling reveals that neural networks are generally poor at estimating their own uncertainty. More-advanced methods try to mitigate this by using alternate means of estimating uncertainty, such as ensemble methods, Monte Carlo dropout, or estimating the loss of the model.

Another issue with uncertainty sampling is that it can be biased toward outliers or data points with incomplete information. While these data points are often the most uncertain, they are not necessarily the most informative. These points are often highly uncertain because the model struggles to predict their labels, but labeling them may not improve the model's understanding of the broader data distribution. Outliers and noisy data can mislead the model, focusing its learning on rare or irrelevant cases rather than general patterns.

You can mitigate this issue by using alternative methods to identify informative samples. These methods include selecting data points based on how much they are expected to change the model (expected model change), how different they are from one another (diversity), or how well they represent the overall data distribution (representativeness). In fact, a combination of these measures can perform better than any single measure.

Adversarial Sampling

To see this in action, you'll explore a combination of uncertainty sampling and diversity sampling by using an adversarial approach; you'll adversarially train a discriminator to distinguish between the embeddings of annotated and unannotated images.

This approach has several advantages because it enhances the uncertainty sampling process by also considering the diversity of the data points. First, the discriminator's choices can indicate the samples' diversity. If the discriminator predicts that an unlabeled image is labeled, that means that the image is similar to already labeled images and might not be very informative. Second, by adversarially training the backbone to fool the discriminator, you're enforcing a structure to the embeddings by using all the data in the dataset. The model learns to organize the data in a way that captures the relationships between different samples, not just focusing on the uncertain ones. This added structure helps the model generalize better, especially when working with small training sets, because it ensures that the model doesn't just memorize individual examples but understands the underlying patterns in the data.

You can implement the adversarial sampling strategy by training a discriminator to identify which samples are most diverse and informative. You'll do this with Listing 12-22.

```
--snip--
adversarial_acc = np.empty((trials, rounds))
for t in range(trials):
❶ discriminator = dl.MultiLayerPerceptron(128, [128, 128], 1,
                                    out_activation=torch.nn.Sigmoid())
❷ discriminator.initialize(dl.initializers.Kaiming())

    adversarial_train_pool = al.ActiveLearningDataset(train_data)
    adversarial_train_pool.annotate_random(budget_per_iteration)
❸ adversarial_strategy = al.AdversarialStrategy(
        backbone=backbone.new(), classification_head=head.new(),
        discriminator_head=discriminator.new(),
        train_pool=adversarial_train_pool, criterion=al.Margin(),
        test=test_data, batch_size=128,
        test_metrics=[Accuracy(task="multiclass", num_classes=10)],
    ).build()

    for r in range(rounds):
        ❹ adversarial_acc[t, r] = al_loop(adversarial_strategy, epochs=5)
```

Listing 12-22: Training with adversarial sampling (by modifying Listing 12-21)

This code snippet implements the adversarial sampling strategy. The discriminator is defined as a multilayer perceptron with an input size of 128 to match the output from the backbone, two hidden layers with 128 units each, and an output size of 1 ❶. The output activation function is set to sigmoid, appropriate for binary classification tasks such as distinguishing between annotated and unannotated samples.

The code then calls the `initialize()` method on the discriminator, using the Kaiming initializer ❷. This initializer is well suited for layers with ReLU activations and helps set up the network weights properly.

The code then initializes the `AdversarialStrategy` class to create the adversarial strategy object ❸. This class takes the backbone, classification head, and discriminator head as input, along with the training data pool, criterion, batch size, and test metrics. The code uses the `backbone.new()` and `head.new()` methods to create new instances of the backbone and classification head, ensuring that each round starts with a fresh model.

The active learning loop runs for the specified number of rounds, each training the model for five epochs ❹. This is fewer epochs compared to the previous strategies because each epoch processes the entire dataset, including both annotated and unannotated data. Furthermore, annotated data points are seen multiple times per epoch since each batch contains an equal number of annotated and unannotated samples, with the smaller set repeated to match the size of the larger one.

This adversarial sampling approach combines uncertainty and diversity by using a discriminator to select informative samples. Specifically, the discriminator primarily accounts for diversity, while the uncertainty is separately measured by the `criterion=al.Margin()` function. These two measures—uncertainty and diversity—are then combined into a single, weighted informativeness score. This combination helps improve the model's generalization ability on small training sets. The resulting accuracies are stored in the `adversarial_acc` array.

Comparing the Performance of the Active Learning Strategies

After running the experiments with all three strategies, you can compare their performance in terms of test accuracy and the number of samples required to reach a certain accuracy level. This comparison will highlight the effectiveness of each active learning strategy and provide insights into their strengths and weaknesses.

You can plot the accuracy as a function of the number of annotated images, using Listing 12-23.

```
import matplotlib.pyplot as plt

❶ x = np.arange(budget_per_iteration, max_budget, budget_per_iteration)

plt.plot(x, np.median(uniform_acc, 0), label="Uniform", linestyle="--")
plt.plot(x, np.median(uncertainty_acc, 0), label="Uncertainty", linestyle="-.")
plt.plot(x, np.median(adversarial_acc, 0), label="Adversarial", linestyle="-")
plt.axhline(full_results[0]["testMulticlassAccuracy_epoch"],
            label="Full Test Accuracy", color="black", linestyle=":")
```

```
plt.xlabel("Number of Annotated Samples")
plt.ylabel("Test Accuracy")
plt.ylim([0, 1])
plt.legend()
plt.show()
```

Listing 12-23: Plotting the accuracy for the three strategies

This code defines the x-axis as the range of annotated samples ❶; plots the median accuracy across trials for the uniform sampling strategy, the uncertainty sampling strategy, and the adversarial sampling strategy; and adds a horizontal line representing the accuracy of the model trained on the full dataset, providing a benchmark for comparison.

Figure 12-9 shows the resulting plot.

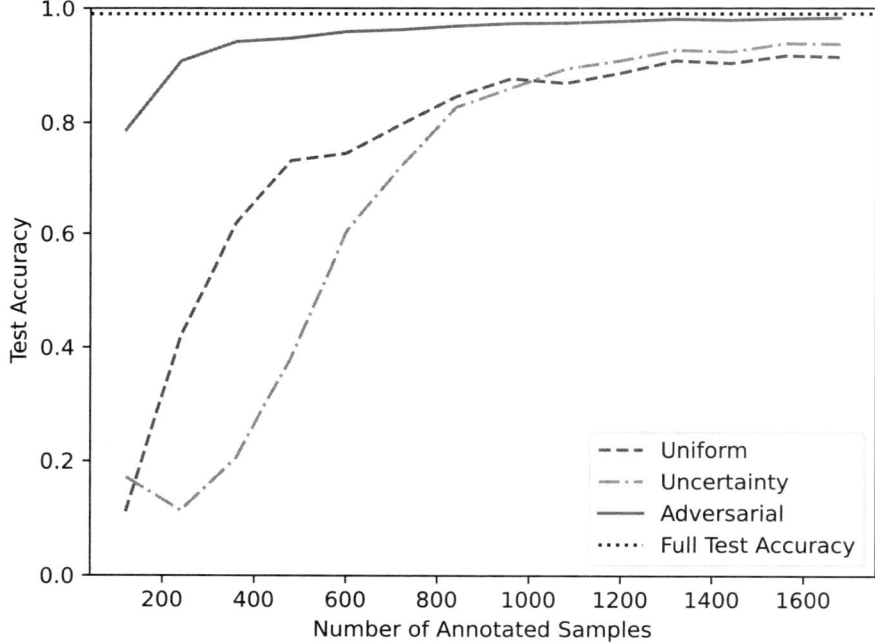

Figure 12-9: Test accuracy as a function of annotated samples

You can observe how the accuracy of each strategy changes as more samples are annotated. Each line represents the median accuracy across multiple trials for each strategy.

The uniform sampling (dashed line) strategy randomly selects samples from the dataset. This approach shows a steady increase in accuracy as more samples are annotated, but it generally requires more samples to reach higher accuracy levels as compared to the other strategies.

The uncertainty sampling (dash-dot line) strategy selects samples about which the model is least certain. After a slow start, this approach shows a faster improvement in accuracy with fewer samples, as compared to uniform sampling, demonstrating the efficiency of selecting informative samples.

The adversarial sampling (solid line) strategy combines uncertainty and diversity by training a discriminator to identify the most informative samples. This strategy reaches high accuracy levels more quickly and consistently than the other two strategies, indicating its effectiveness in selecting diverse and informative samples.

The dotted horizontal line represents the accuracy of the model trained on the full dataset. Adversarial sampling achieves a performance similar to this benchmark while using only 3 percent of the training data.

NOTE   *Code Example 12-A, "Training an MNIST Digits Classifier with Active Learning," is available at* https://github.com/DeepTrackAI/DeepLearningCrashCourse. *Navigate to the* Ch12_AL *folder and then* ec12_A_mnist_al. *The* mnist_al.ipynb *notebook provides a complete code example that uses active learning to train a neural network capable of classifying the MNIST digits.*

Summary

In this chapter, you explored active learning and its application to both binary and multiclass classification problems. Active learning optimizes the labeling process by selectively choosing the most informative samples, reducing the labeling effort while maintaining high model performance. To understand the effectiveness of active learning in binary and multiclass classification, you started by creating simple datasets; you then applied logistic regression models to illustrate the active learning process, using random sampling and uncertainty sampling.

The chapter culminated in a comprehensive project using the MNIST dataset. You used a convolutional neural network and compared the effectiveness of random, uncertainty, and adversarial query strategies. Uncertainty and adversarial sampling strategies significantly outperformed random sampling, achieving high accuracy with fewer annotated samples. The adversarial strategy in particular demonstrated superior efficiency by combining criteria of uncertainty and diversity to select the most informative samples.

As you continue to apply active learning techniques, you'll notice that they not only can enhance the efficiency of the learning process by reducing labeling costs while maintaining or even improving model performance, but also can provide a powerful tool for continuously adapting models to new data and evolving patterns. In fact, although this chapter focused primarily on demonstrating active learning's efficiency in initial training, these techniques are particularly valuable in real-world scenarios with data distributions that may shift over time. By iteratively selecting and labeling the most relevant samples from new or evolving datasets, active learning enables models to remain accurate and up to date without requiring a complete retraining on a vast labeled dataset. This adaptability ensures that your models continue to perform well even as the underlying data changes, making active learning a crucial strategy for maintaining model relevance and robustness in dynamic environments.

Seminal Works and Further Reading

The concept of active learning was proposed in 1994 by David Cohn et al. in "Improving Generalization with Active Learning," published in *Machine Learning* (volume 15, pages 201–221). The authors introduced the idea of query selection in the context of neural networks, focusing on how to actively choose the most informative data points to improve model generalization. Their approach centered on uncertainty sampling, where the model queries instances that it's least certain about, thereby maximizing the learning potential from limited labeled data.

CHALLENGE PROJECTS

12-1: Active learning for text classification   Extend the active learning framework to a text-classification problem. Use a dataset such as the 20 Newsgroups dataset, which consists of news articles categorized into 20 topics. Implement a text classifier by using a neural network and compare active learning strategies. Evaluate the performance in terms of classification accuracy and the number of labeled samples required to achieve a certain accuracy level.

12-2: Advanced text translation with transformer decoders   Implement a transformer decoder model to perform text translation on a public dataset, such as the WMT14 English-German dataset. Preprocess the dataset and train your model to translate sentences from English to German. Evaluate your model's performance by using BLEU scores, and compare your results with those from state-of-the-art models. Additionally, experiment with various active learning strategies to iteratively select the most challenging sentences for labeling, aiming to improve the model's translation accuracy with fewer labeled examples.

12-3: Automated image captioning   Create a neural network model that generates captions for images—for example, by classifying the keywords associated with the objects present in the image. Combining image analysis with NLP, this challenge involves not only recognizing objects in an image but also understanding the context and relationships to generate coherent and accurate descriptions.

12-4: Active learning with vision transformers   Revisit the ViT classification problem introduced in Chapter 8, where achieving high accuracy on the CIFAR-10 dataset required a large number of labeled samples, even with techniques like CutMix. Implement an active learning framework to reduce the number of labeled samples required to achieve high accuracy with ViT. Experiment with active learning strategies, such as uncertainty sampling and adversarial sampling, to identify the most informative images for labeling. Compare the performance of these strategies and evaluate how effectively they reduce the labeling cost while maintaining or improving model accuracy.

13

MASTERING DECISION-MAKING WITH DEEP REINFORCEMENT LEARNING

In this chapter, you'll discover reinforcement learning, a fascinating and powerful branch of machine learning focused on training computers to make decisions and to control systems as agents.

Reinforcement learning has been instrumental in solving complex problems across various domains. For instance, it's used in robotics to enable autonomous navigation, allowing robots to learn how to walk or fly by optimizing their movements through trial and error. In finance, reinforcement learning algorithms are used to manage investment portfolios by adapting to market changes and maximizing returns. In gaming, reinforcement learning has powered agents like AlphaGo, which famously defeated human world champions in the ancient game of Go—a milestone in artificial intelligence.

The history of reinforcement learning dates back to the 1950s and 1960s, with early work by researchers such as Richard Bellman, who developed the Bellman equation, a foundational concept in reinforcement learning. Over the decades, reinforcement learning has evolved from simple rule-based systems to sophisticated algorithms capable of tackling high-dimensional, complex problems. In reinforcement learning, agents learn through interactions with their environment, shaping their behavior to optimize outcomes based on rewards and penalties. This approach is exceptionally well suited for controlling complex systems, especially when predefined rules are inadequate.

You'll start by exploring the foundational concepts of reinforcement learning, including algorithms and strategies that enable agents to learn and adapt, such as Q-learning. You'll apply these principles to play a simplified version of *Tetris* so that you can experience a clear and engaging demonstration of their effectiveness in problem-solving and decision-making tasks.

Moving beyond traditional reinforcement learning, you'll then learn about *deep reinforcement learning*. This advanced variant integrates neural networks in the control cycle, enabling agents to handle high-dimensional input spaces and more-complex decision-making scenarios.

By the end of this chapter, you'll understand both classical and deep reinforcement learning. This knowledge will enable you to address challenges that require you to have adaptive, intelligent control, particularly in high-dimensional and complex environments.

Understanding Reinforcement Learning and Q-Learning

In *reinforcement learning*, an agent learns to make decisions by interacting with an environment through a process of trial and error. The agent's objective is to maximize its cumulative *reward* over time. In this machine learning paradigm, the agent observes the state of the environment, decides which actions to take, receives rewards or penalties as a consequence of its actions, and adjusts its strategy to maximize its reward in the future. In short, reinforcement learning is concerned with decision-making under uncertainty, learning through interaction, and determining the optimal behavior in a given context.

The central elements in reinforcement learning are the *agent*, which is the decision-maker and learner, and the *environment*, which encompasses everything external to the agent that the agent interacts with. The agent perceives the *state*, a representation of the current situation or condition of the environment, and takes an *action*, a choice that impacts the state of the environment. Following the action, the agent receives a *reward*, which is positive or negative (*penalty*) feedback from the environment in response to the action taken. The agent's behavior is guided by a *policy*, a strategy for mapping states to actions, determining its actions based on the current state. Additionally, the agent uses a *value function* to estimate the expected return (cumulative future rewards) of being in a given state or performing a specific action in a given state. The agent's ultimate goal is to learn a policy that maximizes the total expected reward over time.

Q-learning is a type of reinforcement learning: The agent learns an action-value function known as the *Q-function*. This function estimates the expected total reward of taking each possible action in a given state, allowing the agent to choose the optimal policy by selecting the action with the highest expected reward.

The action-value function $Q(s, a)$ represents the expected utility of taking action a in state s. Q-learning aims to determine the function Q that satisfies the *Bellman equation*:

$$Q(s, a) \quad = \quad \underbrace{R(s, a)}_{\text{immediate reward}} \quad + \quad \gamma \quad \underbrace{\max_{a'} Q(s', a')}_{\text{future reward}} \qquad (13.1)$$

Here, $R(s, a)$ denotes the immediate reward received for taking action a while in state s, after which the situation transitions to state s'. The expression $\max_{a'} Q(s', a')$ quantifies the maximum potential value attainable in this subsequent state s'. Including this expression ensures that the agent's decisions optimize cumulative rewards over time, considering both immediate and future gains.

The γ value is the *discount factor*, which balances the importance of immediate versus future rewards. It typically ranges from 0 to 1. A higher γ increases the value of future rewards, leading the agent to prioritize long-term outcomes, while a lower γ favors immediate rewards.

At its core, the Q-learning algorithm iteratively approximates the $Q(s, a)$ function described by the Bellman equation through experience. The algorithm achieves this by executing the *Q-learning update rule*:

$$\tilde{Q}(s, a) \leftarrow \tilde{Q}(s, a) + \alpha \left[\underbrace{R(s, a) + \gamma \max_{a'} \tilde{Q}(s', a')}_{\text{estimated optimal reward}} - \underbrace{\tilde{Q}(s, a)}_{\text{current reward}} \right] \qquad (13.2)$$

Here, $\tilde{Q}(s, a)$ is the agent's current estimate for the true $Q(s, a)$, and α is the learning rate. The term $R(s, a) + \gamma \max_{a'} \tilde{Q}(s', a')$ estimates the optimal future reward. The difference between this estimate and the current reward $\tilde{Q}(s, a)$, scaled by α, determines the magnitude of the update. During this iterative updating process, the agent refines its policy, typically using a *greedy policy*, to select the action with the highest Q-value in the current state based on the current knowledge of the agent captured by $\tilde{Q}(s, a)$. These updates enable the agent to converge on an optimal policy that balances immediate and future rewards, guiding decision-making to achieve the best outcomes over time.

Crucially, Q-learning is a *model-free* reinforcement learning algorithm effective in environments with discrete, finite states and actions. Its model-free nature means that it doesn't require prior knowledge of the environment's dynamics. Furthermore, the versatility of Q-learning makes it suitable for both deterministic and stochastic environments.

In many practical applications, Q-learning performs well in environments with relatively small state-action spaces. For instance, in a simple game like tic-tac-toe, the state space consists of $3^9 = 19{,}683$ possible states, as each of the nine positions on the board can be empty, filled with an X, or filled with an O (note that some of these states are never reached if playing according to the rules of the game). This small state space makes it feasible to maintain and update a Q-table that effectively covers the entire state-action space, allowing the agent to learn optimal policies efficiently.

However, when applied to more-complex environments with vast state spaces, the limitations of Q-learning become evident. The number of possible states can reach astronomical figures, far beyond the capabilities of traditional Q-learning to handle. For example, a grid-based game with a large board and multiple possible tile placements can lead to a combinatorial explosion of states.

Maintaining and updating a Q-table under these conditions would require an immense amount of memory and countless training iterations to explore even a fraction of the state-action space effectively. As you'll see later in the chapter, these challenges require more-advanced approaches, such as deep Q-learning, which can generalize across large state spaces by using neural networks.

EXERCISES

13-1: Implement a Q-learning agent for tic-tac-toe. Recall how you play the game and the strategies you use to win or avoid losing. Most people develop optimal strategies when first learning tic-tac-toe, such as taking the center square, creating forks (two potential winning moves), and blocking your opponent's winning moves. Use these insights to create a Q-learning agent capable of playing the game:

1. Reflect on your winning strategies: List the key strategies you use in tic-tac-toe.
2. Define a state representation: Propose a way to represent the game states that captures these strategies effectively but keeps the state space manageable. Consider simplifying the state space by focusing on critical patterns or board positions.
3. Design a Q-table: Using your state representation, create a simplified Q-table that maps states to actions, incorporating the strategies you've identified.
4. Implement the Q-learning agent: Code a Q-learning agent by using your Q-table structure. Ensure that the agent updates its Q-values based on the rewards from winning, drawing, or losing.
5. Train and evaluate: Train the agent over multiple games against a random player. Observe how the agent's performance improves over time and how effectively it learns to apply your strategies.

13-2: Estimate the total number of possible game states in *Connect Four*, a game played on a seven-column by six-row grid. Discuss how this larger state space affects the feasibility of using traditional Q-learning with a Q-table. Explain why more-advanced methods like deep Q-learning are necessary for such complex environments.

A key challenge in reinforcement learning is balancing *exploration*, or trying new actions to discover their effects, and *exploitation*, or using known information to maximize rewards.

To this end, researchers have recently developed *curiosity-driven exploration*, in which agents have an intrinsic motivation to investigate novel or less understood areas of the environment. This approach uses an intrinsic reward signal based on the *prediction error* or *uncertainty* of the agent's model. Essentially, the agent experiences a form of "boredom" when encountering predictable rewards, while it finds unexpected rewards or penalties more intriguing and worth exploring.

Curiosity-driven exploration is particularly effective in environments with sparse or misleading external rewards, since it promotes comprehensive learning and effective strategy development. By integrating curiosity, agents achieve a more efficient balance between exploration and exploitation, leading to faster learning and improved performance. In the following sections, you'll see how this concept can significantly shape an algorithm's optimization procedure.

Implementing Tetris

A timeless and iconic video game, *Tetris* was created in 1984 by software engineer Alexey Pajitnov. It revolutionized the gaming industry with its simple yet addictive gameplay.

Tetris features a random sequence of "Tetriminos," geometric shapes composed of four square blocks each that descend from the top of the playing field. The player must strategically rotate, move, and drop these pieces to create horizontal lines without gaps. When a player forms such a line, it disappears, and the player earns points. The player loses when the pieces pile up high enough to reach the top of the game board before the player can make them disappear. As the game progresses, the Tetriminos fall more quickly, increasing the challenge.

In this section, you'll implement a simplified version of *Tetris* that you can play yourself.

Constructing a Simplified Tetris

The simplified version of *Tetris* you'll implement captures the fundamental mechanics of the original game, such as tile placement, rotation, dropping, line clearing, and scoring. You'll implement it step-by-step in the Tetris class.

Tiles

Instead of traditional Tetriminos, you'll use a set of simplified tiles consisting of two, three, or four square blocks. Figure 13-1 shows these tiles.

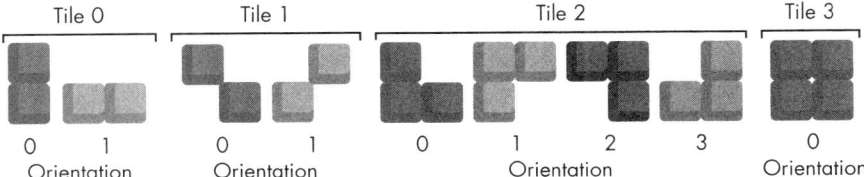

Figure 13-1: The tiles of the simplified Tetris *game*

You can implement these tiles with Listing 13-1.

```
class Tetris:
    """Simplified Tetris."""

    TILES = [
        [
            [[0, 2]],  # Tile 0, orientation 0
            [[0, 1], [0, 1]],  # Tile 0, orientation 1
        ],
        [
            [[1, 2], [0, 1]],  # Tile 1, orientation 0
            [[0, 1], [1, 2]],  # Tile 1, orientation 1
        ],
        [
            [[0, 2], [0, 1]],  # Tile 2, orientation 0
            [[0, 2], [1, 2]],  # Tile 2, orientation 1
            [[1, 2], [0, 2]],  # Tile 2, orientation 2
            [[0, 1], [0, 2]],  # Tile 2, orientation 3
        ],
        [
            [[0, 2], [0, 2]],  # Tile 3, orientation 0
        ],
    ]
```

Listing 13-1: The class implementing Tetris *with a simplified set of tiles*

This code builds the TILES array within the Tetris class. This array represents the types of tiles and their respective orientations. Each tile in the TILES array is a list of orientations. An orientation is itself a list of pairs, in which each pair specifies the blocks occupied by the tile in that pair's corresponding column. The pair values represent the start (inclusive) and end (exclusive) of the occupied blocks. For instance, the pair [0, 2] means that the blocks occupy positions 0 and 1 in that column, while [1, 2] means that the block occupies only position 1 in that column.

The tiles are simplified versions of the traditional Tetriminos:

- Tile 0 has two linear orientations: a vertical line of two blocks and a horizontal line of two blocks.

- Tile 1 has two diagonal orientations: top left to bottom right, and bottom left to top right.

- Tile 2 has four L-shaped orientations, each representing a different rotation.

- Tile 3 is a simple 2×2 square.

Game Board

After you've built your tiles, you can add the game board to the Tetris class, as shown in Listing 13-2.

```
import numpy as np

class Tetris:
    --snip--

    UNDEFINED = -1

    def __init__(self, rows, cols):
        """Initialize Tetris."""
        self.rows, self.cols = rows, cols
        self.restart()

    def restart(self):
        """Restart the game."""
      ❶ self.board = np.full((self.rows, self.cols), Tetris.UNDEFINED)
```

Listing 13-2: Adding the game board to the `Tetris` class (by modifying Listing 13-1)

This code expands the `Tetris` class by introducing the game board, a crucial component of the *Tetris* game. The game board is represented as a 2D NumPy array, with the dimensions specified by rows and cols, defined when initializing the class. The code also sets the constant `UNDEFINED` to -1, to represent empty cells on the board. When the game starts, the restart() method uses this value to initialize the game board to an empty state ❶. This method also provides a convenient way to reset the game, making it easy to start a new game after a game ends.

Gameplay Loop

During gameplay, the player encounters one descending tile at a time. The player can move the tile horizontally, rotate it to change its orientation, and drop it to the bottom of the board. The objective is to place the tiles to make complete horizontal lines running across the board without gaps. When a line is completed, it disappears from the board, and the player earns points. You can implement these functionalities in the `Tetris` class by making the additions shown in Listing 13-3.

```
import numpy as np
import random

class Tetris:
    --snip--
    def restart(self):
        --snip--
        self.current_tile = Tetris.UNDEFINED
        self.tile_x = Tetris.UNDEFINED
        self.tile_y = Tetris.UNDEFINED
        self.tile_orientation = Tetris.UNDEFINED

        self.next_tile()
```

```python
    def next_tile(self):
        """Get the next tile."""
        self.current_tile = random.randint(0, len(Tetris.TILES) - 1)
        self.tile_x = self.cols // 2
        self.tile_y = self.rows
        self.tile_orientation = 0

    def move_left(self):
        """Move current tile to the left."""
        if self.tile_x - 1 >= 0:
            self.tile_x -= 1
            return True
        else:
            return False

    def move_right(self):
        """Move current tile to the right."""
        tilewidth = len(Tetris.TILES[self.current_tile][self.tile_orientation])
        if self.tile_x + 1 <= self.cols - tilewidth:
            self.tile_x += 1
            return True
        else:
            return False

    def rotate(self):
        """Rotate current tile."""
        new_orientation = ((self.tile_orientation + 1)
                           % len(Tetris.TILES[self.current_tile]))
        tilewidth = len(Tetris.TILES[self.current_tile][new_orientation])
        if self.tile_x <= self.cols - tilewidth:
            self.tile_orientation = new_orientation
            return True
        else:
            return False

    def drop(self):
        """Drop current tile and update game board."""
        tile = Tetris.TILES[self.current_tile][self.tile_orientation]

        # Find first location where the tile collides with occupied locations
        self.tile_y = 0
        for tile_column in range(len(tile)):
            # Tile final y position for this tile column
            # if no other columns are taken into account.
            tile_y = -1
```

```
        for y in range(self.rows - 1, -1, -1):
            if self.board[y, self.tile_x + tile_column] > 0:
                tile_y = y + 1 - tile[tile_column][0]
                break
        # Update tile y position
        if tile_y > self.tile_y:
            self.tile_y = tile_y

❶   # Change board entries at the newly placed tile to occupied
    for tile_column in range(len(tile)):
        self.board[self.tile_y + tile[tile_column][0]
                   :self.tile_y + tile[tile_column][1],
                   tile_column + self.tile_x] = 1

❷   # Remove full lines
    removed_lines = 0
    for y in range(self.rows - 1, -1, -1):
        if np.sum(self.board[y, :]) == self.cols:
            removed_lines += 1
            for y1 in range(y, self.rows - 1):
                self.board[y1, :] = self.board[y1 + 1, :]
            self.board[self.rows - 1, :] = Tetris.UNDEFINED

    self.next_tile()
```

Listing 13-3: Adding the gameplay loop to the Tetris *class (by modifying Listing 13-2)*

This code creates the methods that control the movement of the current tile during the gameplay loop, including initialization, lateral movement, rotation, dropping, and updating the game board based on the tile's final position. In addition to the board, the restart() method now sets the values of the current tile (current_tile), its lateral position (tile_x), its vertical position (tile_y), and its orientation (tile_orientation) to UNDEFINED.

The next_tile() method randomly selects the next tile and positions it at the center of the top of the board.

The player can move the current tile left with the move_left() method, move it right with move_right(), or rotate it with rotate(). When the player's action is *legal* (the piece remains within the game-board boundaries and doesn't overlap with already occupied spaces), these methods adjust the position or orientation of the tile within the game board's bounds and return True. Otherwise, they don't change the position or orientation of the tile and return False.

The drop() method moves the tile down until it collides with another tile or the bottom of the board ❶. This method also clears any completed lines, adjusting the game board accordingly ❷. Finally, drop() calls the next_tile() method to choose the next tile.

Game Progression and End Condition

The game progresses by introducing a new tile each time the previous one is placed. Over time, the player either achieves victory by placing the maximum number of tiles or faces defeat when the board fills up to the top.

In this version of the game, the code uses seeded randomness to give the player the option to fix the sequence of new tiles. This predictable sequence is particularly useful for testing and comparing multiple strategies under identical conditions. You can implement these game dynamics with the modifications shown in Listing 13-4.

```
--snip--
class Tetris:
    --snip--
    def __init__(self, rows, cols, max_tiles, random_seed):
        """Initialize Tetris."""
        self.rows, self.cols = rows, cols
        self.max_tiles = max_tiles
        self.random_seed = random_seed

        self.restart()

    def restart(self):
        --snip--
 ❶      self.gameover = False
        self.tile_count = 0

        # Create predefined tile sequence
        rand_state = random.getstate()
        random.seed(self.random_seed)
        self.tile_sequence = [random.randint(0, len(Tetris.TILES) - 1)
                              for _ in range(self.max_tiles)]
        random.setstate(rand_state)

        self.next_tile()

    def next_tile(self):
        """Get the next tile."""
        if self.tile_count < self.max_tiles:
            if self.random_seed is not None:
 ❷              self.current_tile = self.tile_sequence[self.tile_count]
            else:
 ❸              self.current_tile = random.randint(0, len(Tetris.TILES) - 1)

            self.tile_x = self.cols // 2
            self.tile_y = self.rows
            self.tile_orientation = 0

            self.tile_count += 1
```

```
    else:
❹ self.gameover = True

--snip--

def drop(self):
    --snip--
    if self.tile_y + np.max(tile) > self.rows:
❺ self.gameover = True
    else:
        # Change board entries at the newly placed tile to occupied
        --snip--

    self.next_tile()
```

Listing 13-4: Adding the game progression and end condition to the Tetris class (by modifying Listing 13-3)

This code extends the Tetris class to manage game progression by introducing a mechanism to track the number of tiles placed, handle the game's end conditions, and optionally use a seeded random sequence for tile generation, which is useful for consistent testing and strategy comparison.

This revised Tetris class adds a gameover flag ❶, which becomes True under two circumstances: either when the player places the maximum number of tiles (max_tiles) and wins ❹, or when the player fills up the board and loses ❺. Whenever the game restarts, the gameover flag is reset to False ❶, and the tile count is reset to 0.

Importantly, the updated code also adds the random_seed parameter to the class to control the tile sequence. To this end, the restart() method sets up a predefined tile sequence. If random_seed is set to a number, the next tile is taken from this predefined sequence ❷. If random_seed is set to None, the next tile is selected at random, as in the previous version of the class ❸.

Scoring System

To increase the player's engagement and provide a measurable performance indicator, you can introduce a scoring system. Besides motivating human players, this scoring system enables reinforcement learning, which requires quantifiable rewards or penalties to train agents. As shown in Listing 13-5, the addition of this scoring mechanism allows players and agents to gauge their performance and adapt their strategies accordingly.

```
--snip--
class Tetris:
    --snip--
    def restart(self):
        --snip--
        self.reward = 0

        self.next_tile()
```

```
--snip--

def drop(self):
    --snip--
    if self.tile_y + np.max(tile) > self.rows:
        self.gameover = True
    ❶ dreward = -100
    else:
        --snip--
    ❷ dreward = 10 ** (removed_lines - 1) if removed_lines > 0 else 0

    self.next_tile()
    self.reward += dreward
    return dreward
```

Listing 13-5: Adding the scoring system to the Tetris class (by modifying Listing 13-4)

This code modifies the Tetris class to include a scoring system. At the beginning of each game session, the reward variable is set to zero. The player receives a reward for clearing lines ❷; this reward increases exponentially with the number of lines cleared at once, with a reward of 1 for a single line and 10 for two lines. This mechanism creates an incentive to clear multiple lines in a single drop and, hopefully, encourages the player to aim for more-strategic tile placements.

When a player loses because a tile reaches the top row, the player receives a significant penalty ❶. After each tile drop, the code updates the total reward accumulated during the game and returns the incremental reward.

Now that you've implemented the Tetris class, you can create an instance of the game:

```
tetris = Tetris(rows=4, cols=4, max_tiles=50, random_seed=123456)
```

This creates an instance of the game with four rows, four columns, fifty tiles, and a random seed so that the player encounters a consistent tile sequence.

Playing Tetris with the Command Line

It's time to bring the game to life and play it. The simplest way to interact with this implementation is by using the command line, as shown in Listing 13-6.

```
while not tetris.gameover:
    print(f"Tile {tetris.tile_count}/{tetris.max_tiles}")
    print(f"Reward: {tetris.reward}")
    print(f"Current tile {tetris.current_tile} with "
            f"orientation {tetris.tile_orientation} at position {tetris.tile_x}")
    print(tetris.TILES[tetris.current_tile][tetris.tile_orientation])
    print(tetris.board)
```

```
❶ cmd = input("Please enter your command (L, R, O, D, X): ").upper()
  print(f"Your input: {cmd} \n")

  if cmd == "L":
      tetris.move_left()
  elif cmd == "R":
      tetris.move_right()
  elif cmd == "O":
      tetris.rotate()
  elif cmd == "D":
      tetris.drop()
  elif cmd == "X":
      break
```

Listing 13-6: Playing Tetris *with the command line*

This code provides a basic text-based interface to interact with the game. The main gameplay loop continues until the gameover flag is set to True, indicating that the game has ended because the player has either dropped the maximum number of tiles (victory) or filled up the board (loss).

Inside the loop, the game displays relevant information about the current state in text form: the current tile number and the total number of tiles; the current score; details about the current tile, including its number, orientation, and lateral position with respect to the board; and a representation of the current tile's shape and of the game board.

The player is then prompted to press a letter key (L, R, O, D, or X) representing a command to control the game ❶. L moves the current tile to the left; R moves it to the right; O rotates it; D drops it to the bottom of the board; and X exits the game loop and ends the game. Finally, the method of the Tetris object corresponding to the player's command is called to update the game state. For example, if the player inputs L, the move_left() method is called to move the tile leftward.

You can now enjoy playing the game with the command line.

Playing Tetris with a Pygame Graphical Interface

Although playing *Tetris* with the command line can be useful for debugging, this isn't the most user-friendly or enjoyable way to play it. You can create a more visually engaging experience by integrating a graphical interface with Pygame, a popular Python library for game development. This permits you to add colorful graphics, animations, and interactive controls, transforming the text-based game into a dynamic visual experience. In doing so, you'll achieve a more immersive and authentic gameplay similar to the gameplay that has made the original *Tetris* a timeless classic.

You can use Listing 13-7 to implement the play_tetris_with_gui() function to play *Tetris* with a graphical interface.

```python
import pygame

def play_tetris_with_gui(tetris):
    """Play Tetris with GUI for human players."""
    TILE_SIZE = 20
    BLACK = (0, 0, 0)  # RGB code for black color
    GRAY = (128, 128, 128)  # RGB code for gray color
    WHITE = (255, 255, 255)  # RGB code for white color
    RED = (255, 0, 0)  # RGB code for red color

    # Initialize the game engine
    pygame.init()
    pygame.display.set_caption("TETRIS")
    screen = pygame.display.set_mode((200 + tetris.cols * TILE_SIZE,
                                      200 + tetris.rows * TILE_SIZE))
    pygame.key.set_repeat(300, 100)  # Set keyboard delay and interval in ms
    font = pygame.font.SysFont("Calibri", 25, True)

    # Loop until the window is closed
    running = True
    while running:
        # Paint game board
        if pygame.display.get_active():
            screen.fill(WHITE)

            for i in range(tetris.rows):
                for j in range(tetris.cols):
                    ❶ pygame.draw.rect(screen, GRAY,
                                    [100 + TILE_SIZE * j,
                                     80 + TILE_SIZE * (tetris.rows - i),
                                     TILE_SIZE, TILE_SIZE], 1)
                    if tetris.board[i][j] > 0:
                        ❷ pygame.draw.rect(screen, BLACK,
                                        [101 + TILE_SIZE * j,
                                         81 + TILE_SIZE * (tetris.rows - i),
                                         TILE_SIZE - 2, TILE_SIZE - 2])

            tile = tetris.TILES[tetris.current_tile][tetris.tile_orientation]
            for x in range(len(tile)):
                for y in range(tile[x][0], tile[x][1]):
                    ❸ pygame.draw.rect(screen, RED, [
                        101 + TILE_SIZE * (x + tetris.tile_x),
                        81 + TILE_SIZE * (tetris.rows - (y + tetris.tile_y)),
                        TILE_SIZE - 2, TILE_SIZE - 2,
                    ])
```

```
❹ screen.blit(
      font.render(f"Reward: {tetris.reward}", True, BLACK), [0, 0],
  )
❺ screen.blit(
      font.render(f"Tile {tetris.tile_count}/{tetris.max_tiles}",
                    True, BLACK), [0, 30]
  )
  if tetris.gameover:
      screen.blit(font.render("G A M E   O V E R", True, RED),
                    [40, 100 + tetris.rows * TILE_SIZE])
      screen.blit(font.render("Press ESC to try again", True, RED),
                    [10, 100 + tetris.rows * TILE_SIZE + 30])

pygame.display.flip()

# Get user input
for event in pygame.event.get():
    if event.type == pygame.QUIT:
        running = False
    elif event.type == pygame.KEYDOWN:
        if event.key == pygame.K_ESCAPE:
            tetris.restart()
        if not tetris.gameover:
            if event.key == pygame.K_LEFT:
                tetris.move_left()
            elif event.key == pygame.K_RIGHT:
                tetris.move_right()
            elif event.key == pygame.K_UP:
                tetris.rotate()
            elif event.key == pygame.K_DOWN:
                tetris.drop()

pygame.quit()
```

Listing 13-7: The function to play Tetris *with a graphical interface*

After initializing Pygame with `pygame.init()`, this script creates a Pygame window with the title TETRIS and a specified size based on the dimensions of the game board and the tile size. In addition, the script configures the keyboard input settings for smooth gameplay. For this purpose, the script adjusts the *keyboard delay* so that a key can be held down for 300 milliseconds before repeating, and sets the *keyboard interval* between each repeated key event to 100 milliseconds.

During play, the game runs inside a `while` loop that continues until the player closes the window. This loop handles user inputs, updates the game state, and renders the game board.

Inside this game loop, the code first draws the game board on the screen by using Pygame's drawing functions. Each cell of the board is represented by a rectangle ❶, with empty cells outlined in gray and occupied cells filled in black ❷. The current tile is drawn in red ❸.

Then the code displays the game's score (reward) ❹ and the current tile count ❺ on the screen via Pygame's font-rendering capabilities. If the game is over, the Pygame window will display a GAME OVER message and a prompt to restart the game.

At the end of each loop, the script calls the Pygame flip() method to update the Pygame display to reflect the current state of the game board and any messages rendered.

The script captures user inputs through keyboard events: The player presses the left and right arrow keys to move the current tile, the up arrow key to rotate it, and the down arrow key to drop it. Pressing the ESC key restarts the game.

You can now launch the game with the following code:

```
tetris.restart()
play_tetris_with_gui(tetris)
```

Figure 13-2 shows some screenshots of the graphical interface.

Figure 13-2: Screenshots of the simplified Tetris game

You can see the graphical interface as it appears at the beginning of the game (left), during gameplay (middle), and after a victory (right).

By playing on Pygame's rich graphical interface, you can verify that it offers a more immersive and engaging experience compared to the command line version. You should be able to easily get scores well above 60.

EXERCISE

13-3: Using the previous code as a foundation, modify and extend it to implement the classic version of *Tetris*. This requires adjusting the game mechanics to align with the traditional gameplay, including using the original *Tetris* scoring system, implementing the standard tile shapes and rotations, and ensuring that the game's progression and end conditions reflect the classic game's rules.

Making an Agent Play Tetris with Q-Learning

As you've seen in the previous sections, in Q-learning, an agent learns by exploring the environment and receiving rewards or penalties based on its actions. The agent's ultimate goal is to learn a policy that maximizes its cumulative rewards. In this section, you'll adapt the actions of the Tetris class to facilitate an agent's learning process, implement this agent, and then apply the Q-learning procedure.

Adapting the Actions of Tetris for Q-Learning

In the simplified *Tetris* game you implemented with the Tetris class, the player primarily derives rewards from clearing lines. However, line-clearing is a relatively infrequent event, particularly for an untrained agent taking what amounts to random actions. Only after a long series of actions such as moving the tile left and right, rotating it, and dropping it does the agent get the reward. Moreover, clearing a line often requires dropping several tiles, further delaying the possible reward. Consequently, the agent may not receive sufficient immediate feedback to learn effectively—or at all.

To mitigate this issue, you can implement a mechanism that allows the agent to directly position a tile in a specific location and orientation. This approach effectively speeds up the gameplay, functioning as a form of "tile teleportation." With the ability to rapidly experiment with different tile placements and orientations, the agent receives more-immediate feedback on its actions, facilitating a more efficient and effective learning process.

You can implement this modification by creating a child class of the Tetris class, as shown in Listing 13-8.

```
class QLTetris(Tetris):
    """Simplified Tetris for Q-learning."""

    def __init__(self, rows, cols, max_tiles, random_seed):
        """Initialize Tetris for Q-learning."""
        super().__init__(rows, cols, max_tiles, random_seed)

    def teleport(self, new_x, new_orientation):
        """Teleport current tile to new position and orientation."""
❶       if 0 <= new_orientation < len(Tetris.TILES[self.current_tile]):
            tilewidth = len(Tetris.TILES[self.current_tile][new_orientation])
❷           if 0 <= new_x <= self.cols - tilewidth:
                self.tile_x = new_x
                self.tile_orientation = new_orientation
                return True
        return False
```

Listing 13-8: The class to play Tetris *with Q-learning*

By incorporating the teleport() method, the QLTetris class provides a more suitable environment for Q-learning; the agent can rapidly test strategies and receive timely feedback. This method begins by checking the validity of the requested orientation ❶. Then the method calculates the width of the tile in this new orientation. With this new information, the method ensures that the new horizontal position is within the permissible range ❷. If both the new orientation and position are valid, the method instantly updates the tile's horizontal position and orientation, effectively "teleporting" the tile to its new state. The method returns True to indicate the success of the teleport action or False to indicate its failure.

You can now create an instance of this class with Listing 13-9.

```
qltetris = QLTetris(rows=4, cols=4, max_tiles=50, random_seed=123456)
```

Listing 13-9: Creating an instance of Tetris *adapted for Q-learning*

This code creates an instance of the *Tetris* game adapted for Q-learning, which you'll use in the following sections. Note that it uses a fixed sequence of tiles by setting a value for random_seed.

Implementing the Q-Learning Agent

Now that you've built the modified *Tetris* game, you need to create an agent capable of learning to play, using Q-learning. You'll implement the agent step-by-step in this section.

First, you'll define the agent's basic structure, enabling it to interact with the game by taking random actions. Next, you'll implement state tracking, encoding the game board and current tile into a usable format. Then you'll introduce a Q-table for storing and updating expected rewards for state-action pairs, followed by implementing the Q-learning update rule to refine the agent's strategy over time. Finally, you'll train the agent by allowing it to play multiple games, learning from experience and improving its performance as it progresses.

Making the Agent Take Actions

You'll start by defining the basic structure of the QLAgent class, allowing the agent to take random actions in the game by selecting a position and orientation for each tile and then dropping it. You'll also include mechanisms for restarting the game after a loss and handling multiple games in a sequence. Start by creating the QLAgent class, as shown in Listing 13-10.

```
class QLAgent:
    """Q-learning agent to play Tetris."""

    def __init__(self, tetris, games):
        """Initialize the agent."""
        self.tetris = tetris
        self.games, self.game = games, 0

        self.position_num = self.tetris.cols
        self.orientation_num = np.max([len(tile) for tile in Tetris.TILES])
        self.action_num = self.position_num * self.orientation_num
```

```
    def next_turn(self):
        """Execute the next turn in the game."""
        if self.tetris.gameover:
            if self.game + 1 < self.games:
                self.game += 1
    ❶      self.tetris.restart()
            else:
    ❷          return False  # Finish
        else:
    ❸      action = np.random.randint(self.action_num)

            new_x = action // self.position_num
            new_orientation = action % self.orientation_num

    ❹      if self.tetris.teleport(new_x, new_orientation):
                self.tetris.drop()

    ❺  return True  # Continue
```

Listing 13-10: The class representing a Q-learning agent taking a random action

In its initialization, the class receives an instance of QLTetris (tetris) and a number of games to be played (games). The current game (game) is set to 0. Then the initialization method calculates the number of possible actions (action_num) by taking the product of the number of positions (position_num) and the maximum number of possible orientations (orientation_num). The number of positions is equal to the number of rows in the *Tetris* board—in this case, four from the settings in Listing 13-9. In Listing 13-1, the maximum number of possible orientations is four.

When the next_turn() method is called, it randomly selects an action ❸, from which the method gets the tile's potential position (new_x) and orientation (new_orientation). Finally, if this position and orientation are legal ❹, the tile is dropped. Otherwise, nothing happens, and the agent will wait for the next turn.

Once the agent wins or loses a game, it proceeds to start a new game if more games remain to be played ❶, and the next_turn() method returns True ❺. Otherwise, nothing happens, and it returns False ❷.

Observing the Agent Play

After implementing this agent, you might want to observe how it behaves. You can do this by adapting the play_tetris_with_gui() function (Listing 13-7) so that the agent plays in your place, as shown in Listing 13-11.

```
def observe_tetris_with_gui(tetris, agent):
    """Observe a QL agent playing Tetris with GUI."""
    --snip--
    while running:
        --snip--
```

```
    # Get user input
    for event in pygame.event.get():
        if event.type == pygame.QUIT:
            running = False
        elif event.type == pygame.KEYDOWN:
        ❶ running = agent.next_turn()
--snip--
```

Listing 13-11: The function to observe an agent playing Tetris *with a graphical interface (by modifying Listing 13-7)*

This function removes most of the user inputs and keeps only `KEYDOWN`, which now makes the agent take the next turn in the game ❶.

You can use this function with Listing 13-12.

```
qltetris.restart()
agent = QLAgent(qltetris, games=3)
observe_tetris_with_gui(qltetris, agent)
```

Listing 13-12: Observing an agent play

This code restarts the game, creates an agent that will play for three games, and lets you observe what the agent does.

As you push the down arrow key, you'll see that the agent makes random moves, often losing the game quickly. You'll also observe that sometimes nothing happens when you push a key. This is because the randomly selected action is invalid.

Making the Agent Keep Track of the State of the Game

To decide which action to take, the agent must be able to assess the game's current state, which is a representation of the current board situation and the current tile being played. You can make the necessary updates to the `QLAgent` class with Listing 13-13.

```
class QLAgent:
    --snip--
    def __init__(self, tetris, games):
        --snip--
        self.state_size = (
        ❶ self.tetris.cols * self.tetris.rows  # Cells in board
        ❷ + 1 + np.floor(np.log2(len(Tetris.TILES) - 1)).astype(int)  # Tiles
        )
        self.state_num = 2 ** self.state_size

    ❸ self.update_state()

    def update_state(self):
        """Update the state of the agent."""
    ❹ tile = bin(self.tetris.current_tile)[2:]
```

```
⑤ board = np.copy(self.tetris.board.reshape((-1,))).astype(int)
   board[board == Tetris.UNDEFINED] = 0

⑥ self.state_binary = np.append(tile, board)
⑦ self.state = int("".join(str(i) for i in self.state_binary), 2)

def next_turn(self):
    """Execute the next turn in the game."""
    if self.tetris.gameover:
        if self.game + 1 < self.games:
            self.game += 1
            self.tetris.restart()
            self.update_state()
        --snip--
    else:
        action = np.random.randint(self.action_num)
        --snip--
        if self.tetris.teleport(new_x, new_orientation):
            self.tetris.drop()
⑧         self.update_state()
    --snip--
```

Listing 13-13: The class implementing a Q-learning agent with a representation of the state of the game (by modifying Listing 13-10)

This code updates the QLAgent class to include a method for keeping track of the game state. This class calculates a unique representation of the game state by encoding the current board configuration and the current tile, and that state is then used to inform the agent's decisions during gameplay. The state is updated after each turn and when the game restarts.

During its initialization, the updated class calculates the size of the state (state_size) used to represent the state of the game. If you think of the state as a binary number, you can determine state_size by adding the number of cells on the board, each of which can be full or empty (corresponding to 16 bits) ❶, to the logarithm (base 2) of the number of different tiles, rounded down to the nearest integer and incremented by 1 (corresponding to 2 bits) ❷. This second expression represents the additional bits required to encode the current tile in play. The class then calculates the number of states (state_num) as the power of 2 raised to this combined size (2^{16+2}).

The update_state() method updates the state representation of the game. This method first converts the current tile into a binary representation ❹, simplifying the encoding of the tile type by using Python's built-in bin() function. This function returns a string representation of the integer in binary format, prefixed with 0b. The inclusion of [2:] removes this 0b prefix, ensuring that the resulting string contains only binary digits representing the current tile. Next, `update_state()` transforms the game board into a 1D binary list ❺ by flattening the board's cells and converting them to integers; then it sets any undefined cells in the board (represented by `UNDEFINED`) to `zero`, ensuring a consistent binary representation of the state. Next, the binary representations of both the tile and the board ❻ are concatenated, forming a combined binary state representation. Afterward, the method converts this binary state into an integer ❼, providing a unique numerical representation of the entire game state. Ultimately, the Q-learning algorithm needs this state to make decisions based on the game's current situation. Accordingly, the updated code calls the `update_state()` method both when initializing the agent ❽ and after every turn in the game ❾. This means that the agent always has an up-to-date representation of the game state to work with.

You can use Listing 13-12 to verify that this code still works as before. You can also confirm that the number of states is 262,144 by using `print(agent.state_num)`, corresponding to a state size of 18, which you can print using `print(agent.state_size)`. This is a pretty big number for a relatively simple game. You can already see how the state size can scale quickly for more-complex environments.

Adding a Q-Table to the Agent

A *Q-table* is a fundamental data structure in Q-learning, used to store and update the Q-values associated with each state-action pair. The Q-table is essentially a 2D array, with each row representing a possible state the agent can be in, and each column representing a possible action the agent can take.

The entries in the table, known as *Q-values*, quantify the expected future rewards of taking a specific action in a specific state, following the agent's current policy. As the agent explores the environment and experiences various state transitions and rewards, it updates the Q-values in the table, gradually refining its strategy to maximize cumulative rewards.

The Q-table provides the agent with a clear map of its knowledge about the environment, allowing it to select actions that are expected to yield the best outcomes. The size of the Q-table can become large, depending on the number of possible states and actions, which makes it a powerful yet memory-intensive tool in Q-learning.

Once your agent can keep track of the current state, you need to equip it with a Q-table to consult when deciding what action to take, as shown in Listing 13-14.

```
class QLAgent:
    --snip--
    def __init__(self, tetris, games, epsilon):
        --snip--
        self.epsilon = epsilon
        self.Q_table = np.zeros((self.state_num, self.action_num))

        self.update_state()

    def next_turn(self):
        """Execute the next turn in the game."""
```

```
        if self.tetris.gameover:
            --snip--
        else:
            if np.random.rand() < self.epsilon:
             ❶ action = np.random.randint(self.action_num)
            else:
             ❷ action = np.argmax(self.Q_table[self.state, :])
            --snip--
```

Listing 13-14: The class representing a Q-learning agent with a Q-table (by modifying Listing 13-13)

This new iteration of the QLAgent class adds a Q-table and an epsilon parameter to the Q-learning agent. Introduced in the constructor, the epsilon parameter represents the probability of the agent choosing a random action instead of the one suggested by the Q-table. This approach is known as the *epsilon-greedy policy*, which promotes exploration of the state-action space.

The class initializes the Q_table as a 2D NumPy array with dimensions corresponding to the number of possible states (self.state_num) and the number of available actions (self.action_num). The array is filled with 0s so that the table can store the expected rewards for taking different actions in various states. In this case, the array has $262,144 \times 16$ entries, corresponding to 4,194,304 expected rewards. You can verify this with print(agent.Q_table.shape) and print(agent.Q_table.size), respectively.

During each turn, the agent decides whether to take a random action or the best known action based on the current Q-table. The agent makes this decision by comparing a random number to epsilon. If the random number is less than epsilon, the agent chooses a random action ❶. Otherwise, the agent selects the action with the highest expected reward in the current state as indicated by the Q-table ❷. This mechanism balances exploration (trying new actions) and exploitation (using learned knowledge), which is crucial for the Q-agent's effective learning.

You can now use Listing 13-15 to observe how the agent uses the Q-table to play.

```
qltetris.restart()
agent = QLAgent(qltetris, games=3, epsilon=0)
observe_tetris_with_gui(qltetris, agent)
```

Listing 13-15: Observing an agent playing with an epsilon-greedy policy (by modifying Listing 13-12)

This code sets the epsilon-greedy policy to 0, meaning the agent will always choose the strategy from the Q-table without random exploration. Since the Q-table is initially filled with 0s and has not been trained yet, the agent's behavior will be quite simple: It will just teleport all tiles to position 0 and orientation 0 and drop them.

Adding the Code to Train the Agent

Now that you've constructed your Q-table, you need to add the code that makes it possible to train the agent's Q-table according to the Q-learning update rule you saw previously (Equation 13.2). You can do this with the modifications introduced in Listing 13-16.

```
class QLAgent:
    --snip--
    def __init__(self, tetris, games, epsilon, alpha, gamma):
        --snip--
        self.alpha = alpha   # Learning rate
        self.gamma = gamma   # Discount factor
        self.rewards = np.zeros(games)

        self.update_state()

    def next_turn(self):
        """Execute the next turn in the game."""
        if self.tetris.gameover:
    ❶      self.rewards[self.game] = self.tetris.reward
            if self.game > 0 and self.game % 100 == 0:
                av_reward = np.mean(self.rewards[self.game - 100:self.game])
                print(f"game {self.game}/{self.games} reward {av_reward}")

            if self.game + 1 < self.games:
                self.game += 1
                self.tetris.restart()
            else:
    ❷          np.savetxt("Q_table.txt", self.Q_table)
                return False   # Finish
        else:
    ❸      old_state = self.state
            --snip--
            if self.tetris.teleport(new_x, new_orientation):
                reward = self.tetris.drop()

                self.update_state()
    ❹          new_state = self.state

    ❺          dQ = self.alpha * (
                    reward
                    + self.gamma * np.max(self.Q_table[new_state, :])
                    - self.Q_table[old_state, action]
                )

    ❻          self.Q_table[old_state, action] += dQ
            else:   # Penalty for illegal move.
    ❼          self.Q_table[old_state, action] += -50
        --snip--
```

Listing 13-16: The class implementing a Q-learning agent capable of training the Q-table (by modifying Listing 13-14)

This code completes the implementation of the agent. You've now implemented the combination of rewards, penalties, and updating mechanism based on the learning rate and discount factor that will enable the agent to progressively refine its policy and improve its performance in the game.

This code adds two important parameters to the constructor of the QLAgent class. The alpha parameter represents the learning rate, which determines the extent to which the agent updates its knowledge based on new information. The gamma parameter is the discount factor, which balances the importance of immediate and future rewards. You've already seen these parameters in Equation 13.2.

In addition, the agent now maintains an array to store rewards for each game (rewards). This array is used to track the agent's performance over time. During gameplay, the agent checks whether the game is over. If so, the agent logs the received reward for the game ❶ and periodically prints the average reward over the last 100 games, providing insights into its learning progress.

If the number of games played is less than the total number of games specified, the agent starts a new game. Otherwise, the agent saves the Q-table into the *Q_table.txt* file and stops training ❷.

During each turn, the agent records the current state as the old state before making a move ❸. If a move is successful, the agent calculates the reward, updates its state to the new state ❹, and then updates the Q-table. The Q-table update involves calculating the difference in value between the estimated future reward and the current value for the action taken in the old state ❺. This difference, scaled by the learning rate alpha, is added to the current Q-value, allowing the agent to learn from its experience ❻.

If the agent makes an illegal move, the code applies a penalty by subtracting a fixed amount from the Q-value of the [old state, action] pair ❼. This penalty discourages the agent from repeating ineffective or invalid actions, guiding it toward more-successful strategies.

Training the Q-Learning Agent

You can finally train the agent by using Listing 13-17.

```
qltetris.restart()
agent = QLAgent(qltetris, games=1_000, epsilon=0, alpha=0.2, gamma=1)

while agent.next_turn():
    pass
```

Listing 13-17: Training the Q-learning agent

This code trains the Q-learning agent. The code restarts the game, initializes an agent to play 1,000 games without ever taking random moves (epsilon of 0), sets a learning rate of 0.2, and sets a discount factor of 1. The training iterates through a while loop that allows the agent to play, learn, and update its strategy until it completes the specified number of games.

During training, the reward should steadily increase as the Q-learning agent improves its policy. You can visualize this improvement by plotting the rewards over time via Listing 13-18.

```
import matplotlib.pyplot as plt

plt.plot(agent.rewards)
plt.xlabel("Game")
plt.ylabel("Reward")
plt.legend()
plt.show()
```

Listing 13-18: Plotting the reward during training

Figure 13-3 shows the resulting plot.

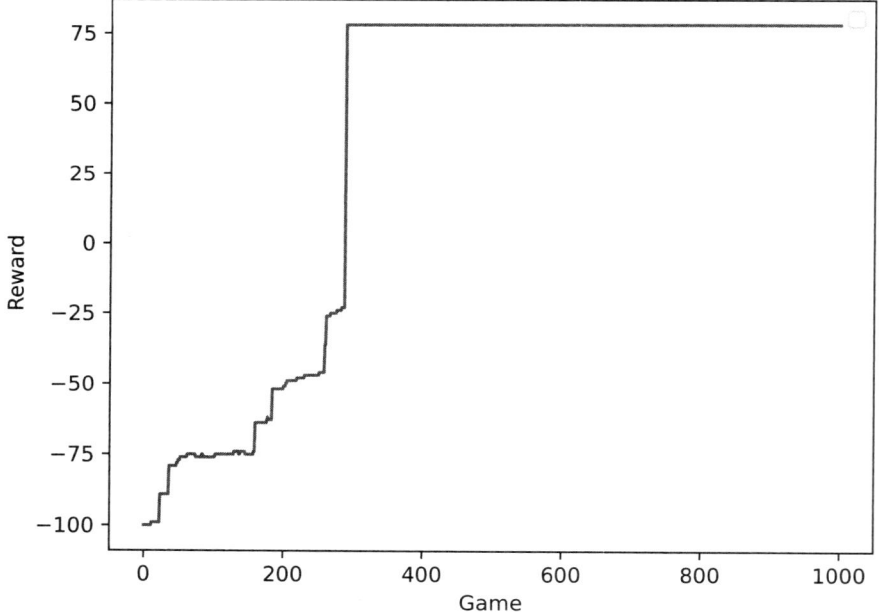

Figure 13-3: The rewards when training a Q-learning agent with a fixed sequence of tiles

As expected, the reward line shows an upward trend, indicating that the agent learns to maximize its cumulative reward over time. Notably, around 350 games, the reward jumps significantly by exactly 100, suggesting that the agent has discovered its first strategy to avoid the −100 penalty for losing the game. However, this result doesn't necessarily mean that the strategy is near optimal. The result simply indicates that the agent has reached a point where it can sustain the game without incurring the game-over penalty.

You can now observe the agent play with the strategy it has learned, using Listing 13-19.

```
qltetris.restart()
agent = QLAgent(qltetris, games=1, epsilon=0, alpha=0.2, gamma=1)
agent.Q_table = np.loadtxt("Q_table.txt")
observe_tetris_with_gui(qltetris, agent)
```

Listing 13-19: Observing a Q-learning agent using a trained Q-table to play Tetris

This code loads the trained Q-table from the *Q_table.txt* file and uses it to initialize the Q-table of the agent. Afterward, you can watch the agent play *Tetris* with the learned strategy. Note that the agent always plays the same strategy, taking advantage of the fixed sequence of tiles.

EXERCISE

13-4: Change the value of epsilon in Listing 13-19 to 0.1 so that on average, one move out of ten is random. Observe that the agent loses its ability to play the game successfully as soon as a random move happens. Can you explain why the policy learned by the agent is so fragile?

To quantify how much the agent learned, you can check the number of Q-table rows that contain nonzero values, which represent the states where the agent has gained some experience. You can do this with Listing 13-20.

```
Q_table = agent.Q_table
non_zero_rows_mask = np.any(Q_table != 0, axis=1)
num_non_zero_rows = np.sum(non_zero_rows_mask)
print(f"Non-zero rows = {num_non_zero_rows}")
```

Listing 13-20: Analyzing the sparsity of the trained Q-table

The output will display a very small number of nonzero rows in the Q-table—typically, around 100 out of the 262,144 Q-table rows corresponding to all possible game states. Such a small number of nonzero rows suggests that the agent has learned to focus its strategy on the subset of states encountered with the fixed sequence of tiles but has not learned to generalize to other situations. Accordingly, the agent is incapable of dealing with even a single random event.

13-5: Introduce randomness in the Q-learning agent's training by setting epsilon to 0.001, allowing occasional exploratory actions. Increase training to 100,000 games for broader state-action learning. Assess the impact on Q-table sparsity, since more-diverse actions might reduce sparsity. Observe the learning curve and final performance, and evaluate whether randomness enhances the agent's policy and ability to learn optimal *Tetris* strategies.

Training with a Random Tile Sequence

You can now assess the performance of Q-learning when the agent is trained with a random sequence of tiles. This introduces a higher level of complexity because of the increased variability in the state space. You can perform this assessment with Listing 13-21.

```
qltetris = QLTetris(rows=4, cols=4, max_tiles=50, random_seed=None)
agent = QLAgent(qltetris, games=200_000, epsilon=0.001, alpha=0.2, gamma=1)

while agent.next_turn():
    pass
```

Listing 13-21: Training the Q-learning agent with random tile sequences (by modifying Listing 13-17)

This code sets the training tile sequence to a random one by selecting None for random_seed, increases the number of games, and introduces additional randomness in the agent by setting epsilon to 0.001.

You can plot the rewards during training by adapting Listing 13-18 to add the smoothed average of the reward over time, as shown in Listing 13-22.

```
smoothed_rewards = np.convolve(agent.rewards, np.ones(100) / 100, mode="valid")

plt.plot(agent.rewards, label="Raw Rewards")
plt.plot(smoothed_rewards, label="Smoothed Rewards")
--snip--
```

Listing 13-22: Plotting the reward during training (by modifying Listing 13-18)

This code uses a convolution operation to calculate the smoothed rewards; this technique helps illustrate the trend more clearly by reducing the noise in the raw rewards. The code should generate a plot similar to Figure 13-4.

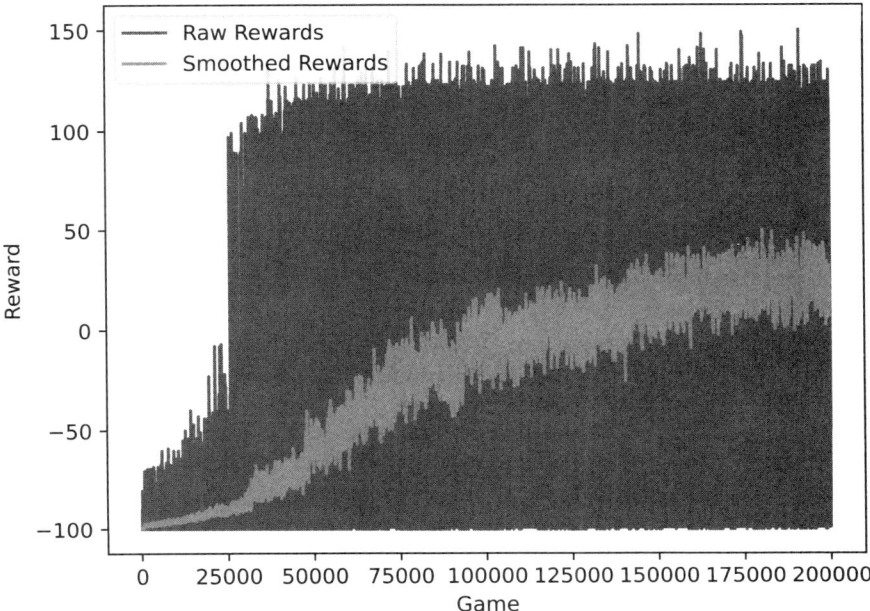

Figure 13-4: The rewards when training a Q-learning agent with random tile sequences

The rewards the agent received don't increase as much as they did during training with the fixed tile sequence, remaining confined around an average of 0 at best. However, the rewards display a very large variability, in part due to the epsilon-greedy policy, which introduces a random action every 1,000 actions on average.

In executing Listing 13-20, the count of nonzero rows in the Q-table increases to about 20,000 thanks to the more random exploration of the space. However, this number is still much smaller than the 262,144 Q-table entries, meaning that the agent hasn't been able to explore the whole state space. As a potential solution, you could try to extend the number of training games.

Making an Agent Play Tetris with Deep Q-Learning

The previous sections highlighted the challenges faced when applying traditional Q-learning to environments with vast state spaces, such as *Tetris* with a random tile sequence. The combinatorial explosion of states makes maintaining and updating a Q-table impractical, since an unfeasible amount of memory and training iterations would be needed to cover a significant portion of the state-action space.

To address these challenges, you can turn to *deep Q-learning*, a powerful variant that combines Q-learning with deep neural networks. Deep Q-learning uses deep learning to approximate the Q-values for state-action pairs, enabling the agent to generalize across similar states and effectively reduce the dimensionality of the state-action space. Instead of a Q-table, a deep Q-learning agent uses a neural network as a function approximator to predict Q-values for all possible actions, given a state. This approach is particularly advantageous for complex environments because it allows the agent to learn in a continuous space and effectively handle a large variety of states.

Understanding Deep Q-Learning

In deep Q-learning, two neural networks play a critical role in the learning process: the Q-network and the target network.

As the main neural network, the *Q-network* (QNet) is actively trained to approximate the Q-value function, predicting the total expected rewards for taking specific actions in a given state. This network undergoes continual learning, updating its weights at each step or after certain intervals during the training process. The QNet bases its updates on the *temporal difference error*, which is the difference between the predicted and target Q-values. The QNet seeks to minimize this discrepancy through backpropagation.

One of the main challenges in deep Q-learning is the inherent instability that can occur if the target Q-values depend on the same network that selects actions. Using the QNet for both purposes can lead to harmful feedback loops where the Q-values might oscillate or diverge. For instance, imagine that the QNet slightly overestimates the value of a particular action in a given state. If this overestimation guides the agent to repeatedly choose that action, the QNet updates might reinforce this mistake, amplifying the error over time. This could cause the Q-values to shift erratically, making it difficult for the agent to learn an optimal policy.

To stabilize the learning process, deep Q-learning uses a *target network* (TargetNet), which shares the QNet's architecture but maintains a separate set of weights. Since the TargetNet doesn't select actions, there's no need to update its weights as frequently. The TargetNet provides stable target Q-values for the QNet to learn from. Updating the TargetNet less frequently reflects the slowly improving policy, avoiding the potential instabilities that might arise from using rapidly changing Q-values as learning targets. Consequently, a separate TargetNet ensures that the QNet has consistent and reliable targets for learning.

NOTE *An intuitive way to understand the relationship between the QNet and TargetNet is through the lens of the* teacher-student learning paradigm. *In this analogy, the QNet is the eager student, constantly learning and updating its knowledge based on new experiences. However, if the student tries to learn solely from their own rapidly changing understanding, they might become confused or develop misconceptions due to overfitting to recent experiences. The TargetNet acts as the wise teacher, providing stable and reliable guidance. By keeping the teacher's knowledge (the TargetNet's weights) fixed for a period, the student can learn effectively from consistent targets* *without being misled by fluctuations in their own learning process. Periodically, the teacher updates their knowledge to reflect the student's progress, ensuring that the learning journey remains on a steady path. This teacher-student dynamic stabilizes the learning process, allowing the QNet to converge more smoothly toward an optimal policy.*

In addition to these networks, deep Q-learning incorporates an *epsilon-greedy strategy* to balance the exploration of untested states with the exploitation of the current knowledge, represented by the Q-values. This strategy initially favors exploration to prevent the agent from becoming trapped in a suboptimal policy early on. As the agent learns more about the environment, the strategy gradually reduces the epsilon value, allowing the agent to transition to exploiting its learned values and refining its policies.

Through these mechanisms, deep Q-learning can approximate the value function for environments with large state spaces, allowing a deep Q-learning agent to learn policies that generalize well across states and lead to high performance levels. This is particularly important in games like *Tetris*, where the number of possible states and sequences of actions is overwhelmingly large, rendering traditional methods ineffective.

Implementing the Deep Q-Learning Agent

With these underlying concepts, you're ready to upgrade the Q-learning agent to a deep Q-learning agent. You'll do this step-by-step in the following sections. First, you'll define the neural networks required for deep Q-learning, including the QNet and the TargetNet. Next, you'll modify the agent to use these networks to select actions and update its policy. Then you'll implement a replay buffer to store and sample experiences, which is essential for training the neural networks. After that, you'll add the training logic for the QNet, ensuring that it learns effectively from the experiences stored in the buffer. Finally, you'll periodically synchronize the TargetNet with the QNet to stabilize the training process. Doing this, you'll implement a fully functional deep Q-learning agent capable of playing *Tetris*.

Adding the Neural Networks

Start by instantiating the necessary neural networks as shown in Listing 13-23.

```
import deeplay as dl
import torch


class DQLAgent(dl.Application):
    """Deep Q-learning agent to play Tetris."""

    def __init__(self, tetris, games, epsilon, alpha, gamma, hidden_units,
                **kwargs):
        --snip--
    ❶ self.q_net = self.get_net(hidden_units)
    ❷ self.target_net = self.get_net(hidden_units)
```

```
❸ super().__init__(
      loss=torch.nn.MSELoss(),
      optimizer=torch.optim.Adam(self.q_net.parameters(), lr=0.001),
      **kwargs,
  )

  self.update_state()

def get_net(self, hidden_units):
    """Create instance of neural network."""
    net = dl.MultiLayerPerceptron(
        in_features=self.state_size,
        hidden_features=hidden_units,
        out_features=self.action_num,
    )
    return net.build()

--snip--
```

Listing 13-23: Adding the neural networks (by modifying Listing 13-14)

This code creates the DQLAgent class with a QNet and TargetNet. In contrast to the traditional Q-learning code, this approach implements this class as a Deeplay Application because it will contain a trainable neural network.

The get_net() method builds a dense neural network that accepts the state as input, has a hidden layer, and returns the predicted Q-values for each possible action. The hidden_units parameter specifies the number of hidden neurons. The activation functions of the hidden layers are set to ReLU by default, but to further stabilize the training, you could also use *GeLU (Gaussian error linear unit)*, a smooth approximation of ReLU that can improve training stability and convergence. When initializing the agent, the code calls this method twice to create the QNet ❶ and the TargetNet ❷.

Finally, the code calls the constructor of the parent Application class to set the loss and optimizer ❸. Notice that only the QNet is optimized in the training cycle, while the weights of the TargetNet will only periodically be updated, as you'll see later. Additional keyword arguments (kwargs) for the Application class can also be passed through the constructor.

You can now inspect the architecture of the QNet and TargetNet via print(agent.q_net) and print(agent.target_net) to confirm that these architectures are identical.

Adapting the State Variable to PyTorch

After defining the QNet and TargetNet, you need to update the state variable to make it compatible with PyTorch, as shown in Listing 13-24.

```
--snip--
class DQLAgent(dl.Application):
    --snip--
```

```
def update_state(self):
    """Update the state of the agent."""
    num_bits = int(np.ceil(np.log2(len(Tetris.TILES))))
❶   tile = bin(self.tetris.current_tile)[2:].zfill(num_bits)
    tile = np.array([int(i) for i in tile])

    board = np.copy(self.tetris.board.reshape((-1,))).astype(int)
    board[board == Tetris.UNDEFINED] = 0

❷   self.state_binary = np.append(tile, board)
    self.state = torch.tensor(self.state_binary, dtype=torch.float32)

--snip--
```

Listing 13-24: Making the state compatible with PyTorch (by modifying Listing 13-23)

To make the state compatible with PyTorch, this code alters the update _state() method to return the state reflecting the current game situation as a PyTorch array. First, the code defines the num_bits variable to determine the number of bits needed to represent all different *Tetris* tiles in binary format. Next, the code converts the current tile into a binary string, removes the 0b prefix, and then zero-pads it to ensure that it has a length equal to the number of bits ❶. This results in a fixed-length binary representation of the current tile type. The code then converts the binary string into an array of integers for further processing.

Like the previous version of this method, the new method represents the game board as a binary list. Each cell of the board is reshaped into a 1D array and converted to integers, just as it was in the corresponding method of the DLAgent class.

Finally, the code concatenates the binary representations of the tile and the board into a representation of the game's complete state ❷. This state is then converted into the state PyTorch tensor to be input into the neural network for further processing and decision-making by the agent.

Updating the Selection of the Action

Once you've modified the method for updating the current state, you can update the selection of the action to use the QNet instead of the Q-table, as shown in Listing 13-25.

```
--snip--
class DQLAgent(dl.Application):
    --snip--

    def next_turn(self):
        """Execute the next turn in the game."""
        if self.tetris.gameover:
            --snip--
```

```
        else:
            old_state = self.state

        with torch.no_grad():
            if np.random.rand() < self.epsilon:
                action = np.random.randint(self.action_num)
            else:
                state = self.state.view(1, self.state_size)
                output = self.q_net(state).detach().numpy()[0]
                action = np.argmax(output)

            new_x = action // self.position_num
            new_orientation = action % self.orientation_num

            self.tetris.teleport(new_x, new_orientation)
            reward = self.tetris.drop()

            self.update_state()
            new_state = self.state

    return True   # Continue
```

Listing 13-25: Updating the selection of the action (by modifying Listing 13-24)

This code modifies the next_turn() method to use the QNet for selecting actions instead of relying on the Q-table. Within a torch.no_grad() context that disables gradient calculations to save memory and computations, the agent decides with an epsilon-greedy strategy whether to take a random action or to choose the best action according to its QNet. In the latter case, the agent's current state is reshaped and passed through the QNet, which outputs the Q-values for each possible action. Then the agent chooses the action with the highest Q-value.

After its selection, the method decomposes the action into rotation and movement components and uses them to manipulate the piece on the game board. The teleport() method moves the piece to the new position and orientation, then drops the piece to update the game state. Note that the if statement to check the legality of the teleport action is now missing; if the teleportation is impossible, the tile will drop in its initial position and orientation. The QNet will have to learn to adapt to this scenario.

Updating the Epsilon-Greedy Strategy

Now that you've applied the QNet to select the action, you need to update the epsilon-greedy strategy so that the value of epsilon gradually decreases across games. This allows the agent to transition from exploring the game environment through random actions to exploiting learned strategies as it gains experience. Listing 13-26 shows how to do this.

```
--snip--
class DQLAgent(dl.Application):
```

```
--snip--

def __init__(self, tetris, games, epsilon_max, epsilon_min, epsilon_scale,
             alpha, gamma, hidden_units, **kwargs):
    --snip--
    self.epsilon_max = epsilon_max
    self.epsilon_min = epsilon_min
    self.epsilon_scale = epsilon_scale
    self.epsilon = self.epsilon_max

    --snip--

def next_turn(self):
    """Execute the next turn in the game."""
    if self.tetris.gameover:
        --snip--
  ❶ self.epsilon = max(
            self.epsilon_min,
            self.epsilon_max - self.game / self.epsilon_scale,
        )
    else:
        --snip--
```

Listing 13-26: Updating the epsilon-greedy strategy (by modifying Listing 13-25)

This code updates the epsilon-greedy policy. Initially, the agent favors exploration by setting a high probability (epsilon_max) of taking random actions. As the agent plays more games, epsilon_scale controls the rate at which the value of epsilon decreases ❶, ensuring that it doesn't fall below the minimum threshold set by epsilon_min. The agent then uses the current value of epsilon to balance exploration and exploitation.

Creating an Experience Buffer

After modifying the epsilon-greedy policy, you need to create a buffer to record the experience accumulated during the game so that you can use it to train the QNet, as shown in Listing 13-27.

```
--snip--
class DQLAgent(dl.Application):
    --snip--

    def __init__(self, tetris, games, epsilon_max, epsilon_min, epsilon_scale,
                 alpha, gamma, hidden_units, replay_buffer_size, **kwargs):
        --snip--
        self.buffer = []
        self.replay_buffer_size = replay_buffer_size

        self.update_state()
```

```
    def next_turn(self):
        """Execute the next turn in the game."""
        if self.tetris.gameover:
            --snip--
        else:
            --snip--
            with torch.no_grad():
                --snip--
                new_state = self.state

        ❶ self.buffer.append({
                "old_state": old_state,
                "action": action,
                "reward": reward,
                "new_state": new_state,
                "gameover": self.tetris.gameover,
            })
            if len(self.buffer) >= self.replay_buffer_size + 1:
              ❷ self.buffer.pop(0)

        return True  # Continue
```

Listing 13-27: Creating a training buffer (by modifying Listing 13-26)

This code adds a buffer to the DQLAgent class. The buffer's size is determined by the replay_buffer_size parameter. During each turn in the game, the code adds a new entry to the buffer. This entry contains all the information needed to train the QNet ❶, including the previous state, the selected action, the reward, the new state, and a flag indicating whether the turn resulted in a game over. When the buffer reaches its capacity, the addition of any new entry will simultaneously remove the oldest one ❷.

Adding the Code to Train the QNet

With all the QNet's components in place, you need to add the code to train it, as shown in Listing 13-28.

```
--snip--
class DQLAgent(dl.Application):
    --snip--

    def __init__(self, tetris, games, epsilon_max, epsilon_min, epsilon_scale,
                 alpha, gamma, hidden_units, replay_buffer_size, batch_size,
                 **kwargs):
        --snip--
        self.buffer = []
        self.replay_buffer_size = replay_buffer_size
        self.batch_size = batch_size
        --snip--
```

```python
def next_turn(self):
    """Execute the next turn in the game."""
    if self.tetris.gameover:
        --snip--
    else:
        --snip--
        if len(self.buffer) >= self.replay_buffer_size:
   ❶         batch = random.sample(self.buffer, self.batch_size)

            # Store states in lists
            states, next_states = [], []
            for sample in batch:
                states.append(sample["old_state"])
                next_states.append(sample["new_state"])

            # Evaluate next state with TargetNet
            with torch.no_grad():
   ❷             q_hat = self.target_net(torch.stack(next_states, dim=0))

            # Compute targets
            targets = torch.zeros(self.batch_size, self.action_num)
            targets_mask = torch.zeros(self.batch_size, self.action_num)
            for idx, sample in enumerate(batch):
                if sample["gameover"]:
                    target = sample["reward"]
                else:
                    target = (sample["reward"]
                                + self.gamma * np.nanmax(q_hat[idx, :]))
                targets[idx, sample["action"]] = target
                targets_mask[idx, sample["action"]] = 1

            # Evaluate predictions, apply mask, and update weights
            self.optimizer.zero_grad()
            preds = self.q_net(torch.stack(states, dim=0))
   ❸         masked_preds = preds * targets_mask
   ❹         loss = self.loss(masked_preds, targets)
            loss.backward()
   ❺         self.optimizer.step()

    return True   # Continue
```

Listing 13-28: Training the QNet (by modifying Listing 13-27)

This code introduces the process for training the QNet by sampling a batch of experiences from the replay buffer. The code uses these samples to compute target Q-values with the TargetNet and then updates the QNet's weights by minimizing the difference between its predicted Q-values and the targets. This allows the agent to learn and improve its performance over time.

The training process begins when the replay buffer reaches the size specified by the `replay_buffer_size` attribute. This ensures that there is enough data to train the network effectively. At this point, the code samples a batch of experiences from the replay buffer ❶. This sampling method helps reduce the correlation between consecutive training samples, which are often similar because of the sequential nature of the task, thus stabilizing the learning process.

Once it has selected a batch, the code gets the current and next states from each experience in the batch and stores them separately in the `states` and `next_states` lists. These will be used to calculate the predicted Q-values for the current states and the maximum Q-value for the next states, in order to update the network.

Next, the code initializes the targets for the Q-value updates (`targets`) alongside a mask that will be used to select the relevant Q-values corresponding to the previously taken actions (`targets_mask`). The code uses the TargetNet to evaluate the next states ❷.

Then, for each sample in the batch, the code computes the target Q-value based on the reward received and, if the game isn't over, the maximum Q-value of the next state. The Bellman equation (Equation 13.2) is applied here by calculating the target as the immediate reward plus the discounted value of the best possible future reward from the next state. Specifically, the code does this by adding the current reward to the product of the discount factor γ and the maximum Q-value from the next state, as predicted by the TargetNet.

The QNet predicts the current Q-values (`preds`), which are then multiplied by the mask ❸ to ensure that the subsequent loss computation focuses only on the Q-values corresponding to the actions actually taken by the agent, effectively ignoring the Q-values of other actions. This masking directs the network's learning only to relevant experiences.

Then the code computes the loss ❹ by comparing these masked predictions with the target Q-values (`targets`). Finally, the network weights are updated using backpropagation ❺.

Updating the TargetNet and Saving the Optimal Weights

Now that you've implemented the main training loop, you're ready to add the finishing touches to the code so that it periodically synchronizes the TargetNet with the QNet and saves the QNet weights in a file whenever the agent achieves a new maximum reward. Listing 13-29 shows how to do this.

```
--snip--
class DQLAgent(dl.Application):
    --snip--

    def __init__(self, tetris, games, epsilon_max, epsilon_min, epsilon_scale,
                alpha, gamma, hidden_units, replay_buffer_size, batch_size,
                sync_target_game_count, **kwargs):
        --snip--
        self.rewards = np.zeros(games)
```

```
            self.max_reward = 0

        self.buffer = []
        self.replay_buffer_size = replay_buffer_size
        self.batch_size = batch_size
        self.sync_target_game_count = sync_target_game_count
        --snip--

def next_turn(self):
    """Execute the next turn in the game."""
    if self.tetris.gameover:
        self.rewards[self.game] = self.tetris.reward
        if self.game > 0 and self.game % 100 == 0:
            av_reward = np.mean(self.rewards[self.game - 100:self.game])
            print(f"game {self.game}/{self.games} reward {av_reward}")
            if av_reward > self.max_reward:
              ❶ self.max_reward = av_reward
              ❷ torch.save(self.q_net.state_dict(), "q_net.pth")
        --snip--
        if self.game + 1 < self.games:
            self.game += 1
            if ((len(self.buffer) >= self.replay_buffer_size)
                and (self.game % self.sync_target_game_count == 0)):
              ❸ self.target_net.load_state_dict(self.q_net.state_dict())

            self.tetris.restart()
            self.update_state()
        else:
          ❹ return False  # Finish
    else:
        --snip--
```

Listing 13-29: Updating the TargetNet and saving the optimal weights (by modifying Listing 13-28)

This code adds the max_reward variable to track the maximum average reward achieved over a window of 100 games, allowing the agent to measure improvements in its performance over time. After achieving a new maximum average reward, the agent updates max_reward with this new value ❶ and saves the current state of the QNet in the *q_net.pth* file ❷. It also adds the sync_target_game_count parameter, which determines how frequently the TargetNet gets synchronized with the QNet ❸.

This version of the code removes the saving of the Q-table ❹, which doesn't exist anymore.

Training the Deep Q-Learning Agent

Finally, train the deep Q-learning agent with Listing 13-30.

```
qltetris = QLTetris(rows=4, cols=4, max_tiles=50, random_seed=None)
agent = DQLAgent(
    qltetris, games=10_000, epsilon_max=1, epsilon_min=0.001,
    epsilon_scale=5_000, alpha=0.001, gamma=1, hidden_units=[128, 128],
    replay_buffer_size=10_000, batch_size=64, sync_target_game_count=100,
)

while agent.next_turn():
    pass
```

Listing 13-30: Training the deep Q-learning agent

To begin, this code creates instances of the `QLTetris` class and the `DQLAgent` agent. Then the training loop is executed until the specified number of games is reached.

To visualize the agent's learning progress over time, you can plot the raw rewards and their smoothed average via Listing 13-22. The result should resemble Figure 13-5.

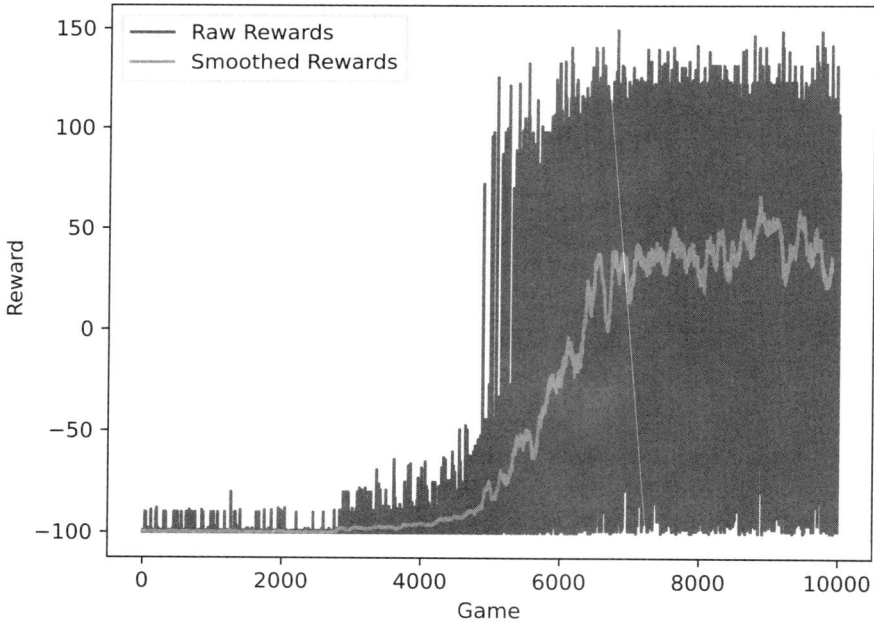

Figure 13-5: The rewards when training a deep Q-learning agent

This plot suggests that the agent has learned a lot. Initially, the rewards start near −100, the minimum achievable. However, after about 4,000 games, the agent starts to learn from its experience and refines its policy. The rewards start to steadily increase, with the average reward reaching around 50. This result would be pretty good for a human player. While the raw rewards keep fluctuating widely, this can be largely attributed to the random moves arising from the value of `epsilon_min=0.001`, which means that roughly one move out of a thousand is random.

Finally, you can observe the behavior of the trained agent via Listing 13-31.

```
qltetris.restart()
agent = DQLAgent(
    qltetris, games=3, epsilon_max=0, epsilon_min=0, epsilon_scale=5_000,
    alpha=0.001, gamma=1, hidden_units=[128, 128], replay_buffer_size=10_000,
    batch_size=64, sync_target_game_count=100,
)
model_state_dict = torch.load("q_net.pth")
agent.q_net.load_state_dict(model_state_dict)
agent.target_net.load_state_dict(model_state_dict)
observe_tetris_with_gui(qltetris, agent)
```

Listing 13-31: Observing the behavior of the trained deep Q-learning agent

This code resets the game, creates a new deep Q-learning agent, loads the saved model state into both the QNet and the TargetNet, and lets you observe how the agent plays the game while using the learned policy.

Importantly, the value of the epsilon-greedy policy is set to zero (by setting both `epsilon_max=0` and `epsilon_min=0`), so the agent always plays the best possible move, without randomness. You'll see the agent playing well enough to compete with the best human players.

NOTE *Code Example 13-1, "Teaching a Deep Q-Learning Agent to Play Tetris," is available at* https://github.com/DeepTrackAI/DeepLearningCrashCourse. *Navigate to the* Ch13_RL *folder and then* ec13_1_tetris. *The* tetris.ipynb *notebook provides a complete code example that trains a deep reinforcement learning model to play Tetris.*

EXERCISES

13-6: Increase the game complexity by changing the board to a 10×20 grid. Note that this would require around $2^{200} \approx 10^{60}$ states, which is impossible to even represent with standard Q-learning. Train a deep Q-learning agent on this new version. Compare its performance with that of the old version, focusing on how it handles increased complexity and the differences in its learning and convergence.

13-7: Use the seven standard Tetrominos to increase tile variety. Update the reinforcement learning environment and train both the Q-learning and deep Q-learning agents. Compare their learning curves, strategies, and highest scores to show that the deep Q-learning's neural network approach has better generalization capabilities.

13-8: Optimize the deep Q-learning agent's performance in *Tetris* by altering the neural network architecture, learning rates, or epsilon decay strategy. Analyze the impact on handling random tiles, and compare the alteration with the original setup to find key factors for improved performance.

Summary

In this chapter, you explored the fascinating world of reinforcement learning, a key branch of machine learning that excels in training computers to make decisions and control systems. You learned the foundational concepts of reinforcement learning, including how agents learn to make optimal decisions by interacting with their environment and adapting their behavior based on a system of rewards and penalties.

You explored Q-learning, a form of reinforcement learning that uses action-value estimation to guide agents toward the best possible actions in a given state. You applied these concepts to make a simplified *Tetris* game, demonstrating reinforcement learning's problem-solving and decision-making capabilities. You explored various game facets, including tile representation, game-board mechanics, gameplay loops, and scoring systems. The application of reinforcement learning highlighted its potential for adaptive system control and continuous performance enhancement.

The chapter also tackled the challenges of large state-space environments. To overcome these hurdles, you used deep reinforcement learning, an advanced variant of Q-learning that combines reinforcement learning with the generalization power of neural networks to manage high-dimensional input spaces and complex decision-making scenarios. These traits are crucial for navigating complex situations with expansive state spaces, possible actions, and eventual outcomes, typical in real-world scenarios.

Whether it's mastering games like *Tetris* or addressing more-complex, real-life challenges such as autonomous driving, robotics, or financial trading, the insights and strategies you learned in this chapter will empower you to solve problems for which adaptive, intelligent control is paramount.

Seminal Works and Further Reading

The principles of reinforcement learning can be traced back to the work of Richard Bellman in his 1957 book *Dynamic Programming* (Princeton University Press). Bellman introduced the Bellman equation, a key recursive relationship used to calculate the value of a policy in Markov decision processes and the basis of many reinforcement learning algorithms.

In 1988, Richard S. Sutton introduced temporal difference learning, bridging the gap between dynamic programming and Monte Carlo methods, in "Learning to Predict by the Methods of Temporal Differences," published in *Machine Learning* (volume 3, pages 9–44). Temporal difference learning became a key algorithm for training agents in environments requiring both prediction and control.

In 1992, Christopher J.C.H. Watkins and Peter Dayan introduced the Q-learning algorithm in "Q-Learning," published in *Machine Learning* (volume 8, pages 279–292). Q-learning is a model-free reinforcement learning method that enables agents to learn the optimal action-value function without needing a model of the environment. Q-learning has become one of the most widely used reinforcement learning methods because of its simplicity and effectiveness.

In 1999, Sutton et al. introduced policy gradient methods in "Policy Gradient Methods for Reinforcement Learning with Function Approximation," published in *Advances in Neural Information Processing Systems* (*NeurIPS*, volume 12). This work made reinforcement learning applicable to environments with continuous actions by directly optimizing the policy rather than the value function, extending the applicability of reinforcement learning to more-complex and high-dimensional scenarios.

The integration of deep learning with reinforcement learning took a major leap in 2013 with "Playing Atari with Deep Reinforcement Learning" by Volodymyr Mnih et al., published on arXiv (article number 1312.5602) and later presented at NeurIPS 2013. This work introduced deep Q-networks, which used deep neural networks to approximate Q-values, allowing agents to play Atari games at a superhuman level. This marked a breakthrough in the practical implementation of reinforcement learning and highlighted the potential of combining neural networks with Q-learning.

A landmark in the application of reinforcement learning was achieved in 2016 by David Silver et al. in "Mastering the Game of Go with Deep Neural Networks and Tree Search," published in *Nature* (volume 529, pages 484–489). This work introduced AlphaGo, a reinforcement learning system that famously defeated the human world champions in the game of Go. AlphaGo combined deep neural networks with Monte Carlo tree search, demonstrating the power of reinforcement learning in solving complex, strategic problems and significantly pushing the boundaries of AI.

CHALLENGE PROJECTS

13-1: Reinforcement learning to play *Space Invasion* Apply reinforcement learning to the *Space Invasion* game, as featured in *Python Crash Course* by Eric Matthes (No Starch Press, 2023). Adapt the game to create an environment suitable for a reinforcement learning agent. Define appropriate states, actions, and rewards that align with the game's objectives, such as avoiding enemies, shooting targets, and maximizing the score. Experiment with both Q-learning and deep Q-learning techniques, comparing their performance.

13-2: Reinforcement learning to play other games Implement and train a reinforcement learning agent to play another classic game, such as *Snake* or *Pac-Man*. Develop the necessary environment for the game, including state representation, actions, and rewards. Experiment with both traditional Q-learning and deep Q-learning approaches to assess their effectiveness.

13-3: Transfer reinforcement learning Investigate the concept of transfer learning in the context of reinforcement learning. Train a deep Q-learning agent on *Tetris* with a specific set of rules or tile shapes. Then modify the game's rules or gradually introduce new tile shapes and observe how the pretrained agent adapts to these changes. Experiment with retraining the agent on the modified game, using the pretrained weights as a starting point.

(continued)

13-4: Impact of various reward functions   Explore the impact of various reward functions on the learning and performance of a reinforcement learning agent that plays *Tetris*. Design and implement alternative reward functions that emphasize different aspects of the game, such as clearing multiple lines simultaneously, maintaining a low stack height, or creating certain patterns. Use these reward functions to train agents, and then compare the functions' strategies and effectiveness. Analyze how the choice of reward function influences the agent's behavior and its ability to master the game.

14

PREDICTING CHAOS WITH RESERVOIR COMPUTING

In this chapter, you'll learn about reservoir computing, which comprises a fixed, randomly generated reservoir of neurons and a trainable output layer. This unique architecture is particularly good at handling dynamic systems and chaotic time series, where traditional methods often struggle.

You'll explore how reservoir computing can efficiently process temporal information with minimal training requirements. You'll also apply reservoir computing to predict complex time-series data, such as weather data, stock market prices, and heart-rate variability. By the end of this chapter, you'll have gained the theoretical insights and practical skills necessary to use reservoir computing to tackle the challenges of dynamic data interpretation.

Introducing Reservoir Computing

The deep learning approaches you've explored in previous chapters, like deep neural networks and backpropagation, often require extensive training and fine-tuning of numerous parameters. In contrast, *reservoir computing* simplifies the training process by using a large, fixed network of randomly generated neurons, called a *reservoir*.

The reservoir acts as a dynamic memory for sequences of input data, projecting the input into a higher-dimensional space where patterns become more distinguishable. The reservoir's weights aren't trained. Instead, a simple readout layer of neurons can be trained to make predictions or classifications.

The advantage of reservoir computing lies in the simplicity of training only the output weights, which drastically reduces the computational burden and avoids the pitfalls of overfitting, common in deep learning. This setup makes reservoir computing particularly adept at tasks involving prediction, classification, and recognition of temporal patterns, offering a robust and efficient alternative for processing sequences and time series.

The basic idea is to harness the rich dynamics of the reservoir to do the heavy lifting, allowing the system to learn from the past and anticipate the future. In other words, the reservoir performs a lot of complex computations, and then the output layer selects those that are most useful to solve the problem at hand.

In the rest of this chapter, you'll apply reservoir computing to predict the dynamics of a classic example of a chaotic system. In a *chaotic system*, or *deterministic chaos*, small changes in initial conditions can lead to vastly different outcomes. This phenomenon is known as the *butterfly effect*. A chaotic system makes long-term predictions extremely difficult. Examples of chaotic systems range from weather patterns to financial markets.

You'll specifically focus on the *Lorenz system*, a simplified model of the weather developed by meteorologist Edward Lorenz in the early 1960s. The model demonstrates how even simple deterministic systems can exhibit unpredictable and chaotic behavior. You'll learn how to construct a reservoir, feed it with data generated from the Lorenz equations, and finally train a readout layer to forecast the system's future states.

Defining the Lorenz System

The Lorenz system is a simplified representation of atmospheric convection; in this process, heat is transferred in the atmosphere through the movement of air. The Lorenz system is expressed as three nonlinear and deterministic differential equations depicting chaotic behavior. These equations describe a 2D fluid layer uniformly warmed from below and cooled from above, representing the air in the atmosphere.

The Lorenz system has three variables: x is proportional to the rate of convection, y represents the horizontal temperature variation, and z corresponds to the vertical temperature variation. The Lorenz equations describe how these variables evolve over time:

$$
\begin{cases}
\frac{dx}{dt} &= \sigma(y - x) \\
\frac{dy}{dt} &= x(\rho - z) - y \\
\frac{dz}{dt} &= xy - \beta z
\end{cases}
\tag{14.1}
$$

The parameters σ, ρ, and β represent physical aspects of the fluid: σ represents the rate of return to equilibrium in the absence of convection; ρ is related to the temperature difference between the bottom and top of the fluid layer; and β is linked with physical dimensions of the fluid layer. These parameters are crucial in determining the system's behavior, highlighting the interplay between fluid dynamics, temperature variations, and length scales.

The Lorenz system is famous for its *Lorenz attractor*, a butterfly-shaped pattern formed by its set of chaotic solutions, which you'll re-create in the following sections. This attractor illustrates the concept of the butterfly effect.

Numerically Integrating the Lorenz System

In this section, you'll first calculate the numerical solution of the Lorenz system. Then you'll use that solution to predict the system's *time evolution*, or how the system's state changes over time, governed by its underlying dynamic equations.

The Lorenz system can be numerically calculated by integrating it step-by-step through a finite difference approach that approximates the continuous time derivatives in the Lorenz equations based on discrete differences over small time intervals. In this method, the state of the system at a future time is estimated based on its current state and the rate of change at the current time. Specifically, for a small time step Δt, you can express the updates as follows:

$$\begin{cases} x_{n+1} &= x_n + \Delta t \cdot \sigma(y_n - x_n) \\ y_{n+1} &= y_n + \Delta t \cdot (x_n(\rho - z_n) - y_n) \\ z_{n+1} &= z_n + \Delta t \cdot (x_n y_n - \beta z_n) \end{cases} \qquad (14.2)$$

Here, x_n, y_n, and z_n represent the state variables at the nth time step, and x_{n+1}, y_{n+1}, and z_{n+1} are the state variables at the subsequent time step. You have to carefully choose Δt: Too large a time step can lead to instability and inaccurate results, while too small a time step can lead to excessive computational cost. Unfortunately, there aren't explicit recipes to choose the right Δt; you have to determine it by trial and error.

NOTE *More-sophisticated methods like the* Runge-Kutta *algorithms* can provide better accuracy and stability for integrating systems like the Lorenz system, especially when dealing with its chaotic behavior.

To perform the numerical integration, start by implementing the `lorenz _step()` function to calculate a single step in the time evolution of the model, as shown in Listing 14-1.

```
def lorenz_step(t, x, y, z, dt, sigma, rho, beta):
    """Calculate the next step in the Lorenz system."""
    dx = sigma * (y - x) * dt
    dy = (x * (rho - z) - y) * dt
    dz = (x * y - beta * z) * dt
    return t + dt, x + dx, y + dy, z + dz
```

Listing 14-1: The function to propagate the Lorenz system one step

This function first calculates the increments of the Lorenz system variables (namely, dx, dy, and dz) and then sums them up to the initial state of the model, while also returning the corresponding updated time.

You can then iterate this function to obtain trajectories starting from specified initial conditions, using the lorenz() function shown in Listing 14-2.

```
import numpy as np

def lorenz(t0, x0, y0, z0, dt, sigma, rho, beta, iter_num):
    """Calculate the evolution of the Lorenz system."""
    t, x, y, z = [np.zeros(iter_num + 1) for _ in range(4)]
    t[0], x[0], y[0], z[0] = t0, x0, y0, z0
    for i in range(iter_num):
        t[i + 1], x[i + 1], y[i + 1], z[i + 1] = \
            lorenz_step(t[i], x[i], y[i], z[i], dt, sigma, rho, beta)
    return t, x, y, z
```

Listing 14-2: The function to obtain a trajectory for the Lorenz system

This function preallocates some NumPy arrays for the trajectory, sets their initial values, and runs a loop to calculate iter_num time steps.

Finally, use this function to calculate the evolution of the Lorenz system for certain initial conditions, as shown in Listing 14-3.

```
t, x, y, z = lorenz(t0=0, x0=1, y0=1, z0=1, dt=0.01,
                    sigma=10, rho=28, beta=8 / 3, iter_num=5_000)
```

Listing 14-3: Integrating the Lorenz system

This code sets the values of the sigma, rho, and beta constants to those originally used by Lorenz.

Visualizing Time Evolution

You can plot the time evolution of the Lorenz system via Listing 14-4.

```
import matplotlib.pyplot as plt

fig, axs = plt.subplots(3, 1, figsize=(8, 6), sharex=True)

axs[0].plot(t, x, "k--", lw=1.1, label="x")
axs[0].set_ylabel("x")
axs[0].legend()

axs[1].plot(t, y, "k--", lw=1.1, label="y")
axs[1].set_ylabel("y")
axs[1].legend()

axs[2].plot(t, z, "k--", lw=1.1, label="z")
axs[2].set_ylabel("z")
```

```
axs[2].legend()
axs[2].set_xlabel("Time Step")

plt.tight_layout()
plt.show()
```

Listing 14-4: Plotting the time evolution of the Lorenz system

This code plots Figure 14-1, which shows the time evolution of the *x*, *y*, and *z* state variables in the Lorenz system.

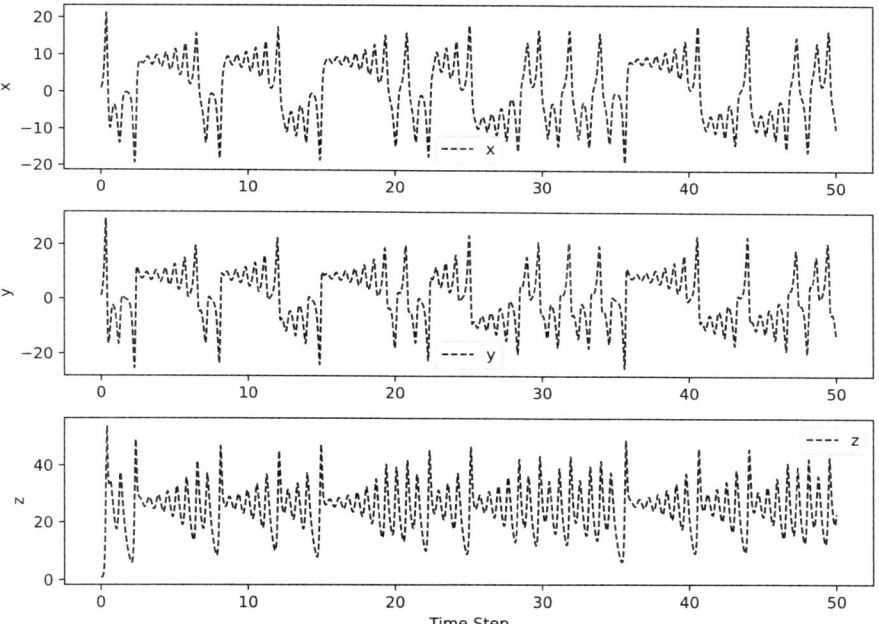

Figure 14-1: The time evolution of the Lorenz system

In the top plot, the variable *x* oscillates over time, displaying a pattern that switches between high and low values with no apparent regularity, suggesting the chaotic nature of the system. In the middle plot, the variable *y* features similar behavior with irregular oscillations, but with a different pattern and frequency, indicating the complex relationship between the variables. In the bottom plot, the variable *z* also features chaotic behavior, with its own distinct amplitude and frequency of oscillations.

The fluctuations in the values of *x*, *y*, and *z* are a graphical representation of the system's inherent unpredictability. Despite the deterministic nature of the underlying equations, each variable influences the others in a dynamic interplay, resulting in the complex, aperiodic patterns captured by these time-series plots.

Visualizing the Lorenz Attractor

Instead of looking at the time evolution of the three individual variables, you can plot the trajectory of the state of the Lorenz system in the 3D space represented by its variables (which is known as a *phase-space plot*). This approach reveals the Lorenz attractor, a captivating geometric shape that illustrates the complex and chaotic behavior of the system. This attractor provides a more holistic view of the system's dynamics than the earlier time-series plots.

You can use Listing 14-5 to plot the Lorenz attractor.

```
fig = plt.figure()
ax = fig.add_subplot(projection="3d")
ax.plot(x, y, z, "k--", lw=0.5)
ax.set_xlabel("X Axis")
ax.set_ylabel("Y Axis")
ax.set_zlabel("Z Axis")
plt.show()
```

Listing 14-5: Plotting the Lorenz attractor

This code produces Figure 14-2.

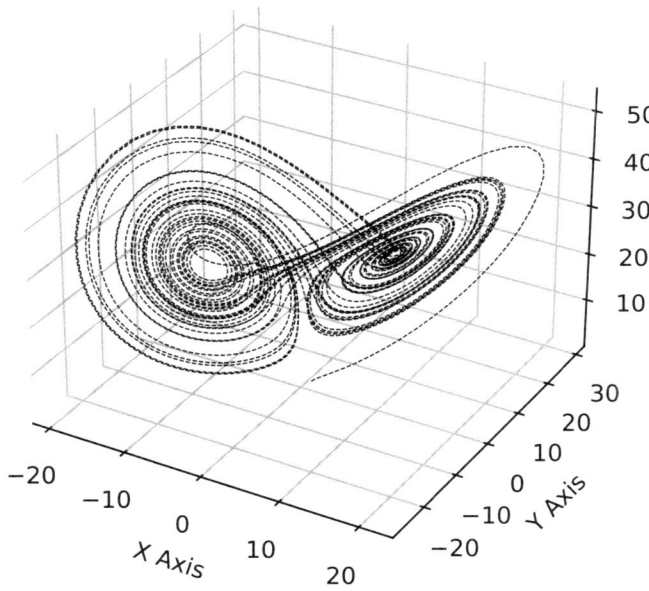

Figure 14-2: The Lorenz attractor

The 3D trajectory of the Lorenz attractor forms a distinctive, nonrepeating pattern with two main lobes (or wings) that appear to be mirrored images of each other. These lobes are where the system's state tends to reside the most, creating a butterfly, or figure-eight, pattern as the trajectory spirals outward before looping back.

Despite its complex structure, the trajectory of the Lorenz attractor never intersects itself, demonstrating the system's deterministic nature (at any given point, the Lorenz system's equations have a unique solution). The path traced by the attractor shows how the system evolves over time, swinging from one lobe to the other unpredictably, which is a classic example of deterministic chaos.

EXERCISES

14-1: Alter the parameters of the Lorenz system (σ, ρ, and β) one at a time and visualize how each change affects the Lorenz attractor. What role does each parameter play in the system's dynamics?

14-2: Extend the simulation of the Lorenz system to a much longer time scale. Do the trajectories settle into a pattern, or do they continue to exhibit chaotic behavior indefinitely?

14-3: Modify the initial conditions of the Lorenz system simulation to observe how different starting points affect the resulting trajectory and Lorenz attractor.

14-4: Investigate the impact of different time-step lengths on the numerical solution of the Lorenz equations. How and why do the trajectories and Lorenz attractor change? What is the largest time step that still provides a stable and accurate solution?

Demonstrating the Butterfly Effect

Now let's introduce a minimal change to the initial conditions and repeat the previous calculations. This will demonstrate the chaotic nature of the Lorenz system and its sensitivity to initial conditions, popularly known as the butterfly effect.

Alter the value of one of the initial conditions from Listing 14-3:

```
t_a, x_a, y_a, z_a = lorenz(t0=0, x0=1 + 0.000_001, y0=1, z0=1, dt=0.01,
                            sigma=10, rho=28, beta=8 / 3, iter_num=5_000)
```

Here, a very small amount is added to the initial condition for the x variable. (Altering the value of some of the other initial conditions would yield qualitatively similar results.)

Then plot the resulting trajectories, adapting Listing 14-4 as shown in Listing 14-6.

```
--snip--
axs[0].plot(t, x, "k--", lw=1.1, label="x")
axs[0].plot(t_a, x_a, color="cyan", lw=0.9, label="x_a")
--snip--
axs[1].plot(t, y, "k--", lw=1.1, label="y")
axs[1].plot(t_a, y_a, color="cyan", lw=0.9, label="y_a")
--snip--
```

```
axs[2].plot(t, z, "k--", lw=1.1, label="z")
axs[2].plot(t_a, z_a, color="cyan", lw=0.9, label="z_a")
--snip--
```

Listing 14-6: Plotting the time evolution of the Lorenz system with a slightly perturbed initial condition (by modifying Listing 14-4)

This code plots the original trajectories as well as those with the slightly perturbed initial condition, producing Figure 14-3.

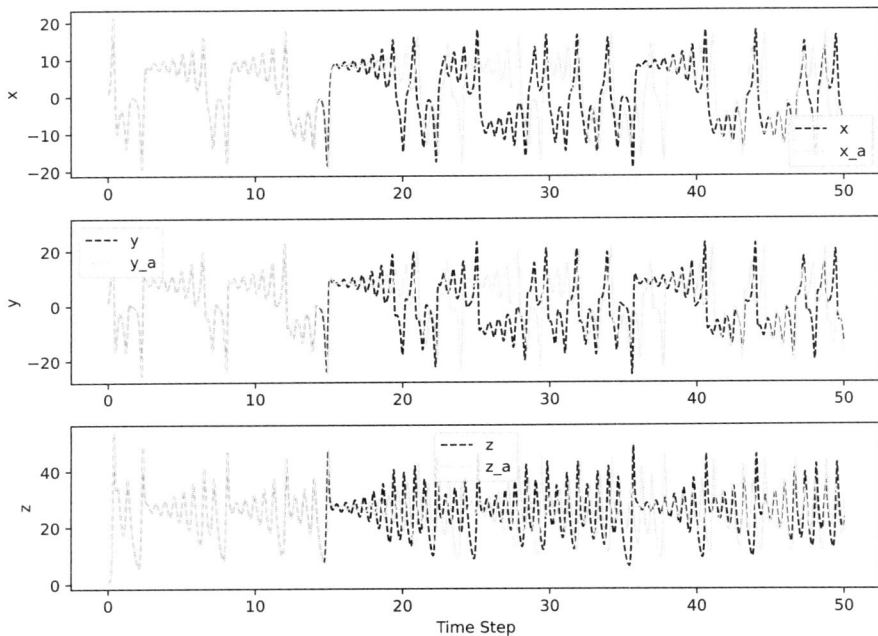

Figure 14-3: The time evolution of the Lorenz system with slightly perturbed initial conditions

This figure plots both the original (dashed lines, x, y, and z) and perturbed (solid lines, x_a, y_a, and z_a) trajectories. Initially, the trajectories of the perturbed and original variables remain close, indicating a low rate of separation. However, as time progresses, the separation increases.

The rate at which the trajectories diverge relates to *Lyapunov exponents*, which measure the rates at which nearby trajectories in a dynamic system diverge or converge. A positive Lyapunov exponent is indicative of chaos, signifying that two infinitesimally close trajectories will diverge exponentially over time. The greater the exponent, the more sensitive the system, and the more quickly the initially close states will diverge.

From the plots, you can infer that the Lorenz system has at least one positive Lyapunov exponent because the perturbed trajectories diverge exponentially from the original ones over time. The rate at which the two trajectories diverge can be used to estimate the largest Lyapunov exponent for the Lorenz system, although for an accurate calculation, a more rigorous mathematical analysis would be required.

You can also plot the Lorenz attractor with Listing 14-7.

```
--snip--
ax.plot(x, y, z, "k--", lw=0.5, label="original")
ax.plot(x_a, y_a, z_a, color="cyan", lw=0.5, label="perturbed")
ax.legend()
--snip--
```

Listing 14-7: Plotting the Lorenz attractor with slightly perturbed initial conditions (by modifying Listing 14-5)

Figure 14-4 shows the resulting attractor.

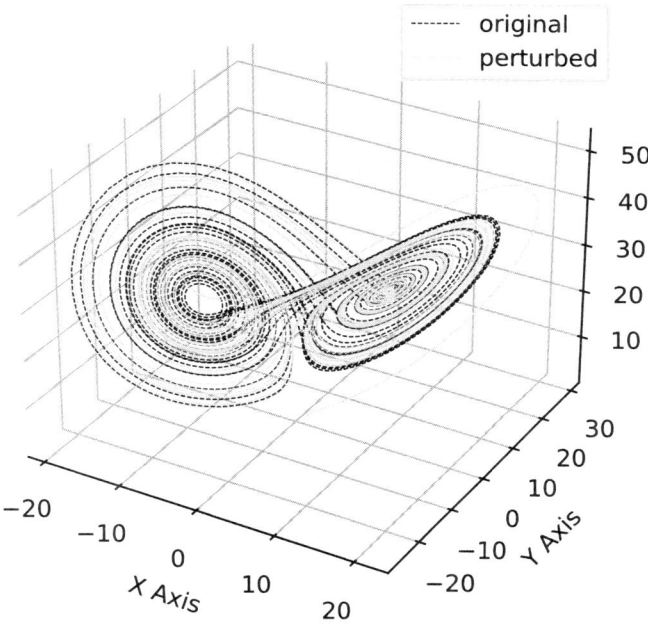

Figure 14-4: The Lorenz attractor with slightly perturbed initial conditions

You can see the Lorenz system's sensitivity to initial conditions as well as its intrinsic deterministic nature. Because of the minute difference in the initial conditions, represented by the original and perturbed trajectories, the two paths evolve distinctly over time, illustrating the chaotic behavior inherent in the system. Remarkably, though, both trajectories converge to the same Lorenz attractor, as you can tell by the two trajectories occupying the same space, a feature that highlights the deterministic aspect of this chaotic system.

This convergence suggests that while the system's short-term behavior is highly sensitive and unpredictable because of its dependence on initial conditions, its long-term dynamics are confined to a specific set of patterns and structures, represented by the Lorenz attractor. This duality—of sensitivity in the short term and determinism in the long term—underscores the complex and fascinating nature of chaotic systems, where unpredictability and order coexist.

EXERCISE

14-5: The Lyapunov exponent measures the rate at which nearby trajectories in a dynamic system diverge over time. A positive Lyapunov exponent indicates sensitive dependence on initial conditions, meaning that small differences in starting points lead to exponentially growing divergence; this is a hallmark of chaotic systems. Estimate the largest Lyapunov exponent of the Lorenz system, using the divergence of two closely started trajectories over time. Implement a computational approach to approximate the Lyapunov exponent and discuss the implications of your findings for the predictability of the system.

Implementing a Reservoir Computer

You're now ready to use reservoir computing to model and predict the behavior of the Lorenz system. You'll first define the size and topology of your reservoir and then initialize the input and reservoir matrices with appropriate scaling. Next, you'll generate data from the Lorenz system to serve as your training and validation datasets.

The training phase adapts the output weights to map the reservoir states to the desired output by using a regularized least squares method. After the training, you'll exploit the reservoir's capability to predict the future states of the Lorenz system, thereby testing the efficacy of your reservoir computer.

Finally, you'll visualize and compare the reservoir's predictions against the actual Lorenz system dynamics.

Setting Up the Reservoir

Figure 14-5 shows the architecture of the reservoir computer you'll use to predict the Lorenz system.

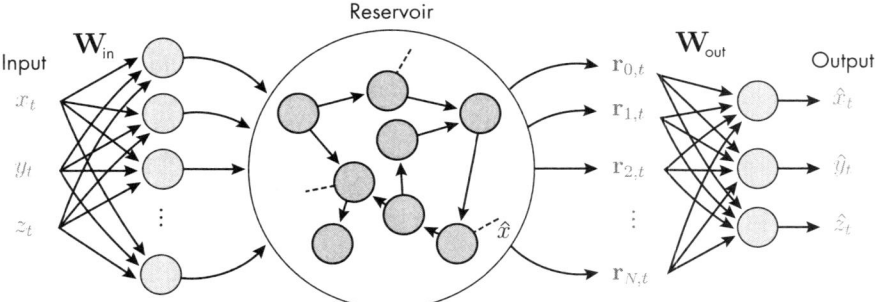

Figure 14-5: The architecture of a reservoir computer for the Lorenz system

The reservoir receives three inputs corresponding to the Lorenz system variables x, y, and z. The reservoir consists of a network of randomly connected neurons. This complex interconnectivity enables the reservoir to process the input signals and predict their temporal evolution. The three outputs correspond to the predicted values of the Lorenz system variables, encapsulating the essence of the dynamic system's behavior.

Input Weights

To implement this reservoir computer, start by defining the connections between the inputs and the reservoir with Listing 14-8.

```
dim_system = 3
dim_reservoir = 300
edge_probability = 0.1


W_in = 2 * edge_probability * (np.random.rand(dim_reservoir, dim_system) - 0.5)
```

Listing 14-8: Defining the reservoir input

This code defines the constants for the dimension of the Lorenz systems (`dim_system`), the dimension of the reservoir with 300 neurons (`dim_reservoir`), and the probability of each possible edge between neurons (`edge_probability`). Then the input weight matrix (`W_in`) is initialized with random values.

Reservoir State and Weights

You can then initialize the state of the reservoir with Listing 14-9.

```
reservoir_state = np.zeros(dim_reservoir)
```

Listing 14-9: Defining the reservoir state

This code sets the states of all neurons in the reservoir to zero.

GRAPH THEORY

To understand the initialization of the reservoir weights, it's helpful to have a basic understanding of some key concepts of *graph theory*, a field of mathematics that studies the properties of graphs.

A *graph* is a collection of nodes with edges that connect pairs of nodes. In the context of reservoir computing, each *node* represents a neuron, and each *edge* represents a connection between neurons. An edge can be assigned a weight that represents the strength of the connection between two nodes.

A *random graph* has connections and weights that are generated by a random process. An *adjacency matrix* is a square matrix used to represent a finite graph. The elements of the matrix indicate whether pairs of nodes are connected (adjacent) in the graph.

The *eigenvalues* of a matrix are a set of values that give important information about the properties of the matrix. The *spectral radius* of a matrix is the largest absolute value of its eigenvalues. In reservoir computing, controlling the spectral radius of the reservoir's adjacency matrix (which represents the connection weights) is crucial to ensure that the reservoir's dynamic behavior is appropriate to process inputs.

Now you're ready to define the connections between the neurons in the reservoir. You'll model the reservoir's random connectivity by using a random graph, represented as an adjacency matrix. You'll define the weights between neurons in the reservoir. Then you'll adjust the spectral radius of the adjacency matrix to control the reservoir's dynamics; this latter step ensures that the reservoir can effectively process and learn from the input data. Let's do this using Listing 14-10.

```
import networkx as nx

scaling_factor = 1.1

graph = nx.gnp_random_graph(dim_reservoir, edge_probability)
graph = nx.to_numpy_array(graph)
❶ A = 2 * (np.random.rand(dim_reservoir, dim_reservoir) - 0.5) * graph
eigenvalues, _ = np.linalg.eig(A)
❷ A = A / np.absolute(np.amax(eigenvalues)) * scaling_factor
```

Listing 14-10: Defining the reservoir connections

This code generates a random graph to represent the reservoir's structure, using the `gnp_random_graph()` function from the NetworkX toolbox for graph theory. This function generates a graph where each possible edge between neurons is included with a probability given by `edge_probability` defined in Listing 14-8. Then the function converts the graph to an adjacency matrix held in a NumPy array, using the `to_numpy_array()` function from NetworkX.

Finally, the code initializes the reservoir's adjacency matrix with random weights ❶, computes its `eigenvalues`, and scales it to control its spectral radius ❷. The spectral radius directly influences the reservoir's dynamics, determining how quickly signals dissipate or amplify within the network. By controlling the spectral radius (typically, keeping it slightly below 1), you ensure that the reservoir is neither too stable (where signals decay too quickly) nor too chaotic (where signals amplify uncontrollably), allowing it to exhibit rich, yet manageable, dynamic behavior. This balance is key for effective temporal pattern processing.

Output Weights

Next, you can initialize the output weights with Listing 14-11.

```
W_out = np.zeros((dim_system, dim_reservoir))
```

Listing 14-11: Defining the output weights

This code initializes the weights of the output layer to zero.

Preparing the Training and Validation Data

To train your reservoir computer, you need a substantial amount of data that captures the complex dynamics of the Lorenz system. To obtain it, generate a long Lorenz trajectory and split it into training and validation data, as shown in Listing 14-12.

```
iter_num = 10_000

t, x, y, z = lorenz(t0=0, x0=1, y0=1, z0=1, dt=0.01,
                    sigma=10, rho=28, beta=8 / 3, iter_num=iter_num)
xyz = list(zip(x, y, z))

split_ratio = 0.50
split_idx = int(iter_num * split_ratio)
```
❶ `t_train, xyz_train = t[:split_idx], np.array(xyz[:split_idx])`
❷ `t_val, xyz_val = t[split_idx:], np.array(xyz[split_idx:])`

Listing 14-12: Generating a long Lorenz trajectory for training and validation

This code uses the `lorenz()` function to simulate a trajectory long enough to represent the Lorenz system's chaotic behavior across its phase space. Then the x, y, and z coordinate lists are combined into a single list of 3-tuples.

Once the trajectory is generated, the code divides it into training and validation sets. The `split_ratio` parameter determines the proportion of data allocated for training ❶, while the remaining data is used for validation ❷.

Training the Reservoir Computer

You're finally ready to train the reservoir to emulate the dynamics of the Lorenz system.

Deriving the Mathematical Formulas

This section covers technical mathematical details that are essential for understanding the theoretical background of the methods used. However, if you prefer to focus on the practical implementation, feel free to skip this section and go directly to the following sections, which include code examples and applications.

The objective of the training is to find the output weights $\mathbf{W}_{out}$ that minimize the regularized MSE between the predicted and actual outputs.

Denote with $\mathbf{R} = [\mathbf{r}_0, \dots, \mathbf{r}_{t-1}, \mathbf{r}_t]$ the matrix of reservoir states, where each column $\mathbf{r}_t$ represents the reservoir state at a specific time step. The update of the reservoir state is given by

$$\mathbf{r}_t = \text{Sigmoid}(\mathbf{A}\mathbf{r}_{t-1} + \mathbf{W}_{in}\mathbf{x}_t) \tag{14.3}$$

where $\mathbf{A}$ is the reservoir matrix, $\mathbf{W}_{in}$ is the input weight matrix, and $\mathbf{x}_t$ is the training input at time t.

The goal is to solve the regularized least squares problem

$$\mathbf{W}_{out} = \arg\min_{\mathbf{W}} \|\mathbf{X} - \mathbf{R}^\top \mathbf{W}\|^2 + \lambda \|\mathbf{W}\|^2 \tag{14.4}$$

where $\mathbf{X}$ is the matrix of training outputs, λ is the regularization factor, and $\|\cdot\|^2$ denotes the *Frobenius norm*, which measures the size of a matrix as the square root of the sum of the absolute squares of its elements.

In Equation 14.4, the regularization factor λ plays a critical role in balancing the model's fit to the training data with the model's complexity. A higher value of λ penalizes larger weights more severely, thus helping to prevent overfitting and ensuring the model's generalization to new data.

The solution of Equation 14.4 is derived by differentiating the regularized least squares objective function with respect to the weight matrix $\mathbf{W}$, setting the derivative equal to 0 to find the minimum, and solving for $\mathbf{W}_{\mathrm{out}}$. This process finally yields the formula for the output weights

$$\mathbf{W}_{\mathrm{out}} = (\mathbf{X}^\top \mathbf{R}^\top)(\mathbf{R}\mathbf{R}^\top + \lambda \mathbf{I})^{-1} \tag{14.5}$$

where $\mathbf{I}$ is the identity matrix.

Implementing a Numerically Stable Sigmoid Function

Before training the reservoir, you need to implement a version of the sigmoid function that carefully handles large positive and negative input values. This is needed to prevent issues with floating-point arithmetic overflow, common in the standard sigmoid function for extreme input values. You can implement it as shown in Listing 14-13.

```
def sigmoid(x):
    """Compute the sigmoid function for the input array."""
    return np.where(x >= 0, 1 / (1 + np.exp(-x)), np.exp(x) / (1 + np.exp(x)))
```

Listing 14-13: The numerically stable sigmoid function

This implementation of the sigmoid function enhances numerical stability by handling large positive and negative values of x differently when x is nonnegative or negative.

Implementing the Training

With the activation function in place, you can train the reservoir computer with Listing 14-14.

```
R = np.zeros((dim_reservoir, xyz_train.shape[0]))
for i in range(xyz_train.shape[0]):
    R[:, i] = reservoir_state
    reservoir_state = sigmoid(np.dot(A, reservoir_state)
                      + np.dot(W_in, xyz_train[i]))

Rt = np.transpose(R)
regularization_factor = 0.0001
inverse_part = np.linalg.inv(np.dot(R, Rt)
                ❶ + regularization_factor * np.identity(R.shape[0]))
W_out = np.dot(np.dot(xyz_train.T, Rt), inverse_part)
```

Listing 14-14: Training the reservoir computer

This code starts by initializing the matrix R to record the evolving internal states of the reservoir over time, capturing its dynamic response to the training inputs. The dimensions of R are the reservoir's size by the length of the training data.

In the subsequent `for` loop, each column of `R` is filled with the current reservoir state, providing a snapshot of the reservoir at each time step. Then the `reservoir_state` is updated (implementing Equation 14.3). This update applies the sigmoid function to a linear combination of the current reservoir state (multiplied by the reservoir matrix `A`) and the current training input (multiplied by the input weight matrix `W_in`). Thanks to the sigmoid function, this step nonlinearly transforms the inputs and the current state of the reservoir to produce the next state, introducing some complex dynamics.

After populating `R`, the code calculates its transpose, `Rt`, and defines a regularization factor. With these elements in place, the code calculates the inverse part of the regularized least squares solution. This is done by taking the inverse of the matrix product of `R` and `Rt`, added to the product of the regularization factor and an identity matrix to ensure numerical stability ❶. This inverse part plays a crucial role in finding a balance between fitting the training data and maintaining model simplicity, enhancing generalization and reducing the risk of overfitting.

Finally, the code computes the output weight matrix `W_out` (Equation 14.5). This is done by first multiplying the transpose of the training data with `Rt` and then multiplying this result with `inverse_part`. The resulting `W_out` matrix, which is fine-tuned through this process, represents the trained weights of the reservoir computer. These weights map the reservoir states to the training outputs in a way that minimizes the regularized MSE between the predicted and actual outputs. The output layer now effectively translates the complex internal dynamics of the reservoir into the desired output, completing the training phase.

Note that the training process of the reservoir computer is entirely deterministic, distinguishing it from the other deep learning techniques you've seen in the previous chapters that often rely on stochastic elements such as random initialization or dropout during training. Instead, in the reservoir computer approach, the initial conditions and the structure of the reservoir are fixed, and the only adaptation occurs through the deterministic optimization of the output weights `W_out` based on the provided training data. This deterministic nature ensures that the training process can be replicated precisely, yielding the same output weights, given the same training data and reservoir configuration.

One advantage of this deterministic training is its potential for simpler and more interpretable models. Since the optimization process is straightforward, analyzing and understanding the relationship between the input data and the trained weights can be easier. Moreover, the absence of random elements in the training can lead to faster convergence and reduce the need for extensive hyperparameter tuning typically associated with stochastic training methods.

However, there are also disadvantages to consider. The deterministic nature means that the reservoir computer model may not explore the full range of possible solutions that could be discovered through stochastic processes, potentially limiting its ability to model very complex patterns or to generalize beyond the training data. Additionally, the fixed structure of the reservoir may not be suitable for all types of problems, and significant expertise may be required to design a reservoir that captures the nuances of a particular dataset or task.

Predicting the Lorenz System

Now you can use the trained reservoir computer to predict the evolution of the Lorenz system with Listing 14-15.

```
steps_to_be_predicted = len(xyz_val)

xyz_pred = np.zeros((steps_to_be_predicted, dim_system))
for i in range(steps_to_be_predicted):
❶ xyz_pred[i] = np.dot(W_out, reservoir_state)
    reservoir_state = sigmoid(np.dot(A, reservoir_state)
                              + np.dot(W_in, xyz_pred[i]))
```

Listing 14-15: Predicting the behavior of the Lorenz system with the trained reservoir computer

This code initializes the xyz_pred array to store the predicted states of the system, with dimensions corresponding to the number of steps to be predicted by the dimensionality of the system.

In the for loop, the reservoir computer makes predictions for each time step. For each iteration, the current prediction is obtained by multiplying the trained output weight matrix with the current reservoir state ❶. This step essentially transforms the internal state of the reservoir into the predicted system state.

After generating the prediction, the reservoir_state is updated for the next time step. This update is similar to the training phase: The sigmoid activation function is applied to a linear combination of the updated reservoir state (multiplied by the reservoir matrix) and the just-predicted system state (multiplied by the input weight matrix). This step ensures that the reservoir state evolves based on both its previous state and the new input derived from the latest prediction.

This process is repeated for all time steps in the validation set, allowing the reservoir computer to generate a sequence of predictions that model the behavior of the Lorenz system over time.

Evaluating the Performance of the Reservoir Computer

Let's examine the effectiveness of the reservoir computer by juxtaposing its predictions against the actual Lorenz system outputs. This comparison is critical to understanding the accuracy of the reservoir computer in capturing the complex dynamics of chaotic systems.

For convenience, you can use

```
x_val, y_val, z_val = xyz_val[:, 0], xyz_val[:, 1], xyz_val[:, 2]
x_pred, y_pred, z_pred = xyz_pred[:, 0], xyz_pred[:, 1], xyz_pred[:, 2]
```

to extract the validation dataset's individual components and the predicted outcomes from the reservoir computer.

Comparing Trajectories

You can then compare the actual and predicted trajectories of each variable over time, using Listing 14-16.

```
--snip--
axs[0].plot(t_val, x_val, "k--", lw=1.1, label="x Lorenz")
axs[0].plot(t_val, x_pred, color="orange", lw=0.9, label="x prediction")
--snip--
axs[1].plot(t_val, y_val, "k--", lw=1.1, label="y Lorenz")
axs[1].plot(t_val, y_pred, color="orange", lw=0.9, label="y prediction")
--snip--
axs[2].plot(t_val, z_val, "k--", lw=1.1, label="z Lorenz")
axs[2].plot(t_val, z_pred, color="orange", lw=0.9, label="z prediction")
--snip--
```

Listing 14-16: Plotting the comparison of the time evolution for the validation and predicted trajectories (by modifying Listing 14-6)

The plot should be similar to Figure 14-6, providing a comparison of the actual Lorenz system trajectories and the predictions made by the reservoir computer, across the three dimensions of the system.

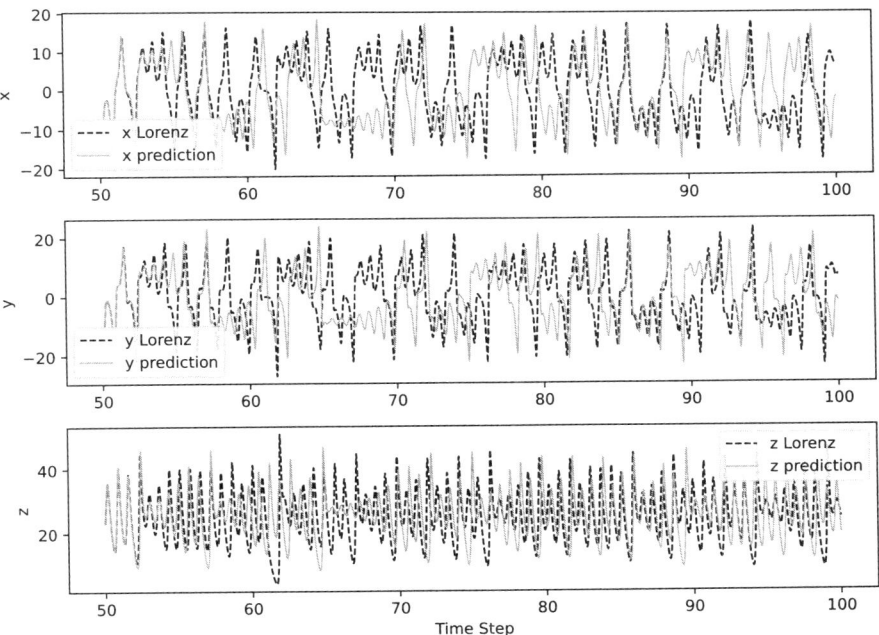

Figure 14-6: Comparison of the time evolution for the validation and predicted trajectories

Initially, the predicted trajectories align closely with the true Lorenz system, indicating that the reservoir computer has captured the system's dynamics well during this phase. However, as time progresses, the predicted paths begin to diverge from the actual trajectories. This divergence highlights the inherent difficulty in predicting chaotic systems over longer time horizons because of their sensitive dependence on initial conditions. This phenomenon, quantified by Lyapunov exponents, measures the rate of separation of infinitesimally close trajectories.

Despite this deviation, the overall shapes and patterns of the predicted trajectories suggest that the reservoir computer still retains some understanding of the Lorenz system's underlying dynamics, but the accuracy of its predictions decreases over time. This happens when the Lyapunov exponents are positive, indicating sensitive dependence on initial conditions and leading to an exponential growth of prediction errors.

Comparing Lorenz Attractors

To verify whether the reservoir computing model has effectively learned the underlying dynamics of the Lorenz system, you can create a 3D plot to visualize the Lorenz attractor, using Listing 14-17.

```
--snip--
ax.plot(x_val, y_val, z_val, "k--", lw=0.5, label="Lorenz system")
ax.plot(x_pred, y_pred, z_pred, lw=0.5, color="orange", label="prediction")
--snip--
```

Listing 14-17: Plotting the Lorenz attractor with validation and predicted trajectories (by modifying Listing 14-7)

This code should generate a plot similar to Figure 14-7.

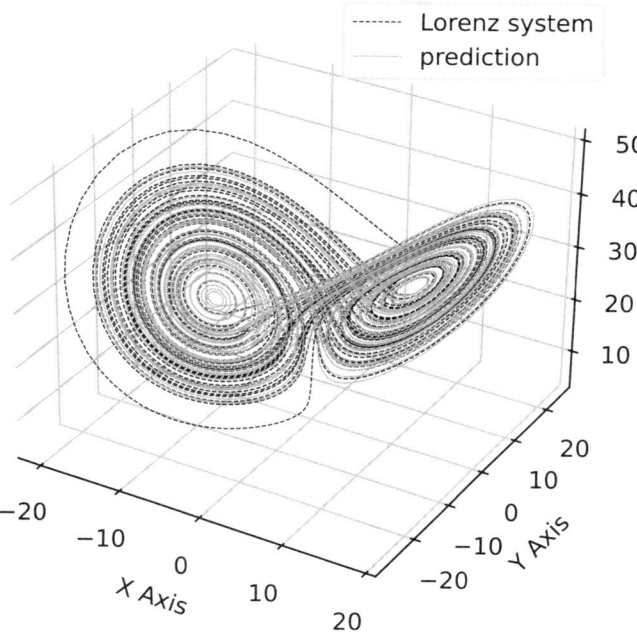

Figure 14-7: Comparison of the Lorenz attractor obtained with validation and predicted trajectories

You can see that the reservoir computer successfully replicates the unique geometry of the Lorenz attractor, demonstrating an understanding of the Lorenz system's chaotic behavior. The similarity in the attractor's shape within the 3D representation implies that the model has internalized the fundamental dynamics sufficiently to mimic the attractor's form, which is a central aspect of the Lorenz system's dynamics.

Thus, even as individual trajectories inevitably part ways over time, reflecting their innate sensitivity to initial conditions, the overall pattern of the attractor prevails. This suggests that the model can be used to forecast the qualitative features of the system's behavior over the long term, despite the inherent challenges of accurate long-range forecasting in chaotic systems. Therefore, the model's consistency in capturing the attractor's topology reflects its ability to understand the underlying dynamics of the Lorenz system despite its chaotic nature.

NOTE *Code Example 14-1, "Training a Reservoir Computer to Predict the Lorenz System," is available at* https://github.com/DeepTrackAI/DeepLearningCrashCourse. *Navigate to the* Ch14_RC *folder and then* ec14_1_lorenz. *The* lorenz.ipynb *notebook provides a complete code example that trains a reservoir computer to predict the evolution of the Lorenz system.*

EXERCISES

14-6: Investigate the sensitivity of the reservoir computer to its hyperparameters. Vary the size of the reservoir, the edge probability, and the scaling factor, and observe how these changes affect the model's ability to predict the Lorenz system. Which are the most critical parameters and their optimal values?

14-7: Assess the robustness of the reservoir computer to noisy input data. Introduce varying levels of noise to the Lorenz system data and evaluate the reservoir computer's predictive performance. Determine the noise threshold at which its predictions begin to significantly diverge from the true system's behavior.

14-8: Experiment with different structures of the reservoir. Replace the random graph with structured alternatives, like small-world or scale-free graphs, and measure how these changes affect the performance.

Summary

In this chapter, you learned about reservoir computing, a paradigm within machine learning that is tailored to deal with complex temporal data. You learned the fundamental concepts that differentiate reservoir computing from other neural network frameworks, like its fixed reservoir of neurons. You also saw how the architecture of reservoir computing simplifies the training process by deterministically adjusting only the output weights, leaving the reservoir's internal structure unchanged.

You then put theory into practice by constructing a reservoir to generate a trajectory of the Lorenz system. Training the reservoir, you saw how the model learned to replicate the chaotic trajectory of the Lorenz system. You also compared the reservoir computer's predictions with the actual behavior of the Lorenz system, using both time-series plots and a 3D representation of the Lorenz attractor. This comparison validated your model, while also highlighting the power of reservoir computing in capturing the underlying laws governing complex systems.

As this chapter ends, you are now equipped with a deep understanding of reservoir computing and its unique place in the world of neural networks. This knowledge will be invaluable as you continue to explore and apply machine learning techniques to ever more challenging problems.

Seminal Works and Further Reading

The foundation for recurrent neural networks and reservoir computing was laid by John J. Hopfield in his seminal 1982 paper "Neural Networks and Physical Systems with Emergent Collective Computational Abilities," published in *Proceedings of the National Academy of Sciences* (volume 79, pages 2,554–2,558). Hopfield introduced Hopfield networks, a form of recurrent neural network with feedback connections. He demonstrated how these networks could settle into stable states that could be used for associative memory tasks. This work paved the way for understanding how dynamics and attractor states could be used in neural computation, and it influenced later developments in both recurrent neural networks and reservoir computing models such as echo state networks and liquid state machines. Hopfield was awarded a share of the 2024 Nobel Prize in Physics for his pioneering work on neural networks.

A major step forward for reservoir computing came in 2004 with "Harnessing Nonlinearity: Predicting Chaotic Systems and Saving Energy in Wireless Communication" by Herbert Jaeger and Harald Haas, published in *Science* (volume 304, pages 78–80). They expanded the application of echo state networks to practical problems such as predicting chaotic time series and optimizing energy use in wireless communication. This work was one of the first to show that reservoir computing could be competitive with other machine learning methods in real-world tasks, bridging the gap between theoretical exploration and practical implementation.

CHALLENGE PROJECTS

14-1: Forecasting with reservoir computing Build and train a reservoir computer to forecast a time series generated by a system other than the Lorenz system. Suggestions include the *Rössler system* (another chaotic system with distinct dynamic properties that can be used to test the ability of the reservoir to capture different types of chaotic behavior) or the *Mackey–Glass equation* (a delayed differential equation known for its complex, chaotic time-series output often used as a benchmark in time-series prediction tasks). Compare the performance of the reservoir computing model with a standard recurrent neural network on the same task to evaluate the effectiveness of the reservoir computing approach in capturing the dynamics of various complex systems.

14-2: Reservoir computing for real-world data Apply reservoir computing to a real-world temporal dataset, such as stock market prices that can be obtained from financial databases like Yahoo! Finance or Google Finance, or weather data that can be accessed through APIs provided by services such as OpenWeatherMap or NOAA Climate Data Online. Process the data, train the reservoir, and evaluate its predictive accuracy. Compare the results with alternative methods, such as recurrent neural networks, to highlight the strengths and weaknesses of reservoir computing in practical applications.

14-3: Memory capacity of reservoir computers Investigate the memory capacity of a reservoir computing system. *Memory capacity* refers to the ability to retain and utilize historical input information for future computations. Design experiments to quantitatively measure the memory capacity of the reservoir by assessing its performance on tasks that require retaining information over different time spans. For instance, you can use the *echo state property* as a metric, which involves presenting the reservoir with a random input signal and then measuring how well the system can reproduce this signal after a certain number of time steps. Analyze how different reservoir configuration parameters, such as the size, connectivity, and spectral radius of the reservoir, affect the memory capacity. Compare the results with theoretical bounds on memory capacity for reservoir computing systems.

CONCLUSION

Congratulations on making it to the end of this book!

By now, you've successfully navigated the world of deep learning and mastered a wide array of concepts and techniques, from the fundamentals of dense neural networks to advanced topics like GANs, transformers, and reservoir computing. You've learned to build and train complex models, you understand the theoretical underpinnings of various architectures, and you know how to apply them to practical tasks. With the hands-on experience you've gained through each project, you now have the skills to tackle real-world problems by using deep learning, setting you up for continued growth and exploration in the field of AI.

But this is just the beginning. Now it's time to experiment and innovate. Use the knowledge and skills you've acquired to work on your own projects. Apply deep learning to new datasets and challenges, and explore creative ways to improve existing models.

Staying updated is crucial in this rapidly evolving field. You can follow the latest research by reading academic journals like *Nature Machine Intelligence* or *IEEE Transactions on Neural Networks and Learning Systems*. Likewise, check the articles submitted to conferences such as NeurIPS, ICML, and CVPR to learn about cutting-edge developments. Most of these papers are available for free through open access repositories like arXiv (*https://arxiv.org*). Participating in online communities like Reddit's r/MachineLearning, Stack Overflow, and specialized forums can also keep you informed and connected.

In addition, consider diving deeper into specific areas of interest. You can find extensive resources on specialized topics such as computer vision, natural language processing, or reinforcement learning across various online platforms. Websites like arXiv provide open access research papers, while platforms such as Coursera, edX, and Udacity offer specialized courses. Furthermore, repositories like GitHub host numerous open source projects and code implementations that can help you explore these topics hands-on. Reading seminal papers and textbooks in these areas can also provide you with deeper insights.

Finally, collaboration and contribution can provide new insights, foster innovation, and expand your network—all vital for growth. Join deep learning communities, contribute to open source projects, and team up with others. Document your projects and share them on platforms like GitHub. A strong portfolio will showcase your skills and help you connect with potential collaborators and employers.

The world of AI and deep learning is vast and full of opportunities. The mastery you've gained from this book has positioned you at the forefront of this field, and it can become your gateway to a future of innovation and discovery. Stay curious, keep learning, and continue pushing the boundaries of what's possible with deep learning.

Thank you for embarking on this journey with us. We hope to stay connected with our readers through our GitHub repository at *https://github .com/DeepTrackAI/DeepLearningCrashCourse*. Please feel free to contribute your thoughts, projects, and suggestions there. We wish you all the best in your continued exploration of deep learning and AI.

INDEX

Note: *Bold page numbers indicate where a term is defined or given extensive treatment. For classes and functions, bold entries show where they are defined; non-bold entries show where they are used.*

Symbols

& (deeptrack operator), 141, 171, 176, 183, 186, 190–192, 194, 200, 215, 230, 235, 242, 256, 269, 286, 308

^ (deeptrack operator), 175, 228, 239

\>\> (deeptrack operator), 140, 141, 170, 175, 176, 181, 186, 190, 198, 215, 227–230, 235, 239–242, 256, 269, 272, 286, 308

@ (dot product), **14**, 17, 23, 28, 32, 33, 58, 62, 63, 64, 69

A

A100 GPU, 386

Abbe, Ernst, 463

Abbe's diffraction limit, 463. *See also* diffraction limit

accuracy, **39**, 203, 211, 533. *See also* binary accuracy

vs. precision, 136

Accuracy (torchmetrics), 548, 550–552

accuracy_score() (sklearn), 203

action (reinforcement learning), **558**

in deep Q-learning, 586

legal, 565

in Q-table, 578–579

action-value function, **559**

activation function, 2, 3, 19–20

Heaviside step, 3, 20

hyperbolic tangent, 19, 20

leaky ReLU, 19, 20

linear, 19, 20

ReLU, 19, 20, 43

sigmoid, 19, 20

softmax, 42

activation potential. **2**, **3**, 23, 26–28, 33, 63

active learning, **530**, 556

with multiple groups, 539–546

with two groups, 531–539

ActiveLearningDataset (deeplay), 550–552

ADALINE (adaptive linear element), 48

Adam (deeplay, torch), 87, 135, 173, 200, 217, 231, 244, 259, 264, 267, 273, 289, 292, 293, 295, 297, 316, 363, 368, 372, 383, 402, 416, 490, 496, 508, 522, 548, 588

Adam optimizer, **45**

β_1 and β_2 parameters, 383

with parameter list, 289

regularization with weight decay, 363

AdamW (deeplay, torch), 356, 440, 458, 461

adaptive average pooling, 148

AdaptiveAvgPool2d (torch), 118, 148, 547

adaptive linear element (ADALINE), 48

adaptive switching circuits, 48

Add (deeplay), 351

Add (deeptrack), 227, 228, 241, 272

additive attention, 335–336

AdditiveAttention, **335**

adjacency matrix, **476–477**, **611**

adversarial learning/training, **376–379**, 423. *See also* generative adversarial networks

adversarial sampling, 549, **552–553**

agent (reinforcement learning), **558**

in deep Q-learning, 585–586

in Q-learning, 574–585, 597

AI (artificial intelligence), xxii

AlexNet, xxii, 165

al_loop(), **549**, 550–552
all_words_in_vocab(), **306**, 307
alpha (parameter LodeSTAR), 275–276
AlphaFold, xxii, 326, 528
AlphaGo, 557, 599
animate(), **510**, 511
Anki decks, 299
annotated data (active learning),
    533–538, 541–545, 548–553
AnnotatedDataset, **133**, 134
anomaly detection, **195**, 375
    with autoencoder, 195–206
        using latent space, 204–206
        using reconstruction error,
        201–203
append() (deeplay), 353, 486, 487,
    495, 547
Application (deeplay), 258, 315,
    587–592, 594
area under the ROC curve
    (AUROC), 117
ArgmaxJI, **217**, 217
artificial intelligence (AI), xxii
artificial neuron, **2–3**, 48. *See also*
    single neuron
AsType (deeptrack), 228, 229, 235,
    241–242
Atari games, 599
attention, 325, **326–336**, 373, 528
    additive, 335–336
    concatenative, 373
    dot-product, 326–331, 373
        standard scaled, 333
        trainable, 333–335
    general, 373
attention head, 343. *See also* multi-head
    attention
attention matrix, **327**, 328–332
    interpretation, 340–342
    visualization, 331–332
attention outputs, **327**, 329–331
attention U-Net, **438–439**
    architecture, 438
    conditional, 447–448, 457–458, 467
AttentionUNet (deeplay), 439, 448,
    458, 467
AUROC (area under the
    ROC curve), 117

autoencoder, 167, 168, 179–207
    for anomaly detection, 195–206
    variational, 179–188
    Wasserstein, 188–195
average pooling, 119, 148, 266,
    487–489
axon, 2

B

Ba, Jimmy, 45
Bachimanchi, Harshith, 472
backbone, 257–258, 265, 335, 552–553
    convolutional, 257–258, 265, 547–548
    message-passing, 501–502
    ViT as, 370–371
backpropagation algorithm, **25–27**,
    48, 145
    implementation, 27–28, 33, 63
    mathematical derivation, 25–27
backward() (torch), 125, 150, 154, 157,
    162, 289, 384, 403, 404, 417, 441,
    462, 593
    sum().backward(), 125
Bahdanau, Dzmitry, 373
Barcelona, 158
batch (in PyTorch), 103
batch processing (graphs), 488–489
batch training/learning, 45, **65–73**
    implementation, 67–68
    increasing batch size, 93
    randomization, 71–73
BCELoss (torch), 182, 383
BCEWithLogitsLoss (torch), 244
Bellman, Richard, 557, 598
Bellman equation, 559, 598
BERT, 374
beta (parameter diffusion model), 433
beta (parameter LodeSTAR), 275–276
beta (parameter VAE), 182–183
beta (regularization factor style
    transfer), 160, 163
Beta distribution, 366
betas (parameter Adam), 363, 368, 383,
    402, 416
bias
    in CNN, 102
    in single neuron, 2, 3, 17–18
bilinear upsampling, 107

BiLingual Evaluation Understudy (BLEU) score, **321–322**, 339

binary accuracy, **116**, 119

BinaryClassifier (deeplay), 115, 119, 356, 522

binary cross-entropy loss, **115**, 116, 119, 182, 244, 356, 377, 379, 383

BioSR (super-resolution) dataset, 463–464

BioSRDataset, **464**, 465

bisectrix, 66, 67, 69, 262, 265, 267

BLEU (BiLingual Evaluation Understudy) score, **321–322**, 339

BLEUScore (torchmetrics), 321

bmm() (torch), 160

boredom (reinforcement learning), 561

bottleneck, **168**, 180, 210, 439

Brightfield (deeptrack), 138, 169

bright-field microscopy, 138, 170, 178, 394, 409

Broad Bioimage Benchmark Collection, 234

Bronte Ciriza, David, 80, 93

Brown, Robert, 426

Brownian motion, 128, 426

Bruna, Joan, 527

buffer (for dataset), 172

buffer (to replay experiences), 591. *See also* replay buffer

build() (deeplay), 267, 273, 363, 368, 372, 381, 382, 391, 392, 400, 401, 414, 415, 439, 467, 501, 548, 550–552, 588

build_vocab_from_iterator(), **304**, 305, 348, 453

butterfly effect, 602, 607–610

bwd_hook_func(), **125**

C

Caicedo, Juan C., 234

Callegari, Agnese, 82

candidate gate (LSTM), 297

Cat (deeplay), 217

CategoricalClassifier (deeplay), 548

categorical cross-entropy loss, **43**, **212**

cell counting dataset, 234–235

cell counting with U-Net, 234–247

cell gate (LSTM), 297

cell localization with LodeSTAR, 268–277

CellTracingDataset, **519**, 521

Cell Tracking Challenge dataset BF-C2DL-HSC, 268–269 DIC-C2DH-HeLa, 512–514

cell trajectory identification with MAGIK, 511–526

centroid (position), 232, 270, 515

chaos, 602, 607, 608

chaotic system, 602

chatbots, 299

ChatGPT, xxii

Chen, Ting, 278

Cho, Kyunghyun, 323

Christiansen, Eric M., 394

Çiçek, Özgün, 248

CIFAR-10 dataset, 358–359

clamp_() (torch), 150

classification head, 362, 370, 522, 548

classification of malaria-infected blood smears, 110–128

classification of MNIST digits with active learning, 547–555 with DNN, 34–47

Classifier (deeplay), 37, 363, 367, 372

classifier-free guidance. 446–453, 458–460

classifier guidance, 446

CLIP (Contrastive Language-Image Pre-training), 326, **450**

Clip (deeptrack), 235, 241

CLIP text encoder, 460–463

CLIPTextModel (transformers), 461

CLIP tokenizer, 460–463

CLIPTokenizer (transformers), 461

clone() (torch), 121, 123, 125, 151, 184, 365, 520

closure(), 161, **161**

closure function, 161–163

code examples
    1-1: *Classifying 1D Data with a Single Neuron*, 9
    1-2: *Classifying 2D Data with a Single Neuron*, 16
    1-3: *Classifying 2D Data with a Two-Layer Neural Network*, 29
    1-A: *Classifying the MNIST Digits*, 47

code examples *(continued)*

2-1: *Regressing 1D Data with a Single Neuron*, 55

2-2: *Regressing 2D Data with a Single Neuron*, 60

2-3: *Regressing 2D Data with a Two-Layer Neural Network*, 64

2-4: *Fitting Data with a Neural Network Trained Using Batch Training*, 73

2-5: *Training a Neural Network Splitting the Data*, 79

2-A: *Simulating the Forces Acting on an Optically Trapped Particle*, 92

3-1: *Implementing Neural Networks in PyTorch*, 110

3-A: *Classifying Blood Smears with a Convolutional Neural Network*, 128

3-B: *Localizing Microscopic Particles*, 145

3-C: *Creating DeepDreams*, 158

3-D: *Transferring Image Styles*, 164

4-1: *Denoising Images*, 178

4-A: *Generating Digit Images*, 188

4-B: *Interpolating Between Images*, 195

4-C: *Detecting ECG Anomalies*, 206

5-1: *Segmenting Biological Tissue Images*, 223

5-A: *Detecting Quantum Dots*, 234

5-B: *Counting Cells with a U-Net*, 247

6-1: *Localizing Particles Using LodeSTAR*, 267

6-A: *Localizing Multiple Cells Using LodeSTAR*, 277

7-1: *Predicting Temperatures using Recurrent Neural Networks*, 298

7-A: *Translating with a Recurrent Neural Network*, 322

8-1: *Understanding Attention*, 336

8-A: *Translating with Attention*, 342

8-B: *Predicting Sentiment Using a Transformer*, 357

8-C: *Classifying Images with a Vision Transformer*, 372

9-1: *Generating New MNIST Digits with a GAN*, 389

9-A: *Generating MNIST Digits On Demand*, 394

9-B: *Virtually Straining a Biological Tissue with a Conditional GAN*, 409

9-C: *Converting Microscopy Images with a CycleGAN*, 422

10-1: *Generating Digits with a Diffusion Model*, 445

10-A: *Generating Bespoke Digits with a Conditional Diffusion Model*, 449

10-B: *Generating Images of Digits from Text Prompts*, 463

10-C: *Generating Super-Resolution Images*, 471

11-1: *Predicting Molecular Properties*, 497

11-A: *Simulating Complex Physical Phenomena*, 511

11-B: *Identifying Trajectories with MAGIK*, 526

12-1: *Training a Binary Classifier with Active Learning*, 539

12-2: *Training a Three-Class Classifier with Active Learning*, 546

12-A: *Training a MNIST Digits Classifier with Active Learning*, 555

13-1: *Teaching a Deep Q-Learning Agent to Play Tetris*, 597

14-1: *Training a Reservoir Computer to Predict the Lorenz System*, 619

Cohn, David, 556

collate(), **349**, 349

comb filter, 280–281

commonsense benchmark, **287**

compiling (a neural network), **37**

Compose (torchvision), 113, 149, 360, 361, 371, 380, 398, 412, 432, 465, 521

computational device, 287–288

computational graph, 91, 121, 184, 385

compute_connectivity(), **503**, 503

compute_graph(), **503**, 506, 509

compute_node_attr(), **502**, 503

ComputeTrajectories, **523**, 524

Compute Unified Device Architecture (CUDA), 288

CompVis, 425

concatenative attention, 373

configure() (deeplay), 36, 42, 44, 45, 118, 199, 353, 400, 401, 522, 547

configure_optimizers() (deeplay, Application method), 368

confusion matrix, **40**

    plotting, 40–41

connected_components() (networkx), 524
Connect Four, 560
connection (graph), 476. *See also* edge
constants() (deeptrack, Source method), 213
context manager, **153–154**. *See also* with
context vector (seq2seq model), **299**, 308–311, 337–338
Contrastive Language-Image Pre-training (CLIP), 326, **450**
contrastive learning, 252–255, 277, 278, 450
contrastive loss, 252
Conv1d (torch), 199
Conv2d (torch), 102, 108, 147–148
convex dataset, 10
convolution, **96–100**
  1D, 96–98
  2D, 98–100
  graph, **476–479**
convolutional base, **109**, 110, 119
ConvolutionalEncoderDecoder2d (deeplay), 173, 199
convolutional layer, **100**, 102–104
  activation, 121–124
ConvolutionalNeuralNetwork (deeplay), 118, 134, 257, 401, 547
ConvTranspose1d (torch), 199
coregistration, 395, 409
corpus file (NLP), 299
corpus iterator (NLP), 302–303
corpus_iterator(), **302**, 305
correlation matrix analysis, 284
Cortes, Corinna, 34
CosineAnnealingLR (torch), 367–368
CPU, xxiv, 38, 91, 244, **287–288**, 312, 381, 386, 387
cpu() (torch), 91, 245, 386, 393, 405, 419, 434, 438, 443, 445, 470, 509
create() (deeplay), 36, 37, 42, 44, 45, 87, 115, 119, 135, 143, 173, 178, 182, 191, 200, 217, 221, 231, 244, 259, 264, 292, 293, 295, 297, 318, 355, 356, 458, 460, 489, 490, 494, 496, 508, 522
create_batch(), **366**, 366, 369
Crop (deeptrack), 235
CropTight (deeptrack), 239

cross-attention, **326**, 326–337, 345, 457, 458. *See also* attention
cross-entropy loss, 211
  binary, **115**, 116, 119, 182, 244, 356, 377, 379, 383
  categorical, **43**, **212**
  sparse, 212
  weighted, 224
CrossEntropyLoss (torch), 217, 231, 363
.csv files, 3, 12, 83, 89, 90, 196, 219, 283
CSVLogger (lightning), 89, 218, 221
CUDA (Compute Unified Device Architecture), 288
cuda (torch), 288
curiosity-driven exploration (reinforcement learning), 560–561
current reward (reinforcement learning), 559, 594
Cursor (matplotlib), 130–131
custom text encoder implementation (NLP), 455–457
CutMix, **365**, 366
CutMix augmentation, **364**
CutMixClassifier, **367**, 368
cutoff (classifier), 116
cutoff (parameter LodeSTAR), 275–276
cvtColor() (cv2), 128
Cybenko, George, 49
Cybenko's theorem, 49
cycle consistency, **410**, 418, 420
CycleGAN, **410**, 424
CycleGANDiscriminator (deeplay), 415
CycleGANResnetGenerator (deeplay), 414
cycle graph, 476–479

D

DALL-E, xxii, 425, 450
Data (torch_geometric), 349, 505–506, 509, 516–517, 519
data augmentation, 214, 252–255, 372, 412, 504, 519–521
  CutMix, 364
  Mixup, 364
  with VAE, 183
DataFrame (pandas), 346, 357
data loader, **38**

DataLoader (deeplay, torch), 38, 39, 45, 88, 115, 134, 142, 172, 177, 183, 186, 191, 200, 218, 222, 232, 235, 244, 260, 267, 272, 286, 308, 349, 361, 364, 372, 383, 403, 416, 440, 468, 547

DataLoader (torch_geometric), 489, 507, 521

data pipeline
  with augmentations, 214–215
  with labels, 186, 190, 215
  to load an image crop, 272
  to load images, 181
  to load text, 307–308
  to load traces, 196–199, 286
  with segmentations, 235, 269

dataset
  BioSR (super-resolution), 463–464
  cell counting, 234–235
  Cell Tracking Challenge
    BF-C2DL-HSC, 268–269
    DIC-C2DH-HeLa, 512–514
  CIFAR-10, 358–359
  electrocardiogram (ECG), 196–197
  English-to-Spanish translations, 299–300
  Fashion-MNIST, 189–191
  Holo2Bright, 411
  Human Motor Neuron, 394–395
  IMDb Large Movie Review, 345–347
  Jena Climate, 282–284
  malaria-infected blood smears, 111–112
  microscopic particle videos, 128–130
  MNIST, 1, 34–35, 181, 380–381, 432–433, 547
    with sentences, 451–452
  optical forces, 80–81
  quantum dot image, 224–225
  SAND (particle simulation), 497–500
  segmented tissue images, 213, 216
  ZINC (molecular properties), 483–486

Dataset (deeptrack), 183, 186, 191, 200, 215, 222, 232, 235, 242, 256, 272, 286, 308

Dataset (torch), 88, 133, 142, 172, 395, 397, 411, 464, 504, 505, 519

Dayan, Peter, 598

DCGANDiscriminator (deeplay), 382, 392

DCGANGenerator (deeplay), 381, 391

DDPM (denoising diffusion probabilistic models) , **427–432**

decision boundary, 15, 20, 535–538, 543, 544

decoder, **168**, 180, 182–185, 188, 199, 218, 299, 310–315, 336–339, 345, 376, 400–401, 501

decoder-only transformer, 345

deep belief nets, 49

deep learning, **xxii**

Deep Learning: A Visual Approach (Glassner), xxiii

deep learning revolution, xxi

deepcopy() (copy), 360, 371

deepdream(), **152**, 153, **154**, 154, **156**, 157

DeepDreams, **145–158**

Deeplay, xxiv, 36, 87, 279, 287, 292, 315, 362, 401, 414, 415, 439, 588

DeeplayModule (deeplay), 309–311, 313, 314, 330, 334, 335, 337, 338, 343, 350, 351, 353, 481, 482, 486–488, 495

DeepTrack2, 137, 286, 308

denoising diffusion probabilistic models (DDPM), **427–432**

denoising encoder-decoder, 169–179

dense neural networks, 20–33, 61–65
  with three layers, 31–33
  with two layers, 20–31, 61–65

dense top, 109, 112, 118–119, 124, 134, 257, 265–266, 353, 361, 362, 487–488, 496

depth (of a neural network), 21

detach() (torch), 91, 103–105, 107, 121, 123, 125, 126, 136, 143, 151, 160, 174, 175, 177, 178, 184, 186, 192–194, 200, 201, 203–205, 232, 245, 260, 262, 264, 267, 273, 312–314, 331, 369, 386, 393, 417, 419, 523, 590

deterministic chaos, 602. *See also* chaos

detransformation, 254

Dhariwal, Prafulla, 472

diffraction limit, 255, 463
  diffraction-limited particle images, 256

Diffusion, **433**, 434, **435**, 440, **444**, **447**, **452**, **467**, 468

diffusion (in physics), 426

diffusion equations, 426

diffusion trajectory, 432

digital twin, 52, 79

  of a physical system, 79–92

directed graph, 477

discount factor (reinforcement learning), 559, 580–581, 594

discriminator, **377–378**, 382, 423

  conditional, **390**, 391–392

distance_matrix() (scipy), 276

Divide (deeptrack), 228, 235, 241

dnn2_clas(), **23**, 24, 29

dnn2_reg(), **62**, 62, 67, 68, 75, 77

dnn3_clas(), **32**, 32

Doersch, Carl, 278

Dosovitskiy, Alexey, 374

dot-product attention, 328–331, 373

  standard scaled, 333

  trainable, 333–335

DotProductAttention, **330**, 330, 337, 338

downsampling layer, 105

DQLAgent, **587–595**, 596, 597

dropout, 148, **295–298**, 355, 387, 551, 615

Dropout (torch), 148, 351, 353

dropout rate, 295

d_sigmoid(), **28**, 28, 33, 63, 68

dying ReLU problem, 105

dynamically learned loss function, 377

E

early stopping, 73, 220–222

EarlyStopping (lightning), 221

Earth mover's distance, 188

eccentricity (of object), 515

edge (graph), 476–479, 611

edge attributes, 491

edge index, 492

eigenvalues (graph), 611

Einstein, Albert, 426

ElasticTransformation (deeptrack), 239

electrocardiogram (ECG) dataset, 196–197

Ellipsoid (deeptrack), 238, 239

Elman, Jeffrey L., 323

Embedding (torch), 309, 310, 353, 455, 487, 495

embedding dimension, 328, 329, 354, 390, 391, 447, 457, 458, 487

embedding layer, 390

encoded distribution, 188

encoder, **168**, 180, 182, 186–188, 199, 218, 299, 308–315, 336, 345, 351–355, 376, 501

encoder-decoder, **168–169**

encoder-only transformer, 345

encoding

  contrastive learning, 252

  geometric learning, 254

  non-contrastive learning, 253

English-to-Spanish translations dataset, 299–300

entropy sampling, 545

environment (reinforcement learning), 558

epoch, **38**

epsilon-greedy policy/strategy, 579, 585, 587, 590, 591, 597

equivariance, 254

error backpropagation.

  See backpropagation algorithm

estimated optimal reward (reinforcement learning), 559

Euclidean norm, 19

Euler integration scheme, 500, 509–510

eval() (torch), 147, 191, 356, 369, 386, 392, 405, 419, 442, 444, 448, 459, 462, 469, 509, 523. *See also* train()

evaluate_model()

  for CycleGAN, **419**, 420

  for virtual staining, **405**, 406

experience buffer, 591.

  See also replay buffer

exploration vs. exploitation (reinforcement learning), 560–561, 579, 587, 591

exposure bias, 314

F

F1 score, 276, 523

f1_score() (sklearn), 523

failure analysis, 46–47

fallout, 117

false-positive rate (FPR), 116
Fashion-MNIST dataset, 189–191
fast forward diffusion process, 429–434
feature map, **99–100**, 103–110, 160, 182, 210–211, 363, 402, 415, 438, 439, 457, 467, 548
feedback (reinforcement learning), 558, 573
feedback loop/mechanism (RNN), 280, 281
filter, 96
  2D, 98–99
    Prewitt, 99
    Sobel, 99
  Gaussian, 97, 98, 99
  matching pattern, 98, 99
  Prewitt, 98
  rectangular, 97
  RGB, 100
  smoothing, 98
  Sobel, 97, 98
  valid complete placements of, 97, 99
filter() (deeptrack), 196
find_contours() (skimage), 525
fit() (torch), 38, 42, 44, 45, 89, 116, 119, 135, 143, 173, 178, 183, 191, 200, 204, 218, 221, 232, 244, 260, 264, 267, 273, 292, 293, 295, 297, 319, 356, 363, 368, 372, 490, 496, 508, 522, 532, 548, 549
flanging, 280
Flatten (torch), 109, 134, 257, 547
FlipLR (deeptrack), 215
flip_transform(), **263**, 263
FlipUD (deeptrack), 215
Fluorescence (deeptrack), 226, 228, 238, 256
fluorescence microscopy, 226, 227, 234, 238, 256, 394
forget gate (LSTM), 297
forward diffusion process, **427**, 427–429
  fast, 429–430
  implementation, 433–435
forward filling, 219
FPR (false-positive rate), 116
from_numpy() (torch), 91, 232, 273, 275, 276

from_pretrained() (transformers), 371, 461
fully connected neural network, 21. *See also* dense neural networks
FuncAnimation (matplotlib), 499, 510, 525
future reward, 558, 559, 578, 581, 594
Fwd_Hook, **153**, 154
fwd_hook_func(), **125**, 125
Fwd_Hooks, **156**, 157, 160, 162

G

GANs. *See* generative adversarial networks
GATs (graph attention networks), 528
gated recurrent unit (GRU), **294–296**
gather() (torch), 315
Gatys, Leon A., 165
Gaudí, Antoni, 158
Gaussian (deeptrack), 241, 256
Gaussian blur, 240
GaussianBlur (deeptrack), 240
Gaussian Error Linear Unit (GeLU), 588
Gaussian filter, 97–99
Gaussian sampling, **179**, **180**
GCL, **481–482**, 486, 487
GCN, **486–488**, 489
GCNs (graph convolutional networks), **486–489**, 527
GeLU (Gaussian Error Linear Unit), 588
GELU (torch), 456
general attention, 335, 373
generative adversarial networks (GANs), 375, 377, **376–379**
  conditional, 390
  training
    algorithm, 379
    implementation, 384–386
generator, **377–379**, 381–382, 423
  conditional, **390**, 390–391
geometric contrastive learning, 278
geometrical–optics approximation (optical tweezers), 79
get_device(), **288**, 288, 381, 400, 414, 433, 466, 508
get_glove_embeddings(), **317**, 318, 328, 355

get_mask(), **242**, 242

Gilmer, Justin, 527

Glassner, Andrew, xxiii

global average pooling, 266, 487–489

Global Vectors for Word Representation (GloVe), 316–318, 328, 332, 355

GNNs (graph neural networks), 475

gnp_random_graph() (networkx), 612

Go (game), xxii, 557, 599

GODataset, **88**, 88

Goodfellow, Ian, 379, 423

Google, 145, 325, 425

Google Colab, xxiv

Google Imagen, 425

GoogLeNet, 165

Google Research, 358

GPT, 374

GPT-4, xxi

GPU, xxiv, 38, 91, 244, **287–288**, 312, 381, 386

   A100, 386

gradient ascent, 149–151

gradient descent, 25

gradient-weighted class activation mapping (Grad-CAM), 124–127

GradualWarmupScheduler (warmup_scheduler), 367

gram(), **160**, 160, 162

Gram matrix, 160–163

Graph (networkx), 524

graph, 476, 611

   directed, 477

   undirected, 477

graph attention network (GAT), 528

graph convolution, **476–479**

GraphConvolution, **480**, 481

graph_convolution(), **478**, 478

graph convolutional network, **486–489**, 527

graph convolution layer, **480–482**

GraphFromSegmentations, **514–516**, 517

graph network–based simulator, 497, 500–502

graph neural networks (GNNs), 475

graph theory, 611

GraphToEdgeMAGIK (deeplay), 522

GraphToNodeMPM (deeplay), 501

Grill, Jean-Bastien, 278

GRU (gated recurrent unit), **294–296**

GRU (torch), 309, 310

guidance strength, 446

GUI for particle position, 130–132

H

Haas, Harald, 620

Hadamard product, 294, 297

handling contractions (NLP), 301

hash table (analogy with dot-product attention), 330

Hassabis, Demis, 528

He, Kaiming, 165

heatmap

   attention, 331–332, 340–342

   with Grad-CAM, 124–127

Heaviside step function, **3**, 19, 20

Helgadottir, Saga, 128, 165

hidden layer, **20**, 27

hidden state, 281, 289, 299, 309, 336, 337

Hinton, Geoffrey E., 49, 207

hist(), **202**, 202–205

history (deeplay, Trainer field), 292, 319, 363

Ho, Jonathan, 431, 472

Hochreiter, Sepp, 323

Hoff, Marcian E., 48

holdout dataset, 74

   Holo2Bright dataset, 411

Holo2BrightDataset, **411**, 413

holographic microscopy, 409

hook_func(), **121**, 122, **123**, **150**, 150

hook function, 121

   backward, 125

   forward, 125

Hopfield, John J., 620

Hopfield networks, 620

Hornik, Kurt, 49

HTML (IPython), 499, 510, 525

Hugging Face (library), 345, 370, 372

Human Motor Neuron dataset, 394–395

hyperbolic tangent function, **19**, 20, 105

hyperparameters, 40, 73

I

IBM Watson, xxii

Identity (numpy), 614

Identity (torch), 134, 199
Image (PIL), 121, 146, 151, 158, 159, 224, 395, 396, 411, 412
image classification with a ViT, 358–372
image conversion with CycleGAN, 409–422
image embedding, 450
ImageFolder (deeptrack), 181, 189, 213, 235
ImageFolder (torchvision), 111, 113
image generation
  conditional
    with diffusion model, 446–450
    with GAN, 389–394
  with diffusion model, 432–445
  with GAN, 379–389
  with VAE, 183–185
  with WAE, 192–193
Imagen (Google), 425
ImageNet Large Scale Visual Recognition Challenge, xxii, 147, 148, 165, 364, 370
image patch embeddings, 362
image segmentation with U-Net, 211–224
image super-resolution, 463–471
image_to_tensor(), **149**, 150, 153, 154, 160
image_translation(), **258**, 259, 263
imbalanced data classes (training), 196
imdb_iterator(), **348**, 348
IMDb Large Movie Review dataset, 345–347
immediate reward, 559, 594
imread() (cv2), 513
imread() (matplotlib), 34, 39, 452
imread() (tiffile), 464
Inception (architecture), 165
Inception (movie), 145
inceptionism, 145
increasing batch size (for training), 93
IndexedPositionalEmbedding (deeplay), 353
inductive bias, 364
input (neuron), 2
input gate (LSTM), 297
InstanceNorm2d (torch), 400, 401
instance segmentation, **211**

interobserver variability, 137
intersection over union (IoU), 216
intraobserver variability, 137
invariance, 254
inverse_flip_transform(), **263**, 264
inverse_translation(), **258**, 259, 264
IOU (intersection over union), 216
Isensee, Fabian, 248
isotropic_erosion() (skimage), 242

J

Jaccard index, 216–217
Jaeger, Herbert, 620
Jena Climate dataset, 282–284
Johnson, Justin, 423
Join (deeptrack), 181, 189, 213
Jumper, John, 528
Jupyter Notebooks, xxiv

K

Kaggle Notebooks, xxiv
Kaiming (deeplay), 552
Kaiming initializer, 553
kernel, 102. *See also* filter
Kingma, Diederik P., 45, 207
Kipf, Thomas N., 527
KL (Kullback–Leibler) divergence, 180, 189
k-nearest neighbors algorithm, 204
Kneusel, Ronald T., xxiii
Krizhevsky, Alex, 165
Kullback–Leibler (KL) divergence, 180, 189

L

L1Loss (torch), 173, 200, 259, 264, 289, 402, 415, 468, 490, 496
l1_loss() (torch), 201, 203
L_1 norm, 19, 416
L_2 norm, 19, 416
L_2-norm pooling, 106
label() (skimage), 232, 236, 245
labeling oracle, 530
label_trans(), **113**, 113, 121
Lambda (deeptrack), 215
large language models (LLMs), xxi
large margin sampling, 545
Latent Diffusion Models, 425, 472

latent representation, 168, 180, 390

latent space, **168**, 180, 188, 204–206, 377

Layer (deeplay), 118, 134, 309, 310, 337, 343, 351, 353, 354, 481, 487, 494, 495, 547

LayerList (deeplay), 36, 353, 486, 487, 495

LayerNorm (torch), 455

LayerNorm (torch_geometric), 351

LazyLinear (torch), 257, 492, 494

LBFGS (torch), 161

L-BFGS (Limited-memory Broyden-Fletcher-Goldfarb-Shanno) algorithm, 161–163

leaky ReLU, **19**, 20, 105

LeakyReLU (torch), 400, 401

learned perceptual image patch similarity (LPIPS), 402

LearnedPerceptualImagePatchSimilarity (torchmetrics), 402

learning rate, 7, **8**

LeCun, Yann, 34, 165

legal action (reinforcement learning), 565

LeNet-5 (architecture), 165

Lenton, Isaac C.D., 93

lerp() (torch), 447

Lightning, xxiv, 287

Limited-memory Broyden-Fletcher-Goldfarb-Shanno (L-BFGS) algorithm, 161–163

Linear (torch), 36, 109, 148, 288, 310, 334, 335, 343, 351, 353, 371, 456, 481, 487

LinearBlock (deeplay), 36

linear function, **19**, 20

linear_sum_assignment() (scipy), 276

link (graph), 476

LLMs (large language models), xxi

load() (json), 451, 498

load() (numpy), 82–83, 133, 498

load() (torch), 508, 597

load_data(), **12**, 12, 22, 30, 52, 56, 57, 61, 65, 74, 77

load_data_1d(), **3**, 4, 10

load_data_file(), **84**, 84, **85**, 86

loader.py, 4, 9, 12, 16, 29, 52, 55, 60, 64, 73, 79

load_from_checkpoint() (lightning), 491, 496

load_glove_embeddings(), **317**, 318, 328, 355

LoadImage (deeptrack), 181, 190, 215, 235, 269

load_images(), **512**, 513, 522

load_npz_data(), **498**, 498

load pretrained embeddings (NLP), 316–318

load_state_dict() (torch), 508, 595, 597

load_video(), **128**, 129

LodeSTAR (deeplay), 267, 273

LodeSTAR (Localization and Detection from Symmetries, Translations, and Rotations), **255–268**, 278

  alpha parameter, 275

  beta parameter, 275

  cutoff parameter, 275

  displacement channels, 266

  mode parameter, 275

  probability channel, 266

  training with flipping, 262–265

  translation equivariant training algorithm, 257

  implementation, 258–260

log() (lightning), 259, 368

logic gates, 22, 32

LogisticRegression (sklearn), 532

logistic regression model, 532–533

logits, 42, 212

log_metrics() (lightning), 368

log_output() (deeplay, Application method), 368

logP (penalized water-octanol partition coefficient), 483

Long, Jonathan, 207

long short-term memory (LSTM), **296–298**, 323

Lorenz, Edward, 602

lorenz(), **604**, 604, 607, 613

Lorenz attractor, 603, 606–607

lorenz_step(), **603**, 604

Lorenz system

  definition, 602–603

  numerical integration, 603–604

  time evolution, 604–605

loss() (deeplay, Application method), 259, 367, 593

loss function, **25**
  dynamically learned, 377
  weighted, 231

LPIPS (learned perceptual image patch similarity), 402

L_p norm, 19

LSTM (long short-term memory), **296–298**, 323

Luong, Minh-Thang, 373

Lyapunov exponent, 608, 610, 618

M

machine learning, **xxii**

Machine Learning with Neural Networks: An Introduction for Scientists and Engineers (Mehlig), xxiii

MAE. *See* mean absolute error

MAGIK, 511, 521–522, 528

malaria-infected blood smears dataset, 111–112

ManualAnnotation, **130**, 131

manual annotation (of particle positions), 130–134

ManyThings.org website, 299

Margin (deeplay), 551, 552

Markov decision process, 598

Markov process, 427

maskedNLL(), **315**, 316

mask_to_positions(), **232**, 232

Math for Deep Learning (Kneusel), xxiii

Matplotlib, xxiv
  %matplotlib inline (standard backend), 132
  %matplotlib ipympl (interactive backend), 131

Matthes, Eric, xxiii

Max Planck Institute for Biogeochemistry, 282

MaxPool1d (torch), 199

MaxPool2d (torch), 105, 108, 109, 118, 134, 147–148, 257, 547

max pooling, 105

McCulloch, Warren S., 48

MeanAbsoluteError (torchmetrics), 87, 135

mean absolute error (MAE), 87, 135, 143, 245, 287, 402, 416, 491, 509

mean percentage error (MPE), 245

mean squared error (MSE), 26, 37, 68, 87, 162, 183, 402, 416, 431, 508, 613, 615

Mehlig, Bernhard, xxiii

memory, 280

message (GNN), 492

message-passing layer, **492–495**

message-passing network, **495–496**, 527

Metal Performance Shaders (MPS), 288. *See also* GPU

MetricCollection (deeplay), 37–38

metrics.csv file, 89, 90, 219

microscopic particle videos dataset, 128–130

Midtvedt, Benjamin, 255, 278

MieSphere (deeplay), 137, 139

mini-batch training. *See* batch training/learning

min pooling, 106

Mixup augmentation, 364

MNIST handwritten digit database, 1, 34–35, 181, 380–381, 432–433, 547
  with sentences, 451–452

mode (parameter LodeSTAR), 275–276

mode collapse, **175–176**, 253, 382, 389, 393, 394, 444

ModelCheckpoint (lightning), 490, 496, 508

model-free reinforcement learning, 559, 598

Module (torch), 370, 455, 480, 492–494

molecular property prediction with GNN, 479–497

MolecularRegressor, **490**, 490, 491, 496

momentum (of an optimizer), 45

Mordvintsev, Alexander, 145

morphing images with WAE, 193–195

MoveAxis (deeptrack), 170, 175, 176, 181, 190, 215, 230, 235, 242, 256, 272

moving average, 96

MPE (mean percentage error), 245

MPN, **495**, 496

MPS (Metal Performance Shaders), 288. *See also* GPU

mps (torch), 288
MSE. *See* mean squared error
MSELoss (torch), 37, 87, 135, 161, 191, 402, 415, 440, 508, 588
MulticlassAccuracy (torch), 37–38
MulticlassJaccardIndex (torchmetrics), 217
multi-head attention, **342–344**, 345
MultiHeadAttentionLayer, **343**, **350**, 351
multilayer perceptron, 21. *See also* dense neural networks
MultiLayerPerceptron (deeplay), 36, 38, 87, 115, 118, 134, 547, 552, 588
multimodal learning, 358
Multiply (deeptrack), 272

N

natural language processing. *See* NLP
NearestNeighbors (sklearn), 204
nearest neighbor upsampling, 107
negative log-likelihood loss, 315
negative pairs (contrastive learning), 252
NetworkX, 612
neural style transfer, **158–164**, 165
neuron. *See also* single neuron
   artificial, **2–3**, 48
   biological, **2**, 48
neuron_clas_1d(), **5**, 6, 8
neuron_clas_2d(), **14**, 14, 15
neuron_clas_2d_bias(), **17**, 18
neuron_reg_1d(), **53**, 53, 54
neuron_reg_2d(), **58**, 59
new() (deeplay), 548, 550–552
NFC (Normalization Form C), 302
NFD (Normalization Form D), 302
n-gram, 321
Nichol, Alexander, 472
NLP (natural language processing), 299
   corpus file, 299
   corpus iterator, 302–303
   custom text encoder implementation, 455–457
   handling contractions, 301
   pretrained embeddings loading, 316–318
   removing noise, 301–302
   tokenization, 300
   vocabulary building, 303–306

nnU-Net, 248
Nobel Prize in Chemistry
   Hassabis, Demis, 528
   Jumper, John, 528
Nobel Prize in Physics
   Hinton, Geoffrey E., 49
   Hopfield, John J., 620
node (graph), 476, 611
node attributes, 476, 477
no_grad() (torch), 290, 314, 338, 339, 405, 435, 444, 509, 590, 592, 593
non-contrastive learning, 277, 278
NonOverlapping (deeptrack), 241
normalization
   output, 42
   weight, 18–19
Normalization Form C (NFC), 302
Normalization Form D (NFD), 302
normalize() (cv2), 128
Normalize (torchvision), 149, 151, 360, 361, 371, 380, 398, 412, 432, 465
normalize() (unicodedata), 301, 302, 307, 320, 348
normalized() (deeplay), 400, 401
normalize_image(), **366**, 366, 369
NormalizeMinMax (deeptrack), 141, 170, 175, 176, 181, 190, 215, 256
.npy files, 82, 83, 133
NumPy, xxiv
numpy() (torch), 91, 114, 122, 126, 136, 143, 151, 184, 186, 260, 262, 264, 267, 273, 369, 386, 393, 399, 405, 413, 419, 434, 438, 443, 445, 470, 484, 509, 523, 524, 590

O

observe_tetris_with_gui(), **575**, 576, 579, 583, 597
OneHot (deeptrack), 229
one-hot encoding, 37, **212**, 229
online network (non-contrastive learning), 253
online training, **65**
open() (PIL, Image method), 121, 146, 158, 159, 224, 396, 411, 412
open() (Python), 3, 12, 81, 84, 85, 302, 307, 317, 451, 453, 498
OpenAI, 425, 450

optical forces dataset, 80–81
optical tweezer, 79
optimal transport theory, 188, 207
optimizer, **37**, 45
   Adam, 45
   momentum of, 45
   RMSprop, 45, 115
   stochastic gradient descent, 37
OTGO (toolbox for optical tweezers
   in the geometrical optics regime),
   82, 84
output (neuron), 2, 3
output gate (LSTM), 297
output layer, **20**
output normalization, 42
overfitting, 39, 73, **77**, 78, 93, 148,
   219–222, 284, 290, 293, 296, 297,
   352, 360, 386, 443, 550, 586, 602,
   614, 615

P

pad(), **306**, 307, 320
Pad (deeptrack), 239
pad_and_process(), **454**, 455, 457, 459
pairwise_distances() (sklearn), 205
Pajitnov, Alexey, 561
Pandas, 89
   read metrics file with, 89
panoptic segmentation, **211**
Parameter (torch), 102
parameters() (torch), 37, 87, 289, 312,
   314, 320, 321, 383, 402, 416, 440,
   458, 461, 462, 588
Parc Güell, 158
ParticleDataset, **504–505**, 507
particle localization (microscopy)
   with convolutional network, 128–145
   with LodeSTAR, 255–268
   with U-Net, 224–234
ParticleLocalizer, **258**, 259, 263
ParticleLocalizerWithFlips, **263**, 264
penalty (reinforcement learning), 558
perceptron, 48
perceptual loss, 402, 404, 407, 423
permute() (torch), 142, 171, 215, 216,
   236, 243, 273, 275, 276, 344, 366,
   369, 405, 413, 419, 443, 445, 465, 470
phase-space plot, 606

Pineda, Jesús, 511, 528
pipeline, **138**. *See also* data pipeline;
   simulation pipeline
pitch shifting, 280
Pitts, Walter, 48
pixel-wise multiclass classification, 211
playing *Tetris*
   with command line, 568–569
   with deep Q-learning, 585–597
   with GUI, 569–572
   with Q-learning, 573–585
play_tetris_with_gui(), **570**, 572
plot_activations(), **122**, 123
plot_attention(), **331**, 331, 340
plot_blood_smears(), **111**, 112, **113**, 114
plot_channels(), **103**, 103–105, 107
plot_class_examples(), **358**, 359
plot_data_1d(), **4**, 5, 52
plot_data_2d(), **13**, 13, 57
plot_image() (Code Example 3-1),
   101, 101
plot_image() (Code Example 4-1), **171**,
   171, 174, 175, 177
plot_model(), **534**, 535, 537
plot_model3(), **542**, 543, 544
plot_mse(), **70**, 70, **72**, 72
plot_mse_train_vs_val(), **76**, 76
plot_position_comparison(), **260**, 261,
   262, 264, 267
plot_pred_1d(), **6**, 6, 54
plot_pred_2d(), **14**, 15, 24, 29, 59, 62,
   75, 77
plot_pred_vs_gt(), **66**, 67, 75, 77
plot_roc(), **117**, 117, 119
plot_simulated_particles(), **138**,
   139, 140
plot_simulated_particles_with
   _positions(), **141**, 141
plotting.py, 5, 6, 9, 12, 14, 16, 29, 52, 53,
   55, 57, 59, 60, 64, 66, 69, 72, 73,
   76, 79
plot_training(), **291**, 291, 292
plot_training_metrics(), **219**, 220, 221
point particle, 255
PointParticle (deeptrack), 227,
   228, 255
Poisson (deeptrack), 140, 170, 240
Poisson noise, 140, 170, 229

policy (reinforcement learning), 558

pooling layer, 105

positional_encoding(), **436**, 437, 440, 442, 444, 455, 468, 469

positional encoding function, 436–438

positional encodings, **352–353**, 362

positive pairs (contrastive learning), 252

precision, 203, 276

  vs. accuracy, 136

precision_score() (sklearn), 203

predicting Lorenz system with reservoir computing, 610–619

prediction error, 560

predictions-versus-ground-truth plot, 65–67

prepare_data() (Code Examples 10-1, 10-A and 10-B), **440**, 441, 448, 459

prepare_data() (Code Example 10-C), **468**, 469

preprocessing(), **348**, 348

pretrained embeddings loading (NLP), 316–318

PretrainedViTModel, **370**, 372

Prewitt filter, 98

prior distribution, 188

process(), **307**, 308

product() (deeptrack, Source method), 213

PropagateLayer, **493**, 494, 495

Pygame, 569–572

Python, xxiv

  documentation, xxiv

  official website, xxiv

Python Crash Course, 3rd edition (Matthes), xxiii

Python package (creating and importing), 4–5

PyTorch, xxiv, **100–110**, 287

  convolutional architectures, 108–109

  convolutional layer, 102–104

  dense layers, 109–110

  pooling layers, 105–106

  ReLU activation, 104–105

  upsampling layers, 106–108

PyTorch tensor (image), 101

Q

Q-function, **558**

Qiao, Chang, 463

QLAgent, **574**, 576, **576**, **578**, 579, **580**, 581, 583, 584

Q-learning, 558–561, 598

QLTetris, **573**, 574, 584, 596

Q-network (deep Q-learning), 586, 599

Q-table, 578–579

quantum dot, 224

  detection, 224–234

quantum dot image dataset, 224–225

query-by-committee sampling, 530

query_random(), **534**, 534, 538, 543, 545

query strategy, 530

query_uncertainty(), **536**, 537, 538, 544, 545

R

Rajaraman, Sivaramakrishnan, 111

RandomCrop (torchvision), 360, 371, 398

random_ellipse_axes(), **238**, 238

RandomFlip, **520**, 521

random graph, 611

RandomHorizontalFlip (torchvision), 360, 371, 398, 412

RandomRotation, **520**, 521

random sampling, 534–536, 543, 548, 550

random_split() (deeptrack, Source method), 196, 213, 285, 308

random_split() (torch), 114, 134

RandomVerticalFlip (torchvision), 398, 412

read_csv() (pandas), 89, 196, 219, 221, 283

recall, 116, 203, 276

recall_score() (sklearn), 203

receiver operating characteristic (ROC), 117

reconstruction error (autoencoder), 196

reconstruction term (loss in VAE), 180

recurrence relations, 279

RecurrentModel (deeplay), 292, 293, 295, 297

recurrent neural networks (RNNs),
281–282
GRU, 294–296
LSTM, 296–298
stacked, 293–294
regionprops() (skimage), 232, 269, 515
register_forward_hook() (torch), 121,
122, 125, 150, 153, 156
register_full_backward_hook()
(torch), 125
regression, **51**
Regressor (deeplay), 87, 135, 173, 200,
217, 231, 244, 292, 293, 295, 297,
490, 508
regularization
for Adam, 363
factor
for reservoir computing, 613
for style transfer, 163
term (VAE), 180–181, 183
training, 73
weight, 18–19
reinforcement learning, 558
ReLU (rectified linear unit), **19**, 20,
104–105
ReLU (torch), 44, 104, 108, 134, 147–
148, 351, 353, 481, 487, 492, 494,
501, 522
ReLU activation function, 43
remove() (os), 111, 269, 317, 512
remove() (torch), 122, 125, 150, 154, 156
removing noise (NLP), 301–302
reparameterization (Gaussian
distribution), 428
replace() (deeplay), 501
replace (in dataset), 172
replay buffer, 587, 591–594
requires_grad_() (torch), 147, 149
requires_grad (torch, Tensor attribute),
319, 355, 462
rescale_intensity() (skimage), 126
reservoir, 601
reservoir computing
implementation, 610–619
introduction, 601–602
reset gate (GRU), 294, 295
residual connection, 165, 344, 351, 352,
414. *See also* skip connections

ResidualMessagePassingNeuralNetwork
(deeplay), 501
resize() (cv2), 128
resize() (skimage), 126, 369
Resize (torchvision), 113, 371, 380
resolve() (deeptrack), 138, 141, 142,
171, 172, 174, 175, 177, 178, 230
reverb, 280
reverse diffusion
implementation, 435–436
process, **427**, 430–432
reward (reinforcement learning), 558
RGB images, 100
RMSprop (deeplay, torch), 45, 115, 119
RMSProp optimizer, **45**
RNN (torch), 288
RNNs. *See* recurrent neural networks
ROC (receiver operating
characteristic), 117
ROC (torchmetrics), 117
ROC curve, 116–118
Rombach, Robin, 472
Ronneberger, Olaf, 210, 248
Rosenblatt, Frank, 48
Rumelhart, David E., 49
Runge-Kutta algorithms, 603

S

Saharia, Chitwan, 472
Salakhutdinov, Ruslan R., 207
SampleToMasks (deeptrack), 229, 242
sampling (active learning)
adversarial, 549, 552–553
entropy, 545
large margin, 545
query-by-committee, 530
random, 534–536, 543, 548, 550
small margin, 545
uncertainty, 530, 536–538, 544, 548,
550–552
sampling process, 428
SAND (particle simulation) dataset,
497–500
save() (numpy), 83, 133
save() (torch), 595
Scarselli, Franco, 527
Schmidhuber, Jürgen, 323
Seaborn, 40

segmentation, **211**, 358
  instance, 211
  panoptic, 211
  semantic, 207, 211
segmented tissue images dataset,
    213, 216
select_labels(), **214**, 215
self-attention, **326**, 332, 342, 343, 362,
    373, 374, 439, 455, 456, 458.
    See also attention
self-loop (graph), 481
self-supervised learning, **252–255**
  contrastive, **252–253**
  geometric, **254–255**
  non-contrastive, **253–254**
semantic segmentation, 207, **211**
sensitive dependence on initial
    conditions, 607. *See also*
    butterfly effect
sensitivity, 116
sentiment analysis, 299
  with a transformer, 342–357
Seq2Seq, **315**, 318
seq2seq (sequence-to-sequence)
    model, 299
seq2seq (sequence-to-sequence)
    transformation, 299
Seq2SeqDecoder (Code Example 7-1),
    310, 312
Seq2SeqDecoder (Code Example 8-A), **337**
Seq2SeqEncoder, **309**, 312
Seq2SeqModel (Code Example 7-1),
    311–314, 316
Seq2SeqModel (Code Example 8-A), **338**
sequence-to-sequence (seq2seq)
    architecture, 311
  combine encoder and decoder,
      311–315
    with attention, 338–339
  define loss, 315
  implement application, 315–316
  implement decoder, 310–311
    with attention, 337–338
  implement encoder, 308–310
  load pretrained embeddings, 316–318
  test, 319–322
    with attention, 339–340
  train, 318–319

sequence-to-sequence (seq2seq)
    model, 299
sequence-to-sequence (seq2seq)
    transformation, 299
Sequential (deeplay, torch), 104, 105,
    107–110, 118, 134, 147–148, 257,
    351, 353, 456, 487, 494, 495, 547
SGD (deeplay, torch), 37, 38
shot noise, 170, 229
sigmoid(), **22**, 23, 28, 32, 33, 62, 63, 69,
    281, 282
sigmoid() (numerically stable), **614**,
    614, 616
sigmoid() (torch), 245
Sigmoid (torch), 36, 115, 118, 353, 401,
    522, 552
sigmoid function, **19**, 20, 105
  simple implementation, **22**, 281
  stable implementation, 614
signal-to-noise ratio (SNR), 140,
    170, 240
Silver, David, 599
Simonyan, Karen, 165
simulate(), **509**, 510
SimulatedDataset (Code Example 3-B),
    142, 142
SimulatedDataset (Code Example 4-1),
    172, 172, 177–178
simulation (with GNN), 497–511
simulation pipeline
  cell images, 237–242
  microscopic particle image, 137–142,
      169–171, 176
  point particle, 255–257
  quantum dots, 225–231
single neuron, 2–19, 52–61
  classification of 1D data with, 3–11
  classification of 2D data with, 11–17
  regression of 1D data with, 52–57
  regression of 2D data with, 57–61
  training algorithm, 7
  training code, 8, 54
skip connections, **209**, 210
sklearn, 203–205, 523, 532
small margin sampling, 545
Smith, Samuel L., 93
SNR (signal-to-noise ratio), 140,
    170, 240

Sobel filter, 97, 98, 99

Softmax (torch), 42, 110, 310, 337

softmax() (torch), 232, 330, 334, 336, 344, 350

softmax activation/function, **42**, 110, 211, 311, 329

Sohl-Dickstein, Jascha, 471

Source (deeptrack), 196, 213, 235, 269, 285, 308

spaCy models, 300

sparse categorical cross-entropy, 212

special tokens, 305–307, 320, 454

spectral radius, 611, 612

Sphere (deeptrack), 169, 176

splitting the data, 73–79

squeeze() (numpy), 136, 138, 141, 184, 214, 230, 434

squeeze() (torch), 47, 101, 151, 190, 192–194, 198, 200, 245, 246, 312–314, 331, 335, 339, 340, 354, 380, 434, 437, 484, 487, 488, 490, 524

Stable Diffusion, 425, 450

stacked recurrent neural networks, 293–294

standard scaled dot-product attention, 333

state (reinforcement learning), 558 in Q-table, 578–579

steepest-descent training, 65

step() (torch), 161, 289, 384, 403, 404, 417, 441, 462, 593

stimulus signals, 2

stochastic differential equations, 426

stochastic gradient descent optimizer, 37

style_transfer(), **160, 161**, 163

Subset (torch), 360

Subtract (deeptrack), 228

sum() (torch), 125

super-resolution, 463–471, 472

super-resolution microscopy, 463

supervised learning, 1

Sutskever, Ilya, 323

Sutton, Richard S., 598, 599

synapse, 2

synaptic potential, 2, 3

synaptic signals, 2

Szegedy, Christian, 165

T

Tanh (torch), 400–401

target network
    deep Q-learning, 586
    non-contrastive learning, 253

teacher forcing, 313

teacher-student learning paradigm, 586

temperature prediction with an RNN, 282–298

temporal difference error, 586

temporal difference learning, 598

tensor processing units (TPUs), xxv

tensor_to_image(), **151**, 152, 153, 161

test() (lightning), 39, 42, 44, 45, 116, 119, 135, 143, 144, 222, 356, 364, 369, 372, 491, 496, 509, 548, 549

test/testing dataset, 39, **74**

Tetriminos, 561

Tetris, 561

Tetris, **562–568**, 568, 573, 576–577, 589

text embeddings, 450

text encoder, 450

TextEncoder, **455**, 457

text-to-image transformation, 450–463

text translation
    with attention, 336–342
    with an RNN, 299–322

textual prompts, 450

threshold (classifier), 116

thresholding (image), 233

tic-tac-toe, 560

tifffile() (tifffile), 464

time evolution, 603

to() (torch), 91, 259, 264, 288–290, 311–314, 320, 322, 339, 381, 382, 384, 386, 391, 392, 400–402, 405, 406, 414, 415, 420, 433–436, 439, 440, 444, 448, 456–462, 467, 468, 482, 490, 509

to_dense_adj() (torch_geometric), 484, 490

to_jshtml() (matplotlib), 499, 510, 525

tokenization (NLP), 300

tokenize(), **300**, 300, **301**, 301, 302, 307, 320, 348, 356, 453, 454

tokenizer, 311

Tolstikhin, Ilya, 207

to_numpy_array() (networkx), 612

ToTensor (deeptrack), 170, 175, 176, 181, 190, 198, 215, 230, 235, 242, 256, 272, 286, 308

ToTensor (torchvision), 113, 149, 360, 361, 371, 380, 398, 412, 432, 465, 547

TPR (true-positive rate), 116

TPUs (tensor processing units), xxv

tqdm() (tqdm), 276, 395–396, 435, 447, 452, 467

train() (torch), 386, 405, 419, 442, 459, 462, 469. *See also* eval()

TrainableAttention, **334**

train_active_learning(), **533**, 534, 537, 538, **541**, 543–545

train_disc(), **403**, 406

trainer, **38**

Trainer (deeplay, lightning), 38, 42, 44, 45, 89, 116, 119, 135, 143, 173, 178, 183, 191, 200, 218, 221, 232, 244, 260, 264, 267, 273, 292, 293, 319, 356, 363, 368, 372, 490, 496, 508, 522, 548, 549

train_gen(), **404**, 406

training dataset, **73**

training a neuron
algorithm, 7
implementation, 8, 54

training an RNN
implementation, 289
monitoring training loss, 290
monitoring validation loss, 290–291

training_step() (deeplay, Application method), 259, 367

train_model() (Code Example 9-C), **416**, 420

train_model() (Code Examples 12-1 and 12-2), **532**, 533, 542

train_preprocess() (deeplay, Application method), 316

transformer, 325, **344–345**
decoder-only, 345
encoder-only, 345

transformer encoder, 345, 351–355, 361, 362

TransformerEncoderLayer, **351**, 353

TransformerEncoderModel, **353**, 355

TransformLayer, **492**, 494, 495

translate() (Code Example 7-A), **320**, 320, 321

translate() (Code Example 8-A), **340**, 340, 341

translate() (kornia), 258

translation, 257
equivariance, 257
translation (NLP), 299

Trencadís Lizard, 158

trilinear upsampling, 108

true-positive rate (TPR), 116

.txt files, 81, 83, 84, 299, 454, 518, 581, 583

U

uncertainty (reinforcement learning), 560

uncertainty sampling, 530, 536–538, 544, 548, 550–552, 556

UncertaintyStrategy (deeplay), 551

underfitting, **77**, 290, 386

undirected graph, 477

U-Net, **210–211**, 248

UNet2d (deeplay), 217, 231, 244, 400

Unicode (encoding standard), 302

UniformStrategy (deeplay), 550

universal approximators (neural network as), 49

unlabeled data, 252

unlabeled pool, 530

unpooling layer, 106

unprocess(), **319**, 320, 322, 339

Unsqueeze (deeptrack), 198

unsqueeze() (torch), 102, 104, 105, 107, 108, 110, 113, 121, 122, 125, 149, 174, 175, 177, 178, 184, 192, 194, 200, 223, 232, 273, 275, 276, 313, 320, 335, 350, 435, 440, 455, 468, 493

unsupervised clustering with VAE, 186–187

unsupervised learning, 167

update() (deeptrack), 138, 141, 142, 171, 172, 174, 175, 177, 178, 227, 230, 238

update gate (GRU), 294, 295

UpdateLayer, **494**, 494, 495

Upsample (torch), 107

upsampling layer, 106

V

VAE (variational autoencoder), **179–188**, 188, 207

validation dataset, 39, **73**

Value (deeptrack), 186, 190, 198, 272, 286, 308

value function (reinforcement learning), 558

vanishing gradient problem, 19, 43, 49, 165, 211, 293, 323, 380

variance schedule, 428

VariationalAutoEncoder (deeplay), 182

variational autoencoder (VAE), **179–188**, 188, 207

Vaswani, Ashish, 373

Velickovic, Petar, 528

vertex (graph), 476

VGG16, 147–149, 159, 402

vgg16() (torchvision), 147

VGG16_Weights (torchvision), 147

VideoCapture (cv2), 128

view() (torch), 160, 204, 205, 263, 315, 344, 366, 590

VirtualStainingDataset, **395–397**, 398, 399

virtual staining with GAN, 394–409

vision transformer (ViT), **361–363**, 374

Visual Studio (VS) Code, xxiv

ViT (deeplay), 362, 368

ViT architecture, **361**

ViTImageProcessor (transformers), 371

ViTModel (transformers), 370–371

Vocab, **303**, 304, 305, 348, 454

vocabulary, 303, 348

vocabulary building (NLP), 303–306, 453–455

Volpe, Giovanni, 472

VS Code (Visual Studio Code), xxiv

W

WassersteinAutoEncoder (deeplay), 191

Wasserstein autoencoder (WAE), **188–195**, 207

Wasserstein distance, 188, 189

Watkins, Christopher J.C.H., 598

weight_decay (parameter Adam), 363, 368

weighted cross-entropy loss, **224**

weighted loss function, 231

weight normalization/regularization, 18–19

weights (neuron), 2, 3

Welling, Max, 207, 527

Werbos, Paul John, 49

where() (numpy), 533, 541, 614

where() (torch), 263

Widrow, Bernard, 48

with (Python), **4**. *See also* context manager

  with Fwd_Hook, 154

  with Fwd_Hooks, 157, 160, 162

  with numpy.load(), 498

  with open(), 3, 12, 81, 84, 85, 302, 307, 317, 451, 453, 498

  with pandas.option_context(), 346, 357

  with torch.no_grad(), 290, 314, 338, 339, 405, 435, 444, 509, 590, 592, 593

Z

Zalando, 189

Zemel, Richard S., 207

zero_() (torch), 150

zero_grad() (torch), 161, 289, 384, 403, 404, 416–417, 441, 462, 593

Zhu, Jun-Yan, 424

ZINC (molecular properties) dataset, 483–486

Zisserman, Andrew, 165

UPDATES

Visit *https://github.com/DeepTrackAI/DeepLearningCrashCourse* for updates, code and data files, and other information.

COLOPHON

The fonts used in *Deep Learning Crash Course* are New Baskerville, Futura, The Sans Mono Condensed, and Dogma. The book was typeset with $\mathrm{\LaTeX}\,2_\varepsilon$ package `nostarch` by Boris Veytsman with many additions by Alex Freed, Miles Bond, and other members of the No Starch Press team *(2023/07/19 v2.4 Typesetting books for No Starch Press).*

RESOURCES

Visit *https://nostarch.com/deep-learning-crash-course* for errata and more information.

More no-nonsense books from **NO STARCH PRESS**

PYTHON CRASH COURSE, 3RD EDITION

A Hands-On, Project-Based Introduction to Programming

BY ERIC MATTHES
552 PP., $49.99
ISBN 978-1-7185-0270-3

DEEP LEARNING

A Visual Approach

BY ANDREW GLASSNER
768 PP., $99.99
ISBN 978-1-7185-0072-3

MATH FOR DEEP LEARNING

What You Need to Know to Understand Neural Networks

BY RONALD T. KNEUSEL
344 PP., $49.99
ISBN 978-1-7185-0190-4

PRACTICAL DEEP LEARNING, 2ND EDITION

A Python-Based Introduction

BY RONALD T. KNEUSEL
584 PP., $69.99
ISBN 978-1-7185-0420-2

MACHINE LEARNING Q AND AI

30 Essential Questions and Answers on Machine Learning and AI

BY SEBASTIAN RASCHKA
264 PP., $49.99
ISBN 978-1-7185-0376-2

NATURAL LANGUAGE PROCESSING WITH PYTHON AND SPACY

A Practical Introduction

BY YULI VASILIEV
216 PP., $39.95
ISBN 978-1-7185-0052-5

PHONE:
800.420.7240 OR
415.863.9900

EMAIL:
SALES@NOSTARCH.COM

WEB:
WWW.NOSTARCH.COM

Never before has the world relied so heavily on the internet to stay connected and informed. That makes the Electronic Frontier Foundation's mission—to ensure that technology supports freedom, justice, and innovation for all people—more urgent than ever.

For over 35 years, EFF has fought for your rights through activism, in the courts, and by developing software because we believe in a better future—one where your device is truly yours, you can speak without being surveilled, and technology helps you connect with the people you care about. With your help, we can realize that vision for a brighter world together.